Maths for Economics

Pearson

At Pearson, we have a simple mission: to help people make more of their lives through learning.

We combine innovative learning technology with trusted content and educational expertise to provide engaging and effective learning experience that serve people wherever and whenever they are learning.

We enable our customers to access a wide and expanding range of market-leading content from world-renowned authors and develop their own tailor-made book. From classroom to boardroom, our curriculum materials, digital learning tools and testing programmes help to educate millions of people worldwide — more than any other private enterprise.

Every day our work helps learning flourish, and wherever learning flourishes, so do people.

To learn more, please visit us at: www.pearson.com/uk

Selected chapters from:

Essential Mathematics for Economic Analysis
Fifth Edition
Knut Sydsæter, Peter Hammond, Arne Strøm and
Andrés Carvajal

Mathematics for Economics and Business
Ninth Edition
Ian Jacques

Pearson

Harlow, England • London • New York • Boston • San Francisco • Toronto • Sydney • Dubai • Singapore • Hong Kong
Tokyo • Seoul • Taipei • New Dehli • Cape Town • São Paulo • Mexico City • Madrid • Amsterdam • Munich • Paris • Milan

Pearson
KAO Two
KAO Park
Harlow
Essex CM17 9NA

And associated companies throughout the world

Visit us on the World Wide Web at:
www.pearson.com/uk

© Pearson Education Limited 2019

Compiled from:

Essential Mathematics for Economic Analysis
Fifth Edition
Knut Sydsæter, Peter Hammond, Arne Strøm and Andrés Carvajal
ISBN 978-1-292-07461-0
© Prentice Hall, Inc. 1995

Mathematics for Economics and Business
Ninth Edition
Ian Jacques
ISBN 978-1-292-19166-9
© Pearson Education Limited 1999, 2009

ISBN 978-1-78764-318-5

Printed and bound in Great Britain by Ashford Colour Press, Gosport, Hampshire.

CONTENTS

Section 1
Introduction

1

ALGEBRA

God made the integers, all else is the work of Man.
—Leopold Kronecker[1]

This chapter deals with elementary algebra, but we also briefly consider a few other topics that you might find that you need to review. Indeed, tests reveal that even students with a good background in mathematics often benefit from a brief review of what they learned in the past. These students should browse through the material and do some of the less simple exercises. Students with a weaker background in mathematics, or who have been away from mathematics for a long time, should read the text carefully and then do most of the exercises. Finally, those students who have considerable difficulties with this chapter should turn to a more elementary book on algebra.

1.1 The Real Numbers

We start by reviewing some important facts and concepts concerning numbers. The basic numbers are the natural numbers:

$$1, \ 2, \ 3, \ 4, \ \ldots$$

also called positive integers. Of these 2, 4, 6, 8, ... are the even numbers, whereas 1, 3, 5, 7, ... are the odd numbers. Though familiar, such numbers are in reality rather abstract and advanced concepts. Civilization crossed a significant threshold when it grasped the idea that a flock of four sheep and a collection of four stones have something in common, namely "fourness". This idea came to be represented by symbols such as the primitive : : (still used on dominoes or playing cards), the Roman numeral IV, and eventually the modern 4. This key notion is grasped and then continually refined as young children develop their mathematical skills.

---

[1] Attributed; circa 1886.

The positive integers, together with 0 and the negative integers $-1, -2, -3, -4, \ldots$, make up the integers, which are

$$0, \pm 1, \pm 2, \pm 3, \pm 4, \ldots$$

They can be represented on a *number line* like the one shown in Fig. 1.1.1, where the arrow gives the direction in which the numbers increase.

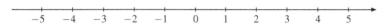

Figure 1.1.1 The number line

The *rational numbers* are those like $3/5$ that can be written in the form a/b, where a and b are both integers. An integer n is also a rational number, because $n = n/1$. Other examples of rational numbers are

$$\frac{1}{2}, \frac{11}{70}, \frac{125}{7}, -\frac{10}{11}, 0 = \frac{0}{1}, -19, -1.26 = -\frac{126}{100}$$

The rational numbers can also be represented on the number line. Imagine that we first mark $1/2$ and all the multiples of $1/2$. Then we mark $1/3$ and all the multiples of $1/3$, and so forth. You can be excused for thinking that "finally" there will be no more places left for putting more points on the line. But in fact this is quite wrong. The ancient Greeks already understood that "holes" would remain in the number line even after all the rational numbers had been marked off. For instance, there are no integers p and q such that $\sqrt{2} = p/q$. Hence, $\sqrt{2}$ is not a rational number.[2]

The rational numbers are therefore insufficient for measuring all possible lengths, let alone areas and volumes. This deficiency can be remedied by extending the concept of numbers to allow for the so-called irrational numbers. This extension can be carried out rather naturally by using decimal notation for numbers, as explained below.

The way most people write numbers today is called the *decimal system*, or the *base 10 system*. It is a positional system with 10 as the base number. Every natural number can be written using only the symbols, $0, 1, 2, \ldots, 9$, which are called *digits*.[3] The positional system defines each combination of digits as a sum of powers of 10. For example,

$$1\,984 = 1 \cdot 10^3 + 9 \cdot 10^2 + 8 \cdot 10^1 + 4 \cdot 10^0$$

Each natural number can be uniquely expressed in this manner. With the use of the signs $+$ and $-$, all integers, positive or negative, can be written in the same way. Decimal points also enable us to express rational numbers other than natural numbers. For example,

$$3.1415 = 3 + 1/10^1 + 4/10^2 + 1/10^3 + 5/10^4$$

Rational numbers that can be written exactly using only a finite number of decimal places are called *finite decimal fractions*.

---

[2] Euclid proved this fact in around the year 300 BCE.

[3] You may recall that a digit is either a finger or a thumb, and that most humans have ten digits.

Each finite decimal fraction is a rational number, but not every rational number can be written as a finite decimal fraction. We also need to allow for *infinite decimal fractions* such as

$$100/3 = 33.333\ldots$$

where the three dots indicate that the digit 3 is repeated indefinitely.

If the decimal fraction is a rational number, then it will always be *recurring* or *periodic*—that is, after a certain place in the decimal expansion, it either stops or continues to repeat a finite sequence of digits. For example,

$$11/70 = 0.1\,\underbrace{571428}\,\underbrace{571428}\,5\ldots$$

with the sequence of six digits 571428 repeated infinitely often.

The definition of a real number follows from the previous discussion. We define a *real number* as an arbitrary infinite decimal fraction. Hence, a real number is of the form $x = \pm m.\alpha_1\alpha_2\alpha_3\ldots$, where m is a nonnegative integer, and for each natural number n, α_n is a digit in the range 0 to 9.

We have already identified the periodic decimal fractions with the rational numbers. In addition, there are infinitely many new numbers given by the nonperiodic decimal fractions. These are called *irrational numbers*. Examples include $\sqrt{2}$, $-\sqrt{5}$, π, $2^{\sqrt{2}}$, and $0.12112111211112\ldots$[4]

We mentioned earlier that each rational number can be represented by a point on the number line. But not all points on the number line represent rational numbers. It is as if the irrational numbers "close up" the remaining holes on the number line after all the rational numbers have been positioned. Hence, an unbroken and endless straight line with an origin and a positive unit of length is a satisfactory model for the real numbers. We frequently state that there is a *one-to-one correspondence* between the real numbers and the points on a number line. Often, too, one speaks of the "real line" rather than the "number line".

The set of rational numbers as well as the set of irrational numbers are said to be "dense" on the number line. This means that between any two different real numbers, irrespective of how close they are to each other, we can always find both a rational and an irrational number—in fact, we can always find infinitely many of each.

When applied to the real numbers, the four basic arithmetic operations always result in a real number. The only exception is that we cannot divide by 0: in the words of American comedian Steven Wright, "Black holes are where God divided by zero."

DIVISION BY ZERO

The ratio $p/0$ is *not* defined for any real number p.

This is very important and should not be confused with the fact that $0/a = 0$, for all $a \neq 0$. Notice especially that $0/0$ is not defined as any real number. For example, if a

---

[4] In general, it is very difficult to decide whether a given number is rational or irrational. It has been known since the year 1776 that π is irrational and since 1927 that $2^{\sqrt{2}}$ is irrational. However, there are many numbers about which we still do not know whether they are irrational or not.

car requires 60 litres of fuel to go 600 kilometres, then its fuel consumption is $60/600 = 10$ litres per 100 kilometres. However, if told that a car uses 0 litres of fuel to go 0 kilometres, we know nothing about its fuel consumption; $0/0$ is completely undefined.

EXERCISES FOR SECTION 1.1

1. Which of the following statements are true?

(a) 1984 is a natural number.

(b) -5 is to the right of -3 on the number line.

(c) -13 is a natural number.

(d) There is no natural number that is not rational.

(e) 3.1415 is not rational.

(f) The sum of two irrational numbers is irrational.

(g) $-3/4$ is rational.

(h) All rational numbers are real.

2. Explain why the infinite decimal expansion

$$1.01001000100001000001\ldots$$

is not a rational number.

1.2   Integer Powers

You should recall that we often write 3^4 instead of the product $3 \cdot 3 \cdot 3 \cdot 3$, that $\frac{1}{2} \cdot \frac{1}{2} \cdot \frac{1}{2} \cdot \frac{1}{2} \cdot \frac{1}{2}$ can be written as $\left(\frac{1}{2}\right)^5$, and that $(-10)^3 = (-10)(-10)(-10) = -1000$. If a is any number and n is any natural number, then a^n is defined by

$$a^n = \underbrace{a \cdot a \cdot \cdots \cdot a}_{n \text{ times}}$$

The expression a^n is called the *n-th power* of a; here a is the *base*, and n is the *exponent*. We have, for example, $a^2 = a \cdot a$, $x^4 = x \cdot x \cdot x \cdot x$, and

$$\left(\frac{p}{q}\right)^5 = \frac{p}{q} \cdot \frac{p}{q} \cdot \frac{p}{q} \cdot \frac{p}{q} \cdot \frac{p}{q}$$

where $a = p/q$, and $n = 5$. By convention, $a^1 = a$, a "product" with only one factor.

We usually drop the multiplication sign if this is unlikely to create misunderstanding. For example, we write abc instead of $a \cdot b \cdot c$, but it is safest to keep the multiplication sign in $1.05^3 = 1.05 \cdot 1.05 \cdot 1.05$.

For any real number $a \neq 0$, we define, further, $a^0 = 1$. Thus, $5^0 = 1$; $(-16.2)^0 = 1$; and $(x \cdot y)^0 = 1$, if $x \cdot y \neq 0$. But if $a = 0$, we do *not* assign a numerical value to a^0: the expression 0^0 is *undefined*.

We also need to define powers with negative exponents. What do we mean by 3^{-2}? It turns out that the sensible definition is to set 3^{-2} equal to $1/3^2 = 1/9$. In general,

$$a^{-n} = \frac{1}{a^n}$$

whenever n is a natural number and $a \neq 0$. In particular, $a^{-1} = 1/a$. In this way we have defined a^x for all integers x.[5]

Properties of Powers

There are some rules for powers that you really must not only know by heart, but understand why they are true. The two most important are:

PROPERTIES OF POWERS

For any real number a, and any integer numbers r and s:

(i) $a^r \cdot a^s = a^{r+s}$ (ii) $(a^r)^s = a^{rs}$

Note carefully what these rules say. According to rule (i), powers with the same base are multiplied by *adding* the exponents. For example,

$$a^3 \cdot a^5 = \underbrace{a \cdot a \cdot a}_{3 \text{ times}} \cdot \underbrace{a \cdot a \cdot a \cdot a \cdot a}_{5 \text{ times}} = \underbrace{a \cdot a \cdot a \cdot a \cdot a \cdot a \cdot a \cdot a}_{3+5 = 8 \text{ times}} = a^8 = a^{3+5}$$

Here is an example of rule (ii):

$$(a^2)^4 = \underbrace{\underbrace{a \cdot a}_{2 \text{ times}} \cdot \underbrace{a \cdot a}_{2 \text{ times}} \cdot \underbrace{a \cdot a}_{2 \text{ times}} \cdot \underbrace{a \cdot a}_{2 \text{ times}}}_{4 \text{ times}} = \underbrace{a \cdot a \cdot a \cdot a \cdot a \cdot a \cdot a \cdot a}_{4 \cdot 2 = 8 \text{ times}} = a^8 = a^{2 \cdot 4}$$

Division of two powers with the same non-zero base goes like this:

$$a^r \div a^s = \frac{a^r}{a^s} = a^r \frac{1}{a^s} = a^r \cdot a^{-s} = a^{r-s}$$

Thus we divide two powers with the same base by *subtracting* the exponent in the denominator from that in the numerator.[6] For example, $a^3 \div a^5 = a^{3-5} = a^{-2}$.

Finally, note that

$$(ab)^r = \underbrace{ab \cdot ab \cdots \cdots ab}_{r \text{ times}} = \underbrace{a \cdot a \cdots \cdots a}_{r \text{ times}} \cdot \underbrace{b \cdot b \cdots \cdots b}_{r \text{ times}} = a^r b^r$$

---

[5] Calculators usually have a power key, denoted by $\boxed{y^x}$ or $\boxed{a^x}$, which can be used to compute powers. Make sure you know how to use it by computing 2^3, which is 8; 3^2, which is 9; and 25^{-3}, which is 0.000064.

[6] An important motivation for introducing the definitions $a^0 = 1$ and $a^{-n} = 1/a^n$ is that we want the rules for powers to be valid for negative and zero exponents as well as for positive ones. For example, we want $a^r \cdot a^s = a^{r+s}$ to be valid when $r = 5$ and $s = 0$. This requires that $a^5 \cdot a^0 = a^{5+0} = a^5$, so we must choose $a^0 = 1$. If $a^n \cdot a^m = a^{n+m}$ is to be valid when $m = -n$, we must have $a^n \cdot a^{-n} = a^{n+(-n)} = a^0 = 1$. Because $a^n \cdot (1/a^n) = 1$, we *must* define a^{-n} to be $1/a^n$.

and

$$\left(\frac{a}{b}\right)^r = \underbrace{\frac{a}{b} \cdot \frac{a}{b} \cdot \cdots \cdot \frac{a}{b}}_{r \text{ times}} = \frac{\overbrace{a \cdot a \cdot \cdots \cdot a}^{r \text{ times}}}{\underbrace{b \cdot b \cdot \cdots \cdot b}_{r \text{ times}}} = \frac{a^r}{b^r} = a^r b^{-r}$$

These rules can be extended to cases where there are several factors. For instance,

$$(abcde)^r = a^r b^r c^r d^r e^r$$

We saw that $(ab)^r = a^r b^r$. What about $(a+b)^r$? One of the most common errors committed in elementary algebra is to equate this to $a^r + b^r$. For example, $(2+3)^3 = 5^3 = 125$, but $2^3 + 3^3 = 8 + 27 = 35$. Thus, in general, $(a+b)^r \neq a^r + b^r$.

EXAMPLE 1.2.1   Simplify the expressions:

(a) $x^p x^{2p}$

(b) $t^s \div t^{s-1}$

(c) $a^2 b^3 a^{-1} b^5$

(d) $\dfrac{t^p t^{q-1}}{t^r t^{s-1}}$

Solution:

(a) $x^p x^{2p} = x^{p+2p} = x^{3p}$

(b) $t^s \div t^{s-1} = t^{s-(s-1)} = t^{s-s+1} = t^1 = t$

(c) $a^2 b^3 a^{-1} b^5 = a^2 a^{-1} b^3 b^5 = a^{2-1} b^{3+5} = a^1 b^8 = ab^8$

(d) $\dfrac{t^p \cdot t^{q-1}}{t^r \cdot t^{s-1}} = \dfrac{t^{p+q-1}}{t^{r+s-1}} = t^{p+q-1-(r+s-1)} = t^{p+q-1-r-s+1} = t^{p+q-r-s}$

EXAMPLE 1.2.2   If $x^{-2}y^3 = 5$, compute $x^{-4}y^6$, $x^6 y^{-9}$, and $x^2 y^{-3} + 2x^{-10}y^{15}$.

Solution: In computing $x^{-4}y^6$, how can we make use of the assumption that $x^{-2}y^3 = 5$? A moment's reflection might lead you to see that $(x^{-2}y^3)^2 = x^{-4}y^6$, and hence $x^{-4}y^6 = 5^2 = 25$. Similarly,

$$x^6 y^{-9} = (x^{-2}y^3)^{-3} = 5^{-3} = 1/125$$

and

$$x^2 y^{-3} + 2x^{-10}y^{15} = (x^{-2}y^3)^{-1} + 2(x^{-2}y^3)^5 = 5^{-1} + 2 \cdot 5^5 = 6250.2$$

EXAMPLE 1.2.3   It is easy to make mistakes when dealing with powers. The following examples highlight some common sources of confusion.

(a) There is an important difference between $(-10)^2 = (-10)(-10) = 100$, and $-10^2 = -(10 \cdot 10) = -100$. The square of minus 10 is not equal to minus the square of 10.

(b) Note that $(2x)^{-1} = 1/(2x)$. Here the product $2x$ is raised to the power of -1. On the other hand, in $2x^{-1}$ only x is raised to the power -1, so $2x^{-1} = 2 \cdot (1/x) = 2/x$.

(c) The volume of a ball with radius r is $\frac{4}{3}\pi r^3$. What will the volume be if the radius is doubled? The new volume is

$$\frac{4}{3}\pi(2r)^3 = \frac{4}{3}\pi(2r)(2r)(2r) = \frac{4}{3}\pi 8r^3 = 8\left(\frac{4}{3}\pi r^3\right)$$

so the volume is 8 times the initial one. If we made the mistake of "simplifying" $(2r)^3$ to $2r^3$, the result would imply only a doubling of the volume; this should be contrary to common sense.

Compound Interest

Powers are used in practically every branch of applied mathematics, including economics. To illustrate their use, recall how they are needed to calculate compound interest.

Suppose you deposit \$1 000 in a bank account paying 8% interest at the end of each year.[7] After one year you will have earned \$1 000 $\cdot$ 0.08 = \$80 in interest, so the amount in your bank account will be \$1 080. This can be rewritten as

$$1000 + \frac{1000 \cdot 8}{100} = 1000\left(1 + \frac{8}{100}\right) = 1000 \cdot 1.08$$

Suppose this new amount of \$1 080 is left in the bank for another year at an interest rate of 8%. After a second year, the extra interest will be \$1 000 $\cdot$ 1.08 $\cdot$ 0.08. So the total amount will have grown to

$$1000 \cdot 1.08 + (1000 \cdot 1.08) \cdot 0.08 = 1000 \cdot 1.08(1 + 0.08) = 1000 \cdot (1.08)^2$$

Each year the amount will increase by the factor 1.08, and we see that at the end of t years it will have grown to \$1 000 $\cdot$ $(1.08)^t$.

If the original amount is \$$K$ and the interest rate is $p\%$ per year, by the end of the first year, the amount will be $K + K \cdot p/100 = K(1 + p/100)$ dollars. The growth factor per year is thus $1 + p/100$. In general, after t (whole) years, the original investment of \$$K$ will have grown to an amount

$$K\left(1 + \frac{p}{100}\right)^t$$

when the interest rate is $p\%$ per year and interest is added to the capital every year—that is, there is compound interest.

This example illustrates a general principle:

EXPONENTIAL GROWTH

A quantity K which increases by $p\%$ per year will have increased to

$$K\left(1 + \frac{p}{100}\right)^t$$

after t years. Here $1 + p/100$ is called the *growth factor* for a growth of $p\%$.

---

[7] Remember that 1% means one in a hundred, or 0.01. So 23%, for example, is 23 $\cdot$ 0.01 = 0.23. To calculate 23% of 4000, we write 4000 $\cdot$ 23/100 = 920 or 4000 $\cdot$ 0.23 = 920.

If you see an expression like $(1.08)^t$ you should immediately be able to recognize it as the amount to which $1 has grown after t years when the interest rate is 8% per year. How should you interpret $(1.08)^0$? You deposit $1 at 8% per year, and leave the amount for 0 years. Then you still have only $1, because there has been no time to accumulate any interest, so that $(1.08)^0$ must necessarily equal 1.[8]

EXAMPLE 1.2.4   A new car has been bought for $15 000 and is assumed to decrease in value (depreciate) by 15% per year over a six-year period. What is its value after six years?

Solution: After one year its value is down to

$$15\,000 - \frac{15\,000 \cdot 15}{100} = 15\,000 \cdot \left(1 - \frac{15}{100}\right) = 15\,000 \cdot 0.85 = 12\,750$$

After two years its value is $15\,000 \cdot (0.85)^2 = \$10\,837.50$, and so on. After six years we realize that its value must be $15\,000 \cdot (0.85)^6 \approx \$5\,657$.

This example illustrates a general principle:

EXPONENTIAL DECLINE

A quantity K which decreases by $p\%$ per year will have decreased to

$$K\left(1 - \frac{p}{100}\right)^t$$

after t years. Here $1 - p/100$ is called the *growth factor* for a decline of $p\%$ a year. (Note that a growth factor that is less than 1 indicates shrinkage.)

Do We Really Need Negative Exponents?

How much money should you have deposited in a bank five years ago in order to have $1 000 today, given that the interest rate has been 8% per year over this period? If we call this amount x, the requirement is that $x \cdot (1.08)^5$ must equal $1 000, or that $x \cdot (1.08)^5 = 1000$. Dividing by 1.08^5 on both sides yields

$$x = \frac{1000}{(1.08)^5} = 1000 \cdot (1.08)^{-5}$$

which is approximately $681. Thus, $\$(1.08)^{-5}$ is what you should have deposited five years ago in order to have $1 today, given the constant interest rate of 8%.

In general, $\$P(1 + p/100)^{-t}$ *is what you should have deposited t years ago in order to have $P today, if the interest rate has been p% every year.*

---

[8] Note that $1000 \cdot (1.08)^5$ is the amount you will have in your account after five years if you invest $1 000 at 8% interest per year. Using a calculator, you find that you will have approximately $1 469.33. A rather common mistake is to put $1000 \cdot (1.08)^5 = (1000 \cdot 1.08)^5 = (1080)^5$. This is a trillion ($10^{12}$) times the right answer!

EXERCISES FOR SECTION 1.2

1. Compute the following numbers: (a) 10^3; (b) $(-0.3)^2$; (c) 4^{-2}; and (d) $(0.1)^{-1}$.

2. Write as powers of 2 the following numbers: (a) 4; (b) 1; (c) 64; and (d) 1/16.

3. Write as powers the following numbers:

   (a) $15 \cdot 15 \cdot 15$ (b) $\left(-\frac{1}{3}\right)\left(-\frac{1}{3}\right)\left(-\frac{1}{3}\right)$ (c) $\frac{1}{10}$ (d) 0.0000001

   (e) $t t t t t t$ (f) $(a-b)(a-b)(a-b)$ (g) $a a b b b b$ (h) $(-a)(-a)(-a)$

4. Expand and simplify the following expressions:

   (a) $2^5 \cdot 2^5$ (b) $3^8 \cdot 3^{-2} \cdot 3^{-3}$ (c) $(2x)^3$ (d) $(-3xy^2)^3$

   (e) $\dfrac{p^{24} p^3}{p^4 p}$ (f) $\dfrac{a^4 b^{-3}}{(a^2 b^{-3})^2}$ (g) $\dfrac{3^4 (3^2)^6}{(-3)^{15} 3^7}$ (h) $\dfrac{p^\gamma (pq)^\sigma}{p^{2\gamma+\sigma} q^{\sigma-2}}$

5. Expand and simplify the following expressions:

   (a) $2^0 \cdot 2^1 \cdot 2^2 \cdot 2^3$ (b) $\left(\dfrac{4}{3}\right)^3$ (c) $\dfrac{4^2 \cdot 6^2}{3^3 \cdot 2^3}$

   (d) $x^5 x^4$ (e) $y^5 y^4 y^3$ (f) $(2xy)^3$

   (g) $\dfrac{10^2 \cdot 10^{-4} \cdot 10^3}{10^0 \cdot 10^{-2} \cdot 10^5}$ (h) $\dfrac{(k^2)^3 k^4}{(k^3)^2}$ (i) $\dfrac{(x+1)^3 (x+1)^{-2}}{(x+1)^2 (x+1)^{-3}}$

6. The surface area of a sphere with radius r is $4\pi r^2$.

   (a) By what factor will the surface area increase if the radius is tripled?

   (b) If the radius increases by 16%, by how many % will the surface area increase?

7. Suppose that a and b are positive, while m and n are integers. Which of the following equalities are true and which are false?

   (a) $a^0 = 0$ (b) $(a+b)^{-n} = 1/(a+b)^n$ (c) $a^m \cdot a^m = a^{2m}$

   (d) $a^m \cdot b^m = (ab)^{2m}$ (e) $(a+b)^m = a^m + b^m$ (f) $a^n \cdot b^m = (ab)^{n+m}$

8. Complete the following implications:

   (a) $xy = 3 \Rightarrow x^3 y^3 = \ldots$ (b) $ab = -2 \Rightarrow (ab)^4 = \ldots$

   (c) $a^2 = 4 \Rightarrow (a^8)^0 = \ldots$ (d) n integer implies $(-1)^{2n} = \ldots$

9. Compute the following: (a) 13% of 150; (b) 6% of 2400; and (c) 5.5% of 200.

10. Give economic interpretations to each of the following expressions and then use a calculator to find the approximate values: (a) $\$50 \cdot (1.11)^8$; (b) $€10\,000 \cdot (1.12)^{20}$; and (c) $£5\,000 \cdot (1.07)^{-10}$.

11. A box containing five balls costs €8.50. If the balls are bought individually, they cost €2.00 each. How much cheaper is it, in percentage terms, to buy the box as opposed to buying five individual balls?

12. (a) £12 000 is deposited in an account earning 4% interest per year. What is the amount after 15 years?

    (b) If the interest rate is 6% each year, how much money should you have deposited in a bank five years ago to have £50 000 today?

13. A quantity increases by 25% each year for three years. How much is the combined percentage growth p over the three-year period?

14. A firm's profit increased from 2010 to 2011 by 20%, but it decreased by 17% from 2011 to 2012.

    (a) Which of the years 2010 and 2012 had the higher profit?

    (b) What percentage decrease in profits from 2011 to 2012 would imply that profits were equal in 2010 and 2012?

1.3 Rules of Algebra

You are certainly already familiar with the most common rules of algebra. We have already used some in this chapter. Nevertheless, it may be useful to recall those that are most important.

RULES OF ALGEBRA

If a, b, and c are arbitrary numbers, then:

(i) $a + b = b + a$ (ii) $(a + b) + c = a + (b + c)$

(iii) $a + 0 = a$ (iv) $a + (-a) = 0$

(v) $ab = ba$ (vi) $(ab)c = a(bc)$

(vii) $1 \cdot a = a$ (viii) $aa^{-1} = 1$ for $a \neq 0$

(ix) $(-a)b = a(-b) = -ab$ (x) $(-a)(-b) = ab$

(xi) $a(b + c) = ab + ac$ (xii) $(a + b)c = ac + bc$

EXAMPLE 1.3.1   These rules are used in the following equalities:

(a) $5 + x^2 = x^2 + 5$

(b) $(a + 2b) + 3b = a + (2b + 3b) = a + 5b$

(c) $x\frac{1}{3} = \frac{1}{3}x$

(d) $(xy)y^{-1} = x(yy^{-1}) = x$

(e) $(-3)5 = 3(-5) = -(3 \cdot 5) = -15$

(f) $(-6)(-20) = 120$

(g) $3x(y + 2z) = 3xy + 6xz$

(h) $(t^2 + 2t)4t^3 = t^2 4t^3 + 2t4t^3 = 4t^5 + 8t^4$

The algebraic rules can be combined in several ways to give:

$$a(b - c) = a[b + (-c)] = ab + a(-c) = ab - ac$$

$$x(a + b - c + d) = xa + xb - xc + xd$$

$$(a + b)(c + d) = ac + ad + bc + bd$$

Figure 1.3.1 provides a geometric argument for the last of these algebraic rules for the case in which the numbers a, b, c, and d are all positive. The area $(a + b)(c + d)$ of the large rectangle is the sum of the areas of the four small rectangles.

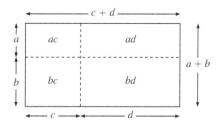

Figure 1.3.1 $(a + b)(c + d) = ac + ad + bc + bd$

Recall the following three "quadratic identities", which are so important that you should definitely memorize them.

$$(a + b)^2 = a^2 + 2ab + b^2$$

$$(a - b)^2 = a^2 - 2ab + b^2$$

$$a^2 - b^2 = (a + b)(a - b)$$

The last of these is called the *difference-of-squares formula*. The proofs are very easy. For example, $(a + b)^2$ means $(a + b)(a + b)$, which equals $aa + ab + ba + bb = a^2 + 2ab + b^2$.

EXAMPLE 1.3.2　　Expand the following expressions:

(a) $(3x + 2y)^2$　　　　(b) $(1 - 2z)^2$　　　　(c) $(4p + 5q)(4p - 5q)$

Solution:

(a) $(3x + 2y)^2 = (3x)^2 + 2(3x)(2y) + (2y)^2 = 9x^2 + 12xy + 4y^2$

(b) $(1 - 2z)^2 = 1 - 2 \cdot 1 \cdot 2 \cdot z + (2z)^2 = 1 - 4z + 4z^2$

(c) $(4p + 5q)(4p - 5q) = (4p)^2 - (5q)^2 = 16p^2 - 25q^2$

We often encounter parentheses with a minus sign in front. Because $(-1)x = -x$,

$$-(a + b - c + d) = -a - b + c - d$$

In words: *When removing a pair of parentheses with a minus in front, change the signs of all the terms within the parentheses — do not leave any out.*

We saw how to multiply two factors, $(a + b)$ and $(c + d)$. How do we compute such products when there are several factors? Here is an example:

$$(a + b)(c + d)(e + f) = [(a + b)(c + d)](e + f)$$
$$= (ac + ad + bc + bd)(e + f)$$
$$= (ac + ad + bc + bd)e + (ac + ad + bc + bd)f$$
$$= ace + ade + bce + bde + acf + adf + bcf + bdf$$

EXAMPLE 1.3.3   Expand the expression $(r + 1)^3$. Use the solution to compute by how much the volume of a ball with radius r metres expands if the radius increases by one metre.

Solution:

$$(r + 1)^3 = [(r + 1)(r + 1)](r + 1) = (r^2 + 2r + 1)(r + 1) = r^3 + 3r^2 + 3r + 1$$

A ball with radius r metres has a volume of $\frac{4}{3}\pi r^3$ cubic metres. If the radius increases by one metre, its volume expands by

$$\frac{4}{3}\pi(r + 1)^3 - \frac{4}{3}\pi r^3 = \frac{4}{3}\pi(r^3 + 3r^2 + 3r + 1) - \frac{4}{3}\pi r^3 = \frac{4}{3}\pi(3r^2 + 3r + 1)$$

Algebraic Expressions

Expressions involving letters such as $3xy - 5x^2y^3 + 2xy + 6y^3x^2 - 3x + 5yx + 8$ are called *algebraic expressions*. We call $3xy$, $-5x^2y^3$, $2xy$, $6y^3x^2$, $-3x$, $5yx$, and 8 the *terms* in the expression that is formed by adding all the terms together. The numbers 3, −5, 2, 6, −3, and 5 are the *numerical coefficients* of the first six terms. Two terms where only the numerical coefficients are different, such as $-5x^2y^3$ and $6y^3x^2$, are called *terms of the same type*. In order to simplify expressions, we collect terms of the same type. Then within each term, we put numerical coefficients first and place the letters in alphabetical order. Thus,

$$3xy - 5x^2y^3 + 2xy + 6y^3x^2 - 3x + 5yx + 8 = x^2y^3 + 10xy - 3x + 8$$

EXAMPLE 1.3.4   Expand and simplify the expression:

$$(2pq - 3p^2)(p + 2q) - (q^2 - 2pq)(2p - q)$$

Solution: The expression equals

$$2pqp + 2pq2q - 3p^3 - 6p^2q - (q^22p - q^3 - 4pqp + 2pq^2)$$
$$= 2p^2q + 4pq^2 - 3p^3 - 6p^2q - 2pq^2 + q^3 + 4p^2q - 2pq^2$$
$$= -3p^3 + q^3$$

Factoring

When we write $49 = 7 \cdot 7$ and $672 = 2 \cdot 2 \cdot 2 \cdot 2 \cdot 2 \cdot 3 \cdot 7$, we have factored these numbers. Algebraic expressions can often be factored in a similar way: to *factor an expression* means to express it as a product of simpler factors. For example, $6x^2y = 2 \cdot 3 \cdot x \cdot x \cdot y$ and $5x^2y^3 - 15xy^2 = 5 \cdot x \cdot y \cdot y(xy - 3)$.[9]

EXAMPLE 1.3.5   Factor each of the following expressions:

(a) $5x^2 + 15x$ (b) $-18b^2 + 9ab$

(c) $K(1 + r) + K(1 + r)r$ (d) $\delta L^{-3} + (1 - \delta)L^{-2}$

Solution:

(a) $5x^2 + 15x = 5x(x + 3)$

(b) $-18b^2 + 9ab = 9ab - 18b^2 = 3 \cdot 3b(a - 2b)$

(c) $K(1 + r) + K(1 + r)r = K(1 + r)(1 + r) = K(1 + r)^2$

(d) $\delta L^{-3} + (1 - \delta)L^{-2} = L^{-3}[\delta + (1 - \delta)L]$

The "quadratic identities" can often be used in reverse for factoring. They sometimes enable us to factor expressions that otherwise appear to have no factors.

EXAMPLE 1.3.6   Factor each of the following expressions:

(a) $16a^2 - 1$ (b) $x^2y^2 - 25z^2$

(c) $4u^2 + 8u + 4$ (d) $x^2 - x + \frac{1}{4}$

Solution:

(a) $16a^2 - 1 = (4a + 1)(4a - 1)$

(b) $x^2y^2 - 25z^2 = (xy + 5z)(xy - 5z)$

(c) $4u^2 + 8u + 4 = 4(u^2 + 2u + 1) = 4(u + 1)^2$

(d) $x^2 - x + \frac{1}{4} = (x - \frac{1}{2})^2$

Sometimes one has to show a measure of inventiveness to find a factoring:

$$4x^2 - y^2 + 6x^2 + 3xy = (4x^2 - y^2) + 3x(2x + y)$$
$$= (2x + y)(2x - y) + 3x(2x + y)$$
$$= (2x + y)(2x - y + 3x)$$
$$= (2x + y)(5x - y)$$

---

[9] Note that $9x^2 - 25y^2 = 3 \cdot 3 \cdot x \cdot x - 5 \cdot 5 \cdot y \cdot y$ does *not* factor $9x^2 - 25y^2$. A correct factoring is $9x^2 - 25y^2 = (3x - 5y)(3x + 5y)$.

Although it might be difficult, sometimes even impossible, to find a factoring, it is very easy to verify that an algebraic expression has been factored correctly by simply multiplying the factors. For example, we check that

$$x^2 - (a + b)x + ab = (x - a)(x - b)$$

by expanding $(x - a)(x - b)$.

Most algebraic expressions *cannot* be factored. For example, there is no way to write $x^2 + 10x + 50$ as a product of simpler factors.[10]

EXERCISES FOR SECTION 1.3

1. Expand and simplify the following expressions:

(a) $-3 + (-4) - (-8)$

(b) $(-3)(2 - 4)$

(c) $(-3)(-12)(-\frac{1}{2})$

(d) $-3[4 - (-2)]$

(e) $-3(-x - 4)$

(f) $(5x - 3y)9$

(g) $2x\left(\frac{3}{2x}\right)$

(h) $0 \cdot (1 - x)$

(i) $-7x\dfrac{2}{14x}$

2. Expand and simplify the following expressions:

(a) $5a^2 - 3b - (-a^2 - b) - 3(a^2 + b)$

(b) $-x(2x - y) + y(1 - x) + 3(x + y)$

(c) $12t^2 - 3t + 16 - 2(6t^2 - 2t + 8)$

(d) $r^3 - 3r^2s + s^3 - (-s^3 - r^3 + 3r^2s)$

3. Expand and simplify the following expressions:

(a) $-3(n^2 - 2n + 3)$

(b) $x^2(1 + x^3)$

(c) $(4n - 3)(n - 2)$

(d) $6a^2b(5ab - 3ab^2)$

(e) $(a^2b - ab^2)(a + b)$

(f) $(x - y)(x - 2y)(x - 3y)$

(g) $(ax + b)(cx + d)$

(h) $(2 - t^2)(2 + t^2)$

(i) $(u - v)^2(u + v)^2$

SM **4.** Expand and simplify the following expressions:

(a) $(2t - 1)(t^2 - 2t + 1)$

(b) $(a + 1)^2 + (a - 1)^2 - 2(a + 1)(a - 1)$

(c) $(x + y + z)^2$

(d) $(x + y + z)^2 - (x - y - z)^2$

5. Expand the following expressions:

(a) $(x + 2y)^2$

(b) $\left(\frac{1}{x} - x\right)^2$

(c) $(3u - 5v)^2$

(d) $(2z - 5w)(2z + 5w)$

6. Complete the following expressions:

(a) $201^2 - 199^2 =$

(b) If $u^2 - 4u + 4 = 1$, then $u =$

(c) $\dfrac{(a + 1)^2 - (a - 1)^2}{(b + 1)^2 - (b - 1)^2} =$

7. Compute $1000^2 / (252^2 - 248^2)$ without using a calculator.

---

[10] Unless we introduce "complex" numbers, that is.

8. Verify the following cubic identities, which are occasionally useful:

   (a) $(a+b)^3 = a^3 + 3a^2b + 3ab^2 + b^3$ (b) $(a-b)^3 = a^3 - 3a^2b + 3ab^2 - b^3$

   (c) $a^3 - b^3 = (a-b)(a^2 + ab + b^2)$ (d) $a^3 + b^3 = (a+b)(a^2 - ab + b^2)$

9. Factor the following expressions:

   (a) $21x^2y^3$ (b) $3x - 9y + 27z$ (c) $a^3 - a^2b$

   (d) $8x^2y^2 - 16xy$ (e) $28a^2b^3$ (f) $4x + 8y - 24z$

   (g) $2x^2 - 6xy$ (h) $4a^2b^3 + 6a^3b^2$ (i) $7x^2 - 49xy$

   (j) $5xy^2 - 45x^3y^2$ (k) $16 - b^2$ (l) $3x^2 - 12$

10. Factor the following expressions:

    (a) $a^2 + 4ab + 4b^2$ (b) $K^2L - L^2K$ (c) $K^{-4} - LK^{-5}$

    (d) $9z^2 - 16w^2$ (e) $-\frac{1}{5}x^2 + 2xy - 5y^2$ (f) $a^4 - b^4$

11. Factor the following expressions:

    (a) $x^2 - 4x + 4$ (b) $4t^2s - 8ts^2$ (c) $16a^2 + 16ab + 4b^2$

    (d) $5x^3 - 10xy^2$ (e) $5x + 5y + ax + ay$ (f) $u^2 - v^2 + 3v + 3u$

    (g) $P^3 + Q^3 + Q^2P + P^2Q$ (h) $K^3 - K^2L$ (i) $KL^3 + KL$

    (j) $L^2 - K^2$ (k) $K^2 - 2KL + L^2$ (l) $K^3L - 4K^2L^2 + 4KL^3$

1.4 Fractions

Recall that

$$a \div b = \frac{a}{b} \begin{array}{l} \leftarrow \text{ numerator} \\ \leftarrow \text{ denominator} \end{array}$$

For example, $5 \div 8 = \frac{5}{8}$. For typographical reasons we often write $5/8$ instead of $\frac{5}{8}$. Of course, $5 \div 8 = 0.625$, in which case we have written the fraction as a decimal number. The fraction $5/8$ is called a *proper fraction* because 5 is less than 8. The fraction $19/8$ is an *improper fraction* because the numerator is larger than (or equal to) the denominator. An improper fraction can be written as a *mixed number*:[11]

$$\frac{19}{8} = 2 + \frac{3}{8} = 2\frac{3}{8}$$

The most important properties of fractions are listed below, with simple numerical examples. It is absolutely essential for you to master these rules, so you should carefully check that you know each of them.

---

[11] Here $2\frac{3}{8}$ means 2 *plus* $\frac{3}{8}$. On the other hand, $2 \cdot \frac{3}{8} = \frac{2 \cdot 3}{8} = \frac{3}{4}$ (by the rules reviewed in what follows). Note, however, that $2\frac{x}{8}$ also means $2 \cdot \frac{x}{8}$; the notation $\frac{2x}{8}$ or $2x/8$ is obviously preferable in this case. Indeed, $\frac{19}{8}$ or $19/8$ is probably better than $2\frac{3}{8}$ because it also helps avoid ambiguity.

PROPERTIES OF FRACTIONS

Let a, b and c be any numbers, with the proviso that $b \neq 0$ and $c \neq 0$ whenever they appear in a denominator. Then,

(i) $\dfrac{a \cdot \cancel{c}}{b \cdot \cancel{c}} = \dfrac{a}{b}$

(ii) $\dfrac{-a}{-b} = \dfrac{(-a) \cdot (-1)}{(-b) \cdot (-1)} = \dfrac{a}{b}$

(iii) $-\dfrac{a}{b} = (-1)\dfrac{a}{b} = \dfrac{(-1)a}{b} = \dfrac{-a}{b}$

(iv) $\dfrac{a}{c} + \dfrac{b}{c} = \dfrac{a+b}{c}$

(v) $\dfrac{a}{b} + \dfrac{c}{d} = \dfrac{a \cdot d + b \cdot c}{b \cdot d}$

(vi) $a + \dfrac{b}{c} = \dfrac{a \cdot c + b}{c}$

(vii) $a \cdot \dfrac{b}{c} = \dfrac{a \cdot b}{c}$

(viii) $\dfrac{a}{b} \cdot \dfrac{c}{d} = \dfrac{a \cdot c}{b \cdot d}$

(ix) $\dfrac{a}{b} \div \dfrac{c}{d} = \dfrac{a}{b} \cdot \dfrac{d}{c} = \dfrac{a \cdot d}{b \cdot c}$

EXAMPLE 1.4.1   The following expressions illustrate the properties of fractions, one by one:

(a) $\dfrac{21}{15} = \dfrac{7 \cdot \cancel{3}}{5 \cdot \cancel{3}} = \dfrac{7}{5}$

(b) $\dfrac{-5}{-6} = \dfrac{5}{6}$

(c) $-\dfrac{13}{15} = (-1)\dfrac{13}{15} = \dfrac{(-1)13}{15} = \dfrac{-13}{15}$

(d) $\dfrac{5}{3} + \dfrac{13}{3} = \dfrac{18}{3} = 6$

(e) $\dfrac{3}{5} + \dfrac{1}{6} = \dfrac{3 \cdot 6 + 5 \cdot 1}{5 \cdot 6} = \dfrac{23}{30}$

(f) $5 + \dfrac{3}{5} = \dfrac{5 \cdot 5 + 3}{5} = \dfrac{28}{5}$

(g) $7 \cdot \dfrac{3}{5} = \dfrac{21}{5}$

(h) $\dfrac{4}{7} \cdot \dfrac{5}{8} = \dfrac{4 \cdot 5}{7 \cdot 8} = \dfrac{\cancel{4} \cdot 5}{7 \cdot 2 \cdot \cancel{4}} = \dfrac{5}{14}$

(i) $\dfrac{3}{8} \div \dfrac{6}{14} = \dfrac{3}{8} \cdot \dfrac{14}{6} = \dfrac{\cancel{3} \cdot \cancel{2} \cdot 7}{\cancel{2} \cdot 2 \cdot 2 \cdot 2 \cdot \cancel{3}} = \dfrac{7}{8}$

Property (i) is very important. It is the rule used to reduce fractions by factoring the numerator and the denominator, then cancelling *common factors*—that is, dividing both the numerator and denominator by the same nonzero quantity.[12]

EXAMPLE 1.4.2   Simplify the expressions:

(a) $\dfrac{5x^2 yz^3}{25xy^2 z}$

(b) $\dfrac{x^2 + xy}{x^2 - y^2}$

(c) $\dfrac{4 - 4a + a^2}{a^2 - 4}$

---

[12] When we use property (i) in reverse, we are *expanding* the fraction. For example, $5/8 = 5 \cdot 125 / 8 \cdot 125 = 625/1000 = 0.625$.

Solution:

(a) $\dfrac{5x^2yz^3}{25xy^2z} = \dfrac{\cancel{5} \cdot \cancel{x} \cdot x \cdot \cancel{y} \cdot \cancel{z} \cdot z \cdot z}{\cancel{5} \cdot 5 \cdot \cancel{x} \cdot \cancel{y} \cdot y \cdot \cancel{z}} = \dfrac{xz^2}{5y}$

(b) $\dfrac{x^2 + xy}{x^2 - y^2} = \dfrac{x(x+y)}{(x-y)(x+y)} = \dfrac{x}{x-y}$

(c) $\dfrac{4 - 4a + a^2}{a^2 - 4} = \dfrac{(a-2)(a-2)}{(a-2)(a+2)} = \dfrac{a-2}{a+2}$

EXAMPLE 1.4.3   When we simplify fractions, only *common* factors can be removed. A frequently occurring error is illustrated in the following expression:

$$\text{Wrong!} \quad \rightarrow \quad \frac{2\cancel{x} + 3y}{\cancel{x}y} = \frac{2 + 3\cancel{y}}{\cancel{y}} = \frac{2 + 3}{1} = 5$$

In fact, the numerator and the denominator in the fraction $(2x + 3y)/xy$ do not have any common factors. But a correct simplification is this: $(2x + 3y)/xy = 2/y + 3/x$.

Another common error is:

$$\text{Wrong!} \quad \rightarrow \quad \frac{x}{x^2 + 2x} = \frac{x}{x^2} + \frac{x}{2x} = \frac{1}{x} + \frac{1}{2}$$

A correct way of simplifying the fraction is to cancel the common factor x, which yields the fraction $1/(x + 2)$.

Properties (iv) to (vi) are those used to add fractions. Note that (v) follows from (i) and (iv). Then we see:

$$\frac{a}{b} + \frac{c}{d} = \frac{a \cdot d}{b \cdot d} + \frac{c \cdot b}{d \cdot b} = \frac{a \cdot d + b \cdot c}{b \cdot d}$$

and we see easily that, for example,

$$\frac{a}{b} - \frac{c}{d} + \frac{e}{f} = \frac{adf}{bdf} - \frac{cbf}{bdf} + \frac{ebd}{bdf} = \frac{adf - cbf + ebd}{bdf} \qquad (*)$$

If the numbers b, d, and f have common factors, the computation carried out in $(*)$ involves unnecessarily large numbers. We can simplify the process by first finding the least common denominator (LCD) of the fractions. To do so, factor each denominator completely; the LCD is the product of all the distinct factors that appear in any denominator, each raised to the highest power to which it gets raised in any denominator. The use of the LCD is demonstrated in the following example.

EXAMPLE 1.4.4   Simplify the following expressions:

(a) $\dfrac{1}{2} - \dfrac{1}{3} + \dfrac{1}{6}$ (b) $\dfrac{2 + a}{a^2 b} + \dfrac{1 - b}{ab^2} - \dfrac{2b}{a^2 b^2}$ (c) $\dfrac{x - y}{x + y} - \dfrac{x}{x - y} + \dfrac{3xy}{x^2 - y^2}$

Solution:

(a) The LCD is 6 and so $\dfrac{1}{2} - \dfrac{1}{3} + \dfrac{1}{6} = \dfrac{1\cdot 3}{2\cdot 3} - \dfrac{1\cdot 2}{2\cdot 3} + \dfrac{1}{2\cdot 3} = \dfrac{3-2+1}{6} = \dfrac{2}{6} = \dfrac{1}{3}$

(b) The LCD is a^2b^2 and so

$$\frac{2+a}{a^2 b} + \frac{1-b}{ab^2} - \frac{2b}{a^2 b^2} = \frac{(2+a)b}{a^2 b^2} + \frac{(1-b)a}{a^2 b^2} - \frac{2b}{a^2 b^2} = \frac{2b+ab+a-ba-2b}{a^2 b^2}$$

$$= \frac{a}{a^2 b^2} = \frac{1}{ab^2}$$

(c) The LCD is $(x+y)(x-y)$ and so

$$\frac{x-y}{x+y} - \frac{x}{x-y} + \frac{3xy}{x^2-y^2} = \frac{(x-y)(x-y)}{(x-y)(x+y)} - \frac{(x+y)x}{(x+y)(x-y)} + \frac{3xy}{(x-y)(x+y)}$$

$$= \frac{x^2 - 2xy + y^2 - x^2 - xy + 3xy}{(x-y)(x+y)}$$

$$= \frac{y^2}{x^2 - y^2}$$

The expression $1 - \frac{5-3}{2}$ means that from the number 1, we subtract the number $\frac{5-3}{2} = \frac{2}{2} = 1$, so $1 - \frac{5-3}{2} = 0$. Alternatively,

$$1 - \frac{5-3}{2} = \frac{2}{2} - \frac{(5-3)}{2} = \frac{2-(5-3)}{2} = \frac{2-5+3}{2} = \frac{0}{2} = 0$$

In the same way,

$$\frac{2+b}{ab^2} - \frac{a-2}{a^2 b}$$

means that we subtract $(a-2)/a^2 b$ from $(2+b)/ab^2$:

$$\frac{2+b}{ab^2} - \frac{a-2}{a^2 b} = \frac{(2+b)a}{a^2 b^2} - \frac{(a-2)b}{a^2 b^2} = \frac{(2+b)a-(a-2)b}{a^2 b^2} = \frac{2(a+b)}{a^2 b^2}$$

It is a good idea first to enclose in parentheses the numerators of the fractions, as in the next example.

EXAMPLE 1.4.5   Simplify the expression:

$$\frac{x-1}{x+1} - \frac{1-x}{x-1} - \frac{-1+4x}{2(x+1)}$$

Solution:

$$\frac{x-1}{x+1} - \frac{1-x}{x-1} - \frac{-1+4x}{2(x+1)} = \frac{(x-1)}{x+1} - \frac{(1-x)}{x-1} - \frac{(-1+4x)}{2(x+1)}$$

$$= \frac{2(x-1)^2 - 2(1-x)(x+1) - (-1+4x)(x-1)}{2(x+1)(x-1)}$$

$$= \frac{2(x^2-2x+1) - 2(1-x^2) - (4x^2-5x+1)}{2(x+1)(x-1)}$$

$$= \frac{x-1}{2(x+1)(x-1)} = \frac{1}{2(x+1)}$$

We prove property (ix) by writing $(a/b) \div (c/d)$ as a ratio of fractions:[13]

$$\frac{a}{b} \div \frac{c}{d} = \frac{\frac{a}{b}}{\frac{c}{d}} = \frac{b \cdot d \cdot \frac{a}{b}}{b \cdot d \cdot \frac{c}{d}} = \frac{\frac{\not{b} \cdot d \cdot a}{\not{b}}}{\frac{b \cdot \not{d} \cdot c}{\not{d}}} = \frac{d \cdot a}{b \cdot c} = \frac{a \cdot d}{b \cdot c} = \frac{a}{b} \cdot \frac{c}{d}$$

When we deal with fractions of fractions, we should be sure to emphasize which is the fraction line of the dominant fraction. For example,

$$\frac{a}{\frac{b}{c}} = a \div \frac{b}{c} = \frac{ac}{b} \qquad (*)$$

whereas

$$\frac{\frac{a}{b}}{c} = \frac{a}{b} \div c = \frac{a}{bc} \qquad (**)$$

Of course, it is safer to write $\frac{a}{b/c}$ or $a/(b/c)$ in the first case, and $\frac{a/b}{c}$ or $(a/b)/c$ in the second case.[14]

EXERCISES FOR SECTION 1.4

1. Simplify the following expressions:

(a) $\dfrac{3}{7} + \dfrac{4}{7} - \dfrac{5}{7}$ (b) $\dfrac{3}{4} + \dfrac{4}{3} - 1$ (c) $\dfrac{3}{12} - \dfrac{1}{24}$ (d) $\dfrac{1}{5} - \dfrac{2}{25} - \dfrac{3}{75}$

(e) $3\dfrac{3}{5} - 1\dfrac{4}{5}$ (f) $\dfrac{3}{5} \cdot \dfrac{5}{6}$ (g) $\left(\dfrac{3}{5} \div \dfrac{2}{15}\right) \cdot \dfrac{1}{9}$ (h) $\left(\dfrac{2}{3} + \dfrac{1}{4}\right) \Big/ \left(\dfrac{3}{4} + \dfrac{3}{2}\right)$

2. Simplify the following expressions:

(a) $\dfrac{x}{10} - \dfrac{3x}{10} + \dfrac{17x}{10}$ (b) $\dfrac{9a}{10} - \dfrac{a}{2} + \dfrac{a}{5}$ (c) $\dfrac{b+2}{10} - \dfrac{3b}{15} + \dfrac{b}{10}$

(d) $\dfrac{x+2}{3} + \dfrac{1-3x}{4}$ (e) $\dfrac{3}{2b} - \dfrac{5}{3b}$ (f) $\dfrac{3a-2}{3a} - \dfrac{2b-1}{2b} + \dfrac{4b+3a}{6ab}$

3. Cancel common factors in the following expressions:

(a) $\dfrac{325}{625}$ (b) $\dfrac{8a^2b^3c}{64abc^3}$ (c) $\dfrac{2a^2 - 2b^2}{3a + 3b}$ (d) $\dfrac{P^3 - PQ^2}{(P+Q)^2}$

---

[13] Illustration: You buy half a litre of a soft drink. Each sip is one fiftieth of a litre. How many sips? Answer: $(1/2) \div (1/50) = 25$. One easily becomes thirsty reading this stuff!

[14] As a numerical example of $(*)$ and $(**)$,

$$\frac{1}{\frac{3}{5}} = \frac{5}{3}, \quad \text{whereas} \quad \frac{\frac{1}{3}}{5} = \frac{1}{15}$$

4. If $x = 3/7$ and $y = 1/14$, find the simplest forms of the following fractions:

(a) $x + y$　　　(b) x/y　　　(c) $(x - y)/(x + y)$　　　(d) $13(2x - 3y)/(2x + 1)$

(SM) **5.** Simplify the following expressions:

(a) $\dfrac{1}{x - 2} - \dfrac{1}{x + 2}$　　　(b) $\dfrac{6x + 25}{4x + 2} - \dfrac{6x^2 + x - 2}{4x^2 - 1}$　　　(c) $\dfrac{18b^2}{a^2 - 9b^2} - \dfrac{a}{a + 3b} + 2$

(d) $\dfrac{1}{8ab} - \dfrac{1}{8b(a + 2)}$　　　(e) $\dfrac{2t - t^2}{t + 2} \cdot \left(\dfrac{5t}{t - 2} - \dfrac{2t}{t - 2} \right)$　　　(f) $2 - \dfrac{a\left(1 - \frac{1}{2a}\right)}{0.25}$

(SM) **6.** Simplify the following expressions:

(a) $\dfrac{2}{x} + \dfrac{1}{x + 1} - 3$　　　(b) $\dfrac{t}{2t + 1} - \dfrac{t}{2t - 1}$　　　(c) $\dfrac{3x}{x + 2} - \dfrac{4x}{2 - x} - \dfrac{2x - 1}{x^2 - 4}$

(d) $\dfrac{1/x + 1/y}{1/xy}$　　　(e) $\dfrac{1/x^2 - 1/y^2}{1/x^2 + 1/y^2}$　　　(f) $\dfrac{a/x - a/y}{a/x + a/y}$

7. Verify that $x^2 + 2xy - 3y^2 = (x + 3y)(x - y)$, and then simplify the expression:

$$\frac{x - y}{x^2 + 2xy - 3y^2} - \frac{2}{x - y} - \frac{7}{x + 3y}$$

(SM) **8.** Simplify the following expressions:

(a) $\left(\dfrac{1}{4} - \dfrac{1}{5} \right)^{-2}$　　　(b) $n - \dfrac{n}{1 - \frac{1}{n}}$　　　(c) $\dfrac{1}{1 + x^{p-q}} + \dfrac{1}{1 + x^{q-p}}$

(d) $\dfrac{\dfrac{1}{x - 1} + \dfrac{1}{x^2 - 1}}{x - \dfrac{2}{x + 1}}$　　　(e) $\dfrac{\dfrac{1}{(x + h)^2} - \dfrac{1}{x^2}}{h}$　　　(f) $\dfrac{\dfrac{10x^2}{x^2 - 1}}{\dfrac{5x}{x + 1}}$

1.5　Fractional Powers

In textbooks and research articles on economics, we constantly see powers with fractional exponents such as $K^{1/4}L^{3/4}$ and $Ar^{2.08}p^{-1.5}$. How do we define a^x when x is a rational number? Of course, we would like the usual rules for powers still to apply.

　　You probably know the meaning of a^x if $x = 1/2$. In fact, if $a \geq 0$ and $x = 1/2$, then we define $a^x = a^{1/2}$ as equal to $\sqrt{a}$, the *square root* of a. Thus, $a^{1/2} = \sqrt{a}$ is defined as the nonnegative number that when multiplied by itself gives a. This definition makes sense because $a^{1/2} \cdot a^{1/2} = a^{1/2+1/2} = a^1 = a$. Note that a real number multiplied by itself must always be nonnegative, whether that number is positive, negative, or zero. Hence, if $a \geq 0$,

$$a^{1/2} = \sqrt{a}$$

For example, $\sqrt{16} = 16^{1/2} = 4$ because $4^2 = 16$ and $\sqrt{1/25} = 1/5$ because

$$\frac{1}{5} \cdot \frac{1}{5} = \frac{1}{25}$$

PROPERTIES OF SQUARE ROOTS

(i) If a and b are nonnegative numbers, then

$$\sqrt{ab} = \sqrt{a}\sqrt{b}$$

(ii) If $a \geq 0$ and $b > 0$, then

$$\sqrt{\frac{a}{b}} = \frac{\sqrt{a}}{\sqrt{b}}$$

Of course, these rules can also be written $(ab)^{1/2} = a^{1/2}b^{1/2}$ and $(a/b)^{1/2} = a^{1/2}/b^{1/2}$. For example, $\sqrt{16 \cdot 25} = \sqrt{16} \cdot \sqrt{25} = 4 \cdot 5 = 20$, and $\sqrt{9/4} = \sqrt{9}/\sqrt{4} = 3/2$.

Note that formulas (i) and (ii) are not valid if a or b or both are negative. For example, $\sqrt{(-1)(-1)} = \sqrt{1} = 1$, whereas $\sqrt{-1} \cdot \sqrt{-1}$ is not defined (unless one uses complex numbers).

It is important to recall that, in general, $(a + b)^r \neq a^r + b^r$. For $r = 1/2$, this implies that we generally have[15]

$$\sqrt{a + b} \neq \sqrt{a} + \sqrt{b}$$

Note also that $(-2)^2 = 4$ and $2^2 = 4$, so both $x = -2$ and $x = 2$ are solutions of the equation $x^2 = 4$. Therefore we have $x^2 = 4$ if and only if $x = \pm\sqrt{4} = \pm 2$. Note, however, that the symbol $\sqrt{4}$ means *only* 2, not -2.

By using a calculator, we find that $\sqrt{2} \div \sqrt{3} \approx 0.816$. Without a calculator, the division $\sqrt{2} \div \sqrt{3} \approx 1.414 \div 1.732$ would be tedious. But if we expand the fraction by rationalizing the denominator—that is, if we multiply both numerator and denominator by the same term in order to remove expressions with roots in the denominator—it becomes easier:

$$\frac{\sqrt{2}}{\sqrt{3}} = \frac{\sqrt{2} \cdot \sqrt{3}}{\sqrt{3} \cdot \sqrt{3}} = \frac{\sqrt{2 \cdot 3}}{3} = \frac{\sqrt{6}}{3} \approx \frac{2.448}{3} = 0.816$$

---

[15] The following observation illustrates just how frequently this fact is overlooked: During an examination in a basic course in mathematics for economists, 22% of 190 students simplified $\sqrt{1/16 + 1/25}$ incorrectly and claimed that it was equal to $1/4 + 1/5 = 9/20$. The correct answer is $\sqrt{41/400} = \sqrt{41}/20$.

Sometimes the difference-of-squares formula of Section 1.3 can be used to eliminate square roots from the denominator of a fraction:

$$\frac{1}{\sqrt{5}+\sqrt{3}} = \frac{\sqrt{5}-\sqrt{3}}{\left(\sqrt{5}+\sqrt{3}\right)\left(\sqrt{5}-\sqrt{3}\right)} = \frac{\sqrt{5}-\sqrt{3}}{5-3} = \frac{1}{2}\left(\sqrt{5}-\sqrt{3}\right)$$

The *n*-th Root

What do we mean by $a^{1/n}$, where n is a natural number, and a is positive? For example, what does $5^{1/3}$ mean? If the rule $(a^r)^s = a^{rs}$ is still to apply in this case, we must have $(5^{1/3})^3 = 5^1 = 5$. This implies that $5^{1/3}$ must be a solution of the equation $x^3 = 5$. Using the intermediate value theorem 7.10.1, this equation can be shown to have a unique positive solution, denoted by $\sqrt[3]{5}$, the *cube root* of 5. Therefore, we must define $5^{1/3}$ as $\sqrt[3]{5}$.

In general, $(a^{1/n})^n = a^1 = a$. Thus, $a^{1/n}$ is a solution of the equation $x^n = a$. Using theorem 7.10.1 again, this equation can be shown to have a unique positive solution denoted by $\sqrt[n]{a}$, the *n-th root* of a:

$$a^{1/n} = \sqrt[n]{a}$$

THE *n*-th ROOT

If a is positive and n is a natural number, then $\sqrt[n]{a}$ is the unique positive number that, raised to the *n*-th power, gives a—that is,

$$\left(\sqrt[n]{a}\right)^n = a$$

EXAMPLE 1.5.1   Compute the following numbers:

(a) $\sqrt[3]{27}$ (b) $(1/32)^{1/5}$ (c) $(0.0001)^{0.25} = (0.0001)^{1/4}$

Solution:

(a) $\sqrt[3]{27} = 3$, because $3^3 = 27$
(b) $(1/32)^{1/5} = 1/2$ because $(1/2)^5 = 1/32$
(c) $(0.0001)^{1/4} = 0.1$ because $(0.1)^4 = 0.0001$

EXAMPLE 1.5.2   An amount \$5 000 in an account has increased to \$10 000 in 15 years. What constant yearly interest rate p has been used?

Solution: After 15 years the amount of \$5 000 has grown to $5000(1 + p/100)^{15}$, so we have the equation

$$5000\left(1 + \frac{p}{100}\right)^{15} = 10\,000$$

or

$$\left(1 + \frac{p}{100}\right)^{15} = 2$$

In general, $(a^t)^{1/t} = a^1 = a$ for $t \neq 0$. Raising each side to the power of 1/15 yields

$$1 + \frac{p}{100} = 2^{1/15}$$

or $p = 100(2^{1/15} - 1)$. With a calculator we find $p \approx 4.73$.

We proceed to define $a^{p/q}$ whenever p is an integer, q is a natural number, and $a > 0$. Consider first $5^{2/3}$. We have already defined $5^{1/3}$. For the second property of powers that we saw in Section 1.2, namely that $(a^r)^s = a^{rs}$, to apply, we must have $5^{2/3} = (5^{1/3})^2$. So we must define $5^{2/3}$ as $\left(\sqrt[3]{5}\right)^2$. In general, for $a > 0$, we define

$$a^{p/q} = \left(a^{1/q}\right)^p = \left(\sqrt[q]{a}\right)^p$$

when p is an integer and q a natural number. From the properties of exponents,

$$a^{p/q} = \left(a^{1/q}\right)^p = \left(a^p\right)^{1/q} = \sqrt[q]{a^p}$$

Thus, to compute $a^{p/q}$, we could either first take the q-th root of a and raise the result to p, or first raise a to the power p and then take the q-th root of the result. We obtain the same answer either way.[16] For example,

$$4^{7/2} = (4^7)^{1/2} = 16384^{1/2} = 128 = 2^7 = (4^{1/2})^7$$

EXAMPLE 1.5.3   Compute the numbers:

(a) $16^{3/2}$ (b) $16^{-1.25}$ (c) $(1/27)^{-2/3}$

Solution:

(a) $16^{3/2} = (16^{1/2})^3 = 4^3 = 64$

(b) $16^{-1.25} = 16^{-5/4} = \frac{1}{16^{5/4}} = \frac{1}{\left(\sqrt[4]{16}\right)^5} = \frac{1}{2^5} = \frac{1}{32}$

(c) $(1/27)^{-2/3} = 27^{2/3} = \left(\sqrt[3]{27}\right)^2 = 3^2 = 9$

---

[16] Tests reveal that many students, while they are able to handle quadratic identities, nevertheless make mistakes when dealing with more complicated powers. Here are examples taken from recent tests:

(a) $(1 + r)^{20}$ is *not* equal to $1^{20} + r^{20}$.
(b) If $u = 9 + x^{1/2}$, it does *not* follow that $u^2 = 81 + x$; instead $u^2 = 81 + 18x^{1/2} + x$.
(c) $(e^x - e^{-x})^p$ is *not* equal to $e^{xp} - e^{-xp}$ (unless $p = 1$).

EXAMPLE 1.5.4   Simplify the following expressions so that the answers contain only positive exponents:

(a) $\dfrac{a^{3/8}}{a^{1/8}}$ (b) $(x^{1/2}x^{3/2}x^{-2/3})^{3/4}$ (c) $\left(\dfrac{10p^{-1}q^{2/3}}{80p^2q^{-7/3}}\right)^{-2/3}$

Solution:

(a) $\dfrac{a^{3/8}}{a^{1/8}} = a^{3/8-1/8} = a^{2/8} = a^{1/4} = \sqrt[4]{a}$

(b) $(x^{1/2}x^{3/2}x^{-2/3})^{3/4} = (x^{1/2+3/2-2/3})^{3/4} = (x^{4/3})^{3/4} = x$

(c) $\left(\dfrac{10p^{-1}q^{2/3}}{80p^2q^{-7/3}}\right)^{-2/3} = (8^{-1}p^{-1-2}q^{2/3-(-7/3)})^{-2/3} = 8^{2/3}p^2q^{-2} = 4\dfrac{p^2}{q^2}$

If q is an odd number and p is an integer, $a^{p/q}$ can be defined even when $a < 0$. For example, $(-8)^{1/3} = \sqrt[3]{-8} = -2$, because $(-2)^3 = -8$. However, in defining $a^{p/q}$ when $a < 0$, q must be odd. If not, we could get contradictions such as "$-2 = (-8)^{1/3} = (-8)^{2/6} = \sqrt[6]{(-8)^2} = \sqrt[6]{64} = 2$".

When computing $a^{p/q}$ it is often easier to find $\sqrt[q]{a}$ first and then raise the result to the p-th power. For example, $(-64)^{5/3} = (\sqrt[3]{-64})^5 = (-4)^5 = -1024$.

EXERCISES FOR SECTION 1.5

1. Compute the following numbers:

(a) $\sqrt{9}$ (b) $\sqrt{1600}$ (c) $(100)^{1/2}$ (d) $\sqrt{9+16}$

(e) $(36)^{-1/2}$ (f) $(0.49)^{1/2}$ (g) $\sqrt{0.01}$ (h) $\sqrt{1/25}$

2. Let a and b be positive numbers. Decide whether each "?" should be replaced by $=$ or $\neq$. Justify your answer.

(a) $\sqrt{25 \cdot 16}$? $\sqrt{25} \cdot \sqrt{16}$ (b) $\sqrt{25+16}$? $\sqrt{25}+\sqrt{16}$

(c) $(a+b)^{1/2}$? $a^{1/2}+b^{1/2}$ (d) $(a+b)^{-1/2}$? $(\sqrt{a+b})^{-1}$

3. Solve for x the following equalities:

(a) $\sqrt{x} = 9$ (b) $\sqrt{x} \cdot \sqrt{4} = 4$ (c) $\sqrt{x+2} = 25$

(d) $\sqrt{3} \cdot \sqrt{5} = \sqrt{x}$ (e) $2^{2-x} = 8$ (f) $2^x - 2^{x-1} = 4$

4. Rationalize the denominator and simplify the following expressions:

(a) $\dfrac{6}{\sqrt{7}}$ (b) $\dfrac{\sqrt{32}}{\sqrt{2}}$ (c) $\dfrac{\sqrt{3}}{4\sqrt{2}}$ (d) $\dfrac{\sqrt{54}-\sqrt{24}}{\sqrt{6}}$

(e) $\dfrac{2}{\sqrt{3}\sqrt{8}}$ (f) $\dfrac{4}{\sqrt{2y}}$ (g) $\dfrac{x}{\sqrt{2x}}$ (h) $\dfrac{x(\sqrt{x}+1)}{\sqrt{x}}$

(SM) **5.** Simplify the following expressions by making the denominators rational:

(a) $\dfrac{1}{\sqrt{7}+\sqrt{5}}$ (b) $\dfrac{\sqrt{5}-\sqrt{3}}{\sqrt{5}+\sqrt{3}}$ (c) $\dfrac{x}{\sqrt{3}-2}$

(d) $\dfrac{x\sqrt{y}-y\sqrt{x}}{x\sqrt{y}+y\sqrt{x}}$ (e) $\dfrac{h}{\sqrt{x+h}-\sqrt{x}}$ (f) $\dfrac{1-\sqrt{x+1}}{1+\sqrt{x+1}}$

6. Compute, without using a calculator, the following numbers:

(a) $\sqrt[3]{125}$ (b) $(243)^{1/5}$ (c) $(-8)^{1/3}$ (d) $\sqrt[3]{0.008}$

(e) $81^{1/2}$ (f) $64^{-1/3}$ (g) $16^{-2.25}$ (h) $\left(\dfrac{1}{3^{-2}}\right)^{-2}$

7. Using a calculator, find approximations to:

(a) $\sqrt[3]{55}$ (b) $(160)^{1/4}$ (c) $(2.71828)^{1/5}$ (d) $(1+0.0001)^{10\,000}$

8. The population of a nation increased from 40 million to 60 million in 12 years. What is the yearly percentage rate of growth p?

9. Simplify the following expressions:

(a) $\left(27x^{3p}y^{6q}z^{12r}\right)^{1/3}$ (b) $\dfrac{(x+15)^{4/3}}{(x+15)^{5/6}}$ (c) $\dfrac{8\sqrt[3]{x^2}\,\sqrt[4]{y}\sqrt{1/z}}{-2\sqrt[3]{x}\sqrt{y^5}\,\sqrt{z}}$

10. Simplify the following expressions, so that each contains only a single exponent:

(a) $\{[(a^{1/2})^{2/3}]^{3/4}\}^{4/5}$ (b) $a^{1/2}\cdot a^{2/3}\cdot a^{3/4}\cdot a^{4/5}$

(c) $\{[(3a)^{-1}]^{-2}(2a^{-2})^{-1}\}/a^{-3}$ (d) $\dfrac{\sqrt[3]{a}\cdot a^{1/12}\cdot\sqrt[4]{a^3}}{a^{5/12}\cdot\sqrt{a}}$

(SM) **11.** Which of the following equations are valid for all x and y?

(a) $(2^x)^2 = 2^{x^2}$ (b) $3^{x-3y} = \dfrac{3^x}{3^{3y}}$

(c) $3^{-1/x} = \dfrac{1}{3^{1/x}}$, with $x\neq 0$ (d) $5^{1/x} = \dfrac{1}{5^x}$, with $x\neq 0$

(e) $a^{x+y} = a^x + a^y$ (f) $2^{\sqrt{x}}\cdot 2^{\sqrt{y}} = 2^{\sqrt{xy}}$ with x and y positive

12. If a firm uses x units of input in process A, it produces $32x^{3/2}$ units of output. In the alternative process B, the same input produces $4x^3$ units of output. For what levels of input does process A produce more than process B?

1.6 Inequalities

The real numbers consist of the positive numbers, 0, and the negative numbers. If a is a positive number, we write $a > 0$ (or $0 < a$), and we say that a is greater than zero. If the number c is negative, we write $c < 0$ (or $0 > c$).

A fundamental property of the positive numbers is that:

$$(a > 0 \text{ and } b > 0) \Rightarrow (a + b > 0 \text{ and } a \cdot b > 0) \tag{1.6.1}$$

In general, we say that *the number a is greater than the number b*, and we write $a > b$ (or $b < a$), if $a - b$ is positive. Thus, $4.11 > 3.12$ because $4.11 - 3.12 = 0.99 > 0$, and $-3 > -5$ because $-3 - (-5) = 2 > 0$. On the number line, Fig. 1.1.1, $a > b$ means that a lies to the right of b.

When $a > b$, we often say that a *is strictly greater than b* in order to emphasize that $a = b$ is ruled out. If $a > b$ or $a = b$, then we write $a \geq b$ (or $b \leq a$) and say that a is *greater than or equal to b*. Thus, $a \geq b$ means that $a - b \geq 0$. For example, $4 \geq 4$ and $4 \geq 2$.[17] We call $>$ and $<$ *strict* inequalities, whereas $\geq$ and $\leq$ are *weak* inequalities. The difference is often very important in economic analysis.

One can prove a number of important properties of $>$ and $\geq$. For example, for any number c

$$a > b \Rightarrow a + c > b + c \tag{1.6.2}$$

The argument is simple: one has $(a + c) - (b + c) = a + c - b - c = a - b$ for all numbers a, b, and c. Hence $a - b > 0$ implies $(a + c) - (b + c) > 0$, so the conclusion follows. On the number line shown in Fig. 1.6.1, this implication is self-evident (here c is chosen to be negative):

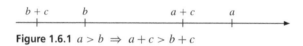

Figure 1.6.1 $a > b \Rightarrow a + c > b + c$

Dealing with more complicated inequalities involves using the following properties:

PROPERTIES OF INEQUALITIES

Let a, b, c, and d be numbers

$$(a > b \text{ and } b > c) \Rightarrow a > c \tag{1.6.3}$$

$$(a > b \text{ and } c > 0) \Rightarrow ac > bc \tag{1.6.4}$$

$$(a > b \text{ and } c < 0) \Rightarrow ac < bc \tag{1.6.5}$$

$$(a > b \text{ and } c > d) \Rightarrow a + c > b + d \tag{1.6.6}$$

All four properties remain valid when each $>$ is replaced by $\geq$, and each $<$ by $\leq$. The properties all follow easily from (1.6.1). For example, property (1.6.5) is proved as

---

[17] Note in particular that it *is* correct to write $4 \geq 2$, because $4 - 2$ *is* positive or 0.

follows: Suppose $a > b$ and $c < 0$. Then $a - b > 0$ and $-c > 0$, so, according to (1.6.1), $(a - b)(-c) > 0$. Hence $-ac + bc > 0$, implying that $ac < bc$.

According to (1.6.4) and (1.6.5):

(a) If the two sides of an inequality are multiplied by a positive number, the direction of the inequality is preserved.

(b) If the two sides of an inequality are multiplied by a negative number, the direction of the inequality is reversed.

It is important that you understand these rules, and realize that they correspond to everyday experience. For instance, (1.6.4) can be interpreted this way: given two rectangles with the same base, the one with the larger height has the larger area.

EXAMPLE 1.6.1   Find what values of x satisfy $3x - 5 > x - 3$.

Solution: Adding 5 to both sides of the inequality yields $3x - 5 + 5 > x - 3 + 5$, or $3x > x + 2$. Adding $(-x)$ to both sides yields $3x - x > x - x + 2$, so $2x > 2$, and after dividing by the positive number 2, we get $x > 1$. The argument can obviously be reversed, so the solution is $x > 1$.

Sign Diagrams

EXAMPLE 1.6.2   Check whether the inequality $(x - 1)(3 - x) > 0$ is satisfied for $x = -3$, $x = 2$, and $x = 5$. Then, find all the values x that satisfy the same inequality.

Solution: For $x = -3$, we have $(x - 1)(3 - x) = (-4) \cdot 6 = -24 < 0$; for $x = 2$, we have $(x - 1)(3 - x) = 1 \cdot 1 = 1 > 0$; and for $x = 5$, we have $(x - 1)(3 - x) = 4 \cdot (-2) = -8 < 0$. Hence, the inequality is satisfied for $x = 2$, but not for $x = -3$ or $x = 5$.

To find the entire solution set, we use a *sign diagram*. The sign variation for each factor in the product is determined. For example, the factor $x - 1$ is negative when $x < 1$, is 0 when $x = 1$, and is positive when $x > 1$. This sign variation is represented in Fig. 1.6.2.

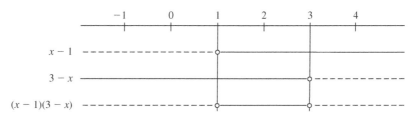

Figure 1.6.2 Sign diagram for $(x - 1)(3 - x)$

The upper dashed line to the left of the vertical line $x = 1$ indicates that $x - 1 < 0$ if $x < 1$; the small circle indicates that $x - 1 = 0$ when $x = 1$; and the solid line to the right of $x = 1$ indicates that $x - 1 > 0$ if $x > 1$. In a similar way, we represent the sign variation for $3 - x$. The sign variation of the product is obtained as follows. If $x < 1$, then $x - 1$ is negative and $3 - x$ is positive, so the product is negative. If $1 < x < 3$, both factors are positive, so the product is positive. If $x > 3$, then $x - 1$ is positive and $3 - x$ is negative, so the product is negative. In conclusion: The solution set consists of those x that are greater than 1, but less than 3. So $(x - 1)(3 - x) > 0 \Leftrightarrow 1 < x < 3$.

EXAMPLE 1.6.3   Find all values of p that satisfy the inequality:

$$\frac{2p - 3}{p - 1} > 3 - p$$

Solution: It is tempting to begin by multiplying each side of the inequality by $p - 1$. However, then we must distinguish between the two cases, $p - 1 > 0$ and $p - 1 < 0$, because if we multiply through by $p - 1$ when $p - 1 < 0$, we have to reverse the inequality sign. There is an alternative method, which makes it unnecessary to distinguish between two different cases. We begin by adding $p - 3$ to both sides. This yields

$$\frac{2p - 3}{p - 1} + p - 3 > 0$$

Making $p - 1$ the common denominator gives

$$\frac{2p - 3 + (p - 3)(p - 1)}{p - 1} > 0$$

Because $2p - 3 + (p - 3)(p - 1) = 2p - 3 + p^2 - 4p + 3 = p^2 - 2p = p(p - 2)$, substituting this in the numerator gives

$$\frac{p(p - 2)}{p - 1} > 0$$

To find the solution set, we again use a sign diagram. On the basis of the sign variations for p, $p - 2$, and $p - 1$, the sign variation for $p(p - 2)/(p - 1)$ is determined. For example, if $0 < p < 1$, then p is positive and $(p - 2)$ is negative, so $p(p - 2)$ is negative. But $p - 1$ is also negative on this interval, so $p(p - 2)/(p - 1)$ is positive. Arguing this way for all the relevant intervals leads to the sign diagram shown in Fig. 1.6.3.[18]

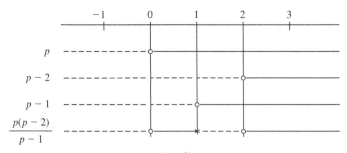

Figure 1.6.3 Sign diagram for $\dfrac{p(p - 2)}{p - 1}$

So the original inequality is satisfied if and only if $0 < p < 1$ or $p > 2$.

---

[18] The original inequality has no meaning when $p = 1$.

Two notes of warning are in order. First, note the most common error committed in solving inequalities, which is precisely that indicated in Example 1.6.3: if we multiply by $p - 1$, the inequality is preserved *only* if $p - 1$ is positive—that is, if $p > 1$. Second, it is vital that you really understand the method of sign diagrams. Another common error is illustrated by the following example.

EXAMPLE 1.6.4   Find all values of x that satisfy the inequality:

$$\frac{(x - 2) + 3(x + 1)}{x + 3} \leq 0$$

"Solution": Suppose we construct the inappropriate sign diagram shown in Fig. 1.6.4.

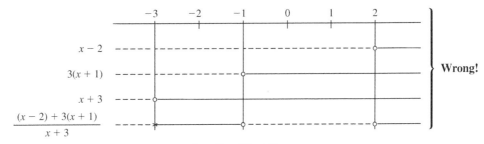

Figure 1.6.4 Wrong sign diagram for $\dfrac{(x - 2) + 3(x + 1)}{x + 3}$

According to this diagram, the inequality should be satisfied for $x < -3$ and for $-1 \leq x \leq 2$. However, for $x = -4$ (< -3), the fraction reduces to 15, which is positive. What went wrong? Suppose $x < -3$. Then $x - 2 < 0$ and $3(x + 1) < 0$ and, therefore, the numerator $(x - 2) + 3(x + 1)$ is negative. Because the denominator $x + 3$ is also negative for $x < -3$, the fraction is positive. The sign variation for the fraction in the diagram is, therefore, completely wrong. The product of two negative numbers is positive, but their sum is negative, and not positive as the wrong sign diagram suggests.

We obtain a correct solution to the given problem by first collecting terms in the numerator so that the inequality becomes $(4x + 1)/(x + 3) \leq 0$. A sign diagram for this inequality reveals the correct answer, which is $-3 < x \leq -1/4$.

Double Inequalities

Two inequalities that are valid simultaneously are often written as a *double inequality*. If, for example, $a \leq z$ and moreover $z < b$, it is natural to write $a \leq z < b$. (On the other hand, if $a \leq z$ and $z > b$, but we do not know which is the larger of a and b, then we cannot write $a \leq b < z$ or $b \leq a \leq z$, and we do *not* write $a \leq z > b$.)

EXAMPLE 1.6.5   One day, the lowest temperature in Buenos Aires was 50°F, and the highest was 77°F. What is the corresponding temperature variation in degrees Celsius? (Recall that if F denotes degrees Fahrenheit and C denotes degrees Celsius, then $F = \frac{9}{5}C + 32$.)

Solution: We have

$$50 \leq \frac{9}{5}C + 32 \leq 77$$

Subtracting 32 from each term yields

$$50 - 32 \leq \frac{9}{5}C \leq 77 - 32$$

or

$$18 \leq \frac{9}{5}C \leq 45$$

Dividing these inequalities by 9/5 yields $10 \leq C \leq 25$. The temperature thus varies between 10°C and 25°C.

EXERCISES FOR SECTION 1.6

1. Decide which of the following inequalities are true:

(a) $-6.15 > -7.16$ (b) $6 \geq 6$ (c) $(-5)^2 \leq 0$ (d) $-\frac{1}{2}\pi < -\frac{1}{3}\pi$

(e) $\frac{4}{5} > \frac{6}{7}$ (f) $2^3 < 3^2$ (g) $2^{-3} < 3^{-2}$ (h) $\frac{1}{2} - \frac{2}{3} < \frac{1}{4} - \frac{1}{3}$

2. Find what values of x satisfy the following inequalities:

(a) $-x - 3 \leq 5$

(b) $3x + 5 < x - 13$

(c) $3x - (x - 1) \geq x - (1 - x)$

(d) $\frac{2x - 4}{3} \leq 7$

(e) $\frac{1}{3}(1 - x) \geq 2(x - 3)$

(f) $\frac{x}{24} - (x + 1) + \frac{3x}{8} < \frac{5}{12}(x + 1)$

(SM) **3.** Solve the following inequalities:

(a) $2 < \frac{3x + 1}{2x + 4}$

(b) $\frac{120}{n} + 1.1 \leq 1.85$

(c) $g^2 - 2g \leq 0$

(d) $\frac{1}{p - 2} + \frac{3}{p^2 - 4p + 4} \geq 0$

(e) $\frac{-n - 2}{n + 4} > 2$

(f) $x^4 < x^2$

4. Solve the following inequalities:

(a) $\frac{x + 2}{x - 1} < 0$

(b) $\frac{2x + 1}{x - 3} > 1$

(c) $5a^2 \leq 125$

(d) $(x - 1)(x + 4) > 0$

(e) $(x - 1)^2(x + 4) > 0$

(f) $(x - 1)^3(x - 2) \leq 0$

(g) $(5x - 1)^{10}(x - 1) < 0$

(h) $(5x - 1)^{11}(x - 1) < 0$

(i) $\frac{3x - 1}{x} > x + 3$

(j) $\frac{x - 3}{x + 3} < 2x - 1$

(k) $x^2 - 4x + 4 > 0$

(l) $x^3 + 2x^2 + x \leq 0$

5. Solve the following inequalities:

   (a) $1 \leq \frac{1}{3}(2x - 1) + \frac{8}{3}(1 - x) < 16$ (b) $-5 < \frac{1}{x} < 0$ (c) $\frac{(1/x) - 1}{(1/x) + 1} \geq 1$

SM 6. Fill in the blanks with "$\Rightarrow$", "$\Leftarrow$", or "$\Leftrightarrow$", when this results in a true statement:

   (a) $x(x + 3) < 0$ ____ $x > -3$ (b) $x^2 < 9$ ____ $x < 3$

   (c) $x^2 > 0$ ____ $x > 0$ (d) $x > y^2$ ____ $x > 0$

7. Decide whether the following inequalities are valid for all x and y:

   (a) $x + 1 > x$ (b) $x^2 > x$ (c) $x + x > x$ (d) $x^2 + y^2 \geq 2xy$

8. Recall the formula to convert Celsius to Fahrenheit, from Example 1.6.5.

   (a) The temperature for storing potatoes should be between 4°C and 6°C. What are the corresponding temperatures in degrees Fahrenheit?

   (b) The freshness of a bottle of milk is guaranteed for seven days if it is kept at a temperature between 36°F and 40°F. Find the corresponding temperature variation in degrees Celsius.

SM 9. If a and b are two positive numbers, define their *arithmetic, geometric,* and *harmonic means,* respectively, by $m_A = \frac{1}{2}(a + b), m_G = \sqrt{ab}$ and

$$m_H = 2\left(\frac{1}{a} + \frac{1}{b}\right)^{-1}$$

Prove that $m_A \geq m_G \geq m_H$, with strict inequalities unless $a = b$.[19]

1.7 Intervals and Absolute Values

Let a and b be any two numbers on the real line. Then we call the set of all numbers that lie between a and b an *interval*. In many situations, it is important to distinguish between the intervals that include their end points and the intervals that do not. When $a < b$, there are four different intervals that all have a and b as end points, as shown in Table 1.1.

Note that an open interval includes neither of its end points, but a closed interval includes both of its end points. A half-open interval contains one of its end points, but not both. All four intervals, however, have the same length, $b - a$. We usually illustrate intervals on the number line as in Fig. 1.7.1, with included end points represented by solid dots, and excluded end points at the tips of arrows.

---

[19] You should first test these inequalities by choosing some specific numbers, using a calculator if you wish. To show that $m_A \geq m_G$, start with the obvious inequality $(\sqrt{a} - \sqrt{b})^2 \geq 0$, and then expand. To show that $m_G \geq m_H$, start by showing that $\sqrt{xy} \leq \frac{1}{2}(x + y)$. Then let $x = 1/a, y = 1/b$.

Table 1.1 Intervals on the real line

Notation	Name	Consists of all x satisfying:
(a, b)	The *open* interval from a to b	$a < x < b$
$[a, b]$	The *closed* interval from a to b	$a \leq x \leq b$
$(a, b]$	A *half-open* interval from a to b	$a < x \leq b$
$[a, b)$	A *half-open* interval from a to b	$a \leq x < b$

Figure 1.7.1 $A = [-4, -2]$, $B = [0, 1)$, and $C = (2, 5)$

The intervals mentioned so far are all *bounded*. We also use the word "interval" to signify certain unbounded sets of numbers. For example, in set notation: $[a, \infty) = \{x : x \geq a\}$ consists of all numbers $x \geq a$; and $(-\infty, b) = \{x : x < b\}$ contains all numbers with $x < b$. Here, "∞" is the common symbol for infinity. This symbol is not a number at all, and therefore the usual rules of arithmetic do not apply to it. In the notation $[a, \infty)$, the symbol ∞ is only intended to indicate that we are considering the collection of *all* numbers larger than or equal to a, without any upper bound on the size of the number. Similarly, $(-\infty, b)$ has no lower bound. From the preceding, it should be apparent what we mean by (a, ∞) and $(-\infty, b]$. The collection of all real numbers is also denoted by the symbol $(-\infty, \infty)$.

Absolute Value

Let a be a real number and imagine its position on the real line. The distance between a and 0 is called the *absolute value* of a. If a is positive or 0, then the absolute value is the number a itself; if a is negative, then because distance must be positive, the absolute value is equal to the positive number $-a$. That is:

ABSOLUTE VALUE

The *absolute value* of the number a is the number $|a|$ defined by

$$|a| = \begin{cases} a & \text{if } a \geq 0 \\ -a & \text{if } a < 0 \end{cases} \tag{1.7.1}$$

For example, $|13| = 13$, $|-5| = -(-5) = 5$, $|-1/2| = 1/2$, and $|0| = 0$. Note in particular that $|-a| = |a|$.[20]

---

[20]   It is a common fallacy to assume that a must denote a positive number, even if this is not explicitly stated. Similarly, on seeing $-a$, many students are led to believe that this expression is always

EXAMPLE 1.7.1   Compute $|x - 2|$ for $x = -3$, $x = 0$, and $x = 4$. Then, rewrite $|x - 2|$ using the definition of absolute value.

Solution: Using the definition, (1.7.1), we have that $|x - 2| = |-3 - 2| = |-5| = 5$, for $x = -3$. For $x = 0$, $|x - 2| = |0 - 2| = |-2| = 2$. Similarly, for $x = 4$, $|x - 2| = |4 - 2| = |2| = 2$.

According, again, to (1.7.1), $|x - 2| = x - 2$ if $x - 2 \geq 0$, that is, $x \geq 2$. However, $|x - 2| = -(x - 2) = 2 - x$ if $x - 2 < 0$, that is, $x < 2$. Hence,

$$|x - 2| = \begin{cases} x - 2, & \text{if } x \geq 2 \\ 2 - x, & \text{if } x < 2 \end{cases}$$

Let x_1 and x_2 be two arbitrary numbers. The *distance* between x_1 and x_2 on the number line is $x_1 - x_2$ if $x_1 \geq x_2$, and $-(x_1 - x_2)$ if $x_1 < x_2$. Therefore, we have:

DISTANCE BETWEEN NUMBERS

The *distance* between x_1 and x_2 on the number line is

$$|x_1 - x_2| = |x_2 - x_1| \tag{1.7.2}$$

In Fig. 1.7.2 we have indicated geometrically that the distance between 7 and 2 is 5, whereas the distance between -3 and -5 is equal to 2, because $|-3 - (-5)| = |-3 + 5| = |2| = 2$.

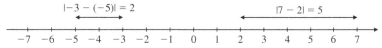

Figure 1.7.2 The distances between 7 and 2 and between -3 and -5.

Suppose $|x| = 5$. What values can x have? There are only two possibilities: either $x = 5$ or $x = -5$, because no other numbers have absolute value equal to 5. Generally, if a is greater than or equal to 0, then $|x| = a$ means that $x = a$ or $x = -a$. Because $|x| \geq 0$ for all x, the equation $|x| = a$ has no solution when $a < 0$.

If a is a positive number and $|x| < a$, then the distance from x to 0 is less than a. Furthermore, when a is nonnegative, and $|x| \leq a$, the distance from x to 0 is less than or equal to a. In symbols:

$$|x| < a \Leftrightarrow -a < x < a \tag{1.7.3}$$

$$|x| \leq a \Leftrightarrow -a \leq x \leq a \tag{1.7.4}$$

---

negative. Observe, however, that the number $-a$ is positive when a itself is negative. For example, if $a = -5$, then $-a = -(-5) = 5$. Nevertheless, it is often a useful convention in economics to define variables so that, as far as possible, their values are positive rather than negative.

EXAMPLE 1.7.2   Check first to see if the inequality $|3x - 2| \leq 5$ holds for $x = -3$, $x = 0$, $x = 7/3$, and $x = 10$. Then, find all the x such that the inequality holds.

Solution: For $x = -3$, $|3x - 2| = |-9 - 2| = 11$; for $x = 0$, $|3x - 2| = |-2| = 2$; for $x = 7/3$, $|3x - 2| = |7 - 2| = 5$; and for $x = 10$, $|3x - 2| = |30 - 2| = 28$. Hence, the given inequality is satisfied for $x = 0$ and $x = 7/3$, but not for $x = -3$ and $x = 10$.

Now, from (1.7.4) the inequality $|3x - 2| \leq 5$ means that $-5 \leq 3x - 2 \leq 5$. Adding 2 to all three expressions gives

$$-5 + 2 \leq 3x - 2 + 2 \leq 5 + 2$$

or $-3 \leq 3x \leq 7$. Dividing by 3 gives $-1 \leq x \leq 7/3$.

EXERCISES FOR SECTION 1.7

1. (a) Calculate $|2x - 3|$ for $x = 0$, $1/2$, and $7/2$.

   (b) Solve the equation $|2x - 3| = 0$.

   (c) Rewrite $|2x - 3|$ by using the definition of absolute value.

2. (a) Calculate $|5 - 3x|$ for $x = -1$, $x = 2$, and $x = 4$.

   (b) Solve the equation $|5 - 3x| = 5$.

   (c) Rewrite $|5 - 3x|$ by using the definition of absolute value.

3. Determine x such that the following expressions hold true:

   (a) $|3 - 2x| = 5$ (b) $|x| \leq 2$ (c) $|x - 2| \leq 1$

   (d) $|3 - 8x| \leq 5$ (e) $|x| > \sqrt{2}$ (f) $|x^2 - 2| \leq 1$

4. A 5-metre iron bar is to be produced. The bar may not deviate by more than 1 mm from its stated length. Write a specification for the bar's length x in metres: (a) by using a double inequality; (b) with the aid of an absolute-value sign.

1.8 Summation

Economists often make use of census data. Suppose, for instance, that a country is divided into six regions. Let N_i denote the population in region i. Then the total population is given by

$$N_1 + N_2 + N_3 + N_4 + N_5 + N_6$$

It is convenient to have an abbreviated notation for such lengthy expressions. The capital Greek letter sigma, Σ, is conventionally used as a *summation symbol*, and the sum is written as

$$\sum_{i=1}^{6} N_i$$

This reads "the sum, from $i = 1$ to $i = 6$, of N_i". If there are n regions, then one possible notation for the total population is

$$N_1 + N_2 + \cdots + N_n \qquad (*)$$

where $\cdots$ indicates that the obvious previous pattern continues, but comes to an end just before the last term N_n. In summation notation, we write

$$\sum_{i=1}^{n} N_i$$

The summation notation tells us to form the sum of all the terms that result when we substitute successive integers for i, starting with its lower limit $i = 1$ and ending with the upper limit $i = n$, respectively, in the example. The symbol i is called the *index of summation*. It is a "dummy variable" that can be replaced by any other letter (which has not already been used for something else). Thus, both $\sum_{j=1}^{n} N_j$ and $\sum_{k=1}^{n} N_k$ represent the same sum as $(*)$.

The upper and lower limits of summation can both vary. For example,

$$\sum_{i=30}^{35} N_i = N_{30} + N_{31} + N_{32} + N_{33} + N_{34} + N_{35}$$

is the total population in the six regions numbered from 30 to 35. More generally, suppose p and q are integers with $q \geq p$. Then,

$$\sum_{i=p}^{q} a_i = a_p + a_{p+1} + \cdots + a_q$$

denotes the sum that results when we substitute successive integers for i, starting with $i = p$ and ending with $i = q$. If the upper and lower limits of summation are the same, then the "sum" reduces to one term. And if the upper limit is less than the lower limit, then there are no terms at all, so the usual convention is that the "sum" reduces to zero.

EXAMPLE 1.8.1   Compute the following summations:

(a) $\sum_{i=1}^{5} i^2$ (b) $\sum_{k=3}^{6}(5k - 3)$ (c) $\sum_{j=0}^{2} \dfrac{(-1)^j}{(j + 1)(j + 3)}$

Solution:

(a) $\sum_{i=1}^{5} i^2 = 1^2 + 2^2 + 3^2 + 4^2 + 5^2 = 1 + 4 + 9 + 16 + 25 = 55$

(b) $\sum_{k=3}^{6}(5k - 3) = (5 \cdot 3 - 3) + (5 \cdot 4 - 3) + (5 \cdot 5 - 3) + (5 \cdot 6 - 3) = 78$

(c) $\sum_{j=0}^{2} \dfrac{(-1)^j}{(j + 1)(j + 3)} = \dfrac{1}{1 \cdot 3} + \dfrac{-1}{2 \cdot 4} + \dfrac{1}{3 \cdot 5} = \dfrac{40 - 15 + 8}{120} = \dfrac{33}{120} = \dfrac{11}{40}$

Sums and the summation notation occur frequently in economics, so it is important to be able to interpret such sums. Often, there are several variables or parameters in addition to the summation index.

EXAMPLE 1.8.2   Expand the following expressions:

(a) $\sum_{i=1}^{n} p_t^{(i)} q^{(i)}$ (b) $\sum_{j=-3}^{1} x^{5-j} y^j$ (c) $\sum_{i=1}^{N} (x_{ij} - \bar{x}_j)^2$

Solution:

(a) $\sum_{i=1}^{n} p_t^{(i)} q^{(i)} = p_t^{(1)} q^{(1)} + p_t^{(2)} q^{(2)} + \cdots + p_t^{(n)} q^{(n)}$

(b) $\sum_{j=-3}^{1} x^{5-j} y^j = x^{5-(-3)} y^{-3} + x^{5-(-2)} y^{-2} + x^{5-(-1)} y^{-1} + x^{5-0} y^0 + x^{5-1} y^1$

(c) $\sum_{i=1}^{N} (x_{ij} - \bar{x}_j)^2 = (x_{1j} - \bar{x}_j)^2 + (x_{2j} - \bar{x}_j)^2 + \cdots + (x_{Nj} - \bar{x}_j)^2$

Note that t is *not* an index of summation in (a), and that j is *not* one in (c).

EXAMPLE 1.8.3   Write the following sums using summation notation:

(a) $1 + 3 + 3^2 + 3^3 + \cdots + 3^{81}$

(b) $a_i^6 + a_i^5 b_j + a_i^4 b_j^2 + a_i^3 b_j^3 + a_i^2 b_j^4 + a_i b_j^5 + b_j^6$

Solution:

(a) This is easy if we note that $1 = 3^0$ and $3 = 3^1$, so that the sum can be written as $3^0 + 3^1 + 3^2 + 3^3 + \cdots + 3^{81}$. The general term is 3^i, and we have

$$1 + 3 + 3^2 + 3^3 + \cdots + 3^{81} = \sum_{i=0}^{81} 3^i$$

(b) This is more difficult. Note, however, that the indices i and j never change. Also, the exponent for a_i decreases step by step from 6 to 0, whereas that for b_j increases from 0 to 6. The general term has the form $a_i^{6-k} b_j^k$, where k varies from 0 to 6. Thus,

$$a_i^6 + a_i^5 b_j + a_i^4 b_j^2 + a_i^3 b_j^3 + a_i^2 b_j^4 + a_i b_j^5 + b_j^6 = \sum_{k=0}^{6} a_i^{6-k} b_j^k$$

EXAMPLE 1.8.4   **(Price Indices).** In order to summarize the overall effect of price changes for several different goods within a country, a number of alternative *price indices* have been suggested. Considering a "basket" of n commodities, define, for $i = 1, \ldots, n$: $q^{(i)}$ as the number of units of good i in the basket; $p_0^{(i)}$ as the price per unit of good i in year 0; and $p_t^{(i)}$ as the price per unit of good i in year t. Then,

$$\sum_{i=1}^{n} p_0^{(i)} q^{(i)} = p_0^{(1)} q^{(1)} + p_0^{(2)} q^{(2)} + \cdots + p_0^{(n)} q^{(n)}$$

is the cost of the basket in year 0, whereas

$$\sum_{i=1}^{n} p_t^{(i)} q^{(i)} = p_t^{(1)} q^{(1)} + p_t^{(2)} q^{(2)} + \cdots + p_t^{(n)} q^{(n)}$$

is the cost of the basket in year t. A price index for year t, with year 0 as the base year, is defined as

$$\frac{\sum_{i=1}^{n} p_t^{(i)} q^{(i)}}{\sum_{i=1}^{n} p_0^{(i)} q^{(i)}} \cdot 100 \qquad \text{(price index)}$$

If the cost of the basket is 1032 in year 0 and the cost of the same basket in year t is 1548, then the price index is $(1548/1032) \cdot 100 = 150$.

In the case where the quantities $q^{(i)}$ are levels of consumption in the base year 0, this is called the *Laspeyres price index*. But if the quantities $q^{(i)}$ are levels of consumption in the year t, this is called the *Paasche price index*.

EXERCISES FOR SECTION 1.8

1. Evaluate the following sums:

(a) $\sum_{i=1}^{10} i$ (b) $\sum_{k=2}^{6} (5 \cdot 3^{k-2} - k)$ (c) $\sum_{m=0}^{5} (2m + 1)$

(d) $\sum_{l=0}^{2} 2^{2^l}$ (e) $\sum_{i=1}^{10} 2$ (f) $\sum_{j=1}^{4} \frac{j+1}{j}$

2. Expand the following sums:

(a) $\sum_{k=-2}^{2} 2\sqrt{k+2}$ (b) $\sum_{i=0}^{3} (x + 2i)^2$

(c) $\sum_{k=1}^{n} a_{ki} b^{k+1}$ (d) $\sum_{j=0}^{m} f(x_j) \, \Delta x_j$

SM 3. Express the following sums in summation notation:

(a) $4 + 8 + 12 + 16 + \cdots + 4n$ (b) $1^3 + 2^3 + 3^3 + 4^3 + \cdots + n^3$

(c) $1 - \frac{1}{3} + \frac{1}{5} - \frac{1}{7} + \cdots + (-1)^n \frac{1}{2n+1}$ (d) $a_{i1} b_{1j} + a_{i2} b_{2j} + \cdots + a_{in} b_{nj}$

(e) $3x + 9x^2 + 27x^3 + 81x^4 + 243x^5$ (f) $a_i^3 b_{i+3} + a_i^4 b_{i+4} + \cdots + a_i^p b_{i+p}$

(g) $a_i^3 b_{i+3} + a_{i+1}^4 b_{i+4} + \cdots + a_{i+p}^{p+3} b_{i+p+3}$ (h) $81\,297 + 81\,495 + 81\,693 + 81\,891$

4. Compute the price index in Example 1.8.4, for $n = 3$, when:

$$p_0^{(1)} = 1, \; p_0^{(2)} = 2, \; p_0^{(3)} = 3, \; p_t^{(1)} = 2, \; p_t^{(2)} = 3, \; p_t^{(3)} = 4, \; q^{(1)} = 3, \; q^{(2)} = 5, \text{ and } q^{(3)} = 7$$

5. Insert the appropriate limits of summation in the right-hand side of the following sums:

(a) $\sum_{k=1}^{10} (k - 2) t^k = \sum_{m=} \quad m t^{m+2}$ (b) $\sum_{n=0}^{N} 2^{n+5} = \sum_{j=} \quad 32 \cdot 2^{j-1}$

6. As of early 2016, the European Economic Area has 31 nations, and officially there is a long-run goal of free mobility of labour throughout the area. For the year 2025, let c_{ij} denote an estimate of the number of persons who will move from nation i to nation j, $i \neq j$. If, say, $i = 25$ and $j = 10$, then we write $c_{25,10}$ for c_{ij}. Explain the meaning of the sums: (a) $\sum_{j=1}^{31} c_{ij}$, and (b) $\sum_{i=1}^{31} c_{ij}$.

(SM) **7.** Decide which of the following equalities are generally valid.

(a) $\sum_{k=1}^{n} ck^2 = c \sum_{k=1}^{n} k^2$ $\qquad\qquad$ (b) $\left(\sum_{i=1}^{n} a_i\right)^2 = \sum_{i=1}^{n} a_i^2$

(c) $\sum_{j=1}^{n} b_j + \sum_{j=n+1}^{N} b_j = \sum_{j=1}^{N} b_j$ $\qquad$ (d) $\sum_{k=3}^{7} 5^{k-2} = \sum_{k=0}^{4} 5^{k+1}$

(e) $\sum_{i=0}^{n-1} a_{i,j}^2 = \sum_{k=1}^{n} a_{k-1,j}^2$ $\qquad\qquad$ (f) $\sum_{k=1}^{n} \dfrac{a_k}{k} = \dfrac{1}{k} \sum_{k=1}^{n} a_k$

1.9 Rules for Sums

The following properties of the summation notation are helpful when manipulating sums:

$$\sum_{i=1}^{n} (a_i + b_i) = \sum_{i=1}^{n} a_i + \sum_{i=1}^{n} b_i \tag{1.9.1}$$

and

$$\sum_{i=1}^{n} ca_i = c \sum_{i=1}^{n} a_i \tag{1.9.2}$$

These properties are known, respectively, as *additivity* and *homogeneity*. Their proofs are straightforward. For example, (1.9.2) is proved by noting that

$$\sum_{i=1}^{n} ca_i = ca_1 + ca_2 + \cdots + ca_n = c(a_1 + a_2 + \cdots + a_n) = c \sum_{i=1}^{n} a_i$$

The homogeneity property states that a constant factor can be moved outside the summation sign. In particular, if $a_i = 1$ for all i, then

$$\sum_{i=1}^{n} c = nc \tag{1.9.3}$$

which just states that a constant c summed n times is equal to n times c.

The summation rules can be applied in combination, to give formulas like

$$\sum_{i=1}^{n} (a_i + b_i - c_i + d) = \sum_{i=1}^{n} a_i + \sum_{i=1}^{n} b_i - \sum_{i=1}^{n} c_i + nd$$

EXAMPLE 1.9.1   Evaluate the sum

$$\sum_{m=2}^{n} \frac{1}{(m-1)m} = \frac{1}{1 \cdot 2} + \frac{1}{2 \cdot 3} + \cdots + \frac{1}{(n-1)n}$$

by using the identity

$$\frac{1}{(m-1)m} = \frac{1}{m-1} - \frac{1}{m}$$

Solution:

$$\sum_{m=2}^{n} \frac{1}{m(m-1)} = \sum_{m=2}^{n} \left(\frac{1}{m-1} - \frac{1}{m} \right)$$

$$= \sum_{m=2}^{n} \frac{1}{m-1} - \sum_{m=2}^{n} \frac{1}{m}$$

$$= \left(\frac{1}{1} + \frac{1}{2} + \frac{1}{3} + \cdots + \frac{1}{n-1} \right) - \left(\frac{1}{2} + \frac{1}{3} + \cdots + \frac{1}{n-1} + \frac{1}{n} \right)$$

$$= 1 - \frac{1}{n}$$

To derive the last equality, note that most of the terms cancel pairwise. The only exceptions are the first term within the first parentheses and the last term within the last parentheses. This powerful trick is commonly used to calculate some special sums of this kind. See Exercise 4, below.

EXAMPLE 1.9.2   The *arithmetic mean* (or *mean*), μ_x, of T numbers $x_1, x_2, \ldots, x_T$ is their average, defined as the sum of all the numbers divided by the number of terms, T. That is,

$$\mu_x = \frac{1}{T} \sum_{i=1}^{T} x_i$$

Prove that $\sum_{i=1}^{T} (x_i - \mu_x) = 0$ and $\sum_{i=1}^{T} (x_i - \mu_x)^2 = \sum_{i=1}^{T} x_i^2 - T\mu_x^2$.

Solution: The difference $x_i - \mu_x$ is the deviation between x_i and the mean. We prove first that the sum of these deviations is 0, using the foregoing definition of μ_x:

$$\sum_{i=1}^{T} (x_i - \mu_x) = \sum_{i=1}^{T} x_i - \sum_{i=1}^{T} \mu_x = \sum_{i=1}^{T} x_i - T\mu_x = T\mu_x - T\mu_x = 0$$

Furthermore, the sum of the squares of the deviations is

$$\sum_{i=1}^{T} (x_i - \mu_x)^2 = \sum_{i=1}^{T} (x_i^2 - 2\mu_x x_i + \mu_x^2) = \sum_{i=1}^{T} x_i^2 - 2\mu_x \sum_{i=1}^{T} x_i + \sum_{i=1}^{T} \mu_x^2$$

$$= \sum_{i=1}^{T} x_i^2 - 2\mu_x T\mu_x + T\mu_x^2 = \sum_{i=1}^{T} x_i^2 - T\mu_x^2$$

Dividing by T, the mean square deviation, $(1/T) \sum_{i=1}^{T} (x_i - \mu_x)^2$, is therefore equal to the mean square, $(1/T) \sum_{i=1}^{T} x_i^2$, minus the square of the mean, μ_x^2.

Useful Formulas

A (very) demanding teacher once asked his students to sum

$$81\,297 + 81\,495 + 81\,693 + \cdots + 100\,899$$

There are one hundred terms and the difference between successive terms is constant and equal to 198. Carl Gauss (1777–1855), later one of the world's leading mathematicians, was in the class, and (at age nine!) is reputed to have given the right answer in only a few minutes. You already took a key step toward finding the solution to this question in Exercise 1.4.1, using mathematical induction. Applied to that easier problem of finding the sum $x = 1 + 2 + \cdots + n$, Gauss' argument was probably different, as follows: First, write the sum x in two ways

$$x = 1 + 2 + \cdots + (n - 1) + n$$
$$x = n + (n - 1) + \cdots + 2 + 1$$

Summing vertically term by term gives

$$2x = (1 + n) + [2 + (n - 1)] + \cdots + [(n - 1) + 2] + (n + 1)$$
$$= (1 + n) + (1 + n) + \cdots + (1 + n) + (1 + n)$$
$$= n(1 + n)$$

Thus, solving for x gives the result:

$$\sum_{i=1}^{n} i = 1 + 2 + \cdots + n = \frac{1}{2}n(n + 1) \tag{1.9.4}$$

The following two summation formulas are occasionally useful in economics.[21] Exercise 1 below asks you to provide their proofs.

$$\sum_{i=1}^{n} i^2 = 1^2 + 2^2 + 3^2 + \cdots + n^2 = \frac{1}{6}n(n + 1)(2n + 1) \tag{1.9.5}$$

$$\sum_{i=1}^{n} i^3 = 1^3 + 2^3 + 3^3 + \cdots + n^3 = \left[\frac{1}{2}n(n + 1)\right]^2 = \left(\sum_{i=1}^{n} i\right)^2 \tag{1.9.6}$$

EXERCISES FOR SECTION 1.9

1. Prove formulas (1.9.5) and (1.9.6), using the principle of mathematical induction seen in Section 1.4.

2. Use results (1.9.1) to (1.9.5) to find $\sum_{k=1}^{n}(k^2 + 3k + 2)$.

3. Prove the summation formula for an *arithmetic series*:

$$\sum_{i=0}^{n-1}(a + id) = na + \frac{n(n - 1)d}{2}$$

Apply the result to find the sum Gauss is supposed to have calculated at age 9.

---

[21] Check to see if they are true for $n = 1, 2, 3$.

4. (a) Prove that $\sum_{k=1}^{n}(a_{k+1} - a_k) = a_{n+1} - a_1$.

   (b) Use the result in (a) to compute the following:

     (i) $\sum_{k=1}^{50}\left(\dfrac{1}{k} - \dfrac{1}{k+1}\right)$ (ii) $\sum_{k=1}^{12}\left(3^{k+1} - 3^k\right)$ (iii) $\sum_{k=1}^{n}\left(ar^{k+1} - ar^k\right)$

1.10 Newton's Binomial Formula

We all know that $(a+b)^1 = a+b$ and $(a+b)^2 = a^2 + 2ab + b^2$. Using the latter equality and writing $(a+b)^3 = (a+b)(a+b)^2$ and $(a+b)^4 = (a+b)(a+b)^3$, we find that

$$(a+b)^1 = a + b$$

$$(a+b)^2 = a^2 + 2ab + b^2$$

$$(a+b)^3 = a^3 + 3a^2b + 3ab^2 + b^3$$

$$(a+b)^4 = a^4 + 4a^3b + 6a^2b^2 + 4ab^3 + b^4$$

The corresponding formula for $(a+b)^m$, where m is any natural number, can be expressed as follows:

NEWTON'S BINOMIAL FORMULA

$$(a+b)^m = a^m + \binom{m}{1}a^{m-1}b + \cdots + \binom{m}{m-1}ab^{m-1} + \binom{m}{m}b^m \qquad (1.10.1)$$

This formula involves the *binomial coefficients* $\binom{m}{k}$, which are defined, for $m = 1, 2, \ldots$ and for $k = 0, 1, 2, \ldots, m$, by

$$\binom{m}{k} = \frac{m(m-1)\cdots(m-k+1)}{k!}$$

where $k!$, read as "k factorial", is standard notation for the product $1 \cdot 2 \cdot 3 \ldots (k-1) \cdot k$ of the first k natural numbers, with the conventions that $0! = 1$, $\binom{m}{0} = 1$, $\binom{m}{1} = m$, and $\binom{m}{m} = 1$.
When $m = 5$, for example, we have

$$\binom{5}{2} = \frac{5 \cdot 4}{1 \cdot 2} = 10, \qquad \binom{5}{3} = \frac{5 \cdot 4 \cdot 3}{1 \cdot 2 \cdot 3} = 10, \qquad \binom{5}{4} = \frac{5 \cdot 4 \cdot 3 \cdot 2}{1 \cdot 2 \cdot 3 \cdot 4} = 5$$

Then (1.10.1) gives $(a+b)^5 = a^5 + 5a^4b + 10a^3b^2 + 10a^2b^3 + 5ab^4 + b^5$.

The coefficients occurring in the expansions for successive powers of $(a+b)$ form the following pattern, called *Pascal's triangle*:[22]

---

[22] Though it was known in China by about the year 1100, long before French mathematician Blaise Pascal (1623–1662) was born.

$$
\begin{array}{ccccccccccccccccccc}
 & & & & & & & & & 1 & & & & & & & & & \\
 & & & & & & & & 1 & & 1 & & & & & & & & \\
 & & & & & & & 1 & & 2 & & 1 & & & & & & & \\
 & & & & & & 1 & & 3 & & 3 & & 1 & & & & & & \\
 & & & & & 1 & & 4 & & 6 & & 4 & & 1 & & & & & \\
 & & & & 1 & & 5 & & 10 & & 10 & & 5 & & 1 & & & & \\
 & & & 1 & & 6 & & 15 & & 20 & & 15 & & 6 & & 1 & & & \\
 & & 1 & & 7 & & 21 & & 35 & & 35 & & 21 & & 7 & & 1 & & \\
 & 1 & & 8 & & 28 & & 56 & & 70 & & 56 & & 28 & & 8 & & 1 & \\
1 & & 9 & & 36 & & 84 & & 126 & & 126 & & 84 & & 36 & & 9 & & 1
\end{array}
$$

This table can be continued indefinitely. The numbers in this triangle are indeed the binomial coefficients. For instance, the numbers in row 6 (when the first row is numbered 0) are

$$
\binom{6}{0}, \quad \binom{6}{1}, \quad \binom{6}{2}, \quad \binom{6}{3}, \quad \binom{6}{4}, \quad \binom{6}{5}, \quad \binom{6}{6}
$$

Note first that the numbers are symmetric about the middle line. This symmetry can be expressed as

$$
\binom{m}{k} = \binom{m}{m-k} \tag{1.10.2}
$$

For example, $\binom{6}{2} = 15 = \binom{6}{4}$. Second, apart from the 1 at both ends of each row, each number is the sum of the two adjacent numbers in the row above. For instance, 56 in the eighth row is equal to the sum of 21 and 35 in the seventh row. In symbols,

$$
\binom{m+1}{k+1} = \binom{m}{k} + \binom{m}{k+1} \tag{1.10.3}
$$

In Exercise 2 you are asked to prove these two properties.

EXERCISES FOR SECTION 1.10

1. Use Newton's binomial formula to find $(a+b)^6$.

2. (a) Prove that $\binom{5}{3} = \dfrac{5!}{2!\,3!}$, and, in general, that

$$
\binom{m}{k} = \frac{m!}{(m-k)!\,k!} \tag{1.10.4}
$$

(b) Verify, by direct computation, that $\binom{8}{3} = \binom{8}{8-3}$ and $\binom{8+1}{3+1} = \binom{8}{3} + \binom{8}{3+1}$.

(c) Use (1.10.4) to verify (1.10.2) and (1.10.3).

1.11 Double Sums

Often one has to combine several summation signs. Consider, for example, the following rectangular array of numbers:

$$
\begin{array}{cccc}
a_{11} & a_{12} & \cdots & a_{1n} \\
a_{21} & a_{22} & \cdots & a_{2n} \\
\vdots & \vdots & & \vdots \\
a_{m1} & a_{m2} & \cdots & a_{mn}
\end{array}
\tag{1.11.1}
$$

The array can be regarded as a *spreadsheet*. A typical number in the array is of the form a_{ij}, where $1 \leq i \leq m$ and $1 \leq j \leq n$.[23] There are $n \cdot m$ numbers in all. Let us find the sum of all the numbers in the array by first finding the sum of the numbers in each of the m rows and then adding all these row sums. The m different row sums can be written in the form $\sum_{j=1}^{n} a_{1j}, \sum_{j=1}^{n} a_{2j}, \ldots, \sum_{j=1}^{n} a_{mj}$.[24] The sum of these m sums is equal to $\sum_{j=1}^{n} a_{1j} + \sum_{j=1}^{n} a_{2j} + \cdots + \sum_{j=1}^{n} a_{mj}$, which can be written as $\sum_{i=1}^{m} \left(\sum_{j=1}^{n} a_{ij} \right)$. If instead we add the numbers in each of the n columns first and then add these sums, we get

$$
\sum_{i=1}^{m} a_{i1} + \sum_{i=1}^{m} a_{i2} + \cdots + \sum_{i=1}^{m} a_{in} = \sum_{j=1}^{n} \left(\sum_{i=1}^{m} a_{ij} \right)
$$

In both these cases, we have calculated the sum of all the numbers in the array.[25] For this reason, we must have

$$
\sum_{i=1}^{m} \sum_{j=1}^{n} a_{ij} = \sum_{j=1}^{n} \sum_{i=1}^{m} a_{ij}
$$

where, according to usual practice, we have deleted the parentheses. This formula says that *in a (finite) double sum, the order of summation is immaterial*. It is important to note that the summation limits for i and j are independent of each other.[26]

EXAMPLE 1.11.1   Compute $\sum_{i=1}^{3} \sum_{j=1}^{4} (i + 2j)$.

Solution:

$$
\sum_{i=1}^{3} \sum_{j=1}^{4} (i + 2j) = \sum_{i=1}^{3} [(i + 2) + (i + 4) + (i + 6) + (i + 8)]
$$

$$
= \sum_{i=1}^{3} (4i + 20) = 24 + 28 + 32 = 84
$$

You should check that the result is the same by summing over i first instead.

---

[23] For example, a_{ij} may indicate the total revenue of a firm from its sales in region i in month j.

[24] In our example, these row sums are the total revenues in each region summed over all the n months.

[25] How do you interpret this sum in our economic example?

[26] Otherwise, changing the order in a double sum like $\sum_{j=1}^{n} \sum_{i=1}^{j} a_{ij}$ to obtain $\sum_{i=1}^{j} \sum_{j=1}^{n} a_{ij}$ results in an expression that makes little sense.

EXERCISES FOR SECTION 1.11

(SM) **1.** Expand and compute the following double sums:

(a) $\sum_{i=1}^{3} \sum_{j=1}^{4} i \cdot 3^j$

(b) $\sum_{s=0}^{2} \sum_{r=2}^{4} \left(\dfrac{rs}{r+s} \right)^2$

(c) $\sum_{i=1}^{m} \sum_{j=1}^{n} (i + j^2)$

(d) $\sum_{i=1}^{m} \sum_{j=1}^{2} i^j$

2. Consider a group of individuals each having a certain number of units of m different goods. Let a_{ij} denote the number of units of good i owned by person j, for $i = 1, \ldots, m$ and $j = 1, \ldots, n$. Explain in words the meaning of the following sums:

(a) $\sum_{j=1}^{n} a_{ij}$

(b) $\sum_{i=1}^{m} a_{ij}$

(c) $\sum_{j=1}^{n} \sum_{i=1}^{m} a_{ij}$

3. Prove that the sum of all the numbers in the triangular table

$$
\begin{array}{ccccc}
a_{11} & & & & \\
a_{21} & a_{22} & & & \\
a_{31} & a_{32} & a_{33} & & \\
\vdots & \vdots & \vdots & \ddots & \\
a_{m1} & a_{m2} & a_{m3} & \cdots & a_{mm}
\end{array}
$$

can be written as $\sum_{i=1}^{m} \left(\sum_{j=1}^{i} a_{ij} \right)$ and also as $\sum_{j=1}^{m} \left(\sum_{i=j}^{m} a_{ij} \right)$.

(SM) **4.** [HARDER] Consider the $m \cdot n$ numbers a_{ij} in the rectangular array (1.11.1). Denote the arithmetic mean of them all by $\bar{a}$, and the mean of all the numbers in the j-th column by $\bar{a}_j$, so that

$$
\bar{a} = \frac{1}{mn} \sum_{r=1}^{m} \sum_{s=1}^{n} a_{rs}
$$

and

$$
\bar{a}_j = \frac{1}{m} \sum_{r=1}^{m} a_{rj}
$$

Prove that $\bar{a}$ is the mean of the column sums $\bar{a}_j$ $(j = 1, \ldots, n)$ and that

$$
\sum_{r=1}^{m} \sum_{s=1}^{m} (a_{rj} - \bar{a})(a_{sj} - \bar{a}) = m^2 (\bar{a}_j - \bar{a})^2 \tag{$*$}
$$

REVIEW EXERCISES

1. (a) What is three times the difference between 50 and x?

(b) What is the quotient between x and the sum of y and 100?

(c) If the price of an item is a including 20% VAT (value added tax), what is the price before VAT?

(d) A person buys x_1, x_2, and x_3 units of three goods whose prices per unit are respectively p_1, p_2, and p_3. What is the total expenditure?

(e) A rental car costs F dollars per day in fixed charges and b dollars per kilometre. How much must a customer pay to drive x kilometres in one day?

(f) A company has fixed costs of F dollars per year and variable costs of c dollars per unit produced. Find an expression for the total cost per unit (total average cost) incurred by the company if it produces x units in one year.

(g) A person has an annual salary of $\$L$ and then receives a raise of $p\%$ followed by a further increase of $q\%$. What is the person's new salary?

2. Express as single real numbers, in decimal notation:

(a) 5^3 (b) 10^{-3} (c) $\dfrac{1}{3^{-3}}$ (d) $\dfrac{-1}{10^{-3}}$

(e) $3^{-2}3^3$ (f) $(3^{-2})^{-3}$ (g) $-\left(\dfrac{5}{3}\right)^0$ (h) $\left(-\dfrac{1}{2}\right)^{-3}$

3. Which of the following expressions are defined, and what are their values?

(a) $(0+2)^0$ (b) 0^{-2} (c) $\dfrac{(10)^0}{(0+1)^0}$ (d) $\dfrac{(0+1)^0}{(0+2)^0}$

4. Simplify the following expressions:

(a) $(2^3 2^{-5})^3$ (b) $\left(\dfrac{2}{3}\right)^{-1} - \left(\dfrac{4}{3}\right)^{-1}$

(c) $(3^{-2} - 5^{-1})^{-1}$ (d) $(1.12)^{-3}(1.12)^3$

(SM) 5. Simplify the following expressions:

(a) $(2x)^4$ (b) $(2^{-1} - 4^{-1})^{-1}$ (c) $\dfrac{24x^3 y^2 z^3}{4x^2 yz^2}$

(d) $\left[-(-ab^3)^{-3}(a^6 b^6)^2\right]^3$ (e) $\dfrac{a^5 \cdot a^3 \cdot a^{-2}}{a^{-3} \cdot a^6}$ (f) $\left[\left(\dfrac{x}{2}\right)^3 \cdot \dfrac{8}{x^{-2}}\right]^{-3}$

6. Complete the following statements:

(a) $x^{-1}y^{-1} = 3 \Rightarrow x^3 y^3 = \cdots$ (b) $x^7 = 2 \Rightarrow (x^{-3})^6 (x^2)^2 = \cdots$

(c) $\left(\dfrac{xy}{z}\right)^{-2} = 3 \Rightarrow \left(\dfrac{z}{xy}\right)^6 = \cdots$ (d) $a^{-1}b^{-1}c^{-1} = 1/4 \Rightarrow (abc)^4 = \cdots$

7. Compute the following numbers: (a) 12% of 300; (b) 5% of 2000; and (c) 6.5% of 1500.

8. Give economic interpretations to each of the following expressions and then use a calculator to find their approximate values: (a) $100 \cdot (1.01)^8 €$; (b) £$50\,000 \cdot (1.15)^{10}$; and (c) $\$6\,000 \cdot (1.03)^{-8}$.

9. (a) $\$100\,000$ is deposited into an account earning 8% interest per year. What is the amount after ten years?

(b) If the interest rate is 8% each year, how much money should you have deposited in a bank six years ago to have $\$25\,000$ today?

(SM) **10.** Expand and simplify the following expressions:

(a) $a(a-1)$

(b) $(x-3)(x+7)$

(c) $-\sqrt{3}\left(\sqrt{3}-\sqrt{6}\right)$

(d) $\left(1-\sqrt{2}\right)^2$

(e) $(x-1)^3$

(f) $(1-b^2)(1+b^2)$

(g) $(1+x+x^2+x^3)(1-x)$

(h) $(1+x)^4$

11. Factor the following expressions:

(a) $25x-5$

(b) $3x^2-x^3y$

(c) $50-x^2$

(d) $a^3-4a^2b+4ab^2$

(SM) **12.** Factor the following expressions:

(a) $5(x+2y)+a(x+2y)$

(b) $(a+b)c-d(a+b)$

(c) $ax+ay+2x+2y$

(d) $2x^2-5yz+10xz-xy$

(e) p^2-q^2+p-q

(f) $u^3+v^3-u^2v-v^2u$

13. Compute the following numbers, without using a calculator:

(a) $16^{1/4}$

(b) $243^{-1/5}$

(c) $5^{1/7}\cdot5^{6/7}$

(d) $(4^8)^{-3/16}$

(e) $64^{1/3}+\sqrt[3]{125}$

(f) $(-8/27)^{2/3}$

(g) $(-1/8)^{-2/3}+(1/27)^{-2/3}$

(h) $\dfrac{1000^{-2/3}}{\sqrt[3]{5^{-3}}}$

14. Solve the following equations for x:

(a) $2^{2x}=8$

(b) $3^{3x+1}=1/81$

(c) $10^{x^2-2x+2}=100$

15. Find the unknown x in each of the following equations:

(a) $25^5\cdot25^x=25^3$

(b) $3^x-3^{x-2}=24$

(c) $3^x\cdot3^{x-1}=81$

(d) $3^5+3^5+3^5=3^x$

(e) $4^{-6}+4^{-6}+4^{-6}+4^{-6}=4^x$

(f) $\dfrac{2^{26}-2^{23}}{2^{26}+2^{23}}=\dfrac{x}{9}$

(SM) **16.** Simplify the following expressions:

(a) $\dfrac{s}{2s-1}-\dfrac{s}{2s+1}$

(b) $\dfrac{x}{3-x}-\dfrac{1-x}{x+3}-\dfrac{24}{x^2-9}$

(c) $\dfrac{\dfrac{1}{x^2y}-\dfrac{1}{xy^2}}{\dfrac{1}{x^2}-\dfrac{1}{y^2}}$

(SM) **17.** Reduce the following fractions:

(a) $\dfrac{25a^3b^2}{125ab}$

(b) $\dfrac{x^2-y^2}{x+y}$

(c) $\dfrac{4a^2-12ab+9b^2}{4a^2-9b^2}$

(d) $\dfrac{4x-x^3}{4-4x+x^2}$

18. Solve the following inequalities:

(a) $2(x-4)<5$

(b) $\dfrac{1}{3}(y-3)+4\geq2$

(c) $8-0.2x\leq\dfrac{4-0.1x}{0.5}$

(d) $\dfrac{x-1}{-3}>\dfrac{-3x+8}{-5}$

(e) $|5-3x|\leq8$

(f) $|x^2-4|\leq2$

19. Using a mobile phone costs \$30 per month, and an additional \$0.16 per minute of use.

    (a) What is the cost for one month if the phone is used for a total of x minutes?

    (b) What are the smallest and largest numbers of *hours* you can use the phone in a month if the monthly telephone bill is to be between \$102 and \$126?

20. If a rope could be wrapped around the Earth's surface at the equator, it would be approximately circular and about 40 million metres long. Suppose we wanted to extend the rope to make it 1 metre above the equator at every point. How many more metres of rope would be needed? (The circumference of a circle with radius r is $2\pi r$.)

21. (a) Prove that

$$a + \frac{a \cdot p}{100} - \frac{\left(a + \frac{a \cdot p}{100}\right) \cdot p}{100} = a\left[1 - \left(\frac{p}{100}\right)^2\right]$$

    (b) An item initially costs \$2 000 and then its price is increased by 5%. Afterwards the price is lowered by 5%. What is the final price?

    (c) An item initially costs a dollars and then its price is increased by p%. Afterwards the (new) price is lowered by p%. What is the final price of the item? (After considering this exercise, look at the expression in part (a).)

    (d) What is the result if one first *lowers* a price by p% and then *increases* it by p%?

22. (a) If $a > b$, is it necessarily true that $a^2 > b^2$?

    (b) Show that if $a + b > 0$, then $a > b$ implies $a^2 > b^2$.

23. (a) If $a > b$, use numerical examples to check whether $1/a > 1/b$, or $1/a < 1/b$.

    (b) Prove that if $a > b$ and $ab > 0$, then $1/b > 1/a$.

24. Prove that, for all real numbers a and b:

    (a) $|ab| = |a| \cdot |b|$ (b) $|a + b| \le |a| + |b|$

    The inequality in (b) is called the *triangle inequality*.

(SM) 25. Consider an equilateral triangle, and let P be an arbitrary point within the triangle. Let h_1, h_2, and h_3 be the shortest distances from P to each of the three sides. Show that the sum $h_1 + h_2 + h_3$ is independent of where point P is placed in the triangle. (*Hint:* Compute the area of the triangle as the sum of three triangles.)

26. Evaluate the following sums:

    (a) $\sum_{i=1}^{4} \frac{1}{i(i+2)}$ (b) $\sum_{j=5}^{9} (2j - 8)^2$ (c) $\sum_{k=1}^{5} \left(\frac{k-1}{k+1}\right)$

    (d) $\sum_{n=2}^{5} (n-1)^2(n+2)$ (e) $\sum_{k=1}^{5} \left(\frac{1}{k} - \frac{1}{k+1}\right)$ (f) $\sum_{i=-2}^{3} (i+3)^i$

27. Express the following sums in summation notation:

(a) $3 + 5 + 7 + \cdots + 199 + 201$

(b) $\dfrac{2}{1} + \dfrac{3}{2} + \dfrac{4}{3} + \cdots + \dfrac{97}{96}$

(c) $4 \cdot 6 + 5 \cdot 7 + 6 \cdot 8 + \cdots + 38 \cdot 40$

(d) $\dfrac{1}{x} + \dfrac{1}{x^2} + \cdots + \dfrac{1}{x^n}$

(e) $1 + \dfrac{x^2}{3} + \dfrac{x^4}{5} + \dfrac{x^6}{7} + \cdots + \dfrac{x^{32}}{33}$

(f) $1 - \dfrac{1}{2} + \dfrac{1}{3} - \dfrac{1}{4} + \cdots - \dfrac{1}{80} + \dfrac{1}{81}$

28. Which of these equalities are always right and which of them are sometimes wrong?

(a) $\sum_{i=1}^{n} a_i = \sum_{j=3}^{n+2} a_{j-2}$

(b) $\sum_{i=1}^{n} (a_i + b_i)^2 = \sum_{i=1}^{n} a_i^2 + \sum_{i=1}^{n} b_i^2$

(c) $\sum_{k=0}^{n} 5 a_{k+1,j} = 5 \sum_{k=1}^{n+1} a_{k,j}$

(d) $\sum_{i=1}^{3} \dfrac{a_i}{b_i} = \dfrac{\sum_{i=1}^{3} a_i}{\sum_{i=1}^{3} b_i}$

SM 29. Find the sums:

(a) $3 + 5 + 7 + \cdots + 197 + 199 + 201$

(b) $1001 + 2002 + 3003 + \cdots + 8008 + 9009 + 10\,010$

2

EQUATIONS

The true mathematician is not a juggler of numbers, but of concepts.
—Ian Stewart (1975)

Virtually all applications of mathematics involve equations that have to be solved. Economics is no exception, so this chapter considers some types of equation that appear frequently in economic models.

Many students are used to dealing with algebraic expressions and equations involving *only one* variable, usually denoted by *x*. Often they have difficulties, at first, in dealing with expressions involving several variables with a wide variety of names, and denoted by different letters. For economists, however, it is very important to be able to handle with ease such algebraic expressions and equations.

2.1 Solving Equations

To *solve* an equation means to find all values of the variables for which the equation is satisfied. Consider the following simple example

$$3x + 10 = x + 4$$

which contains the *variable x*. In order to isolate x on one side of the equation, we add $-x$ to both sides. This gives $2x + 10 = 4$. Adding -10 to both sides of this equation yields $2x = 4 - 10 = -6$. Dividing by 2 we get the solution $x = -3$.

This procedure was probably already familiar to you. The method is summed up next, noting that two equations that have exactly the same solutions are called *equivalent*.

EQUIVALENT EQUATIONS

To get an equivalent equation, do either of the following on both sides of the equality sign:

(i) add (or subtract) the same number;

(ii) multiply (or divide) by the same number different from 0.

When faced with more complicated equations involving parentheses and fractions, we usually begin by multiplying out the parentheses, and then we multiply both sides of the equation by the lowest common denominator for all the fractions.

EXAMPLE 2.1.1   Solve the equation

$$6p - \frac{1}{2}(2p - 3) = 3(1 - p) - \frac{7}{6}(p + 2)$$

Solution: First multiply out the parentheses: $6p - p + \frac{3}{2} = 3 - 3p - \frac{7}{6}p - \frac{7}{3}$. Second, multiply both sides by the lowest common denominator: $36p - 6p + 9 = 18 - 18p - 7p - 14$. Third, gather terms: $55p = -5$. Thus $p = -5/55 = -1/11$.

If a value of a variable makes an expression in an equation undefined, that value is not allowed. For instance, the choice of value 5 for variable z is not allowed in any equation that involves the expression

$$\frac{z}{z - 5}$$

because $5/0$ is undefined. As we shall show in the next example, this fact has implications for the existence of a solution to an equation.

EXAMPLE 2.1.2   Solve the equation

$$\frac{z}{z - 5} + \frac{1}{3} = \frac{-5}{5 - z}$$

Solution: We now know that z cannot be 5. Remembering this restriction, multiply both sides by $3(z - 5)$. This gives $3z + z - 5 = 15$ which has the unique solution $z = 5$. Because we had to assume $z \neq 5$, we must conclude that no solution exists for the original equation.

The next example shows, again, that sometimes a surprising degree of care is needed to find the right solutions.

EXAMPLE 2.1.3   Solve the equation

$$\frac{x+2}{x-2} - \frac{8}{x^2 - 2x} = \frac{2}{x}$$

Solution: Since $x^2 - 2x = x(x-2)$, the common denominator is $x(x-2)$. We see that $x = 2$ and $x = 0$ both make the equation absurd, because then at least one of the denominators becomes 0. If $x \neq 0$ and $x \neq 2$, we can multiply both sides of the equation by the common denominator $x(x-2)$ to obtain

$$\frac{x+2}{x-2} \cdot x(x-2) - \frac{8}{x(x-2)} \cdot x(x-2) = \frac{2}{x} \cdot x(x-2)$$

Cancelling common factors, this reduces to $(x+2)x - 8 = 2(x-2)$ or $x^2 + 2x - 8 = 2x - 4$, and so $x^2 = 4$. Equations of the form $x^2 = a$, where $a > 0$, have two solutions $x = \sqrt{a}$ and $x = -\sqrt{a}$. In our case, $x^2 = 4$ has solutions $x = 2$ and $x = -2$. But $x = 2$ makes the original equation absurd, so *only $x = -2$ is a solution.*

Often, solving a problem in economic analysis requires formulating an appropriate *algebraic* equation.

EXAMPLE 2.1.4   A firm manufactures a commodity that costs $20 per unit to produce. In addition, the firm has fixed costs of $2 000. Each unit is sold for $75. How many units must be sold if the firm is to meet a profit target of $14 500?

Solution: If the number of units produced and sold is denoted by Q, then the revenue of the firm is $75Q$ and the total cost of production is $20Q + 2000$. Because profit is the difference between total revenue and total cost, it can be written as $75Q - (20Q + 2000)$. Since the profit target is $14 500, the equation

$$75Q - (20Q + 2000) = 14\,500$$

must be satisfied. It is now easy to find the solution: $Q = 16\,500/55 = 300$ units.

EXERCISES FOR SECTION 2.1

1. Solve each of the following equations:

   (a) $2x - (5 + x) = 16 - (3x + 9)$ (b) $-5(3x - 2) = 16(1 - x)$

   (c) $4x + 2(x - 4) - 3 = 2(3x - 5) - 1$ (d) $(8x - 7)5 - 3(6x - 4) + 5x^2 = x(5x - 1)$

   (e) $x^2 + 10x + 25 = 0$ (f) $(3x - 1)^2 + (4x + 1)^2 = (5x - 1)(5x + 1) + 1$

2. Solve each of the following equations:

   (a) $3x = \frac{1}{4}x - 7$ (b) $\frac{x-3}{4} + 2 = 3x$ (c) $\frac{1}{2x+1} = \frac{1}{x+2}$ (d) $\sqrt{2x + 14} = 16$

(SM) 3. Solve each of the following equations:

   (a) $\frac{x-3}{x+3} = \frac{x-4}{x+4}$ (b) $\frac{3}{x-3} - \frac{2}{x+3} = \frac{9}{x^2 - 9}$ (c) $\frac{6x}{5} - \frac{5}{x} = \frac{2x-3}{3} + \frac{8x}{15}$

4. Solve the following problems, by first formulating an equation in each case:

(a) The sum of three successive natural numbers is 10 more than twice the smallest of them. Find the numbers.

(b) Jane receives double pay for every hour she works over and above 38 hours per week. Last week, she worked 48 hours and earned a total of $812. What is Jane's regular hourly wage?

(c) James has invested £15 000 at an annual interest rate of 10%. How much additional money should he invest at the interest rate of 12%, if he wants the total interest earned by the end of the year to equal £2 100?

(d) When Mr Barnes passed away, 2/3 of his estate was left to his wife, 1/4 was shared by his children, and the remainder, $100 000, was donated to a charity. How big was Mr Barnes's estate?

(SM) 5. Solve the following equations:

(a) $\dfrac{3y-1}{4} - \dfrac{1-y}{3} + 2 = 3y$

(b) $\dfrac{4}{x} + \dfrac{3}{x+2} = \dfrac{2x+2}{x^2+2x} + \dfrac{7}{2x+4}$

(c) $\dfrac{2 - z/(1-z)}{1+z} = \dfrac{6}{2z+1}$

(d) $\dfrac{1}{2}\left(\dfrac{p}{2} - \dfrac{3}{4}\right) - \dfrac{1}{4}\left(1 - \dfrac{p}{3}\right) - \dfrac{1}{3}(1-p) = -\dfrac{1}{3}$

6. Ms. Preston has y euros to spend on apples, bananas, and cherries. She decides to spend the same amount of money on each kind of fruit. The prices per kilo are 3€ for apples, 2€ for bananas, and 6€ for cherries. What is the total weight of fruit she buys, and how much does she pay per kilo of fruit?[1]

2.2   Equations and Their Parameters

Economists use mathematical models to describe different economic phenomena. These models enable them to explain the interdependence of different economic variables. Macroeconomic models, for instance, are designed to explain the broad outlines of a country's economy; in these models, examples of such variables include the total production of the economy (or gross domestic product), its total consumption, and its total investment.

The simplest kind of relationship between two variables occurs when the response of one of them to a change of one unit in the other one is always the same. In this case, the relationship can be described by a *linear equation*, such as $y = 10x$, $y = 3x + 4$, or

$$y = -\frac{8}{3}x - \frac{7}{2}$$

These three equations have a common structure. This makes it possible to write down a general linear equation covering all the special cases where x and y are the variables:

$$y = ax + b \tag{2.2.1}$$

---

[1] This is an example of "dollar cost" averaging, which we will encounter again in Exercise 11.5.4.

Here a and b are real numbers. For example, letting $a = 3$ and $b = 4$ yields the particular case where $y = 3x + 4$. To accommodate straight lines of the form $x = c$ where c is a constant, it may be necessary to interchange the variables x and y.

The numbers a and b are called *parameters*, as they take on different, but "fixed" values.[2] In economics, parameters often have interesting interpretations.

EXAMPLE 2.2.1   Consider the basic macroeconomic model

$$\text{(i) } Y = C + \bar{I} \qquad \text{and} \qquad \text{(ii) } C = a + bY \qquad (*)$$

where Y is the gross domestic product (GDP), C is consumption, and $\bar{I}$ is total investment, which is treated as fixed. Equation (i) says that GDP is, by definition, the sum of consumption and total investment. Equation (ii) says that consumption is a linear function of GDP. Here, a and b are positive parameters of the model, with $b < 1$.[3] Solve the model for Y in terms of $\bar{I}$ and the parameters.

Solution: Substituting $C = a + bY$ into (i) gives

$$Y = a + bY + \bar{I}$$

Now, we rearrange this equation so that all the terms containing Y are on the left-hand side. This can be done by adding $-bY$ to both sides, thus cancelling the bY term on the right-hand side, to give

$$Y - bY = a + \bar{I}$$

Notice that the left-hand side is equal to $(1 - b)Y$, so $(1 - b)Y = a + \bar{I}$. Dividing both sides by $1 - b$, so that the coefficient of Y becomes 1, gives the answer:

$$Y = \frac{a}{1 - b} + \frac{1}{1 - b}\bar{I} \qquad (**)$$

This solution is a linear equation expressing Y in terms of $\bar{I}$ and the parameters a and b.

Note the power of the approach used here: the model is solved only once, and then numerical answers are found simply by substituting appropriate numerical values for the parameters of the model. For instance, if $\bar{I} = 100$, $a = 500$, $b = 0.8$, then $Y = 3000$.

Economists usually call the equations in $(*)$ the *structural form* of the model, whereas $(**)$ is called its *reduced form*. In the reduced form, the number $1/(1 - b)$ is itself a parameter. This is known as the *investment multiplier*, as it measures the response in income to an "exogenous" increase in investment.

---

[2] Linear equations are studied in more detail in Section 3.4.

[3] Parameter a is often referred to as *autonomous consumption*, as it represents the part of consumption that is *not* determined by the economy's income. The increase of consumption caused by an increase of one unit in income is measured by b; this parameter is, hence, known as *marginal propensity to consume*. Special cases of the model are obtained by choosing particular numerical values for the parameters, such as $\bar{I} = 100$, $a = 500$, $b = 0.8$, or $\bar{I} = 150$, $a = 600$, $b = 0.9$. Thus, $Y = C + 100$ and $C = 500 + 0.8Y$; or $Y = C + 150$ and $C = 600 + 0.9Y$.

Of course, we often need to solve more complicated "non-linear" equations, which often involve "strange" letters denoting their parameters and variables.

EXAMPLE 2.2.2   Suppose that the total demand for money in an economy is given by

$$M = \alpha Y + \beta(r - \gamma)^{-\delta}$$

where M is the quantity of money in circulation, Y is national income and r is the interest rate, while α, β, γ, and δ are positive parameters.

(a) Solve the model for the interest rate, r.

(b) For the USA during the period 1929–1952, the parameters have been estimated as $\alpha = 0.14$, $\beta = 76.03$, $\gamma = 2$, and $\delta = 0.84$. Show that r is then given by

$$r = 2 + \left(\frac{76.03}{M - 0.14Y} \right)^{25/21}$$

Solution:

(a) It follows easily from the given equation that $(r - \gamma)^{-\delta} = (M - \alpha Y)/\beta$. Then, raising each side to the power $-1/\delta$ and adding γ on both sides yields

$$r = \gamma + \left(\frac{\beta}{M - \alpha Y} \right)^{1/\delta} \tag{$*$}$$

where we used the fact that $(a/b)^{-p} = (b/a)^p$.

(b) In this case $1/\delta = 1/0.84 = 100/84 = 25/21$, and the required formula follows immediately from ($*$).

EXERCISES FOR SECTION 2.2

1. Find the value of Y for the case when $Y = C + 150$ and $C = 600 + 0.9Y$ in the model of Example 1. Verify that formula ($**$) gives the same result.

SM 2. Solve the following equations for x:

(a) $\dfrac{1}{ax} + \dfrac{1}{bx} = 2$ (b) $\dfrac{ax + b}{cx + d} = A$ (c) $\frac{1}{2}px^{-1/2} - w = 0$

(d) $\sqrt{1+x} + \dfrac{ax}{\sqrt{1+x}} = 0$ (e) $a^2x^2 - b^2 = 0$ (f) $(3 + a^2)^x = 1$

3. Solve the following equations for the indicated variables:

(a) $q = 0.15p + 0.14$ for p (supply of rice in India);

(b) $S = \alpha + \beta P$ for P (supply function);

(c) $A = \frac{1}{2}gh$ for g (the area of a triangle);

(d) $V = \frac{4}{3}\pi r^3$ for r (the volume of a ball);

(e) $AK^\alpha L^\beta = Y_0$ for L (production function).

SM 4. Solve the following equations for the indicated variables:

(a) $\alpha x - a = \beta x - b$ for x

(b) $\sqrt{pq} - 3q = 5$ for p

(c) $Y = 94 + 0.2(Y - (20 + 0.5Y))$ for Y

(d) $K^{1/2}\left(\dfrac{1}{2}\dfrac{r}{w}K\right)^{1/4} = Q$ for K

(e) $\dfrac{\frac{1}{2}K^{-1/2}L^{1/4}}{\frac{1}{4}L^{-3/4}K^{1/2}} = \dfrac{r}{w}$ for L

(f) $\frac{1}{2}pK^{-1/4}\left(\dfrac{1}{2}\dfrac{r}{w}\right)^{1/4} = r$ for K

5. Solve the following equations for the indicated variables:

(a) $\dfrac{1}{s} + \dfrac{1}{T} = \dfrac{1}{t}$ for s

(b) $\sqrt{KLM} - \alpha L = B$ for M

(c) $\dfrac{x - 2y + xz}{x - z} = 4y$ for z

(d) $V = C\left(1 - \dfrac{T}{N}\right)$ for T

2.3 Quadratic Equations

The general quadratic equation has the form

$$ax^2 + bx + c = 0 \tag{2.3.1}$$

where $a \neq 0$, b, and c are given constants, and variable x is the unknown. If we divide each term by a, we get the equivalent equation $x^2 + (b/a)x + c/a = 0$. If $p = b/a$ and $q = c/a$, the equation is

$$x^2 + px + q = 0 \tag{2.3.2}$$

Two special cases are easy to handle. If $q = 0$, so that there is no "constant term", the equation reduces to $x^2 + px = 0$. This is equivalent to $x(x + p) = 0$, and, since the product of two numbers can be 0 only if at least one of the numbers is 0, we conclude that $x = 0$ or $x = -p$. In short,

$$x^2 + px = 0 \text{ if, and only if, } x = 0 \text{ or } x = -p$$

This means that the equation $x^2 + px = 0$ has the solutions $x = 0$ and $x = -p$, and no others.

If $p = 0$, so that there is no term involving x, Eq. (2.3.2) reduces to $x^2 + q = 0$. Then $x^2 = -q$, and there are two cases to consider. If $q > 0$, the equation has no solutions as no number can be squared to get a negative number. In the alternative case, when $q \leq 0$, both $x = \sqrt{-q}$ and $x = -\sqrt{-q}$ solve the equation. Using the notation $x = \pm\sqrt{-q}$ to express that $\sqrt{-q}$ and $-\sqrt{-q}$ are the values that x can take, we can write, in short, that

$$x^2 + q = 0 \text{ if, and only if, } x = \pm\sqrt{-q} \text{ given that } q \leq 0$$

These results can be applied to solve any instance of the two simple cases.

EXAMPLE 2.3.1   Solve the following equations:

(a) $5x^2 - 8x = 0$ (b) $x^2 - 4 = 0$ (c) $x^2 + 3 = 0$

Solution:

(a) Dividing each term by 5 yields $x^2 - (8/5)x = x(x - 8/5) = 0$, so $x = 0$ or $x = 8/5$.

(b) The equation yields $x^2 = 4$, so $x = \pm\sqrt{4} = \pm 2$. Alternatively, one has $x^2 - 4 = (x + 2)(x - 2)$ so the equation is equivalent to $(x + 2)(x - 2) = 0$. Either way, one concludes that x is either 2 or -2.

(c) Because x^2 is no less than 0, the left-hand side of the equation $x^2 + 3 = 0$ is always strictly positive and, hence, the equation has no solution.

Harder Cases

If (2.3.2) has both coefficients different from 0, solving it becomes harder. Consider, for example,

$$x^2 - (4/3)x - 1/4 = 0$$

We could, of course, try to find the values of x that satisfy the equation by trial and error. However, it is not easy that way to find the only two solutions, which are $x = 3/2$ and $x = -1/6$. Here are two attempts to solve the equation that fail:

(a) A first attempt rearranges $x^2 - (4/3)x - 1/4 = 0$ to give $x^2 - (4/3)x = 1/4$, and so $x(x - 4/3) = 1/4$. Thus, the product of x and $x - 4/3$ must be 1/4. But there are infinitely many pairs of numbers whose product is 1/4, so this is of very little help in finding x.

(b) A second attempt is to divide each term by x to get $x - 4/3 = 1/4x$. Because the equation involves terms in both x and $1/x$, as well as a constant term, we have made no progress whatsoever.

Evidently, we need a completely new idea in order to find the solution of (2.3.2). The following example illustrates the idea that will give us a general method to solve this harder equation.

EXAMPLE 2.3.2   Solve the equation $x^2 + 8x - 9 = 0$.

Solution: It is natural to begin by moving 9 to the right-hand side:

$$x^2 + 8x = 9 \tag{$*$}$$

However, because x occurs in two terms, it is not obvious how to proceed. A method called *completing the square*, one of the oldest tricks in mathematics, turns out to work. In the present case this method involves adding 16 to each side of the equation to get

$$x^2 + 8x + 16 = 9 + 16 \tag{$**$}$$

The point of adding 16 is that the left-hand side is then a complete square: $x^2 + 8x + 16 = (x + 4)^2$. Thus, Eq. (∗∗) takes the form

$$(x + 4)^2 = 25 \qquad\qquad (∗∗∗)$$

The equation $z^2 = 25$ has two solutions, $z = \pm\sqrt{25} = \pm 5$. Thus, (∗∗∗) implies that either $x + 4 = 5$ or $x + 4 = -5$. The required solutions are, therefore, $x = 1$ and $x = -9$.

Alternatively, Eq. (∗∗∗) can be written as $(x+4)^2 - 5^2 = 0$. Using the difference-of-squares formula yields $(x + 4 - 5)(x + 4 + 5) = 0$, which reduces to $(x - 1)(x + 9) = 0$, so we have the following *factorization*

$$x^2 + 8x - 9 = (x - 1)(x + 9)$$

Note that $(x - 1)(x + 9)$ is 0 precisely when $x = 1$ or $x = -9$.

The General Case

We now apply the method of completing the squares to the quadratic equation (2.3.2). This equation obviously has the same solutions as $x^2 + px = -q$. One half of the coefficient of x is $p/2$. Adding the square of this number to each side of the equation yields

$$x^2 + px + \left(\frac{p}{2}\right)^2 = \left(\frac{p}{2}\right)^2 - q$$

The left-hand side is now a complete square, so

$$\left(x + \frac{p}{2}\right)^2 = \frac{p^2}{4} - q \qquad\qquad (∗)$$

Note that if $p^2/4 - q < 0$, then the right-hand side is negative. Because $(x + p/2)^2$ is non-negative for all choices of x, we conclude that Eq. (∗) has no solution in this case. On the other hand, if $p^2/4 - q > 0$, (∗) yields two possibilities:

$$x + p/2 = \sqrt{p^2/4 - q} \qquad \text{and} \qquad x + p/2 = -\sqrt{p^2/4 - q}$$

The values of x are then easily found. These formulas are correct even if $p^2/4 - q = 0$, though then they give just the one solution $x = -p/2$. In conclusion:

SIMPLE QUADRATIC FORMULA

$$x^2 + px + q = 0 \text{ if, and only if, } x = -\frac{p}{2} \pm \sqrt{\frac{p^2}{4} - q}, \text{ provided that } \frac{p^2}{4} \geq q \qquad (2.3.3)$$

Faced with an equation of the type (2.3.1), we can always find its solutions by first dividing the equation by a and then using (2.3.3). Sometimes it is convenient to have the formula for the solution of (2.3.1) in terms of the coefficients a, b, and c. Recall that, by dividing Eq. (2.3.1) by a, we get the equivalent version of Eq. (2.3.2), with $p = b/a$ and $q = c/a$. Substituting these particular values in (2.3.3) gives the solutions $x = -b/2a \pm \sqrt{b^2/4a^2 - c/a}$.

GENERAL QUADRATIC FORMULA

If $b^2 - 4ac \geq 0$ and $a \neq 0$, then

$$ax^2 + bx + c = 0 \text{ if, and only if, } x = \frac{-b \pm \sqrt{b^2 - 4ac}}{2a} \tag{2.3.4}$$

It is probably a good idea to spend a few minutes of your life memorizing this formula, or formula (2.3.3), thoroughly. Once you have done so, you can immediately write down the solutions of any quadratic equation. Only if $b^2 - 4ac \geq 0$ are the solutions real numbers. If we use the formula when $b^2 - 4ac < 0$, the square root of a negative number appears and no real solution exists. The solutions are often called the *roots* of the equation.[4]

EXAMPLE 2.3.3   Use the quadratic formula to find the solutions of the equation

$$2x^2 - 2x - 40 = 0$$

Solution: Write the equation as $2x^2 + (-2)x + (-40) = 0$. Because $a = 2$, $b = -2$, and $c = -40$, the quadratic formula (2.3.4) yields

$$x = \frac{-(-2) \pm \sqrt{(-2)^2 - 4 \cdot 2 \cdot (-40)}}{2 \cdot 2} = \frac{2 \pm \sqrt{4 + 320}}{4} = \frac{2 \pm 18}{4} = \frac{1}{2} \pm \frac{9}{2}$$

The solutions are, therefore, $x = 1/2 + 9/2 = 5$ and $x = 1/2 - 9/2 = -4$.

If we use formula (2.3.3) instead, we divide each term by 2 and get $x^2 - x - 20 = 0$, so $x = 1/2 \pm \sqrt{1/4 + 20} = 1/2 \pm \sqrt{81/4} = 1/2 \pm 9/2$, namely the same solutions as before.

Suppose $p^2/4 - q \geq 0$ and let x_1 and x_2 be the solutions of Eq. (2.3.2). By using the difference-of-squares formula as we did to obtain the factorization in Example 2.3.2, it follows that $(*)$ is equivalent to $(x - x_1)(x - x_2) = 0$. It follows also that:

QUADRATIC FACTORIZATION

If x_1 and x_2 are the solutions of $ax^2 + bx + c = 0$, then

$$ax^2 + bx + c = a(x - x_1)(x - x_2) \tag{2.3.5}$$

---

[4]   The quadratic formula, thus, is very useful, but you should not be a "quadratic formula fanatic" and use it always. If $b = 0$ or $c = 0$, we explained at the beginning of this section how the equation can be solved very easily. During a past exam, one extreme fanatic of the formula, when faced with solving the equation $(x - 4)^2 = 0$, expanded the parentheses to obtain $x^2 - 8x + 16 = 0$, and then used the quadratic formula eventually to get the (correct) answer, $x = 4$. What would you have done?

This is a very important result, because it shows how to factor a general quadratic function. If $b^2 - 4ac < 0$, there is no factorization of $ax^2 + bx + c$. If $b^2 - 4ac = 0$, then $x_1 = x_2$ and $ax^2 + bx + c = a(x - x_1)^2 = a(x - x_2)^2$.

EXAMPLE 2.3.4   Factor, if possible, the following quadratic polynomials:

(a) $\frac{1}{3}x^2 + \frac{2}{3}x - \frac{14}{3}$ (b) $-2x^2 + 40x - 600$

Solution:

(a) $\frac{1}{3}x^2 + \frac{2}{3}x - \frac{14}{3} = 0$ has the same solutions as $x^2 + 2x - 14 = 0$. By formula (2.3.2), its solutions are $x = -1 \pm \sqrt{1 + 14} = -1 \pm \sqrt{15}$, and these are the solutions of the given equation also. Then, from (2.3.5),

$$\frac{1}{3}x^2 + \frac{2}{3}x - \frac{14}{3} = \frac{1}{3}\left[x - \left(-1 + \sqrt{15}\right)\right]\left[x - \left(-1 - \sqrt{15}\right)\right]$$
$$= \frac{1}{3}\left(x + 1 - \sqrt{15}\right)\left(x + 1 + \sqrt{15}\right)$$

(b) We apply (2.3.4) with $a = -2$, $b = 40$, and $c = -600$. In fact $b^2 - 4ac = 1600 - 4800 = -3200 < 0$. Therefore, no factoring exists in this case.

Expanding the right-hand side of the identity $x^2 + px + q = (x - x_1)(x - x_2)$ yields $x^2 + px + q = x^2 - (x_1 + x_2)x + x_1 x_2$. Equating like powers of x gives $x_1 + x_2 = -p$ and $x_1 x_2 = q$. Thus:

RULES FOR QUADRATIC FUNCTIONS

If x_1 and x_2 are the roots of $x^2 + px + q = 0$, then

$$x_1 + x_2 = -p \qquad \text{and} \qquad x_1 x_2 = q \tag{2.3.6}$$

In words, the sum of the roots is minus the coefficient of the first-order term and the product is the constant term. The formulas (2.3.6) can also obtained by adding and multiplying the two solutions found in (2.3.2).

EXERCISES FOR SECTION 2.3

1. Solve the following quadratic equations, if they have solutions:

(a) $15x - x^2 = 0$ (b) $p^2 - 16 = 0$ (c) $(q - 3)(q + 4) = 0$

(d) $2x^2 + 9 = 0$ (e) $x(x + 1) = 2x(x - 1)$ (f) $x^2 - 4x + 4 = 0$

2. Solve the following quadratic equations by using the method of completing the square, and factor, if possible, the left-hand side:

(a) $x^2 - 5x + 6 = 0$

(b) $y^2 - y - 12 = 0$

(c) $2x^2 + 60x + 800 = 0$

(d) $-\frac{1}{4}x^2 + \frac{1}{2}x + \frac{1}{2} = 0$

(e) $m(m - 5) - 3 = 0$

(f) $0.1p^2 + p - 2.4 = 0$

(SM) 3. Solve the following equations, by using the quadratic formula:

(a) $r^2 + 11r - 26 = 0$

(b) $3p^2 + 45p = 48$

(c) $20\,000 = 300K - K^2$

(d) $r^2 + (\sqrt{3} - \sqrt{2})r = \sqrt{6}$

(e) $0.3x^2 - 0.09x = 0.12$

(f) $\frac{1}{24} = p^2 - \frac{1}{12}p$

4. Solve the following equations, by using the quadratic formula:

(a) $x^2 - 3x + 2 = 0$

(b) $5t^2 - t = 3$

(c) $6x = 4x^2 - 1$

(d) $9x^2 + 42x + 44 = 0$

(e) $30\,000 = x(x + 200)$

(f) $3x^2 = 5x - 1$

(SM) 5. (a) Find the lengths of the sides of a rectangle whose perimeter is 40 cm and whose area is 75 cm^2.

(b) Find two successive natural numbers whose sum of squares is 13.

(c) In a right-angled triangle, the hypotenuse is 34 cm. One of the short sides is 14 cm longer than the other. Find the lengths of the two short sides.

(d) A motorist drove 80 km. In order to save 16 minutes, he had to drive 10 km/h faster than usual. What was his usual driving speed?

6. [HARDER] Solve the following equations:

(a) $x^3 - 4x = 0$

(b) $x^4 - 5x^2 + 4 = 0$

(c) $z^{-2} - 2z^{-1} - 15 = 0$

2.4 Nonlinear Equations

We now study a more general form of equation, which encompasses linear and quadratic equations, but for which no general method is readily available. These nonlinear equations are ubiquitous in economics, so we must be able to handle them and obtain as much information from them as possible.

EXAMPLE 2.4.1   Solve each of the following three separate equations:

(a) $x^3\sqrt{x + 2} = 0$

(b) $x(y + 3)(z^2 + 1)\sqrt{w - 3} = 0$

(c) $x^2 - 3x^3 = 0$

Solution:

(a) If $x^3\sqrt{x + 2} = 0$, then either $x^3 = 0$ or $\sqrt{x + 2} = 0$. The equation $x^3 = 0$ has only the solution $x = 0$, while $\sqrt{x + 2} = 0$ gives $x = -2$. The solutions of the equation are therefore $x = 0$ and $x = -2$.

(b) There are four factors in the product. One of the factors, $z^2 + 1$, is never 0. Hence, the solutions are: $x = 0$ or $y = -3$ or $w = 3$.

(c) Start by factoring: $x^2 - 3x^3 = x^2(1 - 3x)$. The product $x^2(1 - 3x)$ is 0 if and only if $x^2 = 0$ or $1 - 3x = 0$. Hence, the solutions are $x = 0$ and $x = 1/3$.[5]

In solving these equations, we have repeatedly used the fact that a product of two or more factors is 0 if and only if at least one of the factors is 0. That is, in general,

$$ab = ac \quad \text{is equivalent to} \quad a = 0 \quad \text{or} \quad b = c \tag{2.4.1}$$

because the equation $ab = ac$ is equivalent to $ab - ac = 0$, or $a(b - c) = 0$. If $ab = ac$ and $a \neq 0$, we conclude from Eq. (2.4.1) that $b = c$.

EXAMPLE 2.4.2   What conclusions about the variables can we draw if

(a) $x(x + a) = x(2x + b)$ (b) $\lambda y = \lambda z^2$ (c) $xy^2(1 - y) - 2\lambda(y - 1) = 0$

Solution:

(a) $x = 0$ or $x + a = 2x + b$. The last equation gives $x = a - b$. The solutions are therefore $x = 0$ and $x = a - b$.

(b) $\lambda = 0$ or $y = z^2$. It is easy to forget the former possibility.

(c) The equation is equivalent to

$$xy^2(1 - y) + 2\lambda(1 - y) = 0$$

which can be written as

$$(1 - y)(xy^2 + 2\lambda) = 0$$

We conclude from the last equation that $1 - y = 0$ or $xy^2 + 2\lambda = 0$, that is $y = 1$ or $\lambda = -\frac{1}{2}xy^2$.

Finally, we consider also some equations involving fractions. Recall that the fraction a/b is not defined if $b = 0$. If $b \neq 0$, then $a/b = 0$ is equivalent to $a = 0$.

EXAMPLE 2.4.3   Solve the following equations:

(a) $\dfrac{1 - K^2}{\sqrt{1 + K^2}} = 0$ (b) $\dfrac{45 + 6r - 3r^2}{(r^4 + 2)^{3/2}} = 0$ (c) $\dfrac{x^2 - 5x}{\sqrt{x^2 - 25}} = 0$

---

[5] When trying to solve an equation, an easy way to make a serious mistake is to cancel a factor which might be zero. It is important to check that the factor being cancelled really is not zero. For instance, suppose one cancels the common factor x^2 in the equation $x^2 = 3x^3$. The result is $1 = 3x$, implying that $x = 1/3$. The solution $x = 0$ has been lost.

Solution:

(a) The denominator is never 0, so the fraction is 0 when $1 - K^2 = 0$, that is when $K = \pm 1$.

(b) Again the denominator is never 0. The fraction is 0 when $45 + 6r - 3r^2 = 0$, that is $3r^2 - 6r - 45 = 0$. Solving this quadratic equation, we find that $r = -3$ or $r = 5$.

(c) The numerator is equal to $x(x - 5)$, which is 0 if $x = 0$ or $x = 5$. At $x = 0$ the denominator is $\sqrt{-25}$, which is not defined, and at $x = 5$ the denominator is 0. We conclude that the equation has no solutions.

EXERCISES FOR SECTION 2.4

1. Solve the following equations:

(a) $x(x + 3) = 0$

(b) $x^3(1 + x^2)(1 - 2x) = 0$

(c) $x(x - 3) = x - 3$

(d) $\sqrt{2x + 5} = 0$

(e) $\dfrac{x^2 + 1}{x(x + 1)} = 0$

(f) $\dfrac{x(x + 1)}{x^2 + 1} = 0$

(SM) **2.** Solve the following equations:

(a) $\dfrac{5 + x^2}{(x - 1)(x + 2)} = 0$

(b) $1 + \dfrac{2x}{x^2 + 1} = 0$

(c) $\dfrac{(x + 1)^{1/3} - \frac{1}{3}x(x + 1)^{-2/3}}{(x + 1)^{2/3}} = 0$

(d) $\dfrac{x}{x - 1} + 2x = 0$

(SM) **3.** Examine what conclusions can be drawn about the variables if:

(a) $z^2(z - a) = z^3(a + b),\ a \neq 0$

(b) $(1 + \lambda)\mu x = (1 + \lambda)y\mu$

(c) $\dfrac{\lambda}{1 + \mu} = \dfrac{-\lambda}{1 - \mu^2}$

(d) $ab - 2b - \lambda b(2 - a) = 0$

2.5 Using Implication Arrows

Implication and equivalence arrows are very useful in helping to avoid mistakes when solving equations. Consider first the following example.

EXAMPLE 2.5.1   Solve the equation $(2x - 1)^2 - 3x^2 = 2\left(\frac{1}{2} - 4x\right)$.

Solution: By expanding $(2x - 1)^2$ and also multiplying out the right-hand side, we obtain a new equation that obviously has the same solutions as the original one:

$$(2x - 1)^2 - 3x^2 = 2\left(\frac{1}{2} - 4x\right) \Leftrightarrow 4x^2 - 4x + 1 - 3x^2 = 1 - 8x$$

Adding $8x - 1$ to each side of the second equation and then gathering terms gives an equivalent equation:

$$4x^2 - 4x + 1 - 3x^2 = 1 - 8x \Leftrightarrow x^2 + 4x = 0$$

Now $x^2 + 4x = x(x + 4)$, and the latter expression is zero if, and only if, $x = 0$ or $x = -4$. That is,

$$x^2 + 4x = 0 \Leftrightarrow x(x + 4) = 0 \Leftrightarrow [x = 0 \text{ or } x = -4]$$

where we have used brackets, for the sake of clarity, in the last expression. Putting everything together, we have derived a chain of equivalence arrows showing that the given equation is satisfied for the two values $x = 0$ and $x = -4$, and for no other values of x.

EXAMPLE 2.5.2   Solve the equation $x + 2 = \sqrt{4 - x}$ for x.[6]

Solution: Squaring both sides of the given equation yields

$$(x + 2)^2 = \left(\sqrt{4 - x}\right)^2$$

Consequently, $x^2 + 4x + 4 = 4 - x$, that is, $x^2 + 5x = 0$. From the latter equation it follows that $x(x + 5) = 0$ which yields $x = 0$ or $x = -5$. Thus, a necessary condition for x to solve $x + 2 = \sqrt{4 - x}$ is that $x = 0$ or $x = -5$. Inserting these two possible values of x into the original equation shows that only $x = 0$ satisfies the equation. The unique solution to the equation is, therefore, $x = 0$.

The method used in solving Example 2.5.2 is the most common. It involves setting up a chain of implications that starts from the given equation and ends with all the possible solutions. By testing each of these trial solutions in turn, we find which of them really do satisfy the equation. Even if the chain of implications is also a chain of equivalences, such a test is always a useful check of both logic and calculations.

EXERCISES FOR SECTION 2.5

1. Using implication arrows, solve the equation

$$\frac{(x + 1)^2}{x(x - 1)} + \frac{(x - 1)^2}{x(x + 1)} - 2\frac{3x + 1}{x^2 - 1} = 0$$

2. Using implication arrows, solve the following equations:
   (a) $x + 2 = \sqrt{4x + 13}$ (b) $|x + 2| = \sqrt{4 - x}$ (c) $x^2 - 2|x| - 3 = 0$

(SM) 3. Using implication arrows, solve the following equations:
   (a) $\sqrt{x - 4} = \sqrt{x + 5} - 9$ (b) $\sqrt{x - 4} = 9 - \sqrt{x + 5}$

---

[6] Recall Example 1.2.1.

4. Consider the following attempt to solve the equation $x + \sqrt{x+4} = 2$:

"From the given equation, it follows that $\sqrt{x+4} = 2 - x$. Squaring both sides gives $x + 4 = 4 - 4x + x^2$. After rearranging the terms, it is seen that this equation implies $x^2 - 5x = 0$. Cancelling x, we obtain $x - 5 = 0$ and this equation is satisfied when $x = 5$."

(a) Mark with arrows the implications or equivalences expressed in the text. Which ones are correct?

(b) Solve the equation correctly.

2.6 Two Linear Equations in Two Unknowns

In the macroeconomic model of Example 2.2.1, we found that two equations were needed to model the economic phenomena at hand. In that example, we focused on the solution for the value of GDP, but economists are interested in the solution of *all* endogenous variables in their models. In the example, total consumption would be solved, too.

For the case of two variables that relate through two linear equations, a general method is easy to develop. An example allows us to develop the ideas before we address the general case.

EXAMPLE 2.6.1   Find the values of x and y that satisfy both of the equations

$$2x + 3y = 18$$
$$3x - 4y = -7$$

Solution:

Method 1: A first possibility is to deal with one of the variables first, as we did in Section 2.2, and then use that variable's solution to solve for the other. That is, to follow a two step procedure: (i) solve one of the equations for one of the variables in terms of the other; (ii) substitute the result into the other equation. This leaves only one equation in one unknown, which is easily solved.[7]

To apply this method to our system, we can solve the first equation for y in terms of x: the first equation, $2x + 3y = 18$, implies that $3y = 18 - 2x$ and, hence, that

---

[7] What we did in Example 2.2.1 was to give the first of these steps. The second step would be to substitute (∗∗) into (ii), to find the solution for C, which is

$$C = \frac{a + b\bar{I}}{1 - b}$$

This equation completes the reduced form of the model, together with (∗∗∗).

$y = 6 - (2/3)x$. Substituting this expression for y into the second equation gives

$$3x - 4\left(6 - \frac{2}{3}x\right) = -7$$

$$3x - 24 + \frac{8}{3}x = -7$$

$$9x - 72 + 8x = -21$$

$$17x = 51$$

so $x = 3$.

Then we find y by using $y = 6 - (2/3)x$ once again to obtain $y = 6 - (2/3) \cdot 3 = 4$. The solution of the system is, therefore, $x = 3$ and $y = 4$.[8]

Method 2: This method is based on eliminating one of the variables by adding or subtracting a multiple of one equation from the other. Suppose we want to eliminate y. Suppose we multiply the first equation in the system by 4 and the second by 3. Then the coefficients of y in both equations will be the same except for the sign. If we then add the transformed equations, the term in y disappears and we obtain

$$8x + 12y = 72$$

$$9x - 12y = -21$$

$$\overline{}$$

$$17x = 51$$

Hence, $x = 3$. To find the value for y, substitute 3 for x in either of the original equations and solve for y. This gives $y = 4$, which agrees with the earlier result.

Systems of two equations and two unknowns are usually known as 2×2 systems. The general 2×2 linear system is

$$ax + by = c \tag{2.6.1}$$

$$dx + ey = f \tag{2.6.2}$$

where a, b, c, d, e, and f are arbitrary given numbers, whereas x and y are the variables, or "unknowns".[9]

Let us first assume that $ae - bd \neq 0$. Using Method 2, we multiply the first equation by e and the second by $-b$, then add, to obtain

$$aex + bey = ce$$

$$-bdx - bey = -bf$$

$$\overline{}$$

$$(ae - bd)x = ce - bf$$

---

[8] A useful check is to verify such a solution by direct substitution. Indeed, substituting $x = 3$ and $y = 4$ in the system gives $2 \cdot 3 + 3 \cdot 4 = 18$ and $3 \cdot 3 - 4 \cdot 4 = -7$.

[9] If $a = 2$, $b = 3$, $c = 18$, $d = 3$, $e = -4$, and $f = -7$, this reduces to the system in the example.

which gives the value for x. We can substitute back in (2.6.1) to find y, and the result is

$$x = \frac{ce - bf}{ae - bd} \quad \text{and} \quad y = \frac{af - cd}{ae - bd}$$

We have found expressions for both x and y.

Evidently, these last formulas break down if the denominator $ae - bd$ in both fractions is equal to 0. In this case the second method fails, and indeed solving the two Eqs (2.6.1) and (2.6.2) requires a special method. We begin by following the first method, assuming that $b \neq 0$.[10] Solving for y in Eq. (2.6.1), we get

$$y = \frac{c}{b} - \frac{a}{b}x \tag{$*$}$$

If we now substitute this solution into (2.6.2), we obtain

$$dx + e\left(\frac{c}{b} - \frac{a}{b}x\right) = f$$

$$dx + \frac{ce}{b} - \frac{ae}{b}x = f$$

$$bd \cdot x + ce - ae \cdot x = bf$$

$$(bd - ae)x = bf - ce$$

The problem is that, since $ae - bd = 0$, the last equation becomes, simply, the statement that $bf - ac = 0$, or that $ac = bf$. Note that we have lost both variables from our analysis, and are left with a statement, which may or may not be true, about the parameters of the system.

If $ae = bd$ and $bf \neq ce$, the system has no solution: it is impossible to find values of x and y that simultaneously satisfy its two equations. Now, suppose that, besides $ae - bd = 0$, we also have that $bf - ce = 0$. Recalling that

$$aex + bey = ce$$

$$-bdx - bey = -bf$$

we can see that our two equations are, in fact, only one. We are dealing with a system where one of the equations repeats the information given by the other, adding nothing new to it. Now, note that if we pick *any* value of x, and let y be determined by $(*)$, the first equation is satisfied immediately, by construction. As for the second equation, using the facts that $ae - bd = 0$, $bf - ce = 0$ and $b \neq 0$, so $ae/b = d$ and $ce/b = f$, we get that

$$dx + ey = dx + e\left(\frac{c}{b} - \frac{a}{b}x\right) = \left(d - \frac{ae}{b}\right)x + \frac{ce}{b} = 0 \cdot x + f = f$$

The second equation is satisfied "for free", and we have found "the" solution for the system—in fact, infinitely many of them: with any value of x, and $y = c/b - (a/b)x$.

---

[10] We only need one of the coefficients a, b, d or e to differ from zero. If all are zero, the problem is trivial and not interesting.

We can summarize these results as follows:

2 × 2 LINEAR SYSTEMS

The solution for system (2.6.1) is

$$x = \frac{ce - bf}{ae - bd} \quad \text{and} \quad y = \frac{af - cd}{ae - bd}, \quad \text{provided that } ae \neq bd \tag{2.6.3}$$

When $ae = bd$ and $bf \neq ce$, the system has no solution.
When $ae = bd$ and $bf = ce$, the system has infinitely many solutions:

$$x \text{ takes } any \text{ value and } y = \frac{c}{b} - \frac{a}{b}x, \quad \text{provided that } b \neq 0 \tag{2.6.4}$$

EXERCISES FOR SECTION 2.6

1. Solve the following systems of equations:

(a) $x - y = 5$ and $x + y = 11$ (b) $4x - 3y = 1$ and $2x + 9y = 4$

(c) $3x + 4y = 2.1$ and $5x - 6y = 7.3$

2. Solve the following systems of equations:

(a)
$$\begin{aligned} 5x + 2y &= 3 \\ 2x + 3y &= -1 \end{aligned}$$

(b)
$$\begin{aligned} x - 3y &= -25 \\ 4x + 5y &= 19 \end{aligned}$$

(c)
$$\begin{aligned} 2x + 3y &= 3 \\ 6x + 6y &= -1 \end{aligned}$$

3. Solve the following systems of equations:

(a)
$$\begin{aligned} 23p + 45q &= 181 \\ 10p + 15q &= 65 \end{aligned}$$

(b)
$$\begin{aligned} 0.01r + 0.21s &= 0.042 \\ -0.25r + 0.55s &= -0.47 \end{aligned}$$

(SM) **4.** (a) Find two numbers whose sum is 52 and whose difference is 26.

(b) Five tables and 20 chairs cost $1 800, whereas two tables and three chairs cost $420. What is the price of each table and each chair?

(c) A firm produces headphones in two qualities, Basic (B) and Premium (P). For the coming year, the estimated output of B is 50% higher than that of P. The profit per unit sold is $300 for P and $200 for B. If the profit target is $180 000 over the next year, how much of each of the two qualities must be produced?

(d) At the beginning of the year a person had a total of $10 000 in two accounts. The interest rates were 5% and 7.2% per year, respectively. If the person has made no transfers during the year, and has earned a total of $676 interest, what was the initial balance in each of the two accounts?

REVIEW EXERCISES

1. Solve each of the following equations:

   (a) $3x - 20 = 16$ (b) $-5x + 8 + 2x = -(4-x)$ (c) $-6(x-5) = 6(2-3x)$

   (d) $\dfrac{4-2x}{3} = -5 - x$ (e) $\dfrac{5}{2x-1} = \dfrac{1}{2-x}$ (f) $\sqrt{x-3} = 6$

SM 2. Solve each of the following equations:

   (a) $\dfrac{x-3}{x-4} = \dfrac{x+3}{x+4}$ (b) $\dfrac{3(x+3)}{x-3} - 2 = 9\dfrac{x}{x^2-9} + \dfrac{27}{(x+3)(x-3)}$

   (c) $\dfrac{2x}{3} = \dfrac{2x-3}{3} + \dfrac{5}{x}$ (d) $\dfrac{x-5}{x+5} - 1 = \dfrac{1}{x} - \dfrac{11x+20}{x^2-5x}$

3. Solve the following equations for the variables specified:

   (a) $x = \frac{2}{3}(y-3) + y$, for y (b) $ax - b = cx + d$, for x

   (c) $AK\sqrt{L} = Y_0$, for L (d) $px + qy = m$, for y

   (e) $\dfrac{\dfrac{1}{1+r} - a}{\dfrac{1}{1+r} + b} = c$, for r (f) $Px(Px+Q)^{-1/3} + (Px+Q)^{2/3} = 0$, for x

SM 4. Solve the following equations for the variables indicated:

   (a) $3K^{-1/2}L^{1/3} = 1/5$, for K (b) $(1+r/100)^t = 2$, for r

   (c) $p - abx_0^{b-1} = 0$, for x_0 (d) $\left[(1-\lambda)a^{-\rho} + \lambda b^{-\rho}\right]^{-1/\rho} = c$, for b

5. Solve the following quadratic equations:

   (a) $z^2 = 8z$ (b) $x^2 + 2x - 35 = 0$ (c) $p^2 + 5p - 14 = 0$

   (d) $12p^2 - 7p + 1 = 0$ (e) $y^2 - 15 = 8y$ (f) $42 = x^2 + x$

6. Solve the following equations:

   (a) $(x^2 - 4)\sqrt{5-x} = 0$ (b) $(x^4 + 1)(4+x) = 0$ (c) $(1-\lambda)x = (1-\lambda)y$

7. Johnson invested \$1 500, part of it at 15% interest and the remainder at 20%. His total yearly income from the two investments was \$275. How much did he invest at each rate?

8. Consider the macro model described by the three equations

$$Y = C + \bar{I} + G, \qquad C = b(Y - T), \qquad T = tY$$

Here the parameters b and t lie in the interval $(0, 1)$, Y is the gross domestic product (GDP), C is consumption, $\bar{I}$ is total investment, T denotes taxes, and G is government expenditure.

   (a) Express Y and C in terms of $\bar{I}$, G, and the parameters.

   (b) What happens to Y and C as t increases?

9. If $5^{3x} = 25^{y+2}$ and $x - 2y = 8$, what is $x - y$?

10. [HARDER] Solve the following systems of equations:

(a)
$$\frac{2}{x} + \frac{3}{y} = 4$$
$$\frac{3}{x} - \frac{2}{y} = 19$$

(b)
$$3\sqrt{x} + 2\sqrt{y} = 2$$
$$2\sqrt{x} - 3\sqrt{y} = \frac{1}{4}$$

(c)
$$x^2 + y^2 = 13$$
$$4x^2 - 3y^2 = 24$$

Section 2
Static Analysis

LINEAR AND NONLINEAR FUNCTIONS

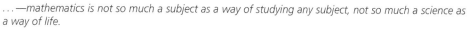

...—mathematics is not so much a subject as a way of studying any subject, not so much a science as a way of life.
—George F.J. Temple (1981)

Functions are important in practically every area of pure and applied mathematics, including mathematics applied to economics. The language of economic analysis is full of terms like demand and supply functions, cost functions, production functions, consumption functions, etc. In this chapter we present a discussion of functions of one real variable, illustrated by some very important economic examples.

3.1 Introduction

One variable is a function of another if the first variable *depends* upon the second. For instance, the area of a circle is a function of its radius. If the radius r is given, then the area A is determined. In fact $A = \pi r^2$, where π is the numerical constant $3.14159\ldots$.

One does not need a mathematical formula to convey the idea that one variable is a function of another: A table can also show the relationship. For instance, Table 3.1 shows the evolution of total final consumption expenditure, measured in current euros, without allowing for inflation, in the European Union (28 countries), from the first quarter of 2013, which we write as 13Q1, to the last quarter of 2014, which we write as 14Q4. This table defines consumption expenditure as a function of the calendar quarter.

In ordinary conversation we sometimes use the word "function" in a similar way. For example, we might say that the infant mortality rate of a country is a function of the quality of its health care, or that a country's national product is a function of the level of investment.

The dependence between two real variables can also be illustrated by means of a graph. In Fig. 3.1.1 we have drawn a curve that allegedly played an important role some years ago in the discussion of "supply side economics". It shows the presumed relationship between a country's income tax rate and its total income tax revenue. Obviously, if the tax rate is 0%, then tax revenue is 0. However, if the tax rate is 100%, then tax revenue will also be (about) 0, since nobody is willing to work if their entire income is going to be confiscated.

Table 3.1 Final consumption expenditure in the EU, 2013Q1–2014Q4 (billions of euros)

Quarter	13Q1	13Q2	13Q3	13Q4	14Q1	14Q2	14Q3	14Q4
Consumption	1 917.5	1 924.9	1 934.3	1 946.0	1 958.6	1 973.4	1 995.1	2 008.2

This curve, which has generated considerable controversy, is supposed to have been drawn on the back of a restaurant napkin by an American economist, Arthur Laffer, who later popularized its message with the public.[1]

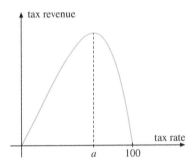

Figure 3.1.1 The "Laffer curve", which relates tax revenue to tax rates

In some instances a graph is preferable to a formula. A case in point is an electrocardiogram (ECG) showing the heartbeat pattern of a patient. Here the doctor studies the pattern of repetitions directly from the graphs; the patient might die before the doctor could understand a formula approximating the ECG picture.

All of the relationships discussed above have one characteristic in common: A definite rule relates each value of one variable to a definite value of another variable. In the ECG example the function is the rule showing electrical activity as a function of time.

In all of our examples it is implicitly assumed that the variables are subject to certain constraints. For instance, in Table 3.1 only the quarters of 2013 and 2014 are relevant.

3.2   Basic Definitions

The examples in the preceding section lead to the following general definition, with D a set of real numbers:

FUNCTION

A (real-valued) *function* of a real variable x with *domain* D is a rule that assigns a unique real number to each real number x in D. As x varies over the whole domain, the set of all possible resulting values $f(x)$ is called the *range* of f.

---

[1]   Actually, there are many economists who previously had the same idea. See, for instance, part (b) in Example 7.2.2.

The word "rule" is used in a very broad sense. *Every* rule with the properties described is called a function, whether that rule is given by a formula, described in words, defined by a table, illustrated by a curve, or expressed by any other means.

Functions are given letter names, such as f, g, F, or φ. If f is a function and x is a number in its domain D, then $f(x)$ denotes the number that the function f assigns to x. The symbol $f(x)$ is pronounced "f of x", or often just "f x". It is important to note the difference between f, which is a symbol for the function (the rule), and $f(x)$, which denotes the value of f at x.

If f is a function, we sometimes let y denote the value of f at x, so $y = f(x)$. Then, we call x the *independent variable*, or the *argument* of f, whereas y is called the *dependent variable*, because the value y (in general) depends on the value of x. The domain of the function f is then the set of all possible values of the independent variable, whereas the range is the set of corresponding values of the dependent variable. In economics, x is often called the *exogenous* variable, which is supposed to be fixed *outside* the economic model, whereas for each given x the equation $y = f(x)$ serves to determine the *endogenous* variable y *inside* the economic model.

A function is often defined by a formula, such as $y = 8x^2 + 3x + 2$. The function is then the rule $x \mapsto 8x^2 + 3x + 2$ that assigns the number $8x^2 + 3x + 2$ to each value of x.

Functional Notation

To become familiar with the relevant notation, it helps to look at some examples of functions that are defined by formulas.

EXAMPLE 3.2.1   A function is defined for all numbers by the following rule:

Assign to any number its third power.

This function will assign $0^3 = 0$ to 0, $3^3 = 27$ to 3, $(-2)^3 = (-2)(-2)(-2) = -8$ to -2, and $(1/4)^3 = 1/64$ to $1/4$. In general, it assigns the number x^3 to the number x. If we denote this third power function by f, then $f(x) = x^3$. So we have $f(0) = 0^3 = 0$, $f(3) = 3^3 = 27$, $f(-2) = (-2)^3 = -8$, and $f(1/4) = (1/4)^3 = 1/64$. In general, substituting a for x in the formula for f gives $f(a) = a^3$, whereas

$$f(a + 1) = (a + 1)^3 = (a + 1)(a + 1)(a + 1) = a^3 + 3a^2 + 3a + 1$$

A common error is to presume that $f(a) = a^3$ implies $f(a + 1) = a^3 + 1$. The error can be illustrated by considering a simple interpretation of f. If a is the edge of a cube measured in metres, then $f(a) = a^3$ is the volume of the cube measured in cubic metres, or m^3. Suppose that each edge of the cube expands by 1 m. Then the volume of the new cube is $f(a + 1) = (a + 1)^3$ m^3. The number $a^3 + 1$ can be interpreted as the number obtained when the volume of a cube with edge a is increased by 1 m^3. In fact, $f(a + 1) = (a + 1)^3$ is quite a bit more than $a^3 + 1$, as illustrated in Figs 3.2.1 and 3.2.2.

EXAMPLE 3.2.2   The total dollar cost of producing x units of a product is given by

$$C(x) = 100x\sqrt{x} + 500$$

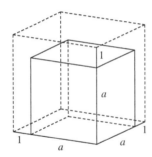

Figure 3.2.1 Volume $f(a+1) = (a+1)^3$

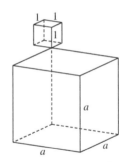

Figure 3.2.2 Volume $a^3 + 1$

for each nonnegative integer x. Find the cost of producing 16 units. Suppose the firm produces a units; find the *increase* in the cost from producing one additional unit.

Solution: The cost of producing 16 units is found by substituting 16 for x in the formula for $C(x)$:

$$C(16) = 100 \cdot 16\sqrt{16} + 500 = 100 \cdot 16 \cdot 4 + 500 = 6900$$

The cost of producing a units is $C(a) = 100a\sqrt{a} + 500$, and the cost of producing $a + 1$ units is $C(a + 1)$. Thus the increase in cost is

$$C(a + 1) - C(a) = 100(a + 1)\sqrt{a + 1} + 500 - 100a\sqrt{a} - 500$$

$$= 100\left[(a + 1)\sqrt{a + 1} - a\sqrt{a}\right]$$

In economic theory, we often study functions that depend on a number of parameters, as well as the independent variable. An obvious generalization of Example 3.2.2 follows.

EXAMPLE 3.2.3   Suppose that the cost of producing x units of a commodity is

$$C(x) = Ax\sqrt{x} + B$$

where A and B are constants. Find the cost of producing 0, 10, and $x + h$ units.

Solution: The cost of producing 0 units is $C(0) = A \cdot 0 \cdot \sqrt{0} + B = 0 + B = B$.[2] Similarly, $C(10) = A10\sqrt{10} + B$. Finally,

$$C(x + h) = A(x + h)\sqrt{x + h} + B$$

which comes from substituting $x + h$ for x in the given formula.

So far we have used x to denote the independent variable, but we could just as well have used almost any other symbol. For example, the following formulas define exactly the same function (and hence we can set $f = g = \varphi$):

$$f(x) = x^4, \qquad g(t) = t^4, \qquad \varphi(\xi) = \xi^4$$

---

[2] Parameter B simply represents fixed costs. These are the costs that must be paid whether or not anything is actually produced, such as a taxi driver's annual licence fee.

For that matter, we could also express this function as $x \mapsto x^4$, or alternatively as $f(\cdot) = (\cdot)^4$. Here it is understood that the dot between the parentheses can be replaced by an arbitrary number, or an arbitrary letter, or even another function (like $1/y$). Thus,

$$1 \mapsto 1^4 = 1, \quad k \mapsto k^4, \quad \text{and} \quad 1/y \mapsto (1/y)^4$$

or alternatively

$$f(1) = 1^4 = 1, \quad f(k) = k^4, \quad \text{and} \quad f(1/y) = (1/y)^4$$

Specifying the Domain and the Range

The definition of a function is not really complete unless its domain is either obvious or specified explicitly. The natural domain of the function f defined by $f(x) = x^3$ is the set of all real numbers. In Example 3.2.2, where $C(x) = 100x\sqrt{x} + 500$ denotes the cost of producing x units of a product, the domain was specified as the set of nonnegative integers. Actually, a more natural domain is the set of numbers $0, 1, 2, \ldots, x_0$, where x_0 is the maximum number of items the firm can produce. For a producer like an iron mine, however, where output x is a continuous variable, the natural domain is the closed interval $[0, x_0]$.

We shall adopt the convention that *if a function is defined using an algebraic formula, the domain consists of all values of the independent variable for which the formula gives a unique value, unless another domain is explicitly mentioned.*

EXAMPLE 3.2.4   Find the domains of

(a) $f(x) = 1/(x + 3)$ (b) $g(x) = \sqrt{2x + 4}$

Solution:

(a) For $x = -3$, the formula reduces to the meaningless expression "$1/0$". For all other values of x, the formula makes $f(x)$ a well-defined number. Thus, the domain consists of all numbers $x \neq -3$.

(b) The expression $\sqrt{2x + 4}$ is uniquely defined for all x such that $2x + 4$ is nonnegative. Solving the inequality $2x + 4 \geq 0$ for x gives $x \geq -2$. The domain of g is therefore the interval $[-2, \infty)$.

Let f be a function with domain D. The set of all values $f(x)$ that the function assumes is called the *range* of f. Often, we denote the domain of f by D_f, and the range by R_f. These concepts are illustrated in Fig. 3.2.3, using the idea of the graph of a function which we formally discuss in Section 3.3.

Alternatively, we can think of any function f as an engine operating so that if x in the domain is an input, the output is $f(x)$. The range of f is then all the numbers we get as output using all numbers in the domain as inputs. If we try to use as an input a number not in the domain, the engine does not work, and there is no output.

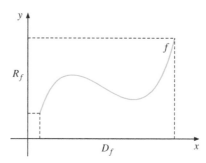

Figure 3.2.3 The domain and range of f

EXAMPLE 3.2.5   Show first that the number 4 belongs to the range of the function defined by $g(x) = \sqrt{2x+4}$. Find the entire range of g. Then, use Example 3.2.4 to show that g has domain $[-2, \infty)$.

Solution: To show that 4 is in the range of g, we must find a number x such that $g(x) = 4$. That is, we must solve the equation $\sqrt{2x+4} = 4$ for x. By squaring both sides of the equation, we get $2x+4 = 4^2 = 16$, that is, $x = 6$. Because $g(6) = 4$, the number 4 does belong to the range R_g.

In order to determine the whole range of g, we must answer the question: As x runs through the whole of the interval $[-2, \infty)$, what are all the possible values of $\sqrt{2x+4}$? For $x = -2$, one has $\sqrt{2x+4} = 0$, and $\sqrt{2x+4}$ can never be negative. We claim that whatever number $y_0 \geq 0$ is chosen, there exists a number x_0 such that $\sqrt{2x_0+4} = y_0$. Indeed, squaring each side of this last equation gives $2x_0 + 4 = y_0^2$. Hence, $2x_0 = y_0^2 - 4$, which implies that $x_0 = \frac{1}{2}(y_0^2 - 4)$. Because $y_0^2 \geq 0$, we have $x_0 = \frac{1}{2}\left(y_0^2 - 4\right) \geq \frac{1}{2}(-4) = -2$. Hence, for every number $y_0 \geq 0$, we have found a number $x_0 \geq -2$ such that $g(x_0) = y_0$. The range of g is, therefore, $[0, \infty)$.

Even if a function is completely specified by a formula, including a specific domain, it is not always easy to find the range of the function. For example, without using the methods of differential calculus, it is hard to find R_f exactly when $f(x) = 3x^3 - 2x^2 - 12x - 3$ and $D_f = [-2, 3]$.

A function f is called *increasing* if $x_1 < x_2$ implies $f(x_1) \leq f(x_2)$, and *strictly increasing* if $x_1 < x_2$ implies $f(x_1) < f(x_2)$. *Decreasing* and *strictly decreasing* functions are defined in the obvious way (see Section 5.3). The function g in Example 3.2.5 is strictly increasing in $[-2, \infty)$.

Calculators (including calculator programs on personal computers or smart phones) often have many special functions built into them. For example, most of them have the key $\boxed{\sqrt{x}}$ which, when given a number x, returns the square root $\sqrt{x}$ of that number. If we enter a nonnegative number such as 25, and then press the square root key, the number 5 appears. If we enter -3, then "Error", or "Not a number" is shown. This is the way the calculator tells us that $\sqrt{-3}$ is not defined within the real number system.

EXERCISES FOR SECTION 3.2

(SM) **1.** Let $f(x) = x^2 + 1$.

    (a) Compute $f(0), f(-1), f(1/2)$, and $f(\sqrt{2})$.

    (b) For what values of x is it true that

        (i) $f(x) = f(-x)$?

        (ii) $f(x + 1) = f(x) + f(1)$?

        (iii) $f(2x) = 2f(x)$?

2. Suppose $F(x) = 10$, for all x. Find $F(0)$, $F(-3)$, and $F(a + h) - F(a)$.

3. Let $f(t) = a^2 - (t - a)^2$, where a is a constant.

    (a) Compute $f(0), f(a), f(-a)$, and $f(2a)$.   (b) Compute $3f(a) + f(-2a)$.

4. Let $f(x) = x/(1 + x^2)$.

    (a) Compute $f(-1/10), f(0), f(1/\sqrt{2}), f(\sqrt{\pi})$, and $f(2)$.

    (b) Show that $f(-x) = -f(x)$ for all x, and that $f(1/x) = f(x)$ for $x \neq 0$.

5. Let $F(t) = \sqrt{t^2 - 2t + 4}$. Compute $F(0)$, $F(-3)$, and $F(t + 1)$.

6. The cost of producing x units of a commodity is given by $C(x) = 1000 + 300x + x^2$.

    (a) Compute $C(0)$, $C(100)$, and $C(101) - C(100)$.

    (b) Compute $C(x + 1) - C(x)$, and explain in words the meaning of the difference.

7. The demand for cotton in the USA, for the period 1915–1919, with appropriate units for the price P and the quantity Q, was estimated to be $Q = D(P) = 6.4 - 0.3P$.

    (a) Find the demand quantity in each case if the price is 8, 10, and 10.22.

    (b) If the demand quantity is 3.13, what is the price?

8. (a) If $f(x) = 100x^2$, show that for all $t, f(tx) = t^2 f(x)$.

    (b) If $P(x) = x^{1/2}$, show that for all $t \geq 0$, $P(tx) = t^{1/2} P(x)$.

9. The cost of removing $p\%$ of the impurities in a lake is given by $b(p) = 10p/(105 - p)$.

    (a) Find $b(0)$, $b(50)$, and $b(100)$.

    (b) What does $b(50 + h) - b(50)$ mean (where $h \geq 0$)?

10. Only for very special "additive" functions is it true that $f(a + b) = f(a) + f(b)$ for all a and b. Determine whether $f(2 + 1) = f(2) + f(1)$ for the following functions:

    (a) $f(x) = 2x^2$ (b) $f(x) = -3x$ (c) $f(x) = \sqrt{x}$

11. (a) If $f(x) = Ax$, show that $f(a + b) = f(a) + f(b)$ for all numbers a and b.

(b) If $f(x) = 10^x$, show that $f(a + b) = f(a) \cdot f(b)$ for all natural numbers a and b.

12. A friend of yours claims that $(x + 1)^2 = x^2 + 1$. Can you use a geometric argument to show that this is wrong?

SM **13.** Find the domains of the functions defined by the following formulas:

(a) $y = \sqrt{5 - x}$ (b) $y = \dfrac{2x - 1}{x^2 - x}$ (c) $y = \sqrt{\dfrac{x - 1}{(x - 2)(x + 3)}}$

14. Let $f(x) = (3x + 6)/(x - 2)$.

(a) Find the domain of the function.

(b) Show that 5 is in the range of f, by finding an x such that $(3x + 6)/(x - 2) = 5$.

(c) Show that 3 is not in the range of f.

15. Find the domain and the range of $g(x) = 1 - \sqrt{x + 2}$.

3.3 Graphs of Functions

Recall that a *rectangular* (or a *Cartesian*) coordinate system is obtained by first drawing two perpendicular lines, called coordinate axes. The two axes are respectively the *x-axis* (or the *horizontal axis*) and the *y-axis* (or the *vertical axis*). The intersection point O is called the *origin*. We measure the real numbers along each of these lines, as shown in Fig. 3.3.1. The unit distance on the *x*-axis is not necessarily the same as on the *y*-axis, although this is the case in Fig. 3.3.1.

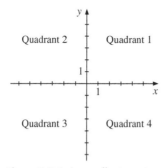

Figure 3.3.1 A coordinate system

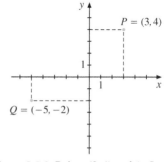

Figure 3.3.2 Points $(3, 4)$ and $(-5, -2)$

The rectangular coordinate system in Fig. 3.3.1 is also called the *xy-plane*. The coordinate axes separate the plane into four quadrants, which traditionally are numbered as in Fig. 3.3.1. Any point P in the plane can be represented by a unique pair (a, b) of real numbers. These can be found by drawing dashed lines, like those in Fig. 3.3.2, which are perpendicular to the two axes. The point represented by (a, b) lies at the intersection of the vertical straight line $x = a$ with the horizontal straight line $y = b$.

Conversely, any pair of real numbers represents a unique point in the plane. For example, in Fig. 3.3.2, if the ordered pair $(3, 4)$ is given, the corresponding point P lies at the intersection of $x = 3$ with $y = 4$. Thus, P lies three units to the right of the y-axis and four units above the x-axis. We call $(3, 4)$ the *coordinates* of P. Similarly, Q lies five units to the left of the y-axis and two units below the x-axis, so the coordinates of Q are $(-5, -2)$.

Note that we call (a, b) an *ordered pair*, because the order of the two numbers in the pair is important. For instance, $(3, 4)$ and $(4, 3)$ represent two different points.

As you surely know, each function of one variable can be represented by a graph in such a rectangular coordinate system. Such a representation helps us visualize the function. This is because the shape of the graph reflects the properties of the function.

GRAPH

The *graph* of a function f is the set of all ordered pairs $(x, f(x))$, where x belongs to the domain of f.

EXAMPLE 3.3.1   Consider the function $f(x) = x^2 - 4x + 3$. The values of $f(x)$ for some special choices of x are given in Table 3.2. If we plot the points $(0, 3)$, $(1, 0)$, $(2, -1)$, $(3, 0)$, and $(4, 3)$, which are obtained from the table, in an xy-plane, and draw a smooth curve through these points, we obtain the graph of the function, as in Fig. 3.3.3.[3]

Table 3.2 Values of $f(x) = x^2 - 4x + 3$

x	0	1	2	3	4
$f(x) = x^2 - 4x + 3$	3	0	−1	0	3

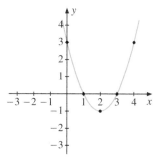

Figure 3.3.3 The graph of $f(x) = x^2 - 4x + 3$

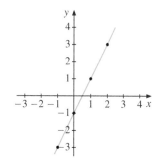

Figure 3.3.4 The graph of $g(x) = 2x - 1$

---

[3] This graph is called a *parabola*, as you will see in Section 3.6.

EXAMPLE 3.3.2   Find some of the points on the graph of $g(x) = 2x - 1$, and sketch it.

Solution: One has $g(-1) = 2 \cdot (-1) - 1 = -3$, $g(0) = 2 \cdot 0 - 1 = -1$, and $g(1) = 2 \cdot 1 - 1 = 1$. Moreover, $g(2) = 3$. There are infinitely many points on the graph, so we cannot write them all down. In Fig. 3.3.4 the four points $(-1, -3)$, $(0, -1)$, $(1, 1)$, and $(2, 3)$ are marked off, and they seem to lie on a straight line. That line is the graph.

Some Important Graphs

Figures 3.3.5–3.3.10 show some special functions that occur so often in applications that you should learn to recognize their graphs. You should in each case make a table of function values to confirm the form of these graphs.

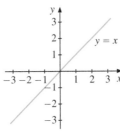

Figure 3.3.5 $y = x$

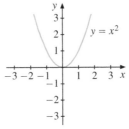

Figure 3.3.6 $y = x^2$

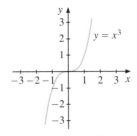

Figure 3.3.7 $y = x^3$

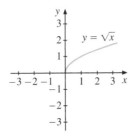

Figure 3.3.8 $y = \sqrt{x}$

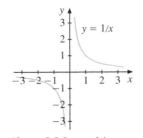

Figure 3.3.9 $y = 1/x$

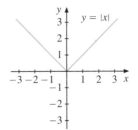

Figure 3.3.10 $y = |x|$

Note that when we try to plot the graph of a function, we must try to include a sufficient number of points, otherwise we might miss some of its important features. Actually, by merely plotting a finite set of points, we can never be entirely sure that there are no wiggles or bumps we have missed. For more complicated functions we have to use differential calculus to decide how many bumps and wiggles there are.

EXERCISES FOR SECTION 3.3

1. Plot all the five points $(2, 3)$, $(-3, 2)$, $(-3/2, -2)$, $(4, 0)$, and $(0, 4)$ in one coordinate system.

2. The graph of function f is given in Fig. 3.3.11.

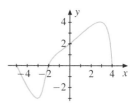

Figure 3.3.11 Exercise 2

(a) Find $f(-5), f(-3), f(-2), f(0), f(3)$, and $f(4)$ by examining the graph.

(b) Determine the domain and the range of f.

3. Fill in the tables and draw the graphs of the following functions:

(a)

x	0	1	2	3	4
$g(x) = -2x + 5$					

(b)

x	-2	-1	0	1	2	3	4
$h(x) = x^2 - 2x - 3$							

(c)

x	-2	-1	0	1	2
$F(x) = 3^x$					

(d)

x	-2	-1	0	1	2	3
$G(x) = 1 - 2^{-x}$						

3.4 Linear Functions

Linear equations occur very often in economics. Recall from Eq. (3.2.1) that they are defined as

$$y = ax + b$$

where a and b are constants. As we saw in Example 3.3.2, the graph of the equation is a straight line. If we let f denote the function that assigns y to x, then $f(x) = ax + b$, and f is called a *linear* function.

Take an arbitrary value of x. Then

$$f(x + 1) - f(x) = a(x + 1) + b - ax - b = a$$

This shows that a measures the change in the value of the function when x increases by one unit. For this reason, the number a is the *slope* of the line (or the function). If the slope a is positive, then the line slants upward to the right, and the larger the value of a, the steeper is the line. On the other hand, if a is negative, then the line slants downward to the right, and the absolute value of a measures the steepness of the line. For example, when $a = -3$, the steepness is 3. In the special case when $a = 0$, the steepness is zero, because the line is horizontal. In this case we have $a = 0$, so the line $y = ax + b$ becomes $y = b$ for all x.

The three different cases are illustrated in Figs 3.4.1 to 3.4.3. If $x = 0$, then $y = ax + b = b$, and b is called the **y**-*intercept*, or often just the intercept.

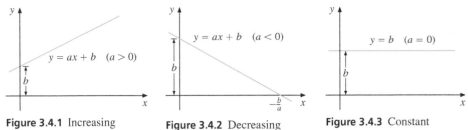

Figure 3.4.1 Increasing   **Figure 3.4.2** Decreasing   **Figure 3.4.3** Constant

EXAMPLE 3.4.1   Find and interpret the slopes of the following straight lines.

(a) The cost function for US Steel Corp. during the period 1917–1938 was estimated to be $C = 55.73x + 182\,100\,000$, where C is the total cost in dollars per year, and x is the production of steel in tons per year.

(b) The demand function for rice in India, for the period 1949–1964, was estimated to be $q = -0.15p + 0.14$, where p is price per kilo in Indian rupees, and q is the annual consumption per person, measured in kilos.

Solution:

(a) The slope is 55.73, which means that if production increases by one ton, then the cost *increases* by \$55.73.

(b) The slope is -0.15, which tells us that if the price increases by one Indian rupee per kilo, then the quantity demanded *decreases* by 0.15 kilos per year.

Computing the slope of a straight line in the plane is easy. Pick two different points on the line $P = (x_1, y_1)$ and $Q = (x_2, y_2)$, as shown in Fig. 3.4.4. The slope of the line is the ratio $(y_2 - y_1)/(x_2 - x_1)$

If we denote the slope by a, then:

SLOPE OF A STRAIGHT LINE

The *slope* of the straight line l is

$$a = \frac{y_2 - y_1}{x_2 - x_1}, \qquad x_1 \neq x_2$$

where (x_1, y_1) and (x_2, y_2) are any two distinct points on l.

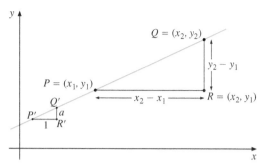

Figure 3.4.4 Slope $a = (y_2 - y_1)/(x_2 - x_1)$

Multiplying both the numerator and the denominator of $(y_2 - y_1)/(x_2 - x_1)$ by -1 gives $(y_1 - y_2)/(x_1 - x_2)$, which does *not* change the ratio. This shows that it does not make any difference which point is P and which is Q. Moreover, the properties of similar triangles imply that the ratios $Q'R'/P'R'$ and QR/PR in Fig. 3.4.4 must be equal. For this reason, the number $a = (y_2 - y_1)/(x_2 - x_1)$ is equal to the change in the value of y when x increases by one unit; this change is the slope.

EXAMPLE 3.4.2   Determine the slopes of the three straight lines l, m, and n in Figs 3.4.5 to 3.4.7.

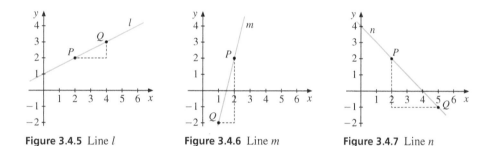

Figure 3.4.5 Line l **Figure 3.4.6** Line m **Figure 3.4.7** Line n

Solution: The lines l, m, and n all pass through $P = (2, 2)$. In Fig. 3.4.5, the point Q is $(4, 3)$, whereas in Fig. 3.4.6 it is $(1, -2)$, and in Fig. 3.4.7 it is $(5, -1)$. Therefore, the respective slopes of the lines l, m, and n are

$$a_l = \frac{3-2}{4-2} = \frac{1}{2}, \qquad a_m = \frac{-2-2}{1-2} = 4, \qquad a_n = \frac{-1-2}{5-2} = -1$$

The Point–slope and Point–point Formulas

Let us find the equation of a straight line l passing through the point $P = (x_1, y_1)$ with slope a. If (x, y) is any other point on the line, the slope a is given by the formula:

$$\frac{y - y_1}{x - x_1} = a$$

Multiplying each side by $x - x_1$, we obtain $y - y_1 = a(x - x_1)$. Hence:

POINT—SLOPE FORMULA OF A STRAIGHT LINE

The equation of the straight line passing through (x_1, y_1) with slope a is

$$y - y_1 = a(x - x_1)$$

Note that when using this formula, x_1 and y_1 are fixed numbers giving the coordinates of the given point. On the other hand, x and y are variables denoting the coordinates of an arbitrary point on the line.

EXAMPLE 3.4.3   Find the equation of the line through $(-2, 3)$ with slope -4. Then find the y-intercept and the point at which this line intersects the x-axis.

Solution: The point–slope formula with $(x_1, y_1) = (-2, 3)$ and $a = -4$ gives the equation $y - 3 = (-4)[x - (-2)]$, or $y - 3 = -4(x + 2)$, which reduces to $4x + y = -5$. The y-intercept has $x = 0$, so $y = -5$. The line intersects the x-axis at the point where $y = 0$, that is, where $4x = -5$, so $x = -5/4$. The point of intersection with the x-axis is therefore $(-5/4, 0)$.[4]

Often we need to find the equation of the straight line that passes through two given distinct points. Combining the slope formula and the point–slope formula, we obtain the following:

POINT—POINT FORMULA OF A STRAIGHT LINE

The equation of the straight line passing through (x_1, y_1) and (x_2, y_2), where $x_1 \neq x_2$, is obtained as follows:

1. Compute the slope of the line,

$$a = \frac{y_2 - y_1}{x_2 - x_1}$$

2. Substitute the expression for a into the point–slope formula. The result is

$$y - y_1 = \frac{y_2 - y_1}{x_2 - x_1}(x - x_1)$$

---

[4] It is a good exercise for you to draw a graph and verify this solution.

EXAMPLE 3.4.4   Find the equation of the line passing through $(-1, 3)$ and $(5, -2)$.

Solution: Let $(x_1, y_1) = (-1, 3)$ and $(x_2, y_2) = (5, -2)$. Then the point–point formula gives

$$y - 3 = \frac{-2 - 3}{5 - (-1)}[x - (-1)] = -\frac{5}{6}(x + 1)$$

or $5x + 6y = 13$.

Graphical Solutions of Linear Equations

Section 2.6 dealt with algebraic methods for solving a system of two linear equations in two unknowns. The equations are linear, so their graphs are straight lines. The coordinates of any point on a line satisfy the equation of that line. Thus, the coordinates of any point of intersection of these two lines will satisfy both equations. This means that any point where these lines intersect will satisfy the equation system.

EXAMPLE 3.4.5   Solve each of the following three pairs of equations graphically:

(a) $x + y = 5$ and $x - y = -1$ (b) $3x + y = -7$ and $x - 4y = 2$

(c) $3x + 4y = 2$ and $6x + 8y = 24$

Solution:

(a) Figure 3.4.8 shows the graphs of the straight lines $x + y = 5$ and $x - y = -1$. There is only one point of intersection, which is $(2, 3)$. The solution of the system is, therefore, $x = 2$, $y = 3$.

(b) Figure 3.4.9 shows the graphs of the straight lines $3x + y = -7$ and $x - 4y = 2$. There is only one point of intersection, which is $(-2, -1)$. The solution of the system is, therefore, $x = -2$, $y = -1$.

(c) Figure 3.4.10 shows the graphs of the straight lines $3x + 4y = 2$ and $6x + 8y = 24$. These lines are parallel and have no point of intersection. The system has no solutions.

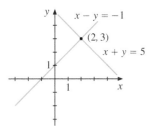

Figure 3.4.8 $x + y = 5$ and $x - y = -1$

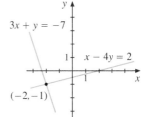

Figure 3.4.9 $3x + y = -7$ and $x - 4y = 2$

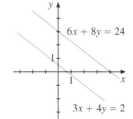

Figure 3.4.10 $3x + 4y = 2$ and $6x + 8y = 24$

Linear Inequalities

This section concludes by discussing how to represent linear inequalities geometrically. We present two examples.

EXAMPLE 3.4.6   Sketch in the xy-plane the set of all pairs of numbers (x, y) that satisfy the inequality $2x + y \leq 4$—that is, using set notation, the set $\{(x, y) : 2x + y \leq 4\}$.

Solution: The inequality can be written as $y \leq -2x + 4$. The set of points (x, y) that satisfy the equation $y = -2x + 4$ is a straight line. Therefore, the set of points (x, y) that satisfy the inequality $y \leq -2x + 4$ must have y-values below those of points on the line $y = -2x + 4$. So it must consist of all points that lie on or below this line. See Fig. 3.4.11.

EXAMPLE 3.4.7   A person has $\$m$ to spend on the purchase of two commodities. The prices of the two commodities are $\$p$ and $\$q$ per unit. Suppose x units of the first commodity and y units of the second commodity are bought. Assuming that negative purchases of either commodity are impossible, one must have both $x \geq 0$ and $y \geq 0$. It follows that the person is restricted to the *budget set* given by

$$B = \{(x, y) : \ px + qy \leq m, \ x \geq 0, \ y \geq 0\}$$

Sketch the budget set B in the xy-plane. Find the slope of the budget line, $px + qy = m$, and its x- and y-intercepts.

Solution: The set of points (x, y) that satisfy $x \geq 0$ and $y \geq 0$ is the first (nonnegative) quadrant. If we impose the additional requirement that $px + qy \leq m$, we obtain the triangular domain B shown in Fig. 3.4.12.

If $px + qy = m$, then $qy = -px + m$ and so $y = (-p/q)x + m/q$. This shows that the slope is $-p/q$. The budget line intersects the x-axis when $y = 0$. Then $px = m$, so $x = m/p$. The budget line intersects the y-axis when $x = 0$. Then $qy = m$, so $y = m/q$. So the two points of intersection are $(m/p, 0)$ and $(0, m/q)$, as shown in Fig. 3.4.12.

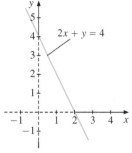

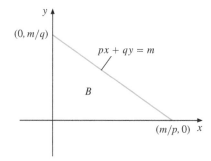

Figure 3.4.11 $\{(x, y) : 2x + y \leq 4\}$ **Figure 3.4.12** Budget set: $px + qy \leq m$, $x \geq 0$, and $y \geq 0$

EXERCISES FOR SECTION 3.4

1. Find the slopes of the lines passing through the following pairs of points:

   (a) $(2, 3)$ and $(5, 8)$ (b) $(-1, -3)$ and $(2, -5)$ (c) $\left(\frac{1}{2}, \frac{3}{2}\right)$ and $\left(\frac{1}{3}, -\frac{1}{5}\right)$

2. Draw graphs for the following straight lines:

   (a) $3x + 4y = 12$ (b) $\dfrac{x}{10} - \dfrac{y}{5} = 1$ (c) $x = 3$

3. Suppose demand D for a good is a linear function of its price per unit, P. When price is $10, demand is 200 units, and when price is $15, demand is 150 units. Find the demand function.

4. Decide which of the following relationships are linear:

   (a) $5y + 2x = 2$ (b) $P = 10(1 - 0.3t)$

   (c) $C = (0.5x + 2)(x - 3)$ (d) $p_1 x_1 + p_2 x_2 = R$, where p_1, p_2, and R constants.

5. A printing company quotes the price of $1\,400$ for producing 100 copies of a report, and $3\,000$ for 500 copies. Assuming a linear relation, what would be the price of printing 300 copies?

6. Find the slopes of the five lines L_1 to L_5 shown in Fig. 3.4.13, and give equations describing them.

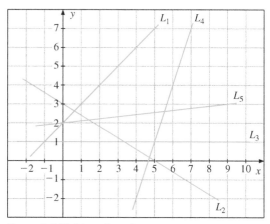

Figure 3.4.13 Lines L_1 to L_5

7. Determine the equations for the following straight lines:

   (a) L_1 passes through $(1, 3)$ and has a slope of 2.

   (b) L_2 passes through $(-2, 2)$ and $(3, 3)$.

   (c) L_3 passes through the origin and has a slope of $-1/2$.

   (d) L_4 passes through $(a, 0)$ and $(0, b)$, with $a \neq 0$.

8. Solve the following systems of equations graphically, where possible:

   (a) $x - y = 5$ and $x + y = 1$ (b) $x + y = 2$, $x - 2y = 2$ and $x - y = 2$

   (c) $3x + 4y = 1$ and $6x + 8y = 6$

9. Sketch in the xy-plane the set of all pairs of numbers (x, y) that satisfy the following inequalities:

(a) $2x + 4y \geq 5$ (b) $x - 3y + 2 \leq 0$ (c) $100x + 200y \leq 300$

(SM) **10.** Sketch in the xy-plane the set of all pairs of numbers (x, y) that satisfy all the following three inequalities: $3x + 4y \leq 12$, $x - y \leq 1$, and $3x + y \geq 3$.

3.5 Linear Models

Linear relations occur frequently in mathematical models. The relationship between the Celsius and Fahrenheit temperature scales is an example of a linear relation between two variables. (Recall that $F = \frac{9}{5}C + 32$, by definition, from Example 2.6.5.) Most of the linear models in economics are approximations to more complicated models. Two illustrations are those shown in Example 3.4.1. Statistical methods have been devised to construct linear functions that approximate the actual data as closely as possible. Let us consider a very naive attempt to construct a linear model based on some population data.

EXAMPLE 3.5.1   A United Nations report estimated that the European population was 606 million in 1960, and 657 million in 1970. Use these estimates to construct a linear function of t that approximates the population in Europe. Then use the function to estimate the population in 1930, 2000, and 2015.

Solution: Let t be the number of years from 1960, so that $t = 0$ is 1960, $t = 1$ is 1961, and so on. If P denotes the population in millions, we construct an equation of the form $P = at + b$. We know that the graph must pass through the points $(t_1, P_1) = (0, 606)$ and $(t_2, P_2) = (10, 657)$. So we use the point–point formula, replacing x and y with t and P, respectively. This gives

$$P - 606 = \frac{657 - 641}{10 - 0}(t - 0) = \frac{51}{10}t$$

or

$$P = 5.1t + 606 \tag{$*$}$$

In Table 3.3, we have compared our estimates with UN forecasts. Note that because $t = 0$ corresponds to 1960, $t = -30$ will correspond to 1930.

Table 3.3 Population estimates for Europe

Year	1930	2000	2015
t	-30	40	55
UN estimates	549	726	738
Formula ($*$) gives	555	810	887

Note that the slope of line $(*)$ is 5.1 This means that if the European population had developed according to $(*)$, then the annual increase in the population would have been constant and equal to 5.1 million.[5]

EXAMPLE 3.5.2　**(The Consumption Function)**　In Keynesian macroeconomic theory, total consumption expenditure on goods and services, C, is assumed to be a function of national income Y, with $C = f(Y)$. Following the work of Keynes's associate Richard F. Kahn, in many models the consumption function is assumed to be linear, so that $C = a + bY$. Then the slope b is called the *marginal propensity to consume*. For example, if C and Y are measured in billions of dollars, the number b tells us by how many billions of dollars consumption would increase if national income were to increase by 1 billion dollars. Following Kahn's insight, the number b is usually thought to lie between 0 and 1.

The Norwegian economist Trygve Haavelmo,[6] in a study of the US economy for the period 1929–1941, estimated the consumption function as $C = 95.05 + 0.712\,Y$. Here, the marginal propensity to consume is equal to 0.712.

EXAMPLE 3.5.3　**(Supply and Demand)**　Over a fixed period of time such as a week, the quantity of a specific good that consumers demand (that is, are willing to buy) will depend on the price of that good. Usually, as the price increases the demand will decrease.[7] Also, the number of units that the producers are willing to supply to the market during a certain period depends on the price they are able to obtain. Usually, the supply will increase as the price increases. So typical demand and supply curves are as indicated in Fig. 3.5.1.

The point E in Fig. 3.5.1, at which demand is equal to supply, represents an *equilibrium*. The price P^e at which this occurs is the *equilibrium price* and the corresponding quantity Q^e is the *equilibrium quantity*. The equilibrium price is thus the price at which consumers will buy the same amount of the good as the producers wish to sell at that price.

As a very simple example, consider the following linear demand and supply functions: $D = 100 - P$ and $S = 10 + 2P$; or, in inverse form, $P = 100 - D$ and $P = \frac{1}{2}S - 5$, as in Fig. 3.5.2.[8] The quantity demanded D equals the quantity supplied S provided $100 - P =$

---

[5] Actually, Europe's population grew unusually fast during the 1960s. Of course, it grew unusually slowly when millions died during the war years 1939–1945. We see that formula $(*)$ does not give very good results compared to the UN estimates. For a better way to model population growth see Example 3.9.1.

[6] (1911–1999). He was awarded the Nobel prize in 1989.

[7] For certain luxury goods like perfume, which are often given as presents, demand might increase as the price increases. For absolutely essential goods, like insulin for diabetics, demand might be almost independent of the price. Occasionally dietary staples could also be "Giffen goods" for which demand rises as price rises. The explanation offered is that these foodstuffs are so essential to a very poor household's survival that a rise in price lowers real income substantially, and so makes alternative sources of nourishment even less affordable.

[8] When specifying a linear supply function, the sign of the constant term can be problematic. In the case we just introduced, a negative constant has the unintuitive implication that supply is positive even when the price is zero—in our case, it is 10 units. One possibility for something like this to occur would be when the producer owns a stock of the product and this is highly perishable. But having the supply be positive and increasing at very low prices can be inconsistent with the producer's behaviour. The difficulty is that a positive constant brings about a problem too: that at

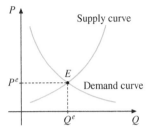

Figure 3.5.1 Demand and supply curves

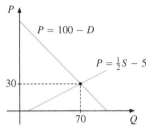

Figure 3.5.2 $D = 100 - P$ and $S = 10 + 2P$

$10 + 2P$, that is, $3P = 90$. So the equilibrium price is $P^e = 30$, with equilibrium quantity $Q^e = 70$.

A peculiarity of Figs 3.5.1 and 3.5.2 is that, although quantity is usually regarded as a function of price, here we measure price on the vertical axis and quantity on the horizontal axis. This has been standard practice in elementary price theory since the fundamental ideas of the French mathematician and economist Antoine-Augustin Cournot (1801–1877) and several other European contemporaries became popularized in the late 19th century by the English economist Alfred Marshall (1842–1924).

EXAMPLE 3.5.4   **(Linear Supply and Demand Functions)**   Consider the following general linear demand and supply schedules: $D = a - bP$ and $S = \alpha + \beta P$, where a and b are positive parameters of the demand function D, while α and β are positive parameters of the supply function.[9]

The equilibrium price P^e occurs where demand equals supply. Hence $D = S$ at $P = P^e$ implying that $a - bP^e = \alpha + \beta P^e$, or $a - \alpha = (\beta + b)P^e$. The corresponding equilibrium quantity is $Q^e = a - bP^e$. So equilibrium occurs at

$$P^e = \frac{a - \alpha}{\beta + b} \quad \text{and} \quad Q^e = a - b\frac{a - \alpha}{\beta + b} = \frac{a\beta + \alpha b}{\beta + b}$$

EXERCISES FOR SECTION 3.5

1. The consumption function $C = 4141 + 0.78Y$ was estimated for the UK during the period 1949–1975. What is the marginal propensity to consume?

2. Find the equilibrium price for each of the following linear models of supply and demand:

(a) $D = 75 - 3P$ and $S = 2P$ (b) $D = 100 - 0.5P$ and $S = -20 + 0.5P$

---

some low prices, the producer's supply is negative. We will overlook these issues here, but they serve as a warning that overly simplified models can sometimes display undesirable features.

[9] Such linear supply and demand functions play an important role in economics. It is often the case that the market for a particular commodity, such as copper, can be represented approximately by suitably estimated linear demand and supply functions.

3. The total cost C of producing x units of some commodity is a linear function of x. Records show that on one occasion, 100 units were made at a total cost of $200, and on another occasion, 150 units were made at a total cost of $275. Express the linear equation for total cost C in terms of the number of units x produced.

4. The expenditure of a household on consumer goods, C, is related to the household's income, y, in the following way: When the household's incomeis $1 000, the expenditure on consumer goods is $900, and whenever income increases by $100, the expenditure on consumer goods increases by $80. Express the expenditure on consumer goods as a function of income, assuming a linear relationship.

5. For most assets such as cars, electronic goods, and furniture, the value decreases, or *depreciates*, each year. If the value of an asset is assumed to decrease by a fixed percentage of the original value each year, it is referred to as *straight line depreciation*.

   (a) Suppose the value of a car which initially costs $20 000 depreciates by 10% of its original value each year. Find a formula for its value $P(t)$ after t years.

   (b) If a $500 washing machine is completely depreciated after ten years (straight line depreciation), find a formula for its value $W(t)$ after t years.

3.6 Quadratic Functions

Economists often find that linear functions are too simple for modelling economic phenomena with acceptable accuracy. Indeed, many economic models involve functions that either decrease down to some minimum value and then increase, or else increase up to some maximum value and then decrease. Some simple functions with this property are the general *quadratic* functions that we first saw in Section 2.3:

$$f(x) = ax^2 + bx + c \tag{3.6.1}$$

where a, b, and c are constants, with $a \neq 0$, otherwise the function would be linear.

In general, the graph of $f(x) = ax^2 + bx + c$ is called a *parabola*. The shape of this parabola roughly resembles $\cap$ when $a < 0$ and $\cup$ when $a > 0$. Three typical cases are illustrated in Figs 3.6.1 to 3.6.3. The graphs are symmetric about the *axis of symmetry*, which is the vertical dashed line in each of the three cases.

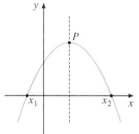

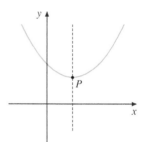

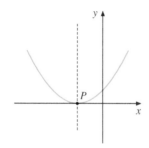

Figure 3.6.1 $a < 0, b^2 > 4ac$ **Figure 3.6.2** $a > 0, b^2 < 4ac$ **Figure 3.6.3** $a > 0, b^2 = 4ac$

In order to investigate the function $f(x) = ax^2 + bx + c$ in more detail, we should find the answers to the following questions:

(a) For which values of x (if any) is $ax^2 + bx + c = 0$?

(b) What are the coordinates of the maximum/minimum point P, also called the *vertex* of the parabola?

The answer to question (a) was given by the quadratic formula (2.3.4) and the subsequent discussion of that formula. The easiest way to handle question (b) is to use derivatives, which is the topic of Chapter 5—see, in particular, Exercise 5.2.7. However, let us briefly consider how the "method of completing the squares" from Section 2.3 can be used to answer question (b).

In fact, this method yields

$$f(x) = ax^2 + bx + c = a\left(x + \frac{b}{2a}\right)^2 - \frac{b^2 - 4ac}{4a} \tag{3.6.2}$$

as is easily verified by expanding the right-hand side and gathering terms. Now, when x varies, only the value of $a(x + b/2a)^2$ changes. This term is equal to 0 only when $x = -b/2a$, and if $a > 0$, it is never less than 0. This means that when $a > 0$, then the function $f(x)$ attains its minimum when $x = -b/2a$, and the value of $f(x)$ is then equal to

$$f(-b/2a) = -(b^2 - 4ac)/4a = c - b^2/4a$$

If $a < 0$ on the other hand, then $a(x + b/2a)^2 \leq 0$ for all x, and the squared term is equal to 0 only when $x = -b/2a$. Hence, $f(x)$ attains its maximum when $x = -b/2a$ in this second case.

To summarize, we have shown the following:

EXTREMA OF QUADRATIC FUNCTIONS

$$\text{If } a > 0, \text{ then } f(x) = ax^2 + bx + c \text{ has its } \textit{minimum} \text{ at } x = -b/2a \tag{3.6.3}$$

$$\text{If } a < 0, \text{ then } f(x) = ax^2 + bx + c \text{ has its } \textit{maximum} \text{ at } x = -b/2a \tag{3.6.4}$$

The axis of symmetry for a parabola is the vertical line through its vertex, which is the point P in all three Figs 3.6.1 to 3.6.3.[10] Indeed, formula (3.6.2) implies that, for any number u, one has

$$f\left(-\frac{b}{2a} + u\right) = au^2 - \frac{b^2 - 4ac}{4a} = f\left(-\frac{b}{2a} - u\right)$$

It follows that the quadratic function $f(x) = ax^2 + bx + c$ is symmetric about the vertical line $x = -b/2a$ which passes through P.

---

[10] The function f is symmetric about $x = x_0$ if $f(x_0 + t) = f(x_0 - t)$ for all x.

Quadratic Optimization Problems in Economics

Much of economic analysis is concerned with optimization problems. Economics, after all, is the science of choice, and optimization problems are the form in which economists usually model choice mathematically. A general discussion of such problems must be postponed until we have developed the necessary tools from calculus. Here we show how the simple results from this section on maximizing quadratic functions can be used to illustrate some basic economic ideas.

EXAMPLE 3.6.1   Suppose the price P per unit obtained by a firm in producing and selling Q units is $P = 102 - 2Q$, and the cost of producing and selling Q units is $C = 2Q + \frac{1}{2}Q^2$. Then the profit is[11]

$$\pi(Q) = PQ - C = (102 - 2Q)Q - \left(2Q + \frac{1}{2}Q^2\right) = 100Q - \frac{5}{2}Q^2$$

Find the value of Q which maximizes profit, and the corresponding maximal profit.

Solution: Using formula (3.6.4), we find that profit is maximized at

$$Q = Q^* = -\frac{100}{2 \cdot (-5/2)} = 20$$

with

$$\pi^* = \pi(Q^*) = 100 \cdot 20 - \frac{5}{2} \cdot 400 = 1000$$

This example is a special case of the monopoly problem studied in the next example.

EXAMPLE 3.6.2   **(A Monopoly Problem)** Consider a firm that is the only seller of the commodity it produces, possibly a patented medicine, and so enjoys a monopoly. The total costs of the monopolist are assumed to be given by the quadratic function

$$C = \alpha Q + \beta Q^2$$

of its output level $Q \geq 0$, where α and β are positive constants. For each Q, the price P at which it can sell its output is assumed to be determined from the linear "inverse" demand function

$$P = a - bQ$$

where a and b are constants with $a > 0$ and $b \geq 0$. So for any nonnegative Q, the total revenue R is given by the quadratic function $R = PQ = (a - bQ)Q$, and profit by the quadratic function

$$\pi(Q) = R - C = (a - bQ)Q - \alpha Q - \beta Q^2 = (a - \alpha)Q - (b + \beta)Q^2$$

Assuming that the monopolist's objective is to maximize the profit function $\pi = \pi(Q)$, find the optimal output level Q^M and the corresponding optimal profit π^M.

---

[11] In mathematics the Greek letter π is used to denote the constant ratio $3.1415\ldots$ between the circumference of a circle and its diameter. In economics, this constant is not used very often. Also, p and P usually denote a price, so π has come to denote profit.

Solution: By using (3.6.4), we see that there is a maximum of π at

$$Q^M = \frac{a - \alpha}{2(b + \beta)} \tag{3.6.5}$$

with

$$\pi^M = \frac{(a - \alpha)^2}{2(b + \beta)} - (b + \beta)\frac{(a - \alpha)^2}{4(b + \beta)^2} = \frac{(a - \alpha)^2}{4(b + \beta)}$$

This result is valid if $a > \alpha$; if $a \le \alpha$, the firm will not produce, but will have $Q^M = 0$ and $\pi^M = 0$. The two cases are illustrated in Figs 3.6.4 and 3.6.5. In Fig. 3.6.5, the part of the parabola to the left of $Q = 0$ is dashed, because it is not really relevant given the natural requirement that $Q \ge 0$. The price and cost associated with Q^M in (3.6.5) can be found by routine algebra.

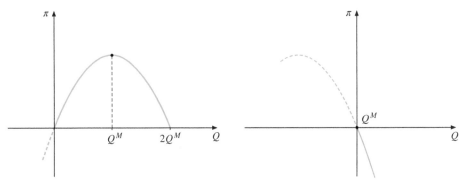

Figure 3.6.4 The profit function, $a > \alpha$ **Figure 3.6.5** The profit function, $a \le \alpha$

If we put $b = 0$ in the price function $P = a - bQ$, then $P = a$ for all Q. In this case, the firm's choice of quantity does not influence the price at all and so the firm is said to be *perfectly competitive*. By replacing a by P in our previous expressions, we see that profit is maximized for a perfectly competitive firm at

$$Q^* = \frac{P - \alpha}{2\beta} \tag{3.6.6}$$

with

$$\pi^* = \frac{(P - \alpha)^2}{4\beta}$$

provided that $P > \alpha$. If $P \le \alpha$, then $Q^* = 0$ and $\pi^* = 0$.

Solving (3.6.6) for P yields $P = \alpha + 2\beta Q^*$. Thus, the equation

$$P = \alpha + 2\beta Q \tag{3.6.7}$$

represents the *supply curve* of this perfectly competitive firm for $P > \alpha$. For $P \le \alpha$, the profit-maximizing output Q^* is 0. The supply curve relating the price on the market to the firm's choice of output quantity is shown in Fig. 3.6.6; it includes all the points of the line segment between the origin and $(0, \alpha)$, where the price is too low for the firm to earn any profit by producing a positive output.

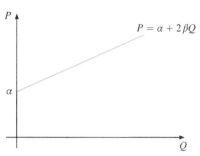

Figure 3.6.6 The supply curve of a perfectly competitive firm

Let us return to the monopoly firm (which has no supply curve). If it could somehow be made to act like a competitive firm, taking price as given, it would be on the supply curve (3.6.7). Given the demand curve $P = a - bQ$, equilibrium between supply and demand occurs when (3.6.7) is also satisfied, and so $P = a - bQ = \alpha + 2\beta Q$. Solving the second equation for Q, and then substituting for P and π in turn, we see that the respective equilibrium levels of output, price, and profit would be

$$Q^e = \frac{a - \alpha}{b + 2\beta}, \qquad P^e = \frac{2a\beta + \alpha b}{b + 2\beta}, \qquad \pi^e = \frac{\beta(a - \alpha)^2}{(b + 2\beta)^2}$$

In order to have the monopolist mimic a competitive firm by choosing to be at (Q^e, P^e), it may be desirable to tax (or subsidize) the output of the monopolist. Suppose that the monopolist is required to pay a specific tax of τ per unit of output. Because the tax payment, $\tau \cdot Q$, is added to the firm's costs, the new total cost function is

$$C = \alpha Q + \beta Q^2 + \tau Q = (\alpha + \tau)Q + \beta Q^2$$

Carrying out the same calculations as before, but with α replaced by $\alpha + \tau$, gives the monopolist's choice of output as

$$Q_\tau^M = \begin{cases} \dfrac{a - \alpha - \tau}{2(b + \beta)}, & \text{if } a \geq \alpha + \tau \\ 0, & \text{otherwise} \end{cases}$$

So $Q_\tau^M = Q^e$ when

$$\frac{a - \alpha - \tau}{2(b + \beta)} = \frac{a - \alpha}{b + 2\beta}$$

Solving this equation for τ yields

$$\tau = -\frac{(a - \alpha)b}{b + 2\beta}$$

Note that τ is actually negative, indicating the desirability of *subsidizing* the output of the monopolist in order to encourage additional production.[12]

---

[12] Of course, subsidizing monopolists is usually felt to be unjust, and many additional complications need to be considered carefully before formulating a desirable policy for dealing with monopolists. Still the previous analysis suggests that if it is desirable to lower a monopolist's price or its profit, this can be done much better directly than by taxing its output.

EXERCISES FOR SECTION 3.6

1. Let $f(x) = x^2 - 4x$.

(a) Complete the following table and use it to sketch the graph of f:

x	-1	0	1	2	3	4	5
$f(x)$							

(b) Using Eq. (3.6.3), determine the minimum point of f.

(c) Solve the equation $f(x) = 0$.

2. Let $f(x) = -\frac{1}{2}x^2 - x + \frac{3}{2}$.

(a) Complete the following table and sketch the graph of f:

x	-4	-3	-2	-1	0	1	2
$f(x)$							

(b) Using Eq. (3.6.4), determine the maximum point of f.

(c) Solve the equation $f(x) = 0$.

(d) Show that $f(x) = -\frac{1}{2}(x - 1)(x + 3)$, and use this to study how the sign of $f(x)$ varies with x. Compare the result with your graph.

3. Determine the maximum/minimum points of the following functions, by using Eqs (3.6.3) or (3.6.4), as appropriate:

(a) $x^2 + 4x$

(b) $x^2 + 6x + 18$

(c) $-3x^2 + 30x - 30$

(d) $9x^2 - 6x - 44$

(e) $-x^2 - 200x + 30\,000$

(f) $x^2 + 100x - 20\,000$

4. Find all the zeros of each quadratic function in Exercise 3, and where possible write each function in the form $a(x - x_1)(x - x_2)$.

5. Find solutions to the following equations, where p and q are parameters.

(a) $x^2 - 3px + 2p^2 = 0$

(b) $x^2 - (p + q)x + pq = 0$

(c) $2x^2 + (4q - p)x = 2pq$

6. A model in the theory of efficient loan markets involves the function

$$U(x) = 72 - (4 + x)^2 - (4 - rx)^2$$

where r is a constant. Find the value of x for which $U(x)$ attains its largest value.

7. A farmer has 1000 metres of fence wire with which to make a rectangular enclosure, as illustrated in the figure below.

(a) Find the areas of the three rectangles whose bases are 100, 250, and 350 metres.

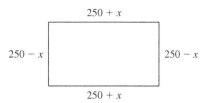

Figure 3.6.7 A plot of land

(b) Let the base have length $250 + x$. Then the height is $250 - x$, as in Fig. 3.6.7. What choice of x gives the maximum area?[13]

8. If a cocoa shipping firm sells Q tons of cocoa in the UK, the price received is given by $P_E = \alpha_1 - \frac{1}{3}Q$. On the other hand, if it buys Q tons from its only source in Ghana, the price it has to pay is given by $P_G = \alpha_2 + \frac{1}{6}Q$. In addition, it costs γ per ton to ship cocoa from its supplier in Ghana to its customers in the UK (its only market). The numbers α_1, α_2, and γ are all positive.

(a) Express the cocoa shipper's profit as a function of Q, the number of tons shipped.

(b) Assuming that $\alpha_1 - \alpha_2 - \gamma > 0$, find the profit-maximizing shipment of cocoa. What happens if $\alpha_1 - \alpha_2 - \gamma \leq 0$?

(c) Suppose the government of Ghana imposes an export tax on cocoa of τ per ton. Find the new expression for the shipper's profits and the new quantity shipped.

(d) Calculate the Ghanaian government's export tax revenue as a function of τ, and compare the graph of this function with the Laffer curve presented in Fig. 3.1.1.

(e) Advise the Ghanaian government on how to obtain as much tax revenue as possible.

(SM) 9. [HARDER] Let $a_1, a_2, \ldots, a_n$ and $b_1, b_2, \ldots, b_n$ be arbitrary real numbers. The inequality

$$\left(a_1 b_1 + a_2 b_2 + \cdots + a_n b_n\right)^2 \leq \left(a_1^2 + a_2^2 + \cdots + a_n^2\right)\left(b_1^2 + b_2^2 + \cdots + b_n^2\right) \tag{3.6.8}$$

is called the *Cauchy–Schwarz inequality*.

(a) Check the inequality for $n = 2$, when $a_1 = -3$, $a_2 = 2$, $b_1 = 5$, and $b_2 = -2$.

(b) Prove (3.6.8) by means of the following trick: first, define f for all x by

$$f(x) = (a_1 x + b_1)^2 + \cdots + (a_n x + b_n)^2$$

It should be obvious that $f(x) \geq 0$ for all x. Write $f(x)$ as $Ax^2 + Bx + C$, where the expressions for A, B, and C are related to the terms in (3.6.8). Because $Ax^2 + Bx + C \geq 0$ for all x, we must have $B^2 - 4AC \leq 0$. Why?

(c) Argue that (3.6.8) then follows.

---

[13] It is reported that certain surveyors in antiquity, when selling rectangular pieces of land to farmers, would write contracts in which only the perimeter was specified. As a result, the lots they sold were long narrow rectangles.

3.7 Polynomials

After considering linear and quadratic functions, the logical next step is to examine *cubic functions* of the form

$$f(x) = ax^3 + bx^2 + cx + d \tag{3.7.1}$$

where a, b, c, and d are constants and $a \neq 0$. It is relatively easy to examine the behaviour of linear and quadratic functions. Cubic functions are considerably more complicated, because the shape of their graphs changes drastically as the coefficients a, b, c, and d vary. Two examples are given in Figs 3.7.1 and 3.7.2. Cubic functions do occasionally appear in economic models.

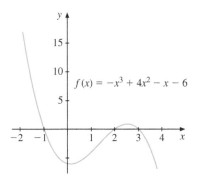

Figure 3.7.1 A cubic function   **Figure 3.7.2** A cubic cost function

EXAMPLE 3.7.1   Consider a firm producing a single commodity. The total cost of producing Q units of the commodity is $C(Q)$. Cost functions often have the following properties: First, $C(0)$ is positive, because an initial fixed expenditure is involved. When production increases, costs also increase. In the beginning, costs increase rapidly, but the rate of increase slows down as production equipment is used for a higher proportion of each working week. However, at high levels of production, costs again increase at a fast rate, because of technical bottlenecks and overtime payments to workers, for example. It can be shown that the cubic cost function $C(Q) = aQ^3 + bQ^2 + cQ + d$ exhibits this type of behaviour provided that $a > 0$, $b < 0$, $c > 0$, $d > 0$, and $3ac > b^2$. Such a function is sketched in Fig. 3.7.2.

Cubic cost functions whose coefficients have a different sign pattern have also been studied. For instance, a study of a particular electric power generating plant revealed that over a certain period, the cost of fuel y as a function of output Q was given by

$$y = -Q^3 + 214.2Q^2 - 7900Q + 320\,700$$

Note, however, that this cost function cannot be valid for all Q, because it suggests that fuel costs would be negative for large enough Q.

The detailed study of cubic functions is made easier by applying differential calculus, as will be seen later.

General Polynomials

Linear, quadratic, and cubic functions are all examples of *polynomials.*

GENERAL POLYNOMIAL

The function P, defined for all x, by

$$P(x) = a_n x^n + a_{n-1} x^{n-1} + \cdots + a_1 x + a_0 \qquad (3.7.2)$$

where $a_0, a_1, \ldots, a_n$ are constants and $a_n \neq 0$, is called the *general polynomial of degree n*, with *coefficients* $a_n, a_{n-1}, \ldots, a_0$.

For instance, when $n = 4$, we obtain $P(x) = a_4 x^4 + a_3 x^3 + a_2 x^2 + a_1 x + a_0$, which is the general *quartic function*, or polynomial of degree 4. Of course, there are many functions like $5 + x^{-2}$ or $1/(x^3 - x + 2)$ that are not polynomials.

Numerous problems in mathematics and its applications involve polynomials. Often, one is particularly interested in finding the number and location of the *zeros* of $P(x)$—that is, the values of x such that $P(x) = 0$. The equation

$$a_n x^n + a_{n-1} x^{n-1} + \cdots + a_1 x + a_0 = 0 \qquad (3.7.3)$$

is called the *general equation of degree n*. It will soon be shown that this equation has *at most n* (real) solutions, also called *roots*, but it need not have any. The corresponding n-th-degree polynomial has a graph which has at most $n - 1$ turning points, but there may be fewer such points. For example, the 100th-degree equation $x^{100} + 1 = 0$ has no solutions because $x^{100} + 1$ is always greater than or equal to 1, and its graph has only one turning point.

According to the *fundamental theorem of algebra*, every polynomial of the form (3.7.2) can be written as a product of polynomials of degree 1 or 2.

Factoring Polynomials

Let $P(x)$ and $Q(x)$ be two polynomials for which the degree of $P(x)$ is greater than or equal to the degree of $Q(x)$. Then, there always exist unique polynomials $q(x)$ and $r(x)$ such that

$$P(x) = q(x)Q(x) + r(x) \qquad (3.7.4)$$

where the degree of $r(x)$ is less than the degree of $Q(x)$. This fact is called the *remainder theorem*. When x is such that $Q(x) \neq 0$, then (3.7.4) can be written in the form

$$\frac{P(x)}{Q(x)} = q(x) + \frac{r(x)}{Q(x)}$$

where $r(x)$ is the remainder. If $r(x) = 0$, we say that $Q(x)$ *is a factor of* $P(x)$, or that $P(x)$ *is divisible by* $Q(x)$. Then $P(x) = q(x)Q(x)$ or $P(x)/Q(x) = q(x)$.

An important special case is when $Q(x) = x - a$. Then $Q(x)$ is of degree 1, so the remainder $r(x)$ must have degree 0, and is therefore a constant. In this special case, for all x,

$$P(x) = q(x)(x - a) + r$$

For $x = a$ in particular, we get $P(a) = r$. Hence, $x - a$ divides $P(x)$ if and only if $P(a) = 0$. This important observation can be formulated as follows:

POLYNOMIAL FACTORIZATION

The polynomial $P(x)$ has the factor $x - a \Leftrightarrow P(a) = 0$.   (3.7.5)

EXAMPLE 3.7.2   Prove that $x - 5$ is a factor of the polynomial $P(x) = x^3 - 3x^2 - 50$.

Solution: $P(5) = 125 - 75 - 50 = 0$, so according to (3.7.5), $x - 5$ divides $P(x)$. In fact, note that $P(x) = (x - 5)(x^2 + 2x + 10)$.

It follows from (3.7.5) that an n-th-degree polynomial $P(x)$ can have *at most n* different zeros. The reason is that each zero gives rise to a different factor of the form $x - a$, so $P(x)$ can have at most n such factors.

Note that each integer m that satisfies the cubic equation

$$-x^3 + 4x^2 - x - 6 = 0 \qquad (*)$$

must satisfy the equation $m(-m^2 + 4m - 1) = 6$. Since $-m^2 + 4m - 1$ is also an integer, m must be a factor of the constant term 6. Thus ± 1, ± 2, ± 3, and ± 6 are the only possible integer solutions. Direct substitution into the left-hand side of Eq. $(*)$ reveals that of these eight possibilities, -1, 2, and 3 are roots of the equation. A third-degree equation has at most three roots, so we have found them all. In fact,

$$-x^3 + 4x^2 - x - 6 = -(x + 1)(x - 2)(x - 3)$$

In general:

INTEGER ROOTS

Suppose that a_n, a_{n-1}, ..., a_1, a_0 are all integers. Then, all possible integer roots of the equation

$$a_n x^n + a_{n-1} x^{n-1} + \cdots + a_1 x + a_0 = 0 \qquad (3.7.6)$$

must be factors of the constant term a_0.

EXAMPLE 3.7.3   Find all possible integer roots of the equation

$$\frac{1}{2}x^3 - x^2 + \frac{1}{2}x - 1 = 0$$

Solution: We multiply both sides of the equation by 2 to obtain an equation whose coefficients are all integers: $x^3 - 2x^2 + x - 2 = 0$. Now, all integer solutions of the equation must be factors of 2, so only ± 1 and ± 2 can be integer solutions. A check shows that $x = 2$ is the only integer solution. In fact, because $x^3 - 2x^2 + x - 2 = (x - 2)(x^2 + 1)$, there is only one real root.

EXAMPLE 3.7.4   Find possible quadratic and cubic functions which have the graphs in Figs 3.7.3 and 3.7.4, respectively.

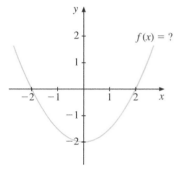

Figure 3.7.3 A quadratic function

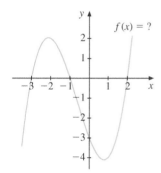

Figure 3.7.4 A cubic function

Solution: For Fig 3.7.3, since the graph intersects the x-axis at the two points $x = -2$ and $x = 2$, we try the quadratic function $f(x) = a(x - 2)(x + 2)$. Then $f(0) = -4a$. According to the graph, $f(0) = -2$, so $a = 1/2$, and hence

$$f(x) = \frac{1}{2}(x - 2)(x + 2) = \frac{1}{2}x^2 - 2$$

For Fig. 3.7.4, because the equation $f(x) = 0$ has roots $x = -3, -1, 2$, we try the cubic function $f(x) = b(x + 3)(x + 1)(x - 2)$. Then $f(0) = -6b$. According to the graph, $f(0) = -3$. So $b = 1/2$, and hence

$$f(x) = \frac{1}{2}(x + 3)(x + 1)(x - 2)$$

Polynomial Division

One can divide polynomials in much the same way as one uses long division to divide numbers. To remind ourselves how long division works, consider a simple numerical example:

$$2735 \div 5 = 500 + 40 + 7$$
$$\underline{2500}$$
$$235$$
$$\underline{200}$$
$$35$$
$$\underline{35}$$
$$0 \qquad \leftarrow \text{ the remainder}$$

Hence, $2735 \div 5 = 547.$[14]

Consider next

$$(-x^3 + 4x^2 - x - 6) \div (x - 2)$$

We write the following:

$$
\begin{array}{ll}
-x^3 + 4x^2 - x - 6 \div \quad x - 2 \quad = -x^2 + 2x + 3 \\
\underline{-x^3 + 2x^2} \qquad\qquad \leftarrow -x^2(x-2) \\
\quad +2x^2 - x - 6 \\
\quad \underline{+2x^2 - 4x} \qquad \leftarrow \quad 2x(x-2) \\
\qquad +3x - 6 \\
\qquad \underline{+3x - 6} \quad \leftarrow \quad 3(x-2) \\
\qquad\qquad 0 \qquad\qquad\qquad \leftarrow \text{ the remainder}
\end{array}
$$

We conclude that $(-x^3 + 4x^2 - x - 6) \div (x - 2) = -x^2 + 2x + 3$. However, it is easy to see that $-x^2 + 2x + 3 = -(x+1)(x-3)$. So

$$-x^3 + 4x^2 - x - 6 = -(x+1)(x-3)(x-2)$$

EXAMPLE 3.7.5   Prove that the polynomial $P(x) = -2x^3 + 2x^2 + 10x + 6$ has a zero at $x = 3$, and factor the polynomial.

Solution: Inserting $x = 3$ yields $P(3) = 0$, so $x = 3$ is a zero. According to (3.7.5), the polynomial $P(x)$ has $x - 3$ as a factor. Performing the division $(-2x^3 + 2x^2 + 10x + 6) \div (x - 3)$, we find that the result is $-2(x^2 + 2x + 1) = -2(x + 1)^2$, and so $P(x) = -2(x - 3)(x + 1)^2$.

Polynomial Division with a Remainder

The division $2734 \div 5$ gives 546 and leaves the remainder 4. So $2734/5 = 546 + 4/5$. We consider a similar form of division for polynomials.

---

[14] Note that the horizontal lines instruct you to subtract the numbers above the lines. You may be more accustomed to a different way of arranging the numbers, but the idea is the same.

EXAMPLE 3.7.6   Perform the division: $(x^4 + 3x^2 - 4) \div (x^2 + 2x)$.

Solution: Proceeding as before,[15]

$$
\begin{array}{l}
x^4 \qquad\; + 3x^2 \qquad\quad - 4 \;\div\quad x^2 + 2x \quad = \; x^2 - 2x + 7 \\
\underline{x^4 + 2x^3 \qquad\qquad\qquad\quad} \leftarrow \;\; x^2(x^2 + 2x) \\
\quad -2x^3 + 3x^2 \qquad\; - 4 \\
\quad \underline{-2x^3 - 4x^2 \qquad\qquad} \leftarrow \; -2x(x^2 + 2x) \\
\qquad\qquad 7x^2 \qquad\; - 4 \\
\qquad\qquad \underline{7x^2 + 14x \qquad} \leftarrow \;\; 7(x^2 + 2x) \\
\qquad\qquad\qquad\;\; -14x - 4 \qquad\qquad\qquad \leftarrow \;\; \text{the remainder}
\end{array}
$$

We conclude that

$$x^4 + 3x^2 - 4 = (x^2 - 2x + 7)(x^2 + 2x) + (-14x - 4)$$

Hence,

$$\frac{x^4 + 3x^2 - 4}{x^2 + 2x} = x^2 - 2x + 7 - \frac{14x + 4}{x^2 + 2x}$$

Rational Functions

A *rational function* is a function $R(x) = P(x)/Q(x)$ that can be expressed as the ratio of two polynomials $P(x)$ and $Q(x)$. This function is defined for all x where $Q(x) \neq 0$. The rational function $R(x)$ is called *proper* if the degree of $P(x)$ is less than the degree of $Q(x)$. When the degree of $P(x)$ is greater than or equal to that of $Q(x)$, then $R(x)$ is called an *improper* rational function. By using polynomial division, any improper rational function can be written as a polynomial plus a proper rational function, as in Example 3.7.6.

EXAMPLE 3.7.7   One of the simplest types of rational function is

$$R(x) = \frac{ax + b}{cx + d}$$

where $c \neq 0$ — otherwise, if $c = 0$, then $R(x)$ is either a linear function in case $d \neq 0$, or else is undefined if $d = 0$ as well.

The graph of R is a *hyperbola*. See Fig. 5.1.7 for a typical example where $R(x) = (3x - 5)/(x - 2)$.[16] A very simple case is $R(x) = a/x$, where $a > 0$. Figure 3.7.5 shows the part of the graph of this function where $x > 0$. Note that the shaded area A always equals a, independent of which point P we choose on the curve, since the area is $A = x_0(a/x_0) = a$.

Studying the behaviour of more complicated rational functions becomes easier once we have developed the proper tools from calculus.[16]

---

[15] The polynomial $x^4 + 3x^2 - 4$ has no terms in x^3 and x, so we inserted some extra space between the powers of x to make room for the terms in x^3 and x that arise in the course of the calculations.

[16] See, for instance, Exercise 7.9.9.

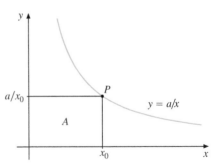

Figure 3.7.5 The area A is independent of P

EXERCISES FOR SECTION 3.7

1. Find all integer roots of the following equations:

(a) $x^4 - x^3 - 7x^2 + x + 6 = 0$ (b) $2x^3 + 11x^2 - 7x - 6 = 0$

(c) $x^4 + x^3 + 2x^2 + x + 1 = 0$ (d) $\frac{1}{4}x^3 - \frac{1}{4}x^2 - x + 1 = 0$

2. Find all integer roots of the following equations:

(a) $x^2 + x - 2 = 0$ (b) $x^3 - x^2 - 25x + 25 = 0$ (c) $x^5 - 4x^3 - 3 = 0$

(SM) 3. Perform the following divisions:

(a) $(2x^3 + 2x - 1) \div (x - 1)$ (b) $(x^4 + x^3 + x^2 + x) \div (x^2 + x)$

(c) $(x^5 - 3x^4 + 1) \div (x^2 + x + 1)$ (d) $(3x^8 + x^2 + 1) \div (x^3 - 2x + 1)$

(SM) 4. Find possible formulas for each of the three polynomials with graphs shown in Figs 3.7.6 to 3.7.8.

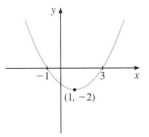

Figure 3.7.6 Exercise 4(a)

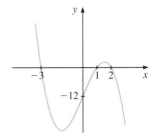

Figure 3.7.7 Exercise 4(b)

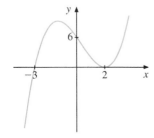

Figure 3.7.8 Exercise 4(c)

5. Perform the following divisions:

(a) $(x^2 - x - 20) \div (x - 5)$ (b) $(x^3 - 1) \div (x - 1)$ (c) $(-3x^3 + 48x) \div (x - 4)$

6. Show that the division $(x^4 + 3x^2 + 5) \div (x - c)$ leaves a remainder for all values of c.

7. Prove that, provided both $c \neq 0$ and $cx + d \neq 0$, one has $\dfrac{ax + b}{cx + d} = \dfrac{a}{c} + \dfrac{bc - ad}{c(cx + d)}$.

(SM) **8.** The following function has been used in demand theory:

$$E = \alpha \frac{x^2 - \gamma x}{x + \beta}$$

with α, β, and γ being constants. Perform the division $(x^2 - \gamma x) \div (x + \beta)$, and use the result to express E as a sum of a linear function and a proper fraction.

3.8 Power Functions

We saw in Section 1.5 how the number x^r can be defined for all rational numbers r. We also need to consider x^r when r is irrational in order for x^r to be defined for all real numbers r. How do we define, say, 5 raised to the irrational power π, that is 5^π? Because π is close to 3.1, we should expect that 5^π is approximately

$$5^{3.1} = 5^{31/10} = \sqrt[10]{5^{31}}$$

which *is* defined. An even better approximation is

$$5^\pi \approx 5^{3.14} = 5^{314/100} = 5^{157/50} = \sqrt[50]{5^{157}}$$

We can continue by taking more decimal places in the representation of $\pi = 3.1415926535\ldots$, and our approximation will be better with every additional decimal digit. Then the meaning of 5^π should be reasonably clear. For the moment, however, let us be content with just using a calculator to find that $5^\pi \approx 156.993$.

POWER FUNCTION

The general *power function* is defined by the formula

$$f(x) = Ax^r \tag{3.8.1}$$

where r and A are constants, for $x > 0$.

When we consider the power function, we assume that $x > 0$. This is because for many values of r, such as $r = 1/2$, the symbol x^r is not defined for negative values of x. And we exclude $x = 0$ because 0^r is undefined if $r \leq 0$.

EXAMPLE 3.8.1   Here are three illustrations of why powers with rational exponents are needed:

(a) The formula $S \approx 4.84 V^{2/3}$ gives the approximate surface area S of a ball as a function of its volume V—see Exercise 6.

(b) The flow of blood, in litres per second, through the heart of an individual is approximately proportional to $x^{0.7}$, where x is the body weight.

(c) Let Y be the net national product, K be capital stock, L be labour, and t be time. The formula $Y = 2.262K^{0.203}L^{0.763}(1.02)^t$ appears in a study of the growth of national product, and shows how powers with fractional exponents can arise in economics.

Graphs of Power Functions

Consider the power function $f(x) = x^r$, defined for all real numbers r provided that $x > 0$. We always have $f(1) = 1^r = 1$, so the graph of the function passes through the point $(1, 1)$ in the xy-plane. The shape of the graph depends crucially on the value of r, as Figs 3.8.1 to 3.8.3 indicate.

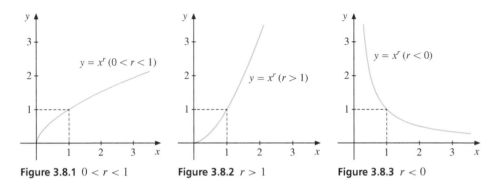

Figure 3.8.1 $0 < r < 1$ **Figure 3.8.2** $r > 1$ **Figure 3.8.3** $r < 0$

If $0 < r < 1$, the graph is like that in Fig. 3.8.1, which resembles the graph of $f(x) = x^{0.5}$ shown in Fig. 3.3.8. For $r > 1$ the graph is like that shown in Fig. 3.8.2; for instance, if $r = 2$ the graph is the right-hand half of the parabola $y = x^2$ shown in Fig. 3.3.6. Finally, for $r < 0$, the graph is shown in Fig. 3.8.3, which, if $r = -1$, is half of the hyperbola $y = 1/x$ shown in Fig. 3.3.9. Fig. 3.8.4 further illustrates how the graph of $y = x^r$ changes with changing positive values of the exponent.

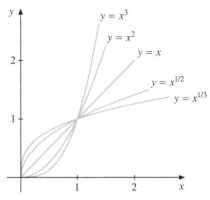

Figure 3.8.4 $y = x^r$

EXERCISES FOR SECTION 3.8

1. Sketch the graphs of $y = x^{-3}$, $y = x^{-1}$, $y = x^{-1/2}$, and $y = x^{-1/3}$, defined for $x > 0$.

2. Use a calculator to find approximate values for $\sqrt{2}^{\sqrt{2}}$ and π^π.

3. Solve the following equations for x:

    (a) $2^{2x} = 8$ (b) $3^{3x+1} = 1/81$ (c) $10^{x^2-2x+2} = 100$

(SM) **4.** Match five of the graphs A–F in Figs 3.8.5 to 3.8.10 with each of the functions (a)–(e) below. Then specify a suitable function in (f) that matches the sixth graph.

    (a) $y = \frac{1}{2}x^2 - x - \frac{3}{2}$ has graph ___   (b) $y = 2\sqrt{2-x}$ has graph ___

    (c) $y = -\frac{1}{2}x^2 + x + \frac{3}{2}$ has graph ___   (d) $y = \left(\frac{1}{2}\right)^x - 2$ has graph ___

    (e) $y = 2\sqrt{x-2}$ has graph ___   (f) $y = $ has graph ___

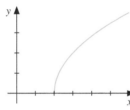

Figure 3.8.5 Graph A

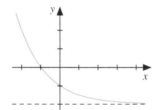

Figure 3.8.6 Graph B

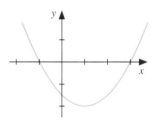

Figure 3.8.7 Graph C

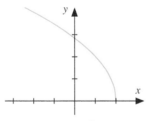

Figure 3.8.8 Graph D

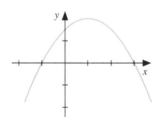

Figure 3.8.9 Graph E

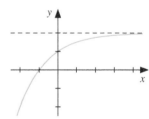

Figure 3.8.10 Graph F

5. Find t when: (a) $3^{5t}9^t = 27$, and (b) $9^t = (27)^{1/5}/3$.

6. The formulas for the surface area S and the volume V of a ball with radius r are $S = 4\pi r^2$ and $V = (4/3)\pi r^3$. Express S as a power function of V.

3.9 Exponential Functions

A quantity that increases (or decreases) by a fixed factor per unit of time is said to *increase* (or *decrease*) *exponentially*. If the fixed factor is a, this leads to the exponential function:

$$f(t) = Aa^t \tag{3.9.1}$$

where $a > 0$ and A are constants. In what follows, we shall consider the case where A is positive, but it will be obvious how to modify the subsequent discussion for the case when A is negative.

Note that if $f(t) = Aa^t$, then $f(t+1) = Aa^{t+1} = Aa^t \cdot a^1 = af(t)$, so the value of f at time $t+1$ is a times the value of f at time t. If $a > 1$, then f is increasing; if $0 < a < 1$, then f is decreasing—see Figs 3.9.1 and 3.9.2. Because $f(0) = Aa^0 = A$, we can always write $f(t) = f(0)a^t$.

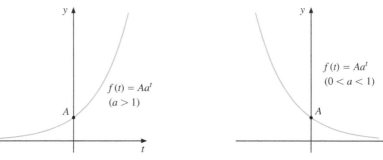

Figure 3.9.1 $f(t) = Aa^t, a > 1$ **Figure 3.9.2** $f(t) = Aa^t, 0 < a < 1$

It is important to recognize the fundamental difference between the exponential functions $f(x) = a^x$ and the typical power function $g(x) = x^a$ that was discussed in Section 3.8. Indeed, for the exponential function a^x, it is the exponent x that varies, while the base a is constant; for the power function x^a, on the other hand, the exponent a is constant, while the base x varies.

Exponential functions appear in many important economic, social, and physical models. For instance, economic growth, population growth, continuously accumulated interest, radioactive decay, and decreasing illiteracy have all been described by exponential functions. In addition, the exponential function is one of the most important functions in statistics. Here is one application:

EXAMPLE 3.9.1   **(Population Growth)** Consider a growing population like that of Europe during the 20th century. In Example 3.5.1, we constructed a linear function $P = 5.1t + 606$, where P denotes the population in millions, $t = 0$ corresponds to the year 1960 when the population was 606 million, and $t = 10$ corresponds to the year 1970 when the population estimate was 657 million. According to this formula, the annual increase in population would be constant and equal to 5.1 million. This is a very unreasonable assumption. After all, the linear function implies that, for $t \leq -119$ (i.e., for years before 1841), the population of Europe was negative!

In fact, according to UN estimates, the European population was to grow by approximately 0.45% annually during the period 1960 to 2000. With a population of 606 million in

1960, the population in 1961 would then be $606 \cdot 1.0045$ (see Section 1.2), which is approximately 609 million. Next year, in 1962, it would have grown to $606 \cdot 1.0045^2$, which is approximately 611 million. If growth were to continue at 0.45% annually, the population figure would grow by the factor 1.0045 each year. Then, t years after 1960, the population would be given by

$$P(t) = 606 \cdot 1.0045^t$$

Thus, $P(t)$ is an exponential function of the form (3.9.1). For the year 2015, corresponding to $t = 55$, the formula yields the estimate $P(55) \approx 776$ million.[17]

Many countries, particularly in Africa, have recently had far faster population growth than Europe. For instance, during the 1970s and 1980s, the growth rate of Zimbabwe's population was close to 3.5% annually. If we let $t = 0$ correspond to the census year 1969 when the population was 5.1 million, the population t years after 1969 is $P(t) = 5.1 \cdot 1.035^t$. If we calculate $P(20)$, $P(40)$, and $P(60)$ using this formula, we get roughly 10, 20, and 40. Thus, the population of Zimbabwe roughly doubles after 20 years; during the next 20 years, it doubles again, and so on. We say that the *doubling time* of the population is approximately 20 years. Of course, this kind of extrapolation is quite dubious, because exponential growth of population cannot go on forever: if the growth rate were to continue at 3.5% annually and there was no emigration, then by year 2296 each Zimbabwean would have only one square metre of land on average—see Exercise 6.

If $a > 1$ and $A > 0$, the exponential function $f(t) = Aa^t$ is increasing. Its *doubling time* is the time it takes for it to double. Its value at $t = 0$ is A, so the doubling time t^* is given by the equation $f(t^*) = Aa^{t^*} = 2A$, or after cancelling A, by $a^{t^*} = 2$. Thus the doubling time of the exponential function $f(t) = Aa^t$ is the power to which a must be raised in order to get 2. In Exercise 7 you will show that the doubling time is independent of which year you take as the base. Ultimately, in Example 3.10.4, we will use the *natural logarithm function*, which is denoted by ln, to determine that $t^* = \ln 2 / \ln a$.

EXAMPLE 3.9.2   Use your calculator to find the doubling time of:

(a) a population, like that of Zimbabwe, increasing at 3.5% annually (thus confirming the earlier calculations);

(b) the population of Kenya in the 1980s, which then had the world's highest annual growth rate of population, 4.2%.

Solution:

(a) The doubling time t^* is given by the equation $1.035^{t^*} = 2$. Using a calculator shows that $1.035^{15} \approx 1.68$, whereas $1.035^{25} \approx 2.36$. Thus, t^* must lie between 15 and 25. Because $1.035^{20} \approx 1.99$, t^* is close to 20. In fact, $t^* \approx 20.15$.

(b) The doubling time t^* is given by the equation $1.042^{t^*} = 2$. Using a calculator, we find that $t^* \approx 16.85$. Thus, with a growth rate of 4.2%, Kenya's population would double in less than 17 years.

---

[17] The actual figure turned out to be about 738 million, which shows the limitations of naive projections.

EXAMPLE 3.9.3   **(Compound Interest)**   A savings account of K that increases by $p\%$ interest each year will have increased after t years to $K(1 + p/100)^t$, as seen in Section 1.2. According to this formula with $K = 1$, a deposit of \$1 earning interest at 8\% per year (so $p = 8$) will have increased after t years to $(1 + 8/100)^t = 1.08^t$ dollars.

Table 3.4 How \$1 of savings increases with time at 8\% annual interest

t	1	2	5	10	20	30	50	100	200
$(1.08)^t$	1.08	1.17	1.47	2.16	4.66	10.06	46.90	2199.76	4 838 949.60

As shown in Table 3.4, after 50 years, \$1 of savings will have increased to more than \$10, and after 200 years, to more than \$4.8 million!

Observe that the expression 1.08^t defines an exponential function of the type (3.9.1), with $a = 1.08$. Even if a is only slightly larger than 1, $f(t)$ will increase very quickly as t becomes large.

EXAMPLE 3.9.4   **(Continuous Depreciation)**   Each year the value of most assets such as cars, electronic goods, or furniture decreases, or *depreciates*. If the value of an asset is assumed to decrease by a fixed percentage each year, then the depreciation is called *continuous*.[18]

Assume that a car, which at time $t = 0$ has the value P_0, depreciates at the rate of 20\% each year over a five-year period. What is its value $A(t)$ at time t, for $t = 1, 2, 3, 4, 5$?

Solution: After one year, its value is $P_0 - (20P_0/100) = P_0(1 - 20/100) = P_0(0.8)^1$. Thereafter, it depreciates each subsequent year by the factor 0.8. Thus, after t years, its value is $A(t) = P_0(0.8)^t$. In particular, $A(5) = P_0(0.8)^5 \approx 0.32P_0$, so after five years its value has decreased to about 32\% of its original value.

The most important properties of the exponential function are summed up by the following:

EXPONENTIAL FUNCTION

The *general exponential function* with base $a > 0$ is

$$f(x) = Aa^x$$

where a is the factor by which $f(x)$ changes when x increases by 1.

If $a = 1 + p/100$, where $p > 0$ and $A > 0$, then $f(x)$ will increase by $p\%$ for each unit increase in x. If $a = 1 - p/100$, where $0 < p < 100$ and $A > 0$, then $f(x)$ will decrease by $p\%$ for each unit increase in x.

---

[18]   Recall the case of linear depreciation discussed in Exercise 3.5.5.

The Natural Exponential Function

Each base a of $f(x) = Aa^x$ gives a different exponential function. In mathematics, one particular value of a gives an exponential function that is far more important than all others. One might guess that $a = 2$ or $a = 10$ would be this special base. Certainly, powers to the base of 2 are important in computing, and powers to the base 10 occur in our usual decimal number system. Nevertheless, once we have studied some calculus, it will turn out that the most important base for an exponential function is an irrational number a little larger than 2.7. In fact, it is so distinguished that it is denoted by the single letter e, possibly because it is the first letter of the word "exponential". Its value to 15 decimal places is[19]

$$e = 2.718281828459045\ldots$$

Many formulas in calculus become much simpler when e is used as the base for exponential functions. Given this base e, the corresponding exponential function

$$f(x) = e^x \tag{3.9.2}$$

is called the *natural exponential function*. In Examples 7.5.4 and 7.6.2 we shall give an explicit way of approximating e^x to an arbitrary degree of accuracy. Of course, all the usual rules for powers apply also to the natural exponential function. In particular,

(a) $e^s e^t = e^{s+t}$ (b) $e^s / e^t = e^{s-t}$ (c) $(e^s)^t = e^{st}$

The graphs of $f(x) = e^x$ and $f(x) = e^{-x}$ are given in Fig. 3.9.3.

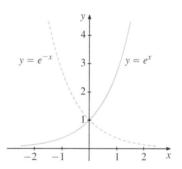

Figure 3.9.3 The graphs of $y = e^x$ and $y = e^{-x}$

Powers with e as their base, even e^1, are difficult to compute by hand. A pocket calculator with an $\boxed{e^x}$ function key can do this immediately, however. For instance, one finds that $e^{1.0} \approx 2.7183$, $e^{0.5} \approx 1.6487$, and $e^{-\pi} \approx 0.0432$.

Sometimes the notation $\exp(u)$, or even $\exp u$, is used in place of e^u. If u is a complicated expression like $x^3 + x\sqrt{x - 1/x} + 5$, it is easier to read and write $\exp(x^3 + x\sqrt{x - 1/x} + 5)$ instead of $e^{x^3 + x\sqrt{x - 1/x} + 5}$.

---

[19] Though this number had been defined implicitly over 100 years earlier, the Swiss scientist and mathematician Leonhard Euler (1707–1783) was the first to denote it by the letter e. He subsequently proved that it was irrational and calculated it to 23 decimal places.

EXERCISES FOR SECTION 3.9

1. If the population of Europe grew at the rate of 0.72% annually, what would be its doubling time?

2. The population of Botswana was estimated to be 1.22 million in 1989, and to be growing at the rate of 3.4% annually. If $t = 0$ denotes 1989, find a formula for the population $P(t)$ at date t. What is the doubling time?

3. A savings account with an initial deposit of $100 earns 12% interest per year. What is the amount of savings after t years? Make a table similar to Table 3.4, stopping at 50 years.

4. Fill in the following table and sketch the graphs of $y = 2^x$ and $y = 2^{-x}$.

x	-3	-2	-1	0	1	2	3
$2x$							
2^{-x}							

5. The *normal density function*

$$\varphi(x) = \frac{1}{\sqrt{2\pi}} e^{-\frac{1}{2}x^2}$$

is one of the most important functions in statistics. Its graph is often called the "bell curve" because of its shape. Use your calculator to fill in the following table:

x	-2	-1	0	1	2
$y = \varphi(x)$					

6. The area of Zimbabwe is approximately $3.91 \cdot 10^{11}$ m^2. Referring to Example 3.9.1 and using a calculator, solve the equation $5.1 \cdot 10^6 \cdot 1.035^t = 3.91 \cdot 10^{11}$ for t, and interpret the solution.

7. With $f(t) = Aa^t$, if $f(t + t^*) = 2f(t)$, prove that $a^{t^*} = 2$. This shows that the doubling time t^* of the general exponential function is independent of the initial time t.

8. Which of the following equations do *not* define exponential functions of x?

   (a) $y = 3^x$ (b) $y = x^{\sqrt{2}}$ (c) $y = (\sqrt{2})^x$

   (d) $y = x^x$ (e) $y = (2.7)^x$ (f) $y = 1/2^x$

9. Suppose that all prices rise at the same proportional (inflation) rate of 19% per year. For an item that currently costs P_0, use the implied formula for the price after t years in order to predict the prices of:

   (a) A 20 kg bag of corn, presently costing $16, after five years.

   (b) A $4.40 can of coffee after ten years.

   (c) A $250 000 house after four years.

10. Find possible exponential functions for the graphs A to C, in Figs 3.9.4 to 3.9.6.

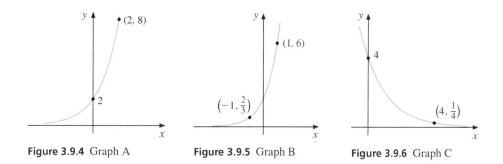

Figure 3.9.4 Graph A   **Figure 3.9.5** Graph B   **Figure 3.9.6** Graph C

3.10 Logarithmic Functions

The doubling time of an exponential function $f(t) = Aa^t$ was defined as the time it takes for $f(t)$ to become twice as large. In order to find the doubling time t^*, we must solve the equation $a^{t^*} = 2$ for t^*. In economics, we often need to solve similar problems:

(a) At the present rate of inflation, how long will it take the price level to triple?

(b) If the world's population grows at 2% per year, how long does it take to double its size?

(c) If \$1 000 is invested in a savings account bearing interest at the annual rate of 8%, how long does it take for the account to reach \$10 000?

All these questions involve solving equations of the form $a^x = b$ for x. For instance, problem (c) reduces to finding which x solves the equation $1000(1.08)^x = 10\,000$.

We begin with equations in which the base of the exponential is e, which was, as you recall, the irrational number $2.718\ldots$. Here are some examples: $e^x = 4$; $5e^{-3x} = 16$; and $A\alpha e^{-\alpha x} = k$. In all these equations, the unknown x occurs as an exponent. We therefore introduce the following useful definition. If $e^u = a$, we call u the *natural logarithm* of a, and we write $u = \ln a$. Hence, we have the following definition of the symbol $\ln a$:

NATURAL LOGARITHM

For any positive number a,

$$e^{\ln a} = a \tag{3.10.1}$$

Thus, $\ln a$ is the power of e you need to get a.

Because e^u is a strictly increasing function of u, it follows that $\ln a$ *is* uniquely determined by the definition (3.10.1). You should memorize this definition. It is the foundation for everything in this section, and for a good part of what comes later. The following example illustrates how to use this definition.

EXAMPLE 3.10.1   Find the following numbers:

(a) $\ln 1$ (b) $\ln e$ (c) $\ln(1/e)$ (d) $\ln 4$ (e) $\ln(-6)$

Solution:

(a) $\ln 1 = 0$, because $e^0 = 1$ and so 0 is the power of e that you need to get 1.

(b) $\ln e = 1$, because $e^1 = e$ and so 1 is the power of e that you need to get e.

(c) $\ln(1/e) = \ln e^{-1} = -1$, because -1 is the power of e that you need to get $1/e$.

(d) $\ln 4$ is the power of e you need to get 4. Because $e^1 \approx 2.7$ and $e^2 = e^1 \cdot e^1 \approx 7.3$, the number $\ln 4$ must lie between 1 and 2. By using the a calculator, you should be able to find a good approximation to $\ln 4$ by trial and error. Of course, it is easier to press 4 and the $\ln x$ key. Then you find that $\ln 4 \approx 1.386$. Thus, $e^{1.386} \approx 4$.

(e) $\ln(-6)$ would be the power of e you need to get -6. Because e^x is positive for all x, it is obvious that $\ln(-6)$ must be undefined. (The same is true for $\ln x$ whenever $x \leq 0$.)

The following box collects some useful rules for natural logarithms.

RULES FOR THE NATURAL LOGARITHMIC FUNCTION

(a) The logarithm of a *product* is the *sum* of the logarithms of the factors: if x and y are positive, then $\ln(xy) = \ln x + \ln y$.

(b) The logarithm of a *quotient* is the *difference* between the logarithms of its numerator and denominator: if x and y are positive, then

$$\ln \frac{x}{y} = \ln x - \ln y$$

(c) The logarithm of a *power* is the exponent multiplied by the logarithm of the base: if x is positive, then $\ln x^p = p \ln x$.

(d) $\ln 1 = 0$, $\ln e = 1$, and, for general x,

$$\ln e^x = x \quad \text{and} \quad x = e^{\ln x} \tag{3.10.2}$$

where the latter expression assumes that $x > 0$.

To show (a), observe first that the definition of $\ln(xy)$ implies that $e^{\ln(xy)} = xy$. Furthermore, $x = e^{\ln x}$ and $y = e^{\ln y}$, so

$$e^{\ln(xy)} = xy = e^{\ln x} e^{\ln y} = e^{\ln x + \ln y} \tag{$*$}$$

where the last step uses the rule $e^s e^t = e^{s+t}$. In general, $e^u = e^v$ implies $u = v$, so we conclude from ($*$) that $\ln(xy) = \ln x + \ln y$.

The proofs of (b) and (c) are based on the rules $e^s/e^t = e^{s-t}$ and $(e^s)^t = e^{st}$, respectively, and are left to the reader. Finally, (d) displays some important properties for convenient reference.

It *is* tempting to replace $\ln(x + y)$ by $\ln x + \ln y$, but this is quite wrong. In fact, $\ln x + \ln y$ is equal to $\ln(xy)$, not to $\ln(x + y)$.

LOG OF A SUM

There are *no* simple formulas for $\ln(x + y)$ and $\ln(x - y)$.

Here are some examples that apply the previous rules.

EXAMPLE 3.10.2   Express in terms of $\ln 2$: (a) $\ln 4$; (b) $\ln \sqrt[3]{2^5}$; and (c) $\ln(1/16)$.

Solution:

(a) $\ln 4 = \ln(2 \cdot 2) = \ln 2 + \ln 2 = 2\ln 2$, or, alternatively $\ln 4 = \ln 2^2 = 2\ln 2$.

(b) We have $\sqrt[3]{2^5} = 2^{5/3}$. Therefore, $\ln \sqrt[3]{2^5} = \ln 2^{5/3} = (5/3)\ln 2$.

(c) $\ln(1/16) = \ln 1 - \ln 16 = 0 - \ln 2^4 = -4\ln 2$. Or, $\ln(1/16) = \ln 2^{-4} = -4\ln 2$.

EXAMPLE 3.10.3   Solve the following equations for x:

(a) $5e^{-3x} = 16$ (b) $A\alpha e^{-\alpha x} = k$ (c) $(1.08)^x = 10$ (d) $e^x + 4e^{-x} = 4$

Solution:

(a) Take $\ln$ of each side of the equation to obtain $\ln(5e^{-3x}) = \ln 16$. The product rule gives $\ln(5e^{-3x}) = \ln 5 + \ln e^{-3x}$. Here, $\ln e^{-3x} = -3x$, by rule (d). Hence, $\ln 5 - 3x = \ln 16$, which gives

$$x = \frac{1}{3}(\ln 5 - \ln 16) = \frac{1}{3}\ln\frac{5}{16}$$

(b) We argue as in (a) and obtain $\ln(A\alpha e^{-\alpha x}) = \ln k$, or $\ln(A\alpha) + \ln e^{-\alpha x} = \ln k$, so $\ln(A\alpha) - \alpha x = \ln k$. Finally, therefore,

$$x = \frac{1}{\alpha}[\ln(A\alpha) - \ln k] = \frac{1}{\alpha}\ln\frac{A\alpha}{k}$$

(c) Again we take the $\ln$ of each side of the equation and obtain $x \ln 1.08 = \ln 10$. So the solution is $x = \ln 10/\ln 1.08$, which is ≈ 29.9. Thus, it takes just short of 30 years for \$1 to increase to \$10 when the interest rate is 8%. (See Table 3.4, in Example 3.9.3.)

(d) It is very tempting to begin with $\ln(e^x + 4e^{-x}) = \ln 4$, but this leads nowhere, because $\ln(e^x + 4e^{-x})$ cannot be further evaluated. Instead, we argue like this: Putting $u = e^x$ gives $e^{-x} = 1/e^x = 1/u$, so the equation is $u + 4/u = 4$, or $u^2 + 4 = 4u$. Solving this quadratic equation for u yields $u = 2$ as the only solution. Hence, $e^x = 2$, and so $x = \ln 2$.

The Function $g(x) = \ln x$

For each positive number x, the number $\ln x$ is defined by $e^{\ln x} = x$. In other words, $u = \ln x$ is the solution of the equation $e^u = x$. This definition is illustrated in Fig. 3.10.1. We call the resulting function

$$g(x) = \ln x \tag{3.10.3}$$

where $x > 0$, the *natural logarithm* of x. Think of x as a point moving upwards on the vertical axis from the origin. As x increases from values less than 1 to values greater than 1, so $g(x)$ increases from negative to positive values. Because e^u tends to 0 as u becomes large and negative, so $g(x)$ becomes large and negative as x tends to 0. Repeating the definition of $\ln x$, then inserting $y = \ln x$ and taking the ln of each side, yields Eq. (3.10.2): $e^{\ln x} = x$ for all $x > 0$; and $\ln e^y = y$ for all y.

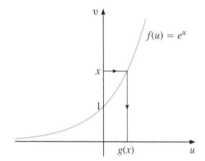

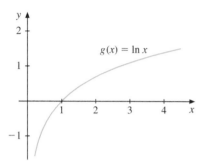

Figure 3.10.1 Construction of $g(x) = \ln x$ **Figure 3.10.2** $g(x) = \ln x$

In Fig. 3.10.2 we have drawn the graph of $g(x) = \ln x$. The shape of this graph ought to be remembered. It can be obtained by reflecting the graph of Fig. 3.10.1 about the 45° line, so that the u- and v-axes are interchanged and become the y- and x-axes of Fig. 3.10.2, respectively. According to Example 3.10.1, we have $g(1/e) = -1, g(1) = 0$, and $g(e) = 1$. Observe that this corresponds well with the graph.

Logarithms with Bases other than e

Recall that we defined $\ln x$ as the exponent to which we must raise the base e in order to obtain x. From time to time, it is useful to have logarithms based on numbers other than e. For many years, until the use of mechanical and then electronic calculators became widespread, tables of logarithms to the base 10 were frequently used to simplify complicated calculations involving multiplication, division, square roots, and so on.

Suppose that a is a fixed positive number (usually chosen larger than 1). If $a^u = x$, then we call u the *logarithm of x to base a* and write $u = \log_a x$. The symbol $\log_a x$ is then defined for every positive number x by the following:

LOGARITHM OF x TO BASE a

$$a^{\log_a x} = x \tag{3.10.4}$$

For instance, $\log_2 32 = 5$, because $2^5 = 32$, whereas $\log_{10}(1/100) = -2$, because $10^{-2} = 1/100$. Note that $\ln x$ is $\log_e x$.

By taking the ln on each side of (3.10.4), we obtain $\log_a x \cdot \ln a = \ln x$, so that

$$\log_a x = \frac{1}{\ln a} \ln x \qquad (3.10.5)$$

This reveals that the logarithm of x in the system with base a is proportional to ln x, with a proportionality factor $1/\ln a$. It follows immediately that $\log_a$ obeys the same rules as ln:

(a) $\log_a(xy) = \log_a x + \log_a y$ (b) $\log_a(x/y) = \log_a x - \log_a y$

(c) $\log_a x^p = p \log_a x$ (d) $\log_a 1 = 0$ and $\log_a a = 1$

Rule (a), for example, follows directly from the corresponding rule for ln, because

$$\log_a(xy) = \frac{1}{\ln a} \ln(xy) = \frac{1}{\ln a}(\ln x + \ln y) = \frac{1}{\ln a} \ln x + \frac{1}{\ln a} \ln y = \log_a x + \log_a y$$

EXAMPLE 3.10.4   Recall from Section 3.9 that the doubling time, t^*, of an exponential function $f(t) = Aa^t$ is given by the formula $a^{t^*} = 2$. Solve this equation for t^*.

Solution: Taking the logarithm to base 2 of both sides of the equation yields $\log_2 a^{t^*} = \log_2 2 = 1$. By rule (c), this implies that $t^* \log_2 a = 1$, and so $t^* = 1/\log_2 a$.

EXERCISES FOR SECTION 3.10

1. Express as multiples of ln 3: (a) $\ln 9$;   (b) $\ln \sqrt{3}$;   (c) $\ln \sqrt[5]{3^2}$;   (d) $\ln(1/81)$.

2. Solve the following equations for x:

(a) $3^x = 8$ (b) $\ln x = 3$ (c) $\ln(x^2 - 4x + 5) = 0$

(d) $\ln[x(x - 2)] = 0$ (e) $\dfrac{x \ln(x + 3)}{x^2 + 1} = 0$ (f) $\ln(\sqrt{x} - 5) = 0$

(SM) **3.** Solve the following equations for x:

(a) $3^x 4^{x+2} = 8$ (b) $3 \ln x + 2 \ln x^2 = 6$ (c) $4^x - 4^{x-1} = 3^{x+1} - 3^x$

(d) $\log_2 x = 2$ (e) $\log_x e^2 = 2$ (f) $\log_3 x = -3$

(SM) **4.** Suppose that $f(t) = Ae^{rt}$ and $g(t) = Be^{st}$, where $A > 0$, $B > 0$, and $r \neq s$. Solve the equation $f(t) = g(t)$ for t.

(SM) **5.** In 1990 the GDP of China was estimated to be $1.2 \cdot 10^{12}$ US dollars, whereas that of the USA was reported to be $5.6 \cdot 10^{12}$ US dollars. The two countries' annual rates of growth were estimated to be 9% and 2% respectively, implying that t years after 1990, their GDP should be Ae^{rt} and Be^{st} respectively, where $r = 0.09$, $s = 0.02$, and A, B are suitable constants. Use the answer to Exercise 4 to determine the date when the two nations' GDP should be the same.

6. Assume that all the variables in the formulas below are positive. Which of them are always true, and which are sometimes false?

(a) $(\ln A)^4 = 4 \ln A$

(b) $\ln B = 2 \ln \sqrt{B}$

(c) $\ln A^{10} - \ln A^4 = 3 \ln A^2$

(d) $\ln \dfrac{A+B}{C} = \ln A + \ln B - \ln C$

(e) $\ln \dfrac{A+B}{C} = \ln(A+B) - \ln C$

(f) $\ln \dfrac{A}{B} + \ln \dfrac{B}{A} = 0$

(g) $p \ln(\ln A) = \ln(\ln A^p)$

(h) $p \ln(\ln A) = \ln(\ln A)^p$

(i) $\dfrac{\ln A}{\ln B + \ln C} = \ln A(BC)^{-1}$

7. Simplify the following expressions:

(a) $\exp[\ln(x)] - \ln[\exp(x)]$

(b) $\ln[x^4 \exp(-x)]$

(c) $\exp[\ln(x^2) - 2 \ln y]$

REVIEW EXERCISES

1. Let $f(x) = 3 - 27x^3$.

(a) Compute $f(0), f(-1), f(1/3)$, and $f(\sqrt[3]{2})$.

(b) Show that $f(x) + f(-x) = 6$ for all x.

2. Let

$$F(x) = 1 + \frac{4x}{x^2 + 4}$$

(a) Compute $F(0)$, $F(-2)$, $F(2)$, and $F(3)$.

(b) What happens to $F(x)$ when x becomes large positive or negative?

(c) Give a rough sketch of the graph of F.

3. Figure 3.R.1 combines the graphs of a quadratic function f and a linear function g. Use the two graphs to find those x where: (a) $f(x) \le g(x)$; (b) $f(x) \le 0$; and (c) $g(x) \ge 0$.

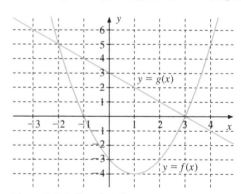

Figure 3.R.1 Two functions

4. Find the domains of the following functions:

(a) $f(x) = \sqrt{x^2 - 1}$

(b) $g(x) = \dfrac{1}{\sqrt{x - 4}}$

(c) $h(x) = \sqrt{(x-3)(5-x)}$

5. The cost of producing x units of a commodity is given by $C(x) = 100 + 40x + 2x^2$.

   (a) Find $C(0)$, $C(100)$, and $C(101) - C(100)$.

   (b) Find $C(x + 1) - C(x)$, and explain in words the meaning of the difference.

6. Find the slopes of the following straight lines:

   (a) $y = -4x + 8$ (b) $3x + 4y = 12$ (c) $\dfrac{x}{a} + \dfrac{y}{b} = 1$.

7. Find equations for the following straight lines:

   (a) L_1 passes through $(-2, 3)$ and has a slope of -3.

   (b) L_2 passes through $(-3, 5)$ and $(2, 7)$.

   (c) L_3 passes through (a, b) and $(2a, 3b)$, where $a \neq 0$.

8. If $f(x) = ax + b$, $f(2) = 3$, and $f(-1) = -3$, then $f(-3) =$?

9. Fill in the following table, then make a rough sketch of the graph of $y = x^2 e^x$.

x	-5	-4	-3	-2	-1	0	1
$y = x^2 e^x$							

10. Find the equation for the parabola $y = ax^2 + bx + c$ that passes through the three points $(1, -3)$, $(0, -6)$, and $(3, 15)$—that is, determine a, b, and c.

11. If a firm sells Q tons of a product, the price P received per ton is $P = 1000 - \frac{1}{3}Q$. The price it has to pay per ton is $P = 800 + \frac{1}{5}Q$. In addition, it has transportation costs of 100 per ton.

    (a) Express the firm's profit π as a function of Q, the number of tons sold, and find the profit-maximizing quantity.

    (b) Suppose the government imposes a tax on the firm's product of 10 per ton. Find the new expression for the firm's profits $\hat{\pi}$ and the new profit-maximizing quantity.

12. In Example 3.6.1, suppose a tax of τ per unit produced is imposed. If $\tau < 100$, what production level now maximizes profits?

13. A firm produces a commodity and receives \$100 for each unit sold. The cost of producing and selling x units is $20x + 0.25x^2$ dollars.

    (a) Find the production level that maximizes profits.

    (b) If a tax of \$10 per unit is imposed, what is the new optimal production level?

    (c) Answer the question in (b) if the sales price per unit is p, the total cost of producing and selling x units is $\alpha x + \beta x^2$, and the tax per unit is τ where $\tau \leq p - \alpha$.

(SM) 14. Write the following polynomials as products of linear factors:

   (a) $p(x) = x^3 + x^2 - 12x$ (b) $q(x) = 2x^3 + 3x^2 - 18x + 8$

15. Suppose that a and b are constants, while n is a natural number. Which of the following divisions leave no remainder?

(a) $(x^3 - x - 1)/(x - 1)$

(b) $(2x^3 - x - 1)/(x - 1)$

(c) $(x^3 - ax^2 + bx - ab)/(x - a)$

(d) $(x^{2n} - 1)/(x + 1)$

16. Find the values of k that make the polynomial $q(x)$ divide the polynomial $p(x)$ in:

(a) $p(x) = x^2 - kx + 4$, $q(x) = x - 2$

(b) $p(x) = k^2x^2 - kx - 6$, $q(x) = x + 2$

(c) $p(x) = x^3 - 4x^2 + x + k$, $q(x) = x + 2$

(d) $p(x) = k^2x^4 - 3kx^2 - 4$, $q(x) = x - 1$

(SM) 17. The cubic function $p(x) = \frac{1}{4}x^3 - x^2 - \frac{11}{4}x + \frac{15}{2}$ has three real zeros. Verify that $x = 2$ is one of them, and find the other two.

18. In 1964 a five-year plan was introduced in Tanzania. One objective was to double the real income per capita over the next 15 years. What is the average annual rate of growth of real income per capita required to achieve this objective?

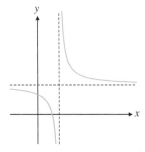

Figure 3.R.2 Graph of $y = \dfrac{ax + b}{x + c}$

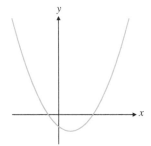

Figure 3.R.3 Graph of $y = px^2 + qx + r$

(SM) 19. Figure 3.R.2 shows the graph of the function $y = f(x) = (ax + b)/(x + c)$. Check which of the constants a, b, and c are positive, zero, or negative.

20. Figure 3.R.3 shows the graph of the function $y = g(x) = px^2 + qx + r$. Check which of the constants p, q, and r are positive, zero, or negative.

21. Recall that: (i) the relationship between the Celsius (C) and Fahrenheit (F) temperature scales is linear; (ii) water freezes at $0°$ C and $32°$ F; and (iii) water boils at $100°$ C and $212°$ F.

(a) Determine the equation that converts C to F.

(b) Which temperature is represented by the same number in both scales?

22. Solve for t in the following equations:

(a) $x = e^{at+b}$

(b) $e^{-at} = 1/2$

(c) $\dfrac{1}{\sqrt{2\pi}}e^{-\frac{1}{2}t^2} = \dfrac{1}{8}$

(SM) **23.** Prove the following equalities, with appropriate restrictions on the variables:

(a) $\ln x - 2 = \ln(x/e^2)$

(b) $\ln x - \ln y + \ln z = \ln \dfrac{xz}{y}$

(c) $3 + 2\ln x = \ln(e^3 x^2)$

(d) $\frac{1}{2}\ln x - \frac{3}{2}\ln \dfrac{1}{x} - \ln(x+1) = \ln \dfrac{x^2}{x+1}$

CHAPTER 4
Matrix Algebra

The impression that you may have gained from reading this text is that mathematics consists of one main topic, calculus, and that every other topic is just a variation on this theme. This is far from the truth. In this chapter, we look at two refreshingly different branches of mathematics. It would be useful for you to have studied Chapter 1, although even this is not essential. There are three sections which need to be read in order.

Section 4.1 introduces the concept of a matrix, which is a convenient mathematical way of representing information displayed in a table. By defining the matrix operations of addition, subtraction and multiplication, it is possible to develop an algebra of matrices. Simple economic examples are used to illustrate these definitions, and it is shown that the rules of matrix manipulation are almost identical to those of ordinary arithmetic. In Section 4.2 you are shown how to calculate the inverse of a matrix. This is analogous to the reciprocal of a number and enables matrix equations to be solved. In particular, inverses provide an alternative way of solving systems of simultaneous linear equations and so can be used to solve problems in statics. Section 4.3 describes Cramer's rule for solving systems of linear equations. This method is a particularly useful way of solving economic models where only a selection of endogenous variables need to be determined.

SECTION 4.1
Basic matrix operations

Objectives

At the end of this section you should be able to:

- Understand the notation and terminology of matrix algebra.
- Find the transpose of a matrix.
- Add and subtract matrices.
- Multiply a matrix by a scalar.
- Multiply matrices together.
- Represent a system of linear equations in matrix notation.

Suppose that a firm produces three types of good, G1, G2 and G3, which it sells to two customers, C1 and C2. The monthly sales for these goods are given in Table 4.1.

During the month the firm sells 3 items of G2 to customer C1, 6 items of G3 to customer C2, and so on. It may well be obvious from the context exactly what these numbers represent. Under these circumstances it makes sense to ignore the table headings and to write this information more concisely as

$$\mathbf{A} = \begin{bmatrix} 7 & 3 & 4 \\ 1 & 5 & 6 \end{bmatrix}$$

which is an example of a matrix. Quite generally, any rectangular array of numbers surrounded by a pair of brackets is called a **matrix** (plural **matrices**), and the individual numbers constituting the array are called **entries** or **elements**. In this text we use square brackets, although it is equally correct to use parentheses (that is, round brackets) instead. It helps to think of a matrix as being made up of rows and columns. The matrix $\mathbf{A}$ has two rows and three columns and is said to have order 2×3. In general, a matrix of **order** $m \times n$ has m rows and n columns.

We denote matrices by capital letters in bold type (that is, $\mathbf{A}, \mathbf{B}, \mathbf{C}, \dots$) and their elements by the corresponding lower-case letter in ordinary type. In fact, we use a rather clever double subscript notation so that a_{ij} stands for the element of $\mathbf{A}$ which occurs in row i and column j. Referring to the matrix $\mathbf{A}$ above, we see that

$a_{12} = 3$ (row 1 and column 2 of $\mathbf{A}$)

and $a_{23} = 6$ (row 2 and column 3 of $\mathbf{A}$)

Table 4.1

		Monthly sales for goods		
		G1	G2	G3
Sold to	C1	7	3	4
customer	C2	1	5	6

A general matrix **D** of order 3 × 2 would be written

$$\begin{bmatrix} d_{11} & d_{12} \\ d_{21} & d_{22} \\ d_{31} & d_{32} \end{bmatrix}$$

Similarly, a 3 × 3 matrix labelled **E** would be written

$$\begin{bmatrix} e_{11} & e_{12} & e_{13} \\ e_{21} & e_{22} & e_{23} \\ e_{31} & e_{32} & e_{33} \end{bmatrix}$$

Practice Problem

1. Let

$$A = \begin{bmatrix} 1 & 2 \\ 3 & 4 \end{bmatrix} \quad B = [1 \ -1 \ 0 \ 6 \ 2] \quad C = \begin{bmatrix} 1 & 0 & 2 & 3 & 1 \\ 5 & 7 & 9 & 0 & 2 \\ 3 & 4 & 6 & 7 & 8 \end{bmatrix} \quad D = [6]$$

(a) State the orders of the matrices **A**, **B**, **C** and **D**.

(b) Write down (if possible) the values of

$$a_{11}, \ a_{22}, \ b_{14}, \ c_{25}, \ c_{33}, \ c_{43}, \ d_{11}$$

All we have done so far is to explain what matrices are and to provide some notation for handling them. A matrix certainly gives us a convenient shorthand to describe information presented in a table. However, we would like to go further than this and to use matrices to solve problems in economics. To do this we describe several mathematical operations that can be performed on matrices, namely:

- transposition;
- addition and subtraction;
- scalar multiplication;
- matrix multiplication.

One obvious omission from the list is matrix division. Strictly speaking, it is impossible to divide one matrix by another, although we can get fairly close to the idea of division by defining something called an inverse, which we consider in Section 4.2.

Advice

If you have not met matrices before, you might like to split this section into two separate parts. You are advised to work through the material as far as 4.1.4 now, leaving matrix multiplication for another session.

4.1.1 Transposition

In Table 4.1 the rows correspond to the two customers and the columns correspond to the three goods. The matrix representation of the table is then

$$\mathbf{A} = \begin{bmatrix} 7 & 3 & 4 \\ 1 & 5 & 6 \end{bmatrix}$$

The same information about monthly sales could easily have been presented the other way round, as shown in Table 4.2. The matrix representation would then be

$$\mathbf{B} = \begin{bmatrix} 7 & 1 \\ 3 & 5 \\ 4 & 6 \end{bmatrix}$$

We describe this situation by saying that **A** and **B** are transposes of each other and write

$$\mathbf{A}^{\mathrm{T}} = \mathbf{B} \qquad \text{read 'A transpose equals B'}$$

or equivalently

$$\mathbf{B}^{\mathrm{T}} = \mathbf{A} \qquad \text{read 'B transpose equals A'}$$

The **transpose** of a matrix is found by replacing rows by columns, so that the first row becomes the first column, the second row becomes the second column, and so on. The number of rows of **A** is then the same as the number of columns of $\mathbf{A}^{\mathrm{T}}$ and vice versa. Consequently, if **A** has order $m \times n$, then $\mathbf{A}^{\mathrm{T}}$ has order $n \times m$.

Example

Write down the transpose of the matrices

$$\mathbf{D} = \begin{bmatrix} 1 & 7 & 0 & 3 \\ 2 & 4 & 6 & 0 \\ 5 & 1 & 9 & 2 \end{bmatrix} \quad \mathbf{E} = \begin{bmatrix} -6 \\ 3 \end{bmatrix}$$

Solution

The transpose of the 3×4 matrix **D** is the 4×3 matrix

$$\mathbf{D}^{\mathrm{T}} = \begin{bmatrix} 1 & 2 & 5 \\ 7 & 4 & 1 \\ 0 & 6 & 9 \\ 3 & 0 & 2 \end{bmatrix}$$

The transpose of the 2×1 matrix **E** is the 1×2 matrix

$$\mathbf{E}^{\mathrm{T}} = [-6 \quad 3]$$

Table 4.2

		Sold to customer	
		C1	C2
Monthly	G1	7	1
sales for	G2	3	5
goods	G3	4	6

Practice Problem

2. Write down the transpose of the following matrices:

$$A = \begin{bmatrix} 1 & 4 & 0 & 1 & 2 \\ 3 & 7 & 6 & 1 & 4 \\ 2 & 1 & 3 & 5 & -1 \\ 2 & -5 & 1 & 8 & 0 \end{bmatrix}$$

$$B = [1 \quad 5 \quad 7 \quad 9]$$

$$C = \begin{bmatrix} 1 & 2 & 3 \\ 2 & 4 & 5 \\ 3 & 5 & 6 \end{bmatrix}$$

There are two particular shapes of matrices which are given special names. A matrix that has only one row, such as

$$c = [5 \quad 2 \quad 1 \quad -4]$$

is called a **row vector**, and a matrix that has only one column, such as

$$d = \begin{bmatrix} -3 \\ 10 \\ 6 \\ -7 \\ 1 \\ 9 \\ 2 \end{bmatrix}$$

is called a **column vector**. It is standard practice to identify vectors using lower-case rather than upper-case letters. In books they are set in bold type. If you are writing them down by hand, then you should underline the letters and put

$\underline{c}$ (or possibly $c̰$)   and $\underline{d}$ (or possibly $d̰$)

This is a useful convention since it helps to distinguish scalar quantities such as x, y, a, b, which denote single numbers, from vector quantities such as $\mathbf{x}, \mathbf{y}, \mathbf{a}, \mathbf{b}$, which denote matrices with one row or column. Incidentally, it is actually quite expensive to print column vectors in books and journals since it is wasteful on space, particularly if the number of elements is large. It is then more convenient to use the transpose notation and write the vector horizontally. For example, the 7×1 matrix $\mathbf{d}$ given previously would be printed as

$$d = [-3 \quad 10 \quad 6 \quad -7 \quad 1 \quad 9 \quad 2]^T$$

where the superscript T tells us that it is the column vector that is intended.

4.1.2 Addition and subtraction

Let us suppose that, for the two-customer three-product example, the matrix

$$A = \begin{bmatrix} 7 & 3 & 4 \\ 1 & 5 & 6 \end{bmatrix}$$

gives the sales for the month of January. Similarly, the monthly sales for February might be given by

$$\mathbf{B} = \begin{bmatrix} 6 & 2 & 1 \\ 0 & 4 & 4 \end{bmatrix}$$

This means, for example, that customer C1 buys 7 items of G1 in January and 6 items of G1 in February. Customer C1 therefore buys a total of

$$7 + 6 = 13$$

items of G1 during the two months. A similar process can be applied to the remaining goods and customers, so that the matrix giving the sales for the two months is

$$\mathbf{C} = \begin{bmatrix} 7+6 & 3+2 & 4+1 \\ 1+0 & 5+4 & 6+4 \end{bmatrix}$$
$$= \begin{bmatrix} 13 & 5 & 5 \\ 1 & 9 & 10 \end{bmatrix}$$

We describe this by saying that **C** is the **sum** of the two matrices **A** and **B** and writing

$$\mathbf{C} = \mathbf{A} + \mathbf{B}$$

In general, to add (or subtract) two matrices of the same size, we simply add (or subtract) their corresponding elements. It is obvious from this definition that, for any two $m \times n$ matrices, **A** and **B**,

$$\mathbf{A} + \mathbf{B} = \mathbf{B} + \mathbf{A}$$

because it is immaterial which way round two numbers are added. Note that in order to combine matrices in this way, it is necessary for them to have the same order. For example, it is impossible to add the matrices

$$\mathbf{D} = \begin{bmatrix} 1 & -7 \\ 1 & 3 \end{bmatrix} \quad \text{and} \quad \mathbf{E} = \begin{bmatrix} 1 & 2 \\ 1 & 1 \\ 3 & 5 \end{bmatrix}$$

because **D** has order 2×2 and **E** has order 3×2.

Example

Let

$$\mathbf{A} = \begin{bmatrix} 9 & -3 \\ 4 & 1 \\ 2 & 0 \end{bmatrix} \quad \text{and} \quad \mathbf{B} = \begin{bmatrix} 5 & 2 \\ -1 & 6 \\ 3 & 4 \end{bmatrix}$$

Find

(a) A + B   **(b)** A − B   **(c)** A − A

Solution

(a) $A + B = \begin{bmatrix} 9 & -3 \\ 4 & 1 \\ 2 & 0 \end{bmatrix} + \begin{bmatrix} 5 & 2 \\ -1 & 6 \\ 3 & 4 \end{bmatrix} = \begin{bmatrix} 14 & -1 \\ 3 & 7 \\ 5 & 4 \end{bmatrix}$

(b) $A - B = \begin{bmatrix} 9 & -3 \\ 4 & 1 \\ 2 & 0 \end{bmatrix} - \begin{bmatrix} 5 & 2 \\ -1 & 6 \\ 3 & 4 \end{bmatrix} = \begin{bmatrix} 4 & -5 \\ 5 & -5 \\ -1 & -4 \end{bmatrix}$

(c) $A - A = \begin{bmatrix} 9 & -3 \\ 4 & 1 \\ 2 & 0 \end{bmatrix} - \begin{bmatrix} 9 & -3 \\ 4 & 1 \\ 2 & 0 \end{bmatrix} = \begin{bmatrix} 0 & 0 \\ 0 & 0 \\ 0 & 0 \end{bmatrix}$

The result of part (c) of this example is a 3×2 matrix in which every entry is zero. Such a matrix is called a **zero matrix** and is written **0**. In fact, there are lots of zero matrices, each corresponding to a particular order. For example,

$$[0] \quad \begin{bmatrix} 0 & 0 \\ 0 & 0 \end{bmatrix} \quad \begin{bmatrix} 0 \\ 0 \\ 0 \\ 0 \end{bmatrix} \quad \begin{bmatrix} 0 & 0 & 0 & 0 & 0 & 0 \\ 0 & 0 & 0 & 0 & 0 & 0 \\ 0 & 0 & 0 & 0 & 0 & 0 \\ 0 & 0 & 0 & 0 & 0 & 0 \end{bmatrix}$$

are the 1×1, 2×2, 4×1 and 4×6 zero matrices, respectively. However, despite this, we shall use the single symbol **0** for all of these since it is usually clear in any actual example what the order is and hence which particular zero matrix is being used. It follows from the definition of addition and subtraction that, for any matrix **A**,

$A - A = 0$

$A + 0 = A$

The role played by the matrix **0** in matrix algebra is therefore similar to that of the number **0** in ordinary arithmetic.

Practice Problem

3. Let

$$A = \begin{bmatrix} 7 & 5 \\ 2 & 1 \end{bmatrix} \quad B = \begin{bmatrix} 5 \\ 4 \end{bmatrix} \quad C = \begin{bmatrix} 2 \\ 2 \end{bmatrix} \quad D = \begin{bmatrix} -6 & 2 \\ 1 & -9 \end{bmatrix} \quad 0 = \begin{bmatrix} 0 \\ 0 \end{bmatrix}$$

Find (where possible)

(a) $A + D$ (b) $A + C$ (c) $B - C$ (d) $C - 0$ (e) $D - D$

4.1.3 Scalar multiplication

Returning to the two-customer three-product example, let us suppose that the sales are the same each month and are given by

$$A = \begin{bmatrix} 7 & 3 & 4 \\ 1 & 5 & 6 \end{bmatrix}$$

This means, for example, that customer C1 buys 7 items of G1 every month, so in a whole year C1 buys

$$12 \times 7 = 84$$

items of G1. A similar process applies to the remaining goods and customers, and the matrix giving the annual sales is

$$B = \begin{bmatrix} 12 \times 7 & 12 \times 3 & 12 \times 4 \\ 12 \times 1 & 12 \times 5 & 12 \times 6 \end{bmatrix} = \begin{bmatrix} 84 & 36 & 48 \\ 12 & 60 & 72 \end{bmatrix}$$

Matrix **B** is found by scaling each element in **A** by 12, and we write

$$B = 12A$$

In general, to multiply a matrix **A** by a scalar k, we simply multiply each element of **A** by k. If

$$A = \begin{bmatrix} 1 & 2 & 3 \\ 4 & 5 & 6 \\ 7 & 8 & 9 \end{bmatrix}$$

then

$$2A = \begin{bmatrix} 2 & 4 & 6 \\ 8 & 10 & 12 \\ 14 & 16 & 18 \end{bmatrix}$$

$$-A = (-1)A = \begin{bmatrix} -1 & -2 & -3 \\ -4 & -5 & -6 \\ -7 & -8 & -9 \end{bmatrix}$$

$$0A = \begin{bmatrix} 0 & 0 & 0 \\ 0 & 0 & 0 \\ 0 & 0 & 0 \end{bmatrix} = 0$$

In ordinary arithmetic we know that

$$a(b + c) = ab + ac$$

for any three numbers a, b and c. It follows from our definitions of matrix addition and scalar multiplication that

$$k(A + B) = kA + kB$$

for any $m \times n$ matrices **A** and **B**, and scalar k.

Another property of matrices is

$$k(lA) = (kl)A$$

for scalars k and l. Again, this follows from the comparable property

$$a(bc) = (ab)c$$

for ordinary numbers.

You are invited to check these two matrix properties for yourself in the following problem.

Practice Problem

4. Let

$$A = \begin{bmatrix} 1 & -2 \\ 3 & 5 \\ 0 & 4 \end{bmatrix} \quad \text{and} \quad B = \begin{bmatrix} 0 & -1 \\ 2 & 7 \\ 1 & 6 \end{bmatrix}$$

(1) Find

   (a) 2A   (b) 2B   (c) A + B   (d) 2(A + B)

   Hence verify that

   $$2(A + B) = 2A + 2B$$

(2) Find

   (a) 3A   (b) –6A

   Hence verify that

   $$-2(3A) = -6A$$

4.1.4 Matrix multiplication

Advice

Hopefully, you have found the matrix operations considered so far in this section easy to understand. We now turn our attention to matrix multiplication. If you have never multiplied matrices before, you may find that it requires a bit more effort to grasp, and you should allow yourself extra time to work through the problems. There is no need to worry. Once you have performed a dozen or so matrix multiplications, you will find that the technique becomes second nature, although the process may appear rather strange and complicated at first sight.

We begin by showing you how to multiply a row vector by a column vector. To illustrate this let us suppose that goods G1, G2 and G3 sell at $50, $30 and $20, respectively, and let us introduce the row vector

$$\mathbf{p} = [50 \quad 30 \quad 20]$$

If the firm sells a total of 100, 200 and 175 goods of type G1, G2 and G3, respectively, then we can write this information as the column vector

$$\mathbf{q} = \begin{bmatrix} 100 \\ 200 \\ 175 \end{bmatrix}$$

The total revenue received from the sale of G1 is found by multiplying the price, $50, by the quantity, 100, to get

$50 \times 100 = \$5000$

Similarly, the revenue from G2 and G3 is

$30 \times 200 = \$6000$

and

$20 \times 175 = \$3500$

respectively. The total revenue of the firm is therefore

$TR = \$5000 + \$6000 + \$3500 = \$14\,500$

The value of TR is a single number and can be regarded as a 1×1 matrix: that is,

[14 500]

This 1×1 matrix is obtained by multiplying together the price vector, **p**, and the quantity vector, **q**, to get

$$[50 \quad 30 \quad 20] \begin{bmatrix} 100 \\ 200 \\ 175 \end{bmatrix} = [14\,500]$$

The value 14 500 is found by multiplying the corresponding elements of **p** and **q** and then adding together: that is,

$$[50 \quad 30 \quad 20] \begin{bmatrix} 100 \\ 200 \\ 175 \end{bmatrix} = [5000 + 6000 + 3500] = [14\,500]$$

In general, if **a** is the row vector

$$[a_{11} \quad a_{12} \quad a_{13} \quad \cdots \quad a_{1s}]$$

and **b** is the column vector

$$\begin{bmatrix} b_{11} \\ b_{21} \\ b_{31} \\ \\ b_{s1} \end{bmatrix}$$

then we define the matrix product

$$\mathbf{ab} = [a_{11} \quad a_{12} \quad a_{13} \quad \cdots \quad a_{1s}] \begin{bmatrix} b_{11} \\ b_{21} \\ b_{31} \\ \\ b_{s1} \end{bmatrix}$$

to be the 1×1 matrix

$$[a_{11}b_{11} + a_{12}b_{21} + a_{13}b_{31} + \ldots + a_{1s}b_{s1}]$$

It is important to notice that the single element in the 1×1 matrix **ab** is found by multiplying each element of **a** by the corresponding element of **b**. Consequently, it is essential that both vectors have the same number of elements. In other words, if **a** has order $1 \times s$ and **b** has order $t \times 1$, then it is only possible to form the product **ab** when $s = t$.

Example

If

$$\mathbf{a} = [1 \quad 2 \quad 3 \quad 4], \quad \mathbf{b} = \begin{bmatrix} 2 \\ 5 \\ -1 \\ 0 \end{bmatrix} \quad \text{and} \quad \mathbf{c} = \begin{bmatrix} 6 \\ 9 \\ 2 \end{bmatrix}$$

find **ab** and **ac**.

Solution

Using the definition of the multiplication of a row vector by a column vector we have

$$\mathbf{ab} = [1 \quad 2 \quad 3 \quad 4] \begin{bmatrix} 2 \\ 5 \\ -1 \\ 0 \end{bmatrix} = [1(2) + 2(5) + 3(-1) + 4(0)] = [9]$$

We have set out the calculations in this way so that you can see how the value, 9, is obtained. There is no need for you to indicate this in your own answers and you may simply write

$$[1 \quad 2 \quad 3 \quad 4] \begin{bmatrix} 2 \\ 5 \\ -1 \\ 0 \end{bmatrix} = [9]$$

without bothering to insert any intermediate steps.

It is impossible to multiply **a** and **c** because **a** has four elements and **c** has only three elements. You can see the problem if you actually try to perform the calculations, since there is no entry in **c** with which to multiply the 4 in **a**.

$$[1 \quad 2 \quad 3 \quad 4] \begin{bmatrix} 6 \\ 9 \\ 2 \end{bmatrix} = [1(6) + 2(9) + 3(2) + 4(?)]$$

Practice Problem

5. Let

$$\mathbf{a} = [1 \;\; -1 \;\; 0 \;\; 3 \;\; 2], \quad \mathbf{b} = [1 \;\; 2 \;\; 9], \quad \mathbf{c} = \begin{bmatrix} 0 \\ -1 \\ 1 \\ 1 \\ 2 \end{bmatrix} \text{ and } \mathbf{d} = \begin{bmatrix} -2 \\ 1 \\ 0 \end{bmatrix}$$

Find (where possible)

(a) ac   (b) bd   (c) ad

We now turn our attention to general matrix multiplication, which is defined as follows. If **A** is an $m \times s$ matrix and **B** is an $s \times n$ matrix, then

C = AB

is an $m \times n$ matrix and c_{ij} is found by multiplying the ith row of **A** into the jth column of **B**.

There are three things to notice about this definition. First, the number of columns of **A** is the same as the number of rows of **B**. Unless this condition is satisfied, it is impossible to form the product **AB**. Secondly, the matrix **C** has order $m \times n$, where m is the number of rows of **A** and n is the number of columns of **B**. Finally, the elements of **C** are found by multiplying row vectors by column vectors.

To illustrate the technique consider what happens when we find the product of the two matrices

$$\mathbf{A} = \begin{bmatrix} 2 & 1 & 0 \\ 1 & 0 & 4 \end{bmatrix} \text{ and } \mathbf{B} = \begin{bmatrix} 3 & 1 & 2 & 1 \\ 1 & 0 & 1 & 2 \\ 5 & 4 & 1 & 1 \end{bmatrix}$$

It is a good idea to check before you begin any detailed calculations that it is possible to multiply these matrices and also to identify the order of the resulting matrix. In this case

A is a 2×3 matrix   and   **B** is a 3×4 matrix

Matrix **A** has three columns and **B** has the same number of rows, so it *is* possible to find **AB**. Moreover, **AB** must have order 2×4 because **A** has two rows and **B** has four columns. Hence

$$\begin{bmatrix} 2 & 1 & 0 \\ 1 & 0 & 4 \end{bmatrix} \begin{bmatrix} 3 & 1 & 2 & 1 \\ 1 & 0 & 1 & 2 \\ 5 & 4 & 1 & 1 \end{bmatrix} = \begin{bmatrix} c_{11} & c_{12} & c_{13} & c_{14} \\ c_{21} & c_{22} & c_{23} & c_{24} \end{bmatrix}$$

All that remains for us to do is to calculate the eight numbers c_{ij}.

The number c_{11} in the top left-hand corner lies in the first row and first column, so to find its value we multiply the first row of **A** into the first column of **B** to get

$$\begin{bmatrix} 2 & 1 & 0 \\ 1 & 0 & 4 \end{bmatrix} \begin{bmatrix} 3 & 1 & 2 & 1 \\ 1 & 0 & 1 & 2 \\ 5 & 4 & 1 & 1 \end{bmatrix} \begin{bmatrix} 7 & c_{12} & c_{13} & c_{14} \\ c_{21} & c_{22} & c_{23} & c_{24} \end{bmatrix}$$

because $2(3) + 1(1) + 0(5) = 7$.

The number c_{12} lies in the first row and second column, so to find its value we multiply the first row of **A** into the second column of **B** to get

$$\begin{bmatrix} 2 & 1 & 0 \\ 1 & 0 & 4 \end{bmatrix} \begin{bmatrix} 3 & 1 & 2 & 1 \\ 1 & 0 & 1 & 2 \\ 5 & 4 & 1 & 1 \end{bmatrix} \begin{bmatrix} 7 & 2 & c_{13} & c_{14} \\ c_{21} & c_{22} & c_{23} & c_{24} \end{bmatrix}$$

because $2(1) + 1(0) + 0(4) = 2$.

The values of c_{13} and c_{14} are then found in a similar way by multiplying the first row of **A** into the third and fourth columns of **B**, respectively, to get

$$\begin{bmatrix} 2 & 1 & 0 \\ 1 & 0 & 4 \end{bmatrix} \begin{bmatrix} 3 & 1 & 2 & 1 \\ 1 & 0 & 1 & 2 \\ 5 & 4 & 1 & 1 \end{bmatrix} \begin{bmatrix} 7 & 2 & 5 & 4 \\ c_{21} & c_{22} & c_{23} & c_{24} \end{bmatrix}$$

because $2(2) + 1(1) + 0(1) = 5$ and $2(1) + 1(2) + 0(1) = 4$.

Finally, we repeat the whole procedure along the second row of **C**. The elements c_{21}, c_{22}, c_{23} and c_{24} are calculated by multiplying the second row of **A** into the four columns of **B** in succession to get

$$\begin{bmatrix} 2 & 1 & 0 \\ 1 & 0 & 4 \end{bmatrix} \begin{bmatrix} 3 & 1 & 2 & 1 \\ 1 & 0 & 1 & 2 \\ 5 & 4 & 1 & 1 \end{bmatrix} \begin{bmatrix} 7 & 2 & 5 & 4 \\ 23 & 17 & 6 & 5 \end{bmatrix}$$

because

$$1(3) + 0(1) + 4(5) = 23$$
$$1(1) + 0(0) + 4(4) = 17$$
$$1(2) + 0(1) + 4(1) = 6$$
$$1(1) + 0(2) + 4(1) = 5$$

In this example we have indicated how to build up the matrix **C** in a step-by-step manner and have used highlights to show you how the calculations are performed. This approach has been adopted merely as a teaching device. There is no need for you to set your calculations out in this way, and you are encouraged to write down your answer in a single line of working.

Advice

Take the trouble to check before you begin that it is possible to form the matrix product and to anticipate the order of the end result. This can be done by jotting down the orders of the original matrices side by side. The product exists if the inner numbers are the same and the order of the answer is given by the outer numbers: that is,

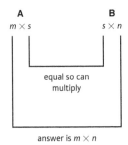

For example, if **A**, **B** and **C** have orders 3×5, 5×2 and 3×4 respectively, then **AB** exists and has order 3×2 because

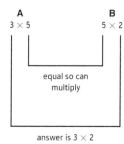

but it is impossible to form **AC** because

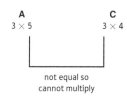

Practice Problem

6. Write down the order of the matrices

$$\mathbf{A} = \begin{bmatrix} 1 & 2 \\ 0 & 1 \\ 3 & 1 \end{bmatrix} \quad \text{and} \quad \mathbf{B} = \begin{bmatrix} 1 & 2 \\ 3 & 4 \end{bmatrix}$$

Hence verify that it is possible to form the matrix product

$$\mathbf{C} = \mathbf{AB}$$

and write down the order of **C**. Calculate all of the elements of **C**.

We have already noted that matrix operations have similar properties to those of ordinary arithmetic. Some particular rules of arithmetic are:

$$a(b + c) = ab + ac \quad \text{(distributive law)}$$
$$(a + b)c = ac + bc \quad \text{(distributive law)}$$
$$a(bc) = (ab)c \quad \text{(associative law)}$$
$$ab = ba \quad \text{(commutative law)}$$

An obvious question to ask is whether they have a counterpart in matrix algebra. It turns out that provided the matrices **A**, **B** and **C** have the correct orders for the appropriate sums and products to exist, then

$$\mathbf{A(B + C)} = \mathbf{AB} + \mathbf{AC}$$
$$\mathbf{(A + B)C} = \mathbf{AC} + \mathbf{BC}$$
$$\mathbf{A(BC)} = \mathbf{(AB)C}$$

However, although it is true that

$$ab = ba$$

for numbers, this result does **not** extend to matrices. Even if **AB** and **BA** both exist, it is not necessarily true that

AB = BA

This is illustrated in the following example.

Example

If

$$A = \begin{bmatrix} 1 & -1 \\ 2 & 1 \end{bmatrix} \quad \text{and} \quad B = \begin{bmatrix} 1 & 3 \\ 1 & 2 \end{bmatrix}$$

evaluate **AB** and **BA**.

Solution

It is easy to check that it is possible to form both products **AB** and **BA** and that they both have order 2×2. In fact

$$AB = \begin{bmatrix} 1 & -1 \\ 2 & 1 \end{bmatrix}\begin{bmatrix} 1 & 3 \\ 1 & 2 \end{bmatrix} = \begin{bmatrix} 0 & 1 \\ 3 & 8 \end{bmatrix}$$

$$BA = \begin{bmatrix} 1 & 3 \\ 1 & 2 \end{bmatrix}\begin{bmatrix} 1 & -1 \\ 2 & 1 \end{bmatrix} = \begin{bmatrix} 7 & 2 \\ 5 & 1 \end{bmatrix}$$

so **AB ≠ BA**.

There are certain pairs of matrices which do commute (that is, for which **AB = BA**) and we shall investigate some of these in the next section. However, these are very much the exception. We therefore have the 'non-property' that, in general,

AB ≠ BA

Practice Problems

7. Let

$$A = \begin{bmatrix} 2 & 1 & 1 \\ 5 & 1 & 0 \\ -1 & 1 & 4 \end{bmatrix}, \quad B = \begin{bmatrix} 1 \\ 2 \\ 1 \end{bmatrix}, \quad C = \begin{bmatrix} 1 & 2 \\ 3 & 1 \end{bmatrix}, \quad D = \begin{bmatrix} 1 & 1 \\ -1 & 1 \\ 2 & 1 \end{bmatrix} \quad \text{and} \quad E = \begin{bmatrix} 1 & 2 & 3 \\ 4 & 5 & 6 \end{bmatrix}$$

Find (where possible)

(a) AB   (b) BA   (c) CD   (d) DC

(e) AE   (f) EA   (g) DE   (h) ED

8. Evaluate the matrix product **Ax**, where

$$A = \begin{bmatrix} 1 & 4 & 7 \\ 2 & 6 & 5 \\ 8 & 9 & 5 \end{bmatrix} \quad \text{and} \quad \mathbf{x} = \begin{bmatrix} x \\ y \\ z \end{bmatrix}$$

Hence show that the system of linear equations

$$x + 4y + 7z = -3$$
$$2x + 6y + 5z = 10$$
$$8x + 9y + 5z = 1$$

can be written as **Ax = b** where

$$\mathbf{b} = \begin{bmatrix} -3 \\ 10 \\ 1 \end{bmatrix}$$

We conclude this section by showing you how to express a familiar problem in matrix notation. For example, we might want to find values of x and y which satisfy

$$2x - 5y = 6$$
$$7x + 8y = -1$$

Motivated by the result of Practice Problem 8, we write this as

$$\mathbf{Ax = b}$$

where

$$A = \begin{bmatrix} 2 & -5 \\ 7 & 8 \end{bmatrix} \quad \mathbf{x} = \begin{bmatrix} x \\ y \end{bmatrix} \quad \mathbf{b} = \begin{bmatrix} 6 \\ -1 \end{bmatrix}$$

It is easy to check that this is correct simply by multiplying out **Ax** to get

$$\begin{bmatrix} 2 & -5 \\ 7 & 8 \end{bmatrix} \begin{bmatrix} x \\ y \end{bmatrix} = \begin{bmatrix} 2x - 5y \\ 7x + 8y \end{bmatrix}$$

and so the matrix equation **Ax = b** reads

$$\begin{bmatrix} 2x - 5y \\ 7x + 8y \end{bmatrix} = \begin{bmatrix} 6 \\ -1 \end{bmatrix}$$

that is,

$$2x - 5y = 6$$
$$7x + 8y = -1$$

Quite generally, any system of n linear equations in n unknowns can be written as

$$\mathbf{Ax = b}$$

where A, x and b are $n \times n$, $n \times 1$ and $n \times 1$ matrices, respectively. The matrix A consists of the coefficients, the vector x consists of the unknowns and the vector b consists of the right-hand sides. The definition of matrix multiplication allows us to write a linear system in terms of matrices, although it is not immediately obvious that there is any advantage in doing so. In the next section we introduce the concept of a matrix inverse and show you how to use this to solve systems of equations expressed in matrix form.

Throughout this section we have noted various properties that matrices satisfy. For convenience these are summarised in the next sub-section.

4.1.5 Summary

Provided that the indicated sums and products make sense,

$$A + B = B + A$$
$$A - A = 0$$
$$A + 0 = A$$
$$k(A + B) = kA + kB$$
$$k(lA) = (kl)A$$
$$A(B + C) = AB + AC$$
$$(A + B)C = AC + BC$$
$$A(BC) = (AB)C$$

We also have the non-property that, in general,

$$AB \neq BA$$

Key Terms

Column vector　A matrix with one column.

Elements　The individual numbers inside a matrix. (Also called **entries**.)

Matrix　A rectangular array of numbers, set out in rows and columns, surrounded by a pair of brackets. (Plural **matrices**.)

Order (of a matrix)　The dimensions of a matrix. A matrix with m rows and n columns has order $m \times n$.

Row vector　A matrix with one row.

Transpose (of a matrix)　The matrix obtained from a given matrix by interchanging rows and columns. The transpose of a matrix A is written A^T.

Zero matrix　A matrix in which every element is zero.

Exercise 4.1

1. The monthly sales (in thousands) of burgers (B1) and bites (B2) in three fast-food restaurants (R1, R2, R3) are as follows:

	R1	R2	R3
B1	35	27	13
B2	42	39	24

January

	R1	R2	R3
B1	31	17	3
B2	25	29	16

February

   (a) Write down two 2×3 matrices **J** and **F**, representing sales in January and February, respectively.

   (b) By finding $\mathbf{J} + \mathbf{F}$, write down the matrix for the total sales over the two months.

   (c) By finding $\mathbf{J} - \mathbf{F}$, write down the matrix for the difference in sales for the two months.

2. If

$$A = \begin{bmatrix} 2 & 3 & 1 & 9 \\ 1 & 0 & 5 & 0 \\ 6 & 7 & 8 & 4 \end{bmatrix} \quad B = \begin{bmatrix} 1 & 7 & 9 & 6 \\ 2 & 1 & 0 & 5 \\ 6 & 4 & 5 & 3 \end{bmatrix}$$

   work out

   (a) $2\mathbf{A}$ (b) $2\mathbf{B}$ (c) $2\mathbf{A} + 2\mathbf{B}$ (d) $2(\mathbf{A} + \mathbf{B})$

   Do you notice any connection between your answers to parts (c) and (d)?

3. If **A**, **B** and **C** are matrices with orders, 3×3, 2×3 and 4×2, respectively, which of the following matrix calculations are possible? If the calculation *is* possible, state the order of the resulting matrix

   $$4\mathbf{B}, \quad \mathbf{A} + \mathbf{B}, \quad 3\mathbf{B}^{\mathrm{T}} + \mathbf{C}, \quad \mathbf{AB}, \quad \mathbf{B}^{\mathrm{T}}\mathbf{A}, \quad (\mathbf{CB})^{\mathrm{T}}, \quad \mathbf{CBA}$$

4. A firm manufactures three products, P1, P2 and P3, which it sells to two customers, C1 and C2. The number of items of each product that are sold to these customers is given by

$$A = \begin{array}{c} \text{C1} \\ \text{C2} \end{array} \begin{bmatrix} 6 & 7 & 9 \\ 2 & 1 & 2 \end{bmatrix} \begin{array}{c} \text{P1 P2 P3} \end{array}$$

   The firm charges both customers the same price for each product according to

   $$\begin{array}{ccc} \text{P1} & \text{P2} & \text{P3} \end{array}$$
   $$B = [100 \quad 500 \quad 200]^{\mathrm{T}}$$

   To make each item of type P1, P2 and P3, the firm uses four raw materials, R1, R2, R3 and R4. The number of tonnes required per item is given by

$$C = \begin{array}{c} \text{P1} \\ \text{P2} \\ \text{P3} \end{array} \begin{bmatrix} 1 & 0 & 0 & 1 \\ 1 & 1 & 2 & 1 \\ 0 & 0 & 1 & 1 \end{bmatrix} \begin{array}{c} \text{R1 R2 R3 R4} \end{array}$$

The cost per tonne of raw materials is

$$\begin{matrix} \text{R1} & \text{R2} & \text{R3} & \text{R4} \end{matrix}$$
$$\mathbf{D} = [20 \quad 10 \quad 15 \quad 15]^{\mathrm{T}}$$

In addition, let

$$\mathbf{E} = [1 \quad 1]$$

Find the following matrix products and give an interpretation of each one.

(a) **AB**　　　(b) **AC**　　(c) **CD**　　(d) **ACD**　　(e) **EAB**

(f) **EACD**　　(g) **EAB – EACD**

5. A firm orders 12, 30 and 25 items of goods G1, G2 and G3. The cost of each item of G1, G2 and G3 is $8, $30 and $15, respectively.

   (a) Write down suitable price and quantity vectors, and use matrix multiplication to work out the total cost of the order.

   (b) Write down the new price vector when the cost of G1 rises by 20%, the cost of G2 falls by 10% and the cost of G3 is unaltered. Use matrix multiplication to work out the new cost of the order and hence find the overall percentage change in total cost.

6. (1) Let

$$\mathbf{A} = \begin{bmatrix} 1 & 2 \\ 3 & 4 \\ 5 & 6 \end{bmatrix} \quad \text{and} \quad \mathbf{B} = \begin{bmatrix} 1 & -1 \\ 2 & 1 \\ -3 & 4 \end{bmatrix}$$

   Find

   (a) $\mathbf{A}^{\mathrm{T}}$　　(b) $\mathbf{B}^{\mathrm{T}}$　　(c) $\mathbf{A} + \mathbf{B}$　　(d) $(\mathbf{A} + \mathbf{B})^{\mathrm{T}}$

   Do you notice any connection between $(\mathbf{A} + \mathbf{B})^{\mathrm{T}}$, $\mathbf{A}^{\mathrm{T}}$ and $\mathbf{B}^{\mathrm{T}}$?

   (2) Let

$$\mathbf{C} = \begin{bmatrix} 1 & 4 \\ 5 & 9 \end{bmatrix} \quad \text{and} \quad \mathbf{D} = \begin{bmatrix} 2 & 1 & 0 \\ -1 & 0 & 1 \end{bmatrix}$$

   Find

   (a) $\mathbf{C}^{\mathrm{T}}$　　(b) $\mathbf{D}^{\mathrm{T}}$　　(c) $\mathbf{CD}$　　(d) $(\mathbf{CD})^{\mathrm{T}}$

   Do you notice any connection between $(\mathbf{CD})^{\mathrm{T}}$, $\mathbf{C}^{\mathrm{T}}$ and $\mathbf{D}^{\mathrm{T}}$?

7. Verify the equations

   (a) $\mathbf{A}(\mathbf{B} + \mathbf{C}) = \mathbf{AB} + \mathbf{AC}$　　(b) $(\mathbf{AB})\mathbf{C} = \mathbf{A}(\mathbf{BC})$

   in the case when

$$\mathbf{A} = \begin{bmatrix} 5 & -3 \\ 2 & 1 \end{bmatrix}, \quad \mathbf{B} = \begin{bmatrix} 1 & 5 \\ 4 & 0 \end{bmatrix} \quad \text{and} \quad \mathbf{C} = \begin{bmatrix} -1 & 1 \\ 1 & 2 \end{bmatrix}$$

8. If

$$\mathbf{A} = [1 \quad 2 \quad -4 \quad 3] \quad \text{and} \quad \mathbf{B} = \begin{bmatrix} 1 \\ 7 \\ 3 \\ 2 \end{bmatrix}$$

   find **AB** and **BA**.

9. (a) Evaluate the matrix product **Ax**, where

$$\mathbf{A} = \begin{bmatrix} 7 & 5 \\ 1 & 3 \end{bmatrix} \quad \text{and} \quad \mathbf{x} = \begin{bmatrix} x \\ y \end{bmatrix}$$

Hence show that the system of linear equations

$$7x + 5y = 3$$
$$x + 3y = 2$$

can be written as $\mathbf{Ax} = \mathbf{b}$ where $\mathbf{b} = \begin{bmatrix} 3 \\ 2 \end{bmatrix}$.

(b) The system of equations

$$2x + 3y - 2z = 6$$
$$x - y + 2z = 3$$
$$4x + 2y + 5z = 1$$

can be expressed in the form $\mathbf{Ax} = \mathbf{b}$. Write down the matrices **A**, **x** and **b**.

Exercise 4.1*

1. Matrices **A**, **B**, **C** and **D** have orders 3×5, 5×2, 5×5 and 3×5, respectively. State whether it is possible to perform the following matrix operations.

If it *is* possible, state the order of the resulting matrix.

(a) 7B   **(b)** $(\mathbf{A} + \mathbf{C})^{\mathrm{T}}$ **(c)** $\mathbf{A} - 2\mathbf{D}$ **(d)** BC

(e) $\mathbf{CB}^{\mathrm{T}}$ **(f)** $\mathbf{D}^{\mathrm{T}}\mathbf{A}$ **(g)** $\mathbf{A}^{\mathrm{T}} + \mathbf{B}^{\mathrm{T}}$

2. Two matrices **A** and **B** are given by

$$\mathbf{A} = \begin{bmatrix} a-1 & b \\ a+b & 3c-b \end{bmatrix} \quad \text{and} \quad \mathbf{B} = \begin{bmatrix} 1 & 3a \\ 2c & d+1 \end{bmatrix}$$

If $\mathbf{A} = \mathbf{B}$, find the values of a, b, c and d.

3. Consider the matrices

$$\mathbf{A} = \begin{bmatrix} a & b & c \\ d & e & f \end{bmatrix} \quad \text{and} \quad \mathbf{B} = \begin{bmatrix} g & h \\ i & j \\ k & l \end{bmatrix}$$

(a) Write down the matrices $\mathbf{A}^{\mathrm{T}}$ and $\mathbf{B}^{\mathrm{T}}$.

(b) Work out the matrix products **AB** and $\mathbf{B}^{\mathrm{T}}\mathbf{A}^{\mathrm{T}}$.

(c) State the relationship between **AB** and $\mathbf{B}^{\mathrm{T}}\mathbf{A}^{\mathrm{T}}$, and use this result to simplify $(\mathbf{A}^{\mathrm{T}}\mathbf{B}^{\mathrm{T}}\mathbf{C}^{\mathrm{T}})^{\mathrm{T}}$.

4. A chain of sports shops, A, B and C, sells T-shirts, trainers and tennis racquets. The weekly sales and profit per item are shown in the tables below:

Sales per week	Shop A	Shop B	Shop C
T-shirts	60	40	25
Trainers	80	123	90
Tennis racquets	10	0	25

Profit per item	Shop A ($)	Shop B ($)	Shop C ($)
T-shirts	1	1	1.50
Trainers	5	8	6
Tennis racquets	20	25	30

The 3×3 matrices formed from the sales and profit tables are denoted by $\mathbf{S}$ and $\mathbf{P}$, respectively.

(a) If $\mathbf{SP}^{\mathrm{T}}$ is denoted by $\mathbf{A}$, find the element a_{11} and give a brief interpretation of this number.

(b) If $\mathbf{S}^{\mathrm{T}}\mathbf{P}$ is denoted by $\mathbf{B}$, find the element b_{33} and give a brief interpretation of this number.

5. On a small island there are supermarkets A, L, S and W. In the current year, 30% of customers buy groceries from A, 20% from L, 40% from S and 10% from W. However, each year,

A retains 80% of its customers but loses 10% to L, 5% to S and 5% to W.
L retains 90% of its customers but loses 5% to A and 5% to S.
S retains 75% of its customers but loses 10% to A, 10% to L and 5% to W.
W retains 85% of its customers losing 5% to A, 5% to L and 5% to S.

(a) If the original market share is represented by the column vector

$$\mathbf{x} = \begin{bmatrix} 0.3 \\ 0.2 \\ 0.4 \\ 0.1 \end{bmatrix}$$

and the matrix representing the transition in supermarket loyalty is

$$\mathbf{T} = \begin{bmatrix} 0.8 & 0.05 & 0.1 & 0.05 \\ 0.1 & 0.9 & 0.1 & 0.05 \\ 0.05 & 0.05 & 0.75 & 0.05 \\ 0.05 & 0 & 0.05 & 0.85 \end{bmatrix}$$

work out the matrix product, $\mathbf{Tx}$, and give an interpretation of the elements of the resulting vector.

(b) Assuming that the same transition matrix applies in subsequent years, work out the percentage of customers who buy groceries in supermarket L after

(i) two years   (ii) three years

6. If $\mathbf{A} = \begin{bmatrix} 3 & -1 & 4 \\ 0 & 2 & 1 \end{bmatrix}$ and $\mathbf{B} = \begin{bmatrix} 4 & 0 & 7 \\ 2 & 5 & 1 \end{bmatrix}$ find the matrix $\mathbf{X}$ which satisfies the matrix equation: $2\mathbf{A} + \mathbf{X}^{\mathrm{T}} = 3\mathbf{B}$.

7. Matrices, **A**, **B** and **C** are given by

$$\mathbf{A} = \begin{bmatrix} 3 & -2 & 4 \\ 6 & 1 & 0 \\ -5 & 9 & 5 \end{bmatrix}, \quad \mathbf{B} = \begin{bmatrix} 1 & 5 & 0 \\ 4 & 4 & 7 \\ 2 & 3 & -9 \end{bmatrix} \text{ and } \mathbf{C} = \begin{bmatrix} 3 & -2 & -7 \\ -4 & 5 & 1 \\ 3 & 0 & 6 \end{bmatrix}$$

If **D** = **A**(2**B** + 3**C**), find d_{23}.

8. Let

$$\mathbf{A} = \begin{bmatrix} a & b \\ c & d \end{bmatrix}, \quad \mathbf{A}^{-1} = \frac{1}{ad - bc} \begin{bmatrix} d & -b \\ -c & a \end{bmatrix} \qquad (ad - bc \neq 0)$$

$$\mathbf{I} = \begin{bmatrix} 1 & 0 \\ 0 & 1 \end{bmatrix} \text{ and } \mathbf{x} = \begin{bmatrix} x \\ y \end{bmatrix}$$

Show that

(a) **AI** = **A** and **IA** = **A**   **(b)** $\mathbf{A}^{-1}\mathbf{A} = \mathbf{I}$ and $\mathbf{A}\mathbf{A}^{-1} = \mathbf{I}$ **(c)** **Ix** = **x**

9. For the commodity market:

$$C = aY + b \quad \text{and} \quad I = cr + d$$

For the money market:

$$M_S = M_S^* \quad \text{and} \quad M_D = k_1 Y + k_2 r + k_3$$

If both markets are in equilibrium, find the matrix, **A**, such that **Ax** = **b**, where $\mathbf{x} = \begin{bmatrix} r \\ Y \end{bmatrix}$ and $\mathbf{b} = \begin{bmatrix} M_s^* - k_3 \\ b + d \end{bmatrix}$.

SECTION 4.2
Matrix inversion

Objectives

At the end of this section you should be able to:

- Write down the 2 × 2 and 3 × 3 identity matrices.
- Detect whether a matrix is singular or non-singular.
- Calculate the determinant and inverse of a 2 × 2 matrix.
- Calculate the cofactors of a 3 × 3 matrix.
- Use cofactors to find the determinant and inverse of a 3 × 3 matrix.
- Use matrix inverses to solve systems of linear equations arising in economics.

In this and the following section we consider **square** matrices, in which the number of rows and columns are equal. For simplicity we concentrate on 2 × 2 and 3 × 3 matrices, although the ideas and techniques apply more generally to $n \times n$ matrices of any size. We have already seen that, with one notable exception, the algebra of matrices is virtually the same as the algebra of numbers. There are, however, two important properties of numbers which we have yet to consider. The first is the existence of a number, 1, which satisfies

$$a1 = a \quad \text{and} \quad 1a = a$$

for any number, a. The second is the fact that corresponding to any non-zero number, a, we can find another number, a^{-1}, with the property that

$$a^{-1}a = 1 \quad \text{and} \quad aa^{-1} = 1 \qquad \boxed{a^{-1} = \frac{1}{a}}$$

If you have worked through Question 8 of Exercise 4.1* you will know how to extend these to 2 × 2 matrices. In part (a) you showed that, for any 2 × 2 matrix, **A**,

$$\mathbf{AI} = \mathbf{A} \quad \text{and} \quad \mathbf{IA} = \mathbf{A}$$

where

$$\mathbf{I} = \begin{bmatrix} 1 & 0 \\ 0 & 1 \end{bmatrix}$$

The matrix **I** is called the **identity** matrix and is analogous to the number 1 in ordinary arithmetic. You also showed in part (b) of Question 8 that corresponding to the 2 × 2 matrix

$$\mathbf{A} = \begin{bmatrix} a & b \\ c & d \end{bmatrix}$$

there is another matrix

$$\mathbf{A}^{-1} = \frac{1}{ad - bc} \begin{bmatrix} d & -b \\ -c & a \end{bmatrix}$$

with the property that

$$\mathbf{A}^{-1}\mathbf{A} = \mathbf{I} \quad \text{and} \quad \mathbf{A}\mathbf{A}^{-1} = \mathbf{I}$$

The matrix $\mathbf{A}^{-1}$ is said to be the **inverse** of $\mathbf{A}$ and is analogous to the reciprocal of a number. The formula for $\mathbf{A}^{-1}$ looks rather complicated, but the construction of $\mathbf{A}^{-1}$ is in fact very easy. Starting with some matrix

$$\mathbf{A} = \begin{bmatrix} a & b \\ c & d \end{bmatrix}$$

we first swap the two numbers on the leading diagonal (that is, the elements along the line joining the top left-hand corner to the bottom right-hand corner of $\mathbf{A}$) to get

$$\begin{bmatrix} d & b \\ c & a \end{bmatrix} \qquad \left(\begin{array}{c} \text{swap} \\ a \text{ and } d \end{array}\right)$$

Secondly, we change the sign of the 'off-diagonal' elements to get

$$\begin{bmatrix} d & -b \\ -c & a \end{bmatrix} \qquad \left(\begin{array}{c} \text{change signs} \\ \text{of } b \text{ and } c \end{array}\right)$$

Finally, we multiply the matrix by the scalar

$$\frac{1}{ad - bc}$$

to get

$$\frac{1}{ad - bc}\begin{bmatrix} d & -b \\ -c & a \end{bmatrix} \qquad \left(\begin{array}{c} \text{divide each element} \\ \text{by } ad - bc \end{array}\right)$$

The number $ad - bc$ is called the **determinant** of $\mathbf{A}$ and is written as

$$\det(\mathbf{A}) \quad \text{or} \quad |\mathbf{A}| \quad \text{or} \quad \begin{vmatrix} a & b \\ c & d \end{vmatrix}$$

Notice that the last step in the calculation is impossible if

$$|\mathbf{A}| = 0$$

because we cannot divide by zero. We deduce that the inverse of a matrix exists only if the matrix has a non-zero determinant. This is comparable to the situation in arithmetic where a reciprocal of a number exists provided the number is non-zero. If the matrix has a non-zero determinant, it is said to be **non-singular**; otherwise it is said to be **singular**.

As an example, consider the matrices

$$\mathbf{A} = \begin{bmatrix} 1 & 2 \\ 3 & 4 \end{bmatrix} \quad \text{and} \quad \mathbf{B} = \begin{bmatrix} 2 & 5 \\ 4 & 10 \end{bmatrix}$$

The determinant of the first matrix is

$$\det(\mathbf{A}) = \begin{vmatrix} 1 & 2 \\ 3 & 4 \end{vmatrix} = 1(4) - 2(3) = 4 - 6 = -2$$

We see that det(**A**) ≠ 0, so the matrix is non-singular and the inverse exists. To find $\mathbf{A}^{-1}$ we swap the diagonal elements, 1 and 4, change the sign of the off-diagonal elements, 2 and 3, and divide by the determinant, −2. Hence

$$\mathbf{A}^{-1} = -\frac{1}{2}\begin{bmatrix} 4 & -2 \\ -3 & 1 \end{bmatrix} = \begin{bmatrix} -2 & 1 \\ 3/2 & -1/2 \end{bmatrix}$$

Of course, if $\mathbf{A}^{-1}$ really is the inverse of **A**, then $\mathbf{A}^{-1}\mathbf{A}$ and $\mathbf{A}\mathbf{A}^{-1}$ should multiply out to give **I**. As a check:

$$\mathbf{A}^{-1}\mathbf{A} = \begin{bmatrix} -2 & 1 \\ 3/2 & -1/2 \end{bmatrix}\begin{bmatrix} 1 & 2 \\ 3 & 4 \end{bmatrix} = \begin{bmatrix} 1 & 0 \\ 0 & 1 \end{bmatrix} \checkmark$$

$$\mathbf{A}\mathbf{A}^{-1} = \begin{bmatrix} 1 & 2 \\ 3 & 4 \end{bmatrix}\begin{bmatrix} -2 & 1 \\ 3/2 & -1/2 \end{bmatrix} = \begin{bmatrix} 1 & 0 \\ 0 & 1 \end{bmatrix} \checkmark$$

To discover whether or not the second matrix

$$\mathbf{B} = \begin{bmatrix} 2 & 5 \\ 4 & 10 \end{bmatrix}$$

has an inverse, we need to find its determinant.

$$\det(\mathbf{B}) = \begin{vmatrix} 2 & 5 \\ 4 & 10 \end{vmatrix} = 2(10) - 5(4) = 20 - 20 = 0$$

We see that det(**B**) = 0, so this matrix is singular and the inverse does not exist.

Practice Problem

1. Find (where possible) the inverse of the following matrices. Are these matrices singular or non-singular?

$$\mathbf{A} = \begin{bmatrix} 6 & 4 \\ 1 & 2 \end{bmatrix} \quad \mathbf{B} = \begin{bmatrix} 6 & 4 \\ 3 & 2 \end{bmatrix}$$

One reason for calculating the inverse of a matrix is that it helps us to solve matrix equations in the same way that the reciprocal of a number is used to solve algebraic equations. We have already seen in Section 4.1 how to express a system of linear equations in matrix form. Any 2 × 2 system

$$ax + by = e$$
$$cx + dy = f$$

can be written as

$$\mathbf{Ax} = \mathbf{b}$$

where

$$\mathbf{A} = \begin{bmatrix} a & b \\ c & d \end{bmatrix} \quad \mathbf{x} = \begin{bmatrix} x \\ y \end{bmatrix} \quad \mathbf{b} = \begin{bmatrix} e \\ f \end{bmatrix}$$

The coefficient matrix, **A**, and right-hand-side vector, **b**, are assumed to be given and the problem is to determine the vector of unknowns, **x**. Multiplying both sides of

$$\mathbf{Ax} = \mathbf{b}$$

by $\mathbf{A}^{-1}$ gives

$$\mathbf{A}^{-1}(\mathbf{Ax}) = \mathbf{A}^{-1}\mathbf{b}$$
$$(\mathbf{A}^{-1}\mathbf{A})\mathbf{x} = \mathbf{A}^{-1}\mathbf{b} \quad \text{(associative property)}$$
$$\mathbf{Ix} = \mathbf{A}^{-1}\mathbf{b} \quad \text{(definition of an inverse)}$$
$$\mathbf{x} = \mathbf{A}^{-1}\mathbf{b} \quad \text{(Question 8(c) in Exercise 4.1*)}$$

The solution vector **x** can therefore be found simply by multiplying $\mathbf{A}^{-1}$ by **b**. We are assuming here that $\mathbf{A}^{-1}$ exists. If the coefficient matrix is singular, then the inverse cannot be found and the system of linear equations does not possess a unique solution; there are either infinitely many solutions or no solution.

The following example illustrates the use of inverses to find equilibrium prices in supply and demand models.

Example

The equilibrium prices P_1 and P_2 for two goods satisfy the equations

$$-4P_1 + P_2 = -13$$
$$2P_1 - 5P_2 = -7$$

Express this system in matrix form and hence find the values of P_1 and P_2.

Solution

Using the notation of matrices, the simultaneous equations

$$-4P_1 + P_2 = -13$$
$$2P_1 - 5P_2 = -7$$

can be written as

$$\begin{bmatrix} -4 & 1 \\ 2 & -5 \end{bmatrix} \begin{bmatrix} P_1 \\ P_2 \end{bmatrix} = \begin{bmatrix} -13 \\ -7 \end{bmatrix}$$

that is, as

$$\mathbf{Ax} = \mathbf{b}$$

where

$$\mathbf{A} = \begin{bmatrix} -4 & 1 \\ 2 & -5 \end{bmatrix} \quad \mathbf{x} = \begin{bmatrix} P_1 \\ P_2 \end{bmatrix} \quad \mathbf{b} = \begin{bmatrix} -13 \\ -7 \end{bmatrix}$$

The matrix **A** has determinant

$$\begin{vmatrix} -4 & 1 \\ 2 & -5 \end{vmatrix} = (-4)(-5) - (1)(2) = 20 - 2 = 18$$

To find $\mathbf{A}^{-1}$ we swap the diagonal elements, -4 and -5, change the sign of the off-diagonal elements, 1 and 2, and divide by the determinant, 18, to get

$$\mathbf{A}^{-1} = \frac{1}{18} \begin{bmatrix} -5 & -1 \\ -2 & -4 \end{bmatrix}$$

Finally, to calculate **x** we multiply $\mathbf{A}^{-1}$ by **b** to get

$$\mathbf{x} = \mathbf{A}^{-1}\mathbf{b} = \frac{1}{18} \begin{bmatrix} -5 & -1 \\ -2 & -4 \end{bmatrix} \begin{bmatrix} -13 \\ -7 \end{bmatrix} = \frac{1}{18} \begin{bmatrix} 72 \\ 54 \end{bmatrix} = \begin{bmatrix} 4 \\ 3 \end{bmatrix}$$

Hence $P_1 = 4$ and $P_2 = 3$.

Practice Problem

2. The equilibrium prices P_1 and P_2 for two goods satisfy the equations

$$9P_1 + P_2 = 43$$
$$2P_1 + 7P_2 = 57$$

Express this system in matrix form and hence find the values of P_1 and P_2.

Simultaneous equations also arise in macroeconomics.

The equilibrium levels of consumption, C, and income, Y, for the simple two-sector macroeconomic model satisfy the structural equations

$$Y = C + I*$$

$$C = aY + b$$

where a and b are parameters in the range $0 < a < 1$ and $b > 0$, and $I*$ denotes investment.

The reduced form of the structural equations for this simple model has already been found in Section 5.3. It is instructive to reconsider this problem using matrices. The objective is to express the endogenous variables, Y and C, in terms of the exogenous variable $I*$ and parameters a and b. The 'unknowns' of this problem are therefore Y and C, and we begin by rearranging the structural equations so that these variables appear on the left-hand sides. Subtracting C from both sides of

$$Y = C + I*$$

gives

$$Y - C = I* \qquad (1)$$

and if we subtract aY from both sides of

$$C = aY + b$$

we get

$$-aY + C = b \tag{2}$$

(It is convenient to put the term involving Y first so that the variables align with those of equation (1).)

In matrix form, equations (1) and (2) become

$$\begin{bmatrix} 1 & -1 \\ -a & 1 \end{bmatrix} \begin{bmatrix} Y \\ C \end{bmatrix} = \begin{bmatrix} I^* \\ b \end{bmatrix}$$

that is,

$$\mathbf{Ax} = \mathbf{b}$$

where

$$\mathbf{A} = \begin{bmatrix} 1 & -1 \\ -a & 1 \end{bmatrix} \quad \mathbf{x} = \begin{bmatrix} Y \\ C \end{bmatrix} \quad \mathbf{b} = \begin{bmatrix} I^* \\ b \end{bmatrix}$$

The matrix $\mathbf{A}$ has determinant

$$\begin{vmatrix} 1 & -1 \\ -a & 1 \end{vmatrix} = 1(1) - (-1)(-a) = 1 - a$$

which is non-zero because $a < 1$.

To find $\mathbf{A}^{-1}$, we swap the diagonal elements, 1 and 1, change the sign of the off-diagonal elements, -1 and $-a$, and divide by the determinant, $1 - a$, to get

$$\mathbf{A}^{-1} = \frac{1}{1-a} \begin{bmatrix} 1 & 1 \\ a & 1 \end{bmatrix}$$

Finally, to determine $\mathbf{x}$ we multiply $\mathbf{A}^{-1}$ by $\mathbf{b}$ to get

$$\mathbf{x} = \mathbf{A}^{-1}\mathbf{b} = \frac{1}{1-a} \begin{bmatrix} 1 & 1 \\ a & 1 \end{bmatrix} \begin{bmatrix} I^* \\ b \end{bmatrix} = \frac{1}{1-a} \begin{bmatrix} I^* + b \\ aI^* + b \end{bmatrix}$$

Hence

$$Y = \frac{I^* + b}{1 - a} \quad \text{and} \quad C = \frac{aI^* + b}{1 - a}$$

The inverse matrix obviously provides a useful way of solving the structural equations of a macroeconomic model. In addition, the elements of the inverse matrix can be given an important economic interpretation. To see this, let us suppose that the investment I^* changes by an amount ΔI^* to become $I^* + \Delta I^*$, with the parameter b held fixed. The new values of Y and C are obtained by replacing I^* by $I^* + \Delta I^*$ in the expressions for Y and C, and are given by

$$\frac{I^* + \Delta I^* + b}{1 - a} \quad \text{and} \quad \frac{a(I^* + \Delta I^*) + b}{1 - a}$$

respectively. The change in the value of Y is therefore

$$\Delta Y = \frac{I^* + \Delta I^* + b}{1 - a} - \frac{I^* + b}{1 - a} = \left(\frac{1}{1-a}\right)\Delta I^*$$

and the change in the value of C is

$$\Delta C = \frac{a(I^* + \Delta I^*) + b}{1 - a} - \frac{aI^* + b}{1 - a} = \left(\frac{a}{1 - a}\right)\Delta I^*$$

In other words, the changes to Y and C are found by multiplying the change in I^* by

$$\frac{1}{1 - a} \quad \text{and} \quad \frac{a}{1 - a}$$

respectively. For this reason we call

$$\frac{1}{1 - a}$$

the investment multiplier for Y and

$$\frac{a}{1 - a}$$

the investment multiplier for C.

Now the inverse matrix is

$$\mathbf{A}^{-1} = \begin{bmatrix} \dfrac{1}{1 - a} & \dfrac{1}{1 - a} \\ \dfrac{a}{1 - a} & \dfrac{1}{1 - a} \end{bmatrix}$$

and we see that these multipliers are precisely the elements that appear in the first column. It is easy to show, using a similar argument, that the second column contains the multipliers for Y and C due to changes in the autonomous consumption, b. The four elements in the inverse matrix can thus be interpreted as follows:

$$\begin{array}{cc} & \begin{array}{cc} I^* & \qquad\qquad b \end{array} \\ \begin{array}{c} Y \\ C \end{array} & \begin{bmatrix} \text{investment multiplier } Y & \text{autonomous consumption multiplier for } Y \\ \text{investment multiplier } C & \text{autonomous consumption multiplier for } C \end{bmatrix} \end{array}$$

Practice Problem

3. The general linear supply and demand equations for a one-commodity market model are given by

$$P = aQ_s + b \qquad (a > 0, b > 0)$$
$$P = -cQ_D + d \quad (c > 0, d > 0)$$

Show that in matrix notation the equilibrium price, P, and quantity, Q, satisfy

$$\begin{bmatrix} 1 & -a \\ 1 & c \end{bmatrix}\begin{bmatrix} P \\ Q \end{bmatrix} = \begin{bmatrix} b \\ d \end{bmatrix}$$

Solve this system to express P and Q in terms of a, b, c and d. Write down the multiplier for Q due to changes in b and deduce that an increase in b leads to a decrease in Q.

The concepts of determinant, inverse and identity matrices apply equally well to 3×3 matrices. The identity matrix is easily dealt with. It can be shown that the 3×3 identity matrix is

$$\mathbf{I} = \begin{bmatrix} 1 & 0 & 0 \\ 0 & 1 & 0 \\ 0 & 0 & 1 \end{bmatrix}$$

You are invited to check that, for any 3×3 matrix **A**,

$$\mathbf{AI} = \mathbf{A} \quad \text{and} \quad \mathbf{IA} = \mathbf{A}$$

Before we can discuss the determinant and inverse of a 3×3 matrix, we need to introduce an additional concept known as a **cofactor**. Corresponding to each element a_{ij} of a matrix **A**, there is a cofactor, A_{ij}. A 3×3 matrix has nine elements, so there are nine cofactors to be computed. The cofactor, A_{ij}, is defined to be the determinant of the 2×2 matrix obtained by deleting row i and column j of **A** (known as a **minor**), prefixed by a '+' or '−' sign according to the following pattern:

$$\begin{bmatrix} + & - & + \\ - & + & - \\ + & - & + \end{bmatrix}$$

For example, suppose we wish to calculate A_{23}, which is the cofactor associated with a_{23} in the matrix

$$\mathbf{A} = \begin{bmatrix} a_{11} & a_{12} & a_{13} \\ a_{21} & a_{22} & a_{23} \\ a_{31} & a_{32} & a_{33} \end{bmatrix}$$

The element a_{23} lies in the second row and third column. Consequently, we delete the second row and third column to produce the 2×2 matrix

$$\begin{bmatrix} a_{11} & a_{12} \\ a_{31} & a_{32} \end{bmatrix}$$

The cofactor, A_{23}, is the determinant of this 2×2 matrix prefixed by a '−' sign because from the pattern

$$\begin{bmatrix} + & - & + \\ - & + & - \\ + & - & + \end{bmatrix}$$

we see that a_{23} is in a minus position. In other words,

$$A_{3} = - \begin{vmatrix} a_{11} & a_{12} \\ a_{31} & a_{32} \end{vmatrix}$$
$$= -(a_{11}a_{32} - a_{12}a_{31})$$
$$= -a_{11}a_{32} + a_{12}a_{31}$$

The '±' pattern can also be worked out using $(-1)^{i+j}$ since when $i + j$ is even, $(-1)^{i+j} = +1$, and when $i + j$ is odd, $(-1)^{i+j} = -1$. For the cofactor A_{23} worked out previously, $(-1)^{2+3} = (-1)^5 = -1$, confirming that the element a_{23} is in the minus position.

Example

Find all the cofactors of the matrix

$$A = \begin{bmatrix} 2 & 4 & 1 \\ 4 & 3 & 7 \\ 2 & 1 & 3 \end{bmatrix}$$

Solution

Let us start in the top left-hand corner and work row by row. For cofactor A_{11}, the element $a_{11} = 2$ lies in the first row and first column, so we delete this row and column to produce the 2×2 matrix

$$\begin{bmatrix} 3 & 7 \\ 1 & 3 \end{bmatrix}$$

Cofactor A_{11} is the determinant of this 2×2 matrix, prefixed by a '+' sign because from the pattern

$$\begin{bmatrix} + & - & + \\ - & + & - \\ + & - & + \end{bmatrix}$$

we see that a_{11} is in a plus position. Hence

$$\begin{aligned} A_{11} &= + \begin{vmatrix} 3 & 7 \\ 1 & 3 \end{vmatrix} \\ &= +(3(3) - 7(1)) \\ &= 9 - 7 \\ &= 2 \end{aligned}$$

For cofactor A_{12}, the element $a_{12} = 4$ lies in the first row and second column, so we delete this row and column to produce the 2×2 matrix

$$\begin{bmatrix} 4 & 7 \\ 2 & 3 \end{bmatrix}$$

Cofactor A_{12} is the determinant of this 2×2 matrix, prefixed by a '−' sign because from the pattern

$$\begin{bmatrix} + & - & + \\ - & + & - \\ + & - & + \end{bmatrix}$$

we see that a_{12} is in a minus position. Hence

$$\begin{aligned} A_{12} &= - \begin{vmatrix} 4 & 7 \\ 2 & 3 \end{vmatrix} \\ &= -(4(3) - 7(2)) \\ &= -(12 - 14) \\ &= 2 \end{aligned}$$

We can continue in this way to find the remaining cofactors:

$$A_{13} = + \begin{vmatrix} 4 & 3 \\ 2 & 1 \end{vmatrix} = -2$$

$$A_{21} = - \begin{vmatrix} 4 & 1 \\ 1 & 3 \end{vmatrix} = -11$$

$$A_{22} = + \begin{vmatrix} 2 & 1 \\ 2 & 3 \end{vmatrix} = 4$$

$$A_{23} = - \begin{vmatrix} 2 & 4 \\ 2 & 1 \end{vmatrix} = 6$$

$$A_{31} = + \begin{vmatrix} 4 & 1 \\ 3 & 7 \end{vmatrix} = 25$$

$$A_{32} = - \begin{vmatrix} 2 & 1 \\ 4 & 7 \end{vmatrix} = -10$$

$$A_{33} = + \begin{vmatrix} 2 & 4 \\ 4 & 3 \end{vmatrix} = -10$$

Practice Problem

4. Find all the cofactors of the matrix

$$\mathbf{A} = \begin{bmatrix} 1 & 3 & 3 \\ 1 & 4 & 3 \\ 1 & 3 & 4 \end{bmatrix}$$

We are now in a position to describe how to calculate the determinant and inverse of a 3×3 matrix. The determinant is found by multiplying the elements in any one row or column by their corresponding cofactors and adding together. It does not matter which row or column is chosen; exactly the same answer is obtained in each case. If we expand along the first row of the matrix

$$\mathbf{A} = \begin{bmatrix} a_{11} & a_{12} & a_{13} \\ a_{21} & a_{22} & a_{23} \\ a_{31} & a_{32} & a_{33} \end{bmatrix}$$

we get

$$\det(\mathbf{A}) = a_{11}A_{11} + a_{12}A_{12} + a_{13}A_{13}$$

Similarly, if we expand down the second column, we get

$$\det(\mathbf{A}) = a_{12}A_{12} + a_{22}A_{22} + a_{32}A_{32}$$

The fact that we get the same answer irrespective of the row and column that we use for expansion is an extremely useful property. It provides us with an obvious check on our calculations. Also, there are occasions when it is more convenient to expand along certain rows or columns than others.

Example

Find the determinants of the following matrices:

$$A = \begin{bmatrix} 2 & 4 & 1 \\ 4 & 3 & 7 \\ 2 & 1 & 3 \end{bmatrix} \quad \text{and} \quad B = \begin{bmatrix} 10 & 7 & 5 \\ 0 & 2 & 0 \\ 2 & 7 & 3 \end{bmatrix}$$

Solution

We have already calculated all nine cofactors of the matrix

$$A = \begin{bmatrix} 2 & 4 & 1 \\ 4 & 3 & 7 \\ 2 & 1 & 3 \end{bmatrix}$$

in the previous example. It is immaterial which row or column we use. Let us choose the second row. The cofactors corresponding to the three elements 4, 3, 7 in the second row were found to be −11, 4, 6, respectively. Consequently, if we expand along this row, we get

$$\begin{vmatrix} 2 & 4 & 1 \\ 4 & 3 & 7 \\ 2 & 1 & 3 \end{vmatrix} = 4(-11) + 3(4) + 7(6) = 10$$

As a check, let us also expand down the third column. The elements in this column are 1, 7, 3 with cofactors −2, 6, −10, respectively. Hence, if we multiply each element by its cofactor and add, we get

$$1(-2) + 7(6) + 3(-10) = 10$$

which is the same as before. If you are interested, you might like to confirm for yourself that the value of 10 is also obtained when expanding along rows 1 and 3, and down columns 1 and 2.

The matrix

$$B = \begin{bmatrix} 10 & 7 & 5 \\ 0 & 2 & 0 \\ 2 & 7 & 3 \end{bmatrix}$$

is entirely new to us, so we have no prior knowledge about its cofactors. In general, we need to evaluate all three cofactors in any one row or column to find the determinant of a 3×3 matrix. In this case, however, we can be much lazier. Observe that all but one of the elements in the second row are zero, so when we expand along this row, we get

$$\begin{aligned} \det(B) &= b_{21}B_{21} + b_{22}B_{22} + b_{23}B_{23} \\ &= 0B_{21} + 2B_{22} + 0B_{23} \\ &= 2B_{22} \end{aligned}$$

Hence B_{22} is the only cofactor that we need to find. This corresponds to the element in the second row and second column, so we delete this row and column to produce the 2×2 matrix

$$\begin{bmatrix} 10 & 5 \\ 2 & 3 \end{bmatrix}$$

The element b_{22} is in a plus position, so

$$B_{22} = + \begin{vmatrix} 10 & 5 \\ 2 & 3 \end{vmatrix} = 20$$

Hence,

$$\det(B) = 2B_{22} = 2 \times 20 = 40$$

Practice Problem

5. Find the determinants of

$$\mathbf{A} = \begin{bmatrix} 1 & 3 & 3 \\ 1 & 4 & 3 \\ 1 & 3 & 4 \end{bmatrix} \quad \text{and} \quad \mathbf{B} = \begin{bmatrix} 270 & -372 & 0 \\ 552 & 201 & 0 \\ 999 & 413 & 0 \end{bmatrix}$$

[Hint: you might find your answer to Practice Problem 4 useful when calculating the determinant of **A**.]

The inverse of the 3×3 matrix

$$\mathbf{A} = \begin{bmatrix} a_{11} & a_{12} & a_{13} \\ a_{21} & a_{22} & a_{23} \\ a_{31} & a_{32} & a_{33} \end{bmatrix}$$

is given by

$$\mathbf{A}^{-1} = \frac{1}{|\mathbf{A}|} \begin{bmatrix} A_{11} & A_{21} & A_{31} \\ A_{12} & A_{22} & A_{32} \\ A_{13} & A_{23} & A_{33} \end{bmatrix}$$

Once the cofactors of **A** have been found, it is easy to construct $\mathbf{A}^{-1}$. We first stack the cofactors in their natural positions

$$\begin{bmatrix} A_{11} & A_{12} & A_{13} \\ A_{21} & A_{22} & A_{23} \\ A_{31} & A_{32} & A_{33} \end{bmatrix}$$ called the adjugate matrix

Secondly, we take the transpose to get

$$\begin{bmatrix} A_{11} & A_{21} & A_{31} \\ A_{12} & A_{22} & A_{32} \\ A_{13} & A_{23} & A_{33} \end{bmatrix}$$ called the adjoint matrix

Finally, we multiply by the scalar

$$\frac{1}{|\mathbf{A}|}$$

to get

$$\mathbf{A}^{-1} = \frac{1}{|\mathbf{A}|} \begin{bmatrix} A_{11} & A_{21} & A_{31} \\ A_{12} & A_{22} & A_{32} \\ A_{13} & A_{23} & A_{33} \end{bmatrix}$$

divide each element by the determinant

The last step is impossible if

$$|\mathbf{A}| = 0$$

because we cannot divide by zero. Under these circumstances, the inverse does not exist and the matrix is singular.

Advice

It is a good idea to check that no mistakes have been made by verifying that

$$\mathbf{A}^{-1}\mathbf{A} = \mathbf{I} \quad \text{and} \quad \mathbf{A}\mathbf{A}^{-1} = \mathbf{I}$$

Example

Find the inverse of

$$\mathbf{A} = \begin{bmatrix} 2 & 4 & 1 \\ 4 & 3 & 7 \\ 2 & 1 & 3 \end{bmatrix}$$

Solution

The cofactors of this particular matrix have already been calculated as

$$A_{11} = 2, \quad A_{12} = 2, \quad A_{13} = -2$$
$$A_{21} = -11, \quad A_{22} = 4, \quad A_{23} = 6$$
$$A_{31} = 25, \quad A_{32} = -10, \quad A_{33} = -10$$

Stacking these numbers in their natural positions gives the adjugate matrix

$$\begin{bmatrix} 2 & 2 & -2 \\ -11 & 4 & 6 \\ 25 & -10 & -10 \end{bmatrix}$$

The adjoint matrix is found by transposing this to get

$$\begin{bmatrix} 2 & -11 & -25 \\ 2 & 4 & -10 \\ -2 & 6 & -10 \end{bmatrix}$$

In the previous example the determinant was found to be 10, so

$$\mathbf{A}^{-1} = \frac{1}{10} \begin{bmatrix} 2 & -11 & 25 \\ 2 & 4 & -10 \\ -2 & 6 & -10 \end{bmatrix} = \begin{bmatrix} 1/5 & -11/10 & 5/2 \\ 1/5 & 2/5 & -1 \\ -1/5 & 3/5 & -1 \end{bmatrix}$$

As a check:

$$\mathbf{A}^{-1}\mathbf{A} = \begin{bmatrix} 1/5 & -11/10 & 5/2 \\ 1/5 & 2/5 & -1 \\ -1/5 & 3/5 & -1 \end{bmatrix} \begin{bmatrix} 2 & 4 & 1 \\ 4 & 3 & 7 \\ 2 & 1 & 3 \end{bmatrix} = \begin{bmatrix} 1 & 0 & 0 \\ 0 & 1 & 0 \\ 0 & 0 & 1 \end{bmatrix} = \mathbf{I} \checkmark$$

$$\mathbf{A}\mathbf{A}^{-1} = \begin{bmatrix} 2 & 4 & 1 \\ 4 & 3 & 7 \\ 2 & 1 & 3 \end{bmatrix} \begin{bmatrix} 1/5 & -11/10 & 5/2 \\ 1/5 & 2/5 & -1 \\ -1/5 & 3/5 & -1 \end{bmatrix} = \begin{bmatrix} 1 & 0 & 0 \\ 0 & 1 & 0 \\ 0 & 0 & 1 \end{bmatrix} = \mathbf{I} \checkmark$$

Practice Problem

6. Find (where possible) the inverses of

$$\mathbf{A} = \begin{bmatrix} 1 & 3 & 3 \\ 1 & 4 & 3 \\ 1 & 3 & 4 \end{bmatrix} \quad \text{and} \quad \mathbf{B} = \begin{bmatrix} 270 & -372 & 0 \\ 552 & 201 & 0 \\ 999 & 413 & 0 \end{bmatrix}$$

[Hint: you might find your answers to Practice Problems 4 and 5 useful.]

Inverses of 3×3 matrices can be used to solve systems of three linear equations in three unknowns. The general system

$$a_{11}x + a_{12}y + a_{13}z = b_1$$
$$a_{21}x + a_{22}y + a_{23}z = b_2$$
$$a_{31}x + a_{32}y + a_{33}z = b_3$$

can be written as

$$\mathbf{Ax} = \mathbf{b}$$

where

$$\mathbf{A} = \begin{bmatrix} a_{11} & a_{12} & a_{13} \\ a_{21} & a_{22} & a_{23} \\ a_{31} & a_{32} & a_{33} \end{bmatrix} \quad \mathbf{x} = \begin{bmatrix} x \\ y \\ z \end{bmatrix} \quad \mathbf{b} = \begin{bmatrix} b_1 \\ b_2 \\ b_3 \end{bmatrix}$$

The vector of unknowns, $\mathbf{x}$, can be found by inverting the coefficient matrix, $\mathbf{A}$, and multiplying by the right-hand-side vector, $\mathbf{b}$, to get

$$\mathbf{x} = \mathbf{A}^{-1}\mathbf{b}$$

Example

Determine the equilibrium prices of three interdependent commodities that satisfy

$$2P_1 + 4P_2 + P_3 = 77$$
$$4P_1 + 3P_2 + 7P_3 = 114$$
$$2P_1 + P_2 + 3P_3 = 48$$

Solution

In matrix notation this system of equations can be written as

$$\mathbf{Ax} = \mathbf{b}$$

where

$$\mathbf{A} = \begin{bmatrix} 2 & 4 & 1 \\ 4 & 3 & 7 \\ 2 & 1 & 3 \end{bmatrix} \quad \mathbf{x} = \begin{bmatrix} P_1 \\ P_2 \\ P_3 \end{bmatrix} \quad \mathbf{b} = \begin{bmatrix} 77 \\ 114 \\ 48 \end{bmatrix}$$

The inverse of the coefficient matrix has already been found in the previous example and is

$$\mathbf{A}^{-1} = \begin{bmatrix} 1/5 & -11/10 & 5/2 \\ 1/5 & 2/5 & -1 \\ -1/5 & 3/5 & -1 \end{bmatrix}$$

so

$$\begin{bmatrix} P_1 \\ P_2 \\ P_3 \end{bmatrix} = \begin{bmatrix} 1/5 & -11/10 & 5/2 \\ 1/5 & 2/5 & -1 \\ -1/5 & 3/5 & -1 \end{bmatrix} \begin{bmatrix} 77 \\ 114 \\ 48 \end{bmatrix} = \begin{bmatrix} 10 \\ 13 \\ 5 \end{bmatrix}$$

The equilibrium prices are therefore given by

$$P_1 = 10, \quad P_2 = 13, \quad P_3 = 5$$

Practice Problem

7. Determine the equilibrium prices of three interdependent commodities that satisfy

$$P_1 + 3P_2 + 3P_3 = 32$$
$$P_1 + 4P_2 + 3P_3 = 37$$
$$P_1 + 3P_2 + 4P_3 = 35$$

[Hint: you might find your answer to Practice Problem 6 useful.]

Throughout this section, we have concentrated on 2×2 and 3×3 matrices. The method described can be extended to larger matrices of order $n \times n$. The cofactor A_{ij} would be the determinant of the $(n-1) \times (n-1)$ matrix left when row i and column j are deleted prefixed by $(-1)^{i+j}$. However, the cofactor approach is very inefficient. The amount of working rises dramatically as n increases, making this method inappropriate for large matrices. The preferred method for solving simultaneous equations is based on the elimination idea. This is easily programmed, and a computer can solve large systems of equations in a matter of seconds.

Key Terms

Cofactor   The cofactor of the element, a_{ij}, is the determinant of the matrix left when row i and column j are deleted, multiplied by $+1$ or -1, depending on whether $i + j$ is even or odd, respectively.

Determinant   A determinant can be expanded as the sum of the products of the elements in any one row or column and their respective cofactors.

Identity matrix   An $n \times n$ matrix, **I**, in which every element on the main diagonal is 1 and the other elements are all 0. If **A** is any $n \times n$ matrix, then $\mathbf{AI} = \mathbf{A} = \mathbf{IA}$.

Inverse matrix   A matrix, $\mathbf{A}^{-1}$, with the property that $\mathbf{A}^{-1}\mathbf{A} = \mathbf{I} = \mathbf{AA}^{-1}$.

Minor   The name given to the cofactor before the '$\pm$' pattern is imposed.

Non-singular matrix   A square matrix with a non-zero determinant.

Singular matrix   A square matrix with a zero determinant. A singular matrix fails to possess an inverse.

Square matrix   A matrix with the same number of rows as columns.

Exercise 4.2

1. **(a)** Find the determinant of

(i) $\begin{bmatrix} 2 & 7 \\ 1 & 4 \end{bmatrix}$ (ii) $\begin{bmatrix} 5 & 6 \\ 3 & 4 \end{bmatrix}$ (iii) $\begin{bmatrix} -2 & -10 \\ 1 & 4 \end{bmatrix}$ (iv) $\begin{bmatrix} -6 & -4 \\ -8 & -7 \end{bmatrix}$

(b) Find the inverse of each matrix in part (a).

2. Let

$$\mathbf{A} = \begin{bmatrix} 2 & 1 \\ 5 & 1 \end{bmatrix} \quad \text{and} \quad \mathbf{B} = \begin{bmatrix} 1 & 0 \\ 2 & 4 \end{bmatrix}$$

(1) Find

(a) $|\mathbf{A}|$ **(b)** $|\mathbf{B}|$ **(c)** $|\mathbf{AB}|$

Do you notice any connection between $|\mathbf{A}|$, $|\mathbf{B}|$ and $|\mathbf{AB}|$?

(2) Find

(a) $\mathbf{A}^{-1}$ **(b)** $\mathbf{B}^{-1}$ **(c)** $(\mathbf{AB})^{-1}$

Do you notice any connection between $\mathbf{A}^{-1}$, $\mathbf{B}^{-1}$ and $(\mathbf{AB})^{-1}$?

3. If the matrices

$$\begin{bmatrix} 2 & -1 \\ 3 & a \end{bmatrix} \quad \text{and} \quad \begin{bmatrix} 2 & b \\ 3 & -4 \end{bmatrix}$$

are singular, find the values of a and b.

4. Evaluate the matrix product, $\begin{bmatrix} 5 & -3 \\ -10 & 8 \end{bmatrix}\begin{bmatrix} 8 & 3 \\ 10 & 5 \end{bmatrix}$.

Hence, or otherwise, write down the inverse of $\begin{bmatrix} 8 & 3 \\ 10 & 5 \end{bmatrix}$.

5. Use matrices to solve the following pairs of simultaneous equations:

   (a) $3x + 4y = -1$ (b) $x + 3y = 8$

   $\ 5x - y = 6$ $\ 4x - y = 6$

6. The demand and supply functions for two interdependent goods are given by

   $$Q_{D_1} = 50 - 2P_1 + P_2$$
   $$Q_{D_2} = 10 + P_1 - 4P_2$$
   $$Q_{S_1} = -20 + P_1$$
   $$Q_{S_2} = -10 + 5P_2$$

   (a) Show that the equilibrium prices satisfy

   $$\begin{bmatrix} 3 & -1 \\ -1 & 9 \end{bmatrix} \begin{bmatrix} P_1 \\ P_2 \end{bmatrix} = \begin{bmatrix} 70 \\ 20 \end{bmatrix}$$

   (b) Find the inverse of the 2×2 matrix in part (a) and hence find the equilibrium prices.

7. If a, b and k are non-zero, show that

   (a) each of these 2×2 matrices is singular:

   (i) $\begin{bmatrix} a & 0 \\ b & 0 \end{bmatrix}$ (ii) $\begin{bmatrix} a & b \\ ka & kb \end{bmatrix}$ (iii) $\begin{bmatrix} a & b \\ \dfrac{1}{b} & \dfrac{1}{a} \end{bmatrix}$

   (b) each of these 2×2 matrices is non-singular:

   (i) $\begin{bmatrix} a & b \\ 0 & k \end{bmatrix}$ (ii) $\begin{bmatrix} 0 & a \\ -a & 0 \end{bmatrix}$ (iii) $\begin{bmatrix} a & b \\ -b & a \end{bmatrix}$

Exercise 4.2*

1. If the matrices

   $$A = \begin{bmatrix} 1 & 2 \\ a & b \end{bmatrix} \quad \text{and} \quad B = \begin{bmatrix} a & 4 \\ 2 & b \end{bmatrix}$$

   are both singular, determine all possible values of a and b.

2. (a) If

   $$A = \begin{bmatrix} a & b \\ c & d \end{bmatrix} \quad \text{and} \quad B = \begin{bmatrix} e & f \\ g & h \end{bmatrix}$$

   work out the matrix product, AB.

   (b) Hence, show that $\det(AB) = \det(A) \times \det(B)$

(c) If **A** is singular and **B** is non-singular, what, if anything, can be deduced about **AB**? Give a brief reason for your answer.

3. Which one of the following matrices has an inverse which is not listed?

$$\mathbf{A} = \begin{bmatrix} 1 & 1 \\ 1 & 0 \end{bmatrix}, \quad \mathbf{B} = \begin{bmatrix} 1 & 0 \\ 0 & 1 \end{bmatrix}, \quad \mathbf{C} = \begin{bmatrix} 0 & 1 \\ 1 & -1 \end{bmatrix}, \quad \mathbf{D} = \begin{bmatrix} 1 & -1 \\ -1 & 0 \end{bmatrix}, \quad \mathbf{E} = \begin{bmatrix} -1 & 0 \\ 0 & 1 \end{bmatrix}$$

4. Find the determinant of the matrix

$$\begin{bmatrix} 5 & -2 & 3 \\ 4 & -1 & -5 \\ 6 & 7 & 9 \end{bmatrix}$$

5. Find the cofactor, A_{23}, of the matrix

$$\mathbf{A} = \begin{bmatrix} 5 & -2 & 7 \\ 6 & 1 & -9 \\ 4 & -3 & 8 \end{bmatrix}$$

6. Find (where possible) the inverse of the matrices

$$\mathbf{A} = \begin{bmatrix} 2 & 1 & -1 \\ 1 & 3 & 2 \\ -1 & 2 & 1 \end{bmatrix} \quad \text{and} \quad \mathbf{B} = \begin{bmatrix} 1 & 4 & 5 \\ 2 & 1 & 3 \\ -1 & 3 & 2 \end{bmatrix}$$

Are these matrices singular or non-singular?

7. For the commodity market

$$C = aY + b \quad (0\ a < 1, b > 0)$$
$$I = cr + d \quad (c < 0, d > 0)$$

For the money market

$$M_S = M_S^*$$
$$M_D = k_1 Y + k_2 r + k_3 \ (k_1, k_3 > 0, k_2 < 0)$$

Show that when the commodity and money markets are both in equilibrium, the income, Y, and interest rate, r, satisfy the matrix equation

$$\begin{bmatrix} 1 - a & -c \\ k_1 & k_2 \end{bmatrix} \begin{bmatrix} Y \\ r \end{bmatrix} = \begin{bmatrix} b + d \\ M_s^* - k_3 \end{bmatrix}$$

and solve this system for Y and r. Write down the multiplier for r due to changes in M_S^* and deduce that interest rates fall as the money supply grows.

8. Find the determinant of the matrix

$$\mathbf{A} = \begin{bmatrix} 2 & 1 & 3 \\ 1 & 0 & a \\ 3 & 1 & 4 \end{bmatrix}$$

in terms of a. Deduce that this matrix is non-singular provided $a \neq 1$ and find $\mathbf{A}^{-1}$ in this case.

9. Find the inverse of

$$\begin{bmatrix} -2 & 2 & 1 \\ 1 & -5 & -1 \\ 2 & -1 & -6 \end{bmatrix}$$

Hence find the equilibrium prices of the three-commodity market model given in Question 6 of Exercise 1.5*.

10. Find the inverse of the matrix

$$A = \begin{bmatrix} 6 & 3 & a \\ 5 & 4 & 2 \\ 7 & 2 & 3 \end{bmatrix}$$

in terms of a.

For what value of a will simultaneous equations of the form

$$6x + 3y + az = b$$
$$5x + 4y + 2z = c$$
$$7x + 2y + 3z = d$$

fail to possess a unique solution?

11. **(a)** Multiply out the brackets in the expression $(a - b)(a - c)(c - b)$.

(b) Show that the determinant of the matrix

$$A = \begin{bmatrix} 1 & 1 & 1 \\ a & b & c \\ a^2 & b^2 & c^2 \end{bmatrix}$$

is $(a - b)(a - c)(c - b)$ and deduce that the simultaneous equations

$$x + y + z = l$$
$$ax + by + cz = m$$
$$a^2x + b^2y + c^2z = n$$

have a unique solution provided, a, b, and c are distinct.

SECTION 4.3
Cramer's rule

Objectives

At the end of this section you should be able to:

- Appreciate the limitations of using inverses to solve systems of linear equations.
- Use Cramer's rule to solve systems of linear equations.
- Apply Cramer's rule to analyse static macroeconomic models.
- Apply Cramer's rule to solve two-country trading models.

In Section 4.2 we described the mechanics of calculating the determinant and inverse of 2×2 and 3×3 matrices. These concepts can be extended to larger systems in an obvious way, although the amount of effort needed rises dramatically as the size of the matrix increases. For example, consider the work involved in solving the system

$$\begin{bmatrix} 1 & 0 & 2 & 3 \\ -1 & 5 & 4 & 1 \\ 0 & 7 & -3 & 6 \\ 2 & 4 & 5 & 1 \end{bmatrix} \begin{bmatrix} x_1 \\ x_2 \\ x_3 \\ x_4 \end{bmatrix} = \begin{bmatrix} -1 \\ 1 \\ -24 \\ 15 \end{bmatrix}$$

using the method of matrix inversion. In this case the coefficient matrix has order 4×4 and so has 16 elements. Corresponding to each of these elements is a cofactor. This is defined to be the 3×3 determinant obtained by deleting the row and column containing the element, prefixed by a '+' or '−' according to the following pattern:

$$\begin{bmatrix} + & - & + & - \\ - & + & - & + \\ + & - & + & - \\ - & + & - & - \end{bmatrix}$$

Determinants are found by expanding along any one row or column, and inverses are found by stacking cofactors as before. However, given that there are 16 cofactors to be calculated, even the most enthusiastic student is likely to view the prospect with some trepidation. To make matters worse, it frequently happens in economics that only a few of the variables x_i are actually needed. For instance, it could be that the variable x_3 is the only one of interest. Under these circumstances, it is clearly wasteful expending a large amount of effort calculating the inverse matrix, particularly since the values of the remaining variables, x_1, x_2 and x_4, are not required.

In this section we describe an alternative method that finds the value of one variable at a time. This new method requires less effort if only a selection of the variables is required. It is known as Cramer's rule and makes use of matrix determinants. **Cramer's rule** for solving any $n \times n$ system, $\mathbf{Ax} = \mathbf{b}$, states that the ith variable, x_i, can be found from

$$x_i = \frac{\det(\mathbf{A}_i)}{\det(\mathbf{A})}$$

where $\mathbf{A}_i$ is the $n \times n$ matrix found by replacing the ith column of $\mathbf{A}$ by the right-hand-side vector $\mathbf{b}$. To understand this, consider the simple 2×2 system

$$\begin{bmatrix} 7 & 2 \\ 4 & 5 \end{bmatrix} \begin{bmatrix} x_1 \\ x_2 \end{bmatrix} = \begin{bmatrix} -6 \\ 12 \end{bmatrix}$$

and suppose that we need to find the value of the second variable, x_2, say. According to Cramer's rule, this is given by

$$x_2 = \frac{\det(\mathbf{A}_2)}{\det(\mathbf{A})}$$

where

$$\mathbf{A} = \begin{bmatrix} 7 & 2 \\ 4 & 5 \end{bmatrix} \quad \text{and} \quad \mathbf{A}_2 = \begin{bmatrix} 7 & -6 \\ 4 & 12 \end{bmatrix}$$

Notice that x_2 is given by the quotient of two determinants. The one on the bottom is that of the original coefficient matrix $\mathbf{A}$. The one on the top is that of the matrix found from $\mathbf{A}$ by replacing the second column (since we are trying to find the second variable) by the right-hand-side vector

$$\begin{bmatrix} -6 \\ 12 \end{bmatrix}$$

In this case the determinants are easily worked out to get

$$\det(\mathbf{A}_2) = \begin{vmatrix} 7 & -6 \\ 4 & 12 \end{vmatrix} = 7(12) - (-6)(4) = 108$$

$$\det(\mathbf{A}) = \begin{vmatrix} 7 & 2 \\ 4 & 5 \end{vmatrix} = 7(5) - 2(4) = 27$$

Hence

$$x_2 = \frac{108}{27} = 4$$

Example

Solve the system of equations

$$\begin{bmatrix} 1 & 2 & 3 \\ -4 & 1 & 6 \\ 2 & 7 & 5 \end{bmatrix} \begin{bmatrix} x_1 \\ x_2 \\ x_3 \end{bmatrix} = \begin{bmatrix} 9 \\ -9 \\ 13 \end{bmatrix}$$

using Cramer's rule to find x_1.

Solution

Cramer's rule gives

$$x_1 = \frac{\det(\mathbf{A}_1)}{\det(\mathbf{A})}$$

where $\mathbf{A}$ is the coefficient matrix

$$\begin{bmatrix} 1 & 2 & 3 \\ -4 & 1 & 6 \\ 2 & 7 & 5 \end{bmatrix}$$

and $\mathbf{A}_1$ is constructed by replacing the first column of $\mathbf{A}$ by the right-hand-side vector

$$\begin{bmatrix} 9 \\ -9 \\ 13 \end{bmatrix}$$

which gives

$$\mathbf{A}_1 = \begin{bmatrix} 9 & 2 & 3 \\ -9 & 1 & 6 \\ 13 & 7 & 5 \end{bmatrix}$$

If we expand each of these determinants along the top row, we get

$$\det(\mathbf{A}_1) = \begin{vmatrix} 9 & 2 & 3 \\ -9 & 1 & 6 \\ 13 & 7 & 5 \end{vmatrix}$$

$$= 9\begin{vmatrix} 1 & 6 \\ 7 & 5 \end{vmatrix} - 2\begin{vmatrix} -9 & 6 \\ 13 & 5 \end{vmatrix} + 3\begin{vmatrix} -9 & 1 \\ 13 & 7 \end{vmatrix}$$

$$= 9(-37) - 2(-123) + 3(-76)$$

$$= -315$$

and

$$\det(\mathbf{A}) = \begin{vmatrix} 1 & 2 & 3 \\ -4 & 1 & 6 \\ 2 & 7 & 5 \end{vmatrix}$$

$$= 1\begin{vmatrix} 1 & 6 \\ 7 & 5 \end{vmatrix} - 2\begin{vmatrix} -4 & 6 \\ 2 & 5 \end{vmatrix} + 3\begin{vmatrix} -4 & 1 \\ 2 & 7 \end{vmatrix}$$

$$= 1(-37) - 2(-32) + 3(-30)$$

$$= -63$$

Hence

$$x_1 = \frac{\det(\mathbf{A}_1)}{\det(\mathbf{A})} = \frac{-315}{-63} = 5$$

Practice Problem

1. **(a)** Solve the system of equations

$$2x_1 + 4x_2 = 16$$
$$3x_1 - 5x_2 = -9$$

using Cramer's rule to find x_2.

(b) Solve the system of equations

$$4x_1 + x_2 + 3x_3 = 8$$
$$-2x_1 + 5x_2 + x_3 = 4$$
$$3x_1 + 2x_2 + 4x_3 = 9$$

using Cramer's rule to find x_3.

We now illustrate the use of Cramer's rule to analyse economic models. We begin by considering the three-sector macroeconomic model involving government activity.

Example

The equilibrium levels of income, Y, disposable income, Y_d, and taxation, T, for a three-sector macroeconomic model satisfy the structural equations

$$Y = C + I^* + G^*$$
$$C = aY_d + b \qquad (0 < a < 1, b > 0)$$
$$Y_d = Y - T$$
$$T = tY + T^* \qquad (t < 1, T^* > 0)$$

Show that this system can be written as $\mathbf{Ax} = \mathbf{b}$, where

$$\mathbf{A} = \begin{bmatrix} 1 & -1 & 0 & 0 \\ 0 & 1 & -a & 0 \\ -1 & 0 & 1 & 1 \\ -t & 0 & 0 & 1 \end{bmatrix} \quad \mathbf{x} = \begin{bmatrix} Y \\ C \\ Y_d \\ T \end{bmatrix} \quad \mathbf{b} = \begin{bmatrix} I^* + G^* \\ b \\ 0 \\ T^* \end{bmatrix}$$

Use Cramer's rule to solve this system for Y.

Solution

In this model the endogenous variables are Y, C, Y_d and T, so we begin by manipulating the equations so that these variables appear on the left-hand sides. Moreover, since the vector of 'unknowns', $\mathbf{x}$, is given to be

$$\begin{bmatrix} Y \\ C \\ Y_d \\ T \end{bmatrix}$$

we need to arrange the equations so that the variables appear in the order Y, C, Y_d, T. For example, in the case of the third equation

$$Y_d = Y - T$$

we first subtract Y and add T to both sides to get

$$Y_d - Y + T = 0$$

but then reorder the terms to obtain

$$-Y + Y_d + T = 0$$

Performing a similar process with the remaining equations gives

$$Y - C = I^* + G^*$$
$$C - aY_d = b$$
$$-Y + Y_d + T = 0$$
$$-tY + T = T^*$$

so that in matrix form they become

$$\begin{bmatrix} 1 & -1 & 0 & 0 \\ 0 & 1 & -a & 0 \\ -1 & 0 & 1 & 1 \\ -t & 0 & 0 & 1 \end{bmatrix} \begin{bmatrix} Y \\ C \\ Y_d \\ T \end{bmatrix} = \begin{bmatrix} I^* + G^* \\ b \\ 0 \\ T^* \end{bmatrix}$$

The variable Y is the first, so Cramer's rule gives

$$Y = \frac{\det(\mathbf{A}_1)}{\det(\mathbf{A})}$$

where

$$\mathbf{A}_1 = \begin{bmatrix} I^* + G^* & -1 & 0 & 0 \\ b & 1 & -a & 0 \\ 0 & 0 & 1 & 1 \\ T^* & 0 & 0 & 1 \end{bmatrix}$$

and

$$\mathbf{A} = \begin{bmatrix} 1 & -1 & 0 & 0 \\ 0 & 1 & -a & 0 \\ -1 & 0 & 1 & 1 \\ -t & 0 & 0 & 1 \end{bmatrix}$$

The calculations are fairly easy to perform, in spite of the fact that both matrices are 4×4, because they contain a high proportion of zeros. Expanding $\mathbf{A}_1$ along the first row gives

$$\det(\mathbf{A}_1) = (I^* + G^*)\begin{vmatrix} 1 & -a & 0 \\ 0 & 1 & 1 \\ 0 & 0 & 1 \end{vmatrix} - (-1)\begin{vmatrix} b & -a & 0 \\ 0 & 1 & 1 \\ T^* & 0 & 1 \end{vmatrix}$$

along the first row the pattern is $+ - + -$

Notice that there is no point in evaluating the last two cofactors in the first row, since the corresponding elements are both zero.

For the first of these 3×3 determinants we choose to expand down the first column, since this column has only one non-zero element. This gives

$$\begin{vmatrix} 1 & -a & 0 \\ 0 & 1 & 1 \\ 0 & 0 & 1 \end{vmatrix} = (1)\begin{vmatrix} 1 & 1 \\ 0 & 1 \end{vmatrix} = 1$$

It is immaterial which row or column we choose for the second 3×3 determinant, since they all contain two non-zero elements. Working along the first row gives

$$\begin{vmatrix} b & -a & 0 \\ 0 & 1 & 1 \\ T^* & 0 & 1 \end{vmatrix} = b\begin{vmatrix} 1 & 1 \\ 0 & 1 \end{vmatrix} - (-a)\begin{vmatrix} 0 & 1 \\ T^* & 1 \end{vmatrix} = b - aT^*$$

Hence

$$\det(\mathbf{A}_1) = (I^* + G^*)(1) - (-1)(b - aT^*) = I^* + G^* + b - aT^*$$

A similar process can be applied to matrix $\mathbf{A}$. Expanding along the top row gives

$$\det(\mathbf{A}) = (1)\begin{vmatrix} 1 & -a & 0 \\ 0 & 1 & 1 \\ 0 & 0 & 1 \end{vmatrix} - (-1)\begin{vmatrix} 0 & -a & 0 \\ -1 & 1 & 1 \\ -t & 0 & 1 \end{vmatrix}$$

The first of these 3×3 determinants has already been found to be 1 in our previous calculations. The second 3×3 determinant is new, and if we expand this along the first row, we get

$$\begin{vmatrix} 0 & -a & 0 \\ -1 & 1 & 1 \\ -t & 0 & 1 \end{vmatrix} = -(-a)\begin{vmatrix} -1 & 1 \\ -t & 1 \end{vmatrix} = a(-1 + t)$$

Hence

$$\det(\mathbf{A}) = (1)(1) - (-1)a(-1 + t) = 1 - a + at$$

Finally, we use Cramer's rule to deduce that

$$Y = \frac{I^* + G^* + b - aT^*}{1 - a + at}$$

Practice Problem

2. Use Cramer's rule to solve the following system of equations for Y_d.

$$\begin{bmatrix} 1 & -1 & 0 & 0 \\ 0 & 1 & -a & 0 \\ -1 & 0 & 1 & 1 \\ -t & 0 & 0 & 1 \end{bmatrix} \begin{bmatrix} Y \\ C \\ Y_d \\ T \end{bmatrix} = \begin{bmatrix} I^* + G^* \\ b \\ 0 \\ T^* \end{bmatrix}$$

[Hint: the determinant of the coefficient matrix has already been evaluated in the previous worked example.]

We conclude this section by introducing foreign trade into our model. In all of our previous macroeconomic models we have implicitly assumed that the behaviour of different countries has no effect on the national income of the other countries. In reality this is clearly not the case, and we now investigate how the economies of trading nations interact. To simplify the situation we shall ignore all government activity and suppose that there are just two countries, labelled 1 and 2, trading with each other but not with any other country. We shall use an obvious subscript notation so that Y_1 denotes the national income of country 1, C_2 denotes the consumption of country 2 and so on. In the absence of government activity, the equation defining equilibrium in country i is

$$Y_i = C_i + I_i + X_i - M_i$$

where I_i is the investment of country i, X_i is the exports of country i and M_i is the imports of country i. As usual, we shall assume that I_i is determined exogenously and takes a known value I_i^*.

Given that there are only two countries, which trade between themselves, the exports of one country must be the same as the imports of the other. In symbols we write

$$X_1 = M_2 \quad \text{and} \quad X_2 = M_1$$

We shall assume that imports are a fraction of national income, so that

$$M_i = m_i Y_i$$

where the marginal propensity to import, m_i, satisfies $0 < m_i < 1$.

Once expressions for C_i and M_i are given, we can derive a system of two simultaneous equations for the two unknowns, Y_1 and Y_2, which can be solved either by using Cramer's rule or by using matrix inverses.

Example

The equations defining a model of two trading nations are given by

$$Y_1 = C_1 + I_1^* + X_1 - M_1 \quad Y_2 = C_2 + I_2^* + X_2 - M_2$$
$$C_1 = 0.8Y_1 + 200 \qquad\qquad C_2 = 0.9Y_2 + 100$$
$$M_1 = 0.2Y_1 \qquad\qquad\qquad M_2 = 0.1Y_2$$

Express this system in matrix form and hence write Y_1 in terms of I_1^* and I_2^*.

Write down the multiplier for Y_1 due to changes in I_2^* and hence describe the effect on the national income of country 1 due to changes in the investment in country 2.

Solution

In this problem there are six equations for six endogenous variables, Y_1, C_1, M_1 and Y_2, C_2, M_2. However, rather than working with a 6×6 matrix, we perform some preliminary algebra to reduce it to only two equations in two unknowns. To do this we substitute the expressions for C_1 and M_1 into the first equation to get

$$Y_1 = 0.8Y_1 + 200 + I_1^* + X_1 - 0.2Y_1$$

Also, since $X_1 = M_2 = 0.1Y_2$, this becomes

$$Y_1 = 0.8Y_1 + 200 + I_1^* + 0.1Y_2 - 0.2Y_1$$

which rearranges as

$$0.4Y_1 - 0.1Y_2 = 200 + I_1^*$$

A similar procedure applied to the second set of equations for country 2 gives

$$-0.2Y_1 + 0.2Y_2 = 100 + I_2^*$$

In matrix form this pair of equations can be written as

$$\begin{bmatrix} 0.4 & -0.1 \\ -0.2 & 0.2 \end{bmatrix} \begin{bmatrix} Y_1 \\ Y_2 \end{bmatrix} = \begin{bmatrix} 200 + I_1^* \\ 100 + I_2^* \end{bmatrix}$$

Cramer's rule gives

$$Y_1 = \frac{\begin{vmatrix} 200 + I_1^* & -0.1 \\ 100 + I_2^* & 0.2 \end{vmatrix}}{\begin{vmatrix} 0.4 & -0.1 \\ -0.2 & 0.2 \end{vmatrix}} = \frac{50 + 0.2I_1^* + 0.1I_2^*}{0.06}$$

To find the multiplier for Y_1 due to changes in I_2^* we consider what happens to Y_1 when I_2^* changes by an amount ΔI_2^*. The new value of Y_1 is obtained by replacing I_2^* by $I_2^* + \Delta I_2^*$ to get

$$\frac{50 + 0.2I_1^* + 0.1(I_2^* + \Delta I_2^*)}{0.06}$$

so the corresponding change in Y_1 is

$$\Delta Y_1 = \frac{50 + 0.2I_1^* + 0.1(I_2^* + \Delta I_2^*)}{0.06} - \frac{50 + 0.2I_1^* + 0.1I_2^*}{0.06}$$

$$= \frac{0.1}{0.06} \Delta I_2^*$$

$$= \frac{5}{3} \Delta I_2^*$$

We deduce that any increase in investment in country 2 leads to an increase in the national income in country 1. Moreover, because $5/3 > 1$, the increase in national income is greater than the increase in investment.

Practice Problem

3. The equations defining a model of two trading nations are given by

$$Y_1 = C_1 + I_1^* + X_1 - M_1 \qquad Y_2 = C_2 + I_2^* + X_2 - M_2$$
$$C_1 = 0.7Y_1 + 50 \qquad\qquad C_2 = 0.8Y_2 + 100$$
$$I_1^* = 200 \qquad\qquad\qquad I_2^* = 300$$
$$M_1 = 0.3Y_1 \qquad\qquad\quad M_2 = 0.1Y_2$$

Express this system in matrix form and hence find the values of Y_1 and Y_2. Calculate the balance of payments between these countries.

Key Term

Cramer's rule   A method of solving simultaneous equations, $\mathbf{Ax} = \mathbf{b}$, by the use of determinants. The ith variable x_i can be computed using $\det(\mathbf{A}_i)/\det(\mathbf{A})$ where $\mathbf{A}_i$ is the determinant of the matrix obtained from $\mathbf{A}$ by replacing the ith column by $\mathbf{b}$.

Exercise 4.3

1. **(a)** Evaluate each of these determinants.

   (i) $\begin{vmatrix} 4 & 2 \\ 1 & 3 \end{vmatrix}$ (ii) $\begin{vmatrix} -7 & 2 \\ 5 & 3 \end{vmatrix}$ (iii) $\begin{vmatrix} 4 & -7 \\ 1 & 5 \end{vmatrix}$

   (b) Use your answers to part (a) to write down the solution of the simultaneous equations

   $$4x + 2x = -7$$
   $$x + 3y = 5$$

2. Use Cramer's rule to find the value of x which satisfies each of the following pairs of simultaneous equations:

   (a) $7x - 3y = 4$ **(b)** $-3x + 4y = 5$ **(c)** $x + 4y = 9$
        $2x + 5y = 7$ $2x + 5y = 12$ $2x - 7y = 3$

3. Use Cramer's rule to find the value of y which satisfies each of the following pairs of simultaneous equations:

   (a) $x + 3y = 9$ **(b)** $5x - 2y = 7$ **(c)** $2x + 3y = 7$
        $2x - 4y = -2$ $2x + 3y = -1$ $3x - 5y = 1$

4. Use Cramer's rule to solve the following sets of simultaneous equations:

   (a) $4x + 3y = 1$ **(b)** $4x + 3y = 1$ **(c)** $4x + 3y = -2$
        $2x + 5y = -3$ $2x + 5y = 11$ $2x + 5y = -36$

5. The demand and supply functions for two interdependent goods are given by

$$Q_{D_1} = 400 - 5P_1 - 3P_2$$
$$Q_{D_2} = 300 - 2P_1 - 3P_2$$
$$Q_{S_1} = -60 + 3P_1$$
$$Q_{S_2} = -100 + 2P_2$$

(a) Show that the equilibrium prices satisfy

$$\begin{bmatrix} 8 & 3 \\ 2 & 5 \end{bmatrix} \begin{bmatrix} P_1 \\ P_2 \end{bmatrix} = \begin{bmatrix} 460 \\ 400 \end{bmatrix}$$

(b) Use Cramer's rule to find the equilibrium price of good 1.

6. Consider the two-sector macroeconomic model

$$Y = C + I^*$$
$$C = aY + b$$

(a) Express this system in the form

$$\mathbf{Ax} = \mathbf{b}$$

where $\mathbf{x} = \begin{pmatrix} Y \\ C \end{pmatrix}$ and $\mathbf{A}$ and $\mathbf{b}$ are 2×2 and 2×1 matrices to be stated.

(b) Use Cramer's rule to solve this system for C.

7. A total revenue function may be modelled by $\text{TR} = aQ + bQ^2$.

(a) If $\text{TR} = 14$ when $Q = 2$ and $\text{TR} = 9$ when $Q = 3$, write down a pair of simultaneous equations for the parameters a and b.

(b) Use Cramer's rule to solve the equations in part (a) and hence find the total revenue when $Q = 1$.

Exercise 4.3*

1. Use Cramer's rule to solve

(a) $\begin{bmatrix} 3 & -2 & 4 \\ 1 & 4 & 0 \\ 5 & 7 & 0 \end{bmatrix} \begin{bmatrix} x \\ y \\ z \end{bmatrix} = \begin{bmatrix} 11 \\ 9 \\ 19 \end{bmatrix}$

for x.

(b) $\begin{bmatrix} 4 & 5 & 0 \\ -1 & 2 & 3 \\ 6 & -1 & 2 \end{bmatrix} \begin{bmatrix} x \\ y \\ z \end{bmatrix} = \begin{bmatrix} 0 \\ 19 \\ -30 \end{bmatrix}$

for y.

(c) $\begin{bmatrix} 4 & -8 & 2 \\ 1 & 0 & 6 \\ -3 & 6 & 2 \end{bmatrix} \begin{bmatrix} x \\ y \\ z \end{bmatrix} = \begin{bmatrix} -43 \\ 0 \\ 34 \end{bmatrix}$

for z.

2. The matrix $\begin{bmatrix} 1 & -1 & 0 & 0 \\ 0 & 1 & -a & 0 \\ -1 & 0 & 1 & 1 \\ -t & 0 & 0 & 1 \end{bmatrix}$ has determinant, $1 - a + at$.

Use Cramer's rule to solve the following system of equations for C:

$$\begin{bmatrix} 1 & -1 & 0 & 0 \\ 0 & 1 & -a & 0 \\ -1 & 0 & 1 & 1 \\ -t & 0 & 0 & 1 \end{bmatrix} \begin{bmatrix} Y \\ C \\ Y_d \\ T \end{bmatrix} = \begin{bmatrix} I^* + G^* \\ b \\ 0 \\ T^* \end{bmatrix}$$

3. Consider the three-sector macroeconomic model:

$$Y = C + I^* + G^*$$
$$C = a(Y - T) + b$$
$$T = tY + T^*$$

(a) Express this system in the form

$$\mathbf{Ax = b}$$

where $\mathbf{x} = \begin{bmatrix} Y \\ C \\ T \end{bmatrix}$ and $\mathbf{A}$ and $\mathbf{b}$ are 3×3 and 3×1 matrices to be stated.

(b) Use Cramer's rule to solve this system for Y.

4. Consider the macroeconomic model defined by

$$Y = C + I^* + G^* + X^* - M$$
$$C = aY + b \qquad\qquad (0 < a < 1, b > 0)$$
$$M = mY + M^* \qquad\qquad (0 < m < 1, M^* > 0)$$

Show that this system can be written as $\mathbf{Ax = b}$, where

$$\mathbf{A} = \begin{bmatrix} 1 & -1 & 1 \\ -a & 1 & 0 \\ -m & 0 & 1 \end{bmatrix} \quad \mathbf{x} = \begin{bmatrix} Y \\ C \\ M \end{bmatrix} \quad \mathbf{b} = \begin{bmatrix} I^* + G^* + X^* \\ b \\ M^* \end{bmatrix}$$

Use Cramer's rule to show that

$$Y = \frac{b + I^* + G^* + X^* - M^*}{1 - a + m}$$

Write down the autonomous investment multiplier for Y and deduce that Y increases as I^* increases.

5. Consider the macroeconomic model defined by

national income: $Y = C + I + G^*$ $(G^* > 0)$

consumption: $C = aY + b$ $(0 < a < 1, b > 0)$

investment: $I = cr + d$ $(c < 0, d > 0)$

money supply: $M_S^* = k_1 Y + k_2 r$ $(k_1 > 0, k_2 < 0, M_S^* > 0)$

Show that this system can be written as $\mathbf{Ax} = \mathbf{b}$, where

$$\mathbf{A} = \begin{bmatrix} 1 & -1 & -1 & 0 \\ -a & 1 & 0 & 0 \\ 0 & 0 & 1 & -c \\ k_1 & 0 & 0 & k_2 \end{bmatrix} \quad \mathbf{x} = \begin{bmatrix} Y \\ C \\ I \\ r \end{bmatrix} \quad \mathbf{b} = \begin{bmatrix} G^* \\ b \\ d \\ M_s^* \end{bmatrix}$$

Use Cramer's rule to show that

$$r = \frac{M_s^*(1 - a) - k_1(b + d + G^*)}{k_2(1 - a) + ck_1}$$

Write down the government expenditure multiplier for r and deduce that the interest rate, r, increases as government expenditure, G^*, increases.

6. The equations defining a model of two trading nations are given by

$Y_1 = C_1 + I_1^* + X_1 - M_1$ $Y_2 = C_2 + I_2^* + X_2 - M_2$

$C_1 = 0.6Y_1 + 50$ $C_2 = 0.8Y_2 + 80$

$M_1 = 0.2Y_1$ $M_2 = 0.1Y_2$

If $I_2^* = 70$, find the value of I_1^* if the balance of payments is zero.

[Hint: construct a system of three equations for the three unknowns, Y_1, Y_2 and I_1^*.]

7. The equations defining a general model of two trading countries are given by

$Y_1 = C_1 + I_1^* + X_1 - M_1$ $Y_2 = C_2 + I_2^* + X_2 - M_2$

$C_1 = a_1Y_1 + b_1$ $C_2 = a_2Y_2 + b_2$

$M_1 = m_1Y_1$ $M_2 = m_2Y_2$

where $0 < a_i < 1$, $b_i > 0$ and $0 < m_i < 1$ $(i = 1, 2)$. Express this system in matrix form and use Cramer's rule to solve this system for Y_1. Write down the multiplier for Y_1 due to changes in I_2^* and hence give a general description of the effect on the national income of one country due to a change in investment in the other.

Formal mathematics

Sigma notation is a convenient shorthand for the summation of series. The sigma notation has an obvious use in matrices where we naturally identify the elements of a matrix using a double subscript notation. In particular it is possible to formally define the operation of matrix multiplication. To motivate this, consider forming the matrix product $\mathbf{C} = \mathbf{AB}$ where $\mathbf{A}$ and $\mathbf{B}$ are general 2×3 and 3×3 matrices with elements, a_{ij} and b_{ij}, respectively:

$$
\begin{bmatrix} c_{11} & c_{12} & c_{13} \\ c_{21} & c_{22} & c_{23} \end{bmatrix} = \begin{bmatrix} a_{11} & a_{12} & a_{13} \\ a_{21} & a_{22} & a_{23} \end{bmatrix} \begin{bmatrix} b_{11} & b_{12} & b_{13} \\ b_{21} & b_{22} & b_{23} \\ b_{31} & b_{32} & b_{33} \end{bmatrix}
$$

If we equate entries in the first row, first column, we get:

$$c_{11} = a_{11}b_{11} + a_{12}b_{21} + a_{13}b_{31}$$

In sigma notation this could be written as $c_{11} = \sum_{k=1}^{3} a_{1k}b_{k1}$

Similarly, for the second row, third column, we get:

$$c_{23} = a_{21}b_{13} + a_{22}b_{23} + a_{23}b_{33}$$

which can be written as $c_{23} = \sum_{k=1}^{3} a_{2k}b_{k3}$.

In general, if $\mathbf{A}$ is an $m \times s$ matrix and $\mathbf{B}$ is an $s \times n$ matrix, then $\mathbf{C} = \mathbf{AB}$ is defined to be an $m \times n$ matrix with

$$c_{ij} = a_{i1}b_{1j} + a_{i2}b_{2j} + a_{i3}b_{3j} + \ldots + a_{is}b_{sj} = \sum_{k=1}^{s} a_{ik}b_{kj}$$

Multiple choice questions

Question 1

If **A, B, C** and **D** are 3×4, 2×3, 4×2 and 3×3 matrices, which one of the following matrix calculations is possible?

A. $(AC)^{-1}$

B. $DA + BD$

C. $D^{-1}B$

D. $5CB - 4D^{-1}$

E. $BD + (AC)^{T}$

Question 2

Find the inverse of the matrix $\begin{bmatrix} 5 & 3 \\ 2 & 1 \end{bmatrix}$.

A. $\begin{bmatrix} -5 & 3 \\ 2 & -1 \end{bmatrix}$

B. $\begin{bmatrix} 1 & -3 \\ -2 & 5 \end{bmatrix}$

C. $\begin{bmatrix} -1 & -3 \\ -2 & -5 \end{bmatrix}$

D. $\begin{bmatrix} -1 & 3 \\ 2 & -5 \end{bmatrix}$

E. $\begin{bmatrix} -1 & 2 \\ 3 & -5 \end{bmatrix}$

Question 3

For what value of a does the following matrix fail to possess an inverse?

$$\begin{bmatrix} -1 & 2 & 1 \\ -2 & 3 & a \\ 0 & 4 & 6 \end{bmatrix}$$

A. 7/2

B. 3/2

C. 17/2

D. 23/2

E. 1/2

Question 4

Find the inverse of $\begin{bmatrix} 3 & 3 & -1 \\ 5 & 4 & 0 \\ 0 & 2 & -3 \end{bmatrix}$

A. $\begin{bmatrix} 12 & -7 & -3 \\ -15 & 9 & -5 \\ -10 & 6 & 3 \end{bmatrix}$

B. $\begin{bmatrix} 12 & -15 & -10 \\ -7 & 9 & 6 \\ -3 & -5 & 3 \end{bmatrix}$

C. $\begin{bmatrix} 12 & -7 & -4 \\ -15 & 9 & 5 \\ -10 & 6 & 3 \end{bmatrix}$

D. $\begin{bmatrix} -12 & 7 & 4 \\ 15 & -9 & -5 \\ 10 & -6 & -3 \end{bmatrix}$

E. $\begin{bmatrix} -12 & 15 & 10 \\ 7 & -9 & -6 \\ 4 & -5 & -3 \end{bmatrix}$

Question 5

The IS-LM model for a two-sector economy is given by

$$0.25Y + 10r - 1040 = 0$$
$$0.10Y - 36r - 256 = 0$$

where Y and r denote the equilibrium values of national income and interest rate, respectively.

If these equations are written in the form $\mathbf{A}x = b$ where $x = \begin{bmatrix} Y \\ r \end{bmatrix}$, work out the inverse of $\mathbf{A}$ and deduce the equilibrium value of r.

A. $\mathbf{A}^{-1} = \begin{bmatrix} 36 & -10 \\ -0.001 & 0.025 \end{bmatrix}$, $r = 5.36$

B. $\mathbf{A}^{-1} = \begin{bmatrix} 3.6 & 1 \\ 0.01 & -0.025 \end{bmatrix}$, $r = 2.8$

C. $\mathbf{A}^{-1} = \begin{bmatrix} 3.6 & 1 \\ 0.01 & -0.025 \end{bmatrix}$, $r = 4$

D. $\mathbf{A}^{-1} = \begin{bmatrix} 3.6 & -1 \\ 0.001 & 0.025 \end{bmatrix}$, $r = 7.44$

E. $\mathbf{A}^{-1} = \begin{bmatrix} 3.6 & -1 \\ 0.001 & 0.025 \end{bmatrix}$, $r = 3.4$

Question 6

If $\mathbf{A} = \begin{bmatrix} 1 & -3 \\ 2 & 1 \\ 0 & -3 \end{bmatrix}$ and $\mathbf{B} = \begin{bmatrix} 3 & 4 & 1 \\ 0 & -1 & 2 \end{bmatrix}$, work out $\mathbf{BA}$.

A. $\begin{bmatrix} 11 & -8 \\ -2 & -6 \end{bmatrix}$

B. $\begin{bmatrix} 11 & -8 \\ -2 & -7 \end{bmatrix}$

C. $\begin{bmatrix} 11 & 8 \\ -2 & -7 \end{bmatrix}$

D. $\begin{bmatrix} 9 & -8 \\ -2 & -7 \end{bmatrix}$

E. $\begin{bmatrix} 11 & -8 \\ 1 & -7 \end{bmatrix}$

Question 7

If $\mathbf{A} = \begin{bmatrix} 3 \\ 2 \\ 0 \\ -1 \end{bmatrix}$ and $\mathbf{B} = [1 \quad 0 \quad -2 \quad 3]$, work out $\mathbf{B}^{\mathrm{T}}\mathbf{A}^{\mathrm{T}}$.

A. $\begin{bmatrix} 3 & 2 & 0 & -1 \\ 0 & 0 & 0 & 0 \\ -6 & -4 & 0 & 2 \\ 9 & 6 & 0 & -3 \end{bmatrix}$

B. $[3 \quad 0 \quad 0 \quad -3]$

C. $[0]$

D. $\begin{bmatrix} 3 & 0 & -6 & 9 \\ 2 & 0 & -4 & 6 \\ 0 & 0 & 0 & 0 \\ -1 & 0 & 2 & -3 \end{bmatrix}$

E. $\begin{bmatrix} 3 \\ 0 \\ 0 \\ -3 \end{bmatrix}$

Question 8

In a macroeconomic model, $\mathbf{A}x = b$ where

$$\mathbf{A} = \begin{bmatrix} 1 & -1 & 0 & 0 \\ 0 & 1 & -a & 0 \\ -1 & 0 & 1 & 1 \\ -t & 0 & 0 & 1 \end{bmatrix}, x = \begin{bmatrix} Y \\ C \\ Y_d \\ T \end{bmatrix}, b = \begin{bmatrix} I^* + G^* \\ b \\ 0 \\ T^* \end{bmatrix} \text{ and } \det(\mathbf{A}) = 1 - a + at.$$

Use Cramer's rule to find C.

A. $\dfrac{b - aT* - a(I* + G*)(1 - t)}{1 - a + at}$

B. $\dfrac{b - aT* - a(I* + G*)(t - 1)}{1 - a + at}$

C. $\dfrac{b + aT* + a(I* + G*)(t - 1)}{1 - a + at}$

D. $\dfrac{b - aT* - at(I* + G*)}{1 - a + at}$

E. $\dfrac{(b - aT*)t - a(I* + G*)}{1 - a + at}$

Question 9

Which one of these 2×2 matrices is not an inverse of any other matrix in the list?

A. $\begin{bmatrix} 4 & 5 \\ 5 & 6 \end{bmatrix}$

B. $\begin{bmatrix} -5 & 6 \\ 4 & -5 \end{bmatrix}$

C. $\begin{bmatrix} -5 & -6 \\ -4 & -5 \end{bmatrix}$

D. $\begin{bmatrix} 4 & -5 \\ -5 & 6 \end{bmatrix}$

E. $\begin{bmatrix} -6 & 5 \\ 5 & -4 \end{bmatrix}$

Question 10

If $\mathbf{A} = \begin{bmatrix} a & b \\ c & d \end{bmatrix}$ and $\mathbf{B} = \begin{bmatrix} p & q \\ r & s \end{bmatrix}$ work out $\mathbf{A}^{\mathrm{T}}\mathbf{B}$

A. $\begin{bmatrix} ap + bs & aq + br \\ cp + ds & cq + dr \end{bmatrix}$

B. $\begin{bmatrix} ap + br & aq + bs \\ cp + dr & cq + ds \end{bmatrix}$

C. $\begin{bmatrix} ap + cr & aq + cs \\ bp + dr & bq + ds \end{bmatrix}$

D. $\begin{bmatrix} ar + cp & aq + cs \\ br + dp & bq + ds \end{bmatrix}$

E. $\begin{bmatrix} ap + cr & as + cq \\ bp + dr & bs + dq \end{bmatrix}$

Examination questions

Question 1

If $\mathbf{A} = \begin{bmatrix} 1 & -2 \\ 0 & 4 \end{bmatrix}$ and $\mathbf{B} = \begin{bmatrix} 6 & -3 \\ -4 & 2 \end{bmatrix}$, work out, where possible:

(a) $\mathbf{A}^{\mathrm{T}} + 2\mathbf{B}$ (b) $\mathbf{AB}$ (c) $\mathbf{A}^{-1}$ (d) $\mathbf{B}^{-1}\mathbf{A}$

Question 2

The demand and supply functions of a good are given by

$$P + 4Q_{\mathrm{D}} = 61$$
$$3P - Q_{\mathrm{S}} = 14$$

Find the equilibrium price and quantity using

(a) the inverse matrix method;

(b) Cramer's rule.

Question 3

$$\mathbf{A} = \begin{bmatrix} 3 & -1 & 0 & 6 \\ -4 & 5 & 2 & 2 \end{bmatrix}, \mathbf{B} = \begin{bmatrix} 4 & -3 \\ 2 & 5 \end{bmatrix}, \mathbf{C} = \begin{bmatrix} 1 & 6 \\ 3 & 0 \\ -2 & 4 \\ -1 & -2 \end{bmatrix}$$

(a) Work out each of the following, where possible:

     (i) $\mathbf{A} + \mathbf{C}$ (ii) $2\mathbf{A} - \mathbf{C}^{\mathrm{T}}$ (iii) $\mathbf{AB}$ (iv) $\mathbf{BA}$

(b) Solve each of the following equations for $\mathbf{X}$:

     (i) $2\mathbf{X} + \mathbf{A}^{\mathrm{T}} = \mathbf{C}$ (ii) $\mathbf{BX} = \mathbf{A}$

Question 4

(a) The demand and supply functions of two interdependent commodities are given by

$$Q_{\mathrm{D}_1} = 40 - 3P_1 - P_2$$
$$Q_{\mathrm{D}_2} = 30 - 4P_1 - 0.5P_2$$
$$Q_{\mathrm{S}_1} = -6 + 5P_1$$
$$Q_{\mathrm{S}_2} = -5 + 2P_2$$

Show that the equilibrium prices satisfy

$$\begin{bmatrix} 8 & 1 \\ 4 & 2.5 \end{bmatrix} \begin{bmatrix} P_1 \\ P_2 \end{bmatrix} = \begin{bmatrix} 46 \\ 35 \end{bmatrix}$$

Solve this system by calculating the inverse of the coefficient matrix.

(b) Use Cramer's rule to find the value of y in the system:

$$\begin{bmatrix} 3 & 5 & 4 \\ 0 & 2 & 7 \\ 1 & 3 & -2 \end{bmatrix} \begin{bmatrix} x \\ y \\ z \end{bmatrix} = \begin{bmatrix} -12 \\ 0 \\ -20 \end{bmatrix}$$

Question 5

Airme and Blight are the only two airlines allowed to operate on the same route. The market share of regular business travellers changes from month to month. Airme retains four-fifths of its customers whilst Blight retains only three-quarters of its customers.

(a) If A_t and B_t, denote the number of customers who fly Airme and Blight in month t explain why

$$\begin{bmatrix} A_t \\ B_t \end{bmatrix} = \begin{bmatrix} 0.8 & 0.25 \\ 0.2 & 0.75 \end{bmatrix} \begin{bmatrix} A_{t-1} \\ B_{t-1} \end{bmatrix}$$

(b) If the number of customers who fly Airme and Blight in the first month are 10 000 and 16 000, respectively use matrix multiplication to work out the number of people who fly Airme

(i) one month later;

(ii) three months later.

(c) If the number of customers flying on Airme and Blight in any month had been 7300 and 5400, respectively, work out how many people flew by each airline the previous month.

Question 6

(a) Find the inverse of the following matrix, in terms of a.

$$\begin{bmatrix} 4 & -2 & -1 \\ -2 & 5 & 1 \\ -4 & 1 & a \end{bmatrix}$$

For what value of a is this matrix singular?

(b) Consider the three-commodity market model defined by:

$$Q_{S_1} = 2P_1 - 7; \quad Q_{D_1} = -2P_1 + 2P_2 + P_3 + 16$$
$$Q_{S_2} = 4P_2 - 4; \quad Q_{D_2} = 2P_1 - P_2 - P_3 + 8$$
$$Q_{S_3} = 2P_3 - 3; \quad Q_{D_3} = 4P_1 - P_2 - 4P_3 + 4$$

By making use of your answer to part (a), or otherwise, find the equilibrium prices.

Question 7

The supply and demand equations of two interdependent commodities are

$$Q_{S_1} = 4(P_1 - t) - 5, \qquad Q_{D_1} = 27 - 3P_1 + P_2$$
$$Q_{S_2} = P_2 - 3, \qquad Q_{D_2} = 25 + 2P_1 - 3P_2$$

where t is the unit tax imposed on good 1.

Show that the market equilibrium prices satisfy a matrix equation of the form $\mathbf{A}x = b$ where $x = \begin{bmatrix} P_1 \\ P_2 \end{bmatrix}$.

Find the inverse of $\mathbf{A}$ and hence solve this system to find P_1 and P_2.

Write down the taxation multiplier for P_2.

Question 8

Consider the following macroeconomic model:

$$Y = C + I^* + G^* + X^* - M^* \quad \text{(equilibrium of national income)}$$
$$C = aY_d + b \quad \text{(consumption; } 0 < a < 1; b > 0)$$
$$T = tY \quad \text{(taxation; } 0 < t < 1)$$

where I^*, G^*, X^*, M^* and Y_d denote investment, government expenditure, exports, imports and disposable income, respectively.

(a) Show that this system can be expressed as $\mathbf{A}x = b$ where

$$\mathbf{A} = \begin{bmatrix} 1 & -1 & 0 \\ -a & 1 & a \\ -t & 0 & 1 \end{bmatrix}, b = \begin{bmatrix} I + G^* + X^* - M^* \\ b \\ 0 \end{bmatrix} \text{ and } x = \begin{bmatrix} Y \\ C \\ T \end{bmatrix}.$$

(b) Show that the determinant of $\mathbf{A}$ is $1 - a(1 - t)$

(c) By using Cramer's rule, or otherwise, show that $Y = \dfrac{b + I^* + G^* + X^* - M^*}{1 - a(1 - t)}$.

(d) Write down the autonomous investment multiplier for Y and deduce that the change in national income exceeds any increase in investment.

(e) Work out the marginal propensity to consume multiplier for Y and hence state the direction of change in Y due to an increase in a.

Question 9

The trace of a 2×2 matrix $\mathbf{A} = \begin{bmatrix} a & b \\ c & d \end{bmatrix}$ is defined to be $\text{tr}(\mathbf{A}) = a + d$.

(a) Work out the trace of $\begin{bmatrix} 7 & 4 \\ -2 & -5 \end{bmatrix}$

(b) Prove that if $\mathbf{A}$ and $\mathbf{B}$ are any 2×2 matrices, then $\text{tr}(\alpha\mathbf{A} + \beta\mathbf{B}) = \alpha\,\text{tr}(\mathbf{A}) + \beta\,\text{tr}(\mathbf{B})$ for any numbers α and β.

(c) Decide whether following results are true or false for general 2×2 matrices. If the result is true, prove it, and if the result is false, provide a counter-example.

(i) $\text{tr}(\mathbf{A}^{-1}) = (\text{tr}(\mathbf{A}))^{-1}$

(ii) $\text{tr}(\mathbf{AB}) = \text{tr}(\mathbf{BA})$

Section 3
Comparative-static Analysis

5

DIFFERENTIATION

To think of it [differential calculus] merely as a more advanced technique is to miss its real content. In it, mathematics becomes a dynamic mode of thought, and that is a major mental step in the ascent of man.
—Jacob Bronowski (1973)

An important topic in many scientific disciplines, including economics, is the study of how quickly quantities change over time. In order to compute the future position of a planet, to predict the growth in population of a biological species, or to estimate the future demand for a commodity, we need information about rates of change.

The concept used to describe the rate of change of a function is the derivative, which is *the* central concept in mathematical analysis. This chapter defines the derivative of a function and presents some of the important rules for calculating it.

Isaac Newton (1642–1727) and Gottfried Wilhelm Leibniz (1646–1716) discovered most of these general rules independently of each other. This initiated differential calculus, which has been the foundation for the development of modern science. It has also been of central importance to the theoretical development of modern economics.

5.1 Slopes of Curves

We begin this chapter with a geometrical motivation for the concept. When we study the graph of a function, we would like to have a precise measure of its steepness at a point. We know that for the line $y = px + q$, the number p denotes its slope. If p is large and positive, then the line rises steeply from left to right; if p is large and negative, the line falls steeply. But for an arbitrary function f, what is the steepness of its graph? A natural answer is to define the steepness or *slope* of a curve *at a particular point* as the slope of the tangent to the curve at that point—that is, as the slope of the straight line which just touches the curve at that point. For the curve in Fig. 5.1.1 the steepness at point P is seen to be $1/2$, because the slope of the tangent line L is $1/2$.

In Fig. 5.1.1, point P has coordinates $(a, f(a))$. The slope of the tangent to the graph at P is called the *derivative* of $f(x)$ at $x = a$, and we denote this number by $f'(a)$, read as "f prime a". In Fig. 5.1.1, we have $f'(a) = 1/2$. In general,

$f'(a)$ is the slope of the tangent to the curve $y = f(x)$ at the point $(a, f(a))$

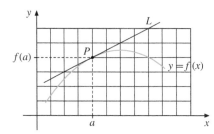

Figure 5.1.1 $f'(a) = 1/2$

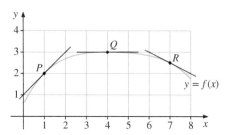

Figure 5.1.2 Example 5.1.1

EXAMPLE 5.1.1   Find $f'(1), f'(4)$, and $f'(7)$ for the function whose graph is shown in Fig. 5.1.2.

Solution: At the point $P = (1, 2)$, the tangent goes through the point $(0, 1)$, and so has slope 1. At the point $Q = (4, 3)$ the tangent is horizontal, and so has slope 0. At the point $R = (7, 2\frac{1}{2})$, the tangent goes through $(8, 2)$, and so has slope $-1/2$. Hence, $f'(1) = 1$, $f'(4) = 0$, and $f'(7) = -1/2$.

EXERCISES FOR SECTION 5.1

1. Figure 5.1.3 shows the graph of a function f. Find the values of $f(3)$ and $f'(3)$.

2. Figure 5.1.4 shows the graph of a function g. Find the values of $g(5)$ and $g'(5)$.

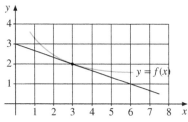

Figure 5.1.3 Exercise 1

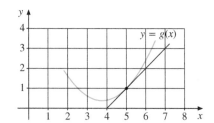

Figure 5.1.4 Exercise 2

5.2   Tangents and Derivatives

The previous section gave a rather vague definition of the tangent to a curve at a point. All we said is that it is a straight line which just touches the curve at that point. We now give a more formal definition of the same concept.

The geometric idea behind the definition is easy to understand. Consider a point P on a curve in the xy-plane — see Fig. 5.2.1. Take another point Q on the curve. The entire straight line through P and Q is called a *secant*. If we keep P fixed, but let Q move along the curve toward P, then the secant will rotate around P, as indicated in Fig. 5.2.2. The limiting straight line PT toward which the secant tends is called the *tangent (line)* to the curve at P. Suppose that the curve in Figs 5.2.1 and 5.2.2 is the graph of a function f. The approach illustrated in Fig. 5.2.2 allows us to find the slope of the tangent PT to the graph of f at the point P.

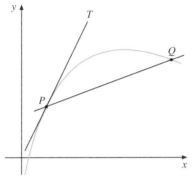

Figure 5.2.1 A secant   **Figure 5.2.2** Secants and the tangent

Figure 5.2.3 reproduces the curve, the points P and Q, and the tangent PT in Fig. 5.2.2. Point P in Fig. 5.2.3 has coordinates $(a, f(a))$. Point Q lies close to P and is also on the graph of f. Suppose that the x-coordinate of Q is $a + h$, where h is a small number different from 0. Then the x-coordinate of Q is not a (because $Q \neq P$), but a number close to a. Because Q lies on the graph of f, the y-coordinate of Q is equal to $f(a + h)$. Hence, the point Q has coordinates $(a + h, f(a + h))$.

The slope of the secant PQ is, therefore,

$$\frac{f(a + h) - f(a)}{h} \tag{5.2.1}$$

This fraction is called a *Newton quotient* of f. Note that when $h = 0$, the fraction becomes 0/0 and so is undefined. But choosing $h = 0$ corresponds to letting $Q = P$. When Q moves toward P along the graph of f, the x-coordinate of Q, which is $a + h$, must tend to a, and so h tends to 0. Simultaneously, the secant PQ tends to the tangent to the graph at P. This suggests that we ought to *define* the slope of the tangent at P as the number that the slope of the secant approaches as h tends to 0. In the previous section we called this number $f'(a)$, so we propose the following definition of $f'(a)$: $f'(a)$ is the limit, as h *tends to 0, of the Newton quotient.*

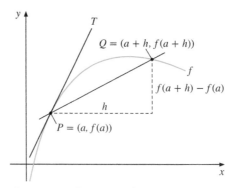

Figure 5.2.3 Newton quotient

It is common to use the abbreviated notation $\lim_{h \to 0}$ for "the limit as h tends to zero" of an expression involving h. We therefore have the following definition:

DEFINITION OF DERIVATIVE

The derivative of function f at point a, denoted by $f'(a)$, is

$$f'(a) = \lim_{h \to 0} \frac{f(a+h) - f(a)}{h} \tag{5.2.2}$$

The number $f'(a)$ gives the slope of the tangent to the curve $y = f(x)$ at the point $(a, f(a))$. The equation for a straight line passing through (x_1, y_1) and having a slope b is given by $y - y_1 = b(x - x_1)$. Hence, we obtain:

DEFINITION OF TANGENT

The equation for the tangent to the graph of $y = f(x)$ at the point $(a, f(a))$ is

$$y - f(a) = f'(a)(x - a) \tag{5.2.3}$$

So far the concept of a limit in the definition of $f'(a)$ is somewhat imprecise. Section 5.5 discusses the concept of limit in more detail. Because it is relatively complicated, we rely on intuition for the time being. Consider a simple example.

EXAMPLE 5.2.1   Use (5.2.2) to compute $f'(a)$ when $f(x) = x^2$. Find in particular $f'(1/2)$ and $f'(-1)$. Give geometric interpretations, and find the equation for the tangent at each of the points $(1/2, 1/4)$ and $(-1, 1)$.

Solution: For $f(x) = x^2$, we have $f(a+h) = (a+h)^2 = a^2 + 2ah + h^2$, and so

$$f(a+h) - f(a) = (a^2 + 2ah + h^2) - a^2 = 2ah + h^2$$

Hence, for all $h \neq 0$, we obtain

$$\frac{f(a+h) - f(a)}{h} = \frac{2ah + h^2}{h} = \frac{h(2a+h)}{h} = 2a + h \qquad (*)$$

because we can cancel h whenever $h \neq 0$. But as h tends to 0, so $2a + h$ obviously tends to $2a$. Thus, we can write

$$f'(a) = \lim_{h \to 0} \frac{f(a+h) - f(a)}{h} = \lim_{h \to 0} (2a + h) = 2a$$

This shows that when $f(x) = x^2$, then $f'(a) = 2a$. For the special case when $a = 1/2$, we obtain $f'(1/2) = 2 \cdot 1/2 = 1$. Similarly, $f'(-1) = 2 \cdot (-1) = -2$.

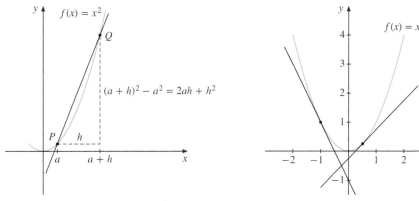

Figure 5.2.4 A secant of $f(x) = x^2$ **Figure 5.2.5** Tangents of $f(x) = x^2$

Figure 5.2.4 provides a geometric interpretation of $(*)$. In Fig. 5.2.5, we have drawn the tangents to the curve $y = x^2$ corresponding to the values $a = 1/2$ and $a = -1$ of x. At $a = 1/2$, we have $f(a) = (1/2)^2 = 1/4$ and $f'(1/2) = 1$. According to (5.2.3), the equation of the tangent is $y - 1/4 = 1 \cdot (x - 1/2)$ or $y = x - 1/4$.[1] Note that the formula $f'(a) = 2a$ shows that $f'(a) < 0$ when $a < 0$, and $f'(a) > 0$ when $a > 0$. Does this agree with the graph?

If f is a relatively simple function, we can find $f'(a)$ by using the following recipe:

COMPUTING THE DERIVATIVE

(i) Add h to a and compute $f(a + h)$.

(ii) Compute the corresponding change in the function value: $f(a + h) - f(a)$.

(iii) For $h \neq 0$, form the Newton quotient (5.2.1).

(iv) Simplify the fraction in step (iii) as much as possible. Wherever possible, cancel h from the numerator and denominator.

(v) Then $f'(a)$ is the limit, as h tends to 0, of the Newton quotient.

---

[1] Can you show that the other tangent drawn in Fig. 5.2.5 has the equation $y = -2x - 1$?

Let us apply this recipe to another example.

EXAMPLE 5.2.2   Compute $f'(a)$ when $f(x) = x^3$.

Solution: We follow the recipe step by step:

(i) $f(a+h) = (a+h)^3 = a^3 + 3a^2h + 3ah^2 + h^3$

(ii) $f(a+h) - f(a) = (a^3 + 3a^2h + 3ah^2 + h^3) - a^3 = 3a^2h + 3ah^2 + h^3$

(iii)–(iv) $\dfrac{f(a+h) - f(a)}{h} = \dfrac{3a^2h + 3ah^2 + h^3}{h} = 3a^2 + 3ah + h^2$

(v) As h tends to 0, so $3ah + h^2$ also tends to 0; hence, the entire expression $3a^2 + 3ah + h^2$ tends to $3a^2$. Therefore, $f'(a) = 3a^2$.

We have thus shown that the graph of the function $f(x) = x^3$ at the point $x = a$ has a tangent with slope $3a^2$. Note that $f'(a) = 3a^2 > 0$ when $a \neq 0$, and $f'(0) = 0$. The tangent points upwards to the right for all $a \neq 0$, and is horizontal at the origin. You should look at the graph of $f(x) = x^3$ in Fig. 4.3.7 to confirm this behaviour.

The recipe works well for simple functions like those in Examples 5.2.1 and 5.2.2. But for more complicated functions such as $f(x) = \sqrt{3x^2 + x + 1}$ it is unnecessarily cumbersome. The powerful rules explained in Section 5.6 allow the derivatives of even quite complicated functions to be found quite easily. Understanding these rules, however, relies on the more precise concept of limits that we will provide in Section 5.5.

On Notation

We showed in Example 5.2.1 that if $f(x) = x^2$, then for every a we have $f'(a) = 2a$. We frequently use x as the symbol for a quantity that can take any value, so we write $f'(x) = 2x$. Using this notation, our results from the two last examples are as follows:

$$f(x) = x^2 \Rightarrow f'(x) = 2x \tag{5.2.4}$$

$$f(x) = x^3 \Rightarrow f'(x) = 3x^2 \tag{5.2.5}$$

The result in (5.2.4) is a special case of the following rule, which you are asked to show in Exercise 7: given constants a, b and c,

$$f(x) = ax^2 + bx + c \Rightarrow f'(x) = 2ax + b \tag{5.2.6}$$

Here are some applications of (5.2.6):

$$f(x) = 3x^2 + 2x + 5 \Rightarrow f'(x) = 2 \cdot 3x + 2 = 6x + 2$$

$$f(x) = -16 + \frac{1}{2}x - \frac{1}{16}x^2 \Rightarrow f'(x) = \frac{1}{2} - \frac{1}{8}x$$

$$f(x) = (x - p)^2 = x^2 - 2px + p^2 \Rightarrow f'(x) = 2x - 2p$$

where p is a constant. If we use y to denote the typical value of the function $y = f(x)$, we often denote the derivative simply by y'. We can then write

$$y = x^3 \Rightarrow y' = 3x^2$$

Several other forms of notation for the derivative are often used in mathematics and its applications. One of them, originally due to Leibniz, is called the *differential notation*. If $y = f(x)$, then in place of $f'(x)$, we write

$$\frac{dy}{dx}, \quad \frac{df(x)}{dx} \quad \text{or} \quad \frac{d}{dx}f(x)$$

For instance, if $y = x^2$, then

$$\frac{dy}{dx} = 2x \quad \text{or} \quad \frac{d}{dx}(x^2) = 2x$$

We can think of the symbol "d/dx" as an instruction to differentiate what follows with respect to x. Differentiation occurs so often in mathematics that it has become standard to use *w.r.t.* as an abbreviation for *with respect to*.[2]

When we use letters other than f, x, and y, the notation for the derivative changes accordingly. For example:

$$P(t) = t^2 \Rightarrow P'(t) = 2t; \quad Y = K^3 \Rightarrow Y' = 3K^2; \quad \text{and } A = r^2 \Rightarrow \frac{dA}{dr} = 2r$$

EXERCISES FOR SECTION 5.2

1. Let $f(x) = 4x^2$. Show that $f(5 + h) - f(5) = 40h + 4h^2$, implying that $\dfrac{f(5+h) - f(5)}{h} = 40 + 4h$ for $h \neq 0$. Use this result to find $f'(5)$. Compare the answer with (5.2.6).

2. Let $f(x) = 3x^2 + 2x - 1$.

    (a) Show that $\dfrac{f(x+h) - f(x)}{h} = 6x + 2 + 3h$ for $h \neq 0$, and use this result to find $f'(x)$.

    (b) Find in particular $f'(0)$, $f'(-2)$, and $f'(3)$. Find also the equation of the tangent to the graph at the point $(0, -1)$.

3. The demand function for a commodity with price P is given by the formula $D(P) = a - bP$. Use rule (5.2.6) to find $dD(P)/dP$.

4. The cost of producing x units of a commodity is given by the formula $C(x) = p + qx^2$. Use rule (5.2.6) to find $C'(x)$.[3]

5. Show that $[f(x + h) - f(x)]/h = -1/x(x + h)$, and use this to show that

$$f(x) = \frac{1}{x} = x^{-1} \Rightarrow f'(x) = -\frac{1}{x^2} = -x^{-2}$$

---

[2] At this point, we will only think of the symbol "dy/dx" as meaning $f'(x)$ and will not consider how it might relate to dy divided by dx.

[3] In Section 5.4, this is interpreted as the *marginal cost*.

SM **6.** In each case below, find the slope of the tangent to the graph of f at the specified point:

(a) $f(x) = 3x + 2$, at $(0, 2)$ (b) $f(x) = x^2 - 1$, at $(1, 0)$ (c) $f(x) = 2 + 3/x$, at $(3, 3)$

(d) $f(x) = x^3 - 2x$, at $(0, 0)$ (e) $f(x) = x + 1/x$, at $(-1, -2)$ (f) $f(x) = x^4$, at $(1, 1)$

7. Let $f(x) = ax^2 + bx + c$.

(a) Show that $[f(x + h) - f(x)]/h = 2ax + b + ah$. Use this to show that $f'(x) = 2ax + b$.

(b) For what value of x is $f'(x) = 0$? Explain this result in the light of (3.6.3) and (3.6.4).

8. Figure 5.2.6 shows the graph of a function f. Determine the sign of the derivative $f'(x)$ at each of the four points a, b, c, and d.

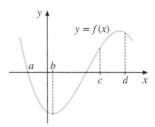

Figure 5.2.6 Exercise 8

SM **9.** Let $f(x) = \sqrt{x}$.

(a) Show that $(\sqrt{x + h} - \sqrt{x})(\sqrt{x + h} + \sqrt{x}) = h$.

(b) Use the result in part (a) to show that the Newton quotient of $f(x)$ is $1/(\sqrt{x + h} + \sqrt{x})$.

(c) Use the result in part (b) to show that for $x > 0$ one has $f'(x) = \dfrac{1}{2\sqrt{x}} = \dfrac{1}{2}x^{-1/2}$.

10. Let $f(x) = ax^3 + bx^2 + cx + d$.

(a) Show that $\dfrac{f(x + h) - f(x)}{h} = 3ax^2 + 2bx + c + 3axh + ah^2 + bh$ for $h \neq 0$, and find $f'(x)$.

(b) Show that the result in part (a) generalizes Example 5.2.2 and Exercise 7.

11. [HARDER] Apply the results of Exercise 8 to prove first that

$$\left[(x + h)^{1/3} - x^{1/3} \right] \left[(x + h)^{2/3} + (x + h)^{1/3} x^{1/3} + x^{2/3} \right] = h$$

Then follow the argument used to solve Exercise 9 to show that $f(x) = x^{1/3} \Rightarrow f'(x) = \frac{1}{3}x^{-2/3}$.

5.3 Increasing and Decreasing Functions

The terms *increasing* and *decreasing* functions have been used previously to describe the behaviour of a function as we travel from *left to right* along its graph. In order to establish a definite terminology, we introduce the following definitions. We assume that f is defined in an interval I and that x_1 and x_2 are numbers from that interval.

INCREASING AND DECREASING FUNCTIONS

(i) If $f(x_2) \geq f(x_1)$ whenever $x_2 > x_1$, then f is *increasing* in I.

(ii) If $f(x_2) > f(x_1)$ whenever $x_2 > x_1$, then f is *strictly increasing* in I.

(iii) If $f(x_2) \leq f(x_1)$ whenever $x_2 > x_1$, then f is *decreasing* in I.

(iv) If $f(x_2) < f(x_1)$ whenever $x_2 > x_1$, then f is *strictly decreasing* in I

Figures 5.3.1–5.3.4 illustrate these definitions. Note that we allow an increasing, or decreasing, function to have sections where the graph is horizontal. This does not quite agree with common language: few people would say that their salary increases when it stays constant! For this reason, therefore, sometimes an increasing function is called non-decreasing, and a decreasing function is called nonincreasing.

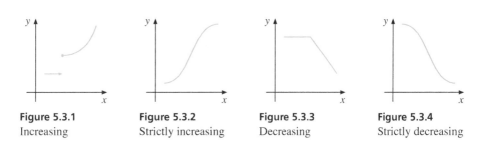

Figure 5.3.1   **Figure 5.3.2**   **Figure 5.3.3**   **Figure 5.3.4**
Increasing   Strictly increasing   Decreasing   Strictly decreasing

To find out on which intervals a function is (strictly) increasing or (strictly) decreasing using the definitions, we have to consider the sign of $f(x_2) - f(x_1)$ whenever $x_2 > x_1$. This is usually quite difficult to do directly by checking the values of $f(x)$ at different points x, but we already know a good test of whether a function is increasing or decreasing, in terms of the sign of its derivative:

$$f'(x) \geq 0 \text{ for all } x \text{ in the interval } I \iff f \text{ is increasing in } I \qquad (5.3.1)$$

$$f'(x) \leq 0 \text{ for all } x \text{ in the interval } I \iff f \text{ is increasing in } I \qquad (5.3.2)$$

Using the fact that the derivative of a function is the slope of the tangent to its graph, the equivalences in (5.3.1) and (5.3.2) seem almost obvious. An observation which is equally correct is the following:

$$f'(x) = 0 \text{ for all } x \text{ in the interval } I \iff f \text{ is constant in } I \qquad (5.3.3)$$

A precise proof of (5.3.1)– (5.3.3) relies on the mean-value theorem, which we will study in Section 7.4.

EXAMPLE 5.3.1   Use result (5.2.6) to find the derivative of $f(x) = \frac{1}{2}x^2 - 2$. Then examine where f is increasing/decreasing.

Solution: We find that $f'(x) = x$, which is nonnegative for $x \geq 0$, and nonpositive if $x \leq 0$, and thus $f'(0) = 0$. We conclude that f is increasing in $[0, \infty)$ and decreasing in $(-\infty, 0]$. Draw the graph of f to confirm this.

EXAMPLE 5.3.2   Use the result in Exercise 5.2.10 in order to find the derivative of the cubic function $f(x) = -\frac{1}{3}x^3 + 2x^2 - 3x + 1$. Then examine where f is increasing/decreasing.

Solution: The formula in the exercise can be used with $a = -1/3$, $b = 2$, $c = -3$, and $d = 1$. Thus $f'(x) = -x^2 + 4x - 3$. Solving the equation $f'(x) = -x^2 + 4x - 3 = 0$ yields $x = 1$ and $x = 3$, and thus $f'(x) = -(x - 1)(x - 3) = (x - 1)(3 - x)$. A sign diagram for $(x - 1)(3 - x)$ reveals that $f'(x) = (x - 1)(3 - x)$ is nonnegative in the interval $[1, 3]$, and nonpositive in $(-\infty, 1]$ and in $[3, \infty)$.[4] We conclude that $f(x)$ is increasing in $[1, 3]$, but decreasing in $(-\infty, 1]$ and in $[3, \infty)$. See Fig. 5.3.5.

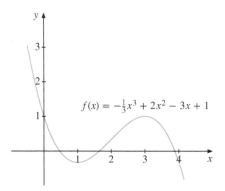

Figure 5.3.5 $f(x) = -\frac{1}{3}x^3 + 2x^2 - 3x + 1$

If $f'(x)$ is strictly positive in an interval, the function should be strictly increasing. Indeed,

$$f'(x) > 0 \text{ for all } x \text{ in the interval } I \implies f \text{ is strictly increasing in } I \qquad (5.3.4)$$

$$f'(x) < 0 \text{ for all } x \text{ in the interval } I \implies f \text{ is strictly decreasing in } I \qquad (5.3.5)$$

The implications in (5.3.4) and (5.3.4) give sufficient conditions for f to be strictly increasing or decreasing. They cannot be reversed to give necessary conditions. For example, if $f(x) = x^3$, then $f'(0) = 0$. Yet f is strictly increasing — see Exercise 3.[5]

---

[4] See Example 2.6.2.

[5] The following statement is often seen: "Suppose that f is strictly increasing — that is, $f'(x) > 0$." The example $f(x) = x^3$ shows that the statement is wrong. A function can be strictly increasing even though the derivative is 0 at certain points. In fact, suppose that $f'(x) \geq 0$ for all x in I and $f'(x) = 0$ at only a finite number of points in I. Then $f'(x) > 0$ in the subinterval between any two adjacent zeros of $f'(x)$, and so f is strictly increasing on each such subinterval. It follows that f is strictly increasing on the whole interval.

1. Use (5.2.6), (5.3.1), and (5.3.2) to examine where $f(x) = x^2 - 4x + 3$ is increasing/decreasing. Compare with Fig. 4.3.3.

2. Use the result in Exercise 5.2.10 to examine where $f(x) = -x^3 + 4x^2 - x - 6$ is increasing/decreasing. Compare with Fig. 4.7.1.

3. Show algebraically that $f(x) = x^3$ is strictly increasing by studying the sign of

$$x_2^3 - x_1^3 = (x_2 - x_1)(x_1^2 + x_1 x_2 + x_2^2) = (x_2 - x_1)\left[\left(x_1 + \frac{1}{2}x_2\right)^2 + \frac{3}{4}x_2^2\right]$$

5.4 Rates of Change

The derivative of a function at a particular point was defined as the slope of the tangent to its graph at that point. Economists interpret the derivative in many important ways, starting with the rate of change of an economic variable.

Suppose that a quantity y is related to a quantity x by $y = f(x)$. If x has the value a, then the value of the function is $f(a)$. Suppose that a is changed to $a + h$. The new value of y is $f(a + h)$, and the change in the value of the function when x is changed from a to $a + h$ is $f(a + h) - f(a)$. The change in y per unit change in x has a particular name; it is called the *average rate of change of f over the interval from a to $a + h$*. It is equal to

$$\frac{f(a + h) - f(a)}{h}$$

Note that this fraction is precisely the Newton quotient of f at a. Taking the limit as h tends to 0 gives the derivative of f at a, which we interpret as follows:

The *instantaneous rate of change of f* at a is $f'(a)$.

This very important concept appears whenever we study quantities that change. When time is the independent variable, we often use the "dot notation" for differentiation with respect to time. For example, if $x(t) = t^2$, we write $\dot{x}(t) = 2t$.

Sometimes we are interested in studying the proportion $f'(a)/f(a)$. This proportion can be interpreted as follows:

The *relative rate of change of f* at a is $\dfrac{f'(a)}{f(a)}$.

In economics, such relative rates of change are often seen. Sometimes they are called *proportional rates of change*. They are usually quoted in percentages per unit of time—for example, percentages per year.[6] Often we will describe a variable as increasing at, say, 3% a year if there is a relative rate of change of $3/100 = 0.03$ each year.

EXAMPLE 5.4.1   Let $N(t)$ be the number of individuals in a population of animals at time t. If t increases to $t + h$, then the change in population is equal to $N(t + h) - N(t)$ individuals. Hence,

$$\frac{N(t + h) - N(t)}{h}$$

is *the average rate of change*. Taking the limit as h tends to 0 gives $\dot{N}(t) = dN/dt$ for *the rate of change of population at time t*.

In Example 4.5.1, the formula $P = 5.1t + 606$ was used as an (inaccurate) estimate of Europe's population, in millions, at a date which comes t years after 1960. In this case, the rate of change is $dP/dt = 5.1$ million per year, the same for all t.

EXAMPLE 5.4.2   Let $K(t)$ be the capital stock in an economy at time t. The rate of change $\dot{K}(t)$ of $K(t)$ is called the *net rate of investment* at time t,[7] and is usually denoted by $I(t)$:

$$\dot{K}(t) = I(t) \tag{5.4.1}$$

EXAMPLE 5.4.3   Consider a firm producing some commodity in a given period, and let $C(x)$ denote its cost of producing x units. The derivative $C'(x)$ at x is called the *marginal cost* at x. According to the definition, it is equal to

$$C'(x) = \lim_{h \to 0} \frac{C(x + h) - C(x)}{h} \tag{5.4.2}$$

When h is small in absolute value, we obtain the approximation

$$C'(x) \approx \frac{C(x + h) - C(x)}{h} \tag{5.4.3}$$

The difference $C(x + h) - C(x)$ is called the *incremental cost* of producing h units of extra output. For h small, a linear approximation to this incremental cost is $hC'(x)$, the product of the marginal cost and the change in output. This is true even when $h < 0$, signifying a decrease in output and, provided that $C'(x) > 0$, a lower cost.

Note that putting $h = 1$ in (5.4.3) makes marginal cost *approximately* equal to

$$C'(x) \approx C(x + 1) - C(x) \tag{5.4.4}$$

---

[6] Or per annum, for those who think Latin is still a useful language.

[7] This differs from gross investment because some investment is needed to replace depreciated capital.

Marginal cost is then approximately equal to the *incremental cost* $C(x+1) - C(x)$, that is, the *additional cost of producing one more unit than x*. In elementary economics books marginal cost is often defined as the difference $C(x+1) - C(x)$ because more appropriate concepts from differential calculus cannot be used.

In this book, we will sometimes offer comparable economic interpretations that consider the change in a function when a variable x is increased by one unit; it would be more accurate to consider the change in the function per unit increase, for small increases. Here is an example.

EXAMPLE 5.4.4   Let $C(x)$ denote the cost in millions of dollars for removing $x\%$ of the pollution in a lake. Give an economic interpretation of the equality $C'(50) = 3$.

Solution: Because of the linear approximation $C(50 + h) - C(50) \approx hC'(50)$, the precise interpretation of $C'(50) = 3$ is that, starting at 50%, for each extra 1% of pollution that is removed, the extra cost is about 3 million dollars. Much less precisely, $C'(50) = 3$ means that it costs about 3 million dollars extra to remove 51% instead of 50% of the pollution.

Following these examples, economists often use the word "marginal" to indicate a derivative. To mention just two of many examples we shall encounter, the *marginal propensity to consume* is the derivative of the consumption function with respect to income; similarly, the *marginal product*, or *productivity*, of labour is the derivative of the production function with respect to labour input.

The concept is so important that it underlies most of our understanding of economics. For example, Adam Smith, seen by many as the founder of the science, struggled to understand why a non-essential commodity such as a diamond could be worth so much more than an essential one, such as water. Using marginal analysis, Carl Menger (1840–1921), Leon Walras (1834–1910) and Stanley Jevons (1835–1882) explained this seeming paradox: if offered a choice between *only* water or *only* diamonds, people would surely choose water, as it is essential; but, given the water and the diamonds a person already owns, they may value one *extra* glass of water less than one *extra* diamond. This fundamental understanding of optimal decisions led to the three economists being considered founders of the "Marginalist" school of economic thought.

EXERCISES FOR SECTION 5.4

1. Let $C(x) = x^2 + 3x + 100$ be the cost function of a firm. Show that when x is changed from 100 to $100 + h$, where $h \neq 0$, the average rate of change per unit of output is

$$\frac{C(100 + h) - C(100)}{h} = 203 + h$$

What is the marginal cost $C'(100)$? Then use (5.2.6) to find $C'(x)$ and, in particular, $C'(100)$.

2. If the cost function of a firm is $C(x) = \bar{C} + cx$, give economic interpretations of the parameters c and $\bar{C}$.

3. If the total saving of a country is a function $S(Y)$ of the national product Y, then $S'(Y)$ is called the *marginal propensity to save*, or MPS. Find the MPS for the following functions:

   (a) $S(Y) = \bar{S} + sY$ (b) $S(Y) = 100 + 0.1Y + 0.0002Y^2$

4. Let $T(y)$ denote the income tax a person is liable to pay, as a function of its income y. Then $T'(y)$ is called the *marginal tax rate*. Consider the case when $T(y) = ty$, where t is a constant number in the interval $(0, 1)$. Characterize this tax function by determining its marginal rate.

5. Let $x(t)$ denote the number of barrels of oil left in a well at time t, where time is measured in minutes. What is the interpretation of the equation $x'(0) = -3$?

6. The total cost of producing $x \geq 0$ units of a commodity is $C(x) = x^3 - 90x^2 + 7500x$.

   (a) Use the result in Exercise 5.2.10 to compute the marginal cost function $C'(x)$.

   (b) For what value of x is the marginal cost the least?

7. (a) A firm's profit function is $\pi(Q) = 24Q - Q^2 - 5$. Find the marginal profit, and the value Q^* of Q which maximizes profits.

   (b) A firm's revenue function is $R(Q) = 500Q - \frac{1}{3}Q^3$. Find the marginal revenue.

   (c) For the particular cost function $C(Q) = -Q^3 + 214.2Q^2 - 7900Q + 320\,700$ which was considered in Example 4.7.1, find the marginal cost.

8. Referring to the definition given in Example 5.4.3, compute the marginal cost in the following cases:

   (a) $C(x) = a_1x^2 + b_1x + c_1$ (b) $C(x) = a_1x^3 + b_1$

5.5   A Dash of Limits

In Section 5.2, we defined the derivative of a function based on the concept of a limit. The same concept has many other uses in mathematics, as well as in economic analysis, so now we should take a closer look. Here we give a preliminary definition and formulate some important rules for limits.

EXAMPLE 5.5.1   Consider the function F defined by the formula

$$F(x) = \frac{e^x - 1}{x}$$

where the number $e \approx 2.718$ is the base for the natural exponential function that was introduced in Section 3.9. Note that if $x = 0$, then $e^0 = 1$, and the fraction collapses to the absurd expression "0/0". Thus, the function F is not defined for $x = 0$. Yet one can still ask what happens to $F(x)$ when x is close to 0. Using a calculator, we find the values shown in Table 5.1.

From the table, it appears that as x gets closer and closer to 0, so the fraction $F(x)$ gets closer and closer to 1. It therefore seems reasonable to assume that $F(x)$ tends to 1 in

Table 5.1 Values of $F(x) = (e^x - 1)/x$ when x is close to 0

x	-1	-0.1	-0.001	-0.0001	0	0.0001	0.001	0.1	1
$F(x)$	0.632	0.956	0.999	1.000	Not defined	1.000	1.001	1.052	1.718

the limit as x tends to 0. Indeed, as we argue later, our definition of e is motivated by the requirement that this limit equal 1. So we write:

$$\lim_{x \to 0} \frac{e^x - 1}{x} = 1 \quad \text{or} \quad \frac{e^x - 1}{x} \to 1 \quad \text{as} \quad x \to 0$$

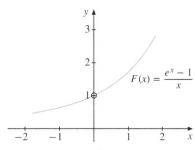

Figure 5.5.1 $y = \dfrac{e^x - 1}{x}$

Figure 5.5.1 shows a portion of the graph of F. The function F is defined for all x, except at $x = 0$, and $\lim_{x \to 0} F(x) = 1$. A small circle is used to indicate that the corresponding point $(0, 1)$ is not in the graph of F.

Suppose, in general, that a function f is defined for all x near a, but not necessarily at $x = a$. *Then we say that the number A is the limit of $f(x)$ as x tends to a if $f(x)$ tends to A as x tends to (but is not equal to) a.* We write:

$$\lim_{x \to a} f(x) = A, \quad \text{or} \quad f(x) \to A \text{ as } x \to a$$

It is possible, however, that the value of $f(x)$ does not tend to any fixed number as x tends to a. Then we say that $\lim_{x \to a} f(x)$ *does not exist*, or that $f(x)$ *does not have a limit as x tends to a.*

EXAMPLE 5.5.2   Using a calculator, examine the limit

$$\lim_{h \to 0} \frac{\sqrt{h + 1} - 1}{h}$$

Solution: By choosing numbers h close to 0, we construct Table 5.2.

Table 5.2 Values of $F(h) = (\sqrt{h + 1} - 1)/h$ when h is close to 0

h	-0.5	-0.2	-0.1	-0.01	0	0.01	0.1	0.2	0.5
$F(h)$	0.586	0.528	0.513	0.501	Not defined	0.499	0.488	0.477	0.449

This suggests that the desired limit is 0.5.

The limits that we claimed to have found in Examples 5.5.1 and 5.5.2 are both based on a rather shaky numerical procedure. For instance, in Example 5.5.2, how can we really be certain that our guess is correct? Could it be that if we chose h values even closer to 0, the fraction would tend to a limit other than 0.5, or maybe not have any limit at all? Further numerical computations will support our belief that the initial guess is correct, but we can never make a table that has *all* the values of h close to 0, so numerical computation alone can never establish with certainty what the limit is.

This illustrates the need to have a rigorous procedure for finding limits, based on a precise mathematical definition of the limit concept. Here we merely give a preliminary definition which will convey the right idea.

LIMIT

The expression

$$\lim_{x \to a} f(x) = A \tag{5.5.1}$$

means that we can make $f(x)$ as close to A as we want for all x sufficiently close to, but not equal to, a.

We emphasize:

(a) The number $\lim_{x \to a} f(x)$ depends on how $f(x)$ behaves for values of x close to a, but not on what happens to f at the precise value $x = a$. Indeed, when finding $\lim_{x \to a} f(x)$, we are simply not interested in the value $f(a)$, or even in whether f is defined at a.

(b) When computing $\lim_{x \to a} f(x)$, we must consider values of x on both sides of a.

Rules for Limits

Since limits cannot really be determined merely by numerical computations, we use simple rules instead. Their validity can be shown later once we have a precise definition of the limit concept. These rules are very straightforward; we have even used a few of them already in the previous section.

Suppose that f and g are defined as functions of x in a neighbourhood of a (but not necessarily at a). Then we have the following rules, written down in a way that makes them easy to refer to later:[8]

---

[8] Because of the identities $f(x) - g(x) = f(x) + (-1)g(x)$, and $f(x)/g(x) = f(x)(g(x))^{-1}$, it is clear that some of these rules follow from others.

RULES FOR LIMITS

If $\lim_{x \to a} f(x) = A$ and $\lim_{x \to a} g(x) = B$, then

$$\lim_{x \to a} [f(x) \pm g(x)] = A \pm B \tag{5.5.2}$$

$$\lim_{x \to a} [f(x) \cdot g(x)] = A \cdot B \tag{5.5.3}$$

$$\lim_{x \to a} \frac{f(x)}{g(x)} = \frac{A}{B}, \quad \text{if } B \neq 0 \tag{5.5.4}$$

$$\lim_{x \to a} [f(x)]^r = A^r, \quad \text{if } A^r \text{ is defined and } r \text{ is a real number} \tag{5.5.5}$$

It is easy to give intuitive explanations for these rules. Suppose that $\lim_{x \to a} f(x) = A$ and that $\lim_{x \to a} g(x) = B$. These equations imply that, when x is close to a, then $f(x)$ is close to A and $g(x)$ is close to B. So intuitively the sum $f(x) + g(x)$ is close to $A + B$, the difference $f(x) - g(x)$ is close to $A - B$, the product $f(x)g(x)$ is close to $A \cdot B$, and so on.

These rules can be used repeatedly to obtain new extended rules such as

$$\lim_{x \to a} \left[f_1(x) + f_2(x) + \cdots + f_n(x) \right] = \lim_{x \to a} f_1(x) + \lim_{x \to a} f_2(x) + \cdots + \lim_{x \to a} f_n(x)$$

$$\lim_{x \to a} \left[f_1(x) \cdot f_2(x) \cdots f_n(x) \right] = \lim_{x \to a} f_1(x) \cdot \lim_{x \to a} f_2(x) \cdots \lim_{x \to a} f_n(x)$$

In words: *the limit of a sum is the sum of the limits, and the limit of a product is equal to the product of the limits.*

There are two special cases when the limit is obvious. First, suppose the function $f(x)$ is equal to the same constant value c for every x. Then, at every point a, $\lim_{x \to a} c = c$. Second, it is also evident that if $f(x) = x$, then, again at every point a, $\lim_{x \to a} f(x) = \lim_{x \to a} x = a$. Combining these two simple limits with the general rules allows easy computation of the limits for certain combinations of functions.

EXAMPLE 5.5.3   Use the rules specified in (5.5.2) to (5.5.5) to compute the following limits:

(a) $\lim_{x \to -2} (x^2 + 5x)$ (b) $\lim_{x \to 4} \dfrac{2x^{3/2} - \sqrt{x}}{x^2 - 15}$ (c) $\lim_{x \to a} Ax^n$

Solution:

(a) By the first rule, $\lim_{x \to -2}(x^2 + 5x)$ equals $\lim_{x \to -2}(x \cdot x) + \lim_{x \to -2}(5 \cdot x)$. Using the second rule twice, the latter can be computed as

$$\lim_{x \to -2} x \cdot \lim_{x \to -2} x + \lim_{x \to -2} 5 \cdot \lim_{x \to -2} x$$

so it follows that

$$\lim_{x \to -2} (x^2 + 5x) = (-2)(-2) + 5 \cdot (-2) = -6$$

(b) $\lim_{x \to 4} \dfrac{2x^{3/2} - \sqrt{x}}{x^2 - 15} = \dfrac{2\lim_{x \to 4} x^{3/2} - \lim_{x \to 4} \sqrt{x}}{\lim_{x \to 4} x^2 - 15} = \dfrac{2 \cdot 4^{3/2} - \sqrt{4}}{4^2 - 15} = \dfrac{2 \cdot 8 - 2}{16 - 15} = 14$

(c) $\lim_{x \to a} Ax^n = \lim_{x \to a} A \cdot \lim_{x \to a} x^n = A \cdot \left(\lim_{x \to a} x \right)^n = A \cdot a^n$, where n is a natural number.

This last example was straightforward. Examples 5.5.1 and 5.5.2 were more difficult, as they involved a fraction whose numerator and denominator both tend to 0. A simple observation can sometimes help us find such limits, provided that they exist. Because $\lim_{x \to a} f(x)$ can only depend on the values of f when x is close to, but not equal to a, we have the following:

If the functions f and g are equal for all x close to a, but not necessarily at $x = a$, then

$$\lim_{x \to a} f(x) = \lim_{x \to a} g(x) \tag{5.5.6}$$

whenever either limit exists.

Here are some examples of how this rule works.

EXAMPLE 5.5.4   Compute the limit $\lim_{x \to 2} \dfrac{3x^2 + 3x - 18}{x - 2}$.

Solution: We see that both numerator and denominator tend to 0 as x tends to 2. Because the numerator $3x^2 + 3x - 18$ is equal to 0 for $x = 2$, it has $x - 2$ as a factor. In fact, $3x^2 + 3x - 18 = 3(x - 2)(x + 3)$. Hence,

$$f(x) = \frac{3x^2 + 3x - 18}{x - 2} = \frac{3(x - 2)(x + 3)}{x - 2}$$

For $x \neq 2$, we can cancel $x - 2$ from both numerator and denominator to obtain $3(x + 3)$. So the functions $f(x)$ and $g(x) = 3(x + 3)$ are equal for all $x \neq 2$. By (5.5.6), it follows that

$$\lim_{x \to 2} \frac{3x^2 + 3x - 18}{x - 2} = \lim_{x \to 2} 3(x + 3) = 3(2 + 3) = 15$$

EXAMPLE 5.5.5   Compute the limits: (a) $\lim_{h \to 0} \dfrac{\sqrt{h + 1} - 1}{h}$;   (b) $\lim_{x \to 4} \dfrac{x^2 - 16}{4\sqrt{x} - 8}$.

Solution:

(a) The numerator and the denominator both tend to 0 as h tends to 0. Here we must use a little trick. We multiply both numerator and denominator by $\sqrt{h + 1} + 1$ to get

$$\frac{\sqrt{h + 1} - 1}{h} = \frac{\left(\sqrt{h + 1} - 1 \right) \left(\sqrt{h + 1} + 1 \right)}{h \left(\sqrt{h + 1} + 1 \right)} = \frac{h + 1 - 1}{h \left(\sqrt{h + 1} + 1 \right)} = \frac{1}{\sqrt{h + 1} + 1}$$

for all $h \neq 0$, after cancelling the common factor h. For all $h \neq 0$ (and $h \geq -1$), the given function is equal to $1/(\sqrt{h+1}+1)$, which tends to $1/2$ as h tends to 0. We conclude that the limit of our function is equal to $1/2$, which confirms the result in Example 5.5.2.

(b) We must try to simplify the fraction, because $x = 4$ gives $0/0$. Again we can use a trick to factorize the fraction as follows:

$$\frac{x^2 - 16}{4\sqrt{x} - 8} = \frac{(x+4)(x-4)}{4\left(\sqrt{x}-2\right)} = \frac{(x+4)\left(\sqrt{x}+2\right)\left(\sqrt{x}-2\right)}{4\left(\sqrt{x}-2\right)} \qquad (*)$$

Here we have used the factorization $x - 4 = \left(\sqrt{x}+2\right)\left(\sqrt{x}-2\right)$, which is correct for $x \geq 0$. In the last fraction of $(*)$, we can cancel $\sqrt{x} - 2$ when $\sqrt{x} - 2 \neq 0$ — that is, when $x \neq 4$. Using (5.5.6) again gives

$$\lim_{x \to 4} \frac{x^2 - 16}{4\sqrt{x} - 8} = \lim_{x \to 4} \frac{1}{4}(x+4)(\sqrt{x}+2) = \frac{1}{4}(4+4)(\sqrt{4}+2) = 8$$

EXERCISES FOR SECTION 5.5

1. Determine the following by using the rules for limits:

   (a) $\lim_{x \to 0} (3 + 2x^2)$

   (b) $\lim_{x \to -1} \frac{3 + 2x}{x - 1}$

   (c) $\lim_{x \to 2} (2x^2 + 5)^3$

   (d) $\lim_{t \to 8} \left(5t + t^2 - \frac{1}{8}t^3\right)$

   (e) $\lim_{y \to 0} \frac{(y+1)^5 - y^5}{y + 1}$

   (f) $\lim_{z \to -2} \frac{1/z + 2}{z}$

2. Examine the following limits numerically by using a calculator:

   (a) $\lim_{h \to 0} \frac{1}{h}(2^h - 1)$

   (b) $\lim_{h \to 0} \frac{1}{h}(3^h - 1)$

   (c) $\lim_{\lambda \to 0} \frac{1}{\lambda}(3^\lambda - 2^\lambda)$

3. Consider the limit $\lim_{x \to 1} \frac{x^2 + 7x - 8}{x - 1}$.

   (a) Examine the limit numerically by making a table of values of the fraction when x is close to 1.

   (b) Find the limit precisely by using the method in Example 5.5.4.

4. Compute the following limits, where $h \neq 0$ in (f):

   (a) $\lim_{x \to 2} (x^2 + 3x - 5)$

   (b) $\lim_{y \to -3} \frac{1}{y + 8}$

   (c) $\lim_{x \to 0} \frac{x^3 - 2x - 1}{x^5 - x^2 - 1}$

   (d) $\lim_{x \to 0} \frac{x^3 + 3x^2 - 2x}{x}$

   (e) $\lim_{h \to 0} \frac{(x+h)^3 - x^3}{h}$

   (f) $\lim_{x \to 0} \frac{(x+h)^3 - x^3}{h}$

(SM) 5. Compute the following limits:

   (a) $\lim_{h \to 2} \frac{\frac{1}{3} - \frac{2}{3h}}{h - 2}$

   (b) $\lim_{x \to 0} \frac{x^2 - 1}{x^2}$

   (c) $\lim_{t \to 3} \frac{\sqrt[3]{32t - 96}}{t^2 - 2t - 3}$

   (d) $\lim_{h \to 0} \frac{\sqrt{h + 3} - \sqrt{3}}{h}$

   (e) $\lim_{t \to -2} \frac{t^2 - 4}{t^2 + 10t + 16}$

   (f) $\lim_{x \to 4} \frac{2 - \sqrt{x}}{4 - x}$

(SM) **6.** If $f(x) = x^2 + 2x$, compute the following limits:

(a) $\lim\limits_{x \to 1} \dfrac{f(x) - f(1)}{x - 1}$ (b) $\lim\limits_{x \to 2} \dfrac{f(x) - f(1)}{x - 1}$ (c) $\lim\limits_{h \to 0} \dfrac{f(2 + h) - f(2)}{h}$

(d) $\lim\limits_{x \to a} \dfrac{f(x) - f(a)}{x - a}$ (e) $\lim\limits_{h \to 0} \dfrac{f(a + h) - f(a)}{h}$ (f) $\lim\limits_{h \to 0} \dfrac{f(a + h) - f(a - h)}{h}$

7. [HARDER] Compute the following limits, where in part (c) n denotes any natural number:

(a) $\lim\limits_{x \to 2} \dfrac{x^2 - 2x}{x^3 - 8}$ (b) $\lim\limits_{h \to 0} \dfrac{\sqrt[3]{27 + h} - 3}{h}$ (*Hint*: Put $u = \sqrt[3]{27 + h}$.)   (c) $\lim\limits_{x \to 1} \dfrac{x^n - 1}{x - 1}$

5.6 Simple Rules for Differentiation

Recall that the derivative of a function f was defined by the formula

$$f'(x) = \lim_{h \to 0} \frac{f(x + h) - f(x)}{h} \qquad (*)$$

If this limit exists, we say that f is *differentiable* at x. The process of finding the derivative of a function is called *differentiation*. It is useful to think of this as an operation that transforms one function f into a new function f'. The function f' is then defined for the values of x where the limit in $(*)$ exists. If $y = f(x)$, we can use the symbols y' and dy/dx as alternatives to $f'(x)$.

In Section 5.2 we used formula $(*)$ to find the derivatives of some simple functions. However, it is difficult and time consuming to apply the definition directly in each separate case. We now embark on a systematic programme to find general rules which ultimately will give mechanical and efficient procedures for finding the derivative of very many differentiable functions specified by a formula, even one that is complicated. We start with some simple rules.

If f is a constant function, then its derivative is 0:

$$f(x) = A \implies f'(x) = 0 \qquad (5.6.1)$$

The result is easy to see geometrically. The graph of $f(x) = A$ is a straight line parallel to the x-axis. The tangent to the graph is the line itself, which has slope 0 at each point—see Fig. 5.6.1. You should now use the definition of $f'(x)$ to get the same answer.

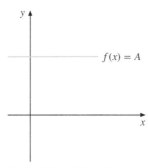

Figure 5.6.1 $f(x) = A$

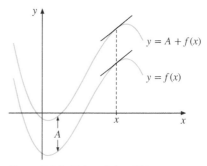

Figure 5.6.2 $f(x)$ and $A + f(x)$

The next two rules are also very useful.

SIMPLE RULES

When taking derivatives, additive constants disappear while multiplicative constants are preserved:

$$y = A + f(x) \Rightarrow y' = f'(x) \tag{5.6.2}$$

$$y = Af(x) \Rightarrow y' = Af'(x) \tag{5.6.3}$$

Rule (5.6.2) is illustrated in Fig. 5.6.2, where A is positive. The graph of $A + f(x)$ is that of $f(x)$ shifted upwards by A units in the direction of the y-axis. So the tangents to the two curves $y = f(x)$ and $y = f(x) + A$ at the same value of x must be parallel. In particular, they must have the same slope. Again you should try to use the definition of $f'(x)$ to give a formal proof of this assertion.

Let us prove rule (5.6.3) by using the definition of a derivative. If $g(x) = Af(x)$, then

$$g(x + h) - g(x) = Af(x + h) - Af(x) = A\left[f(x + h) - f(x)\right]$$

and so

$$g'(x) = \lim_{h \to 0} \frac{g(x + h) - g(x)}{h} = A \lim_{h \to 0} \frac{f(x + h) - f(x)}{h} = Af'(x)$$

For an economic illustration of rule (5.6.3), suppose that $R(t)$ denotes the revenue at time t of firm A, and firm B's revenue $S(t)$ at each time is three times larger than that of A. Then the absolute growth rate of B's revenue is three times larger than that of A. In mathematical notation: $S(t) = 3R(t) \Rightarrow S'(t) = 3R'(t)$. Nevertheless, the firms' *relative* growth rates $R'(t)/R(t)$ and $S'(t)/S(t)$ will be equal.

In Leibniz's notation, the results (5.6.1), (5.6.2), and (5.6.3) are as follows:

$$\frac{d}{dx}A = 0, \quad \frac{d}{dx}[A + f(x)] = \frac{d}{dx}f(x), \quad \frac{d}{dx}[Af(x)] = A\frac{d}{dx}f(x)$$

EXAMPLE 5.6.1   Suppose we know $f'(x)$. Find the derivatives of:

(a) $5 + f(x)$　　　　(b) $f(x) - \frac{1}{2}$　　　　　　　　(c) $4f(x)$

(d) $-\frac{1}{5}f(x)$　　　　(e) $\dfrac{Af(x) + B}{C}$, where $C \neq 0$

Solution: Applying rules (5.6.2) and (5.6.3), we obtain:

(a) $\dfrac{d}{dx}(5 + f(x)) = f'(x)$

(b) $\dfrac{d}{dx}\left(f(x) - \dfrac{1}{2}\right) = \dfrac{d}{dx}\left(-\dfrac{1}{2} + f(x)\right) = f'(x)$

(c) $\dfrac{d}{dx}(4f(x)) = 4f'(x)$

(d) $\dfrac{d}{dx}\left(-\dfrac{1}{5}f(x)\right) = \dfrac{d}{dx}\left(-\dfrac{1}{5}f(x)\right) = -\dfrac{1}{5}f'(x)$

(e) $\dfrac{d}{dx}\left(\dfrac{Af(x) + B}{C}\right) = \dfrac{d}{dx}\left(\dfrac{A}{C}f(x) + \dfrac{B}{C}\right) = \dfrac{A}{C}f'(x)$

Few rules of differentiation are more useful than the following:

THE POWER RULE

Given any constant a,

$$f(x) = x^a \Rightarrow f'(x) = ax^{a-1} \tag{5.6.4}$$

For $a = 2$ and $a = 3$ this rule was confirmed in Section 5.2. The method used in these two examples can be generalized to the case where a is an arbitrary natural number. Later we shall see that the rule is valid for all real numbers a.

EXAMPLE 5.6.2   Use rule (5.6.4) to compute the derivatives of:

(a) $y = x^5$　　　　(b) $y = 3x^8$　　　　(c) $y = \dfrac{x^{100}}{100}$

Solution:

(a) $y = x^5 \Rightarrow y' = 5x^{5-1} = 5x^4$

(b) $y = 3x^8 \Rightarrow y' = 3 \cdot 8x^{8-1} = 24x^7$

(c) $y = \dfrac{x^{100}}{100} = \dfrac{1}{100}x^{100} \Rightarrow y' = \dfrac{1}{100}100x^{100-1} = x^{99}$

EXAMPLE 5.6.3   Use rule (5.6.4) to compute:

(a) $\dfrac{d}{dx}\left(x^{-0.33}\right)$　　(b) $\dfrac{d}{dr}(-5r^{-3})$　　(c) $\dfrac{d}{dp}(Ap^\alpha + B)$　　(d) $\dfrac{d}{dx}\left(\dfrac{A}{\sqrt{x}}\right)$

Solution:

(a) $\dfrac{d}{dx}\left(x^{-0.33}\right) = -0.33x^{-0.33-1} = -0.33x^{-1.33}$

(b) $\dfrac{d}{dr}(-5r^{-3}) = (-5)(-3)r^{-3-1} = 15r^{-4}$

(c) $\dfrac{d}{dp}(Ap^{\alpha} + B) = A\alpha p^{\alpha-1}$

(d) $\dfrac{d}{dx}\left(\dfrac{A}{\sqrt{x}}\right) = \dfrac{d}{dx}(Ax^{-1/2}) = A\left(-\dfrac{1}{2}\right)x^{-1/2-1} = -\dfrac{1}{2}Ax^{-3/2} = \dfrac{-A}{2x\sqrt{x}}$

EXAMPLE 5.6.4   Let $r > 0$ denote a household's income measured in, say, dollars per year. The *Pareto income distribution* is described by the formula

$$f(r) = \frac{B}{r^{\beta}} = Br^{-\beta} \tag{5.6.5}$$

where B and β are positive constants. As explained more fully in Section 10.4, $f(r)\Delta r$ is approximately the proportion of the population whose income is between r and $r + \Delta r$. The distribution function gives a good approximation for incomes above a certain threshold level. For these, empirical estimates of β have usually been in the interval $2.4 < \beta < 2.6$.

Using (5.6.4), we find that $f'(r) = -\beta Br^{-\beta-1} = -\beta B/r^{\beta+1}$ so $f'(r) < 0$, and $f(r)$ is strictly decreasing.

EXERCISES FOR SECTION 5.6

1. Compute the derivatives of the following functions:

(a) $y = 5$ (b) $y = x^4$ (c) $y = 9x^{10}$ (d) $y = \pi^7$

2. Suppose we know $g'(x)$. Find expressions for the derivatives of the following:

(a) $2g(x) + 3$ (b) $-\frac{1}{6}g(x) + 8$ (c) $\dfrac{g(x) - 5}{3}$

3. Find the derivatives of the following:

(a) x^6 (b) $3x^{11}$ (c) x^{50} (d) $-4x^{-7}$

(e) $\dfrac{x^{12}}{12}$ (f) $\dfrac{-2}{x^2}$ (g) $\dfrac{3}{\sqrt[3]{x}}$ (h) $\dfrac{-2}{x\sqrt{x}}$

4. Compute the following:

(a) $\dfrac{d}{dr}(4\pi r^2)$ (b) $\dfrac{d}{dy}\left(Ay^{b+1}\right)$ (c) $\dfrac{d}{dA}\left(\dfrac{1}{A^2\sqrt{A}}\right)$

5. Explain why $f'(a) = \lim\limits_{x \to a} \dfrac{f(x) - f(a)}{x - a}$. Then use this formula to find $f'(a)$ when $f(x) = x^2$.

6. For each of the following functions, find a function $F(x)$ having $f(x)$ as its derivative—that is, a function that satisfies $F'(x) = f(x)$.[9]

(a) $f(x) = x^2$ (b) $f(x) = 2x + 3$ (c) $f(x) = x^a$, for $a \neq -1$

---

[9] Note that you are not asked to find $f'(x)$.

7. [HARDER] The following limits all take the form $\lim_{h \to 0}[f(a+h) - f(a)]/h$. Use your knowledge of derivatives to find the limits.

(a) $\lim_{h \to 0} \dfrac{(5+h)^2 - 5^2}{h}$ (b) $\lim_{s \to 0} \dfrac{(s+1)^5 - 1}{s}$ (c) $\lim_{h \to 0} \dfrac{5(x+h)^2 + 10 - 5x^2 - 10}{h}$

5.7   Sums, Products, and Quotients

If we know $f'(x)$ and $g'(x)$, then what are the derivatives of the four functions $f(x) + g(x)$, $f(x) - g(x), f(x) \cdot g(x)$, and $f(x)/g(x)$? You will probably guess the first two correctly, but are less likely to be right about the last two, unless you have already learned the answers.

Sums and Differences

Suppose f and g are both defined on a set A of real numbers.

DERIVATIVES OF SUMS AND DIFFERENCES

If both f and g are differentiable at x, then the sum $f + g$ and the difference $f - g$ are both differentiable at x, with

$$F(x) = f(x) \pm g(x) \Rightarrow F'(x) = f'(x) \pm g'(x) \tag{5.7.1}$$

In Leibniz's notation:

$$\frac{\mathrm{d}}{\mathrm{d}x}\left(f(x) \pm g(x)\right) = \frac{\mathrm{d}}{\mathrm{d}x}f(x) \pm \frac{\mathrm{d}}{\mathrm{d}x}g(x)$$

We can give a formal proof of (5.7.1).

Consider the case when $F(x) = f(x) + g(x)$, The Newton quotient of F is

$$\frac{F(x+h) - F(x)}{h} = \frac{(f(x+h) + g(x+h)) - (f(x) + g(x))}{h}$$

$$= \frac{f(x+h) - f(x)}{h} + \frac{g(x+h) - g(x)}{h}$$

When $h \to 0$, the last two fractions tend to $f'(x)$ and $g'(x)$, respectively, and thus the sum of the fractions tends to $f'(x) + g'(x)$. Hence,

$$F'(x) = \lim_{h \to 0} \frac{F(x+h) - F(x)}{h} = f'(x) + g'(x)$$

This proves (5.7.1) for the sum. The proof of the result for the difference is similar—only some of the signs change in an obvious way.

EXAMPLE 5.7.1   Compute $\dfrac{d}{dx}\left(3x^8 + x^{100}/100\right)$.

Solution: Using (5.7.1) and the results from Example 5.6.2,

$$\frac{d}{dx}\left(3x^8 + x^{100}/100\right) = \frac{d}{dx}(3x^8) + \frac{d}{dx}\left(x^{100}/100\right) = 24x^7 + x^{99}$$

EXAMPLE 5.7.2   In Example 5.4.3, $C(x)$ denoted the cost of producing x units of some commodity in a given period. If $R(x)$ is the revenue from selling those x units, then the profit function $\pi(x) = R(x) - C(x)$ is the difference between the revenue and the cost. According to (5.7.1), $\pi'(x) = R'(x) - C'(x)$. In particular, $\pi'(x) = 0$ when $R'(x) = C'(x)$. In words: *Marginal profit is 0 when marginal revenue is equal to marginal cost.*

Rule (5.7.1) can be extended to sums of an arbitrary number of terms. For example,

$$\frac{d}{dx}(f(x) - g(x) + h(x)) = f'(x) - g'(x) + h'(x)$$

which we see by writing $f(x) - g(x) + h(x)$ as $(f(x) - g(x)) + h(x)$, and then using (5.7.1) twice. Using the rules (5.6.2)–(5.6.4) and (5.7.1) makes it easy to differentiate any polynomial.

Products

Suppose $f(x) = x$ and $g(x) = x^2$, then $(f \cdot g)(x) = x^3$. Here $f'(x) = 1$, $g'(x) = 2x$, and $(f \cdot g)'(x) = 3x^2$. Hence, the derivative of $(f \cdot g)(x)$ is *not* equal to $f'(x) \cdot g'(x) = 2x$. The correct rule for differentiating a product is a little more complicated.

DERIVATIVE OF A PRODUCT

If both f and g are differentiable at the point x, then so is $F = f \cdot g$, and

$$F(x) = f(x) \cdot g(x) \Rightarrow F'(x) = f'(x) \cdot g(x) + f(x) \cdot g'(x) \qquad (5.7.2)$$

Formulated in words: *The derivative of the product of two functions is equal to the derivative of the first times the second, plus the first times the derivative of the second.* The formula, however, is much easier to digest than these words.

In Leibniz's notation, the product rule is expressed as:

$$\frac{d}{dx}[f(x) \cdot g(x)] = \left[\frac{d}{dx}f(x)\right] \cdot g(x) + f(x) \cdot \left[\frac{d}{dx}g(x)\right]$$

Before demonstrating why (5.7.2) is valid, here are two examples.

EXAMPLE 5.7.3   Find $h'(x)$ when $h(x) = (x^3 - x) \cdot (5x^4 + x^2)$. Confirm the answer by expanding $h(x)$ as a single polynomial, then differentiating the result.

Solution: We see that $h(x) = f(x) \cdot g(x)$ with $f(x) = x^3 - x$ and $g(x) = 5x^4 + x^2$. Here $f'(x) = 3x^2 - 1$ and $g'(x) = 20x^3 + 2x$. Thus, from (5.7.2)

$$h'(x) = f'(x) \cdot g(x) + f(x) \cdot g'(x) = (3x^2 - 1) \cdot (5x^4 + x^2) + (x^3 - x) \cdot (20x^3 + 2x)$$

Usually we simplify the answer by expanding to obtain just one polynomial. Simple computations give $h'(x) = 35x^6 - 20x^4 - 3x^2$.

Alternatively, expanding $h(x)$ as a single polynomial gives $h(x) = 5x^7 - 4x^5 - x^3$, whose derivative, from rules (5.6.4) and (5.7.1), is $h'(x) = 35x^6 - 20x^4 - 3x^2$.

EXAMPLE 5.7.4   Let $D(P)$ denote the demand function for a product. By selling $D(P)$ units at price P per unit, the producer earns revenue $R(P)$ given by $R(P) = PD(P)$. Usually $D'(P)$ is negative because demand goes down when the price increases. According to the product rule for differentiation,

$$R'(P) = D(P) + PD'(P) \tag{$*$}$$

For an economic interpretation, suppose P increases by one dollar. The revenue $R(P)$ changes for two reasons. First, $R(P)$ increases by $1 \cdot D(P)$, because each of the $D(P)$ units brings in one dollar more. But a one dollar increase in the price per unit causes demand to change by $D(P + 1) - D(P)$ units, which is approximately $D'(P)$. The (positive) loss due to a one dollar increase in the price per unit is then $-PD'(P)$, which must be subtracted from $D(P)$ to obtain $R'(P)$, as in Eq. ($*$). The resulting expression merely expresses the simple fact that $R'(P)$, the total rate of change of $R(P)$, is what you gain minus what you lose.

Now we proceed with the proof of (5.7.2):

Suppose f and g are differentiable at x, so that the two Newton quotients

$$\frac{f(x + h) - f(x)}{h} \quad \text{and} \quad \frac{g(x + h) - g(x)}{h}$$

tend to the limits $f'(x)$ and $g'(x)$, respectively, as h tends to 0. We must show that the Newton quotient of F also tends to a limit, which is given by $f'(x)g(x) + f(x)g'(x)$. The Newton quotient of F is

$$\frac{F(x + h) - F(x)}{h} = \frac{f(x + h)g(x + h) - f(x)g(x)}{h} \tag{$*$}$$

To proceed further we must somehow transform the right-hand side (RHS) to involve the Newton quotients of f and g. We use a trick: The numerator of the RHS is unchanged if we both subtract and add the number $f(x)g(x + h)$. Hence, with a suitable regrouping of terms, we have

$$\frac{F(x + h) - F(x)}{h} = \frac{f(x + h)g(x + h) - f(x)g(x + h) + f(x)g(x + h) - f(x)g(x)}{h}$$

$$= \frac{f(x + h) - f(x)}{h}g(x + h) + f(x)\frac{g(x + h) - g(x)}{h}$$

As h tends to 0, the two Newton quotients tend to $f'(x)$ and $g'(x)$, respectively. Now we can write $g(x + h)$ for $h \neq 0$ as

$$g(x + h) = \left[\frac{g(x + h) - g(x)}{h}\right]h + g(x)$$

By the product rule for limits and the definition of $g'(x)$, this tends to $g'(x) \cdot 0 + g(x) = g(x)$ as h tends to 0. It follows that the Newton quotient of F tends to $f'(x)g(x) + f(x)g'(x)$ as h tends to 0.

To conclude, now that we have seen how to differentiate products of two functions, let us consider products of more than two functions. For example, suppose that $y = f(x)g(x)h(x)$. What is y'? We extend the same technique shown earlier and put $y = [f(x)g(x)]h(x)$. Then the product rule gives

$$y' = [f(x)g(x)]' \, h(x) + [f(x)g(x)] \, h'(x)$$

$$= [f'(x)g(x) + f(x)g'(x)] \, h(x) + f(x)g(x)h'(x)$$

$$= f'(x)g(x)h(x) + f(x)g'(x)h(x) + f(x)g(x)h'(x)$$

If none of the three functions is equal to 0, we can write the result as follows:[10]

$$\frac{(fgh)'}{fgh} = \frac{f'}{f} + \frac{g'}{g} + \frac{h'}{h}$$

By analogy, it is easy to write down the corresponding result for a product of n functions. In words, the relative rate of growth of the product is the sum of the relative rates at which each factor is changing.

Quotients

Suppose $F(x) = f(x)/g(x)$, where f and g are differentiable in x with $g(x) \neq 0$. Bearing in mind the complications in the formula for the derivative of a product, one should be somewhat reluctant to make a quick guess as to the correct formula for $F'(x)$.

In fact, it is quite easy to find the formula for $F'(x)$ if we *assume* that $F(x)$ *is* differentiable. From $F(x) = f(x)/g(x)$ it follows that $f(x) = F(x)g(x)$. Thus, the product rule gives $f'(x) = F'(x) \cdot g(x) + F(x) \cdot g'(x)$. Solving for $F'(x)$ yields $F'(x) \cdot g(x) = f'(x) - F(x) \cdot g'(x)$, and so

$$F'(x) = \frac{f'(x) - F(x)g'(x)}{g(x)} = \frac{f'(x) - [f(x)/g(x)] \, g'(x)}{g(x)}$$

Multiplying both numerator and denominator of the last fraction by $g(x)$ gives the following important formula.

DERIVATIVE OF A QUOTIENT

If f and g are differentiable at x and $g(x) \neq 0$, then $F = f/g$ is differentiable at x, and

$$F(x) = \frac{f(x)}{g(x)} \Rightarrow F'(x) = \frac{f'(x) \cdot g(x) - f(x) \cdot g'(x)}{(g(x))^2} \tag{5.7.3}$$

---

[10] If all the functions are positive, this result is easier to show using logarithmic differentiation. See Section 5.11.

In words: *The derivative of a quotient is equal to the derivative of the numerator times the denominator minus the numerator times the derivative of the denominator, this difference then being divided by the square of the denominator.* In simpler notation, we have $(f/g)' = (f'g - fg')/g^2$.

Note that in the product rule formula, the two functions appear symmetrically, so that it is easy to remember. In the formula for the derivative of a quotient, the expressions in the numerator must be in the right order. Here is one way to check that you have the order right. Write down the formula you believe is correct. Put $g \equiv 1$. Then $g' \equiv 0$, and your formula ought to reduce to f'. If you get $-f'$, then your signs are wrong.

EXAMPLE 5.7.5   Compute $F'(x)$ and $F'(4)$ when

$$F(x) = \frac{3x - 5}{x - 2}$$

Solution: We apply (5.7.3), with $f(x) = 3x - 5$, $g(x) = x - 2$. Then $f'(x) = 3$ and $g'(x) = 1$. So we obtain, for $x \neq 2$:

$$F'(x) = \frac{3 \cdot (x - 2) - (3x - 5) \cdot 1}{(x - 2)^2} = \frac{3x - 6 - 3x + 5}{(x - 2)^2} = \frac{-1}{(x - 2)^2}$$

To find $F'(4)$, we put $x = 4$ in the formula for $F'(x)$ to get $F'(4) = -1/(4 - 2)^2 = -1/4$. Note that $F'(x) < 0$ for all $x \neq 2$. Hence F is strictly decreasing both for $x < 2$ and for $x > 2$. Note that $(3x - 5)/(x - 2) = 3 + 1/(x - 2)$. The graph is shown in Fig. 5.1.7.

EXAMPLE 5.7.6   Let $C(x)$ be the total cost of producing x units of a commodity. Then $C(x)/x$ is the *average cost* of producing x units. Find an expression for $\dfrac{d}{dx}[C(x)/x]$.

Solution:

$$\frac{d}{dx}\left(\frac{C(x)}{x}\right) = \frac{C'(x)x - C(x)}{x^2} = \frac{1}{x}\left(C'(x) - \frac{C(x)}{x}\right) \tag{5.7.4}$$

Note that the marginal cost $C'(x)$ exceeds the average cost $C(x)/x$ if, and only if, average cost increases as output increases.[11]

The formula for the derivative of a quotient becomes more symmetric if we consider relative rates of change. By using (5.7.3), simple computation shows that

$$F(x) = \frac{f(x)}{g(x)} \implies \frac{F'(x)}{F(x)} = \frac{f'(x)}{f(x)} - \frac{g'(x)}{g(x)} \tag{5.7.5}$$

That is, *the relative rate of change of a quotient is equal to the relative rate of change of the numerator minus the relative rate of change of the denominator.*

Let $W(t)$ be the nominal wage rate and $P(t)$ the price index at time t. Then $w(t) = W(t)/P(t)$ is called the *real wage rate*. According to (5.7.5),

$$\frac{\dot{w}(t)}{w(t)} = \frac{\dot{W}(t)}{W(t)} - \frac{\dot{P}(t)}{P(t)}$$

---

[11] In a similar way, if a basketball team recruits a new player, the average height of the team increases if and only if the new player's height exceeds the old average height.

The relative rate of change of the real wage rate is equal to the difference between the relative rates of change of the nominal wage rate and the price index. Thus, if nominal wages increase at the rate of 5% per year but prices rise by 6% per year, then real wages fall by 1%. Also, if inflation leads to wages and prices increasing at the same relative rate, then the real wage rate is constant.

EXERCISES FOR SECTION 5.7

1. Differentiate w.r.t x the following functions:

   (a) $x + 1$ (b) $x + x^2$ (c) $3x^5 + 2x^4 + 5$

   (d) $8x^4 + 2\sqrt{x}$ (e) $\frac{1}{2}x - \frac{3}{2}x^2 + 5x^3$ (f) $1 - 3x^7$

2. Differentiate w.r.t x the following functions:

   (a) $\frac{3}{5}x^2 - 2x^7 + \frac{1}{8} - \sqrt{x}$ (b) $(2x^2 - 1)(x^4 - 1)$ (c) $\left(x^5 + \dfrac{1}{x}\right)(x^5 + 1)$

SM   3. Differentiate w.r.t x the following functions:

   (a) $\dfrac{1}{x^6}$ (b) $x^{-1}(x^2 + 1)\sqrt{x}$ (c) $\dfrac{1}{\sqrt{x^3}}$ (d) $\dfrac{x + 1}{x - 1}$

   (e) $\dfrac{x + 1}{x^5}$ (f) $\dfrac{3x - 5}{2x + 8}$ (g) $3x^{-11}$ (h) $\dfrac{3x - 1}{x^2 + x + 1}$

4. Differentiate w.r.t x the following functions:

   (a) $\dfrac{\sqrt{x} - 2}{\sqrt{x} + 1}$ (b) $\dfrac{x^2 - 1}{x^2 + 1}$ (c) $\dfrac{x^2 + x + 1}{x^2 - x + 1}$

5. Let $x = f(L)$ be the output when L units of labour are used as input. Assume that $f(0) = 0$ and that $f'(L) > 0, f''(L) < 0$ for all $L > 0$. Average productivity is defined by the formula $g(L) = f(L)/L$.

   (a) Let $L^* > 0$. Indicate on a figure the values of $f'(L^*)$ and $g(L^*)$. Which is larger?

   (b) How does the average productivity change when labour input increases?

SM   6. For each of the following functions, determine the intervals where it is increasing.

   (a) $y = 3x^2 - 12x + 13$ (b) $y = \frac{1}{4}(x^4 - 6x^2)$ (c) $y = \dfrac{2x}{x^2 + 2}$ (d) $y = \dfrac{x^2 - x^3}{2(x + 1)}$

SM   7. Find the equations for the tangents to the graphs of the following functions at the specified points:

   (a) $y = 3 - x - x^2$ at $x = 1$ (b) $y = \dfrac{x^2 - 1}{x^2 + 1}$ at $x = 1$

   (c) $y = \left(\dfrac{1}{x^2} + 1\right)(x^2 - 1)$ at $x = 2$ (d) $y = \dfrac{x^4 + 1}{(x^2 + 1)(x + 3)}$ at $x = 0$

8. Consider an oil well where $x(t)$ denotes the rate of extraction in barrels per day and $p(t)$ denotes the price in dollars per barrel, both at time t. Then $R(t) = p(t)x(t)$ is the revenue in dollars per day. Find an expression for $\dot{R}(t)$, and give it an economic interpretation in the case when $p(t)$ and $x(t)$ are both increasing. (*Hint*: $R(t)$ increases for two reasons.)

(SM) 9. Differentiate the following functions w.r.t. t:

(a) $\dfrac{at + b}{ct + d}$ (b) $t^n \left(a\sqrt{t} + b \right)$ (c) $\dfrac{1}{at^2 + bt + c}$

10. If $f(x) = \sqrt{x}$, then $f(x) \cdot f(x) = x$. Differentiate this equation using the product rule in order to find a formula for $f'(x)$. Compare this with the result in Exercise 5.2.9.

11. Suppose that $a = -n$ where n is any natural number. By using the relation $x^{-n} = 1/x^n$ and the quotient rule (5.7.3), prove the power rule stating that $y = x^a \Rightarrow y' = ax^{a-1}$.

5.8 The Chain Rule

Suppose that y is a function of u, and that u is a function of x. Then y is a composite function of x. Suppose that x changes. This gives rise to a two-stage "chain reaction": first, u reacts directly to the change in x; second, y reacts to this change in u. If we know the rates of change du/dx and dy/du, then what is the rate of change dy/dx? It turns out that the relationship between these rates of change is simple.

THE CHAIN RULE

If y is a differentiable function of u, and u is a differentiable function of x, then y is a differentiable function of x, and

$$\frac{dy}{dx} = \frac{dy}{du} \cdot \frac{du}{dx} \tag{5.8.1}$$

It is easier to remember the chain rule when using Leibniz's notation, as the left-hand side of 5.8.1 is exactly what results if we "cancel" the du on the right-hand side. Of course this is just a mnemonic and one must be careful: because dy/du and du/dx are not fractions, but merely symbols for derivatives, and du is not a number, cancelling is *not* defined![12]

---

[12] It has been suggested that proving (5.8.1) by cancelling du is not much better than proving that $64/16 = 4$ by cancelling the two sixes: $\not{6}4/1\not{6} = 4$.

An important special case is when y is a power function.

THE GENERALIZED POWER RULE

If $y = u^a$ and u is a differentiable function of x, then

$$y' = au^{a-1}u' \tag{5.8.2}$$

The chain rule is very powerful. Facility in applying it comes from a lot of practice.

EXAMPLE 5.8.1   Find dy/dx when:

(a) $y = u^5$ and $u = 1 - x^3$ (b) $y = \dfrac{10}{(x^2 + 4x + 5)^7}$

Solution:

(a) Here we can use (5.8.1) directly. Since $dy/du = 5u^4$ and $du/dx = -3x^2$, we have

$$\frac{dy}{dx} = \frac{dy}{du} \cdot \frac{du}{dx} = 5u^4(-3x^2) = -15x^2u^4 = -15x^2(1 - x^3)^4$$

(b) If we write $u = x^2 + 4x + 5$, then $y = 10u^{-7}$. By the generalized power rule (5.8.2), one has

$$\frac{dy}{dx} = 10(-7)u^{-8}u' = -70u^{-8}(2x + 4) = \frac{-140(x + 2)}{(x^2 + 4x + 5)^8}$$

After a little training, the intermediate steps become unnecessary. For example, to differentiate the compound function

$$y = (\underbrace{1 - x^3}_{u})^5$$

suggested by part (a) of Example 5.8.1, we can *think* of y as $y = u^5$, where $u = 1 - x^3$. Now we can differentiate both u^5 and $1 - x^3$ in our heads, and so write down $y' = 5(1 - x^3)^4(-3x^2)$ immediately.

Note that if you differentiate $y = x^5/5$ using the quotient rule, you obtain the right answer, but commit a small "mathematical crime". This is because it is much easier to write y as $y = (1/5)x^5$ to get $y' = (1/5)5x^4 = x^4$. In the same way, it is unnecessarily cumbersome to apply quotient rule to the function given in part (b) of Example 5.8.1. The generalized power rule is much more effective.

EXAMPLE 5.8.2   Differentiate the functions:

(a) $y = (x^3 + x^2)^{50}$ (b) $y = \left(\dfrac{x-1}{x+3}\right)^{1/3}$ (c) $y = \sqrt{x^2 + 1}$

Solution:

(a) $y = (x^3 + x^2)^{50} = u^{50}$ where $u = x^3 + x^2$, so $u' = 3x^2 + 2x$. Then (5.8.2) gives

$$y' = 50u^{50-1} \cdot u' = 50(x^3 + x^2)^{49}(3x^2 + 2x)$$

(b) Again, we use (5.8.2):

$$y = \left(\frac{x-1}{x+3}\right)^{1/3} = u^{1/3}$$

where $u = (x-1)/(x+3)$. The quotient rule gives

$$u' = \frac{1 \cdot (x+3) - (x-1) \cdot 1}{(x+3)^2} = \frac{4}{(x+3)^2}$$

and hence

$$y' = \frac{1}{3}u^{(1/3)-1} \cdot u' = \frac{1}{3}\left(\frac{x-1}{x+3}\right)^{-2/3} \cdot \frac{4}{(x+3)^2} = \frac{4}{3}(x+1)^{-2/3}(x+3)^{-4/3}$$

(c) Note first that $y = \sqrt{x^2 + 1} = (x^2 + 1)^{1/2}$, so $y = u^{1/2}$ where $u = x^2 + 1$. Hence,

$$y' = \frac{1}{2}u^{(1/2)-1} \cdot u' = \frac{1}{2}(x^2 + 1)^{-1/2} \cdot 2x = \frac{x}{\sqrt{x^2 + 1}}$$

The formulation of the chain rule may appear abstract and difficult. However, when we interpret the derivatives involved in (5.8.1) as rates of change, the chain rule becomes rather intuitive, as the next example from economics will indicate.

EXAMPLE 5.8.3   The demand quantity x for a commodity depends on price p. Suppose that price p is not constant, but depends on time t. Then x is a composite function of t, and according to the chain rule,

$$\frac{dx}{dt} = \frac{dx}{dp} \cdot \frac{dp}{dt}$$

Suppose, for instance, that the demand for butter decreases by 5000 pounds if the price goes up by one dollar per pound. So $dx/dp \approx -5000$. Suppose further that the price per pound increases by five cents per month, so $dp/dt \approx 0.05$. What is the decrease in demand in pounds per month?

Solution: Because the price per pound increases by \$0.05 per month, and the demand decreases by 5000 pounds for every dollar increase in the price, the demand *decreases* by approximately $5000 \cdot 0.05 = 250$ pounds per month. This means that $dx/dt \approx -250$, measured in pounds per month.

The next example uses the chain rule several times.

EXAMPLE 5.8.4   Find $x'(t)$ when $x(t) = 5\left(1 + \sqrt{t^3 + 1}\right)^{25}$.

Solution: The initial step is easy: let $x(t) = 5u^{25}$, where $u = 1 + \sqrt{t^3 + 1}$, to obtain

$$x'(t) = 5 \cdot 25u^{24}\frac{du}{dt} = 125u^{24}\frac{du}{dt} \tag{$*$}$$

The new feature in this example is that we cannot write down du/dt at once. Finding du/dt requires using the chain rule a second time. Let $u = 1 + \sqrt{v} = 1 + v^{1/2}$, where $v = t^3 + 1$. Then

$$\frac{du}{dt} = \frac{1}{2}v^{(1/2)-1} \cdot \frac{dv}{dt} = \frac{1}{2}v^{-1/2} \cdot 3t^2 = \frac{1}{2}(t^3+1)^{-1/2} \cdot 3t^2 \qquad (**)$$

From $(*)$ and $(**)$, we get

$$x'(t) = 125\left(1 + \sqrt{t^3+1}\right)^{24} \cdot \tfrac{1}{2}(t^3+1)^{-1/2} \cdot 3t^2$$

Suppose, as in the last example, that x is a function of u, u is a function of v, and v is in turn a function of t. Then x is a composite function of t, and the chain rule can be used twice to obtain

$$\frac{dx}{dt} = \frac{dx}{du} \cdot \frac{du}{dv} \cdot \frac{dv}{dt}$$

This is precisely the formula used in the last example. Again the notation is suggestive because the left-hand side is exactly what results if we "cancel" both du and dv on the right-hand side.

An Alternative Formulation of the Chain Rule

Although Leibniz's notation makes it very easy to remember the chain rule, it suffers from the defect of not specifying where each derivative is evaluated. We remedy this by introducing names for the functions involved. So let $y = f(u)$ and $u = g(x)$. Then y can be written as

$$y = f(g(x))$$

Here y is a *composite function* of x with $g(x)$ as the *kernel*, and f as the *exterior function*.

THE CHAIN RULE

If g is differentiable at x_0 and f is differentiable at $u_0 = g(x_0)$, then the composite function $F(x) = f(g(x))$ is differentiable at x_0, and

$$F'(x_0) = f'(u_0)g'(x_0) = f'(g(x_0))g'(x_0) \qquad (5.8.3)$$

In words: *to differentiate a composite function, first differentiate the exterior function w.r.t. the kernel, and then multiply by the derivative of the kernel.*

EXAMPLE 5.8.5   Find the derivative of the compound function $F(x) = f(g(x))$ at $x_0 = -3$ in case $f(u) = u^3$ and $g(x) = 2 - x^2$.

Solution: In this case one has $f'(u) = 3u^2$ and $g'(x) = -2x$. So according to (5.8.3), one has $F'(-3) = f'(g(-3)) g'(-3)$. Now $g(-3) = 2 - (-3)^2 = 2 - 9 = -7$; $g'(-3) = 6$; and $f'(g(-3)) = f'(-7) = 3(-7)^2 = 3 \cdot 49 = 147$. So $F'(-3) = f'(g(-3)) g'(-3) = 147 \cdot 6 = 882$.

Finally, we prove that the Chain Rule is correct. Using this alternative formulation, it is tempting to try to argue (5.8.3) as follows:

In simplified notation, with $y = F(x) = f(u)$ and $u = g(x)$, as above, it is tempting to argue as follows: Since $u = g(x)$ is continuous, $\Delta u = g(x) - g(x_0) \to 0$ as $x \to x_0$, and so

$$F'(x_0) = \lim_{\Delta x \to 0} \frac{\Delta y}{\Delta x} = \lim_{\Delta x \to 0} \left(\frac{\Delta y}{\Delta u} \cdot \frac{\Delta u}{\Delta x} \right) = \lim_{\Delta u \to 0} \frac{\Delta y}{\Delta u} \cdot \lim_{\Delta x \to 0} \frac{\Delta u}{\Delta x} = \frac{dy}{du} \cdot \frac{du}{dx} = f'(u_0)g'(x_0)$$

There is a catch, however, because Δu may be equal to 0 for values of x arbitrarily close to x_0, and then $\Delta y / \Delta u$ will be undefined. A correct argument goes as follows:

Define functions φ and γ as:

$$\varphi(u) = \begin{cases} \dfrac{f(u) - f(u_0)}{u - u_0} & \text{if } u \neq u_0 \\ f'(u_0) & \text{if } u = u_0 \end{cases} \quad \text{and} \quad \gamma(x) = \begin{cases} \dfrac{g(x) - g(x_0)}{x - x_0} & \text{if } x \neq x_0 \\ g'(x_0) & \text{if } x = x_0 \end{cases}$$

Then, by definition of the derivatives $f'(u_0)$ and $g'(x_0)$, one has $\lim_{u \to u_0} \varphi(u) = \varphi(u_0)$ and $\lim_{x \to x_0} \gamma(x) = \gamma(x_0)$. Moreover,

$$f(u) - f(u_0) = \varphi(u)(u - u_0) \text{ and } g(x) - g(x_0) = \gamma(x)(x - x_0)$$

for all u in an interval around u_0 and all x in an interval around x_0. So for h close to 0, it follows that

$$\begin{aligned} F(x_0 + h) - F(x_0) &= f(g(x_0 + h)) - f(g(x_0)) \\ &= \varphi(g(x_0 + h)) \cdot [g(x_0 + h) - g(x_0)] \\ &= \varphi(g(x_0 + h)) \cdot \gamma(x_0 + h) \cdot h \end{aligned}$$

Hence

$$F'(x_0) = \lim_{h \to 0} \varphi(g(x_0 + h))\gamma(x_0 + h) = \varphi(g(x_0))\gamma(x_0) = f'(g(x_0))g'(x_0)$$

EXERCISES FOR SECTION 5.8

1. Use the chain rule (5.8.1) to find dy/dx for the following:

(a) $y = 5u^4$, where $u = 1 + x^2$

(b) $y = u - u^6$, where $u = 1 + 1/x$

2. Compute the following:

(a) dY/dt, when $Y = -3(V + 1)^5$ and $V = \frac{1}{3}t^3$.

(b) dK/dt, when $K = AL^a$ and $L = bt + c$, where A, a, b, and c are positive constants.

(SM) **3.** Find the derivatives of the following functions, where a, p, q, and b are constants:

(a) $y = \dfrac{1}{(x^2 + x + 1)^5}$ (b) $y = \sqrt{x + \sqrt{x + \sqrt{x}}}$ (c) $y = x^a(px + q)^b$

4. If Y is a function of K, and K is a function of t, find the formula for the derivative of Y with respect to t at $t = t_0$.

5. If $Y = F(K)$ and $K = h(t)$, find the formula for dY/dt.

6. Consider the demand function $x = b - \sqrt{ap - c}$, where a, b, and c are positive constants, x is the quantity demanded, and p is the price, for $p > c/a$. Compute dx/dp.

7. Find a formula for $h'(x)$ when: (a) $h(x) = f(x^2)$; and (b) $h(x) = f(x^n g(x))$.

8. Let $s(t)$ be the distance in kilometres a car goes in t hours. Let $B(s)$ be the number of litres of fuel the car uses to go s kilometres. Provide an interpretation of the function $b(t) = B(s(t))$, and find a formula for $b'(t)$.

9. Suppose that $C = 20q - 4q\left(25 - \frac{1}{2}x\right)^{1/2}$, where q is a constant and $x < 50$. Find dC/dx.

10. Differentiate each of the following in two different ways:

(a) $y = (x^4)^5 = x^{20}$ (b) $y = (1 - x)^3 = 1 - 3x + 3x^2 - x^3$

11. Suppose you invest €1 000 at $p\%$ interest per year. Let $g(p)$ denote how many euros you will have after ten years.

(a) Give economic interpretations of: (i) $g(5) \approx 1629$; and (ii) $g'(5) \approx 155$.

(b) To check the numbers in (a), find a formula for $g(p)$, then compute $g(5)$ and $g'(5)$.

12. If f is differentiable at x, find expressions for the derivatives of the following functions:

(a) $x + f(x)$ (b) $[f(x)]^2 - x$ (c) $[f(x)]^4$ (d) $x^2 f(x) + [f(x)]^3$

(e) $xf(x)$ (f) $\sqrt{f(x)}$ (g) $\dfrac{x^2}{f(x)}$ (h) $\dfrac{[f(x)]^2}{x^3}$

5.9 Higher-Order Derivatives

The derivative f' of a function f is often called the *first derivative* of f. If f' is also differentiable, then we can differentiate f' in turn. The result $(f')'$ is called the *second derivative*, written more concisely as f''. We use $f''(x)$ to denote the second derivative of f evaluated at the particular point x.

EXAMPLE 5.9.1   Find $f'(x)$ and $f''(x)$ when $f(x) = 2x^5 - 3x^3 + 2x$.

Solution: The rules for differentiating polynomials imply that $f'(x) = 10x^4 - 9x^2 + 2$. Then we differentiate each side of this equality to get $f''(x) = 40x^3 - 18x$.

The different forms of notation for the second derivative are analogous to those for the first derivative. For example, we write $y'' = f''(x)$ in order to denote the second derivative of $y = f(x)$. The Leibniz notation for the second derivative is also used. In the notation dy/dx or $df(x)/dx$ for the first derivative, we interpreted the symbol d/dx as an operator indicating that what follows is to be differentiated with respect to x. The second derivative is obtained by using the operator d/dx twice: $f''(x) = (d/dx)(d/dx)f(x)$. We usually think of this as $f''(x) = (d/dx)^2 f(x)$, and so write

$$f''(x) = \frac{d^2 f(x)}{dx^2} \quad \text{or} \quad y'' = \frac{d^2 y}{dx^2}$$

Pay special attention to where the superscripts are placed! Of course, the notation for the second derivative must change if the variables have other names.

EXAMPLE 5.9.2   Find:

(a) Y'' when $Y = AK^a$ is a function of $K > 0$, with A and a as constants.

(b) $d^2 L/dt^2$ when $L = \dfrac{t}{t+1}$, and $t \geq 0$.

Solution:

(a) Differentiating $Y = AK^a$ once with respect to K gives $Y' = AaK^{a-1}$. Differentiating a second time with respect to K yields $Y'' = Aa(a-1)K^{a-2}$.

(b) First, use the quotient rule to find that $\dfrac{dL}{dt} = \dfrac{d}{dt}\left(\dfrac{t}{t+1}\right) = \dfrac{1 \cdot (t+1) - t \cdot 1}{(t+1)^2}$
$= (t+1)^{-2}$. Then,

$$\frac{d^2 L}{dt^2} = -2(t+1)^{-3} = \frac{-2}{(t+1)^3}$$

Convex and Concave Functions

Recall from Section 5.3 how the sign of the first derivative determines whether a function is increasing or decreasing on an interval I. If $f'(x) \geq 0$ ($f'(x) \leq 0$) on I, then f is increasing (decreasing) on I, and conversely. The second derivative $f''(x)$ is the derivative of $f'(x)$. Hence:

$$f''(x) \geq 0 \text{ on } I \iff f' \text{ is increasing on } I \tag{5.9.1}$$

$$f''(x) \leq 0 \text{ on } I \iff f' \text{ is decreasing on } I \tag{5.9.2}$$

The equivalence in (5.9.1) is illustrated in Fig. 5.9.1. The slope of the tangent, $f'(x)$, is increasing as x increases. On the other hand, the slope of the tangent to the graph in Fig. 5.9.2 is decreasing as x increases, which illustrates (5.9.2).

To help visualize this, imagine sliding a ruler along the curve and keeping it aligned with the tangent to the curve at each point. As the ruler moves along the curve from left to right, the tangent rotates anti-clockwise in Fig. 5.9.1, clockwise in Fig. 5.9.2.

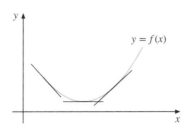

Figure 5.9.1 The slope of the tangent line increases as x increases

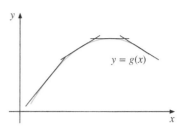

Figure 5.9.2 The slope of the tangent line decreases as x increases

Suppose that f is continuous in the interval I and twice differentiable in the interior of I. Then we can introduce the following definitions:

CONVEX AND CONCAVE FUNCTIONS

$$f \text{ is } convex \text{ on } I \iff f''(x) \geq 0 \text{ for all } x \text{ in } I \qquad (5.9.3)$$

$$f \text{ is } concave \text{ on } I \iff f''(x) \leq 0 \text{ for all } x \text{ in } I \qquad (5.9.4)$$

These properties are illustrated in Figs 5.9.3–5.9.6, which should be studied carefully. Whether a function is concave or convex is crucial to many results in economic analysis, especially the many that involve maximization or minimization problems. We note that often I is the whole real line, in which case the interval is not mentioned explicitly.

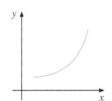

Figure 5.9.3
Increasing convex

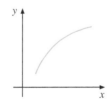

Figure 5.9.4
Increasing concave

Figure 5.9.5
Decreasing convex

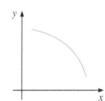

Figure 5.9.6
Decreasing concave

EXAMPLE 5.9.3   Check the convexity/concavity of the following functions:

(a) $f(x) = x^2 - 2x + 2$ (b) $f(x) = ax^2 + bx + c$

Solution:

(a) Here $f'(x) = 2x - 2$ so $f''(x) = 2$. Because $f''(x) > 0$ for all x, the function f is convex.

(b) Here $f'(x) = 2ax + b$, so $f''(x) = 2a$. If $a = 0$, then f is linear. In this case, the function f meets both the definitions in (5.9.3) and (5.9.4), so it is both concave and convex. If $a > 0$, then $f''(x) > 0$, so f is convex. If $a < 0$, then $f''(x) < 0$, so f is concave. The last two cases are illustrated by the graphs in Figs 4.6.1 and 4.6.2.

We consider two typical examples of convex and concave functions. Fig. 5.9.7 shows a rough graph of the function P, for dates between 1500 and 2000, where $P(t)$ measures the world population (in billions) in year t. It appears from the figure that not only is $P(t)$ increasing, but the rate of increase increases: each year the *increase* becomes larger. So, for the last five centuries, $P(t)$ has been convex.

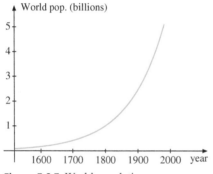

Figure 5.9.7 World population   **Figure 5.9.8** Wheat production

The graph in Fig. 5.9.8 shows the crop of wheat $Y(N)$ when N pounds of fertilizer per acre are used. The curve is based on fertilizer experiments in Iowa during 1952. The function has a maximum at $N = N_0 \approx 172$. Increasing the amount of fertilizer beyond N_0 will cause wheat production to decline. Moreover, $Y(N)$ is concave. If $N < N_0$, increasing N by one unit will *increase* $Y(N)$ by less, the larger is N. On the other hand, if $N > N_0$, increasing N by one unit will *decrease* $Y(N)$ by more, the larger is N.

EXAMPLE 5.9.4   Examine the concavity/convexity of the production function $Y = AK^a$, defined for all $K \geq 0$, where $A > 0$ and $a > 0$.

Solution: From Example 5.9.2, one has $Y'' = Aa(a - 1)K^{a-2}$.

If $a \in (0, 1)$, then the coefficient $Aa(a - 1) < 0$, so that $Y'' < 0$ for all $K > 0$. Hence, the function is concave. The graph of $Y = AK^a$ for $0 < a < 1$, is shown in Fig. 5.9.9.

On the other hand, if $a > 1$, then $Y'' > 0$ and Y is a convex function of K, as shown in Fig. 5.9.10.

Finally, if $a = 1$, then Y is linear, so it is both concave and convex.

EXAMPLE 5.9.5   Suppose that the two functions U and g are both increasing and concave, with $U' \geq 0$, $U'' \leq 0$, $g' \geq 0$, and $g'' \leq 0$. Prove that the composite function $f(x) = g(U(x))$ is also increasing and concave.

Solution: Using the chain rule yields

$$f'(x) = g'(U(x)) \cdot U'(x) \qquad (*)$$

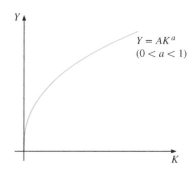

Figure 5.9.9 Concave production function   **Figure 5.9.10** Convex production function

Because g' and U' are both ≥ 0, so $f'(x) \geq 0$. Hence, f is increasing. In words: *an increasing transformation of an increasing function is increasing.*

In order to compute $f''(x)$, we must differentiate the product of the two functions $g'(U(x))$ and $U'(x)$. According to the chain rule, the derivative of $g'(U(x))$ is equal to $g''(U(x)) \cdot U'(x)$. Hence,

$$f''(x) = g''(U(x)) \cdot [U'(x)]^2 + g'(U(x)) \cdot U''(x) \qquad (**)$$

Because $g'' \leq 0$, $g' \geq 0$, and $U'' \leq 0$, it follows that $f''(x) \leq 0$. Again, in words: *an increasing concave transformation of a concave function is concave.*

Third and Higher Derivatives

If $y = f(x)$, the derivative of $y'' = f''(x)$ is called the *third derivative*, customarily denoted by $y''' = f'''(x)$. It is notationally cumbersome to continue using more and more primes to indicate repeated differentiation, so the *fourth derivative* is usually denoted by $y^{(4)} = f^{(4)}(x)$.[13] The same derivative can be expressed as d^4y/dx^4. In general, let

$$y^{(n)} = f^{(n)}(x) \quad \text{or} \quad \frac{d^n y}{dx^n}$$

denote the *n-th derivative* of f at x. The number n is called the *order* of the derivative. For example, $f^{(6)}(x_0)$ denotes the sixth derivative of f calculated at x_0, found by differentiating six times.

EXAMPLE 5.9.6   Compute all the derivatives up to and including order 4 of

$$f(x) = 3x^{-1} + 6x^3 - x^2$$

where $x \neq 0$.

Solution: Repeated differentiation gives

$$f'(x) = -3x^{-2} + 18x^2 - 2x, \qquad f''(x) = 6x^{-3} + 36x - 2$$
$$f'''(x) = -18x^{-4} + 36, \qquad f^{(4)}(x) = 72x^{-5}$$

---

[13] We put the number 4 in parentheses in order to avoid confusion with y^4, the fourth power of y.

EXERCISES FOR SECTION 5.9

1. Compute the second derivatives of:

    (a) $y = x^5 - 3x^4 + 2$ (b) $y = \sqrt{x}$ (c) $y = (1 + x^2)^{10}$

2. Find d^2y/dx^2 when $y = \sqrt{1 + x^2} = (1 + x^2)^{1/2}$.

3. Compute:

    (a) y'' for $y = 3x^3 + 2x - 1$ (b) Y''' for $Y = 1 - 2x^2 + 6x^3$

    (c) d^3z/dt^3 for $z = 120t - (1/3)t^3$ (d) $f^{(4)}(1)$ for $f(z) = 100z^{-4}$

4. Find $g''(2)$ when $g(t) = \dfrac{t^2}{t - 1}$.

5. Find formulas for y'' and y''' when $y = f(x)g(x)$.

6. Find d^2L/dt^2 when $L = 1/\sqrt{2t - 1}$.

7. If $u(y)$ denotes an individual's utility of having income (or consumption) y, then $R = -yu''(y)/u'(y)$ is the coefficient of *relative risk aversion*.[14] Compute R for the following utility functions, where A_1, A_2, and ρ are positive constants with $\rho \neq 1$, and we assume that $y > 0$:

    (a) $u(y) = A_1 y$ (b) $u(y) = \sqrt{y}$ (c) $u(y) = A_1 - A_2 y^{-2}$ (d) $u(y) = A_1 + A_2 \dfrac{y^{1-\rho}}{1 - \rho}$

8. Let $U(x) = \sqrt{x}$ and $g(u) = u^3$. Then $f(x) = g(U(x)) = x^{3/2}$, which is not a concave function. Why does this not contradict the conclusion in Example 5.9.5?

9. The US defence secretary claimed in 1985 that Congress had reduced the defence budget. Representative Gray pointed out that the budget had not been reduced; Congress had only reduced the rate of increase. If P denotes the size of the defence budget, translate the statements into statements about the signs of P' and P''.

10. Sentence in a newspaper: "The rate of increase of bank loans is increasing at an increasing rate". If $L(t)$ denotes total bank loans at time t, represent the sentence by a mathematical statement about the sign of an appropriate derivative of L.

5.10 Exponential Functions

Exponential functions were introduced in Section 3.9. They were shown to be well suited to describing certain economic phenomena such as growth and compound interest. In particular we introduced the *natural* exponential function $f(x) = e^x$, where $e \approx 2.71828$, as well as the alternative notation $\exp x$.

---

[14] By contrast, $R_A = -u''(y)/u'(y)$ is the coefficient of *absolute risk aversion*.

Now we explain why this particular exponential function deserves to be called "natural". Consider the Newton quotient of $f(x) = e^x$, which is

$$\frac{f(x+h) - f(x)}{h} = \frac{e^{x+h} - e^x}{h} \qquad (*)$$

If this fraction tends to a limit as h tends to 0, then $f(x) = e^x$ is differentiable and $f'(x)$ is precisely equal to this limit.

To simplify the right-hand side of $(*)$, we make use of the rule $e^{x+h} = e^x \cdot e^h$ to write $e^{x+h} - e^x$ as $e^x(e^h - 1)$. So $(*)$ can be rewritten as

$$\frac{f(x+h) - f(x)}{h} = e^x \cdot \frac{e^h - 1}{h}$$

We now evaluate the limit of the right-hand side as $h \to 0$. Note that e^x is a constant when we vary only h. As for $(e^h - 1)/h$, in Example 5.5.1 we argued that this fraction tends to 1 as h tends to 0, although in that example the variable was x and not h. It follows that

DERIVATIVE OF THE NATURAL EXPONENTIAL FUNCTION

$$f(x) = e^x \quad \Longrightarrow \quad f'(x) = e^x \qquad (5.10.1)$$

Thus the *natural exponential function $f(x) = e^x$ has the remarkable property that its derivative is equal to the function itself*. This is the main reason why the function appears so often in mathematics and applications. An implication of (5.10.1) is that $f''(x) = e^x$. Because $e^x > 0$ for all x, both $f'(x)$ and $f''(x)$ are positive. Hence, both f and f' are strictly increasing. This confirms the increasing convex shape indicated in Fig. 4.9.3.

Combining (5.10.1) with the other rules of differentiation, we can differentiate many expressions involving the exponential function e^x.

EXAMPLE 5.10.1   Find the first and second derivatives of:

(a) $y = x^3 + e^x$ (b) $y = x^5 e^x$ (c) $y = e^x/x$

Solution:

(a) We find that $y' = 3x^2 + e^x$ and $y'' = 6x + e^x$.

(b) By the product rule, $y' = 5x^4 e^x + x^5 e^x = x^4 e^x(5 + x)$. To find y'', differentiate $y' = 5x^4 e^x + x^5 e^x$ once more to obtain $y'' = 20x^3 e^x + 5x^4 e^x + 5x^4 e^x + x^5 e^x = x^3 e^x(x^2 + 10x + 20)$.

(c) The quotient rule yields

$$y = \frac{e^x}{x} \Rightarrow y' = \frac{e^x x - e^x \cdot 1}{x^2} = \frac{e^x(x-1)}{x^2}$$

Differentiating $y' = \dfrac{e^x x - e^x}{x^2}$ once more w.r.t. x gives

$$y'' = \frac{(e^x x + e^x - e^x)x^2 - (e^x x - e^x)2x}{(x^2)^2} = \frac{e^x(x^2 - 2x + 2)}{x^3}$$

Combining (5.10.1) with the chain rule (5.8.1) allows some rather complicated functions to be differentiated. First, note that $y = e^{g(x)}$ can be rewritten as $y = e^u$, where $u = g(x)$. Then $y' = e^u \cdot u'$ and $u' = g'(x)$, so that:

$$y = e^{g(x)} \implies y' = e^{g(x)} g'(x) \tag{5.10.2}$$

EXAMPLE 5.10.2   Differentiate the functions:

(a) $y = e^{-x}$ (b) $y = x^p e^{ax}$, where p and a are constants   (c) $y = \sqrt{e^{2x} + x}$

Solution:

(a) Direct use of (5.10.2) gives $y = e^{-x} \Rightarrow y' = e^{-x} \cdot (-1) = -e^{-x}$. This derivative is always negative, so the function is strictly decreasing. Furthermore, $y'' = e^{-x} > 0$, so the function is convex. This, again, agrees with the graph shown in Fig. 4.9.3.

(b) By the chain rule, the derivative of e^{ax} is ae^{ax}. Hence, using the product rule,

$$y' = px^{p-1} e^{ax} + x^p a e^{ax} = x^{p-1} e^{ax}(p + ax)$$

(c) Let $y = \sqrt{e^{2x} + x} = \sqrt{u}$, with $u = e^{2x} + x$. Then $u' = 2e^{2x} + 1$, where we used the chain rule. Using the chain rule again with $v = e^{2x} + x$, we obtain

$$y = \sqrt{e^{2x} + x} = \sqrt{v} \Rightarrow y' = \frac{1}{2\sqrt{v}} \cdot v' = \frac{2e^{2x} + 1}{2\sqrt{e^{2x} + x}}$$

EXAMPLE 5.10.3   For each of the following functions, find the intervals where they are increasing:

(a) $y = \dfrac{e^x}{x}$ (b) $y = x^4 e^{-2x}$ (c) $y = xe^{-\sqrt{x}}$

Solution:

(a) According to part (c) of Example 5.10.1, $y' = e^x(x - 1)/x^2$, so $y' \geq 0$ if and only if $x \geq 1$. Thus y is increasing in $[1, \infty)$.

(b) According to part (b) of Example 5.10.2, with $p = 4$ and $a = -2$, we have $y' = x^3 e^{-2x}(4 - 2x)$. A sign diagram reveals that y is increasing in $[0, 2]$.

(c) The function is only defined for $x \geq 0$. Using the chain rule, for $x > 0$ the derivative of $e^{-\sqrt{x}}$ is $-e^{-\sqrt{x}}/2\sqrt{x}$, so by the product rule, the derivative of $y = xe^{-\sqrt{x}}$ is

$$y' = 1 \cdot e^{-\sqrt{x}} - \frac{xe^{-\sqrt{x}}}{2\sqrt{x}} = e^{-\sqrt{x}}\left(1 - \frac{1}{2}\sqrt{x}\right)$$

where we have used the fact that $x/\sqrt{x} = \sqrt{x}$. It follows that y is increasing when $x > 0$ and $1 - \frac{1}{2}\sqrt{x} \geq 0$. Because $y = 0$ when $x = 0$ and $y > 0$ when $x > 0$, it follows that y is increasing in $[0, 4]$.

A common error when differentiating exponential functions is to believe that the derivative of e^x w.r.t x is "xe^{x-1}". Actually, this is the derivative of e^x w.r.t e. The exponential function e^x of x has been confused with the power function e^x of e!

SURVEY OF THE PROPERTIES OF THE NATURAL EXPONENTIAL FUNCTION

The natural exponential function

$$f(x) = \exp(x) = e^x \; (e = 2.71828\ldots)$$

is differentiable, strictly increasing and convex. In fact,

$$f(x) = e^x \Rightarrow f'(x) = f(x) = e^x$$

The following properties hold for all exponents s and t:

$$e^s e^t = e^{s+t}, \; e^s/e^t = e^{s-t} \; \text{and} \; (e^s)^t = e^{st}$$

Moreover,

$$\lim_{x \to -\infty} e^x = 0 \; \text{and} \; \lim_{x \to \infty} e^x = \infty$$

Differentiating Other Exponential Functions

So far we have considered only the derivative of e^x, where $e = 2.71828\ldots$. How can we differentiate $y = a^x$, where a is any other positive number? According to definition (3.10.1), we have $a = e^{\ln a}$. So, using the general property $(e^r)^s = e^{rs}$, we have the formula

$$a^x = \left(e^{\ln a}\right)^x = e^{(\ln a)x}$$

This shows that in functions involving the expression a^x, we can just as easily work with the special exponential function e^{bx}, where b is a constant equal to $\ln a$. In particular, we can differentiate a^x by differentiating $e^{x \ln a}$. According to (5.10.2), with $g(x) = (\ln a)x$, we have

$$y = a^x \Rightarrow y' = a^x \ln a \qquad\qquad (5.10.3)$$

EXAMPLE 5.10.4   Find the derivatives of: (a) $f(x) = 10^{-x}$; and (b) $g(x) = x2^{3x}$.

Solution:

(a) Rewrite $f(x) = 10^{-x} = 10^u$, where $u = -x$. Using (5.10.3) and the chain rule gives
$f'(x) = -10^{-x} \ln 10$.

(b) Rewrite $y = 2^{3x} = 2^u$, where $u = 3x$. By (5.10.3) and the chain rule,

$$y' = (2^u \ln 2)u' = (2^{3x} \ln 2) \cdot 3 = 3 \cdot 2^{3x} \ln 2$$

Finally, using the product rule we obtain

$$g'(x) = 1 \cdot 2^{3x} + x \cdot 3 \cdot 2^{3x} \ln 2 = 2^{3x}(1 + 3x \ln 2)$$

EXERCISES FOR SECTION 5.10

1. Find the first-order derivatives of:

(a) $y = e^x + x^2$ (b) $y = 5e^x - 3x^3 + 8$ (c) $y = \dfrac{x}{e^x}$ (d) $y = \dfrac{x + x^2}{e^x + 1}$

(e) $y = -x - 5 - e^x$ (f) $y = x^3 e^x$ (g) $y = e^x x^{-2}$ (h) $y = (x + e^x)^2$

2. Find the first derivatives w.r.t. t of the following functions, where a, b, c, p, and q are constants:

(a) $x = (a + bt + ct^2)e^t$ (b) $x = \dfrac{p + qt^3}{te^t}$ (c) $x = \dfrac{(at + bt^2)^2}{e^t}$

3. Find the first and second derivatives of:

(a) $y = e^{-3x}$ (b) $y = 2e^{x^3}$ (c) $y = e^{1/x}$ (d) $y = 5e^{2x^2 - 3x + 1}$

(SM) **4.** Find the intervals where the following functions are increasing:

(a) $y = x^3 + e^{2x}$ (b) $y = 5x^2 e^{-4x}$ (c) $y = x^2 e^{-x^2}$

5. Find the intervals where the following functions are increasing:

(a) $y = x^2 / e^{2x}$ (b) $y = e^x - e^{3x}$ (c) $y = \dfrac{e^{2x}}{x + 2}$

6. Find:

(a) $\dfrac{d}{dx}\left(e^{(e^x)}\right)$ (b) $\dfrac{d}{dt}\left(e^{t/2} + e^{-t/2}\right)$ (c) $\dfrac{d}{dt}\left(\dfrac{1}{e^t + e^{-t}}\right)$ (d) $\dfrac{d}{dz}\left(e^{z^3} - 1\right)^{1/3}$

7. Differentiate:

(a) $y = 5^x$ (b) $y = x2^x$ (c) $y = x^2 2^{x^2}$ (d) $y = e^x 10^x$

5.11 Logarithmic Functions

In Section 3.10 we introduced the natural logarithmic function, $g(x) = \ln x$. It is defined for all $x > 0$ and has the graph shown in Fig. 4.10.2.

This function has $f(x) = e^x$ as its *inverse*. If we *assume* that $g(x) = \ln x$ has a derivative for all $x > 0$, we can easily find that derivative. To do so, we differentiate w.r.t x the equation defining $g(x) = \ln x$, which is

$$e^{g(x)} = x \qquad\qquad (*)$$

Using (5.10.2) to differentiate each side of $(*)$, we obtain $e^{g(x)} g'(x) = 1$. Since $e^{g(x)} = x$, this implies $xg'(x) = 1$, and thus the derivative of $\ln x$ at x is simply the number $1/x$.

DERIVATIVE OF THE NATURAL LOGARITHMIC FUNCTION

$$g(x) = \ln x \Rightarrow g'(x) = \frac{1}{x} \qquad (5.11.1)$$

For $x > 0$, we have $g'(x) > 0$, so that $g(x)$ is *strictly* increasing. Note moreover that $g''(x) = -1/x^2$, which is less than 0 for all $x > 0$, so that $g(x)$ is concave. This confirms the shape of the graph in Fig. 4.10.2. In fact, the growth of $\ln x$ is quite slow: for example, $\ln x$ does not attain the value 10 until $x > 22\,026$, because $\ln x = 10$ gives $x = e^{10} \approx 22\,026.5$.

EXAMPLE 5.11.1   Compute y' and y'' when:

(a) $y = x^3 + \ln x$ (b) $y = x^2 \ln x$ (c) $y = \ln x / x$

Solution:

(a) We find easily that $y' = 3x^2 + 1/x$. Furthermore, $y'' = 6x - 1/x^2$.

(b) The product rule gives $y' = 2x \ln x + x^2(1/x) = 2x \ln x + x$. Differentiating the last expression w.r.t. x gives $y'' = 2 \ln x + 2x(1/x) + 1 = 2 \ln x + 3$.

(c) Here we use the quotient rule:

$$y' = \frac{(1/x)x - (\ln x) \cdot 1}{x^2} = \frac{1 - \ln x}{x^2}$$

Differentiating again yields

$$y'' = \frac{-(1/x)x^2 - (1 - \ln x)2x}{(x^2)^2} = \frac{2 \ln x - 3}{x^3}$$

Often, we need to consider composite functions involving natural logarithms. Because $\ln u$ is defined only when $u > 0$, a composite function of the form $y = \ln h(x)$ will only be defined for values of x satisfying $h(x) > 0$.

Combining the rule for differentiating $\ln x$ with the chain rule allows us to differentiate many different types of function. Suppose, for instance, that $y = \ln h(x)$, where $h(x)$ is differentiable and positive. By the chain rule, $y = \ln u$ with $u = h(x)$ implies that $y' = (1/u)u' = (1/h(x)) h'(x)$, so:

$$y = \ln h(x) \Rightarrow y' = \frac{h'(x)}{h(x)} \qquad (5.11.2)$$

Note that if $N(t)$ is a function of t, then the derivative of its natural logarithm

$$\frac{\mathrm{d}}{\mathrm{d}t} \ln N(t) = \frac{1}{N(t)} \frac{\mathrm{d}N(t)}{\mathrm{d}t} = \frac{\dot{N}(t)}{N(t)}$$

is the relative rate of growth of $N(t)$.

EXAMPLE 5.11.2   Find the domains of the following functions and compute their derivatives:

(a) $y = \ln(1 - x)$ (b) $y = \ln(4 - x^2)$ (c) $y = \ln\left(\dfrac{x-1}{x+1}\right) - \dfrac{1}{4}x$

Solution:

(a) $\ln(1 - x)$ is defined if $1 - x > 0$, that is if $x < 1$. To find its derivative, we use (5.11.2), with $h(x) = 1 - x$. Then $h'(x) = -1$, and

$$y' = \frac{-1}{1-x} = \frac{1}{x-1}$$

(b) $\ln(4 - x^2)$ is defined if $4 - x^2 > 0$, that is if $(2 - x)(2 + x) > 0$. This is satisfied if and only if $-2 < x < 2$. Formula (5.11.2) gives

$$y' = \frac{-2x}{4 - x^2} = \frac{2x}{x^2 - 4}$$

(c) We can write $y = \ln u - \frac{1}{4}x$, where $u = (x - 1)/(x + 1)$. For the function to be defined, we require that $u > 0$. A sign diagram shows that this is satisfied if $x < -1$ or $x > 1$. Using (5.11.2), we obtain

$$y' = \frac{u'}{u} - \frac{1}{4}$$

where

$$u' = \frac{1 \cdot (x + 1) - 1 \cdot (x - 1)}{(x + 1)^2} = \frac{2}{(x + 1)^2}$$

So

$$y' = \frac{2(x + 1)}{(x + 1)^2(x - 1)} - \frac{1}{4} = \frac{9 - x^2}{4(x^2 - 1)} = \frac{(3 - x)(3 + x)}{4(x - 1)(x + 1)}$$

EXAMPLE 5.11.3   Find the intervals where the following functions are increasing:

(a) $y = x^2 \ln x$ (b) $y = 4x - 5\ln(x^2 + 1)$ (c) $y = 3\ln(1 + x) + x - \frac{1}{2}x^2$

Solution:

(a) The function is defined for $x > 0$, and

$$y' = 2x \ln x + x^2(1/x) = x(2 \ln x + 1)$$

Hence, $y' \geq 0$ when $\ln x \geq -1/2$, that is, when $x \geq e^{-1/2}$. That is, y is increasing in the interval $[e^{-1/2}, \infty)$.

(b) We find that

$$y' = 4 - \frac{10x}{x^2 + 1} = 4(x - 2)\left(x - \frac{1}{2}\right)x^2 + 1$$

A sign diagram reveals that y is increasing in each of the intervals $(-\infty, \frac{1}{2}]$ and $[2, \infty)$.

(c) The function is defined for $x > -1$, and

$$y' = \frac{3}{1+x} + 1 - x = \frac{(2-x)(2+x)}{x+1}$$

A sign diagram reveals that y is increasing in $(-1, 2]$.

SURVEY OF THE PROPERTIES OF THE NATURAL LOGARITHMIC FUNCTION

The natural logarithmic function

$$g(x) = \ln x$$

is differentiable, strictly increasing and concave in $(0, \infty)$. In fact,

$$g'(x) = 1/x, \quad g''(x) = -1/x^2$$

By definition, $e^{\ln x} = x$ for all $x > 0$, and $\ln e^x = x$ for all x. The following properties hold for all $x > 0$, $y > 0$:

$$\ln(xy) = \ln x + \ln y, \ \ln(x/y) = \ln x - \ln y, \ \text{and} \ \ln x^p = p \ln x$$

Moreover,

$$\ln x \to -\infty \ \text{as} \ x \to 0 \ \text{from the right}$$

while

$$\ln x \to +\infty \ \text{as} \ x \to +\infty$$

Logarithmic Differentiation

When differentiating an expression containing products, quotients, roots, powers, and combinations of these, it is often an advantage to use *logarithmic differentiation*. The method is illustrated by two examples:

EXAMPLE 5.11.4   Find the derivative of $y = x^x$ defined for all $x > 0$.

Solution: The power rule of differentiation, $y = x^a \Rightarrow y' = ax^{a-1}$, requires the exponent a to be a constant, while the rule $y = a^x \Rightarrow y' = a^x \ln a$ requires that the base a is constant. In the expression x^x both the exponent and the base vary with x, so neither of the two rules can be used.

Begin by taking the natural logarithm of each side, $\ln y = x \ln x$. Differentiating w.r.t x gives $y'/y = 1 \cdot \ln x + x(1/x) = \ln x + 1$. Multiplying by $y = x^x$ gives us the result:

$$y = x^x \Rightarrow y' = x^x(\ln x + 1)$$

EXAMPLE 5.11.5   Find the derivative of $y = [A(x)]^\alpha [B(x)]^\beta [C(x)]^\gamma$, where α, β, and γ are constants and A, B, and C are positive functions.

Solution: First, take the natural logarithm of each side to obtain

$$\ln y = \alpha \ln(A(x)) + \beta \ln(B(x)) + \gamma \ln(C(x))$$

Differentiation w.r.t. x yields

$$\frac{y'}{y} = \alpha \frac{A'(x)}{A(x)} + \beta \frac{B'(x)}{B(x)} + \gamma \frac{C'(x)}{C(x)}$$

Multiplying by y, we have

$$y' = \left[\alpha \frac{A'(x)}{A(x)} + \beta \frac{B'(x)}{B(x)} + \gamma \frac{C'(x)}{C(x)} \right] [A(x)]^\alpha [B(x)]^\beta [C(x)]^\gamma$$

In Eq. (3.10.5), we showed that the logarithm of x in the system with base a, denoted by $\log_a x$, satisfies $\log_a x = (1/\ln a) \ln x$. Differentiating each side w.r.t x, it follows immediately that:

$$y = \log_a x \Rightarrow y' = \frac{1}{\ln a} \frac{1}{x} \tag{5.11.3}$$

Approximating the Number e

If $g(x) = \ln x$, then $g'(x) = 1/x$, and, in particular, $g'(1) = 1$. We use in turn: (i) the definition of $g'(1)$; (ii) the fact that $\ln 1 = 0$; (iii) the rule $\ln x^p = p \ln x$. The result is

$$1 = g'(1) = \lim_{h \to 0} \frac{\ln(1+h) - \ln 1}{h} = \lim_{h \to 0} \frac{1}{h} \ln(1+h) = \lim_{h \to 0} \ln(1+h)^{1/h}$$

Because $\ln(1+h)^{1/h}$ tends to 1 as h tends to 0 and the exponential mapping is continuous, it follows that $(1+h)^{1/h} = \exp\left[\ln(1+h)^{1/h}\right]$ itself must tend to $\exp 1 = e$. That is,

$$e = \lim_{h \to 0} (1+h)^{1/h} \tag{5.11.4}$$

To illustrate this limit, Table 5.3 gives some function values that were computed using a calculator. These numbers seem to confirm that the decimal expansion 2.718281828 ... we gave for e starts out correctly. Of course, this by no means proves that the limit exists, but it does suggest that closer and closer approximations to e can be obtained by choosing h smaller and smaller.[15]

Table 5.3 Values of $(1+h)^{1/h}$ when h gets smaller and smaller

h	1	1/2	1/10	1/1000	1/100 000	1/1 000 000
$(1+h)^{1/h}$	2	2.25	2.5937 ...	2.7169 ...	2.71825 ...	2.718281828 ...

---

[15] A better way to approximate e^x, for general real x, is suggested in Examples 7.5.4 and 7.6.2.

Power Functions

In Section 5.6 we claimed that, for all real numbers a,

$$f(x) = x^a \Rightarrow f'(x) = ax^{a-1} \qquad\qquad (*)$$

This important rule has only been established for certain special values of a, particularly the rational numbers. Because $x = e^{\ln x}$, we have $x^a = (e^{\ln x})^a = e^{a \ln x}$. Using the chain rule, we obtain

$$\frac{d}{dx}(x^a) = \frac{d}{dx}(e^{a \ln x}) = e^{a \ln x} \cdot \frac{a}{x} = x^a \frac{a}{x} = ax^{a-1}$$

This justifies using the same power rule even when a is an irrational number.

EXERCISES FOR SECTION 5.11

1. Compute the first and second derivatives of:

  (a) $y = \ln x + 3x - 2$ (b) $y = x^2 - 2 \ln x$ (c) $y = x^3 \ln x$ (d) $y = \dfrac{\ln x}{x}$

2. Find the derivatives of:

  (a) $y = x^3 (\ln x)^2$ (b) $y = \dfrac{x^2}{\ln x}$ (c) $y = (\ln x)^{10}$ (d) $y = (\ln x + 3x)^2$

SM **3.** Find the derivatives of:

  (a) $\ln(\ln x)$ (b) $\ln \sqrt{1 - x^2}$ (c) $e^x \ln x$ (d) $e^{x^3} \ln x^2$

  (e) $\ln(e^x + 1)$ (f) $\ln(x^2 + 3x - 1)$ (g) $2(e^x - 1)^{-1}$ (h) $e^{2x^2 - x}$

4. Determine the domains of the functions defined by:

  (a) $y = \ln(x + 1)$ (b) $y = \ln\left(\dfrac{3x - 1}{1 - x}\right)$ (c) $y = \ln |x|$

SM **5.** Determine the domains of the functions defined by:

  (a) $y = \ln(x^2 - 1)$ (b) $y = \ln(\ln x)$ (c) $y = \dfrac{1}{\ln(\ln x) - 1}$

SM **6.** Find the intervals where the following functions are increasing:

  (a) $y = \ln(4 - x^2)$ (b) $y = x^3 \ln x$ (c) $y = \dfrac{(1 - \ln x)^2}{2x}$

7. Find the equation for the tangent to the graph of

  (a) $y = \ln x$ at the three points with x-coordinates: 1, $\frac{1}{2}$, and e;

  (b) $y = xe^x$ at the three points with x-coordinates: 0, 1, and -2.

8. Use logarithmic differentiation to find $f'(x)/f(x)$ when:

  (a) $f(x) = x^{2x}$ (b) $f(x) = \sqrt{x - 2}(x^2 + 1)(x^4 + 6)$ (c) $f(x) = \left(\dfrac{x + 1}{x - 1}\right)^{1/3}$

(SM) **9.** Differentiate the following functions using logarithmic differentiation:

(a) $y = (2x)^x$ (b) $y = x^{\sqrt{x}}$ (c) $y = \left(\sqrt{x}\right)^x$

10. Prove that if u and v are differentiable functions of x, and $u > 0$, then

$$y = u^v \Rightarrow y' = u^v \left(v' \ln u + \frac{vu'}{u} \right)$$

(SM) **11.** [HARDER] If $f(x) = e^x - 1 - x$, then $f'(x) = e^x - 1 > 0$ for all $x > 0$. The function $f(x)$ is there-fore strictly increasing in the interval $[0, \infty)$. Since $f(0) = 0$, it follows that $f(x) > 0$ for all $x > 0$, and so $e^x > 1 + x$ for all $x > 0$. Use the same method to prove the following inequalities:

(a) $e^x > 1 + x + x^2/2$ for $x > 0$ (b) $\frac{1}{2}x < \ln(1 + x) < x$ for $0 < x < 1$

(c) $\ln x < 2(\sqrt{x} - 1)$ for $x > 1$

REVIEW EXERCISES

1. Let $f(x) = x^2 - x + 2$. Show that $[f(x + h) - f(x)]/h = 2x - 1 + h$, and use this result to find $f'(x)$.

2. Let $f(x) = -2x^3 + x^2$. Compute $[f(x + h) - f(x)]/h$, and find $f'(x)$.

3. Compute the first- and second-order derivatives of the following functions:

(a) $y = 2x - 5$ (b) $y = \frac{1}{3}x^9$ (c) $y = 1 - \frac{1}{10}x^{10}$ (d) $y = 3x^7 + 8$

(e) $y = \dfrac{x - 5}{10}$ (f) $y = x^5 - x^{-5}$ (g) $y = \frac{1}{4}x^4 + \frac{1}{3}x^3 + \frac{1}{2}5^2$ (h) $y = \dfrac{1}{x} + \dfrac{1}{x^3}$

4. Let $C(Q)$ denote the cost of producing Q units per month of a commodity. What is the interpretation of $C'(1000) = 25$? Suppose the price obtained per unit is fixed at 30 and that the current output per month is 1000. Is it profitable to increase production?

5. For each of the following functions, find the equation for the tangent to the graph at the specified point:

(a) $y = -3x^2$ at $x = 1$ (b) $y = \sqrt{x} - x^2$ at $x = 4$ (c) $y = \dfrac{x^2 - x^3}{x + 3}$ at $x = 1$

6. Let $A(x)$ denote the dollar cost of building a house with a floor area of x square metres. What is the interpretation of $A'(100) = 250$?

7. Differentiate the following functions:

(a) $f(x) = x(x^2 + 1)$ (b) $g(w) = w^{-5}$ (c) $h(y) = y(y - 1)(y + 1)$

(d) $G(t) = \dfrac{2t + 1}{t^2 + 3}$ (e) $\varphi(\xi) = \dfrac{2\xi}{\xi^2 + 2}$ (f) $F(s) = \dfrac{s}{s^2 + s - 2}$

8. Find the derivatives:

   (a) $\dfrac{d}{da}(a^2 t - t^2)$ (b) $\dfrac{d}{dt}(a^2 t - t^2)$ (c) $\dfrac{d}{d\varphi}\left(x\varphi^2 - \sqrt{\varphi}\right)$

9. Use the chain rule to find dy/dx for the following:

   (a) $y = 10u^2$ where $u = 5 - x^2$ (b) $y = \sqrt{u}$ where $u = \dfrac{1}{x} - 1$

10. Compute the following:

    (a) dZ/dt when $Z = (u^2 - 1)^3$ and $u = t^3$ (b) dK/dt when $K = \sqrt{L}$ and $L = 1 + 1/t$

11. If $a(t)$ and $b(t)$ are positive valued differentiable functions of t, and if A, α, and β are constants, find expressions for $\dot{x}/x$ where:

    (a) $x = a(t)^2 \cdot b(t)$ (b) $x = A \cdot a(t)^\alpha \cdot b(t)^\beta$ (c) $x = A \cdot [a(t)^\alpha + b(t)^\beta]^{\alpha+\beta}$

12. If $R = S^\alpha$, $S = 1 + \beta K^\gamma$, and $K = At^p + B$, find an expression for dR/dt.

13. Find the derivatives of the following functions, where a, b, p, and q are constants:

    (a) $h(L) = (L^a + b)^p$ (b) $C(Q) = aQ + bQ^2$ (c) $P(x) = \left(ax^{1/q} + b\right)^q$

14. Find the first derivatives of:

    (a) $y = -7e^x$ (b) $y = e^{-3x^2}$ (c) $y = \dfrac{x^2}{e^x}$ (d) $y = e^x \ln(x^2 + 2)$

    (e) $y = e^{5x^3}$ (f) $y = 2 - x^4 e^{-x}$ (g) $y = (e^x + x^2)^{10}$ (h) $y = \ln\left(\sqrt{x} + 1\right)$

(SM) 15. Find the intervals where the following functions are increasing:

    (a) $y = (\ln x)^2 - 4$ (b) $y = \ln(e^x + e^{-x})$ (c) $y = x - \frac{3}{2}\ln(x^2 + 2)$

16. (a) Suppose $\pi(Q) = QP(Q) - cQ$, where P is a differentiable function and c is a constant. Find an expression for $d\pi/dQ$.

    (b) Suppose $\pi(L) = PF(L) - wL$, where F is a differentiable function and P and w are constants. Find an expression for $d\pi/dL$.

SECTION 5.3
Marginal functions

Objectives

At the end of this section you should be able to:

- Calculate marginal revenue and marginal cost.
- Derive the relationship between marginal and average revenue for both a monopoly and perfect competition.
- Calculate marginal product of labour.
- State the law of diminishing marginal productivity using the notation of calculus.
- Calculate marginal propensity to consume and marginal propensity to save.

At this stage you may be wondering what on earth differentiation has to do with economics. In fact, we cannot get very far with economic theory without making use of calculus. In this section we concentrate on three main areas that illustrate its applicability:

- revenue and cost;
- production;
- consumption and savings.

We consider each of these in turn.

5.3.1 Revenue and cost

In Chapter 2 we investigated the basic properties of the revenue function, TR. It is defined to be PQ, where P denotes the price of a good and Q denotes the quantity demanded. In practice, we usually know the demand function, which provides a relationship between P and Q. This enables a formula for TR to be written down solely in terms of Q. For example, if

$$P = 100 - 2Q$$

then

$$\text{TR} = PQ = (100 - 2Q)Q = 100Q - 2Q^2$$

The formula can be used to calculate the value of TR corresponding to any value of Q. Not content with this, we are also interested in the effect on TR of a change in the value of Q from some existing level. To do this we introduce the concept of marginal revenue. The **marginal revenue**, MR, of a good is defined by

$$\text{MR} = \frac{d(\text{TR})}{dQ}$$

marginal revenue is the derivative of total revenue with respect to demand

For example, the marginal revenue function corresponding to

$$TR = 100Q - 2Q^2$$

is given by

$$\frac{d(TR)}{dQ} = 100 - 4Q$$

If the current demand is 15, say, then

$$MR = 100 - 4(15) = 40$$

You may be familiar with an alternative definition often quoted in elementary economics textbooks. Marginal revenue is sometimes taken to be the change in TR brought about by a 1 unit increase in Q. It is easy to check that this gives an acceptable approximation to MR, although it is not quite the same as the exact value obtained by differentiation. For example, substituting $Q = 15$ into the total revenue function considered previously gives

$$TR = 100(15) - 2(15)^2 = 1050$$

An increase of 1 unit in the value of Q produces a total revenue

$$TR = 100(16) - 2(16)^2 = 1088$$

This is an increase of 38, which, according to the non-calculus definition, is the value of MR when Q is 15. This compares with the exact value of 40 obtained by differentiation.

It is instructive to give a graphical interpretation of these two approaches. In Figure 5.12 the point A lies on the TR curve corresponding to a quantity Q_0. The exact value of MR at this point is equal to the derivative

$$\frac{d(TR)}{dQ}$$

and so is given by the slope of the tangent at A. The point B also lies on the curve but corresponds to a 1-unit increase in Q. The vertical distance from A to B therefore equals the change in TR when Q increases by 1 unit. The slope of the line joining A and B (known as a **chord**) is

$$\frac{\Delta(TR)}{\Delta Q} = \frac{\Delta(TR)}{1} = \Delta(TR)$$

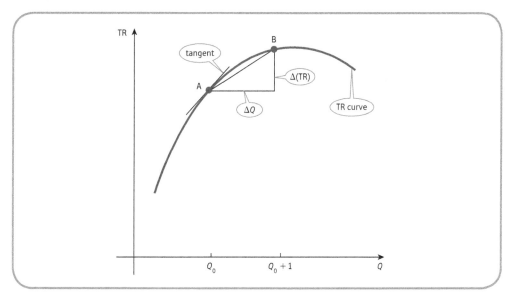

Figure 5.12

In other words, the slope of the chord is equal to the value of MR obtained from the non-calculus definition. Inspection of the diagram reveals that the slope of the tangent is approximately the same as that of the chord joining A and B. In this case the slope of the tangent is slightly the larger of the two, but there is not much in it. We therefore see that the 1-unit-increase approach produces a reasonable approximation to the exact value of MR given by

$$\frac{d(TR)}{dQ}$$

Practice Problem

1. If the demand function is

    $$P = 60 - Q$$

    find an expression for TR in terms of Q.

    (1) Differentiate TR with respect to Q to find a general expression for MR in terms of Q. Hence write down the exact value of MR at $Q = 50$.

    (2) Calculate the value of TR when

    (a) $Q = 50$ **(b)** $Q = 51$

    and hence confirm that the 1-unit-increase approach gives a reasonable approximation to the exact value of MR obtained in part (1).

The approximation indicated by Figure 5.12 holds for any value of ΔQ. The slope of the tangent at A is the marginal revenue, MR. The slope of the chord joining A and B is $\Delta(TR)/\Delta Q$. It follows that

$$MR \cong \frac{\Delta(TR)}{\Delta Q}$$

This equation can be transposed to give

$$\Delta(TR) \cong MR \times \Delta Q \qquad \left(\begin{array}{c}\text{multiply both}\\\text{sides by } \Delta Q\end{array}\right)$$

that is,

change in total revenue $\cong$ marginal revenue $\times$ change in demand

Moreover, Figure 5.12 shows that the smaller the value of ΔQ, the better the approximation becomes.

> ## Example
>
> If the total revenue function of a good is given by
>
> $$100Q - Q^2$$
>
> write down an expression for the marginal revenue function. If the current demand is 60, estimate the change in the value of TR due to a 2-unit increase in Q.
>
> ### Solution
>
> If
>
> $$\text{TR} = 100Q - Q^2$$
>
> then
>
> $$\text{MR} = \frac{d(\text{TR})}{dQ}$$
> $$= 100 - 2Q$$
>
> When $Q = 60$
>
> $$\text{MR} = 100 - 2(60) = -20$$
>
> If Q increases by 2 units, $\Delta Q = 2$ and the formula
>
> $$\Delta(\text{TR}) \cong \text{MR} \times \Delta Q$$
>
> shows that the change in total revenue is approximately
>
> $$(-20) \times 2 = -40$$
>
> A 2-unit increase in Q therefore leads to a decrease in TR of about 40.

> ## Practice Problem
>
> 2. If the total revenue function of a good is given by
>
> $$1000Q - 4Q^2$$
>
>   write down an expression for the marginal revenue function. If the current demand is 30, find the approximate change in the value of TR due to a
>
>   (a) 3-unit increase in Q;
>
>   (b) 2-unit decrease in Q.

The simple model of demand assumed that price, P, and quantity, Q, are linearly related according to an equation,

$$P = aQ + b$$

where the slope, a, is negative and the intercept, b, is positive. A downward-sloping demand curve such as this corresponds to the case of a **monopolist**. A single firm, or possibly a group

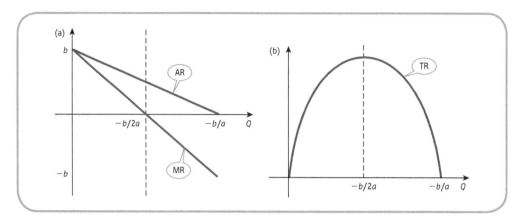

Figure 5.13

of firms forming a cartel, is assumed to be the only supplier of a particular product and so has control over the market price. As the firm raises the price, so demand falls. The associated total revenue function is given by

$$TR = PQ$$
$$= (aQ + b)Q$$
$$= aQ^2 + bQ$$

An expression for marginal revenue is obtained by differentiating TR with respect to Q to get

$$MR = 2aQ + b$$

It is interesting to notice that, on the assumption of a linear demand equation, the marginal revenue is also linear with the same intercept, b, but with slope $2a$. The marginal revenue curve slopes downhill exactly twice as fast as the demand curve. This is illustrated in Figure 5.13(a).

The **average revenue**, AR, is defined by

$$AR = \frac{TR}{Q}$$

and, since $TR = PQ$, we have

$$AR = \frac{PQ}{Q} = P$$

For this reason the demand curve is labelled average revenue in Figure 5.13(a). The above derivation of the result $AR = P$ is independent of the particular demand function. Consequently, the terms 'average revenue curve' and 'demand curve' are synonymous.

Figure 5.13(a) shows that the marginal revenue takes both positive and negative values. This is to be expected. The total revenue function is a quadratic, and its graph has the familiar parabolic shape indicated in Figure 5.13(b). To the left of $-b/2a$ the graph is uphill, corresponding to a positive value of marginal revenue, whereas to the right of this point it is downhill, giving a negative value of marginal revenue. More significantly, at the maximum point of the TR curve, the tangent is horizontal with zero slope, and so MR is zero.

At the other extreme from a monopolist is the case of **perfect competition**. For this model we assume that there are a large number of firms all selling an identical product and that

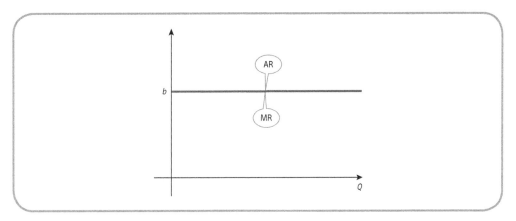

F igure 5.14

there are no barriers to entry into the industry. Since any individual firm produces a tiny proportion of the total output, it has no control over price. The firm can sell only at the prevailing market price and, because the firm is relatively small, it can sell any number of goods at this price. If the fixed price is denoted by b, then the demand function is

$P = b$

and the associated total revenue function is

$\text{TR} = PQ = bQ$

An expression for marginal revenue is obtained by differentiating TR with respect to Q and, since b is just a constant, we see that

$\text{MR} = b$

In the case of perfect competition, the average and marginal revenue curves are the same. They are horizontal straight lines, b units above the Q axis, as shown in Figure 5.14.

So far we have concentrated on the total revenue function. Exactly the same principle can be used for other economic functions. For instance, we define the **marginal cost**, MC, by

$$\text{MC} = \frac{d(\text{TC})}{dQ}$$

marginal cost is the derivative of total cost with respect to output

Again, using a simple geometrical argument, it is easy to see that if Q changes by a small amount ΔQ, then the corresponding change in TC is given by

$\Delta(\text{TC}) \cong \text{MC} \times \Delta Q$

change in total cost $\cong$ marginal cost $\times$ change in output

In particular, putting $\Delta Q = 1$ gives

$\Delta(\text{TC}) \cong \text{MC}$

so that MC gives the approximate change in TC when Q increases by 1 unit.

Example

If the average cost function of a good is

$$AC = 2Q + 6 + \frac{13}{Q}$$

find an expression for MC. If the current output is 15, estimate the effect on TC of a 3-unit decrease in Q.

Solution

We first need to find an expression for TC using the given formula for AC. Now we know that the average cost is just the total cost divided by Q: that is,

$$AC = \frac{TC}{Q}$$

Hence

$$TC = (AC)Q$$

$$= \left(2Q + 6 + \frac{13}{Q} \right)Q$$

and, after multiplying out the brackets, we get

$$TC = 2Q^2 + 6Q + 13$$

In this formula the last term, 13, is independent of Q and so must denote the fixed costs. The remaining part, $2Q^2 + 6Q$, depends on Q and so represents the total variable costs. Differentiating gives

$$MC = \frac{d(TC)}{dQ}$$

$$= 4Q + 6$$

Notice that because the fixed costs are constant, they differentiate to zero and so have no effect on the marginal cost. When $Q = 15$,

$$MC = 4(15) + 6 = 66$$

Also, if Q decreases by 2 units, then $\Delta Q = -2$. Hence the change in TC is given by

$$\Delta(TC) \cong MC \times \Delta Q = 66 \times (-2) = -132$$

so TC decreases by 132 units approximately.

Practice Problem

3. Find the marginal cost given the average cost function

$$AC = \frac{100}{Q} + 2$$

Deduce that a 1-unit increase in Q will always result in a 2-unit increase in TC, irrespective of the current level of output.

5.3.2 Production

Production functions were introduced in Section 2.3. In the simplest case output, Q, is assumed to be a function of labour, L, and capital, K. Moreover, in the short run the input K can be assumed to be fixed, so Q is then only a function of one input L. (This is not a valid assumption in the long run, and in general, Q must be regarded as a function of at least two inputs. The variable L is usually measured in terms of the number of workers or possibly in terms of the number of worker hours. Motivated by our previous work, we define the **marginal product of labour**, MP_L, by

$$MP_L = \frac{dQ}{dL}$$

marginal product of labour is the derivative of output with respect to labour

As before, this gives the approximate change in Q that results from using 1 more unit of L.

It is instructive to work out numerical values of MP_L for the particular production function

$$Q = 300L^{1/2} - 4L$$

where L denotes the actual size of the workforce.

Differentiating Q with respect to L gives

$$
\begin{aligned}
MP_L &= \frac{dQ}{dL} \\
&= 300(\tfrac{1}{2} L^{-1/2}) - 4 \\
&= 150L^{-1/2} - 4 \\
&= \frac{150}{\sqrt{L}} - 4
\end{aligned}
$$

Substituting $L = 1, 9, 100$ and 2500 in turn into the formula for MP_L gives:

(a) When $L = 1$

$$MP_L = \frac{150}{\sqrt{9}} - 4 = 146$$

(b) When $L = 9$

$$MP_L = \frac{150}{\sqrt{1}} - 4 = 46$$

(c) When $L = 100$

$$MP_L = \frac{150}{\sqrt{100}} - 4 = 11$$

(d) When $L = 2500$

$$MP_L = \frac{150}{\sqrt{2500}} - 4 = -1$$

Notice that the values of MP_L decline with increasing L. Part (a) shows that if the workforce consists of only one person then to employ two people would increase output by approximately 146. In part (b) we see that to increase the number of workers from 9 to 10 would result in about 46 additional units of output. In part (c) we see that a 1-unit increase in labour from a level of 100 increases output by only 11. In part (d) the situation is even worse. This indicates that to increase staff actually reduces output! The latter is a rather surprising result, but it is borne out by what occurs in real production processes. This may be due to problems of overcrowding on the shopfloor or to the need to create an elaborate administration to organise the larger workforce.

This production function illustrates the **law of diminishing marginal productivity** (sometimes called the **law of diminishing returns**). It states that the increase in output due to a 1-unit increase in labour will eventually decline. In other words, once the size of the workforce has reached a certain threshold level, the marginal product of labour will get smaller. For the production function

$$Q = 300L^{1/2} - 4L$$

the value of MP_L continually goes down with rising L. This is not always so. It is possible for the marginal product of labour to remain constant or to go up to begin with for small values of L. However, if it is to satisfy the law of diminishing marginal productivity, then there must be some value of L above which MP_L decreases.

A typical product curve is sketched in Figure 5.15, which has slope

$$\frac{\mathrm{d}Q}{\mathrm{d}L} = \mathrm{MP}_L$$

Between 0 and L_0 the curve bends upwards, becoming progressively steeper, and so the slope function, MP_L, increases. Mathematically, this means that the slope of MP_L is positive: that is,

$$\frac{\mathrm{d}(\mathrm{MP}_L)}{\mathrm{d}Q} > 0$$

Now MP_L is itself the derivative of Q with respect to L, so we can use the notation for the second-order derivative and write this as

$$\frac{\mathrm{d}^2Q}{\mathrm{d}L^2} > 0$$

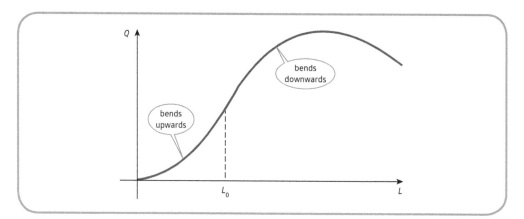

Figure 5.15

Similarly, if L exceeds the threshold value of L_0 then Figure 5.15 shows that the product curve bends downwards and the slope decreases. In this region, the slope of the slope function is negative, so that

$$\frac{d^2Q}{dL^2} < 0$$

The law of diminishing returns states that this must happen eventually: that is,

$$\frac{d^2Q}{dL^2} < 0$$

for sufficiently large L.

Practice Problem

4. A Cobb–Douglas production function is given by

$$Q = 5L^{1/2}K^{1/2}$$

Assuming that capital, K, is fixed at 100, write down a formula for Q in terms of L only. Calculate the marginal product of labour when

(a) $L = 1$ (b) $L = 9$ (c) $L = 10\,000$

Verify that the law of diminishing marginal productivity holds in this case.

5.3.3 Consumption and savings

If we assume that national income (Y) is only used up in consumption (C) and savings (S) then

$$Y = C + S$$

Of particular interest is the effect on C and S due to variations in Y. Expressed simply, if national income rises by a certain amount, are people more likely to go out and spend their extra income on consumer goods, or will they save it? To analyse this behaviour we use the concepts **marginal propensity to consume**, MPC, and **marginal propensity to save**, MPS, which are defined by

$$\text{MPC} = \frac{dC}{dY} \quad \text{and} \quad \text{MPS} = \frac{dS}{dY}$$

marginal propensity to consume is the derivative of consumption with respect to income

marginal propensity to save is the derivative of savings with respect to income

These definitions are consistent, where MPC and MPS were taken to be the slopes of the linear consumption and savings curves, respectively. At first sight it appears that, in general, we need to work out two derivatives in order to evaluate MPC and MPS. However, this is not strictly necessary. Recall that we can do whatever we like to an equation provided we do the same thing to both sides. Consequently, we can differentiate both sides of the equation

$$Y = C + S$$

with respect to Y to deduce that

$$\frac{dY}{dY} = \frac{dC}{dY} + \frac{dS}{dY} = MPC + MPS$$

Now we are already familiar with the result that when we differentiate x with respect to x, the answer is 1. In this case Y plays the role of x, so

$$\frac{dY}{dY} = 1$$

Hence

$$1 = MPC + MPS$$

This formula is identical to the result given in Section 1.7 for simple linear functions. In practice, it means that we need only work out one of the derivatives. The remaining derivative can then be calculated directly from this equation.

Example

If the consumption function is

$$C = 0.01Y^2 + 0.2Y + 50$$

calculate MPC and MPS when $Y = 30$.

Solution

In this example the consumption function is given, so we begin by finding MPC. To do this we differentiate C with respect to Y. If

$$C = 0.01Y^2 + 0.2Y + 50$$

then

$$\frac{dC}{dY} = 0.02Y + 0.2$$

so, when $Y = 30$,

$$MPC = 0.02(30) + 0.2 = 0.8$$

To find the corresponding value of MPS we use the formula

$$MPC + MPS = 1$$

which gives

$$MPS = 1 - MPC = 1 - 0.8 = 0.2$$

This indicates that when national income increases by 1 unit (from its current level of 30), consumption rises by approximately 0.8 units, whereas savings rise by only about 0.2 units. At this level of income the nation has a greater propensity to consume than it has to save.

Practice Problem

5. If the savings function is given by

$$S = 0.02Y^2 - Y + 100$$

calculate the values of MPS and MPC when $Y = 40$. Give a brief interpretation of these results.

Key Terms

Average revenue   Total revenue per unit of output: $AR = TR/Q = P$.

Chord   A straight line joining two points on a curve.

Law of diminishing marginal productivity (law of diminishing returns)   Once the size of the workforce exceeds a particular value, the increase in output due to a 1-unit increase in labour will decline: $d^2Q/dL^2 < 0$ for sufficiently large L.

Marginal cost   The cost of producing 1 more unit of output: $MC = d(TC)/dQ$.

Marginal product of labour   The extra output produced by 1 more unit of labour: $MP_L = dQ/dL$.

Marginal propensity to consume   The fraction of a rise in national income which goes into consumption: $MPC = dC/dY$.

Marginal propensity to save   The fraction of a rise in national income which goes into savings: $MPS = dS/dY$.

Marginal revenue   The extra revenue gained by selling 1 more unit of a good: $MR = d(TR)/dQ$.

Monopolist   The only firm in the industry.

Perfect competition   A situation in which there are no barriers to entry in an industry where there are many firms selling an identical product at the market price.

Exercise 5.3

1. If the demand function is

   $$P = 100 - 4Q$$

   find expressions for TR and MR in terms of Q. Hence estimate the change in TR brought about by a 0.3-unit increase in output from a current level of 12 units.

2. If the demand function is

   $$P = 80 - 3Q$$

   show that

   $$MR = 2P - 80$$

3. A monopolist's demand function is given by

   $$P + Q = 100$$

   Write down expressions for TR and MR in terms of Q and sketch their graphs. Find the value of Q which gives a marginal revenue of zero and comment on the significance of this value.

4. If the average cost function of a good is

$$AC = \frac{15}{Q} + 2Q + 9$$

find an expression for TC. What are the fixed costs in this case? Write down an expression for the marginal cost function.

5. A firm's production function is

$$Q = 50L - 0.01L^2$$

where L denotes the size of the workforce. Find the value of MP_L in the case when

(a) $L = 1$ (b) $L = 10$ (c) $L = 100$ (d) $L = 1000$

Does the law of diminishing marginal productivity apply to this particular function?

6. If the consumption function is

$$C = 50 + 2\sqrt{Y}$$

calculate MPC and MPS when $Y = 36$ and give an interpretation of these results.

7. If the consumption function is

$$C = 0.02Y^2 + 0.1Y + 25$$

find the value of Y when MPS = 0.38.

8. The price of a company's shares, P, recorded in dollars at midday is a function of time, t, measured in days since the beginning of the year. Give an interpretation of the statement:

$$\frac{dP}{dt} = 0.25$$

when $t = 6$.

9. If the demand function is

$$P = 3000 - 2\sqrt{Q}$$

find expressions for TR and MR. Calculate the marginal revenue when $Q = 9$ and give an interpretation of this result.

Exercise 5.3*

1. A firm's demand function is given by

$$P = 100 - 4\sqrt{Q} - 3Q$$

(a) Write down an expression for total revenue, TR, in terms of Q.

(b) Find an expression for the marginal revenue, MR, and find the value of MR when $Q = 9$.

(c) Use the result of part (b) to *estimate* the change in TR when Q increases by 0.25 units from its current level of 9 units and compare this with the exact change in TR.

2. The consumption function is

    $$C = 0.01Y^2 + 0.8Y + 100$$

    (a) Calculate the values of MPC and MPS when $Y = 8$.

    (b) Use the fact that $C + S = Y$ to obtain a formula for S in terms of Y. By differentiating this expression, find the value of MPS at $Y = 8$ and verify that this agrees with your answer to part (a).

3. The fixed costs of producing a good are 100 and the variable costs are $2 + Q/10$ per unit.

    (a) Find expressions for TC and MC.

    (b) Evaluate MC at $Q = 30$ and hence estimate the change in TC brought about by a 2-unit increase in output from a current level of 30 units.

    (c) At what level of output does MC = 22?

4. Show that the law of diminishing marginal productivity holds for the production function

    $$Q = 6L^2 - 0.2L^3$$

5. A firm's production function is given by

    $$Q = 5\sqrt{L} - 0.1L$$

    (a) Find an expression for the marginal product of labour, MP_L.

    (b) Solve the equation $MP_L = 0$ and briefly explain the significance of this value of L.

    (c) Show that the law of diminishing marginal productivity holds for this function.

6. A firm's average cost function takes the form

    $$AC = 4Q + a + \frac{6}{Q}$$

    and it is known that MC = 35 when $Q = 3$. Find the value of AC when $Q = 6$.

7. The total cost of producing a good is given by

    $$TC = 250 + 20Q$$

    The marginal revenue is 18 at $Q = 219$. If production is increased from its current level of 219, would you expect profit to increase, decrease or stay the same? Give reasons for your answer.

8. Given the demand and total cost functions

    $$P = 150 - 2Q \qquad \text{and} \qquad TC = 40 + 0.5Q^2$$

    find the marginal profit when $Q = 25$ and give an interpretation of this result.

9. If the total cost function is given by $TC = aQ^2 + bQ + c$, show that

    $$\frac{d(AC)}{dQ} = \frac{MC - AC}{Q}$$

SECTION 5.5
Elasticity

Objectives

At the end of this section you should be able to:

- Calculate price elasticity averaged along an arc.
- Calculate price elasticity evaluated at a point.
- Decide whether supply and demand are inelastic, unit elastic or elastic.
- Understand the relationship between price elasticity of demand and revenue.
- Determine the price elasticity for general linear demand functions.

One important problem in business is to determine the effect on revenue of a change in the price of a good. Let us suppose that a firm's demand curve is downward-sloping. If the firm lowers the price, then it will receive less for each item, but the number of items sold increases. The formula for total revenue, TR, is

$$TR = PQ$$

and it is not immediately obvious what the net effect on TR will be as P decreases and Q increases. The crucial factor here is not the absolute changes in P and Q but rather the proportional or percentage changes. Intuitively, we expect that if the percentage rise in Q is greater than the percentage fall in P, then the firm experiences an increase in revenue. Under these circumstances we say that demand is **elastic**, since the demand is relatively sensitive to changes in price. Similarly, demand is said to be **inelastic** if demand is relatively insensitive to price changes. In this case, the percentage change in quantity is less than the percentage change in price. A firm can then increase revenue by raising the price of the good. Although demand falls as a result, the increase in price more than compensates for the reduced volume of sales and revenue rises. Of course, it could happen that the percentage changes in price and quantity are equal, leaving revenue unchanged. We use the term **unit elastic** to describe this situation.

We quantify the responsiveness of demand to price change by defining the **price elasticity of demand** to be

$$E = \frac{\text{percentage change in demand}}{\text{percentage change in price}}$$

Notice that because the demand curve slopes downwards, a positive change in price leads to a negative change in quantity and vice versa. Consequently, the value of E is always negative. It is usual for economists to ignore the negative sign and consider just the magnitude of elasticity. If this positive value is denoted by $|E|$, then the previous classification of demand functions can be restated more succinctly as:

Demand is said to be

- inelastic if $|E| < 1$
- unit elastic if $|E| = 1$
- elastic if $|E| > 1$

As usual, we denote the changes in P and Q by ΔP and ΔQ respectively, and seek a formula for E in terms of these symbols. To motivate this, suppose that the price of a good is \$12 and that it rises to \$18. A moment's thought should convince you that the percentage change in price is then 50%. You can probably work this out in your head without thinking too hard. However, it is worthwhile identifying the mathematical process involved. To obtain this figure we first express the change

$$18 - 12 = 6$$

as a fraction of the original to get

$$\frac{6}{12} = 0.5$$

and then multiply by 100 to express it as a percentage. This simple example gives us a clue as to how we might find a formula for E. In general, the percentage change in price is

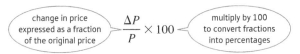

Similarly, the percentage change in quantity is

$$\frac{\Delta Q}{Q} \times 100$$

Hence

$$E = \left(\frac{\Delta Q}{Q} \times 100 \right) \div \left(\frac{\Delta P}{P} \times 100 \right)$$

Now, when we divide two fractions, we turn the denominator upside down and multiply, so

$$E = \left(\frac{\Delta Q}{Q} \times \cancel{100} \right) \times \left(\frac{P}{\cancel{100} \times \Delta P} \right)$$

$$= \frac{P}{Q} \times \frac{\Delta Q}{\Delta P}$$

A typical demand curve is illustrated in Figure 5.17, in which a price fall from P_1 to P_2 causes an increase in demand from Q_1 to Q_2.

To be specific, let us suppose that the demand function is given by

$$P = 200 - Q^2$$

with $P_1 = 136$ and $P_2 = 119$.

The corresponding values of Q_1 and Q_2 are obtained from the demand equation

$$P = 200 - Q^2$$

by substituting $P = 136$ and 119, respectively, and solving for Q. For example, if $P = 136$, then

$$136 = 200 - Q^2$$

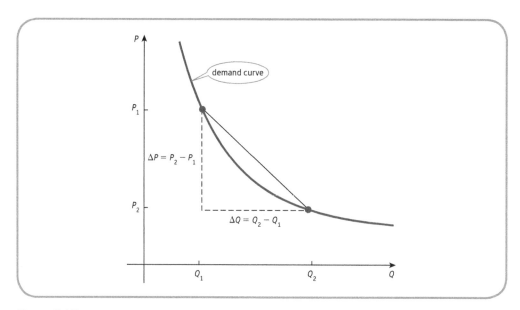

Figure 5.17

which rearranges to give

$$Q^2 = 200 - 136 = 64$$

This has solution $Q = \pm 8$ and, since we can obviously ignore the negative quantity, we have $Q_1 = 8$. Similarly, setting $P = 119$ gives $Q_2 = 9$. The elasticity formula is

$$E = \frac{P}{Q} \times \frac{\Delta Q}{\Delta P}$$

and the values of ΔP and ΔQ are easily worked out to be

$$\Delta P = 119 - 136 = -17$$

$$\Delta Q = 9 - 8 = 1$$

However, it is not at all clear what to take for P and Q. Do we take P to be 136 or 119? Clearly we are going to get two different answers depending on our choice. A sensible compromise is to use their average and take

$$P = {}^1\!/_2(136 + 119) = 127.5$$

Similarly, averaging the Q values gives

$$Q = {}^1\!/_2(8 + 9) = 8.5$$

Hence

$$E = \frac{127.5}{8.5} \times \left(\frac{1}{-17} \right) = -0.88$$

This value is an estimate of elasticity averaged over a section of the demand curve between (Q_1, P_1) and (Q_2, P_2). For this reason, it is called **arc elasticity** and is obtained by replacing P by ${}^1\!/_2(P_1 + P_2)$ and Q by ${}^1\!/_2(Q_1 + Q_2)$ in the general formula.

Practice Problem

1. Given the demand function

$$P = 1000 - 2Q$$

calculate the arc elasticity as P falls from 210 to 200.

A disappointing feature of this approach is the need to compromise and calculate the elasticity averaged along an arc rather than calculate the exact value at a point. A formula for the latter can easily be deduced from

$$E = \frac{P}{Q} \times \frac{\Delta Q}{\Delta P}$$

by considering the limit as ΔQ and ΔP tend to zero in Figure 5.17. All that happens is that the arc shrinks to a point and the ratio $\Delta Q/\Delta P$ tends to dQ/dP. The price elasticity at a point (**point elasticity**) may therefore be found from

$$E = \frac{P}{Q} \times \frac{dQ}{dP}$$

Example

Given the demand function

$$P = 50 - 2Q$$

find the elasticity when the price is 30. Is demand inelastic, unit elastic or elastic at this price?

Solution

To find dQ/dP we need to differentiate Q with respect to P. However, we are actually given a formula for P in terms of Q, so we need to transpose

$$P = 50 - 2Q$$

for Q. Adding $2Q$ to both sides gives

$$P + 2Q = 50$$

and if we subtract P, then

$$2Q = 50 - P$$

Finally, dividing through by 2 gives

$$Q = 25 - \tfrac{1}{2}P$$

Hence

$$\frac{dQ}{dP} = -\tfrac{1}{2}$$

We are given that $P = 30$, so at this price, demand is

$$Q = 25 - \tfrac{1}{2}(30) = 10$$

These values can now be substituted into

$$E = \frac{P}{Q} \times \frac{dQ}{dP}$$

to get

$$E = \frac{30}{10} \times \left(-\frac{1}{2}\right) = -1.5$$

Moreover, since $|1.5| > 1$, demand is elastic at this price.

Practice Problem

2. Given the demand function

$$P = 100 - Q$$

calculate the magnitude of the price elasticity of demand when the price is

(a) 10   **(b)** 50   **(c)** 90

Is the demand inelastic, unit elastic or elastic at these prices?

It is quite common in economics to be given the demand function in the form

$$P = f(Q)$$

where P is a function of Q. In order to evaluate elasticity, it is necessary to find

$$\frac{dQ}{dP}$$

which assumes that Q is actually given as a function of P. Consequently, we may have to transpose the demand equation and find an expression for Q in terms of P before we perform the differentiation. This was the approach taken in the previous example. Unfortunately, if $f(Q)$ is a complicated expression, it may be difficult, if not impossible, to carry out the initial rearrangement to extract Q. An alternative approach is based on the fact that

$$\frac{dQ}{dP} = \frac{1}{dP/dQ}$$

A proof of this can be obtained via the chain rule, although we omit the details. This result shows that we can find dQ/dP by just differentiating the original demand function to get dP/dQ and reciprocating.

Example

Given the demand function

$$P = -Q^2 - 4Q + 96$$

find the price elasticity of demand when $P = 51$. If this price rises by 2%, calculate the corresponding percentage change in demand.

Solution

We are given that $P = 51$, so to find the corresponding demand we need to solve the quadratic equation

$$-Q^2 - 4Q + 96 = 51$$

that is,

$$-Q^2 - 4Q + 45 = 0$$

To do this we use the standard formula

$$\frac{-b \pm \sqrt{b^2 - 4ac}}{2a}$$

which gives

$$Q = \frac{-(-4) \pm \sqrt{((-4)^2 - 4(-1)(45))}}{2(-1)}$$

$$= \frac{4 \pm \sqrt{196}}{-2}$$

$$= \frac{4 \pm 14}{-2}$$

The two solutions are −9 and 5. As usual, the negative value can be ignored, since it does not make sense to have a negative quantity, so $Q = 5$.

To find the value of E we also need to calculate

$$\frac{dQ}{dP}$$

from the demand equation, $P = -Q^2 - 4Q + 96$. It is not at all easy to transpose this for Q. Indeed, we would have to use the formula for solving a quadratic, as before, replacing the number 51 with the letter P. Unfortunately, this expression involves square roots and the subsequent differentiation is quite messy. (You might like to have a go at this yourself!) However, it is easy to differentiate the given expression with respect to Q to get

$$\frac{dP}{dQ} = -2Q - 4$$

and so

$$\frac{dQ}{dP} = \frac{1}{dP/dQ} = \frac{1}{-2Q - 4}$$

Finally, putting $Q = 5$ gives

$$\frac{dQ}{dP} = -\frac{1}{14}$$

The price elasticity of demand is given by

$$E = \frac{P}{Q} \times \frac{dQ}{dP}$$

and if we substitute $P = 51$, $Q = 5$ and $dQ/dP = -1/14$, we get

$$E = \frac{51}{5} \times \left(-\frac{1}{14} \right) = -0.73$$

To discover the effect on Q due to a 2% rise in P, we return to the original definition

$$E = \frac{\text{percentage change in demand}}{\text{percentage change in price}}$$

We know that $E = -0.73$ and that the percentage change in price is 2%, so

$$-0.73 = \frac{\text{percentage change in demand}}{2\%}$$

which shows that demand changes by

$$-0.73 \times 2\% = -1.46\%$$

A 2% rise in price therefore leads to a fall in demand of 1.46%.

Practice Problem

3. Given the demand equation

    $$P = -Q^2 - 10Q + 150$$

    find the price elasticity of demand when $Q = 4$. Estimate the percentage change in price needed to increase demand by 10%.

The **price elasticity of supply** is defined in an analogous way to that of demand. We define

$$E = \frac{\text{percentage change in supply}}{\text{percentage change in price}}$$

An increase in price leads to an increase in supply, so E is positive.

Example

Given the supply function

$$P = 10 + \sqrt{Q}$$

find the price elasticity of supply

(a) averaged along an arc between $Q = 100$ and $Q = 105$;

(b) at the point $Q = 100$.

Solution

(a) We are given that

$$Q_1 = 100, \ Q_2 = 105$$

so that

$$P_1 = 10 + \sqrt{100} = 20 \text{ and } P_2 = 10 + \sqrt{105} = 20.247$$

Hence

$$\Delta P = 20.247 - 20 = 0.247, \qquad \Delta Q = 105 - 100 = 5$$

$$P = \frac{1}{2}(20 + 20.247) = 20.123, \qquad Q = \frac{1}{2}(100 + 105) = 102.5$$

The formula for arc elasticity gives

$$E = \frac{P}{Q} \times \frac{\Delta Q}{\Delta P} = \frac{20.123}{102.5} \times \frac{5}{0.247} = 3.97$$

(b) To evaluate the elasticity at the point $Q = 100$, we need to find the derivative, $\dfrac{dQ}{dP}$. The supply equation

$$P = 10 + Q^{1/2}$$

differentiates to give

$$\frac{dP}{dQ} = \frac{1}{2}Q^{-1/2} = \frac{1}{2\sqrt{Q}}$$

so that

$$\frac{dQ}{dP} = 2\sqrt{Q}$$

At the point $Q = 100$, we get

$$\frac{dQ}{dP} = 2\sqrt{100} = 20$$

The formula for point elasticity gives

$$E = \frac{P}{Q} \times \frac{dQ}{dP} = \frac{20}{100} \times 20 = 4$$

Notice that, as expected, the answers to parts (a) and (b) are nearly the same.

Practice Problem

4. If the supply equation is

$$Q = 150 + 5P + 0.1P^2$$

calculate the price elasticity of supply

(a) averaged along an arc between $P = 9$ and $P = 11$;

(b) at the point $P = 10$.

Advice

The concept of elasticity can be applied to more general functions. For the moment we investigate the theoretical properties of demand elasticity. The following material is more difficult to understand than the foregoing, so you may prefer just to concentrate on the conclusions and skip the intermediate derivations.

We begin by analysing the relationship between elasticity and marginal revenue. Marginal revenue, MR, is given by

$$\text{MR} = \frac{d(\text{TR})}{dQ}$$

Now, TR is equal to the product PQ, so we can apply the product rule to differentiate it. If

$$u = P \quad \text{and} \quad v = Q$$

then

$$\frac{du}{dQ} = \frac{dP}{dQ} \text{ and } \frac{dv}{dQ} = \frac{dQ}{dQ} = 1$$

By the product rule

$$\text{MR} = u\frac{dv}{dQ} + v\frac{du}{dQ}$$

$$= P + Q \times \frac{dP}{dQ}$$

$$= P\left(1 + \frac{Q}{P} \times \frac{dP}{dQ}\right)$$

check this by multiplying out the brackets

Now

$$\frac{P}{Q} \times \frac{dQ}{dP} = E$$

so

$$\frac{Q}{P} \times \frac{dP}{dQ} = \frac{1}{E}$$

turn both sides upside down

This can be substituted into the expression for MR to get

$$\text{MR} = P\left(1 + \frac{1}{E}\right)$$

The connection between marginal revenue and demand elasticity is now complete, and this formula can be used to justify the intuitive argument that we gave at the beginning of this section concerning revenue and elasticity. Observe that if $-1 < E < 0$ then $1/E < -1$, so MR is negative for any value of P. It follows that the revenue function is decreasing in regions where demand is inelastic, because MR determines the slope of the revenue curve. Similarly, if $E < -1$, then $1/E > -1$, so MR is positive for any price, P, and the revenue curve is upwards. In other words, the revenue function is increasing in regions where demand is elastic. Finally, if $E = -1$, then MR is 0, and so the slope of the revenue curve is horizontal at points where demand is unit elastic.

Throughout this section we have taken specific functions and evaluated the elasticity at particular points. It is more instructive to consider general functions and to deduce general expressions for elasticity. Consider the standard linear downward-sloping demand function

$$P = aQ + b$$

when $a < 0$ and $b > 0$. This typifies the demand function faced by a monopolist. To transpose this equation for Q, we subtract b from both sides to get

$$aQ = P - b$$

and then divide through by a to get

$$Q = \frac{1}{a}(P - b)$$

Hence

$$\frac{dQ}{dP} = \frac{1}{a}$$

The formula for elasticity of demand is

$$E = \frac{P}{Q} \times \frac{dQ}{dP}$$

so replacing Q by $(1/a)(P - b)$ and dQ/dP by $1/a$ gives

$$E = \frac{P}{(1/a)(P - b)} \times \frac{1}{a}$$

$$= \frac{P}{P - b}$$

Notice that this formula involves P and b but not a. Elasticity is therefore independent of the slope of linear demand curves. In particular, this shows that, corresponding to any price P, the elasticities of the two demand functions sketched in Figure 5.18 are identical. This is perhaps a rather surprising result. We might have expected demand to be more elastic at point A than at point B, since A is on the steeper curve. However, the mathematics shows that this is not the case. (Can you explain, in economic terms, why this is so?)

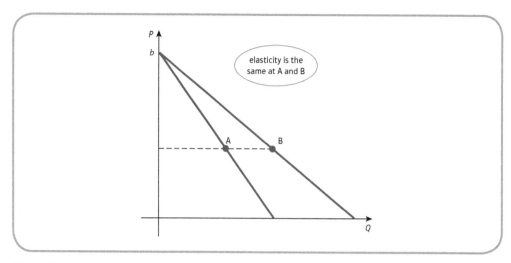

Figure 5.18

Another interesting feature of the result

$$E = \frac{P}{P - b}$$

is the fact that b occurs in the denominator of this fraction, so that corresponding to any price, P, the larger the value of the intercept, b, the smaller the magnitude of the elasticity. In Figure 5.19, the magnitude of the elasticity at C is smaller than that at D because C lies on the curve with the larger intercept.

The dependence of E on P is also worthy of note. It shows that elasticity varies along a linear demand curve. This is illustrated in Figure 5.20. At the left-hand end, $P = b$, so

$$E = \frac{b}{b - b} = \frac{b}{0} = \infty \quad \text{(read 'infinity')}$$

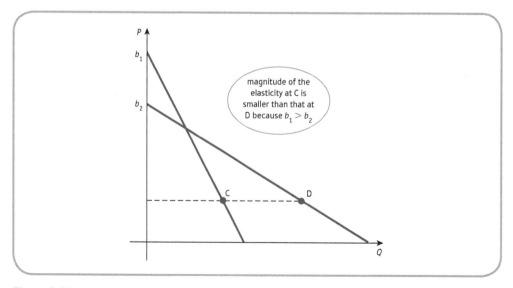

Figure 5.19

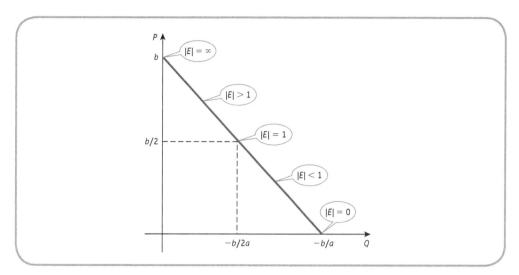

Figure 5.20

At the right-hand end, $P = 0$, so

$$E = \frac{0}{0 - b} = \frac{0}{-b} = 0$$

As you move down the demand curve, the magnitude of elasticity decreases from ∞ to 0, taking all possible values. Demand is unit elastic when $E = -1$ and the price at which this occurs can be found by solving

$$\frac{P}{P - b} = -1 \quad \text{for} \quad P$$
$$P = b - P \quad \text{(multiply both sides by } P - b\text{)}$$
$$2P = b \quad \text{(add } P \text{ to both sides)}$$
$$P = \frac{b}{2} \quad \text{(divide both sides by 2)}$$

The corresponding quantity can be found by substituting $P = b/2$ into the transposed demand equation to get

$$Q = \frac{1}{a}\left(\frac{b}{2} - b\right) = -\frac{b}{2a}$$

Demand is unit elastic exactly halfway along the demand curve. To the left of this point, $|E| > 1$ and demand is elastic, whereas to the right, $|E| < 1$ and demand is inelastic.

In our discussion of general demand functions, we have concentrated on those which are represented by straight lines since these are commonly used in simple economic models. There are other possibilities, and Question 4 in Exercise 5.5* investigates a class of functions that have constant elasticity.

Key Terms

Arc elasticity   Elasticity measured between two points on a curve.

Elastic demand   Where the percentage change in demand is more than the corresponding percentage change in price: $|E| > 1$.

Inelastic demand   Where the percentage change in demand is less than the corresponding percentage change in price: $|E| < 1$.

Point elasticity   Elasticity measured at a particular point on a curve: $E = \dfrac{P}{Q} \times \dfrac{dQ}{dP}$.

Price elasticity of demand   A measure of the responsiveness of the change in demand due to a change in price: (percentage change in demand) ÷ (percentage change in price).

Price elasticity of supply   A measure of the responsiveness of the change in supply due to a change in price: (percentage change in supply) ÷ (percentage change in price).

Unit elasticity of demand   Where the percentage change in demand is the same as the percentage change in price: $|E| = 1$.

Exercise 5.5

1. Given the demand function

   $$P = 500 - 4Q^2$$

   calculate the price elasticity of demand averaged along an arc joining $Q = 8$ and $Q = 10$.

2. Find the price elasticity of demand at the point $Q = 9$ for the demand function

   $$P = 500 - 4Q^2$$

   and compare your answer with that of Question 1.

3. Find the price elasticity of demand at $P = 6$ for each of the following demand functions:

   (a) $P = 30 - 2Q$

   (b) $P = 30 - 12Q$

   (c) $P = \sqrt{(100 - 2Q)}$

4. (a) If an airline increases prices for business class flights by 8%, demand falls by about 2.5%. Estimate the elasticity of demand. Is demand elastic, inelastic or unit elastic?

   (b) Explain whether you would expect a similar result to hold for economy class flights.

5. The demand function of a good is given by

   $$Q = \frac{1000}{P^2}$$

   (a) Calculate the price elasticity of demand at $P = 5$ and hence estimate the percentage change in demand when P increases by 2%.

   (b) Comment on the accuracy of your estimate in part (a) by calculating the exact percentage change in demand when P increases from 5 to 5.1.

6. **(a)** Find the elasticity of demand in terms of Q for the demand function, $P = 20 - 0.05Q$.

   (b) For what value of Q is demand unit elastic?

   (c) Find an expression for MR and verify that MR = 0 when demand is unit elastic.

7. Consider the supply equation

   $$Q = 4 + 0.1P^2$$

   (a) Write down an expression for dQ/dP.

   (b) Show that the supply equation can be rearranged as

   $$P = \sqrt{(10Q - 40)}$$

   Differentiate this to find an expression for dP/dQ.

   (c) Use your answers to parts (a) and (b) to verify that

   $$\frac{dQ}{dP} = \frac{1}{dP/dQ}$$

   (d) Calculate the elasticity of supply at the point $Q = 14$.

8. If the supply equation is

   $$Q = 7 + 0.1P + 0.004P^2$$

   find the price elasticity of supply if the current price is 80.

   (a) Is supply elastic, inelastic or unit elastic at this price?

   (b) Estimate the percentage change in supply if the price rises by 5%.

Exercise 5.5*

1. Find the elasticity for the demand function

   $$Q = 80 - 2P - 0.5P^2$$

   averaged along an arc joining $Q = 32$ to $Q = 50$. Give your answer to 2 decimal places.

2. Consider the supply equation

   $$P = 7 + 2Q^2$$

   By evaluating the price elasticity of supply at the point $P = 105$, estimate the percentage increase in supply when the price rises by 7%.

3. If the demand equation is

   $$Q + 4P = 60$$

   find a general expression for the price elasticity of demand in terms of P. For what value of P is demand unit elastic?

4. Show that the price elasticity of demand is constant for the demand functions

   $$P = \frac{A}{Q^n}$$

   where A and n are positive constants.

5. Find a general expression for the point elasticity of supply for the function

$$Q = aP + b \ (a > 0)$$

Deduce that the supply function is

(a) unit elastic when $b = 0$;

(b) elastic when $b < 0$.

Give a brief geometrical interpretation of these results.

6. A supply function is given by

$$Q = 40 + 0.1P^2$$

(1) Find the price elasticity of supply averaged along an arc between $P = 11$ and $P = 13$. Give your answer correct to three decimal places.

(2) Find an expression for price elasticity of supply at a general point, P.

Hence:

(a) Estimate the percentage change in supply when the price increases by 5% from its current level of 17. Give your answer correct to one decimal place.

(b) Find the price at which supply is unit elastic.

7. (a) Show that the elasticity of the supply function

$$P = aQ + b$$

is given by

$$E = \frac{P}{P - b}$$

(b) Consider the two supply functions

$$P = 2Q + 5 \text{ and } P = aQ + b$$

The quantity supplied is the same for both functions when $P = 10$, and at this point, the price elasticity of supply for the second function is five times larger than that for the first function. Find the values of a and b.

8. (a) If E denotes the elasticity of a general supply function, $Q = f(P)$, show that the elasticity of:

(i) $Q = [f(P)]^n$ is nE **(ii)** $Q = \lambda f(P)$ is E **(iii)** $Q = \lambda + f(P)$ is $\dfrac{f(P)E}{\lambda + f(P)}$

where n and λ are positive constants.

(b) Show that the elasticity of the supply function $Q = P$ is 1 and use the results of part (a) to write down the elasticity of

(i) $Q = P^3$ **(ii)** $Q = 10P\sqrt{P}$ **(iii)** $Q = 5\sqrt{P} - 2$

6

PARTIAL DIFFERENTIATION

Mathematics is not a careful march down a well-cleared highway, but a journey into a strange wilderness, where the explorers often get lost.
—W.S. Anglin (1992)

So far, this book has been concerned almost exclusively with functions of one variable. Yet a realistic description of economic phenomena often requires considering a large number of variables. For example, one consumer's demand for a good like orange juice depends on its price, on the consumer's income, and on the prices of substitutes like other soft drinks, or complements like some kinds of food.

Previous chapters have presented important properties of functions of one variable. For functions of several variables, most of what economists need to know consists of relatively simple extensions of properties presented in the previous chapters for functions of one variable. Moreover, most of the difficulties already arise in the transition from one variable to two variables. To help readers see how to overcome these difficulties, Sections 6.1 to 6.3 deal exclusively with functions of two variables. These have graphs in three dimensions, which it is possible to represent even in two-dimensional figures—though with some difficulty. However, as the previous example of the demand for orange juice suggests, there are many interesting economic problems that can only be represented mathematically by functions of many variables. These are discussed in Sections 6.4 to 6.7. The final section, 6.8, is devoted to the economically important topic of elasticity.

6.1 Functions of Two Variables

We begin with the following definition, where D is a subset of the xy-plane.

FUNCTIONS OF TWO VARIABLES

A function f of two real variables, x and y, with domain D is a rule that assigns a specified number

$$f(x, y) \text{ to each point } (x, y) \text{ in } D \tag{6.1.1}$$

If f is a function of two variables, we often let a letter like z denote the value of f at point (x, y), so $z = f(x, y)$. Then we call x and y the *independent variables*, or the *arguments* of f, whereas z is called the *dependent variable*, because the value z, in general, depends on the values of x and y. The domain of function f is then the set of all possible pairs of the independent variables, whereas its *range* is the set of corresponding values of the dependent variable. In economics, x and y are often called the *exogenous* variables, whereas z is the *endogenous* variable.[1]

EXAMPLE 6.1.1   Consider the function f that, to every pair of numbers (x, y), assigns the number $2x + x^2 y^3$. The function f is thus defined by

$$f(x, y) = 2x + x^2 y^3$$

What are $f(1, 0), f(0, 1), f(-2, 3)$, and $f(a + 1, b)$?

Solution: First, $f(1, 0)$ is the value when $x = 1$ and $y = 0$. So $f(1, 0) = 2 \cdot 1 + 1^2 \cdot 0^3 = 2$. Similarly, we have $f(0, 1) = 2 \cdot 0 + 0^2 \cdot 1^3 = 0$, and $f(-2, 3) = 2(-2) + (-2)^2 \cdot 3^3 = -4 + 4 \cdot 27 = 104$. Finally, we find $f(a + 1, b)$ by replacing x with $a + 1$ and y with b in the formula for $f(x, y)$, giving $f(a + 1, b) = 2(a + 1) + (a + 1)^2 b^3$.

EXAMPLE 6.1.2   A study of the demand for milk found the relationship

$$x = A \frac{m^{2.08}}{p^{1.5}}$$

where x is milk consumption, p is the relative price of milk, m is income per family, and A is a positive constant. This equation defines x as a function of p and m. Note that milk consumption goes up when income increases, and down when the price of milk increases—which seems reasonable.

EXAMPLE 6.1.3   A function of two variables appearing in many economic models is

$$F(x, y) = A x^a y^b \tag{6.1.2}$$

where A, a, and b are constants. Usually, one assumes that F is defined only for $x > 0$ and $y > 0$.

---

[1]   In economic models with several simultaneous equations, the distinction between exogenous and endogenous variables is much more nuanced.

A function F of the form (6.1.2) is generally called a *Cobb–Douglas function*.[2] It is most often used to describe certain production processes. Then x and y are called *input factors*, while $F(x, y)$ is the number of units produced, or the *output*. In this case, F is called a *production function*.

Note that the function defined in Example 6.1.2 is also a Cobb–Douglas function, because we have $x = Ap^{-1.5}m^{2.08}$.

It is important to become thoroughly familiar with standard functional notation.

EXAMPLE 6.1.4   For the function F given in Example 6.1.3, find an expression for $F(2x, 2y)$ and for $F(tx, ty)$, where t is an arbitrary positive number. Find also an expression for $F(x + h, y) - F(x, y)$. Give economic interpretations.

Solution: We find that

$$F(2x, 2y) = A(2x)^a(2y)^b = A2^a x^a 2^b y^b = 2^a 2^b A x^a y^b = 2^{a+b} F(x, y)$$

When F is a production function, this shows that if each of the input factors is doubled, then the output is 2^{a+b} times as large. For example, if $a + b = 1$, then doubling both factors of production implies doubling the output. In the general case,

$$F(tx, ty) = A(tx)^a(ty)^b = At^a x^a t^b y^b = t^a t^b A x^a y^b = t^{a+b} F(x, y) \qquad (*)$$

(How do you formulate this result in your own words?)[3]

Finally, we see that

$$F(x + h, y) - F(x, y) = A(x + h)^a y^b - Ax^a y^b = Ay^b[(x + h)^a - x^a] \qquad (**)$$

This shows the change in output when the first input factor is changed by h units while the other input factor is unchanged. For example, suppose $A = 100$, $a = 1/2$, and $b = 1/4$, in which case $F(x, y) = 100x^{1/2}y^{1/4}$. If we choose $x = 16$, $y = 16$, and $h = 1$, Eq. (**) implies that

$$F(16 + 1, 16) - F(16, 16) = 100 \cdot 16^{1/4}[17^{1/2} - 16^{1/2}] = 100 \cdot 2[\sqrt{17} - 4] \approx 24.6$$

Hence, if we increase the input of the first factor from 16 to 17, while keeping the input of the second factor constant at 16 units, then we increase production by about 24.6 units.

Domains

For functions studied in economics, there are usually explicit or implicit restrictions on the domain where the function is defined. For instance, if $f(x, y)$ is a production function, we

---

[2] The function in (6.1.2) is named after American researchers C.W. Cobb and P.H. Douglas, who applied it, with $a + b = 1$, in a paper that appeared in 1927 on the estimation of production functions. The function, however, should properly be called a "Wicksell function", because Swedish economist K. Wicksell (1851–1926) introduced such production functions before 1900.

[3] Because of property (*), we call function F *homogeneous of degree $a + b$*.

usually assume that the input quantities are nonnegative, so $x \geq 0$ and $y \geq 0$. In economics, it is often crucially important to be clear what are the domains of the functions being used.

In the same way as for functions of one variable, we assume, unless otherwise stated, that the domain of a function defined by a formula is the largest set of points in which the formula gives a meaningful and unique value.

Sometimes it is helpful to draw a graph of the domain D in the xy-plane.

EXAMPLE 6.1.5   Determine the domains of the functions given by the following formulas, then draw the sets in the xy-plane.

(a) $f(x, y) = \sqrt{x - 1} + \sqrt{y}$ (b) $g(x, y) = \dfrac{2}{(x^2 + y^2 - 4)^{1/2}} + \sqrt{9 - (x^2 + y^2)}$

Solution:

(a) We must require that $x \geq 1$ and $y \geq 0$, for only then do $\sqrt{x - 1}$ and $\sqrt{y}$ have any meaning. The (unbounded) domain is indicated in Fig. 6.1.1.

(b) $(x^2 + y^2 - 4)^{1/2} = \sqrt{x^2 + y^2 - 4}$ is only defined if $x^2 + y^2 \geq 4$. Moreover, we must have $x^2 + y^2 \neq 4$; otherwise, the denominator is equal to 0. Furthermore, we must require that $9 - (x^2 + y^2) \geq 0$, or $x^2 + y^2 \leq 9$. All in all, therefore, we must have $4 < x^2 + y^2 \leq 9$. Because the graph of $x^2 + y^2 = r^2$ consists of all the points on the circle with centre at the origin and radius r, the domain is the set of points (x, y) that lie outside, but not on, the circle $x^2 + y^2 = 4$; and inside or on the circle $x^2 + y^2 = 9$. This set is shown in Fig. 6.1.2, where the solid circle is in the domain, but the dashed circle is not.

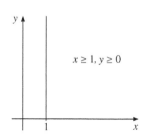

Figure 6.1.1 Domain of $\sqrt{x - 1} + \sqrt{y}$

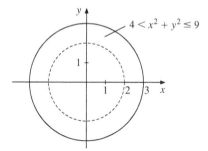

Figure 6.1.2 Domain of $2/(x^2 + y^2 - 4)^{1/2} + \sqrt{9 - (x^2 + y^2)}$

EXERCISES FOR SECTION 6.1

1. Let $f(x, y) = x + 2y$. Find $f(0, 1), f(2, -1), f(a, a)$, and $f(a + h, b) - f(a, b)$.

2. Let $f(x, y) = xy^2$. Find the respective values of $f(0, 1), f(-1, 2), f(10^4, 10^{-2}), f(a, a)$, $f(a + h, b)$, and $f(a, b + k) - f(a, b)$.

3. Let $f(x, y) = 3x^2 - 2xy + y^3$. Find $f(1, 1)$, $f(-2, 3)$, $f(1/x, 1/y)$, $p = [f(x + h, y) - f(x, y)]/h$, and $q = [f(x, y + k) - f(x, y)]/k$.

4. Let $f(x, y) = x^2 + 2xy + y^2$.

   (a) Find $f(-1, 2)$, $f(a, a)$, and $f(a + h, b) - f(a, b)$.

   (b) Prove that $f(2x, 2y) = 2^2 f(x, y)$, and that $f(tx, ty) = t^2 f(x, y)$ for all t.

5. Let $F(K, L) = 10K^{1/2}L^{1/3}$, for $K \geq 0$ and $L \geq 0$. Find $F(1, 1)$, $F(4, 27)$, $F(9, 1/27)$, $F(3, \sqrt{2})$, $F(100, 1000)$, and $F(2K, 2L)$.

6. Examine the domains of the functions given by the following formulas, and then draw them in the xy-plane:

   (a) $\dfrac{x^2 + y^3}{y - x + 2}$ (b) $\sqrt{2 - (x^2 + y^2)}$ (c) $\sqrt{(4 - x^2 - y^2)(x^2 + y^2 - 1)}$

7. Find the domains of the functions defined by the following formulas:

   (a) $1/(e^{x+y} - 3)$ (b) $\ln(x - a)^2 + \ln(y - b)^2$ (c) $2\ln(x - a) + 2\ln(y - b)$

6.2   Partial Derivatives with Two Variables

For a function $y = f(x)$ of one variable, the derivative $f'(x)$ is a number that measures the function's rate of change as x changes. For functions of two variables, such as $z = f(x, y)$, we also want to examine how quickly the value of the function changes w.r.t. changes in the values of the independent variables. For example, if $f(x, y)$ is a firm's profit when it uses quantities x and y of two different inputs, we want to know whether and by how much profit can increase as either x or y is varied.

Consider the function

$$z = x^3 + 2y^2 \qquad (*)$$

Suppose first that y is held constant. Then, $2y^2$ is constant and, really, there is only one variable now. Of course, the rate of change of z w.r.t. x is given by

$$\frac{\mathrm{d}z}{\mathrm{d}x} = 3x^2$$

On the other hand, we can keep x fixed in $(*)$ and examine how z varies as y varies. This involves taking the derivative of z w.r.t. y while keeping x constant. The result is

$$\frac{\mathrm{d}z}{\mathrm{d}y} = 4y$$

Obviously, there are many other variations we could study. For example, x and y could vary simultaneously. But in this section, we restrict our attention to variations in *either x or y*.

When we consider functions of two variables, mathematicians (and economists) usually write $\partial z/\partial x$ instead of $\mathrm{d}z/\mathrm{d}x$ for the derivative of z w.r.t. x when y is held fixed. This slight change of notation, replacing d by ∂, is intended to remind the reader that only one independent variable is changing, with the other(s) held fixed. In the same way, we write $\partial z/\partial y$ instead of dz/dy when y varies and x is held fixed. Hence, we have

$$z = x^3 + 2y^2 \implies \frac{\partial z}{\partial x} = 3x^2 \text{ and } \frac{\partial z}{\partial y} = 4y$$

In general, we introduce the following definitions:

PARTIAL DERIVATIVES

If $z = f(x, y)$, then

$\partial z/\partial x$ is the derivative of $f(x, y)$ w.r.t. x, when y is held constant $\qquad$ (6.2.1)

$\partial z/\partial y$ is the derivative of $f(x, y)$ w.r.t. y, when x is held constant $\qquad$ (6.2.2)

When $z = f(x, y)$, we also denote the derivative $\partial z/\partial x$ by $\partial f/\partial x$, and this is called the *partial derivative of z (or f) w.r.t. x*; $\partial z/\partial y = \partial f/\partial y$ is the *partial derivative of z (or f) w.r.t. y*. Note that $\partial f/\partial x$ is the rate of change of $f(x, y)$ w.r.t. x when y is constant, and correspondingly for $\partial f/\partial y$. Of course, because there are two variables, there are two partial derivatives.

It is usually easy to find the partial derivatives of a function $z = f(x, y)$. To find $\partial f/\partial x$, just think of y as a constant and differentiate $f(x, y)$ w.r.t. x as if f were a function only of x. The rules for finding derivatives of functions of one variable can all be used when we want to compute $\partial f/\partial x$. The same is true for $\partial f/\partial y$. Let us look at some further examples.

EXAMPLE 6.2.1 $\qquad$ Find the partial derivatives of the following functions:

(a) $f(x, y) = x^3 y + x^2 y^2 + x + y^2$ $\qquad\qquad$ (b) $f(x, y) = \dfrac{xy}{x^2 + y^2}$

Solution:

(a) We find, holding y constant,

$$\frac{\partial f}{\partial x} = 3x^2 y + 2xy^2 + 1$$

while, holding x constant,

$$\frac{\partial f}{\partial y} = x^3 + 2x^2 y + 2y$$

(b) For this function the quotient rule gives

$$\frac{\partial f}{\partial x} = \frac{y(x^2 + y^2) - xy \cdot 2x}{(x^2 + y^2)^2} = \frac{y^3 - x^2 y}{(x^2 + y^2)^2}, \qquad \frac{\partial f}{\partial y} = \frac{x^3 - y^2 x}{(x^2 + y^2)^2}$$

Observe that the function is symmetric in x and y, in the sense that its value is unchanged if we interchange x and y. By interchanging x and y in the formula for $\partial f/\partial x$, therefore, we will find the correct formula for $\partial f/\partial y$.

It is a good exercise for you to find $\partial f/\partial y$ in the usual way and check that the foregoing answer is correct.

Several other forms of notation are often used to indicate the partial derivatives of $z = f(x, y)$. Some of the most common are

$$\frac{\partial f}{\partial x} = \frac{\partial z}{\partial x} = z'_x = f'_x(x, y) = f'_1(x, y) = \frac{\partial f(x, y)}{\partial x} = \frac{\partial f}{\partial x}(x, y)$$

$$\frac{\partial f}{\partial y} = \frac{\partial z}{\partial y} = z'_y = f'_y(x, y) = f'_2(x, y) = \frac{\partial f(x, y)}{\partial y} = \frac{\partial f}{\partial y}(x, y)$$

Among these, we find $f'_1(x, y)$ and $f'_2(x, y)$ to be the most satisfactory. Here the numerical subscript refers to the position of the argument in the function. Thus, f'_1 indicates the partial derivative w.r.t. the first variable, and f'_2 w.r.t. the second variable. This notation also reminds us that the partial derivatives themselves are functions of x and y. Finally, $f'_1(a, b)$ and $f'_2(a, b)$ are suitable designations of the values of the partial derivatives at point (a, b) instead of at (x, y). For example, given the function $f(x, y) = x^3y + x^2y^2 + x + y^2$ in Example 6.2.1(a), one has

$$f'_1(x, y) = 3x^2y + 2xy^2 + 1, \quad f'_1(a, b) = 3a^2b + 2ab^2 + 1$$

In particular, $f'_1(0, 0) = 1$ and $f'_1(-1, 2) = 3(-1)^2 2 + 2(-1)2^2 + 1 = -1$.

We note that the alternative notation $f'_x(x, y)$ and $f'_y(x, y)$ is often used, but it is sometimes too ambiguous in connection with composite functions. For instance, what does $f'_x(x^2y, x - y)$ mean?

Remember that the numbers $f'_1(x, y)$ and $f'_2(x, y)$ measure the rate of change of f w.r.t. x and y, respectively. For example, if $f'_1(x, y) > 0$, then a small increase in x will lead to an increase in $f(x, y)$.

EXAMPLE 6.2.2   In Example 6.1.2 we studied the function $x = Ap^{-1.5}m^{2.08}$. Find the partial derivatives of x w.r.t. p and m, and discuss their signs.

Solution: We find that $\partial x/\partial p = -1.5Ap^{-2.5}m^{2.08}$ and $\partial x/\partial m = 2.08Ap^{-1.5}m^{1.08}$. Because A, p, and m are positive, $\partial x/\partial p < 0$ and $\partial x/\partial m > 0$. These signs are in accordance with the final remarks in the example.

Formal Definitions of Partial Derivatives

So far the functions have been given by explicit formulas and we have found the partial derivatives by using the ordinary rules for differentiation. If these rules cannot be used, however, we must resort to the formal definition of partial derivative. This is derived from the definition of derivative for functions of one variable in the following rather obvious way.

If $z = f(x, y)$, then with $g(x) = f(x, y)$ (y fixed), the partial derivative of $f(x, y)$ w.r.t. x is simply $g'(x)$. Now, by definition, $g'(x) = \lim_{h \to 0}[g(x + h) - g(x)]/h$. Because $f'_1(x, y) = g'(x)$, it follows that:

PARTIAL DERIVATIVES

Given $f(x, y)$,

$$f_1'(x, y) = \lim_{h \to 0} \frac{f(x + h, y) - f(x, y)}{h} \tag{6.2.3}$$

and, similarly,

$$f_2'(x, y) = \lim_{k \to 0} \frac{f(x, y + k) - f(x, y)}{k} \tag{6.2.4}$$

provided that the limits exist.

If the limit in (6.2.3) does not exist, we say that $f_1'(x, y)$ *does not exist*, or that z is *not differentiable* w.r.t. x at the point. Similarly, if the limit in (6.2.2) does not exist, then $f_2'(x, y)$ does not exist and z is not differentiable w.r.t. y at that point. For instance, the function $f(x, y) = |x| + |y|$ is not differentiable, w.r.t. either x or y, at the point $(x, y) = (0, 0)$.

If h is small in absolute value, then from Eq. (6.2.1) we obtain the approximation

$$f_1'(x, y) \approx \frac{f(x + h, y) - f(x, y)}{h} \tag{6.2.5}$$

Similarly, if k is small in absolute value,

$$f_2'(x, y) \approx \frac{f(x, y + k) - f(x, y)}{k} \tag{6.2.6}$$

These approximations can be interpreted as follows:

PARTIAL DERIVATIVES

Given $f(x, y)$:

(i) The partial derivative $f_1'(x, y)$ is approximately equal to the change in $f(x, y)$ per unit increase in x, holding y constant.

(ii) The partial derivative $f_2'(x, y)$ is approximately equal to the change in $f(x, y)$ per unit increase in y, holding x constant.

These approximations must be used with caution. Roughly speaking, they will not be too inaccurate provided that the partial derivatives do not vary too much over the actual intervals. This warning is true also for the one-variable case. But it applies more forcefully here, as even a seemingly small variation in, say, y, can change $f_1'(x, y)$ in a significant manner.

EXAMPLE 6.2.3   Let $Y = F(K, L)$ be the number of units produced when K units of capital and L units of labour are used as inputs in a production process. What is the economic interpretation of $F_K'(100, 50) = 5$?

Solution: $F_K'(100, 50) = 5$ means that, starting from $K = 100$ and holding labour input fixed at 50, a small increase in K increases output by five units per unit increase in K.

Higher-Order Partial Derivatives

If $z = f(x, y)$, then $\partial f/\partial x$ and $\partial f/\partial y$ are called *first-order partial derivatives*. These partial derivatives are, in general, again functions of the two variables. From $\partial f/\partial x$, provided this derivative is itself differentiable, we can generate two new functions by taking the partial derivatives w.r.t. x and y. In the same way, we can take the partial derivatives of $\partial f/\partial y$ w.r.t. x and y. The four functions we obtain by differentiating twice in this way are called *second-order partial derivatives* of $f(x, y)$. They are expressed as

$$\frac{\partial}{\partial x}\left(\frac{\partial f}{\partial x}\right) = \frac{\partial^2 f}{\partial x^2}, \quad \frac{\partial}{\partial x}\left(\frac{\partial f}{\partial y}\right) = \frac{\partial^2 f}{\partial x \partial y}, \quad \frac{\partial}{\partial y}\left(\frac{\partial f}{\partial x}\right) = \frac{\partial^2 f}{\partial y \partial x}, \quad \text{and} \quad \frac{\partial}{\partial y}\left(\frac{\partial f}{\partial y}\right) = \frac{\partial^2 f}{\partial y^2}$$

For brevity, we sometimes refer to the first- and second-order "partials", suppressing the word "derivatives".

EXAMPLE 6.2.4   For the function in part (a) of Example 6.2.1, we obtain

$$\frac{\partial^2 f}{\partial x^2} = 6xy + 2y^2, \quad \frac{\partial^2 f}{\partial y \partial x} = 3x^2 + 4xy, \quad \frac{\partial^2 f}{\partial x \partial y} = 3x^2 + 4xy, \quad \text{and} \quad \frac{\partial^2 f}{\partial y^2} = 2x^2 + 2$$

As with first-order partial derivatives, several other kinds of notation are also frequently used for second-order partial derivatives. For example, $\partial^2 f/\partial x^2$ is also denoted by $f''_{11}(x, y)$ or $f''_{xx}(x, y)$. In the same way, $\partial^2 f/\partial y \partial x$ can also be written as $f''_{12}(x, y)$ or $f''_{xy}(x, y)$. Note that $f''_{12}(x, y)$ means that we differentiate $f(x, y)$ first w.r.t. the first argument x and then w.r.t. the second argument y. To find $f''_{21}(x, y)$, we must differentiate in the reverse order. In Example 6.2.4, these two "cross" second-order partial derivatives (or "mixed-partials") are equal. For most functions $z = f(x, y)$, it will actually be the case that

$$\frac{\partial^2 f}{\partial x \partial y} = \frac{\partial^2 f}{\partial y \partial x} \tag{6.2.7}$$

Sufficient conditions for this equality are given in Theorem 6.6.1.

It is very important to note the exact meaning of the different symbols that have been introduced. If we consider Eq. (6.2.7), for example, it would be a serious mistake to believe that the two expressions are equal because $\partial x \partial y$ is the same as $\partial y \partial x$. Here the expression on the left-hand side is in fact the derivative of $\partial f/\partial y$ w.r.t. x, and the right-hand side is the derivative of $\partial f/\partial x$ w.r.t. y. It is a remarkable fact, and not a triviality, that the two are usually equal.

It is also important to observe that $\partial^2 z/\partial x^2$ is quite different from $(\partial z/\partial x)^2$. For example, if $z = x^2 + y^2$, then $\partial z/\partial x = 2x$. Therefore, $\partial^2 z/\partial x^2 = 2$, whereas $(\partial z/\partial x)^2 = 4x^2$.

Analogously, we define partial derivatives of the third, fourth, and higher orders. For example, we write $\partial^4 z/\partial x \partial y^3 = z^{(4)}_{yyyx}$ when we first differentiate z three times w.r.t. y and then differentiate the result once more w.r.t. x. Here is an additional example.

EXAMPLE 6.2.5   If $f(x, y) = x^3 e^{y^2}$, find the first- and second-order partial derivatives at the point $(x, y) = (1, 0)$.

Solution: To find $f'_1(x, y)$, we differentiate $x^3 e^{y^2}$ w.r.t. x while treating y as a constant. When y is a constant, so is e^{y^2}. Hence, $f'_1(x, y) = 3x^2 e^{y^2}$ and so

$$f'_1(1, 0) = 3 \cdot 1^2 e^{0^2} = 3$$

To find $f'_2(x, y)$, we differentiate $f(x, y)$ w.r.t. y while treating x as a constant:

$$f'_2(x, y) = x^3 2y e^{y^2} = 2x^3 y e^{y^2}$$

and so $f'_2(1, 0) = 0$.

To find the second-order partial $f''_{11}(x, y)$, we must differentiate $f'_1(x, y)$ w.r.t. x once more, while treating y as a constant. Hence, $f''_{11}(x, y) = 6x e^{y^2}$ and so

$$f''_{11}(1, 0) = 6 \cdot 1 e^{0^2} = 6$$

To find $f''_{22}(x, y)$, we must differentiate $f'_2(x, y) = 2x^3 y e^{y^2}$ w.r.t. y once more, while treating x as a constant. Because $y e^{y^2}$ is a product of two functions, each involving y, we use the product rule to obtain

$$f''_{22}(x, y) = (2x^3)(1 \cdot e^{y^2} + y 2y e^{y^2}) = 2x^3 e^{y^2} + 4x^3 y^2 e^{y^2}$$

Evaluating this at $(1, 0)$ gives $f''_{22}(1, 0) = 2$. Moreover,

$$f''_{12}(x, y) = \frac{\partial}{\partial y}\left[f'_1(x, y)\right] = \frac{\partial}{\partial y}(3x^2 e^{y^2}) = 3x^2 2y e^{y^2} = 6x^2 y e^{y^2}$$

and

$$f''_{21}(x, y) = \frac{\partial}{\partial x}\left[f'_2(x, y)\right] = \frac{\partial}{\partial x}(2x^3 y e^{y^2}) = 6x^2 y e^{y^2}$$

Hence, $f''_{12}(1, 0) = f''_{21}(1, 0) = 0$.

EXERCISES FOR SECTION 6.2

1. Find $\partial z/\partial x$ and $\partial z/\partial y$ for the following functions:

    (a) $z = 2x + 3y$ (b) $z = x^2 + y^3$ (c) $z = x^3 y^4$ (d) $z = (x + y)^2$

2. Find $\partial z/\partial x$ and $\partial z/\partial y$ for the following functions:

    (a) $z = x^2 + 3y^2$ (b) $z = xy$ (c) $z = 5x^4 y^2 - 2xy^5$ (d) $z = e^{x+y}$

    (e) $z = e^{xy}$ (f) $z = e^x/y$ (g) $z = \ln(x + y)$ (h) $z = \ln(xy)$

3. Find $f'_1(x, y), f'_2(x, y)$, and $f''_{12}(x, y)$ for the following functions:

    (a) $f(x, y) = x^7 - y^7$ (b) $f(x, y) = x^5 \ln y$ (c) $f(x, y) = (x^2 - 2y^2)^5$

4. Find all first- and second-order partial derivatives for the following functions:

    (a) $z = 3x + 4y$ (b) $z = x^3 y^2$ (c) $z = x^5 - 3x^2 y + y^6$

    (d) $z = x/y$ (e) $z = (x - y)/(x + y)$ (f) $z = \sqrt{x^2 + y^2}$

(SM) **5.** Find all the first- and second-order partial derivatives for the following functions:

(a) $z = x^2 + e^{2y}$ (b) $z = y \ln x$ (c) $z = xy^2 - e^{xy}$ (d) $z = x^y$

6. The estimated production function for a certain fishery is $F(S, E) = 2.26 \, S^{0.44} E^{0.48}$, where S denotes the stock of lobsters, E the harvesting effort, and $F(S, E)$ the catch.

(a) Find $F'_S(S, E)$ and $F'_E(S, E)$.

(b) Show that $SF'_S + EF'_E = kF$ for a suitable constant k.

7. Prove that if $z = (ax + by)^2$, then $xz'_x + yz'_y = 2z$.

8. Let $z = \frac{1}{2} \ln(x^2 + y^2)$. Show that $\partial^2 z / \partial x^2 + \partial^2 z / \partial y^2 = 0$.

9. Suppose that if a household consumes x units of one good and y units of a second good, its satisfaction is measured by the function $s(x, y) = 2 \ln x + 4 \ln y$. Suppose that the household presently consumes 20 units of the first good and 30 units of the second. What is the approximate increase in satisfaction from consuming one extra unit of: (a) the first good? (b) the second good?

6.3   Geometric Representation

When studying functions of one variable, we saw how useful it was to represent the function by its graph in a coordinate system in the plane. This section considers how to visualize functions of two variables as having graphs which form surfaces in a three-dimensional space. We begin by introducing a coordinate system in the space.

Recall how any point in a plane can be represented by a pair of real numbers by using two mutually orthogonal coordinate lines: a rectangular coordinate system in the plane. In a similar way, points in three-dimensional space can be represented by triples of real numbers using three mutually orthogonal coordinate lines. In Fig. 6.3.1 we have drawn such a coordinate system. The three lines that are orthogonal to each other and intersect at the point O in Fig. 6.3.1 are called *coordinate axes*. They are usually called the x-axis, y-axis, and z-axis. We choose units to measure the length along each axis, and select a positive direction on each of them as indicated by the arrows.

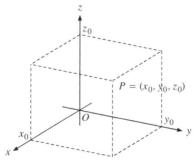

Figure 6.3.1   A coordinate system

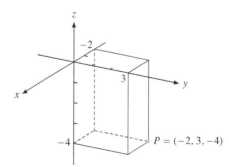

Figure 6.3.2 $P = (-2, 3, -4)$

The equation $x = 0$ is satisfied by all points in a *coordinate plane* spanned by the y-axis and the z-axis. This is called the yz-plane. There are two other coordinate planes: the xy-plane on which $z = 0$; and the xz-plane on which $y = 0$. We often think of the xy-plane as horizontal, with the z-axis passing vertically through it.

Each coordinate plane divides the space into two *half-spaces*. For example, the xy-plane separates the space into the regions where $z > 0$, above the xy-plane, and $z < 0$, below the xy-plane. The three coordinate planes together divide up the space into eight *octants*. The octant which has $x \geq 0$, $y \geq 0$, and $z \geq 0$ is called the *nonnegative octant*.

Every point P in space now has an associated triple of numbers (x_0, y_0, z_0) that describes its location, as suggested in Fig. 6.3.1. Conversely, it is clear that every triple of numbers also represents a unique point in space in this way. Note in particular that when z_0 is negative, the point (x_0, y_0, z_0) lies below the xy-plane in which $z = 0$. In Fig. 6.3.2, we have constructed the point P with coordinates $(-2, 3, -4)$. Point P in Fig. 6.3.1 lies in the positive octant.

The Graph of a Function of Two Variables

Suppose $z = f(x, y)$ is a function of two variables defined over a domain D in the xy-plane. The *graph* of the function f is the set of all points $(x, y, f(x, y))$ in the space obtained by letting (x, y) "run through" the whole of D. If f is a sufficiently "nice" function, the graph of f will be a connected surface in the space, like the graph in Fig. 6.3.3. In particular, if (x_0, y_0) is a point in the domain D, we see how the point $P = (x_0, y_0, f(x_0, y_0))$ on the surface is obtained by letting $f(x_0, y_0)$ be the "height" of f at (x_0, y_0).

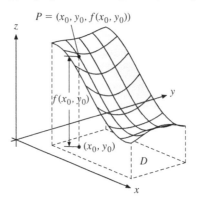

Figure 6.3.3   Graph of $y = f(x, y)$

A talented sculptor with plenty of time and resources could in principle construct this three-dimensional graph of the function $z = f(x, y)$. So could a 3D printer. Even drawing a figure like Fig. 6.3.3, which represents this graph in two dimensions, requires considerable artistic ability.[4]

We now describe a second kind of geometric representation that often does better when we are confined to two dimensions, as we are in the pages of this book.

---

[4] Using modern computer graphics, however, complicated functions of two variables can have their graphs drawn fairly easily, and these can be rotated or transformed to display the shape of the graph better.

Level Curves

Map makers can describe some topographical features of the earth's surface such as hills and valleys even in a plane map. The usual way of doing so is to draw a set of *level curves* or contours connecting points on the map that represent places on the earth's surface with the same elevation above sea level. For instance, there may be such contours corresponding to 100 metres above sea level, others for 200, 300, and 400 metres above sea level, and so on. Off the coast, or in places like the valley of the River Jordan, which drains into the Dead Sea, there may be contours for 100 metres below sea level, etc. Where the contours are closer together, that indicates a hill with a steeper slope. Thus, studying a contour map carefully can give a good idea how the altitude varies on the ground.

The same idea can be used to give a geometric representation of an arbitrary function $z = f(x, y)$. The graph of the function in the three-dimensional space is visualized as being cut by horizontal planes parallel to the xy-plane. The resulting intersection between each plane and the graph is then projected onto the xy-plane. If the intersecting plane is $z = c$, then the projection of the intersection onto the xy-plane is called the *level curve* at height c for f. This level curve will consist of points satisfying the equation $f(x, y) = c$. Figure 6.3.4 illustrates the construction of such a level curve.

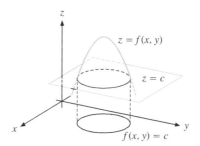

Figure 6.3.4 The graph of $z = f(x, y)$ and one of its level curves

EXAMPLE 6.3.1   Consider the function of two variables defined by the equation

$$z = x^2 + y^2 \qquad (*)$$

What are the level curves? Draw both a set of level curves and the graph of the function.

Solution: The variable z can only assume values ≥ 0. Each level curve has the equation

$$x^2 + y^2 = c \qquad (**)$$

for some $c \geq 0$. We see that these are circles in the xy-plane centred at the origin and with radius $\sqrt{c}$, as in Fig. 6.3.5.

As for the graph of $(*)$, all the level curves are circles. For $y = 0$, we have $z = x^2$. This shows that the graph of $(*)$ cuts the xz-plane (where $y = 0$) in a parabola. Similarly, for $x = 0$, we have $z = y^2$, which is the graph of a parabola in the yz-plane. In fact, the graph of $(*)$ is obtained by rotating the parabola $z = x^2$ around the z-axis. This surface of revolution is called a *paraboloid*, with its lowest part shown in Fig. 6.3.6. Five of the level curves in the xy-plane are also indicated.

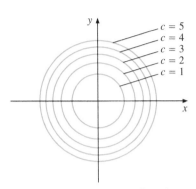

Figure 6.3.5 Solutions of $x^2 + y^2 = c$

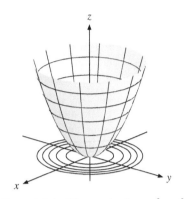

Figure 6.3.6 The graph of $z = x^2 + y^2$

EXAMPLE 6.3.2   Suppose $F(K, L)$ denotes a firm's output when its inputs of capital and labour are, respectively, K and L. A level curve for this production function is a curve in the KL-plane given by $F(K, L) = Y_0$, where Y_0 is a constant. This curve is called an *isoquant*, signifying "equal quantity". For a Cobb–Douglas function, $F(K, L) = AK^a L^b$, with $a + b < 1$ and $A > 0$, Figs 6.3.7 and 6.3.8, respectively, show a part of the graph near the origin, and three of the isoquants.

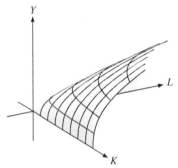

Figure 6.3.7 Graph of a
Cobb–Douglas production function

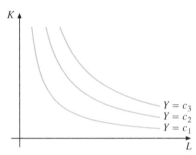

Figure 6.3.8 Isoquants of a
Cobb–Douglas production function

EXAMPLE 6.3.3   Show that all points (x, y) satisfying $xy = 3$ lie on a level curve for the function

$$g(x, y) = \frac{3(xy + 1)^2}{x^4 y^4 - 1}$$

Solution: By substituting $xy = 3$ in the expression for g, we find

$$g(x, y) = \frac{3(xy + 1)^2}{(xy)^4 - 1} = \frac{3(3 + 1)^2}{3^4 - 1} = \frac{48}{80} = \frac{3}{5}$$

This shows that, for all (x, y) where $xy = 3$, the value of $g(x, y)$ is a constant $3/5$. Hence, any point (x, y) satisfying $xy = 3$ is on a level curve (at height $3/5$) for g.[5]

---

[5] In fact, $g(x, y) = 3(c + 1)^2/(c^4 - 1)$ whenever $xy = c \neq \pm 1$, so this equation represents a level curve for g for every value of c except $c \neq \pm 1$.

Geometric Interpretations of Partial Derivatives

Partial derivatives of the first order have an interesting geometric interpretation. Let $z = f(x, y)$ be a function of two variables, with its graph as shown in Fig. 6.3.9. Let us keep the value of y fixed at y_0. The points $(x, y, f(x, y))$ on the graph of f that have $y = y_0$ are those that lie on the curve K_y indicated in the figure. The partial derivative $f'_x(x_0, y_0)$ is the derivative of $z = f(x, y_0)$ w.r.t. x at the point $x = x_0$, and is therefore the slope of the tangent line l_y to the curve K_y at $x = x_0$. In the same way, $f'_y(x_0, y_0)$ is the slope of the tangent line l_x to the curve K_x at $y = y_0$.

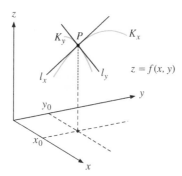

Figure 6.3.9 Partial derivatives

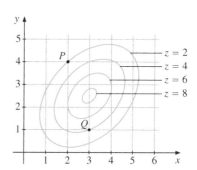

Figure 6.3.10 Level curves

This geometric interpretation of the two partial derivatives can be explained in another way. Imagine that the graph of f looks like the surface of a mountain, as in Fig. 6.3.9, and suppose that we are standing at point P with coordinates $(x_0, y_0, f(x_0, y_0))$ in three dimensions, where the height is $f(x_0, y_0)$ units above the xy-plane. The slope of the terrain at P varies as we look in different directions. In particular, suppose we look in the direction parallel to the positive x-axis. Then $f'_x(x_0, y_0)$ is a measure of the "steepness" in this direction. In the figure, $f'_x(x_0, y_0)$ is negative, because moving from P in the direction given by the positive x-axis will take us downwards. In the same way, we see that $f'_y(x_0, y_0)$ is a measure of the "steepness" in the direction parallel to the positive y-axis. We see that $f'_y(x_0, y_0)$ is positive, meaning that the slope is upward in this direction.

Let us now briefly consider the geometric interpretation of the "direct" second-order derivatives f''_{xx} and f''_{yy}. Consider the curve K_y on the graph of f in Fig. 6.3.9. It seems that along this curve, $f''_{xx}(x, y_0)$ is negative, because $f'_x(x, y_0)$ decreases as x increases. In particular, $f''_{xx}(x_0, y_0) < 0$. In the same way, we see that moving along K_x makes $f'_y(x_0, y)$ decrease as y increases, so $f''_{yy}(x_0, y) < 0$ along K_x. In particular, $f''_{yy}(x_0, y_0) < 0$. The cross-partials, f''_{xy} and f''_{yx}, do not have such easy geometric interpretations.[6]

---

[6] Consider again the curve K_y, and recall that its position is determined by the value of y, namely y_0, which we are keeping fixed when we compute the partial w.r.t. x. The first partial is $f'_x(x, y_0)$, which we can see as the slope of line l_y in the direction of the x-axis. Now, imagine that you increase y_0 slightly, so that the curve K_y gets pushed in the direction of the y-axis. Of course, the l_y lines gets pushed too, and its slope may change. The cross-partial f''_{xy} measures the magnitude of that change.

EXAMPLE 6.3.4   Consider Fig. 6.3.10 which shows some level curves of a function $z = f(x\ y)$. On the basis of this figure, answer the following questions:

(a) What are the signs of $f_x'(x, y)$ and $f_y'(x, y)$ at the points P and Q? Estimate also the *value* of $f_x'(3, 1)$.

(b) What are the solutions of the equations: (i) $f(3, y) = 4$; and (ii) $f(x, 4) = 6$?

(c) What is the largest value that $f(x, y)$ can attain when $x = 2$, and for which y value does this maximum occur?

Solution:

(a) If you stand at P, you are on the level curve $f(x, y) = 2$. If you look in the direction of the positive x-axis, along the line $y = 4$, then you will see the terrain sloping upwards, because the nearest level curves will correspond to larger z values. Hence, $f_x' > 0$. If you stand at P and look in the direction of the positive y-axis, along $x = 2$, the terrain will slope downwards. Thus, at P, we must have $f_y' < 0$. At Q, we find similarly that $f_x' < 0$ and $f_y' > 0$. To estimate $f_x'(3, 1)$, we use $f_x'(3, 1) \approx f(4, 1) - f(3, 1) = 2 - 4 = -2$.[7]

(b) Equation (i) has the solutions $y = 1$ and $y = 4$, because the line $x = 3$ cuts the level curve $f(x, y) = 4$ at $(3, 1)$ and at $(3, 4)$. Equation (ii) has no solutions, because the line $y = 4$ does not meet the level curve $f(x, y) = 6$ at all.

(c) The highest value of c for which the level curve $f(x, y) = c$ has a point in common with the line $x = 2$ is $c = 6$. The largest value of $f(x, y)$ when $x = 2$ is therefore 6, and we see from Fig. 6.3.10 that this maximum value is attained when $y \approx 2.2$.

Gradients

We conclude this section by giving a geometric interpretation of the two partial derivatives on the xy-plane. At any point $(x, y) = (a, b)$, the two partials can be written together as the pair

$$(f_1'(a, b), f_2'(a, b)) \tag{$*$}$$

This pair, of course, can itself be represented in the plane, as in Fig. 6.3.11. In the figure, we have used $Df(a, b)$ to denote the pair $(*)$, and have indicated it by a line that connects the point with these coordinates to the origin. Suppose we add (a, b) to the pair $(*)$, giving $(a, b) + Df(a, b) = (a + f_1'(a, b), b + f_2'(a, b))$. Then we are moving the line from the origin to the point (a, b). In the figure, we have also transformed the line into an arrow, and have drawn a line that is perpendicular to it and goes through the point (a, b). We also have the level curve of function f going through that point. We will elaborate more on this in FMEA, but there are three important ideas to remember:

1. The line that is perpendicular to the arrow is also tangent to the level curve; this implies that a small change to (x, y) in the direction of that line leaves the value of the function unchanged.

---

[7] This approximation is actually far from exact. If we keep $y = 1$ and *decrease* x by one unit, then $f(2, 1) \approx 4$, which should give the estimate $f_x'(3, 1) \approx 4 - 4 = 0$. The "map" is not sufficiently finely graded around Q.

2. A small change to (x, y) in the direction of the arrow, on the other hand, induces the fastest possible increase in the value of the function. A step in the direction opposite to the arrow would induce the fastest possible decrease in the value of the function.

3. The length of the arrow indicates the rate of change by which the function would increase after a perturbation to (x, y) in that direction. The longer the arrow, the faster the increase.

The pair $Df(a, b) = (f_1'(a, b), f_2'(a, b))$ is a very useful object. In more advanced differential calculus, it allows our analysis to be generalized to changes in (x, y) in any direction on the plane, and not just parallel to one of the two axes. Then $Df(a, b)$ is usually thought of as an arrow, or "vector", which is called *the gradient vector of the function f at the point* (a, b).

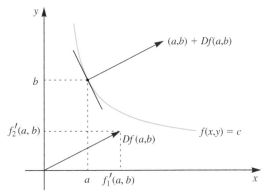

Figure 6.3.11   The gradient vector

EXERCISES FOR SECTION 6.3

1. Draw a three-dimensional coordinate system, including a box like those shown in Figs 6.3.1 and 6.3.2, and mark the points $P = (3, 0, 0)$, $Q = (0, 2, 0)$, $R = (0, 0, -1)$, and $S = (3, -2, 4)$.

2. Describe geometrically the set of points (x, y, z) in three dimensions, where: (a) $y = 2$ and $z = 3$ while x varies freely; (b) $y = x$ while z varies freely.

3. Show that $x^2 + y^2 = 6$ is a level curve of $f(x, y) = \sqrt{x^2 + y^2} - x^2 - y^2 + 2$.

4. Show that $x^2 - y^2 = c$ is a level curve of $f(x, y) = e^{x^2} e^{-y^2} + x^4 - 2x^2 y^2 + y^4$ for all values of the constant c.

5. Explain why two level curves of the function $z = f(x, y)$ corresponding to different values of z cannot intersect.

6. Let $f(x)$ represent a function of one variable. If we let $g(x, y) = f(x)$, then we have defined a function of two variables, but y is not present in its formula. Explain how the graph of g is obtained from the graph of f. Illustrate with $f(x) = x$ and also with $f(x) = -x^3$.

7. Draw the graphs of the following functions in three-dimensional space, and draw a set of level curves for each of them:

   (a) $z = 3 - x - y$ (b) $z = \sqrt{3 - x^2 - y^2}$

8. Figure 6.3.12 shows some level curves for the function $z = f(x, y)$.

(a) What is $f(2, 3)$? Solve the equation $f(x, 3) = 8$ for x.

(b) Find the smallest value of $z = f(x, y)$ if $x = 2$. What is the corresponding value of y?

(c) What are the signs of $f_1'(x, y)$ and $f_2'(x, y)$ at the points A, B, and C? Estimate the values of these two partial derivatives at A.

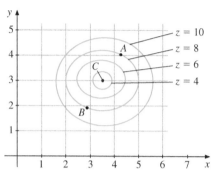

Figure 6.3.12 Exercise 8   **Figure 6.3.13** Exercise 9

(SM) **9.** Figure 6.3.13 shows some level curves for $z = f(x, y)$, together with the line $2x + 3y = 12$.

(a) What are the signs of f_x' and f_y' at the points P and Q?

(b) Find possible solutions of the equations (i) $f(1, y) = 2$; and (ii) $f(x, 2) = 2$.

(c) What is the largest value of $f(x, y)$ among those (x, y) that satisfy $2x + 3y = 12$?

(SM) **10.** [HARDER] Suppose $F(x, y)$ is a function about which nothing is known except that $F(0, 0) = 0$, as well as that $F_1'(x, y) \geq 2$ for all (x, y), and $F_2'(x, y) \leq 1$ for all (x, y). What can be said about the relative sizes of $F(0, 0)$, $F(1, 0)$, $F(2, 0)$, $F(0, 1)$, and $F(1, 1)$? Write down the inequalities that have to hold between these numbers.

6.4 Surfaces and Distance

An equation in *two* variables, such as $f(x, y) = c$, can be represented by a set of points in the plane, called the graph of the equation. In a similar way, an equation in *three* variables x, y, and z, such as $g(x, y, z) = c$, can be represented by a point set in the three-dimensional space, also called the *graph* of the equation. This graph consists of all triples (x, y, z) satisfying the equation, and will usually form what can be called a *surface* in the space.

One of the simplest types of equation in three variables is

$$ax + by + cz = d \tag{6.4.1}$$

with a, b, and c not all 0. This is the general equation for a plane in three-dimensional space. Assuming that a and b are not both 0, the graph of this equation intersects the xy-plane when $z = 0$. Then $ax + by = d$, which is a straight line in the xy-plane unless $a = b = 0$. In the same way we see that, provided at most one of a, b, and c is equal to zero, the graph intersects the two other coordinate planes in straight lines.

Let us rename the coefficients and consider the equation

$$px + qy + rz = m \qquad (6.4.2)$$

where p, q, r, m are all positive. This equation can be given an economic interpretation. Suppose a household has a total budget of m to spend on three commodities, whose prices are respectively p, q, and r per unit. If the household buys x units of the first, y units of the second, and z units of the third commodity, then the total expense is $px + qy + rz$. Hence, Eq. (6.4.2) is the household's *budget equation*: only triples (x, y, z) that satisfy (6.4.2) can be bought if expenditure must equal m. The budget equation represents a *plane* in space, called the *budget plane*. Because in most cases one also has $x \geq 0$, $y \geq 0$, and $z \geq 0$, the interesting part of the plane is the triangle with vertices at $P = (m/p, 0, 0)$, $Q = (0, m/q, 0)$, and $R = (0, 0, m/r)$, as shown in Fig. 6.4.1. If we allow the household to underspend, the *budget set* is defined as

$$B = \{ (x, y, z) : px + qy + rz \leq m, \ x \geq 0, \ y \geq 0, \ z \geq 0 \}$$

This represents the three-dimensional body bounded by the three coordinate planes and the budget plane. It generalizes the two-commodity budget set discussed in Example 3.4.7.

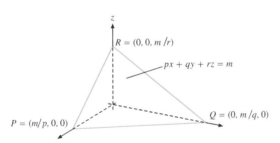

Figure 6.4.1 A budget set when there are three goods

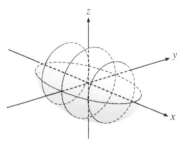

Figure 6.4.2 $x^2/a^2 + y^2/b^2 + z^2/c^2 = 1$ where $a > b = c$ (a rugby ball)

Another rather interesting surface appears in Fig. 6.4.2. This surface is called an *ellipsoid*, which some readers may recognize as having the shape of a rugby ball.

The Distance Formula

In Section 5.5 we gave the formula for the distance between two points in the plane.

Consider a rectangular box with edges of length a, b, and c, as shown in Fig. 6.4.3. By Pythagoras's theorem, $(PR)^2 = a^2 + b^2$, and $(PQ)^2 = (PR)^2 + (RQ)^2 = a^2 + b^2 + c^2$, so that the box has diagonal of length $PQ = \sqrt{a^2 + b^2 + c^2}$.

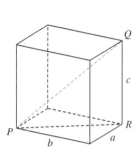

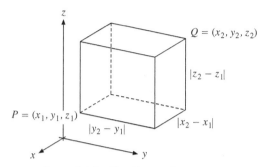

Figure 6.4.3   The distance between points P and Q, denoted PQ

Figure 6.4.4   The distance between two typical points

Next we find the distance between two typical points $P = (x_1, y_1, z_1)$ and $Q = (x_2, y_2, z_2)$ in space, as illustrated in Fig. 6.4.4. These two points lie precisely at the corners of a rectangular box with edges of lengths $a = |x_2 - x_1|$, $b = |y_2 - y_1|$, and $c = |z_2 - z_1|$. Hence

$$(PQ)^2 = a^2 + b^2 + c^2 = |x_2 - x_1|^2 + |y_2 - y_1|^2 + |z_2 - z_1|^2$$
$$= (x_2 - x_1)^2 + (y_2 - y_1)^2 + (z_2 - z_1)^2$$

This motivates the following definition:

DISTANCE BETWEEN TWO POINTS

The *distance* between the two points (x_1, y_1, z_1) and (x_2, y_2, z_2) is

$$d = \sqrt{(x_2 - x_1)^2 + (y_2 - y_1)^2 + (z_2 - z_1)^2} \tag{6.4.3}$$

EXAMPLE 6.4.1   Calculate the distance, d, between the points $(1, 2, -3)$ and $(-2, 4, 5)$.

Solution: According to formula (6.4.3),

$$d = \sqrt{(-2 - 1)^2 + (4 - 2)^2 + (5 - (-3))^2} = \sqrt{(-3)^2 + 2^2 + 8^2} = \sqrt{77} \approx 8.77$$

Let (a, b, c) be a point in space. The sphere with radius r and centre at (a, b, c) is the set of all points (x, y, z) whose distance from (a, b, c) is equal to r. Using the distance formula, we obtain

$$\sqrt{(x - a)^2 + (y - b)^2 + (z - c)^2} = r$$

Squaring each side yields:

EQUATION FOR A SPHERE

The equation for the *sphere* with centre at (a, b, c) and radius r is

$$(x - a)^2 + (y - b)^2 + (z - c)^2 = r^2 \tag{6.4.4}$$

EXAMPLE 6.4.2   Find the equation for the sphere with centre at $(-2, -2, -2)$ and radius 4.

Solution: According to formula (6.4.4), the equation is

$$(x - (-2))^2 + (y - (-2))^2 + (z - (-2))^2 = 4^2$$

or

$$(x + 2)^2 + (y + 2)^2 + (z + 2)^2 = 16$$

EXAMPLE 6.4.3   How do you interpret the expression $(x + 4)^2 + (y - 3)^2 + (z + 5)^2$? As: (i) the sphere with centre at the point $(-4, 3, -5)$, (ii) the distance between the points (x, y, z) and $(-4, 3, -5)$, or (iii) the square of the distance between the points (x, y, z) and $(-4, 3, -5)$?

Solution: Only (iii) is correct.

EXERCISES FOR SECTION 6.4

1. Sketch graphs of the surfaces in space described by each of the following three equations:

(a) $x = a$ (b) $y = b$ (c) $z = c$

2. Find the distances between the following two pairs of points:

(a) $(-1, 2, 3)$ and $(4, -2, 0)$ (b) (a, b, c) and $(a + 1, b + 1, c + 1)$

3. Find the equation for the sphere with centre at $(2, 1, 1)$ and radius 5.

4. What is the geometric interpretation of the equation $(x + 3)^2 + (y - 3)^2 + (z - 4)^2 = 25$?

5. The graph of $z = x^2 + y^2$ is a paraboloid—see Fig. 6.3.6. If the point (x, y, z) lies on this paraboloid, interpret the expression $(x - 4)^2 + (y - 4)^2 + (z - 1/2)^2$.

6.5   Functions of More Variables

Many of the most important functions we study in economics, such as the GDP of a country, depend on a very large number of variables. Mathematicians and economists express this dependence by saying that GDP is a *function* of the different variables.

Any ordered collection of n numbers $(x_1, x_2, \ldots, x_n)$ is called an *n-vector*. To save space, n-vectors are often denoted by bold letters. For example, we write $\mathbf{x} = (x_1, x_2, \ldots, x_n)$.

FUNCTIONS OF n VARIABLES

Given a set D of n-vectors, *a function f of n variables, $x_1, \ldots, x_n$, with domain D is a rule* that assigns a specified number

$$f(\mathbf{x}) = f(x_1, \ldots, x_n) \tag{6.5.1}$$

to each n-vector $\mathbf{x} = (x_1, \ldots, x_n)$ in D.

EXAMPLE 6.5.1

(a) The demand for sugar in the USA in the period 1929–1935 was estimated to be described, approximately, by the formula

$$x = 108.83 - 6.0294p + 0.164w - 0.4217t$$

where x is the demand for sugar, p is its price, w is a production index, and t is the date (where $t = 0$ corresponds to 1929).

(b) The following formula is an estimate for the demand for beer in the UK:

$$x = 1.058x_1^{0.136}x_2^{-0.727}x_3^{0.914}x_4^{0.816}$$

Here the quantity demanded, x, is a function of four variables: x_1, the income of the individual; x_2, the price of beer; x_3, a general price index for all other commodities; and x_4, the strength of the beer.

The simpler of the functions in Example 6.5.1 is the one in part (a). The variables p, w, and t occur here only to the first power, and they are only multiplied by constants, not by each other. Such functions are called *linear*. In general,

$$f(x_1, x_2, \ldots, x_n) = a_1 x_1 + a_2 x_2 + \cdots + a_n x_n + b \tag{6.5.2}$$

where $a_1, a_2, \ldots, a_n$, and b are constants, is a *linear function* in n variables.[8]

The function in part (b) of the example is a special case of the general Cobb–Douglas function

$$F(x_1, x_2, \ldots, x_n) = A x_1^{a_1} x_2^{a_2} \cdots x_n^{a_n} \tag{6.5.3}$$

where $A > 0$, $a_1, \ldots, a_n$ are constants, defined for $x_1 > 0, x_2 > 0, \ldots, x_n > 0$. We use this function very often in this book.

Note that taking the natural logarithm of each side of Eq. (6.5.3) gives

$$\ln F = \ln A + a_1 \ln x_1 + a_2 \ln x_2 + \cdots + a_n \ln x_n \tag{6.5.4}$$

This shows that the Cobb–Douglas function is *log-linear* (or ln-linear), because $\ln F$ is a linear function of $\ln x_1, \ln x_2, \ldots, \ln x_n$.

EXAMPLE 6.5.2   Suppose an economist interested in the price of apples records n observations in different stores. Suppose the results are the n positive numbers $x_1, x_2, \ldots, x_n$. In statistics, several different measures for their average value are used. Some of the most common are generalized versions of the ones seen in Exercise 2.6.9:

(a) the *arithmetic* mean: $\bar{x}_A = \frac{1}{n}(x_1 + x_2 + \cdots + x_n)$

(b) the *geometric* mean: $\bar{x}_G = \sqrt[n]{x_1 x_2 \cdots x_n}$

---

[8] This is rather common terminology, although many mathematicians would insist that f should really be called *affine* if $b \neq 0$, and *linear* only if $b = 0$.

(c) the *harmonic* mean: $\bar{x}_H = \dfrac{1}{\frac{1}{n}\left(\frac{1}{x_1} + \frac{1}{x_2} + \cdots + \frac{1}{x_n}\right)}$

Note that $\bar{x}_A$ is a linear function of $x_1, \ldots, x_n$, whereas $\bar{x}_G$ and $\bar{x}_H$ are nonlinear functions. ($\bar{x}_G$ is log-linear.) For example, if four observations are $x_1 = 1, x_2 = 2, x_3 = 3$, and $x_4 = 4$, then

$$\bar{x}_A = (1 + 2 + 3 + 4)/4 = 2.5, \quad \bar{x}_G = \sqrt[4]{1 \cdot 2 \cdot 3 \cdot 4} = \sqrt[4]{24} \approx 2.21$$

$$\text{and} \quad \bar{x}_H = [(1/1 + 1/2 + 1/3 + 1/4)/4]^{-1} = 48/25 = 1.92$$

In this case $\bar{x}_H < \bar{x}_G < \bar{x}_A$. It turns out that the corresponding weak inequalities

$$\bar{x}_H \leq \bar{x}_G \leq \bar{x}_A \tag{6.5.5}$$

are valid in general.[9]

EXAMPLE 6.5.3   An individual must decide what quantities of n different commodities to buy during a given time period. Consumer demand theory often assumes that the individual has a utility function $U(x_1, x_2, \ldots, x_n)$ representing preferences, and that this measures the satisfaction the individual obtains by acquiring x_1 units of good 1, x_2 units of good 2, and so on. This is an important economic example of a function of n variables, to which we return several times.

One model of consumer demand is the *linear expenditure system*, which is based on the particular utility function

$$U\left(x_1, x_2, \ldots, x_n\right) = a_1 \ln\left(x_1 - c_1\right) + a_2 \ln\left(x_2 - c_2\right) + \cdots + a_n \ln(x_n - c_n)$$

that depends on the $2n$ nonnegative parameters $a_1, a_2, \ldots, a_n$ and $c_1, c_2, \ldots, c_n$. Here, each c_i represents the quantity of the commodity numbered i that the consumer needs to survive. Some, or even all, of the constants c_i could be 0.

Because $\ln z$ is only defined when $z > 0$, we see that all n inequalities $x_1 > c_1, x_2 > c_2, \ldots, x_n > c_n$ must be satisfied if $U(x_1, x_2, \ldots, x_n)$ is to be defined. Of course, the condition $a_i > 0$ implies that the consumer prefers more of the particular good i.

Continuity

The concept of continuity for functions of one variable may be generalized to functions of several variables. Roughly speaking, a function of n variables is *continuous* if small changes in the independent variables induce small changes in the function value. Just as in the one-variable case, we have the following useful rule:

PRESERVATION OF CONTINUITY

Any function of n variables that can be constructed from continuous functions by combining the operations of addition, subtraction, multiplication, division, and functional composition is continuous wherever it is defined.

---

[9] Recall that Exercise 2.6.9 asked you to show Eq. (6.5.5) for the case $n = 2$.

If a function of one variable is continuous, it will also be continuous when considered as a function of several variables. For example, $f(x, y, z) = x^2$ is a continuous function of x, y, and z: small changes in x, y, and z give at most small changes in x^2.

EXAMPLE 6.5.4   Where are the functions given by the following formulas continuous?

(a) $f(x, y, z) = x^2y + 8x^2y^5z - xy + 8z$ (b) $g(x, y) = \dfrac{xy - 3}{x^2 + y^2 - 4}$

Solution:

(a) As the sum of products of positive powers, f is defined and continuous for all x, y, and z.

(b) The function g is defined and continuous for all pairs (x, y) except those that lie on the circle $x^2 + y^2 = 4$. There the denominator is zero, and so $g(x, y)$ is not defined.

Euclidean *n*-Dimensional Space

No concrete geometric interpretation is possible for functions of three or more variables. Yet we can still use *geometric language* when dealing with functions of n variables. It is usual to call the set of all possible n-vectors $\mathbf{x} = (x_1, x_2, \ldots, x_n)$ of real numbers the *Euclidean n-dimensional space*, or *n-space*, and to denote it by $\mathbb{R}^n$. For $n = 1$, $n = 2$, and $n = 3$, we have geometric representations of $\mathbb{R}^n$ as a line, a plane, and a three-dimensional space, respectively. But for $n \geq 4$, there is no geometric representation.

If $z = f(x_1, x_2, \ldots, x_n) = f(\mathbf{x})$ represents a function of n variables, we define the *graph* of f as the set of all points $(\mathbf{x}, f(\mathbf{x}))$ in $\mathbb{R}^{n+1}$ for which $\mathbf{x}$ belongs to the domain of f. We also call the graph a *surface* (or sometimes a *hypersurface*) in $\mathbb{R}^{n+1}$. For $z = z_0$ (constant), the set of points in $\mathbb{R}^n$ satisfying $f(\mathbf{x}) = z_0$ is called a *level surface* of f. When $f(x)$ is a linear function such as $a_1x_1 + a_2x_2 + \cdots + a_nx_n + b$, this surface, which would be a plane if $n = 3$, is called a *hyperplane* when $n > 3$.

In both producer and consumer theory, it is usual to give level surfaces a different name. If $x = f(\mathbf{v}) = f(v_1, v_2, \ldots, v_n)$ is the amount produced when the input quantities of n different factors of production are respectively v_1, v_2, ..., v_n, the level surfaces where $f(v_1, v_2, \ldots, v_n) = x_0$ (constant) are called *isoquants*, as in Example 6.3.2. On the other hand, if $u = U(\mathbf{x})$ is a utility function that represents the consumer's preferences, the level surface where $U(x_1, x_2, \ldots, x_n) = u_0$ is called an *indifference surface*.

EXERCISES FOR SECTION 6.5

1. Let $f(x, y, z) = xy + xz + yz$.

(a) Find $f(-1, 2, 3)$ and $f(a + 1, b + 1, c + 1) - f(a, b, c)$.

(b) Show that $f(tx, ty, tz) = t^2 f(x, y, z)$ for all t.

2. A study of milk production found that

$$y = 2.90 \, x_1^{0.015} x_2^{0.250} x_3^{0.350} x_4^{0.408} x_5^{0.030}$$

where y is the output of milk, and x_1, ..., x_5 are the quantities of five different input factors.

(a) If all the factors of production were doubled, what would happen to y?

(b) Write the relation in log-linear form.

(SM) **3.** A pension fund decides to invest \$720 million in the shares of XYC Inc., a company with a volatile share price. Rather than invest all the money at once and so risk paying an unduly high price, the fund practises "dollar cost averaging" by investing \$120 million per week in six successive weeks. The prices it pays are \$50 per share in the first week, then \$60, \$45, \$40, \$75, and finally \$80 in the sixth week.

(a) How many shares in total does it buy?

(b) Which is the most accurate representation of the average price: the arithmetic mean, the geometric mean, or the harmonic mean?

4. An American bank, A, and a European bank, E, agree a currency swap. In n successive weeks $w = 1, 2, \ldots, n$, bank A will buy \$100 million worth of euros from bank E, at a price of p_w dollars per euro determined by the spot exchange rate at the end of week w. After n weeks:

(a) How many euros will bank A have bought?

(b) What is the dollar price per euro it will have paid, on average?

5. [HARDER] It is observed that three machines A, B, and C produce, respectively, 60, 80, and 40 units of a product during one workday lasting eight hours. The average output is then 60 units per day. We see that A, B, and C use, respectively, eight, six, and 12 minutes to make one unit.

(a) If all machines were equally efficient and jointly produced $60 + 80 + 40 = 180$ units during a day, then how much time would be required to produce each unit?[10]

(b) Suppose that n machines $A_1, A_2, \ldots, A_n$ produce the same product simultaneously during a time interval of length T. Given that the production times per unit are respectively $t_1, t_2, \ldots, t_n$, find the total output Q. Show that if all the machines were equally efficient and together had produced exactly the same total amount Q in the time span T, then the time needed for each machine to produce one unit would be precisely the harmonic mean $\bar{t}_H$ of $t_1, t_2, \ldots, t_n$.

6.6   Partial Derivatives with More Variables

The last section gave several economic examples of functions involving many variables. Accordingly, we need to extend the concept of partial derivative to functions of more than two variables.

PARTIAL DERIVATIVES IN n VARIABLES

If $z = f(\mathbf{x}) = f(x_1, x_2, \ldots, x_n)$, then $\partial f / \partial x_i$, for $i = 1, 2, \ldots, n$, means the partial derivative of $f(x_1, x_2, \ldots, x_n)$ w.r.t. x_i, when all the other variables x_j, for $j \neq i$, are held constant.

---

[10] Note that the answer is not $(8 + 6 + 12)/3$.

So, provided that they all exist, there are n partial derivatives of first order, one for each variable x_i, for $i = 1, \ldots, n$. Other notation used for the first-order partials of $z = f(x_1, x_2, \ldots, x_n)$ includes

$$\frac{\partial f}{\partial x_i} = \frac{\partial z}{\partial x_i} = \partial z/\partial x_i = z_i' = f_i'\left(x_1, x_2, \ldots, x_n\right)$$

EXAMPLE 6.6.1   Find the three first-order partials of $f(x_1, x_2, x_3) = 5x_1^2 + x_1x_2^3 - x_2^2x_3^2 + x_3^3$.

Solution: We find that

$$f_1' = 10x_1 + x_2^3, \ f_2' = 3x_1x_2^2 - 2x_2x_3^2, \ f_3' = -2x_2^2x_3 + 3x_3^2$$

As in (6.2.5), we have the following rough approximation:

APPROXIMATE PARTIAL DERIVATIVE

The partial derivative $\partial z/\partial x_i$ is approximately equal to the per-unit change in $z = f(x_1, x_2, \ldots, x_n)$ caused by an increase in x_i, while holding constant all the other x_j for $j \neq i$.

In symbols, for small h one has

$$f_i'(x_1, \ldots, x_n) \approx \frac{f(x_1, \ldots, x_{i-1}, x_i + h, x_{i+1}, \ldots, x_n) - f(x_1, \ldots, x_{i-1}, x_i, x_{i+1}, \ldots, x_n)}{h}$$

(6.6.1)

For each of the n first-order partials of f, we have n second-order partials:

$$\frac{\partial}{\partial x_j}\left(\frac{\partial f}{\partial x_i}\right) = \frac{\partial^2 f}{\partial x_j \partial x_i} = z_{ij}''$$

provided that all the derivatives exist. Here both i and j may take any value $1, 2, \ldots, n$, so altogether there are n^2 second-order partials.

It is usual to display these second-order partials in an $n \times n$ square array as follows

$$f''(\mathbf{x}) = \begin{pmatrix} f_{11}''(\mathbf{x}) & f_{12}''(\mathbf{x}) & \ldots & f_{1n}''(\mathbf{x}) \\ f_{21}''(\mathbf{x}) & f_{22}''(\mathbf{x}) & \ldots & f_{2n}''(\mathbf{x}) \\ \vdots & \vdots & \ddots & \vdots \\ f_{n1}''(\mathbf{x}) & f_{n2}''(\mathbf{x}) & \ldots & f_{nn}''(\mathbf{x}) \end{pmatrix}$$

(6.6.2)

Such rectangular arrays of numbers (or symbols) are called *matrices*, and (6.6.2) is called the *Hessian matrix* of f at $\mathbf{x} = (x_1, x_2, \ldots, x_n)$.

The n second-order partial derivatives f_{ii}'' found by differentiating twice w.r.t. the same variable are called *direct second-order partials*; the others, f_{ij}'' where $i \neq j$, are *mixed* or *cross* partials.

EXAMPLE 6.6.2   Find the Hessian matrix of the function f defined in Example 6.6.1.

Solution: We differentiate the first-order partials found in Example 6.6.1. The resulting Hessian is

$$\begin{pmatrix} f_{11}'' & f_{12}'' & f_{13}'' \\ f_{21}'' & f_{22}'' & f_{23}'' \\ f_{31}'' & f_{32}'' & f_{33}'' \end{pmatrix} = \begin{pmatrix} 10 & 3x_2^2 & 0 \\ 3x_2^2 & 6x_1x_2 - 2x_3^2 & -4x_2x_3 \\ 0 & -4x_2x_3 & -2x_2^2 + 6x_3 \end{pmatrix}$$

Young's Theorem

If $z = f(x_1, x_2, \ldots, x_n)$, then the two second-order cross-partial derivatives z_{ij}'' and z_{ji}'' are usually equal. That is,

$$\frac{\partial}{\partial x_j}\left(\frac{\partial f}{\partial x_i}\right) = \frac{\partial}{\partial x_i}\left(\frac{\partial f}{\partial x_j}\right)$$

This implies that the order of differentiation does not matter. The next theorem makes precise a more general result.

THEOREM 6.6.1 (YOUNG'S THEOREM)

Suppose that all the m-th-order partial derivatives of the function $f(x_1, x_2, \ldots, x_n)$ are continuous. If any two of them involve differentiating w.r.t. each of the variables the same number of times, then they are necessarily equal.

The content of this result can be explained as follows: Let $m = m_1 + \cdots + m_n$, and suppose that $f(x_1, x_2, \ldots, x_n)$ is differentiated m_1 times w.r.t. x_1, m_2 times w.r.t. x_2, ..., and m_n times w.r.t. x_n.[11] Suppose that the continuity condition is satisfied for these m-th-order partial derivatives. Then we end up with the same result no matter what is the order of differentiation, because each of the final partial derivatives is equal to

$$\frac{\partial^m f}{\partial x_1^{m_1} \partial x_2^{m_2} \ldots \partial x_n^{m_n}}$$

In particular, for the case when $m = 2$, for $i = 1, \ldots, n$ and $j = 1, \ldots, n$,

$$\frac{\partial^2 f}{\partial x_j \partial x_i} = \frac{\partial^2 f}{\partial x_i \partial x_j}$$

if both these partials are continuous. A proof of Young's theorem is given in most advanced calculus books. Exercise 11 shows that the crossed partial derivatives are not always equal.

---

[11]   Some of the integers $m_1, \ldots, m_n$ can be zero, of course.

Formal Definitions of Partial Derivatives

In Section 6.2, we gave a formal definition of partial derivatives for functions of two variables. This was done by modifying the definition of the derivative for a function of one variable. The same modification works for a function of n variables.

Indeed, if $z = f(x_1, \ldots, x_n)$, then with

$$g(x_i) = f(x_1, \ldots, x_{i-1}, x_i, x_{i+1}, \ldots, x_n)$$

we have $\partial z / \partial x_i = g'(x_i)$, where we think of all the variables x_j other than x_i as constants. If we use the definition of $g'(x_i)$, as in (6.2.2), we obtain

$$\frac{\partial z}{\partial x_i} = \lim_{h \to 0} \frac{f(x_1, \ldots, x_i + h, \ldots, x_n) - f(x_1, \ldots, x_i, \ldots, x_n)}{h} \tag{6.6.3}$$

if the limit exists.

As in Section 6.2, if the limit in (6.6.3) does not exist, then we say that $\partial z / \partial x_i$ *does not exist*, or that z is not differentiable w.r.t. x_i at the point. Similarly, the approximation in (6.6.1) holds because the fraction on the right-hand side of Eq. (6.6.3) is close to the limit if $h \neq 0$ is small enough.

Virtually all the functions we consider have continuous partial derivatives everywhere in their domains. If $z = f(x_1, x_2, \ldots, x_n)$ has continuous partial derivatives of first order in a domain D, we call f *continuously differentiable* in D. In this case, f is also called a C^1 *function* on D. If all partial derivatives up to order k exist and are continuous, then f is called a C^k *function*.

EXERCISES FOR SECTION 6.6

1. Calculate $F_1'(1, 1, 1)$, $F_2'(1, 1, 1)$, and $F_3'(1, 1, 1)$ for $F(x, y, z) = x^2 e^{xz} + y^3 e^{xy}$.

(SM) **2.** Calculate all first-order partials of the following functions:

    (a) $f(x, y, z) = x^2 + y^3 + z^4$ (b) $f(x, y, z) = 5x^2 - 3y^3 + 3z^4$ (c) $f(x, y, z) = xyz$

    (d) $f(x, y, z) = x^4 / yz$ (e) $f(x, y, z) = (x^2 + y^3 + z^4)^6$ (f) $f(x, y, z) = e^{xyz}$

3. Let x and y be the populations of two cities and d the distance between them. Suppose that the number of travellers T between the cities is given by $T = kxy/d^n$, where k and n are positive constants. Find $\partial T/\partial x$, $\partial T/\partial y$, and $\partial T/\partial d$, and discuss their signs.

4. Let g be defined by

$$g(x, y, z) = 2x^2 - 4xy + 10y^2 + z^2 - 4x - 28y - z + 24$$

for all (x, y, z).

    (a) Calculate $g(2, 1, 1)$, $g(3, -4, 2)$, and $g(1, 1, a + h) - g(1, 1, a)$.

    (b) Find all partial derivatives of the first and second orders.

5. Let $\pi(p, r, w) = \frac{1}{4} p^2 (1/r + 1/w)$. Find the partial derivatives of π w.r.t. p, r, and w.

6. Find all first- and second-order partials of $w(x, y, z) = 3xyz + x^2y - xz^3$.

7. If $f(x, y, z) = p(x) + q(y) + r(z)$, what are f_1', f_2', and f_3'?

8. Find the Hessian matrices of: (a) $f(x, y, z) = ax^2 + by^2 + cz^2$; (b) $g(x, y, z) = Ax^a y^b z^c$.

9. Prove that if $w = \left(\dfrac{x - y + z}{x + y - z}\right)^h$, then $x\dfrac{\partial w}{\partial x} + y\dfrac{\partial w}{\partial y} + z\dfrac{\partial w}{\partial z} = 0$.

(SM) 10. Define the function $f(x, y, z) = x^{y^z}$ for $x > 0$, $y > 0$, and $z > 0$. Find its first-order partial derivatives by differentiating $\ln f$.

(SM) 11. [HARDER] Define the function $f(x, y) = xy(x^2 - y^2)/(x^2 + y^2)$ when $(x, y) \neq (0, 0)$, and $f(0, 0) = 0$. Find expressions for $f_1'(0, y)$ and $f_2'(x, 0)$, then show that $f_{12}''(0, 0) = -1$ and $f_{21}''(0, 0) = 1$. Check that Young's theorem is not contradicted because f_{12}'' and f_{21}'' are both discontinuous at point $(0, 0)$.

6.7 Economic Applications

This section considers several economic applications of partial derivatives.

EXAMPLE 6.7.1   Consider an agricultural production function $Y = F(K, L, T)$, where Y is the number of units produced, K is capital invested, L is labour input, and T is the area of agricultural land that is used. Then $\partial Y/\partial K = F_K'$ is called the *marginal product of capital*. It is the rate of change of output Y w.r.t. K when L and T are held fixed. Similarly, $\partial Y/\partial L = F_L'$ and $\partial Y/\partial T = F_T'$ are the *marginal products of labour and of land*, respectively. For example, if K is the value of capital equipment measured in dollars, and $\partial Y/\partial K = 5$, then increasing capital input by h units would increase output by approximately $5h$ units.

Suppose, in particular, that F is the Cobb–Douglas function $F(K, L, T) = AK^a L^b T^c$, where A, a, b, and c are positive constants. Find the marginal products, and the second-order partials. Discuss their signs.

Solution: The marginal products are

$$F_K' = AaK^{a-1}L^bT^c, \quad F_L' = AbK^aL^{b-1}T^c, \quad \text{and} \quad F_T' = AcK^aL^bT^{c-1}$$

Assuming K, L, and T are all positive, the marginal products are positive. Thus, an increase in capital, labour, or land will increase the number of units produced.

The cross second-order partials, also called mixed partials, are:[12]

$$F_{KL}'' = AabK^{a-1}L^{b-1}T^c, \quad F_{KT}'' = AacK^{a-1}L^bT^{c-1}, \quad \text{and} \quad F_{LT}'' = AbcK^aL^{b-1}T^{c-1}$$

---

[12] Check for yourself that F_{LK}'', F_{TK}'', and F_{TL}'' give, respectively, the same results.

Note that these partials are positive. We call each pair of factors *complementary*, because more of one increases the marginal product of the other.

The direct second-order partials are

$$F''_{KK} = Aa(a-1)K^{a-2}L^bT^c, \quad F''_{LL} = Ab(b-1)K^aL^{b-2}T^c, \quad F''_{TT} = Ac(c-1)K^aL^bT^{c-2}$$

For instance, F''_{KK} is the partial derivative of the marginal product of capital, F'_K, w.r.t. K. If $a < 1$, then $F''_{KK} < 0$, and there is a diminishing marginal product of capital—that is, a small increase in the capital invested will lead to a decrease in the marginal product of capital. We can interpret this to mean that, although small increases in capital cause output to rise, so that $F'_K > 0$, this rise occurs at a decreasing rate, since $F''_{KK} < 0$. Similarly for labour if $b < 1$, and for land if $c < 1$.

EXAMPLE 6.7.2   Let x be the GDP of a country, and let y be a measure of its level of pollution. If the function $u(x, y)$ purports to measure the total well-being of the society, what signs do you expect $u'_x(x, y)$ and $u'_y(x, y)$ to have? Can you guess what economists usually assume about the sign of $u''_{xy}(x, y)$?

Solution: It is reasonable to expect that well-being increases as GDP increases, but decreases as the level of pollution increases. Hence, we will usually have $u'_x(x, y) > 0$ and $u'_y(x, y) < 0$. According to (6.6.2), $u''_{xy} = (\partial/\partial y)(u'_x)$ is approximately equal to the change in u'_x per unit increase in y, the level of pollution. Moreover, u'_x is, approximately, the increase in welfare per unit increase in x.

It is often assumed that $u''_{xy} < 0$. This implies that the increase in welfare obtained by an extra unit of x will decrease when the level of pollution increases.[13] Because of Young's Theorem, 6.6.1, the inequality $u''_{xy} < 0$ also implies that $u''_{yx} < 0$. Thus the increase in welfare obtained from being exposed to one unit less pollution, which is approximately $-u'_y$, increases with consumption x. This accords with the controversial view that as people can afford to consume more, they also become less tolerant of pollution.

EXERCISES FOR SECTION 6.7

1. The demand for money, M, in the USA for the period 1929–1952 has been estimated as

$$M = 0.14Y + 76.03(r-2)^{-0.84}$$

where Y is the annual national income, and the interest rate is $r\%$ per year, with $r > 2$. Find $\partial M/\partial Y$ and $\partial M/\partial r$, then discuss their signs.

(SM) 2. If a and b are constants, compute the expression $KY'_K + LY'_L$ for the following:

(a) $Y = AK^a + BL^a$ (b) $Y = AK^aL^b$ (c) $Y = \dfrac{K^2L^2}{aL^3 + bK^3}$

---

[13] An analogy: When a confirmed nonsmoker sits in a room filled with tobacco smoke, the extra satisfaction from one more piece of cake will decrease if the concentration of smoke increases too much.

3. The demand for a product, D, depends on the price p of the product and on the price q charged by a competing producer. It is $D(p, q) = a - bpq^{-\alpha}$, where a, b, and α are positive constants with $\alpha < 1$. Find $D_p'(p, q)$ and $D_q'(p, q)$, and comment on the signs of the partial derivatives.

4. Let $F(K, L, M) = AK^a L^b M^c$. Show that $KF_K' + LF_L' + MF_M' = (a + b + c)F$.

5. Let $D(p, q)$ and $E(p, q)$ be the demands for two commodities when the prices per unit are p and q, respectively. Suppose the commodities are *substitutes* in consumption, such as butter and margarine. What are the normal signs of the partial derivatives of D and E w.r.t. p and q?

6. Find $\partial U / \partial x_i$ when $U(x_1, x_2, \ldots, x_n) = 100 - e^{-x_1} - e^{-x_2} - \cdots - e^{-x_n}$.

(SM) 7. [HARDER] Calculate the expression $KY_K' + LY_L'$ for the CES function $Y = Ae^{\lambda t} \left[aK^{-\rho} + bL^{-\rho} \right]^{-\mu/\rho}$.

6.8 Partial Elasticities

Section 7.7 introduced the concept of elasticity for functions of one variable. Here we study the corresponding concept for functions of several variables. This enables us to distinguish between, for instance, the price and income elasticities of demand, as well as between different price elasticities.

Two Variables

If $z = f(x, y)$, we define the partial elasticity of z w.r.t. x and y by

$$\text{El}_x z = \frac{x}{z} \frac{\partial z}{\partial x}, \qquad \text{El}_y z = \frac{y}{z} \frac{\partial z}{\partial y} \qquad (6.8.1)$$

Often economists just refer to the elasticity rather than the partial elasticity. Thus, $\text{El}_x z$ is the elasticity of z w.r.t. x when y is held constant, and $\text{El}_y z$ is the elasticity of z w.r.t. y when x is held constant. The number $\text{El}_x z$ is, approximately, the percentage change in z caused by a 1% increase in x when y is held constant, and $\text{El}_y z$ has a corresponding interpretation.

When all the variables are positive, elasticities can be expressed as logarithmic derivatives. Accordingly,

$$\text{El}_x z = \frac{\partial \ln z}{\partial \ln x}, \quad \text{and} \quad \text{El}_y z = \frac{\partial \ln z}{\partial \ln y} \qquad (6.8.2)$$

EXAMPLE 6.8.1   Find the (partial) elasticities of z w.r.t. x when: (a) $z = Ax^a y^b$; (b) $z = xye^{x+y}$.

Solution:

(a) When finding the elasticity of $Ax^a y^b$ w.r.t. x, the variable y, and thus Ay^b, is held constant. From Example 7.7.1 we obtain $\text{El}_x z = a$. In the same way, $\text{El}_y z = b$.

(b) It is convenient here to use Eq. (6.8.2). Assuming all variables are positive, taking appropriate natural logarithms gives $\ln z = \ln x + \ln y + x + y = \ln x + \ln y + e^{\ln x} + y$. Hence $\text{El}_x z = \partial \ln z / \partial \ln x = 1 + e^{\ln x} = 1 + x$.

EXAMPLE 6.8.2   The demand D_1 for potatoes in the USA, for the period 1927 to 1941, was estimated to be $D_1 = Ap^{-0.28}m^{0.34}$, where p is the price of potatoes and m is mean income. The demand for apples was estimated to be $D_2 = Bq^{-1.27}m^{1.32}$, where q is the price of apples.

Find the price elasticities of demand, $\text{El}_p D_1$ and $\text{El}_q D_2$, as well as the income elasticities of demand $\text{El}_m D_1$ and $\text{El}_m D_2$, and comment on their signs.

Solution: According to part (a) of Example 6.8.1, $\text{El}_p D_1 = -0.28$. If the price of potatoes increases by 1%, demand decreases by approximately 0.28%. Furthermore, $\text{El}_q D_2 = -1.27$, $\text{El}_m D_1 = 0.34$, and $\text{El}_m D_2 = 1.32$.

Both price elasticities $\text{El}_p D_1$ and $\text{El}_q D_2$ are negative, so demand decreases when the price increases in both cases, as seems reasonable. Both income elasticities $\text{El}_m D_1$ and $\text{El}_m D_2$ are positive, so demand increases when mean income increases—as seems reasonable. Note that the demand for apples is more sensitive to both price and income increases than is the demand for potatoes. This also seems reasonable, since at that time potatoes were a more essential commodity than apples for most consumers.

More Variables

If $z = f(x_1, x_2, \ldots, x_n) = f(\mathbf{x})$, we define the *(partial) elasticity* of z, or of f, w.r.t. x_i as the elasticity of z w.r.t. x_i when all the other variables are held constant. Thus, assuming all the variables are positive, we can write

$$\text{El}_i z = \frac{x_i}{f(\mathbf{x})} \frac{\partial f(\mathbf{x})}{\partial x_i} = \frac{x_i}{z} \frac{\partial z}{\partial x_i} = \frac{\partial \ln z}{\partial \ln x_i} \tag{6.8.3}$$

The number $\text{El}_i z$ is approximately equal to the percentage change in z caused by a 1% increase in x_i, the i-th variable, keeping all the other x_j constant. Among other forms of notation commonly used instead of $\text{El}_i z$, we mention: $\text{El}_i f(\mathbf{x})$, $\text{El}_{x_i} z$, ε_i, e_i, and $\hat{z}_i$. The latter, of course, is pronounced "z hat i".

EXAMPLE 6.8.3   Suppose $D = Ax_1^{a_1} x_2^{a_2} \cdots x_n^{a_n}$ is defined for all $x_1 > 0$, $x_2 > 0$, $\ldots$, $x_n > 0$, where $A > 0$ and $a_1, a_2, \ldots, a_n$ are constants. Find the elasticity of D w.r.t. x_i, for $i = 1, \ldots, n$.

Solution: Because all the factors except $x_i^{a_i}$ are constant, we can apply Eq. (7.7.3) to obtain the result $\text{El}_i D = a_i$.

As a special case of this example, suppose that $D_i = Am^{\alpha}p_i^{-\beta}p_j^{\gamma}$, where m is income, p_i is the own price, and p_j is the price of a substitute good. Then α is the income elasticity of demand defined as in Example 6.8.2. On the other hand, $-\beta$ is the elasticity of demand w.r.t. changes in its own price p_i, so it is called the *own-price elasticity* of demand. However, because own-price elasticities of demand are usually negative, one often describes

β rather than $-\beta$ as being the own-price elasticity of demand. Finally, γ is the elasticity of demand w.r.t. the price of the specified substitute. By analogy with the cross-partial derivatives defined in Section 6.6, it is called a *cross-price elasticity* of demand.

Note that the proportion of income spent on good i is

$$\frac{p_i D_i}{m} = Am^{\alpha-1} p_i^{1-\beta} p_j^{\gamma}$$

When the income elasticity $\alpha < 1$, this proportion is a decreasing function of income. Economists describe a good with this property as a *necessity*. On the other hand, when $\alpha > 1$, the proportion of income spent on good i rises with income, in which case economists describe good i as a *luxury*. Referring back to Example 6.8.2, these definitions imply that during the period 1927–1941, which includes the years of the Great Depression, potatoes were a necessity, but apples a (relative) luxury.

Exercise 4 considers this distinction between necessities and luxuries for more general demand functions.

EXERCISES FOR SECTION 6.8

1. Find the partial elasticities of z w.r.t. x and y in the following cases:

(a) $z = xy$ (b) $z = x^2 y^5$ (c) $z = x^n e^x y^n e^y$ (d) $z = x + y$

2. Let $z = (ax_1^d + bx_2^d + cx_3^d)^g$, where a, b, c, d, and g are constants. Find $\sum_{i=1}^3 \text{El}_i z$.

3. Let $z = x_1^p \cdots x_n^p \exp(a_1 x_1 + \cdots + a_n x_n)$, where $a_1, \ldots, a_n$, and p are constants. Find the partial elasticities of z w.r.t. $x_1, \ldots, x_n$.

(SM) **4.** Let $D(p, m)$ indicate a typical consumer's demand for a particular commodity, as a function of its price p and the consumer's own income m. Show that the proportion pD/m of income spent on the commodity increases with income if $\text{El}_m D > 1$ (in which case the good is a "luxury", whereas it is a "necessity" if $\text{El}_m D < 1$).

REVIEW EXERCISES

1. Let $f(x, y) = 3x - 5y$. Calculate $f(0, 1), f(2, -1), f(a, a)$, and $f(a + h, b) - f(a, b)$.

2. Let $f(x, y) = 2x^2 - 3y^2$. Calculate $f(-1, 2), f(2a, 2a), f(a, b + k) - f(a, b)$, and $f(tx, ty) - t^2 f(x, y)$.

3. Let $f(x, y, z) = \sqrt{x^2 + y^2 + z^2}$. Calculate $f(3, 4, 0), f(-2, 1, 3)$, and $f(tx, ty, tz)$ for $t \geq 0$.

4. Let $Y = F(K, L) = 15K^{1/5} L^{2/5}$ denote the number of units produced when K units of capital and L units of labour are used as inputs.

(a) Compute $F(0, 0)$, $F(1, 1)$, and $F(32, 243)$.

(b) Find an expression for $F(K + 1, L) - F(K, L)$, and give an economic interpretation.

(c) Compute $F(32 + 1, 243) - F(32, 243)$, and compare the result with what you get by calculating $F'_K(32, 243)$.

(d) Show that $F(tK, tL) = t^k F(K, L)$ for a constant k.

5. According to a study of industrial fishing, the annual herring catch is given by the production function $Y(K, S) = 0.06157K^{1.356}S^{0.562}$ involving the catching effort K and the herring stock S.

(a) Find $\partial Y/\partial K$ and $\partial Y/\partial S$.

(b) If K and S are both doubled, what happens to the catch?

6. For which pairs of numbers (x, y) are the functions given by the following formulas defined?

(a) $3xy^3 - 45x^4 - 3y$ (b) $\sqrt{1 - xy}$ (c) $\ln(2 - (x^2 + y^2))$

7. For which pairs of numbers (x, y) are the functions given by the following formulas defined?

(a) $1/\sqrt{x + y - 1}$ (b) $\sqrt{x^2 - y^2} + \sqrt{x^2 + y^2 - 1}$ (c) $\sqrt{y - x^2} - \sqrt{\sqrt{x} - y}$

8. Complete the following implications:

(a) $z = (x^2y^4 + 2)^5 \Rightarrow \dfrac{\partial z}{\partial x} =$

(b) $F(K, L) = (\sqrt{K} + \sqrt{L})^2 \Rightarrow \sqrt{K}\dfrac{\partial F}{\partial K} =$

(c) $F(K, L) = (K^a + L^a)^{1/a} \Rightarrow KF'_K(K, L) + LF'_L(K, L) =$

(d) $g(t, w) = \dfrac{3t}{w} + wt^2 \Rightarrow \dfrac{\partial^2 g}{\partial w \partial t} =$

(e) $g(t_1, t_2, t_3) = (t_1^2 + t_2^2 + t_3^2)^{1/2} \Rightarrow g'_3(t_1, t_2, t_3) =$

(f) $f(x, y, z) = 2x^2yz - y^3 + x^2z^2 \Rightarrow f'_1(x, y, z) =$, and $f''_{13}(x, y, z) =$

9. Let f be defined for all (x, y) by $f(x, y) = (x - 2)^2(y + 3)^2$.

(a) Calculate $f(0, 0), f(-2, -3)$, and $f(a + 2, b - 3)$.

(b) Find f'_x and f'_y.

10. Verify that the two points $(-1, 5)$ and $(1, 1)$ both lie on the same level curve for the function $g(x, y) = (2x + y)^3 - 2x + 5/y$.

11. For each $c \neq 0$, verify that $x - y = c$ is a level curve for $F(x, y) = \ln(x^2 - 2xy + y^2) + e^{2x-2y}$.

SM 12. Let f be defined for all (x, y) by $f(x, y) = x^4 + 2y^2 - 4x^2y + 4y$.

(a) Find $f'_1(x, y)$ and $f'_2(x, y)$.

(b) Find all pairs (x, y) which solve both equations $f'_1(x, y) = 0$ and $f'_2(x, y) = 0$.

13. Find the partial elasticities of z w.r.t. x and y in the following cases:

(a) $z = x^3y^{-4}$ (b) $z = \ln(x^2 + y^2)$ (c) $z = e^{x+y}$ (d) $z = (x^2 + y^2)^{1/2}$

14. (a) If $F(x, y) = e^{2x}(1 - y)^2$, find $\partial F/\partial y$.

    (b) If $F(K, L, M) = (\ln K)(\ln L)(\ln M)$, find F'_L and F''_{LM}.

    (c) If $w = x^y y^x z^x$, with x, y, and z positive, find w'_x using logarithmic differentiation.

15. [HARDER] Compute $\partial^{p+q} z / \partial y^q \partial x^p$ at $(0, 0)$ for the following:

    (a) $z = e^x \ln(1 + y)$

    (b) $z = e^{x+y}(xy + y - 1)$ (*Hint:* First prove by, induction on n that $\dfrac{d^n}{du^n} e^u u = e^u(u + n)$.)

16. [HARDER] Show that, if $u = Ax^a y^b$, then $u''_{xy}/u'_x u'_y$ can be expressed as a function of u alone. Use this to prove that

$$\frac{1}{u'_x} \frac{\partial}{\partial x} \left(\frac{u''_{xy}}{u'_x u'_y} \right) = \frac{1}{u'_y} \frac{\partial}{\partial y} \left(\frac{u''_{xy}}{u'_x u'_y} \right)$$

Section 4
Optimisation Problems

7

OPTIMISATION

If you want literal realism, look at the world around you; if you want understanding, look at theories.
—Robert Dorfman (1964)

Finding the best way to do a specific task involves what is called an *optimization problem*. Examples abound in almost all areas of human activity. A manager seeks those combinations of inputs, such as capital and labour, that maximize profit or minimize cost. A doctor might want to know when is the best time of day to inject a drug, so as to avoid the concentration in the bloodstream becoming dangerously high. A farmer might want to know what amount of fertilizer per square yard will maximize profits. An oil company may wish to find the optimal rate of extraction from its wells.

Studying an optimization problem of this sort systematically requires a mathematical model. Constructing one is usually not easy, and only in simple cases will the model lead to the problem of maximizing or minimizing a function of a single variable—the main topic of this chapter.

In general, no mathematical methods are more important in economics than those designed to solve optimization problems. Though economic optimization problems usually involve several variables, the examples of quadratic optimization in Section 3.6 indicate how useful economic insights can be gained even from simple one-variable optimization.

7.1 Extreme Points

Those points in the domain of a function where it reaches its largest and its smallest values are usually referred to as maximum and minimum points. If we do not need to bother about the distinction between maxima and minima, we call them *extreme points*, or *extrema*. Thus, if $f(x)$ has domain D, then

$$c \in D \text{ is a } maximum \ point \text{ for } f \Leftrightarrow f(x) \le f(c) \text{ for all } x \in D \tag{7.1.1}$$

$$d \in D \text{ is a } minimum \ point \text{ for } f \Leftrightarrow f(x) \ge f(d) \text{ for all } x \in D \tag{7.1.2}$$

In (7.1.1), we call $f(c)$ the *maximum value*, and in (7.1.2), we call $f(d)$ the *minimum value*.[1] If the value of f at c is strictly larger than at any other point in D, then c is a *strict maximum* point. Similarly, d is a *strict minimum* point if $f(x) > f(d)$ for all $x \in D$, $x \ne d$. As collective names, we use the terms *optimal points* and *values*, or *extreme points* and *values*.

If f is a function with domain D, then the function $-f$ is defined in D by $(-f)(x) = -f(x)$. Note that $f(x) \le f(c)$ for all x in D if and only if $-f(x) \ge -f(c)$ for all x in D. Thus, point c maximizes f in D if and only if it minimizes $-f$ in D. This simple observation, which is illustrated in Fig. 7.1.1, can be used to convert maximization problems to minimization problems and vice versa.

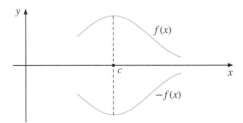

Figure 7.1.1 Point c is a maximum point for $f(x)$, and a minimum point for $-f(x)$

Sometimes we can find the maximum and minimum points of a function simply by studying the formula that defines it.

EXAMPLE 7.1.1   Find possible maximum and minimum points for:

(a) $f(x) = 3 - (x - 2)^2$ (b) $g(x) = \sqrt{x - 5} - 100$, for $x \ge 5$

Solution:

(a) Because $(x - 2)^2 \ge 0$ for all x, it follows that $f(x) \le 3$ for all x. But $f(x) = 3$ when $(x - 2)^2 = 0$ at $x = 2$. Therefore, $x = 2$ is a maximum point for f. Because $f(x) \to -\infty$ as $x \to \infty$, f has no minimum.

(b) Since $\sqrt{x - 5}$ is ≥ 0 for all $x \ge 5$, it follows that $f(x) \ge -100$ for all $x \ge 5$. Since $f(5) = -100$, we conclude that $x = 5$ is a minimum point. Since $f(x) \to \infty$ as $x \to \infty$, f has no maximum.

---

[1] Some authors use different terminology, referring to the extreme values as the maximum or minimum, and to the points where these values are reached as *maximizers* or *minimizers*.

Rarely can we find extreme points as simply as in Example 7.1.1. The main task of this chapter is to explain how to locate possible extreme points in more complicated cases.

Suppose that c is a point in some interval I. If c is not an end point of I, it is possible to construct another interval, perhaps very small, that contains points on both sides of c, but which is completely included in I. Suppose, for instance, that c lies in $I = (a, b]$. If $c < b$, then the smaller of the two numbers $c - a$ and $b - c$ will be larger than zero. Let us denote that smaller number by δ and define the interval $J = (c - \delta, c + \delta)$. Then we will have numbers in J on both sides of c, while $J \subseteq I$. The same is not true if $c = b$, as any interval that includes numbers to the right of c will have elements outside of I. In order to distinguish these two situations, we say that any $c < b$ that lies in I is *interior* to I, while b is on the *boundary* of I, as is a. To make this idea explicit:

INTERIOR OF AN INTERVAL

Let a and b be real numbers. All the points in the open interval (a, b) are *interior* to the intervals $[a, b]$, $[a, b)$, $(a, b]$ and (a, b). For the intervals $[a, b)$ and (a, b), the end point b can be ∞; for the intervals $(a, b]$ and (a, b), the end point a can be $-\infty$.

An essential observation is that if f is a differentiable function that has a maximum or minimum at an interior point c of its domain, then the tangent line to its graph must be horizontal (parallel to the x-axis) at that point. Hence, $f'(c) = 0$. Points c at which f is differentiable and $f'(c) = 0$ are called *critical*, or *stationary*, *points* for f. Precisely formulated, one has the following theorem:

THEOREM 7.1.1 (NECESSARY FIRST-ORDER CONDITION)

Suppose that a function f is differentiable in an interval I and that c is an interior point of I. For $x = c$ to be a maximum or minimum point for f in I, a necessary condition is that it is a critical point for f—i.e., $x = c$ is a solution of

$$f'(x) = 0 \tag{7.1.3}$$

A proof of the theorem is as follows:

Suppose that f has a maximum at c. If the absolute value of h is sufficiently small, then $c + h \in I$ because c is an interior point of I. Because c is a maximum point, $f(c + h) - f(c) \leq 0$. If h is sufficiently small and positive, the Newton quotient satisfies $[f(c + h) - f(c)]/h \leq 0$. The limit of this quotient as $h \to 0^+$ is therefore ≤ 0 as well. But because $f'(c)$ exists, this limit is equal to $f'(c)$, so $f'(c) \leq 0$. For small negative values of h, on the other hand, we get $[f(c + h) - f(c)]/h \geq 0$. The limit of this expression as $h \to 0^-$ is therefore ≥ 0. So $f'(c) \geq 0$. We have now proved that $f'(c) \leq 0$ and $f'(c) \geq 0$, so $f'(c) = 0$.

The proof in the case when c is a minimum point is similar.

Before starting to explore systematically other properties of maxima and minima, we provide some geometric examples. They will indicate for us the role played by the critical points of a function in the theory of optimization. Figure 7.1.2 shows the graph of a function f defined in an interval $[a, b]$ and having two critical points, c and d. At c, there is a maximum; at d, there is a minimum.

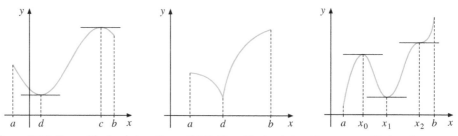

Figure 7.1.2 Two critical points   **Figure 7.1.3** No critical points   **Figure 7.1.4** No interior extrema

In Fig. 7.1.3, the function has no critical points. There is a maximum at the end point b and a minimum at d. At d, the function is not differentiable. At b, the derivative (the left-hand derivative) is not 0.

Condition (7.1.3) is known as a first-order condition, or FOC, as it refers to the function's first derivative. Theorem 7.1.1 implies that (7.1.3) is a *necessary* condition for a differentiable function f to have a maximum or minimum at an interior point x in its domain. The condition is far from sufficient. This is illustrated in Fig. 7.1.4, where f has three critical points, x_0, x_1, and x_2, but none of them are extrema. At the end point a there is a minimum, whereas at end point b there is a maximum.[2] At the critical point x_0 the function f has a "local maximum", in the sense that its value at that point is higher than at all neighbouring points. Similarly, at x_1 it has a local "minimum", whereas at x_2 there is a critical point that is neither a local minimum nor a local maximum—in fact, x_2 is a special case of an *inflection point*.

The situation suggested in Fig. 7.1.2 is the most typical for problems arising in applications, since maximum and minimum points usually will be attained at critical points. But Figs 7.1.3 and 7.1.4 illustrate situations that *can* occur, also in economic problems. Actually, the three figures represent important aspects of single-variable optimization problems. Because the theory is so important in economics, we must not simply rely on vague geometric insights. Instead, we must develop a firmer analytical foundation by formulating precise mathematical results.

---

[2] Or, if you prefer, suppose that b is not in the domain of the function, and that $f(x)$ approaches ∞ as x tends to b.

1. Use arguments similar to those in Example 7.1.1 to find the maximum or minimum points for the following functions:

(a) $f(x) = \dfrac{8}{3x^2 + 4}$ (b) $g(x) = 5(x + 2)^4 - 3$ (c) $h(x) = \dfrac{1}{1 + x^4}$ for $x \in [-1, 1]$

(d) $F(x) = \dfrac{-2}{2 + x^2}$ (e) $G(x) = 2 - \sqrt{1 - x}$ (f) $H(x) = 100 - e^{-x^2}$

7.2 Simple Tests for Extreme Points

In many cases we can find maximum or minimum values for a function just by studying the sign of its first derivative. Suppose $f(x)$ is differentiable in an interval I and that it has only one critical point, $x = c$. Suppose $f'(x) \geq 0$ for all x in I such that $x \leq c$, whereas $f'(x) \leq 0$ for all x in I such that $x \geq c$. Then $f(x)$ is increasing to the left of c and decreasing to the right of c. It follows that $f(x) \leq f(c)$ for all $x \leq c$, and $f(c) \geq f(x)$ for all $x \geq c$. Hence, $x = c$ is a maximum point for f in I, as illustrated in Fig. 7.2.1.

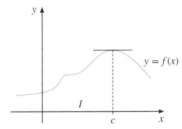 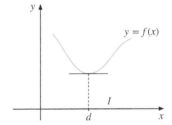

Figure 7.2.1 $x = c$ is a maximum point   **Figure 7.2.2** $x = d$ is a minimum point

With obvious modifications, a similar result holds for minimum points, as illustrated in Fig. 7.2.2. Briefly stated:[3]

THEOREM 7.2.1 (FIRST-DERIVATIVE TEST FOR EXTREMA)

Suppose the function $f(x)$ is differentiable in an interval I that includes c.

(i) If $f'(x) \geq 0$ for $x \leq c$ and $f'(x) \leq 0$ for $x \geq c$, then $x = c$ is a maximum point for f in I.

(ii) If $f'(x) \leq 0$ for $x \leq c$ and $f'(x) \geq 0$ for $x \geq c$, then $x = c$ is a minimum point for f in I.

---

[3] Many books in mathematics for economists instruct students always to check so-called second-order conditions, even when this first-derivative test is much easier to use.

EXAMPLE 7.2.1   Measured in milligrams per litre, the concentration of a drug in the bloodstream, t hours after injection, is given by the formula

$$c(t) = \frac{t}{t^2 + 4}, \ t \geq 0$$

Find the time of maximum concentration.

Solution: Differentiating with respect to t yields

$$c'(t) = \frac{1 \cdot (t^2 + 4) - t \cdot 2t}{(t^2 + 4)^2} = \frac{4 - t^2}{(t^2 + 4)^2} = \frac{(2 + t)(2 - t)}{(t^2 + 4)^2}$$

For $t \geq 0$, the term $2 - t$ alone determines the sign of the fraction, because the other terms are positive: if $t \leq 2$, then $c'(t) \geq 0$; whereas if $t \geq 2$, then $c'(t) \leq 0$. We conclude that $t = 2$ maximizes $c(t)$. Thus, the concentration of the drug is highest two hours after injection. Because $c(2) = 0.25$, the maximum concentration is 0.25 mg.

EXAMPLE 7.2.2   Consider the function f that is defined for all x by

$$f(x) = e^{2x} - 5e^x + 4 = (e^x - 1)(e^x - 4)$$

(a) Find the zeros of $f(x)$ and compute $f'(x)$.

(b) Find the intervals where f increases and decreases, and determine its possible extreme points and values.

(c) Examine $\lim_{x \to -\infty} f(x)$, and sketch the graph of f.

Solution:

(a) $f(x) = (e^x - 1)(e^x - 4) = 0$ when $e^x = 1$ and when $e^x = 4$. Hence $f(x) = 0$ for $x = 0$ and for $x = \ln 4$. By differentiating $f(x)$, we obtain $f'(x) = 2e^{2x} - 5e^x$.

(b) $f'(x) = 2e^{2x} - 5e^x = e^x(2e^x - 5)$. Thus $f'(x) = 0$ for $e^x = 5/2 = 2.5$; that is, $x = \ln 2.5$. Furthermore, $f'(x) \leq 0$ for $x \leq \ln 2.5$, and $f'(x) \geq 0$ for $x \geq \ln 2.5$. So $f(x)$ is decreasing in the interval $(-\infty, \ln 2.5]$ and increasing in $[\ln 2.5, \infty)$. Hence $f(x)$ has a minimum at $x = \ln 2.5$, and $f(\ln 2.5) = (2.5 - 1)(2.5 - 4) = -2.25$. Since $f(x) \to \infty$ as $x \to \infty$, $f(x)$ has no maximum.

(c) When $x \to -\infty$, then e^x tends to 0, and $f(x)$ tends to 4. The graph is drawn in Fig. 7.2.3. Note that $y = 4$ is an asymptote as $x \to -\infty$.

Extreme Points for Concave and Convex Functions

Recall the definitions of concave and convex functions in Section 5.9. Suppose that f is concave with $f''(x) \leq 0$ for all x in an interval I. Then $f'(x)$ is decreasing in I. If $f'(c) = 0$ at an interior point c of I, then $f'(x)$ must be nonnegative to the left of c, and nonpositive to the right of c. This implies that the function itself is increasing to the left of c and decreasing to the right of c. We conclude that $x = c$ is a maximum point for f in I. We obviously get a corresponding result for a minimum of a convex function.

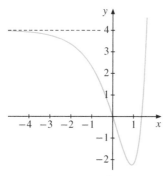

Figure 7.2.3 $f(x) = e^{2x} - 5e^x + 4$

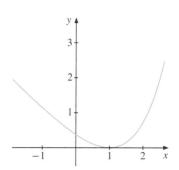

Figure 7.2.4 $f(x) = e^{x-1} - x$

THEOREM 7.2.2 (EXTREMA FOR CONCAVE AND CONVEX FUNCTIONS)

Suppose that f is a function defined in an interval I and that c is a critical point for f in the interior of I.

(i) If f is concave, then c is a maximum point for f in I.

(ii) If f is convex, then c is a minimum point for f in I.

EXAMPLE 7.2.3   Consider the function f defined for all x by $f(x) = e^{x-1} - x$. Show that f is convex and find its minimum point. Sketch the graph.

Solution: $f'(x) = e^{x-1} - 1$ and $f''(x) = e^{x-1} > 0$, so f is convex. Note that $f'(x) = e^{x-1} - 1 = 0$ for $x = 1$. From Theorem 7.2.2 it follows that $x = 1$ minimizes f. See Fig. 7.2.4 for the graph of f, which confirms the result.

EXERCISES FOR SECTION 7.2

1. Let y denote the weekly average quantity of pork produced in Chicago during 1948, in millions of pounds, and let x be the total weekly work effort, in thousands of hours. A study estimated the relation $y = -2.05 + 1.06x - 0.04x^2$. Determine the value of x that maximizes y by studying the sign variation of y'.

(SM) **2.** Find the derivative of the function h, defined for all x by the formula $h(x) = 8x/(3x^2 + 4)$. Note that $h(x) \to 0$ as $x \to \pm\infty$. Use the sign variation of $h'(x)$ to find the extreme points of $h(x)$.

3. The height of a flowering plant after t months is given by $h(t) = \sqrt{t} - \frac{1}{2}t$, for $t \in [0, 3]$. At what time is the plant at its tallest?

4. Show that

$$f(x) = \frac{2x^2}{x^4 + 1} \Rightarrow f'(x) = \frac{4x(1 + x^2)(1 + x)(1 - x)}{(x^4 + 1)^2}$$

and find the maximum value of f on $[0, \infty)$.

5. Find possible extreme points for $g(x) = x^3 \ln x$, for $x \in (0, \infty)$.

6. Find possible extreme points for $f(x) = e^{3x} - 6e^x$, for $x \in (-\infty, \infty)$.

7. Find the maximum of $y = x^2 e^{-x}$ on $[0, 4]$.

(SM) 8. Use Theorem 7.2.2 to find the values of x that maximize/minimize the functions given by the following formulas:

   (a) $y = e^x + e^{-2x}$ (b) $y = 9 - (x - a)^2 - 2(x - b)^2$ (c) $y = \ln x - 5x$, for $x > 0$

9. Consider n numbers $a_1, a_2, \ldots, a_n$. Find the number $\bar{x}$ which gives the best approximation to these numbers, in the sense of minimizing the distance function

$$d(x) = (x - a_1)^2 + (x - a_2)^2 + \cdots + (x - a_n)^2$$

(SM) 10. [HARDER] After the North Sea flood catastrophe in 1953, the Dutch government initiated a project to determine the optimal height of the dykes. One of the models involved finding the value of x minimizing $f(x) = I_0 + kx + Ae^{-\alpha x}$, for $x \geq 0$. Here x denotes the extra height in metres that should be added to the dykes, $I_0 + kx$ is the construction cost, and $Ae^{-\alpha x}$ is an estimate of the expected loss caused by flooding. The parameters I_0, k, A, and α are all positive constants.

   (a) Suppose that $A\alpha > k$ and find $x_0 > 0$ that minimizes $f(x)$.

   (b) The constant A is defined as $A = p_0 V(1 + 100/\delta)$, where p_0 is the probability that the dykes will be flooded if they are not rebuilt, V is an estimate of the cost of flood damage, and δ is an interest rate. Show that

$$x_0 = \frac{1}{\alpha} \ln \left[\frac{\alpha p_0 V}{k} \left(1 + \frac{100}{\delta} \right) \right]$$

   Examine what happens to x_0 when one of the variables p_0, V, δ, or k increases. Comment on the reasonableness of the results.[4]

7.3 Economic Examples

This section presents some interesting instances of economic optimization problems.

EXAMPLE 7.3.1   Suppose $Y(N)$ bushels of wheat are harvested per acre of land when N pounds of fertilizer per acre are used. If P is the dollar price per bushel of wheat and q is the dollar price per pound of fertilizer, then profits in dollars per acre are

$$\pi(N) = PY(N) - qN$$

for $N \geq 0$. Suppose there exists N^* such that $\pi'(N) \geq 0$ for $N \leq N^*$, whereas $\pi'(N) \leq 0$ for $N \geq N^*$. Then N^* maximizes profits, and $\pi'(N^*) = 0$. That is, $PY'(N^*) - q = 0$, so

$$PY'(N^*) = q \tag{$*$}$$

---

[4] This problem is discussed in D. van Dantzig, "Economic Decision Problems for Flood Prevention". *Econometrica*, 24 (1956): 276–287.

Let us give an economic interpretation of this condition. Suppose N^* units of fertilizer are used and we contemplate increasing N^* by one unit. What do we gain? If N^* increases by one unit, then $Y(N^* + 1) - Y(N^*)$ more bushels are produced. Now $Y(N^* + 1) - Y(N^*) \approx Y'(N^*)$. For each of these bushels, we get P dollars, so *by increasing N^* by one unit, we gain approximately $PY'(N^*)$ dollars*. On the other hand, *by increasing N^* by one unit, we lose q dollars*, because this is the cost of one unit of fertilizer. Hence, we can interpret (∗) as follows: In order to maximize profits, you should increase the amount of fertilizer to the level N^* at which an additional pound of fertilizer equates the changes in your gains and losses from the extra pound.

(a) In an (unrealistic) example, suppose that $Y(N) = \sqrt{N}$, $P = 10$, and $q = 0.5$. Find the amount of fertilizer which maximizes profits in this case.

(b) An agricultural study in Iowa estimated the yield function $Y(N)$ for the year 1952 as

$$Y(N) = -13.62 + 0.984N - 0.05N^{1.5}$$

If the price of wheat is $1.40 per bushel and the price of fertilizer is $0.18 per pound, find the amount of fertilizer that maximizes profits.

Solution:

(a) The profit function is

$$\pi(N) = PY(N) - qN = 10N^{1/2} - 0.5N, \ N \geq 0$$

Then $\pi'(N) = 5N^{-1/2} - 0.5$. We see that $\pi'(N^*) = 0$ when $(N^*)^{-1/2} = 0.1$, hence $N^* = 100$. Moreover, it follows that $\pi'(N) \geq 0$ when $N \leq 100$ and $\pi'(N) \leq 0$ when $N \geq 100$. We conclude that $N^* = 100$ maximizes profits. See Fig. 7.3.1.

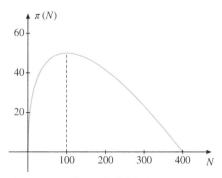

Figure 7.3.1 Example 7.3.1(a)

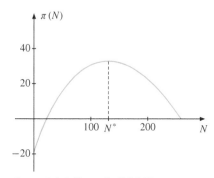

Figure 7.3.2 Example 7.3.1(b)

(b) In this case,

$$\pi(N) = 1.4(-13.62 + 0.984N - 0.05N^{1.5}) - 0.18N$$

$$= -19.068 + 1.1976N - 0.07N^{1.5}$$

so that

$$\pi'(N) = 1.1976 - 0.07 \cdot 1.5N^{0.5} = 1.1976 - 0.105\sqrt{N}$$

Hence $\pi'(N^*) = 0$ when $0.105\sqrt{N^*} = 1.1976$. This implies that

$$\sqrt{N^*} = 1.1976/0.105 \approx 11.4 \quad \text{and so} \quad N^* \approx (11.4)^2 \approx 130$$

By studying the expression for $\pi'(N)$, we see that $\pi'(N)$ is positive to the left of N^* and negative to the right of N^*. Hence, $N^* \approx 130$ maximizes profits. The graph of $\pi(N)$ is shown in Fig. 7.3.2.

EXAMPLE 7.3.2   Suppose that the total cost of producing $Q > 0$ units of a commodity is $C(Q) = aQ^2 + bQ + c$, where a, b, and c are positive constants.

(a) Find the value of Q that minimizes the average cost defined by $A(Q) = C(Q)/Q$ in the special case when $C(Q) = 2Q^2 + 10Q + 32$.

(b) Show that in the general case, the average cost function has a minimum at $Q^* = \sqrt{c/a}$. In the same coordinate system, draw the graphs of the average cost, the marginal cost, and the straight line $P = aQ + b$.

Solution: ·

(a) We find that here $A(Q) = 2Q + 10 + 32/Q$, so $A'(Q) = 2 - 32/Q^2$ and $A''(Q) = 64/Q^3$. Since $A''(Q) > 0$ for all $Q > 0$, the function A is convex, and since $A'(Q) = 0$ for $Q = 4$, this is a minimum point.

(b) We find that here $A(Q) = aQ + b + c/Q$, $A'(Q) = a - c/Q^2$ and $A''(Q) = 2c/Q^3$. Since $A''(Q) > 0$ for all $Q > 0$, the function A is convex, and since $A'(Q) = 0$ for $Q^* = \sqrt{c/a}$, this is a minimum point. The graphs are drawn in Fig. 7.3.3. Note that at the minimum point Q^*, marginal cost is equal to average cost. This is no coincidence, because it is true in general that $A'(Q) = 0$ if and only if $C'(Q) = A(Q)$.[5]

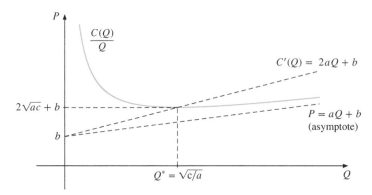

Figure 7.3.3 Average cost function

The following example is typical of how economists use implicit differentiation in connection with optimization problems.

---

[5] See Example 6.7.6. The minimum average cost is $A(Q^*) = a\sqrt{c/a} + b + c/\sqrt{c/a} = \sqrt{ac} + b + \sqrt{ac} = 2\sqrt{ac} + b$.

EXAMPLE 7.3.3   A monopolist is faced with the inverse demand function $P(Q)$ denoting the price when output is Q. The monopolist has a constant average cost k per unit produced.

(a) Find the profit function $\pi(Q)$, and prove that the first-order condition for maximal profit at $Q^* > 0$ is

$$P(Q^*) + Q^* P'(Q^*) = k \qquad (*)$$

(b) By implicit differentiation of $(*)$ find how the monopolist's choice of optimal production is affected by changes in k.

(c) How does the optimal profit react to a change in k?

Solution:

(a) The profit function is $\pi(Q) = QP(Q) - kQ$, so $\pi'(Q) = P(Q) + QP'(Q) - k$. In order for $Q^* > 0$ to maximize $\pi(Q)$, one must have $\pi'(Q^*) = 0$, or equivalently $(*)$.

(b) Assuming that Eq. $(*)$ defines Q^* as a differentiable function of k, we obtain

$$P'(Q^*)\frac{\mathrm{d}Q^*}{\mathrm{d}k} + \frac{\mathrm{d}Q^*}{\mathrm{d}k}P'(Q^*) + Q^*P''(Q^*)\frac{\mathrm{d}Q^*}{\mathrm{d}k} = 1$$

Solving for $\mathrm{d}Q^*/\mathrm{d}k$ gives

$$\frac{\mathrm{d}Q^*}{\mathrm{d}k} = \frac{1}{Q^*P''(Q^*) + 2P'(Q^*)}$$

(c) Because $\pi(Q^*) = Q^*P(Q^*) - kQ^*$, differentiating w.r.t. k gives

$$\frac{\mathrm{d}\pi(Q^*)}{\mathrm{d}k} = \frac{\mathrm{d}Q^*}{\mathrm{d}k}P(Q^*) + Q^*P'(Q^*)\frac{\mathrm{d}Q^*}{\mathrm{d}k} - Q^* - k\frac{\mathrm{d}Q^*}{\mathrm{d}k}$$

But the three terms containing $\mathrm{d}Q^*/\mathrm{d}k$ all cancel because of the first-order condition $(*)$. So $\mathrm{d}\pi^*/\mathrm{d}k = -Q^*$. Thus, if the cost increases by one unit, the optimal profit will decrease by approximately Q^*, the optimal output level.

EXERCISES FOR SECTION 7.3

1. (a) A firm produces $Q = 2\sqrt{L}$ units of a commodity when L units of labour are employed. If the price obtained per unit is €160, and the price per unit of labour is €40, what value of L maximizes profits $\pi(L)$?

(b) A firm produces $Q = f(L)$ units of a commodity when L units of labour are employed. Assume that $f'(L) > 0$ and $f''(L) < 0$. If the price obtained per unit is 1 and price per unit of labour is w, what is the first-order condition for maximizing profits at $L = L^*$?

(c) By implicitly differentiating the first-order condition in (b) w.r.t. w, find how L^* changes when w changes.

(SM) **2.** In Example 7.3.3, suppose that $P(Q) = a - Q$, and assume that $0 < k < a$.

(a) Find the profit maximizing output Q^* and the associated monopoly profit $\pi(Q^*)$.

(b) How does the monopoly profit react to changes in k? Find $\mathrm{d}\pi(Q^*)/\mathrm{d}k$.

(c) The government argues that the monopoly produces too little. It wants to induce the monopolist to produce $\hat{Q} = a - k$ units by granting a subsidy s per unit of output. Calculate the subsidy s required to reach the target.

3. A square tin plate whose edges are 18 cm long is to be made into an open square box of depth x cm by cutting out equally sized squares of width x in each corner and then folding over the edges. Draw a figure, and show that the volume of the box is, for $x \in [0, 9]$:

$$V(x) = x(18 - 2x)^2 = 4x^3 - 72x^2 + 324x$$

Also find the maximum point of V in $[0, 9]$.

4. In an economic model, the proportion of families whose income is no more than x, and who have a home computer, is given by

$$p(x) = a + k(1 - e^{-cx})$$

where a, k, and c are positive constants. Determine $p'(x)$ and $p''(x)$. Does $p(x)$ have a maximum? Sketch the graph of p.

5. Suppose the tax T a person pays on income w is given by $T = a(bw + c)^p + kw$, where a, b, c, and k are positive constants, and $p > 1$. Then the average tax rate is

$$\bar{T}(w) = \frac{T}{w} = a\frac{(bw + c)^p}{w} + k$$

Find the value of income that minimizes the average tax rate.

7.4   The Extreme Value Theorem

The main theorems used so far in this chapter to locate extreme points require the function to be steadily increasing on one side of the point and steadily decreasing on the other side. Many functions with a derivative whose sign varies in a more complicated way may still have a maximum or minimum. This section shows how to locate possible extreme points for an important class of such functions.

It is not difficult to think of functions that have no extreme points. Example 7.2.3 illustrates one such function, but there are even simpler cases such as, for instance, the function $f(x) = x$, defined over the whole real line. The following theorem gives important sufficient conditions for extreme points to exist.

THEOREM 7.4.1   (THE EXTREME VALUE THEOREM)

Suppose that f is a continuous function over a closed and bounded interval $[a, b]$. Then there exists a point d in $[a, b]$ where f has a minimum, and a point c in $[a, b]$ where f has a maximum—that is, one has $f(d) \leq f(x) \leq f(c)$ for all x in $[a, b]$.

One of the most common misunderstandings of the extreme value theorem is illustrated by the following statement from a student's exam paper: "The function is continuous, but since it is not defined on a closed, bounded interval, the extreme value theorem shows that there is no maximum." The misunderstanding here is that, although the conditions of the theorem are sufficient, they certainly are not *necessary* for the existence of an extreme point. In Exercise 9, you will study a function defined in an interval that is neither closed nor bounded, and moreover the function is not even continuous. Even so, it has both a maximum and a minimum.

This observation does not mean, however, that we can dispense with the assumptions of the theorem. Figures 7.4.1 to 7.4.3 display cases where two of the assumptions of Theorem 7.4.1 are satisfied, but the remaining one is not. In each case, the function fails to attain a maximum—even though it possesses a minimum.

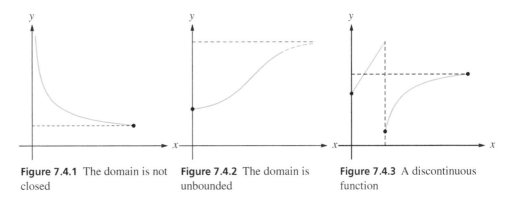

Figure 7.4.1 The domain is not closed

Figure 7.4.2 The domain is unbounded

Figure 7.4.3 A discontinuous function

The proof of the extreme value theorem is surprisingly difficult.[6] Yet the result is not hard to believe. Imagine, for example, a mountainous stage of a cycle race like the Tour de France. Since roads avoid going over cliffs, the height of the road above sea level is a continuous function of the distance travelled, as illustrated in Fig. 7.4.4. As the figure also shows, the stage must take the cyclist over some highest point P, as well as through a lowest point Q. Of course, these points could also be at the start or finish of the ride, and the ride must finish eventually!

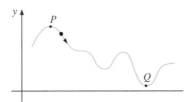

Figure 7.4.4 Altitude as a function of distance

---

[6] The original proof was given by German mathematician Karl Weierstrass (1815–1897). Essentially, the argument is that the range of a continuous function defined over a closed and bounded interval is, itself, closed and bounded. The end points of the range, which are the extreme values of the function, therefore exist.

How to Search for Maxima and Minima

Suppose we know that a function f has a maximum and/or a minimum in some bounded interval I. The optimum must occur either at an interior point of I or else at one of the end points. If it occurs inside the interval I—namely at an interior point—and if f is differentiable, then the derivative f' is zero at that point. In addition, there is the possibility that the optimum occurs at a point where f is not differentiable. Hence, every extreme point must belong to one of the following three different sets:

(a) interior points in I where $f'(x) = 0$;

(b) end points of I, if included in I; and

(c) interior points in I where f' does not exist.

Points satisfying any one of these three conditions will be called *candidate extreme points*. Whether they are actual extreme points depends on a careful comparison of function values, as explained below. A typical example showing that a minimum can occur at a point of type (c) is shown in Fig. 7.1.3. However, most functions that economists study are differentiable everywhere, so the following recipe covers most problems of interest.

FINDING THE EXTREMA OF FUNCTIONS

In order to find the maximum and minimum values of a differentiable function f defined on a closed, bounded interval $[a, b]$.

(i) Find all critical points of f in (a, b) — that is, find all points x in (a, b) that satisfy the FOC, Eq. (7.1.3).

(ii) Evaluate f at the end points a and b of the interval and also at all critical points.

(iii) The largest function value found in (ii) is the maximum value, and the smallest function value is the minimum value of f in $[a, b]$.

A differentiable function is continuous, so the extreme value theorem assures us that maximum and minimum points do exist, provided that its domain is closed and bounded. Following the procedure just given, we can, in principle, find these extreme points.

EXAMPLE 7.4.1   Find the maximum and minimum values, for $x \in [0, 3]$, of:

$$f(x) = 3x^2 - 6x + 5$$

Solution: The function is differentiable everywhere, and $f'(x) = 6x - 6 = 6(x - 1)$. Hence $x = 1$ is the only critical point. The candidate extreme points are the end points 0 and 3, as well as $x = 1$. We calculate the value of f at these three points. The results are $f(0) = 5$, $f(3) = 14$, and $f(1) = 2$. We conclude that the maximum value is 14, obtained at $x = 3$, and the minimum value is 2 at $x = 1$.

EXAMPLE 7.4.2   Find the maximum and minimum values, for $x \in [-1, 3]$, of

$$f(x) = \frac{1}{4}x^4 - \frac{5}{6}x^3 + \frac{1}{2}x^2 - 1$$

Solution: The function is differentiable everywhere, and

$$f'(x) = x^3 - \frac{5}{2}x^2 + x = x\left(x^2 - \frac{5}{2}x + 1\right)$$

Solving the quadratic equation $x^2 - \frac{5}{2}x + 1 = 0$, we get the roots $x = 1/2$ and $x = 2$. Thus $f'(x) = 0$ for $x = 0, x = 1/2$, and $x = 2$. These three points, together with the two end points $x = -1$ and $x = 3$ of the interval, constitute the five candidate extreme points. We find that $f(-1) = 7/12, f(0) = -1, f(1/2) = -185/192, f(2) = -5/3$ and $f(3) = 5/4$. Thus, the maximum value of f is $5/4$, at $x = 3$; the minimum value is $-5/3$, at $x = 2$.

Note that it was unnecessary to study the sign variation of $f'(x)$ or to use other tests, such as second-order conditions, in order to verify that we have found the maximum and minimum values. In the two previous examples, we had no trouble in finding the solutions to the equation $f'(x) = 0$. However, in some cases, finding all the solutions to $f'(x) = 0$ might constitute a formidable, or even insuperable, problem. For instance, the function,

$$f(x) = x^{26} - 32x^{23} - 11x^5 - 2x^3 - x + 28$$

defined for x in $[-1, 5]$ is continuous, so it does have a maximum and a minimum in $[-1, 5]$. Yet it is impossible to find any exact solution to the equation $f'(x) = 0$.

Difficulties of this kind are often encountered in practical optimization problems. In fact, only in very special cases can the equation $f'(x) = 0$ be solved exactly. Fortunately, there are standard numerical methods for use on a computer that in most cases will find points arbitrarily close to the actual solutions of such equations.

The Mean Value Theorem

This section deals with the mean value theorem, which is a principal tool for the precise demonstration of results in calculus. The section is a bit more advanced than the rest of the book, and hence may be considered optional.

Consider a function f defined on an interval $[a, b]$, and suppose that the graph of f is connected and lacks kinks, as illustrated in Fig. 7.4.5. Because the graph of f joins A to B by a connected curve having a tangent at each point, it is geometrically plausible that for at least one value of x between a and b, the tangent to the graph at x should be parallel to the line AB. In Fig. 7.4.5, x^* appears to be such a value of x. The line AB has slope $[f(b) - f(a)]/(b - a)$. So the condition for the tangent line at $(x^*, f(x^*))$ to be parallel to the line AB is that $f'(x^*) = [f(b) - f(a)]/(b - a)$. In fact, x^* can be chosen so that the vertical distance between the graph of f and AB is as large as possible. The proof that follows is based on this fact.

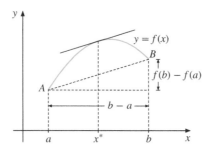

Figure 7.4.5 The mean value theorem

THEOREM 7.4.2 (THE MEAN VALUE THEOREM)

If f is continuous in the closed and bounded interval $[a, b]$, and differentiable in the open interval (a, b), then there exists at least one point x^* in (a, b) such that

$$f'(x^*) = \frac{f(b) - f(a)}{b - a} \qquad (7.4.1)$$

We can prove this theorem as follows:

According to the point–point formula, the straight line through A and B in Fig. 7.4.5 has the equation

$$y - f(a) = \frac{f(b) - f(a)}{b - a}(x - a)$$

The function

$$g(x) = f(x) - f(a) - \frac{f(b) - f(a)}{b - a}(x - a)$$

therefore measures the vertical distance between the graph of f and that line segment. Note that

$$g'(x) = f'(x) - \frac{f(b) - f(a)}{b - a} \qquad (*)$$

Obviously, $g(a) = g(b) = 0$. The function $g(x)$ inherits from f the properties of being continuous in $[a, b]$ and differentiable in (a, b). By the extreme value theorem, $g(x)$ has a maximum and a minimum over $[a, b]$. Because $g(a) = g(b)$, at least one of these extreme points x^* must lie in (a, b). Theorem 7.1.1 tells us that $g'(x^*) = 0$, and the conclusion follows from $(*)$.

EXAMPLE 7.4.3   Test the mean value theorem on the function $f(x) = x^3 - x$, defined over $[0, 2]$.

Solution: We find that $[f(2) - f(0)]/(2 - 0) = 3$ and $f'(x) = 3x^2 - 1$. The equation $f'(x) = 3$ has two solutions, $x = \pm 2\sqrt{3}/3$. The positive root $x^* = 2\sqrt{3}/3 \in (0, 2)$, and

$$f'(x^*) = \frac{f(2) - f(0)}{2 - 0}$$

This confirms the mean value theorem in this case.

Recall from Section 5.3 that a function f is *increasing* in I if $f(x_2) \geq f(x_1)$ whenever $x_2 > x_1$ with x_1 and x_2 in I. Using the definition of the derivative, we see easily that if $f(x)$ is increasing and differentiable, then $f'(x) \geq 0$. The mean value theorem can be used to make this statement precise, and to prove the converse. Let f be a function which is continuous in the interval I and differentiable in the interior of I. Suppose $f'(x) \geq 0$ for all x in the interior of I. Let $x_2 > x_1$ be two arbitrary numbers in I. According to the mean value theorem, there exists a number x^* in (x_1, x_2) such that

$$f(x_2) - f(x_1) = f'(x^*)(x_2 - x_1) \tag{7.4.2}$$

Because $x_2 > x_1$ and $f'(x^*) \geq 0$, it follows that $f(x_2) \geq f(x_1)$, so $f(x)$ is increasing. This proves statement (5.3.1). The equivalence in (5.3.2) can be proved by considering the condition for $-f$ to be increasing. Finally, (5.3.3) involves both f and $-f$ being increasing.[7]

We can also use the mean value theorem to prove Lagrange's remainder formula (7.6.2):

We start by proving that the formula is correct for $n = 1$. This means that we want to prove formula (7.6.4). For $x \neq 0$, define the function $S(x)$ implicitly by the equation

$$f(x) = f(0) + f'(0)x + \tfrac{1}{2}S(x)x^2 \tag{$*$}$$

If we can prove that there exists a number c between 0 and x such that $S(x) = f''(c)$, then (7.6.4) is established. Keep x fixed and define the function g, for all t between 0 and x, by

$$g(t) = f(x) - [f(t) + f'(t)(x-t) + \tfrac{1}{2}S(x)(x-t)^2] \tag{$**$}$$

Then $(*)$ and $(**)$ imply that $g(0) = f(x) - [f(0) + f'(0)x + \tfrac{1}{2}S(x)x^2] = 0$ and that $g(x) = f(x) - [f(x) + 0 + 0] = 0$. So, by the mean value theorem, there exists a number c strictly between 0 and x such that $g'(c) = 0$. Differentiating $(**)$ with respect to t, with x fixed, we get

$$g'(t) = -f'(t) + f'(t) - f''(t)(x-t) + S(x)(x-t)$$

Thus, $g'(c) = -f''(c)(x-c) + S(x)(x-c)$. Because $g'(c) = 0$ and $c \neq x$, it follows that $S(x) = f''(c)$. Hence, we have proved (7.6.4).

The proof for the case when $n > 1$ is based on the same idea, generalizing $(*)$ and $(**)$ in the obvious way.

EXERCISES FOR SECTION 7.4

1. Find the maximum and minimum and draw the graph of $f(x) = 4x^2 - 40x + 80$, for $x \in [0, 8]$.

(SM) **2.** Find the maximum and minimum of each function over the indicated interval:

(a) $f(x) = -2x - 1$ over $[0, 3]$ (b) $f(x) = x^3 - 3x + 8$ over $[-1, 2]$

(c) $f(x) = (x^2 + 1)/x$ over $[1/2, 2]$ (d) $f(x) = x^5 - 5x^3$ over $[-1, \sqrt{5}]$

(e) $f(x) = x^3 - 4500x^2 + 6 \cdot 10^6 x$ over $[0, 3000]$

3. Suppose the function g is defined for all $x \in [-1, 2]$ by $g(x) = \tfrac{1}{5}(e^{x^2} + e^{2-x^2})$. Calculate $g'(x)$ and find the extreme points of g.

---

[7] Alternatively it follows easily by using Eq. (7.4.2).

4. A sports club plans to charter a plane, and charge its members 10% commission on the price they pay to buy seats. That price is arranged by the charter company. The standard fare for each passenger is $800. For each additional person above 60, all travellers (including the first 60) get a discount of $10. The plane can take at most 80 passengers.

(a) How much commission is earned when there are 61, 70, 80, and $60 + x$ passengers?

(b) Find the number of passengers that maximizes the total commission earned by the sports club.

5. Let the function f be defined for $x \in [1, e^3]$ by $f(x) = (\ln x)^3 - 2(\ln x)^2 + \ln x$.

(a) Compute $f(e^{1/3}), f(e^2)$, and $f(e^3)$. Find the zeros of $f(x)$.

(b) Find the extreme points of f.

(c) Show that f defined over $[e, e^3]$ has an inverse function g and determine $g'(2)$.

(SM) **6.** [HARDER] For the following functions determine all numbers x^* in the specified intervals such that $f'(x^*) = [f(b) - f(a)]/(b - a)$:

(a) $f(x) = x^2$, in $[1, 2]$ (b) $f(x) = \sqrt{1 - x^2}$, in $[0, 1]$

(c) $f(x) = 2/x$, in $[2, 6]$ (d) $f(x) = \sqrt{9 + x^2}$, in $[0, 4]$

7. [HARDER] You are supposed to sail from point A in a lake to point B. What does the mean value theorem have to say about your trip?

8. [HARDER] Consider the function f defined, for all $x \in [-1, 1]$, by

$$f(x) = \begin{cases} x, & \text{for } x \in (-1, 1) \\ 0, & \text{for } x = -1 \text{ and for } x = 1 \end{cases}$$

Is this function continuous? Does it attain a maximum or minimum?

9. [HARDER] Let f be defined for all x in $(0, \infty)$ by

$$f(x) = \begin{cases} x + 1, & \text{for } x \in (0, 1] \\ 1, & \text{for } x \in (1, \infty) \end{cases}$$

Prove that f attains maximum and minimum values. Verify that, nevertheless, *none* of the conditions in the extreme value theorem is satisfied.

7.5 Further Economic Examples

EXAMPLE 7.5.1   A firm that produces a single commodity wants to maximize its profits. The total revenue generated in a certain period by producing and selling Q units is $R(Q)$ dollars, whereas $C(Q)$ denotes the associated total dollar cost. The profit obtained as a result of producing and selling Q units is, then,

$$\pi(Q) = R(Q) - C(Q) \tag{$*$}$$

Suppose that because of technical limitations, there is a maximum quantity $\bar{Q}$ that can be produced by the firm in a given period. Assume that R and C are differentiable functions in the interval $(0, \bar{Q})$. The profit function is then differentiable, so it is also continuous. Consequently π does have a maximum value. In special cases, that maximum might occur at $Q = 0$ or at $Q = \bar{Q}$. If not, it has an "interior maximum" where the production level Q^* satisfies $\pi'(Q^*) = 0$, and so

$$R'(Q^*) = C'(Q^*) \qquad\qquad (**)$$

Hence, *production should be adjusted to a point where the marginal revenue is equal to the marginal cost.*

Let us assume that the firm gets a fixed price P per unit sold. Then $R(Q) = PQ$, and $(**)$ takes the form

$$P = C'(Q^*) \qquad\qquad (7.5.1)$$

Thus, in the case when the firm has no control over the price, *production should be adjusted to a level at which the marginal cost is equal to the price per unit of the commodity*—assuming an interior maximum.

It is quite possible that the firm has functions $R(Q)$ and $C(Q)$ for which Eq. $(**)$ has several solutions. If so, the maximum profit occurs at that point Q^* among the solutions of $(**)$ which gives the highest value of $\pi(Q^*)$.

Equation $(**)$ has an economic interpretation rather like that for the corresponding optimality condition in Example 7.3.1. Indeed, suppose we contemplate increasing production from the level Q^* by one unit. We would increase revenue by the amount $R(Q^* + 1) - R(Q^*) \approx R'(Q^*)$. We would increase cost by the amount $C(Q^* + 1) - C(Q^*) \approx C'(Q^*)$. Equation $(**)$ equates $R'(Q^*)$ and $C'(Q^*)$, so that the approximate extra revenue earned by selling an extra unit is offset by the approximate extra cost of producing that unit.

EXAMPLE 7.5.2   Suppose that the firm in the preceding example obtains a fixed price $P = 121$ per unit, and that the cost function is $C(Q) = 0.02Q^3 - 3Q^2 + 175Q + 500$. The firm can produce at most $\bar{Q} = 110$ units.

(a) Make a table of the values of the functions $R(Q) = 121Q$, $C(Q)$, and $\pi(Q) = R(Q) - C(Q)$, for Q taking the values 0, 10, 30, 50, 70, 90, and 110. Draw the graphs of $R(Q)$ and $C(Q)$ in the same coordinate system.

(b) Answer the following questions, approximately, by using the graphs in (a):
   (i) How many units must be produced in order for the firm to make a profit?
   (ii) How many units must be produced for the profit to be $2 000?
   (iii) Which production level maximizes profits?

(c) Answer the question in (b.iii) by computation.

(d) What is the smallest price per unit the firm must charge in order not to lose money, if capacity is fully utilized—that is, if it produces 110 units?

Solution:

(a) We form the following table:

Q	0	10	30	50	70	90	110
$R(Q) = 121Q$	0	1 210	3 630	6 050	8 470	10 890	13 310
$C(Q)$	500	1 970	3 590	4 250	4 910	6 530	10 070
$\pi(Q) = R(Q) - C(Q)$	−500	−760	40	1 800	3 560	4 360	3 240

The graphs of $R(Q)$ and $C(Q)$ are shown in Fig. 7.5.1.

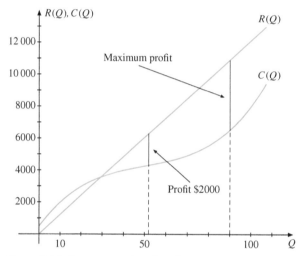

Figure 7.5.1 Revenue, cost, and profit

(b) (i) The firm earns a profit if $\pi(Q) > 0$, that is when $R(Q) > C(Q)$. On the figure we see that $R(Q) > C(Q)$ when Q is larger than, approximately, 30.

(ii) We must find where the "gap" between $R(Q)$ and $C(Q)$ is $2 000. This occurs when $Q \approx 52$.

(iii) The profit is largest when the gap between $R(Q)$ and $C(Q)$ is largest. This seems to occur when $Q \approx 90$.

(c) When the formula for $C'(Q)$ is inserted into Eq. (7.5.1) with $P = 121$, the result is $121 = 0.06Q^2 - 6Q + 175$. Solving this quadratic equation yields $Q = 10$ and $Q = 90$. We know that $\pi(Q)$ must have a maximum point in $[0, 110]$, and there are four candidates: $Q = 0$, $Q = 10$, $Q = 90$, and $Q = 110$. Using the table from part (a), we see that

$$\pi(0) = -500, \ \pi(10) = -760, \ \pi(90) = 4360, \ \pi(110) = 3240$$

The firm therefore attains maximum profit by producing 90 units.

(d) If the price per unit is P, the profit from producing 110 units is

$$\pi(110) = P \cdot 110 - C(110) = 110P - 10\,070$$

The smallest price P which ensures that the firm does not lose money when producing 110 units, satisfies $\pi(110) = 0$, that is $110P = \$10\,070$ with solution $P \approx \$91.55$. This is the average cost of producing 110 units. The price must be at least \$91.55 if revenue is going to be enough to cover the cost of producing at full capacity.

EXAMPLE 7.5.3   In the model of the previous example, the firm took the price as given. Consider an example at the other extreme, where the firm has a monopoly in the sale of the commodity. Assume that the price $P(Q)$ per unit varies with Q according to the formula $P(Q) = 100 - \frac{1}{3}Q$ for $Q \in [0, 300]$. Suppose now the cost function is

$$C(Q) = \frac{1}{600}Q^3 - \frac{1}{3}Q^2 + 50Q + \frac{1000}{3}$$

The profit is, then,

$$\pi(Q) = QP(Q) - C(Q) = -\frac{1}{600}Q^3 + 50Q - \frac{1000}{3}$$

Find the production level that maximizes profit, and compute the maximum profit.

Solution: The derivative of $\pi(Q)$ is $\pi'(Q) = -\frac{1}{200}Q^2 + 50$. Hence, $\pi'(Q) = 0$ for $Q^2 = 10\,000$. Because $Q < 0$ is not permissible, the maximum is at $Q = 100$.

The values of $\pi(Q)$ at the end points of $[0, 300]$ are $\pi(0) = -1000/3$ and $\pi(300) = -91\,000/3$. Since $\pi(100) = 3000$, we conclude that $Q = 100$ maximizes profit, and the maximum profit is 3000.

EXAMPLE 7.5.4   (**Either a borrower or a lender be**)[8]   Recall Example 7.1.5, and suppose that a student has current income y_1 and expects future income y_2. She plans current consumption, $c_1 > 0$, and future consumption, $c_2 > 0$, in order to maximize the utility function

$$U = \ln c_1 + \frac{1}{1+\delta} \ln c_2$$

where δ is her discount rate.[9] If she borrows now, so that $c_1 > y_1$, then future consumption, after repaying the loan amount $c_1 - y_1$ with interest charged at rate r, will be

$$c_2 = y_2 - (1 + r)(c_1 - y_1)$$

Alternatively, if she saves now, so that $c_1 < y_1$, then future consumption will be

$$c_2 = y_2 + (1 + r)(y_1 - c_1)$$

after receiving interest at rate r on her savings. Find the optimal borrowing or saving plan.

---

[8]   According to Shakespeare, Polonius's advice to Hamlet was: "Neither a borrower nor a lender be".
[9]   In terms of Example 7.1.5, $\beta = 1/(1 + \delta)$.

Solution: Whether the student borrows or saves, second period consumption is

$$c_2 = y_2 - (1+r)(c_1 - y_1)$$

in either case. So the student will want to maximize, by choosing c_1,

$$U = \ln c_1 + \frac{1}{1+\delta} \ln[y_2 - (1+r)(c_1 - y_1)] \qquad (*)$$

We can obviously restrict attention to the interval $0 < c_1 < y_1 + (1+r)^{-1}y_2$, where both c_1 and c_2 are positive. Differentiating $(*)$ w.r.t. the choice variable c_1 gives

$$\frac{dU}{dc_1} = \frac{1}{c_1} - \frac{1+r}{1+\delta} \cdot \frac{1}{y_2 - (1+r)(c_1 - y_1)}$$

Rewriting the fractions so that they have a common denominator yields

$$\frac{dU}{dc_1} = \frac{(1+\delta)[y_2 - (1+r)(c_1 - y_1)] - (1+r)c_1}{c_1(1+\delta)[y_2 - (1+r)(c_1 - y_1)]}$$

Rearranging the numerator and equating the derivative to 0, we have

$$\frac{dU}{dc_1} = \frac{(1+\delta)[(1+r)y_1 + y_2] - (2+\delta)(1+r)c_1}{c_1(1+\delta)[y_2 - (1+r)(c_1 - y_1)]} = 0 \qquad (**)$$

The unique solution of this equation is

$$c_1^* = \frac{(1+\delta)[(1+r)y_1 + y_2]}{(2+\delta)(1+r)} = y_1 + \frac{(1+\delta)y_2 - (1+r)y_1}{(2+\delta)(1+r)}$$

From $(**)$, we see that for $c_1 < c_1^*$ one has $dU/dc_1 > 0$, whereas for $c_1 > c_1^*$ one has $dU/dc_1 < 0$. We conclude that c_1^* indeed maximizes U. Moreover, the student lends if and only if $(1+\delta)y_2 < (1+r)y_1$. In the more likely case when $(1+\delta)y_2 > (1+r)y_1$ because future income is considerably higher than present income, she will borrow. Only if by some chance $(1+\delta)y_2$ is exactly equal to $(1+r)y_1$ will she be neither a borrower nor a lender. However, this discussion has neglected the difference between borrowing and lending rates of interest that one always observes in reality.

EXERCISES FOR SECTION 7.5

1. With reference to Example 7.5.1, suppose that $R(Q) = 10Q - Q^2/1000$ for $Q \in [0, 10\,000]$ and $C(Q) = 5000 + 2Q$ for all $Q \geq 0$. Find the value of Q that maximizes profit.

2. With reference to Example 7.5.1, let $R(Q) = 80Q$ and $C(Q) = Q^2 + 10Q + 900$. The firm can produce at most 50 units.

(a) Draw the graphs of R and C in the same coordinate system.

(b) Answer the following questions both graphically and by computation:

(i) How many units must be produced for the firm to make a profit?

(ii) How many units must be produced for the firm to maximize profit?

3. A pharmaceutical firm produces penicillin. The sales price per unit is 200, while the cost of producing x units is given by $C(x) = 500\,000 + 80x + 0.003x^2$. The firm can produce at most $30\,000$ units. What value of x maximizes profits?

(SM) **4.** Consider Example 7.5.1 and find the production level which maximizes profits when

   (a) $R(Q) = 1840Q$ and $C(Q) = 2Q^2 + 40Q + 5000$

   (b) $R(Q) = 2240Q$ and $C(Q) = 2Q^2 + 40Q + 5000$

   (c) $R(Q) = 1840Q$ and $C(Q) = 2Q^2 + 1940Q + 5000$

5. The price a firm obtains for a commodity varies with demand Q according to the formula $P(Q) = 18 - 0.006Q$. Total cost is $C(Q) = 0.004Q^2 + 4Q + 4500$.

   (a) Find the firm's profit $\pi(Q)$ and the value of Q which maximizes profit.

   (b) Find a formula for the elasticity of $P(Q)$ w.r.t. Q, and find the particular value Q^* of Q at which the elasticity is equal to -1.

   (c) Show that the marginal revenue is 0 at Q^*.

6. With reference to Example 7.5.1, let $R(Q) = PQ$ and $C(Q) = aQ^b + c$, where P, a, b, and c are positive constants, and $b > 1$. Find the value of Q which maximizes the profit $\pi(Q) = PQ - (aQ^b + c)$. Make use of Theorem 7.2.2.

7.6 Local Extreme Points

So far this chapter has discussed what are often referred to as *global* optimization problems. The reason for this terminology is that we have been seeking the largest or smallest values of a function when we compare the function values at *all* points in the domain, without exception. In applied optimization problems, especially those arising in economics, it is usually these global extrema that are of interest. However, sometimes one is interested in the local maxima and minima of a function. In this case, we compare the function value at the point in question only with alternative function values at nearby points.

Consider Fig. 7.6.1 and think of the graph as representing the profile of a landscape. Then the mountain tops P_1 and P_2 represent local maxima, whereas the valley bottoms Q_1 and Q_2 represent local minima. The precise definitions are as follows:

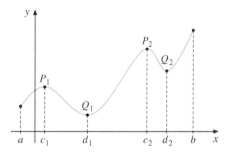

Figure 7.6.1 c_1, c_2, and b are local maximum points; a, d_1, and d_2 are local minimum points

LOCAL EXTREMA

The function f has a *local maximum* at c if there exists an interval (α, β) about c such that

$$f(x) \leq f(c) \text{ for all } x \text{ in } (\alpha, \beta) \text{ which are in the domain of } f \qquad (7.6.1)$$

It has a *local minimum* at c if there exists an interval (α, β) about c such that

$$f(x) \geq f(c) \text{ for all } x \text{ in } (\alpha, \beta) \text{ which are in the domain of } f \qquad (7.6.2)$$

These definitions imply that point a in Fig. 7.6.1 is a local minimum point, while b is a local (and global) maximum point.[10] Function values corresponding to local maximum (minimum) points are called *local maximum (minimum) values*. As collective names we use *local extreme points* and *local extreme values*.

In searching for (global) maximum and minimum points, Theorem 7.1.1 was very useful. Actually, the same result is valid for local extreme points:

At a local extreme point in the interior of the domain of a differentiable function, the derivative must be zero.

This is clear if we recall that the proof of Theorem 7.1.1 needed to consider the behaviour of the function in only a small interval about the optimal point. Consequently, in order to find possible local maxima and minima for a function f defined in an interval I, we can again search among the following types of point:

(i)   interior points in I where $f'(x) = 0$;

(ii) end points of I, if included in I; and

(iii) interior points in I where f' does not exist.

We have thus established *necessary* conditions for a function f defined in an interval I to have a local extreme point. But how do we decide whether a point satisfying the necessary conditions is a local maximum, a local minimum, or neither? In contrast to global extreme points, it does not help to calculate the function value at the different points satisfying these necessary conditions. To see why, consider again the function whose graph is given in Fig. 7.6.1. Point P_1 is a local maximum point and Q_2 is a local minimum point, but the function value at P_1 is *smaller* than the function value at Q_2.

---

[10] Some authors restrict the definition of local maximum/minimum points only to *interior* points of the domain of the function. According to this definition, a global maximum point that is not an interior point of the domain is not a local maximum point. It seems desirable that a global maximum/minimum point should always be a local maximum/minimum point as well, so we stick to definitions (7.6.1) and (7.6.2).

The First-Derivative Test

There are two main ways of determining whether a given critical point is a local maximum, a local minimum, or neither. One of them is based on studying the sign of the first derivative about the critical point, and is an easy modification of Theorem 7.2.1.

THEOREM 7.6.1 (FIRST-DERIVATIVE TEST FOR LOCAL EXTREMA)

Suppose c is a critical point for $y = f(x)$.

  (i) If $f'(x) \geq 0$ throughout some interval (a, c) to the left of c and $f'(x) \leq 0$ throughout some interval (c, b) to the right of c, then $x = c$ is a local maximum point for f.

  (ii) If $f'(x) \leq 0$ throughout some interval (a, c) to the left of c and $f'(x) \geq 0$ throughout some interval (c, b) to the right of c, then $x = c$ is a local minimum point for f.

  (iii) If $f'(x) > 0$ both throughout some interval (a, c) to the left of c and throughout some interval (c, b) to the right of c, then $x = c$ is not a local extreme point for f. The same conclusion holds if $f'(x) < 0$ on both sides of c.

Only case (iii) is not already covered by Theorem 7.2.1. In fact, if $f'(x) > 0$ in (a, c) and also in (c, b), then $f(x)$ is strictly increasing in $(a, c]$ as well as in $[c, b)$. Then $x = c$ cannot be a local extreme point.

EXAMPLE 7.6.1   Classify the critical points of $f(x) = \frac{1}{9}x^3 - \frac{1}{6}x^2 - \frac{2}{3}x + 1$.

Solution: We get $f'(x) = \frac{1}{3}(x + 1)(x - 2)$, so $x = -1$ and $x = 2$ are the critical points. The sign diagram for $f'(x)$ is:

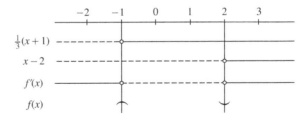

We conclude from this sign diagram that $x = -1$ is a local maximum point whereas $x = 2$ is a local minimum point.

EXAMPLE 7.6.2   Classify the critical points of $f(x) = x^2 e^x$.

Solution: Differentiating, we get $f'(x) = 2xe^x + x^2 e^x = xe^x(2 + x)$. Then $f'(x) = 0$ for $x = 0$ and for $x = -2$. A sign diagram shows that f has a local maximum point at $x = -2$ and a local, as well as global, minimum point at $x = 0$. The graph of f is given in Fig. 7.6.2.

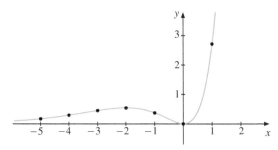

Figure 7.6.2 $f(x) = x^2 e^x$

The Second-Derivative Test

For most problems of practical interest in which an explicit function is specified, the first-derivative test on its own will determine whether a critical point is a local maximum, a local minimum, or neither. Note that the theorem requires knowing the sign of $f'(x)$ at points both to the left and to the right of the given critical point. The next test requires knowing the first two derivatives of the function, but only at the critical point itself.

THEOREM 7.6.2   (SECOND-DERIVATIVE TEST FOR LOCAL EXTREMA)

Let f be a twice differentiable function in an interval I, and let c be an interior point of I.

(i) If $f'(c) = 0$ and $f''(c) < 0$, then $x = c$ is a strict local maximum point.

(ii) If $f'(c) = 0$ and $f''(c) > 0$, then $x = c$ is a strict local minimum point.

(iii) If $f'(c) = 0$ and $f''(c) = 0$, the character of $x = c$ remains undetermined.

The proof is as follows:

To prove part (i), assume $f'(c) = 0$ and $f''(c) < 0$. By definition of $f''(c)$ as the derivative of $f'(x)$ at c,

$$f''(c) = \lim_{h \to 0} \frac{f'(c+h) - f'(c)}{h} = \lim_{h \to 0} \frac{f'(c+h)}{h}$$

Because $f''(c) < 0$, it follows that $f'(c+h)/h < 0$ if $|h|$ is sufficiently small. In particular, if h is a small positive number, then $f'(c+h) < 0$, so f' is negative in an interval to the right of c. In the same way, we see that f' is positive in some interval to the left of c. But then c is a strict local maximum point for f.

Part (ii) can be proved in the same way.

For the inconclusive part (iii), where $f'(c) = f''(c) = 0$, "anything" can happen. Each of three functions, $f(x) = x^4$, $f(x) = -x^4$, and $f(x) = x^3$, satisfies $f'(0) = f''(0) = 0$. At $x = 0$, they have, as shown in Figs 7.6.3 to 7.6.5, respectively, a minimum, a maximum, and what will be called a point of inflection in Section 7.7. Usually, as here, the first-derivative test can be used to classify critical points at which $f'(c) = f''(c) = 0$.

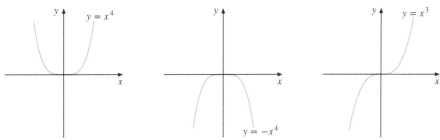

Figure 7.6.3 Minimum point   **Figure 7.6.4** Maximum point   **Figure 7.6.5** Inflection point

EXAMPLE 7.6.3   Classify the critical points of $f(x) = \frac{1}{9}x^3 - \frac{1}{6}x^2 - \frac{2}{3}x + 1$, by using the second-derivative test.

Solution: We saw in Example 7.6.1 that

$$f'(x) = \frac{1}{3}x^2 - \frac{1}{3}x - \frac{2}{3} = \frac{1}{3}(x+1)(x-2)$$

with two critical points $x = -1$ and $x = 2$. Furthermore, $f''(x) = \frac{2}{3}x - \frac{1}{3}$, so that $f''(-1) = -1$ and $f''(2) = 1$. From Theorem 7.6.2 it follows that $x = -1$ is a local maximum point and $x = 2$ is a local minimum point. This confirms the results in Example 7.6.1.

EXAMPLE 7.6.4   Classify the critical points of $f(x) = x^2 e^x$, using the second-derivative test.

Solution: From Example 7.6.2, $f'(x) = 2xe^x + x^2 e^x$, with $x = 0$ and $x = -2$ as the two critical points. The second derivative of f is

$$f''(x) = 2e^x + 2xe^x + 2xe^x + x^2 e^x = e^x(2 + 4x + x^2)$$

We find that $f''(0) = 2 > 0$ and $f''(-2) = -2e^{-2} < 0$. From Theorem 7.6.2, it follows that $x = 0$ is a local minimum point and $x = -2$ is a local maximum point. This confirms the results in Example 7.6.2.

Theorem 7.6.2 can be used to obtain a useful necessary condition for local extrema. Suppose that f is twice differentiable in the interval I and that c is an interior point of I where there is a local maximum. Then $f'(c) = 0$. Moreover, $f''(c) > 0$ is impossible, because by part (ii) in Theorem 7.6.2, this inequality would imply that c is a strict local minimum. Hence, $f''(c)$ has to be ≤ 0. In the same way, we see that $f''(c) \geq 0$ is a necessary condition for local minimum. Briefly formulated:

NECESSARY SECOND-ORDER CONDITIONS

$$\text{Point } c \text{ is a local maximum for } f \;\Rightarrow\; f''(c) \le 0 \qquad (7.6.3)$$

$$\text{Point } c \text{ is a local minimum for } f \;\Rightarrow\; f''(c) \ge 0 \qquad (7.6.4)$$

Many results in economic analysis rely on postulating an appropriate sign for the second derivative rather than suitable variations in the sign of the first derivative.

EXAMPLE 7.6.5   Suppose that the firm in Example 7.5.1 faces a sales tax of τ dollars per unit. The firm's profit from producing and selling Q units is, then, $\pi(Q) = R(Q) - C(Q) - \tau Q$. In order to maximize profits at some quantity Q^* satisfying $0 < Q^* < \bar{Q}$, one must have $\pi'(Q^*) = 0$. Hence,

$$R'(Q^*) - C'(Q^*) - \tau = 0 \qquad (*)$$

Suppose $R''(Q^*) < 0$ and $C''(Q^*) > 0$. Equation $(*)$ implicitly defines Q^* as a differentiable function of τ. Find an expression for $dQ^*/d\tau$ and discuss its sign. Also compute the derivative w.r.t. τ of the optimal value $\pi(Q^*)$ of the profit function, and show that $d\pi(Q^*)/d\tau = -Q^*$.

Solution: Differentiating $(*)$ with respect to τ yields

$$R''(Q^*)\frac{dQ^*}{d\tau} - C''(Q^*)\frac{dQ^*}{d\tau} - 1 = 0$$

Solving for $dQ^*/d\tau$ gives

$$\frac{dQ^*}{d\tau} = \frac{1}{R''(Q^*) - C''(Q^*)} \qquad (**)$$

The sign assumptions on R'' and C'' imply that $dQ^*/d\tau < 0$. Thus, the optimal number of units produced will decline if the tax rate τ increases.

The optimal value of the profit function is $\pi(Q^*) = R(Q^*) - C(Q^*) - \tau Q^*$. Taking into account the dependence of Q^* on τ, we get

$$\frac{d\pi(Q^*)}{d\tau} = R'(Q^*)\frac{dQ^*}{d\tau} - C'(Q^*)\frac{dQ^*}{d\tau} - Q^* - \tau\frac{dQ^*}{d\tau}$$

$$= \left[R'(Q^*) - C'(Q^*) - \tau\right]\frac{dQ^*}{d\tau} - Q^*$$

$$= -Q^*$$

Note how the square bracket disappears from this last expression because of the FOC $(*)$. This is an instance of the "envelope theorem", which will be discussed in Section 9.7. For each 1¢ increase in the sales tax, profit decreases by approximately Q^* cents, where Q^* is the number of units produced at the optimum.

EXERCISES FOR SECTION 7.6

(SM) **1.** Consider the function f defined for all x by $f(x) = x^3 - 12x$. Find the critical points of f, and classify them by using both the first- and second-derivative tests.

(SM) **2.** Determine possible local extreme points and values for the following functions:

(a) $f(x) = -2x - 1$ (b) $f(x) = x^3 - 3x + 8$ (c) $f(x) = x + \dfrac{1}{x}$

(d) $f(x) = x^5 - 5x^3$ (e) $f(x) = \frac{1}{2}x^2 - 3x + 5$ (f) $f(x) = x^3 + 3x^2 - 2$

(SM) **3.** Let function f be given by the formula $f(x) = (1 + 2/x)\sqrt{x + 6}$.

(a) Find the domain of f and the intervals where $f(x)$ is positive.

(b) Find possible local extreme points.

(c) Examine $f(x)$ as $x \to 0^-$, $x \to 0^+$, and $x \to \infty$. Also determine the limit of $f'(x)$ as $x \to \infty$. Does f have a maximum or a minimum in the domain?

4. Figure 7.6.6 graphs the *derivative* of a function f. Which of points a, b, c, d, and e are local maximum points for f, local minimum points for f, or neither?

5. Let $f(x) = x^3 + ax^2 + bx + c$. What requirements must be imposed on the constants a, b, and c in order that f will have: (a) a local minimum at $x = 0$? (b) critical points at $x = 1$ and $x = 3$?

6. Find the local extreme points for: (a) $f(x) = x^3 e^x$; and (b) $g(x) = x^2 2^x$.

(SM) **7.** [HARDER] Find the local extreme points of $f(x) = x^3 + ax + b$. Use the answer to show that the equation $f(x) = 0$ has three different real roots if, and only if, $4a^3 + 27b^2 < 0$.

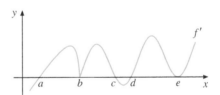

Figure 7.6.6 Exercise 4

7.7 Inflection Points, Concavity, and Convexity

Recall that in Section 5.9 we defined a twice differentiable function $f(x)$ to be concave in an interval I if $f''(x) \leq 0$ for all x in I, and convex if $f''(x) \geq 0$ for all x in I. Points at which a function changes from being convex to being concave, or *vice versa*, are called *inflection points*.[11] For twice differentiable functions they can be defined this way:

---

[11] We note that what a mathematician would call a turning point of a function f, which is a point at which the sign of $f'(x)$ changes, is often erroneously called an inflection point in popular parlance. Perhaps it is too much to expect popular parlance to take account of changes in the sign of the second derivative!

INFLECTION POINTS

If the function f is twice differentiable, the point c is called an *inflection point* for f if there exists an interval (a, b) about c such that:

(a) $f''(x) \geq 0$ in (a, c) and $f''(x) \leq 0$ in (c, b); *or*

(b) $f''(x) \leq 0$ in (a, c) and $f''(x) \geq 0$ in (c, b).

Briefly, $x = c$ is an inflection point if $f''(x)$ *changes sign* at $x = c$, and we refer to the point $(c, f(c))$ as an inflection point on the graph. Figure 7.7.1 gives an abstract example from mathematics, while Fig. 7.7.2 gives a sporting example: it shows the profile of a ski jump. The point P, where the slope is steepest, is an inflection point.

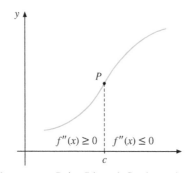

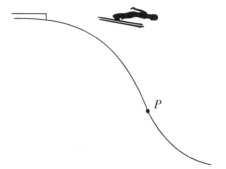

Figure 7.7.1 Point P is an inflection point on the graph; $x = c$ is an inflection point for the function

Figure 7.7.2 The point P, where the slope is steepest, is an inflection point

When looking for possible inflection points of a function, we usually use part (ii) in the following theorem:

THEOREM 7.7.1 (TEST FOR INFLECTION POINTS)

Let f be a function with a continuous second derivative in an interval I, and let c be an interior point of I.

(i) If c is an inflection point for f, then $f''(c) = 0$.

(ii) If $f''(c) = 0$ and f'' changes sign at c, then c is an inflection point for f.

The proof of this theorem is rather simple:

(i) Because $f''(x) \leq 0$ on one side of c and $f''(x) \geq 0$ on the other, and because f'' is continuous, it must be true that $f''(c) = 0$.

(ii) If f'' changes sign at c, then c is an inflection point for f, by definition.

This theorem implies that $f''(c) = 0$ is a *necessary* condition for c to be an inflection point. It is not a sufficient condition, however, because $f''(c) = 0$ does not imply that f'' changes sign at $x = c$. A typical case is given in the next example.

EXAMPLE 7.7.1   Show that the function $f(x) = x^4$ does not have an inflection point at $x = 0$, even though $f''(0) = 0$.

Solution: Here $f'(x) = 4x^3$ and $f''(x) = 12x^2$, so that $f''(0) = 0$. But $f''(x) > 0$ for all $x \neq 0$, and so f'' does not change sign at $x = 0$. Hence, $x = 0$ is not an inflection point—in fact, it is a global minimum, as shown in Fig. 7.6.3.

EXAMPLE 7.7.2   Find possible inflection points for $f(x) = \frac{1}{9}x^3 - \frac{1}{6}x^2 - \frac{2}{3}x + 1$.

Solution: From Example 7.6.1, we have $f''(x) = \frac{2}{3}x - \frac{1}{3} = \frac{2}{3}\left(x - \frac{1}{2}\right)$. Hence, $f''(x) \leq 0$ for $x \leq 1/2$, whereas $f''(1/2) = 0$ and $f''(x) \geq 0$ for $x > 1/2$. According to part (ii) in Theorem 7.7.1, $x = 1/2$ is an inflection point for f.

EXAMPLE 7.7.3   Find possible inflection points for $f(x) = x^6 - 10x^4$.

Solution: In this case $f'(x) = 6x^5 - 40x^3$ and

$$f''(x) = 30x^4 - 120x^2 = 30x^2(x^2 - 4) = 30x^2(x - 2)(x + 2)$$

A sign diagram for f'' is as follows:

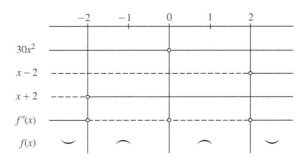

From the sign diagram we see that f'' changes sign at $x = -2$ and at $x = 2$, so these are inflection points. Since f'' does not change sign at $x = 0$, it is not an inflection point, even though $f''(0) = 0$.

Economic models often involve functions having inflection points. The cost function in Fig. 4.7.2 is a typical example. Here is another.

EXAMPLE 7.7.4   A firm produces a commodity using only one input. Let $y = f(x)$, for $x \geq 0$, be the output obtained when x units of the input are used. Then f is called a *production function*. Its first derivative measures the increase in output that is obtained by increasing the input used infinitesimally; this derivative is called the firm's *marginal product*. It is often assumed that the graph of a production function is "S-shaped". That is, the marginal product, $f'(x)$, is increasing up to a certain production level c, and then decreasing. Such a production function is indicated in Fig. 7.7.1. If f is twice differentiable, then $f''(x) \geq 0$ in $[0, c]$, and $f'(x) \leq 0$ in $[c, \infty)$. Hence, f is first convex and then concave, with c as an inflection point. Note that at $x = c$ a unit increase in input gives the maximum increase in output.

More General Definitions of Concave and Convex Functions

So far the convexity and concavity properties of functions have been defined by looking at the sign of the second derivative. An alternative geometric characterization of convexity and concavity suggests a more general definition that is valid even for functions that are not differentiable.

CONCAVE AND CONVEX FUNCTIONS

A function f is called *concave* if the line segment joining any two points on the graph is below the graph, or on it. It is called *convex* if any such line segment lies above, or on the graph.

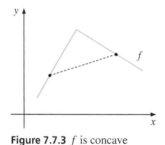

Figure 7.7.3 f is concave

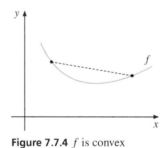

Figure 7.7.4 f is convex

These definitions are illustrated in Figs 7.7.3 and 7.7.4. Because the graph has a "kink" in Fig. 7.7.3, this function is not even differentiable, let alone twice differentiable. For twice differentiable functions, one can prove that this general definition is equivalent to the definitions in (5.9.3) and (5.9.4). Now, in order to use the definition to examine the convexity or concavity of a given function, we need an algebraic formulation. This will be discussed in FMEA.

Strictly Concave and Strictly Convex Functions

A function f is called *strictly concave* if the line segment joining any two points on the graph is strictly below the graph, except at the end points of the segment; it is called *strictly convex* if any such segment lies strictly above the graph, again except at the end points of the segment. For instance, the function whose graph is shown in Fig. 7.7.3 has two linear pieces, on which line segments joining two points coincide with part of the graph. Thus this function is concave, but not strictly concave. By contrast, the function graphed in Fig. 7.7.4 is strictly convex.

Fairly obvious sufficient conditions for strict concavity/convexity are the following, which will be further discussed in FMEA:

$$f''(x) < 0 \text{ for all } x \in (a, b) \implies f \text{ is strictly concave in } (a, b) \qquad (7.7.1)$$

$$f''(x) > 0 \text{ for all } x \in (a, b) \implies f \text{ is strictly convex in } (a, b) \qquad (7.7.2)$$

The reverse implications are not correct. For instance, one can prove that $f(x) = x^4$ is strictly convex in the interval $(-\infty, \infty)$, but $f''(x)$ is not > 0 everywhere, because $f''(0) = 0$—see Fig. 7.6.3.

For twice differentiable functions, it is usually much easier to check concavity/convexity by considering the sign of the second derivative than by using the definitions of the properties. However, in theoretical arguments the definitions are often very useful, especially because they generalize easily to functions of several variables. (See FMEA.)

EXERCISES FOR SECTION 7.7

1. Let f be defined for all x by $f(x) = x^3 + \frac{3}{2}x^2 - 6x + 10$.

(a) Find the critical points of f and determine the intervals where f increases.

(b) Find the inflection point for f.

2. Decide where the following functions are convex and determine possible inflection points:

(a) $f(x) = \dfrac{x}{1 + x^2}$ (b) $g(x) = \dfrac{1 - x}{1 + x}$ (c) $h(x) = xe^x$

(SM) **3.** Find local extreme points and inflection points for the functions defined by the following formulas:

(a) $y = (x + 2)e^{-x}$ (b) $y = \ln x + 1/x$ (c) $y = x^3 e^{-x}$

(d) $y = \dfrac{\ln x}{x^2}$ (e) $y = e^{2x} - 2e^x$ (f) $y = (x^2 + 2x)e^{-x}$

4. A competitive firm receives a price p for each unit of its output, and pays a price w for each unit of its only variable input. It also incurs set up costs of F. Its output from using x units of variable input is $f(x) = \sqrt{x}$.

(a) Determine the firm's revenue, cost, and profit functions.

(b) Write the first-order condition for profit maximization, and give it an economic interpretation. Check whether profit really is maximized at a point satisfying the first-order condition.

5. Find the extreme points and the inflection points of the function f whose graph is shown in Fig. 7.7.5.

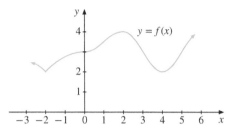

Figure 7.7.5 Exercise 5

6. Find numbers a and b such that the graph of $f(x) = ax^3 + bx^2$ passes through $(-1, 1)$ and has an inflection point at $x = 1/2$.

7. Consider the following cubic cost function, defined for $x \geq 0$: $C(x) = ax^3 + bx^2 + cx + d$, where $a > 0$, $b < 0$, $c > 0$, and $d > 0$. Find the intervals where the function is convex and where it is concave. Find also the unique inflection point.

8. Use the same coordinate system to draw the graphs of two concave functions f and g, both defined for all x. Let the function h be defined by $h(x) = \min\{f(x), g(x)\}$—that is, for each given x, the number $h(x)$ is the smaller of $f(x)$ and $g(x)$. Draw the graph of h and explain why it is also concave.

REVIEW EXERCISES

1. Let $f(x) = \dfrac{x^2}{x^2 + 2}$.

   (a) Compute $f'(x)$ and determine where $f(x)$ is increasing/decreasing.

   (b) Find possible inflection points.

   (c) Determine the limit of $f(x)$ as $x \to \pm\infty$, and sketch the graph of $f(x)$.

2. A firm's production function is $Q(L) = 12L^2 - \frac{1}{20}L^3$, where L denotes the number of workers, with $L \in [0, 200]$.

   (a) What size of the work force maximizes output $Q(L)$?

   (b) What size of the work force maximizes output per worker, $Q(L)/L$? Letting L^* denote such size, note that $Q'(L^*) = Q(L^*)/L^*$. Is this a coincidence?

3. A farmer has one thousand metres of fence wire to make a rectangular enclosure, as in Exercise 4.6.7, but this time no fencing is needed on one side of the enclosure that is a straight canal bank. What should be the dimensions of the enclosure in order to maximize area?

4. By producing and selling Q units of some commodity a firm earns a total revenue $R(Q) = -0.0016Q^2 + 44Q$ and incurs a cost of $C(Q) = 0.0004Q^2 + 8Q + 64\,000$.

   (a) What production level maximizes profits?

   (b) The elasticity $\text{El}_Q\, C(Q) \approx 0.12$ for $Q = 1000$. Interpret this result.

5. The unit price P obtained by a firm in producing and selling $Q \geq 0$ units is $P(Q) = a - bQ^2$, and the cost of producing and selling Q units is $C(Q) = \alpha - \beta Q$. All constants are positive. Find the level of production that maximizes profits.

6. Let $g(x) = x - 2\ln(x + 1)$.

   (a) Where is g defined?

   (b) Find $g'(x)$ and $g''(x)$.

   (c) Find possible extreme points and inflection points, and sketch the graph.

7. Let $f(x) = \ln(x + 1) - x + \frac{1}{2}x^2 - \frac{1}{6}x^3$.

   (a) Find the domain of the function and prove that, for x in the domain:

   $$f'(x) = \frac{x^2 - x^3}{2(x + 1)}$$

   (b) Find possible extreme points and inflection points.

   (c) Check $f(x)$ as $x \to (-1)^+$, and sketch the graph on the interval $(-1, 2]$.

SM 8. Consider the function defined, for all x, by $h(x) = e^x/(2 + e^{2x})$.

   (a) Where is h increasing/decreasing? Find possible maximum and minimum points for h.

   (b) If one restricts the domain of h to $(-\infty, 0]$, it has an inverse. Why? Find an expression for the inverse function.

9. Let $f(x) = \left(e^{2x} + 4e^{-x}\right)^2$.

   (a) Find $f'(x)$ and $f''(x)$.

   (b) Determine where f is increasing/decreasing, and show that f is convex.

   (c) Find possible global extreme points for f.

SM 10. [HARDER] Letting $a > 0$, consider the function

   $$f(x) = \frac{x}{\sqrt[3]{x^2 - a}}$$

   (a) Find the domain D_f of f and the intervals where $f(x)$ is positive. Show that the graph of f is symmetric about the origin.

   (b) Where is f increasing and where is it decreasing? Find possible local extreme points.

   (c) Find possible inflection points for f.

SM 11. [HARDER] Classify the critical points of

   $$f(x) = \frac{6x^3}{x^4 + x^2 + 2}$$

   by using the first-derivative test. Sketch the graph of f.

MULTIVARIABLE OPTIMISATION

At first sight it is curious that a subject as pure and passionless as mathematics can have anything useful to say about that messy, ill-structured, chancy world in which we live.

Fortunately we find that whenever we comprehend what was previously mysterious, there is at the centre of everything order, pattern and common sense.
—Patrick (B.H.P.) Rivett (1978)

Chapter 8 was concerned with optimization problems involving functions of one variable. Most interesting economic optimization problems, however, require the simultaneous choice of several variables. For example, a profit-maximizing producer of a single commodity chooses not only its output level, but also the quantities of many different inputs. A consumer chooses what quantities of the many different goods available for her to buy.

Most of the mathematical difficulties arise already in the transition from one to two variables. On the other hand, textbooks in economics often illustrate economic problems by using functions of only two variables, for which one can at least draw level curves in the plane. We therefore begin this chapter by studying the two-variable case. The first section presents the basic results, illustrated by relatively simple examples and problems. Then, we give a more systematic presentation of the theory with two variables. Subsequently we consider how the theory can be generalized to functions of several variables.

Much of economic analysis involves seeing how the solution to an optimization problem responds when the situation changes—for example, if some relevant parameters change. Thus, the theory of the firm considers how a change in the price of a good that is either an input or an output can affect the optimal quantities of all the inputs and outputs, as well as the maximum profit. Some simple results of this kind are briefly introduced at the end of the chapter.

8.1 Two Choice Variables: Necessary Conditions

Consider a differentiable function $z = f(x, y)$ defined on a set S in the xy-plane. Suppose that f attains its largest value (its maximum) at an "interior" point (x_0, y_0) of S, as indicated in Fig. 8.1.1. If we keep y fixed at y_0, then the function $g(x) = f(x, y_0)$ depends only on x

and has its maximum at $x = x_0$. Geometrically, if P is the highest point on the surface in Fig. 8.1.1, then P is certainly also the highest point on the curve through P that has $y = y_0$—i.e. on the curve which is the intersection of the surface with the plane $y = y_0$. From Theorem 8.1.1, we know that $g'(x_0) = 0$. But for all x, the derivative $g'(x)$ is exactly the same as the partial derivative $f_1'(x, y_0)$. At $x = x_0$, therefore, one has $f_1'(x_0, y_0) = 0$. In the same way, we see that (x_0, y_0) must satisfy $f_2'(x_0, y_0) = 0$, because the function $h(y) = f(x_0, y)$ has its maximum at $y = y_0$. A point (x_0, y_0) where both the partial derivatives are 0 is called a *critical* (or *stationary*) *point* of f.

If f attains its smallest value (its minimum) at an interior point (x_0, y_0) of S, a similar argument shows that the point again must be a critical point. So we have the following important result:[1]

THEOREM 8.1.1 (NECESSARY FIRST-ORDER CONDITIONS)

A differentiable function $z = f(x, y)$ can have a maximum or minimum at an interior point (x_0, y_0) of its domain only if it is a *critical point*—that is, if the point $(x, y) = (x_0, y_0)$ satisfies the two equations

$$f_1'(x, y) = 0 \text{ and } f_2'(x, y) = 0$$

which are known as first-order conditions, or FOCS.

In Fig. 8.1.2, the three points P, Q, and R are all critical points, but only P is a maximum.[2] In the following examples and problems only the first-order conditions are considered. Section 8.2 explains how to verify that we have found the optimum.

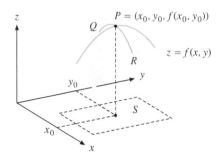

Figure 8.1.1 Maximum point, P, is critical

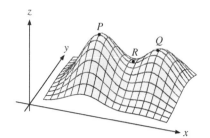

Figure 8.1.2 Only P is a maximum

EXAMPLE 8.1.1   The function f is defined for all (x, y) by

$$f(x, y) = -2x^2 - 2xy - 2y^2 + 36x + 42y - 158$$

Assume that f has a maximum point. Find it.

---

[1]   The concept of interior point is defined precisely in Section 8.5.
[2]   Later, we shall call Q a *local maximum*, whereas R is a *saddle point*.

Solution: Theorem 8.1.1 applies, so a maximum point (x, y) must be a critical point, satisfying the first-order conditions:

$$f_1'(x, y) = -4x - 2y + 36 = 0 \text{ and } f_2'(x, y) = -2x - 4y + 42 = 0$$

These are two linear equations which determine x and y. We find that $(x, y) = (5, 8)$ is the only pair of numbers which satisfies both equations. Assuming there is a maximum point, these must be its coordinates. The maximum value is $f(5, 8) = 100$.[3]

EXAMPLE 8.1.2   A firm produces two different kinds, A and B, of a commodity. The daily cost of producing x units of A and y units of B is

$$C(x, y) = 0.04x^2 + 0.01xy + 0.01y^2 + 4x + 2y + 500$$

Suppose that the firm sells all its output at a price per unit of \$15 for A and \$9 for B. Find the daily production levels x and y that maximize profit per day.

Solution: Profit per day is $\pi(x, y) = 15x + 9y - C(x, y)$, so

$$\pi(x, y) = 15x + 9y - 0.04x^2 - 0.01xy - 0.01y^2 - 4x - 2y - 500$$

$$= -0.04x^2 - 0.01xy - 0.01y^2 + 11x + 7y - 500$$

If $x > 0$ and $y > 0$ maximize profit, then (x, y) must satisfy

$$\frac{\partial \pi}{\partial x} = -0.08x - 0.01y + 11 = 0, \quad \frac{\partial \pi}{\partial y} = -0.01x - 0.02y + 7 = 0$$

These two linear equations in x and y have the unique solution $x = 100$, $y = 300$, with $\pi(100, 300) = 1100$. (We have not proved that this actually is a maximum. For that, see Exercise 8.2.1).

EXAMPLE 8.1.3   **(Profit maximization)** Suppose that $Q = F(K, L)$ is a production function with K as the capital input and L as the labour input. The price per unit of output is p, the cost (or rental) per unit of capital is r, and the wage rate is w. The constants p, r, and w are all positive. The profit, π, from producing and selling $F(K, L)$ units is then given by the function

$$\pi(K, L) = pF(K, L) - rK - wL$$

If F is differentiable and π has a maximum with $K > 0$, $L > 0$, then the FOCs are

$$\pi_K'(K, L) = pF_K'(K, L) - r = 0 \text{ and } \pi_L'(K, L) = pF_L'(K, L) - w = 0$$

Thus, a necessary condition for profit to be a maximum when $K = K^*$ and $L = L^*$ is that

$$pF_K'(K^*, L^*) = r \text{ and } pF_L'(K^*, L^*) = w \qquad (*)$$

---

[3] In Example 8.2.2 we prove that $(5, 8)$ *really is* a maximum point.

The first equation says that r, the cost of capital, must equal the value, at price p per unit, of the marginal product of capital. The second equation has a similar interpretation.

Suppose we think of increasing capital input from the level K^* by k units. How much would be gained? Production would increase by approximately $F'_K(K^*, L^*)k$ units. Because each extra unit is priced at p, the revenue gain is approximately $pF'_K(K^*, L^*)k$. How much is lost? The answer is rk, because r is the cost of each unit of capital. These two must be equal.

The second equation in $(*)$ has a similar interpretation: Increasing labour input by ℓ units from level L^* will lead to the approximate gain $pF'_L(K^*, L^*)\ell$ in revenue, whereas the extra labour cost is $w\ell$. The profit-maximizing pair (K^*, L^*) thus has the property that the extra revenue from increasing either input is just offset by the extra cost.

Economists often divide the first-order conditions $(*)$ by the positive price p to reach the alternative form $F'_K(K, L) = r/p$ and $F'_L(K, L) = w/p$. So, to obtain maximum profit, the firm must choose K and L to equate the marginal productivity of capital to its "relative" price, r/p, and also to equate the marginal productivity of labour to its relative price, w/p.

Note that the conditions in $(*)$ are necessary, but generally not sufficient for an interior maximum.[4]

EXAMPLE 8.1.4   Find the only possible solution to the following special case of Example 8.1.3:

$$\max \pi(K, L) = 12K^{1/2}L^{1/4} - 1.2K - 0.6L$$

Solution: The first-order conditions are

$$\pi'_K(K, L) = 6K^{-1/2}L^{1/4} - 1.2 = 0 \quad \text{and} \quad \pi'_L(K, L) = 3K^{1/2}L^{-3/4} - 0.6 = 0$$

These equations imply that $K^{-1/2}L^{1/4} = K^{1/2}L^{-3/4} = 0.2 = 1/5$. Multiplying each side of the first equation here by $K^{1/2}L^{3/4}$ reduces it to $L = K$. Hence $K^{-1/4} = L^{-1/4} = 1/5$. It follows that $K = L = 5^4 = 625$ is the only possible solution.[5]

EXAMPLE 8.1.5   A firm is a monopolist in the domestic market, but takes as given the price, p_w, of its product in the world market. The quantities sold in the two markets are denoted by x_d and x_w, respectively. The price obtained in the domestic market, as a function of its sales, is given by the inverse demand function $p_d = P(x_d)$. The cost of producing x units is $C(x)$, regardless of how this output is distributed between the domestic and world markets.

(a) Find the profit function $\pi(x_d, x_w)$ and write down the first-order conditions for profit to be maximized at $x_d > 0$, $x_w > 0$. Give economic interpretations of these conditions.

(b) Suppose that in the domestic market the firm is faced with a demand curve whose price elasticity is constant, equal to -2. What is the relationship between the prices in the domestic and world markets?

---

[4] Sufficient conditions for an optimum are given in Example 8.3.3.
[5] See Example 8.2.3 for a proof that this is indeed a maximum point.

Solution:

(a) The revenue from selling x_d units in the domestic market at the price $p_d = P(x_d)$ is $P(x_d) \cdot x_d$. In the world market the revenue is $p_w x_w$. The profit function is $\pi = \pi(x_d, x_w) = P(x_d)x_d + p_w x_w - C(x_d + x_w)$. Thus, the first-order conditions are

$$\pi'_1 = p_d + P'(x_d) \cdot x_d - C'(x_d + x_w) = 0 \tag{$*$}$$

$$\pi'_2 = p_w - C'(x_d + x_w) = 0 \tag{$**$}$$

According to ($**$), the marginal cost in the world market must equal the price, which is the marginal revenue in this case. In the domestic market the marginal cost must also equal the marginal revenue. Suppose the firm contemplates producing and selling a little extra in its domestic market. The extra revenue per unit increase in output equals p_d minus the loss that arises because of the induced price reduction for all domestic sales. The latter loss is approximately $P'(x_d) \cdot x_d$. Since the cost of an extra unit of output is approximately the marginal cost $C'(x_d + x_w)$, condition ($*$) expresses the requirement that, per unit of extra output, the domestic revenue gain is just offset by the cost increase.

(b) The price elasticity of demand is -2, meaning that $\mathrm{El}_{p_d} x_d = (p_d/x_d)(dx_d/dp_d) = -2$. By the rule for differentiating inverse functions one has $dp_d/dx_d = 1/(dx_d/dp_d)$. It follows that

$$P'(x_d) \cdot x_d = \frac{dp_d}{dx_d}x_d = -\frac{1}{2}p_d$$

Then ($*$) and ($**$) imply that $\frac{1}{2}p_d = C'(x_d + x_w) = p_w$, so the domestic market price is twice the world market price.

EXERCISES FOR SECTION 8.1

1. The function f defined for all (x, y) by $f(x, y) = -2x^2 - y^2 + 4x + 4y - 3$ has a maximum. Find the corresponding values of x and y.

2. Consider the function f defined for all (x, y) by $f(x, y) = x^2 + y^2 - 6x + 8y + 35$.

   (a) The function has a minimum point. Find it.

   (b) Show that $f(x, y)$ can be written in the form $f(x, y) = (x - 3)^2 + (y + 4)^2 + 10$. Explain why this shows that you have really found the minimum in part (a).

3. In the profit-maximizing problem of Example 8.1.3, let $p = 1$, $r = 0.65$, $w = 1.2$, and

   $$F(K, L) = 80 - (K - 3)^2 - 2(L - 6)^2 - (K - 3)(L - 6)$$

   Find the only possible values of K and L that maximize profits.

4. Annual profits for a firm are given by

   $$P(x, y) = -x^2 - y^2 + 22x + 18y - 102$$

   where x is the amount spent on research, and y is the amount spent on advertising.

   (a) Find the profits when $x = 10$, $y = 8$ and when $x = 12$, $y = 10$.

(b) Find the only possible values of x and y that can maximize profits, and the corresponding profit.

8.2 Two Choice Variables: Sufficient Conditions

Suppose f is a function of one variable defined in an interval I. Recall from Theorem 8.2.2 that, if f is twice differentiable, in this case a very simple sufficient condition for a critical point in I to be a maximum point is that $f''(x) \leq 0$ for all x in I. Shorthand for this sufficient condition is to say that the function f is concave.

For functions of two variables there is a corresponding test for concavity based on the second-order *partial* derivatives. Provided the function has an interior critical point, this test implies that its graph is a surface shaped like the one in Fig. 8.1.1.

Consider any curve parallel to the xz-plane which lies in the surface, like QPR in that figure. Any such curve is the graph of a concave function of one variable, implying that $f_{11}''(x, y) \leq 0$. A similar argument holds for any curve parallel to the yz-plane which lies in the surface, implying that $f_{22}''(x, y) \leq 0$. In general, however, having these two second-order partial derivatives be nonpositive is *not* sufficient on its own to ensure that the surface is shaped like the one in Fig. 8.1.1. This is clear from the next example.

EXAMPLE 8.2.1   The function $f(x, y) = 3xy - x^2 - y^2$ has $f_{11}''(x, y) = f_{22}''(x, y) = -2$. Each curve parallel to the xz-plane that lies in the surface defined by the graph has the equation $z = 3xy_0 - x^2 - y_0^2$ for some fixed y_0. It is therefore a concave parabola. So is each curve parallel to the yz-plane that lies in the surface. But along the line $y = x$ the function reduces to $f(x, x) = x^2$, whose graph is a convex rather than a concave parabola. It follows that f has no maximum (or minimum) at $(0, 0)$, which is its only critical point.

What Example 8.2.1 shows is that conditions ensuring that the graph of f looks like the one in Fig. 8.1.1 cannot ignore the second-order cross partial derivative $f_{12}''(x\ y)$. The following result is analogous to Theorem 8.2.2. We leave a detailed discussion of it to FMEA, but present a proof of its local version in Section 8.3. To formulate the theorem, however, we need a new concept: a set S in the xy-plane is *convex* if for each pair of points P and Q in S, the whole line segment between P and Q lies in S.

THEOREM 8.2.1 (SUFFICIENT CONDITIONS FOR A MAXIMUM OR MINIMUM)

Suppose that (x_0, y_0) is an interior critical point for a C^2 function $f(x, y)$ defined in a convex set S in $\mathbb{R}^2$.

(a) If for all (x, y) in S, one has

$$f_{11}''(x, y) \leq 0, \quad f_{22}''(x, y) \leq 0, \quad \text{and}$$

$$f_{11}''(x, y)f_{22}''(x, y) - \left[f_{12}''(x, y)\right]^2 \geq 0$$

then (x_0, y_0) is a maximum point for $f(x, y)$ in S.

(b) If for all (x, y) in S, one has

$$f_{11}''(x, y) \geq 0, \ f_{22}''(x, y) \geq 0, \ \text{and}$$

$$f_{11}''(x, y)f_{22}''(x, y) - \left[f_{12}''(x, y)\right]^2 \geq 0$$

then (x_0, y_0) is a minimum point for $f(x, y)$ in S.

The conditions in part (a) of Theorem 8.2.1 are sufficient for a critical point to be a maximum point. They are far from being necessary. This is clear from the function whose graph is shown in Fig. 8.1.2, which *has* a maximum at P, but where the conditions in (a) are certainly not satisfied in the whole of its domain.

Importantly, if a twice differentiable function $z = f(x, y)$ satisfies the inequalities in (a) throughout a convex set S, it is called *concave*, whereas it is called *convex* if it satisfies the inequalities in (b) throughout S. It follows from these definitions that f is concave if and only if $-f$ is convex, just as in the one-variable case. There are more general definitions of concave and convex functions which apply to functions that are not necessarily differentiable. These are presented in FMEA.[6]

EXAMPLE 8.2.2   Show that we have found a maximum in Example 8.1.1.

Solution: We found that $f_1'(x, y) = -4x - 2y + 36$ and $f_2'(x, y) = -2x - 4y + 42$. Furthermore, $f_{11}'' = -4, f_{12}'' = -2$, and $f_{22}'' = -4$. Thus, $f_{11}''(x, y) \leq 0, f_{22}''(x, y) \leq 0$, and

$$f_{11}''(x, y)f_{22}''(x, y) - \left[f_{12}''(x, y)\right]^2 = 16 - 4 = 12 \geq 0$$

According to part (a) in Theorem 8.2.1, these inequalities guarantee that the critical point $(5, 8)$ is a maximum point.

EXAMPLE 8.2.3   Show that we have found the maximum in Example 8.1.4.

Solution: If $K > 0$ and $L > 0$, we find that

$$\pi_{KK}'' = -3K^{-3/2}L^{1/4}, \ \pi_{KL}'' = \tfrac{3}{2}K^{-1/2}L^{-3/4}, \ \text{and} \ \pi_{LL}'' = -\tfrac{9}{4}K^{1/2}L^{-7/4}$$

Clearly, $\pi_{KK}'' < 0, \pi_{LL}'' < 0$, and moreover,

$$\pi_{KK}''\pi_{LL}'' - (\pi_{KL}'')^2 = \tfrac{27}{4}K^{-1}L^{-3/2} - \tfrac{9}{4}K^{-1}L^{-3/2} = \tfrac{9}{2}K^{-1}L^{-3/2} > 0$$

It follows that the critical point $(K, L) = (625, 625)$ maximizes profit.

This section concludes with two examples of optimization problems where the choice of variables is subject to constraints. Nevertheless, a simple transformation can be used to convert the problem into the form we have been discussing, without any constraints.

---

[6] The one-variable case was briefly discussed in Section 8.7.

EXAMPLE 8.2.4   Suppose that any production by the firm in Example 8.1.2 creates pollution, so it is legally restricted to produce a total of 320 units of the two kinds of output. The firm's problem is then

$$\max -0.04x^2 - 0.01xy - 0.01y^2 + 11x + 7y - 500 \text{ subject to } x + y = 320$$

What are the optimal quantities of the two kinds of output now?

Solution: The firm still wants to maximize its profits. But because of the restriction $y = 320 - x$, the new profit function is

$$\hat{\pi}(x) = -0.04x^2 - 0.01x(320 - x) - 0.01(320 - x)^2 + 11x + 7(320 - x) - 500$$

We easily find $\hat{\pi}'(x) = -0.08x + 7.2$, so $\hat{\pi}'(x) = 0$ for $x = 7.2/0.08 = 90$. Since $\hat{\pi}''(x) = -0.08 < 0$ for all x, the point $x = 90$ does maximize $\hat{\pi}$. The corresponding value of y is $y = 320 - 90 = 230$. The maximum profit is 1040.

EXAMPLE 8.2.5   A firm has three factories producing the same item. Let x, y, and z denote the respective output quantities that the three factories produce in order to fulfil an order for 2000 units in total. Hence, $x + y + z = 2000$. The cost functions for the three factories are

$$C_1(x) = 200 + \frac{1}{100}x^2, \ C_2(y) = 200 + y + \frac{1}{300}y^3, \ \text{and } C_3(z) = 200 + 10z$$

The total cost of fulfilling the order is, thus,

$$C(x, y, z) = C_1(x) + C_2(y) + C_3(z)$$

Find the values of x, y, and z that minimize C.

Solution: Solving the equation $x + y + z = 2000$ for z yields $z = 2000 - x - y$. Substituting this expression for z in the expression for C yields, after simplifying,

$$\hat{C}(x, y) = C(x, y, 2000 - x - y) = \frac{1}{100}x^2 - 10x + \frac{1}{300}y^3 - 9y + 20\,600$$

Any critical points of $\hat{C}$ must satisfy the two equations

$$\hat{C}_1'(x, y) = \frac{1}{50}x - 10 = 0 \text{ and } \hat{C}_2'(x, y) = \frac{1}{100}y^2 - 9 = 0$$

The only economically sensible solution is $x = 500$ and $y = 30$, implying that $z = 1470$. The corresponding value of C is $17\,920$.

The second-order partials are $\hat{C}_{11}''(x, y) = \frac{1}{50}$, $\hat{C}_{12}''(x, y) = 0$, and $\hat{C}_{22}''(x, y) = \frac{1}{50}y$. It follows that for all $x \geq 0$, $y \geq 0$, one has $\hat{C}_{11}''(x, y) \geq 0$, $\hat{C}_{22}''(x, y) \geq 0$, and

$$\hat{C}_{11}''(x, y)\hat{C}_{22}''(x, y) - \hat{C}_{12}''(x, y)^2 = \frac{y}{2500} \geq 0$$

Part (b) of Theorem 8.2.1 implies that $(500, 30)$ is a minimum point of $\hat{C}$ within the convex domain of points (x, y) satisfying $x \geq 0$, $y \geq 0$, and $x + y \leq 2000$. It follows that $(500, 30, 1470)$ is a minimum point of C within the domain of (x, y, z) satisfying $x \geq 0$, $y \geq 0$, $z \geq 0$, and $x + y + z = 2000$.

EXERCISES FOR SECTION 8.2

1. Prove that the true maximum has been found in: (a) Example 8.1.2; (b) Exercise 8.1.1; (c) Exercise 8.1.3.

2. A firm produces two different kinds, A and B, of a commodity. The daily cost of producing x units of A and y units of B is

$$C(x, y) = 2x^2 - 4xy + 4y^2 - 40x - 20y + 514$$

Suppose that the firm sells all its output at a price per unit of $24 for A and $12 for B.

(a) Find the daily production levels x and y that maximize profit.

(b) The firm is required to produce exactly 54 units per day of the two kinds combined. What is the optimal production plan now?

SM 3. Maximize the utility function $U(x, y, z) = xyz$, subject to $x + 3y + 4z = 108$ and $x, y, z > 0$, by eliminating the variable x and defining an appropriate function of only y and z.

4. The demands for a monopolist's two products are determined by the equations $p = 25 - x$ and $q = 24 - 2y$, where p and q are prices per unit of the two goods, and x and y are the corresponding quantities. The costs of producing x units of the first good and y units of the other are

$$C(x, y) = 3x^2 + 3xy + y^2$$

(a) Find the monopolist's profit $\pi(x, y)$ from producing and selling x units of the first good and y units of the other.

(b) Find the values of x and y that maximize $\pi(x, y)$. Verify that you have found the maximum profit.

5. A firm produces two goods. The cost of producing x units of good 1 and y units of good 2 is

$$C(x, y) = x^2 + xy + y^2 + x + y + 14$$

Suppose that the firm sells all its output of each good at prices per unit of p and q respectively. Find the values of x and y that maximize profits, under the assumptions that $\frac{1}{2}p + \frac{1}{2} < q < 2p - 1$ and $p > 1$.

6. The profit function of a firm is $\pi(x, y) = px + qy - \alpha x^2 - \beta y^2$, where p and q are the prices per unit and $\alpha x^2 + \beta y^2$ are the costs of producing and selling x units of the first good and y units of the other. The constants are all positive.

(a) Find the values of x and y that maximize profits. Denote them by x^* and y^*. Verify that the second-order conditions are satisfied.

(b) Define $\pi^*(p, q) = \pi(x^*, y^*)$. Verify that $\partial\pi^*(p, q)/\partial p = x^*$ and $\partial\pi^*(p, q)/\partial q = y^*$. Give these results economic interpretations.

7. Find the smallest value of $x^2 + y^2 + z^2$ when we require that $4x + 2y - z = 5$.[7]

8. Let A, a, and b be positive constants, and p, q, and r be arbitrary constants. Show that the function $f(x, y) = Ax^a y^b - px - qy - r$ is concave for $x > 0$, $y > 0$ provided that $a + b \leq 1$.

8.3   Local Extreme Points

Sometimes one needs to consider *local* extreme points of a function. The point (x_0, y_0) is said to be a *local maximum point* of f in S if $f(x, y) \leq f(x_0, y_0)$ for all pairs (x, y) in S that lie sufficiently close to (x_0, y_0). More precisely, the definition is that there exists a positive number r such that $f(x, y) \leq f(x_0, y_0)$ for all (x, y) in S that lie inside the circle with centre (x_0, y_0) and radius r. If the inequality is strict for $(x, y) \neq (x_0, y_0)$, then (x_0, y_0) is a *strict* local maximum point.

A *(strict) local minimum* point is defined in the obvious way, and it should also be clear what we mean by *local maximum and minimum values, local extreme points*, and *local extreme values*. Note how these definitions imply that a global extreme point is also a local extreme point; the converse is not true, of course.

In searching for maximum and minimum points, the first-order conditions were very useful. The same result also applies to the local extreme points: *Any local extreme point in the interior of the domain of a differentiable function must be critical.* This observation follows because in the argument for Theorem 8.1.1 it was sufficient to consider the behaviour of the function in a small neighbourhood of the optimal point.

These first-order conditions are necessary for a differentiable function to have a local extreme point. However, a critical point does not have to be a local extreme point. A critical point (x_0, y_0) of f which, like point R in Fig. 8.1.2, is neither a local maximum nor a local minimum point, is called a *saddle point* of f. Hence: *A saddle point (x_0, y_0) is a critical point with the property that there exist points (x, y) arbitrarily close to (x_0, y_0) with $f(x, y) < f(x_0, y_0)$, and there also exist such points with $f(x, y) > f(x_0, y_0)$.*

EXAMPLE 8.3.1   Show that $(0, 0)$ is a saddle point of $f(x, y) = x^2 - y^2$.

Solution: It is easy to check that $(0, 0)$ is a critical point at which $f(0, 0) = 0$. Moreover, $f(x, 0) = x^2$ and $f(0, y) = -y^2$, so $f(x, y)$ takes positive and negative values arbitrarily close to the origin. Hence, $(0, 0)$ is a saddle point. See the graph in Fig. 8.3.1.

Local extreme points and saddle points can be illustrated by thinking of the mountains in the Himalayas. Every summit is a local maximum, but only the highest (Mount Everest) is the (global) maximum. The deepest points of the lakes or glaciers are local minima. In every mountain pass there will be a saddle point that is the highest point in one compass

---

[7] Geometrically, the problem is to find the point in the plane $4x + 2y - z = 5$ which is closest to the origin.

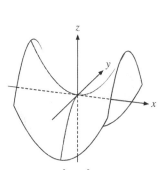

Figure 8.3.1 $z = x^2 - y^2$, with saddle point at $(0, 0)$

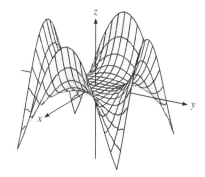

Figure 8.3.2 $z = x^4 - 3x^2y^2 + y^4$, with saddle point at $(0, 0)$

direction and the lowest in another. That said, the surface in Fig. 8.3.2 shows that not all saddle points have graphs that look as neat as the one shown in Fig. 8.3.1.

The critical points of a function thus fall into three categories: local maximum points, local minimum points, and saddle points. How do we distinguish between these three cases?

Consider first the case when $z = f(x, y)$ has a local maximum at (x_0, y_0). The functions $g(x) = f(x, y_0)$ and $h(y) = f(x_0, y)$ describe the behaviour of f along the straight lines $y = y_0$ and $x = x_0$, respectively, as in Fig. 8.1.1. These functions must achieve local maxima at x_0 and y_0, respectively, so $g''(x_0) = f_{11}''(x_0, y_0) \leq 0$ and $h''(y_0) = f_{22}''(x_0, y_0) \leq 0$.

On the other hand, if $g''(x_0) < 0$ and $h''(y_0) < 0$, then we know that g and h really do achieve local maxima at x_0 and y_0, respectively. Stated differently, the conditions $f_{11}''(x_0, y_0) < 0$ and $f_{22}''(x_0, y_0) < 0$ will ensure that $f(x, y)$ has a local maximum in the directions through (x_0, y_0) that are parallel to the x-axis and the y-axis. Note, however, that the signs of $f_{11}''(x_0, y_0)$ and $f_{22}''(x_0, y_0)$ on their own do not reveal much about the behaviour of the graph of $z = f(x, y)$ when we move away from (x_0, y_0) in directions other than the two mentioned. Example 8.3.1 illustrated the problem.

It turns out that in order to have a correct second-derivative test for functions f of two variables, the mixed second-order partial $f_{12}''(x_0, y_0)$ must also be considered, just as it had to be in Section 8.2. The following theorem can be used to determine the nature of the critical points in most cases. (A proof is given at the end of this section.)

THEOREM 8.3.1 (SECOND-DERIVATIVE TEST FOR LOCAL EXTREMA)

Suppose that $f(x, y)$ is a C^2 function in a domain S, and let (x_0, y_0) be an interior critical point of S. Write

$$A = f_{11}''(x_0, y_0), \ B = f_{12}''(x_0, y_0), \ \text{and} \ C = f_{22}''(x_0, y_0)$$

Now:

(a) if $A < 0$ and $AC - B^2 > 0$, then (x_0, y_0) is a strict local maximum point.

(b) if $A > 0$ and $AC - B^2 > 0$, then (x_0, y_0) is a strict local minimum point.

(c) if $AC - B^2 < 0$, then (x_0, y_0) is a saddle point.

(d) if $AC - B^2 = 0$, then (x_0, y_0) could be a local maximum, a local minimum, or a saddle point.

Note that $AC - B^2 > 0$ in (a) implies that $AC > B^2 \geq 0$, and so $AC > 0$. Thus, if $A < 0$, then also $C < 0$. The condition $C = f_{22}''(x_0, y_0) < 0$ is, thus, indirectly included in the assumptions in (a). The corresponding observation for (b) is also valid.

The conditions in (a), (b), and (c) are usually called local *second-order conditions*. Note that these are sufficient conditions for a critical point to be, respectively, a *strict local* maximum point, a *strict local* minimum point, or a saddle point. None of these conditions is necessary. The results in Exercise 5 will confirm (d), because it shows that a critical point where $AC - B^2 = 0$ can fall into any of the three categories. The second-derivative test is inconclusive in this case.

EXAMPLE 8.3.2   Find the critical points and classify them when $f(x, y) = x^3 - x^2 - y^2 + 8$.

Solution: The critical points must satisfy the two equations

$$f_1'(x, y) = 3x^2 - 2x = 0 \text{ and } f_2'(x, y) = -2y = 0$$

Because $3x^2 - 2x = x(3x - 2)$, we see that the first equation has the solutions $x = 0$ and $x = 2/3$. The second equation has the solution $y = 0$. We conclude that $(0, 0)$ and $(2/3, 0)$ are the only critical points.

Furthermore, $f_{11}''(x, y) = 6x - 2, f_{12}''(x, y) = 0$, and $f_{22}''(x, y) = -2$. A convenient way of classifying the critical points is to make a table like the following:

(x, y)	A	B	C	$AC - B^2$	Type of point
$(0, 0)$	-2	0	-2	4	Local maximum point
$(2/3, 0)$	2	0	-2	-4	Saddle point

with A, B, and C defined in Theorem 8.3.1.

EXAMPLE 8.3.3   Consider Example 8.1.3 and suppose that the production function F is twice differentiable. Define

$$\Delta(K, L) = F_{KK}''(K, L)F_{LL}''(K, L) - \left[F_{KL}''(K, L)\right]^2$$

and let (K^*, L^*) be an input pair satisfying the first-order conditions $(*)$ in the example.

(a) Prove that if

$$F_{KK}''(K, L) \leq 0, \ F_{LL}''(K, L) \leq 0 \ \text{ and } \ \Delta(K, L) \geq 0 \ \text{ for all } K \geq 0 \text{ and } L \geq 0 \qquad (*)$$

so that the product function F is concave, then (K^*, L^*) maximizes profit.

(b) Prove also that if

$$F''_{KK}(K^*, L^*) < 0 \quad \text{and} \quad \Delta(K^*, L^*) > 0 \tag{8.3.1}$$

then (K^*, L^*) is a strict local maximum for the profit function.

Solution:

(a) The second-order partials of the profit function are:

$$\pi''_{KK}(K, L) = pF''_{KK}(K, L); \quad \pi''_{KL}(K, L) = pF''_{KL}(K, L); \quad \pi''_{LL}(K, L) = pF''_{LL}(K, L)$$

Since $p > 0$, the conclusion follows from part (a) in Theorem 8.2.1.

(b) In this case the conclusion follows from part (a) in Theorem 8.3.1.

Proof of the Second-Derivative Test

We now want to prove sufficiency Theorem 8.3.1, and will do this based on our understanding of the one-dimensional case studied in Theorem 8.6.2. Before doing that, it is instructive to develop some intuition by determining some *necessary conditions* for local optimization.

Let $z = f(x, y)$ be the function graphed in Fig. 8.3.3, with (x_0, y_0) as a local maximum point. For fixed values of h and k, define the function g of one variable by

$$g(t) = f(x_0 + th, y_0 + tk)$$

This function tells us what happens to f as one moves away from (x_0, y_0) in the direction (h, k) when $t > 0$, or in the reverse direction $(-h, -k)$ when $t < 0$.

If f has a local maximum at (x_0, y_0), then $g(t)$ must certainly have a local maximum at $t = 0$. From Theorem 8.1.1 and formula (8.6.3), necessary conditions for this are that $g'(0) = 0$ and $g''(0) \leq 0$. The first- and second-order derivatives of $g(t)$ can be calculated as in Example 12.1.5. At $t = 0$, the second derivative of g is

$$g''(0) = f''_{11}(x_0, y_0)h^2 + 2f''_{12}(x_0, y_0)hk + f''_{22}(x_0, y_0)k^2 \tag{8.3.2}$$

So if f has a local maximum at (x_0, y_0), the expression in (8.3.2) must be nonpositive for all choices of (h, k).

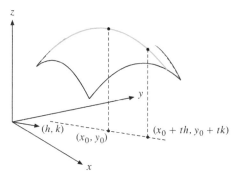

Figure 8.3.3 The second derivative test

In this way we have obtained a *necessary* condition for f to have a local maximum at (x_0, y_0). We now proceed to find *sufficient* conditions for a local maximum. For the one-variable case, we know from part (i) in Theorem 8.6.2 that the conditions $g'(0) = 0$ and $g''(0) < 0$ are sufficient for g to have a local maximum at $t = 0$. It is therefore reasonable to conjecture that we have the following result:

If $f_1'(x_0, y_0) = f_2'(x_0, y_0) = 0$ and the expression in (8.3.2) for the second derivative $g''(0)$ is negative for all directions $(h, k) \neq (0, 0)$, then (x_0, y_0) is a (strict) local maximum point for f.

This turns out to be correct, as will be proved in FMEA. Exercise 7, however, shows that the expression in (8.3.2) really must be negative for *all* directions (h, k), without exception. Relying on this result, we can prove part (a) of Theorem 8.3.1:

It suffices to verify that $A < 0$ and $AC - B^2 > 0$ imply that

$$Ah^2 + 2Bhk + Ck^2 < 0 \text{ for all } (h, k) \neq (0, 0) \tag{8.3.3}$$

To this end we complete the square:

$$Ah^2 + 2Bhk + Ck^2 = A\left[\left(h + \frac{B}{A}k\right)^2 + \frac{AC - B^2}{A^2}k^2\right] \tag{8.3.4}$$

The expression in square brackets is obviously non-negative, and equals 0 only if both $h + Bk/A = 0$ and $k = 0$, implying that $h = k = 0$. Because $A < 0$, the right-hand side of Eq. (8.3.4) is negative for all $(h, k) \neq (0, 0)$, so we have proved (8.3.3).

EXERCISES FOR SECTION 8.3

1. Consider the function f defined for all (x, y) by $f(x, y) = 5 - x^2 + 6x - 2y^2 + 8y$.

(a) Find its partial derivatives of first and second order.

(b) Find the only critical point and classify it by using the second-derivative test. What does Theorem 8.2.1 tell us?

2. Consider the function f defined for all (x, y) by $f(x, y) = x^2 + 2xy^2 + 2y^2$.

(a) Find its partial derivatives of first and second order.

(b) Show that its critical points are $(0, 0)$, $(-1, 1)$ and $(-1, -1)$, and classify them.

(SM) **3.** Let f be a function of two variables, given by

$$f(x, y) = (x^2 - axy)e^y$$

where $a \neq 0$ is a constant.

(a) Find the critical points of f and decide for each of them if it is a local maximum point, a local minimum point, or a saddle point.

(b) Let (x^*, y^*) be the critical point where $x^* \neq 0$, and let $f^*(a) = f(x^*, y^*)$. Find $df^*(a)/da$. Show that if we let $\hat{f}(x, y, a) = (x^2 - axy)e^y$, then

$$\hat{f}_3'(x^*, y^*, a) = \frac{df^*(a)}{da}$$

(SM) **4.** Suppose in Example 10.3.2 that the market value of the tree at time t is a function $f(t, x)$ of the amount x spent on trimming the tree at time 0, as well as of t. Assuming continuous compounding at the interest rate r, the present discounted value of the profit earned on the tree is then $V(t, x) = f(t, x)e^{-rt} - x$.

  (a) What are the first-order conditions for $V(t, x)$ to have a maximum at $t^* > 0$, $x^* > 0$?

  (b) What are the first-order conditions if $f(t, x)$ takes the separable form $f(t, x) = g(t)h(x)$, with $g(t) > 0$ and $h(x) > 0$? (Note that in this case t^* does not depend on the function h.)

  (c) In the separable case, prove that $g''(t^*) < r^2 g(t^*)$ and $h''(x^*) < 0$ are sufficient conditions for a critical point (t^*, x^*) to be a local maximum point for V.

  (d) Find t^* and x^* when $g(t) = e^{\sqrt{t}}$ and $h(x) = \ln(x + 1)$, and check the local second-order conditions.

5. Consider the three functions: (i) $z = -x^4 - y^4$;   (ii) $z = x^4 + y^4$;   (iii) $z = x^3 + y^3$.

  (a) Prove that the origin is a critical point for each one of these functions, and that $AC - B^2 = 0$ at the origin in each case.

  (b) By studying the functions directly, prove that the origin is respectively a maximum point for (i), a minimum point for (ii), and a saddle point for (iii).

(SM) **6.** [HARDER] Consider the function $f(x, y) = \ln(1 + x^2 y)$.

  (a) Find its domain.

  (b) Prove that the critical points are all the points on the y-axis.

  (c) Show that the second-derivative test fails.

  (d) Classify the critical points by looking directly at the sign of the value of $f(x, y)$.

7. [HARDER] The graph of $f(x, y) = (y - x^2)(y - 2x^2)$ intersects the xy-plane $z = 0$ in two parabolas.

  (a) In the xy-plane, draw the domains where f is negative, and where f is positive. Show that $(0, 0)$ is the only critical point, and that it is a saddle point.

  (b) Suppose $(h, k) \neq (0, 0)$ is any direction vector. Let $g(t) = f(th, tk)$ and show that g has a local minimum at $t = 0$, whatever the direction (h, k) may be.[8]

8.4   Linear Models with Quadratic Objectives

In this section we consider some other interesting economic applications of optimization theory when there are two variables. Versions of the first example have already appeared in Example 8.1.5 and Exercise 8.2.4.

EXAMPLE 8.4.1   **(Discriminating Monopolist)** Consider a firm that sells a product in two isolated geographical areas. If it wants to, it can then charge different prices in the two different

---

[8] Thus, although $(0, 0)$ is a saddle point, the function has a local minimum at the origin in each direction.

areas because what is sold in one area cannot easily be resold in the other.[9] Suppose that such a firm also has some monopoly power to influence the different prices it faces in the two separate markets by adjusting the quantity it sells in each. Economists generally use the term "discriminating monopolist" to describe a firm having this power.

Faced with two such isolated markets, the discriminating monopolist has two independent demand curves. Suppose that, in inverse form, these are

$$P_1 = a_1 - b_1 Q_1 \text{ and } P_2 = a_2 - b_2 Q_2 \qquad (*)$$

for market areas 1 and 2, respectively. Suppose, too, that the total cost is proportional to total production: $C(Q) = \alpha Q$, for some positive constant α.[10] As a function of Q_1 and Q_2, total profits are

$$\pi(Q_1, Q_2) = P_1 Q_1 + P_2 Q_2 - C(Q_1 + Q_2)$$
$$= (a_1 - b_1 Q_1)Q_1 + (a_2 - b_2 Q_2)Q_2 - \alpha(Q_1 + Q_2)$$
$$= (a_1 - \alpha)Q_1 + (a_2 - \alpha)Q_2 - b_1 Q_1^2 - b_2 Q_2^2$$

We want to find the values of $Q_1 \geq 0$ and $Q_2 \geq 0$ that maximize profits. The first-order conditions are

$$\pi_1'(Q_1, Q_2) = (a_1 - \alpha) - 2b_1 Q_1 = 0 \text{ and } \pi_2'(Q_1, Q_2) = (a_2 - \alpha) - 2b_2 Q_2 = 0$$

with the solutions $Q_1^* = (a_1 - \alpha)/2b_1$ and $Q_2^* = (a_2 - \alpha)/2b_2$. Furthermore, one has $\pi_{11}''(Q_1, Q_2) = -2b_1$, $\pi_{12}''(Q_1, Q_2) = 0$, and $\pi_{22}''(Q_1, Q_2) = -2b_2$. Hence, for all (Q_1, Q_2), it follows that

$$\pi_{11}'' \leq 0, \ \pi_{22}'' \leq 0, \ \text{and} \ \pi_{11}'' \pi_{22}'' - (\pi_{12}'')^2 = 4b_1 b_2 \geq 0$$

We conclude from Theorem 8.2.1 that if Q_1^* and Q_2^* are both positive, implying that (Q_1^*, Q_2^*) is an interior point in the domain of π, then the pair (Q_1^*, Q_2^*) really does maximize profits.

The corresponding prices can be found by inserting these values in $(*)$ to get

$$P_1^* = a_1 - b_1 Q_1^* = \tfrac{1}{2}(a_1 + \alpha) \text{ and } P_2^* = a_2 - b_2 Q_2^* = \tfrac{1}{2}(a_2 + \alpha)$$

The maximum profit is

$$\pi^* = \frac{(a_1 - \alpha)^2}{4b_1} + \frac{(a_2 - \alpha)^2}{4b_2}$$

Both sales quantities Q_1^* and Q_2^* are positive provided $a_1 > \alpha$ and $a_2 > \alpha$. In this case, P_1^* and P_2^* are both greater than α. This implies that there is no "dumping", with the price in

---

[9] As an example, it seems that express mail or courier services find it possible to charge much higher prices in Europe than they can in North America. Another example is that pharmaceutical firms often charge much more for the same medication in the USA than they do in Europe or Canada.

[10] It is true that this cost function neglects transport costs. But the point to be made is that, even though supplies to the two areas are perfect substitutes in production, the monopolist will generally be able to earn higher profits by charging different prices, if this is allowed.

one market less than the cost α. Nor is there any "cross-subsidy", with the losses due to dumping in one market being subsidized out of profits in the other market. It is notable that the optimal prices are independent of b_1 and b_2. More important, note that the prices are *not* the same in the two markets, except in the special case when $a_1 = a_2$. Indeed, $P_1^* > P_2^*$ if, and only if, $a_1 > a_2$. This says that the price is higher in the market where consumers are willing to pay a higher price for each unit when the quantity is close to zero.

EXAMPLE 8.4.2   Suppose that the monopolist in Example 8.4.1 has the demand functions $P_1 = 100 - Q_1$ and $P_2 = 80 - Q_2$, and that the cost function is $C(Q) = 6Q$.

(a) How much should be sold in the two markets to maximize profits? What are the corresponding prices?

(b) How much profit is lost if it becomes illegal to discriminate?

(c) The authorities impose a tax of τ per unit sold in the first market. Discuss the consequences.

Solution:

(a) Here $a_1 = 100$, $a_2 = 80$, $b_1 = b_2 = 1$, and $\alpha = 6$. Example 8.4.1 gives the answers

$$Q_1^* = (100 - 6)/2 = 47, \ Q_2^* = 37, \ P_1^* = \tfrac{1}{2}(100 + 6) = 53, \ \text{and} \ P_2^* = 43$$

The corresponding profit is $P_1^* Q_1^* + P_2^* Q_2^* - 6(Q_1^* + Q_2^*) = 3578$.

(b) If price discrimination is not permitted, then $P_1 = P_2 = P$, and $Q_1 = 100 - P$, $Q_2 = 80 - P$, with total demand $Q = Q_1 + Q_2 = 180 - 2P$. Then $P = 90 - \tfrac{1}{2}Q$, so profits are

$$\pi = \left(90 - \tfrac{1}{2}Q\right)Q - 6Q = 84Q - \tfrac{1}{2}Q^2$$

This has a maximum at $Q = 84$ when $P = 48$. The corresponding profit is now $\pi = 3528$, so the loss in profit is $3578 - 3528 = 50$.

(c) With the introduction of the tax, the new profit function is

$$\hat{\pi} = (100 - Q_1)Q_1 + (80 - Q_2)Q_2 - 6(Q_1 + Q_2) - \tau Q_1$$

We easily see that this has a maximum at $\hat{Q}_1 = 47 - \tfrac{1}{2}\tau$, $\hat{Q}_2 = 37$, with corresponding prices $\hat{P}_1 = 53 + \tfrac{1}{2}\tau$, $\hat{P}_2 = 43$. The tax therefore has no influence on the sales in market 2, while the amount sold in market 1 is lowered and the price in market 1 goes up. The optimal profit π^* is easily worked out: it equals

$$(53 + \tfrac{1}{2}\tau)(47 - \tfrac{1}{2}\tau) + 43 \cdot 37 - 6(84 - \tfrac{1}{2}\tau) - \tau(47 - \tfrac{1}{2}\tau) = 3578 - 47\tau + \tfrac{1}{4}\tau^2$$

So, compared to (a), introducing the tax makes the profit fall by $47\tau - \tfrac{1}{4}\tau^2$. The authorities in market 1 obtain a tax revenue which is

$$T = \tau \hat{Q}_1 = \tau(47 - \tfrac{1}{2}\tau) = 47\tau - \tfrac{1}{2}\tau^2$$

Thus we see that profits fall by $\tfrac{1}{4}\tau^2$ more than the tax revenue. This amount $\tfrac{1}{4}\tau^2$ represents the so-called deadweight loss from the tax.

A monopolistic firm faces a downward-sloping demand curve. A *discriminating monopolist* such as in Example 8.4.1 faces separate downward-sloping demand curves in two or more isolated markets. A *monopsonistic firm*, on the other hand, faces an upward-sloping supply curve for one or more of its factors of production. Then, by definition, a *discriminating monopsonist* faces two or more upward-sloping supply curves for different kinds of the same input—for example, workers of different race or gender. Of course, discrimination by race or gender is illegal in many countries. The following example, however, suggests one possible reason why firms might want to discriminate if they were allowed to.

EXAMPLE 8.4.3   **(Discriminating Monopsonist)** Consider a firm using quantities L_1 and L_2 of two kinds of labour as its only inputs in order to produce output Q according to the simple production function $Q = L_1 + L_2$. Thus, both output and labour supply are measured so that each unit of labour produces one unit of output. Note especially how the two kinds of labour are essentially indistinguishable, because each unit of each type makes an equal contribution to the firm's output. Suppose, however, that there are two segmented labour markets, with different inverse supply functions specifying the wage that must be paid to attract a given labour supply. Specifically, suppose that

$$w_1 = \alpha_1 + \beta_1 L_1; \quad w_2 = \alpha_2 + \beta_2 L_2$$

Assume moreover that the firm is competitive in its output market, taking price P as fixed. Then the firm's profits are

$$\pi(L_1, L_2) = PQ - w_1 L_1 - w_2 L_2 = P(L_1 + L_2) - (\alpha_1 + \beta_1 L_1)L_1 - (\alpha_2 + \beta_2 L_2)L_2$$
$$= (P - \alpha_1)L_1 - \beta_1 L_1^2 + (P - \alpha_2)L_2 - \beta_2 L_2^2$$

The firm wants to maximize profits. The first-order conditions are

$$\pi_1'(L_1, L_2) = (P - \alpha_1) - 2\beta_1 L_1 = 0 \quad \text{and} \quad \pi_2'(L_1, L_2) = (P - \alpha_2) - 2\beta_2 L_2 = 0$$

These have the solutions

$$L_1^* = \frac{P - \alpha_1}{2\beta_1} \quad \text{and} \quad L_2^* = \frac{P - \alpha_2}{2\beta_2}$$

It is easy to see that the conditions for maximum in Theorem 8.2.1 are satisfied, so that L_1^*, L_2^* really do maximize profits if $P > \alpha_1$ and $P > \alpha_2$. The maximum profit is

$$\pi^* = \frac{(P - \alpha_1)^2}{4\beta_1} + \frac{(P - \alpha_2)^2}{4\beta_2}$$

The corresponding wages are

$$w_1^* = \alpha_1 + \beta_1 L_1^* = \tfrac{1}{2}(P + \alpha_1) \quad \text{and} \quad w_2^* = \alpha_2 + \beta_2 L_2^* = \tfrac{1}{2}(P + \alpha_2)$$

Hence, $w_1^* = w_2^*$ only if $\alpha_1 = \alpha_2$. Generally, the wage is higher for the type of labour that demands a higher wage for very low levels of labour supply. Perhaps this is the type of labour with better job prospects elsewhere.

EXAMPLE 8.4.4   (**Econometrics: Linear Regression**) Empirical economics is concerned with analysing data in order to try to discern some pattern that helps in understanding the past, and possibly in predicting the future. For example, price and quantity data for a particular commodity such as natural gas may be used in order to try to estimate a demand function. This might then be used to predict how demand will respond to future price changes. The most commonly used technique for estimating such a function is *linear regression*.

Suppose it is thought that variable y depends upon variable x. Suppose that we have observations (x_t, y_t) of both variables at times $t = 1, 2, \ldots, T$. Then the technique of linear regression seeks to fit a linear function

$$y = \alpha + \beta x$$

to the data, as indicated in Fig. 8.4.1.

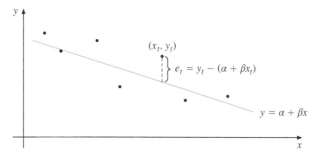

Figure 8.4.1 Linear regression

Of course, an exact fit is possible only if there exist numbers α and β for which $y_t = \alpha + \beta x_t$ for $t = 1, 2, \ldots, T$. This is rarely possible. Generally, however α and β may be chosen, one has instead

$$y_t = \alpha + \beta x_t + e_t, \ t = 1, 2, \ldots, T$$

where e_t is an *error* or *disturbance* term. Obviously, one hopes that the errors will be small, on average. So the parameters α and β are chosen to make the errors as "small as possible", somehow. One idea would be to make the sum $\sum_{t=1}^{T}(y_t - \alpha - \beta x_t)$ equal to zero. However, in this case, large positive discrepancies would cancel large negative discrepancies. Indeed, the sum of errors could be zero even though the line is very far from giving a perfect or even a good fit. We must somehow prevent large positive errors from cancelling large negative errors. Usually, this is done by minimizing the quadratic "loss" function

$$L(\alpha, \beta) = \frac{1}{T} \sum_{t=1}^{T} e_t^2 = \frac{1}{T} \sum_{t=1}^{T} \left(y_t - \alpha - \beta x_t\right)^2 \tag{$*$}$$

which equals the mean (or average) square error. Expanding the square gives

$$L(\alpha, \beta) = \frac{1}{T} \sum_{t=1}^{T} \left(y_t^2 + \alpha^2 + \beta^2 x_t^2 - 2\alpha y_t - 2\beta x_t y_t + 2\alpha\beta x_t\right)$$

This is a quadratic function of α and β. We shall show how to derive the *ordinary least-squares* estimates of α and β. To do so it helps to introduce some standard notation. Write

$$\mu_x = \frac{x_1 + \cdots + x_T}{T} = \frac{1}{T}\sum_{t=1}^{T} x_t, \qquad \mu_y = \frac{y_1 + \cdots + y_T}{T} = \frac{1}{T}\sum_{t=1}^{T} y_t$$

for the *statistical means* of x_t and y_t, and

$$\sigma_{xx} = \frac{1}{T}\sum_{t=1}^{T}(x_t - \mu_x)^2, \; \sigma_{yy} = \frac{1}{T}\sum_{t=1}^{T}(y_t - \mu_y)^2, \; \sigma_{xy} = \frac{1}{T}\sum_{t=1}^{T}(x_t - \mu_x)(y_t - \mu_y)$$

for their *statistical variances*, as well as their *covariance*, respectively. In what follows, we shall assume that the x_t are not all equal. Then, in particular, $\sigma_{xx} > 0$.

Using the result in Example 2.9.2, we have

$$\sigma_{xx} = \frac{1}{T}\sum_{t=1}^{T} x_t^2 - \mu_x^2 \quad \text{and} \quad \sigma_{yy} = \frac{1}{T}\sum_{t=1}^{T} y_t^2 - \mu_y^2$$

while you can verify that, similarly,

$$\sigma_{xy} = \frac{1}{T}\sum_{t=1}^{T} x_t y_t - \mu_x \mu_y$$

Then, the expression for $L(\alpha, \beta)$ becomes

$$L(\alpha, \beta) = \left(\sigma_{yy} + \mu_y^2\right) + \alpha^2 + \beta^2\left(\sigma_{xx} + \mu_x^2\right) - 2\alpha\mu_y - 2\beta\left(\sigma_{xy} + \mu_x\mu_y\right) + 2\alpha\beta\mu_x$$
$$= \alpha^2 + \mu_y^2 + \beta^2\mu_x^2 - 2\alpha\mu_y - 2\beta\mu_x\mu_y + 2\alpha\beta\mu_x + \beta^2\sigma_{xx} - 2\beta\sigma_{xy} + \sigma_{yy}$$

The first-order conditions for a minimum of $L(\alpha, \beta)$ take the form

$$L_1'(\alpha, \beta) = 2\alpha - 2\mu_y + 2\beta\mu_x = 0$$
$$L_2'(\alpha, \beta) = 2\beta\mu_x^2 - 2\mu_x\mu_y + 2\alpha\mu_x + 2\beta\sigma_{xx} - 2\sigma_{xy} = 0$$

Note that $L_2'(\alpha, \beta) = \mu_x L_1'(\alpha, \beta) + 2\beta\sigma_{xx} - 2\sigma_{xy}$. So the unique critical point of $L(\alpha, \beta)$ is $(\hat{\alpha}, \hat{\beta})$ where

$$\hat{\beta} = \frac{\sigma_{xy}}{\sigma_{xx}} \quad \text{and} \quad \hat{\alpha} = \mu_y - \hat{\beta}\mu_x = \mu_y - \left(\frac{\sigma_{xy}}{\sigma_{xx}}\right)\mu_x \qquad (**)$$

Furthermore, $L_{11}'' = 2$, $L_{12}'' = 2\mu_x$, $L_{22}'' = 2\mu_x^2 + 2\sigma_{xx}$. Thus $L_{11}'' \geq 0$, $L_{22}'' \geq 0$, and

$$L_{11}'' L_{22}'' - (L_{12}'')^2 = 2(2\mu_x^2 + 2\sigma_{xx}) - (2\mu_x)^2 = 4\sigma_{xx} = 4T^{-1}\sum_{t=1}^{T}(x_t - \mu_x)^2 \geq 0$$

We conclude that the conditions in part (b) of Theorem 8.2.1 are satisfied, and therefore the pair $(\hat{\alpha}, \hat{\beta})$ given by $(**)$ minimizes $L(\alpha, \beta)$. The problem is then completely solved: *The straight line that best fits the observations* (x_1, y_1), (x_2, y_2), ..., (x_T, y_T), *in the sense of minimizing the mean square error in* $(*)$, *is* $y = \hat{\alpha} + \hat{\beta}x$ *where* $\hat{\alpha}$ *and* $\hat{\beta}$ *are given by* $(**)$.

Note in particular that this estimated straight line passes through the mean (μ_x, μ_y) of the observed pairs (x_t, y_t), $t = 1, \ldots, T$. Also, with a little bit of tedious algebra we obtain

$$L(\alpha, \beta) = \left(\alpha + \beta\mu_x - \mu_y\right)^2 + \sigma_{xx}\left(\beta - \sigma_{xy}/\sigma_{xx}\right)^2 + \left(\sigma_{xx}\sigma_{yy} - \sigma_{xy}^2\right)/\sigma_{xx}$$

The first two terms on the right are always nonnegative, and with $\alpha = \hat{\alpha}$ and $\beta = \hat{\beta}$, they are zero, confirming that $\hat{\alpha}$ and $\hat{\beta}$ do give the minimum value of $L(\alpha, \beta)$.

EXERCISES FOR SECTION 8.4

1. Suppose that the monopolist in Example 8.4.1 faces the two inverse demand functions $P_1 = 200 - 2Q_1$ and $P_2 = 180 - 4Q_2$, and that the cost function is $C = 20(Q_1 + Q_2)$.

   (a) How much should be sold in the two markets to maximize total profit? What are the corresponding prices?

   (b) How much profit is lost if it becomes illegal to discriminate?

   (c) Discuss the consequences of imposing a tax of $\tau = 5$ per unit on the product sold in market 1.

(SM) 2. A firm produces and sells a product in two separate markets. When the price in market A is p per ton, and the price in market B is q per ton, the demand in tons per week in the two markets are, respectively,
$$Q_A = a - bp, \quad Q_B = c - dq$$

   The cost function is $C(Q_A, Q_B) = \alpha + \beta(Q_A + Q_B)$, and all constants are positive.

   (a) Find the firm's profit π as a function of the prices p and q, and then find the pair (p^*, q^*) that maximizes profit.

   (b) Suppose it becomes unlawful to discriminate by price, so that the firm must charge the same price in the two markets. What price $\hat{p}$ will now maximize profit?

   (c) In the case $\beta = 0$, find the firm's loss of profit if it has to charge the same price in both markets. Comment.

3. In Example 8.4.1, discuss the effects of a tax imposed in market 1 of τ per unit of Q_1.

(SM) 4. The following table shows the Norwegian gross national product (GNP) and spending on foreign aid (FA) for the period 1970–1973, in millions of crowns:

Year	1970	1971	1972	1973
GNP	79 835	89 112	97 339	110 156
FA	274	307	436	524

Growth of both GNP and FA was almost exponential during the period. So, approximately, one has $GNP = Ae^{a(t-t_0)}$, with $t_0 = 1970$. Define $x = t - t_0$ and $b = \ln A$. Then $\ln(GNP) = ax + b$. On the basis of the table above, one gets the following

Year	1970	1971	1972	1973
$y = \ln(GNP)$	11.29	11.40	11.49	11.61

   (a) Using the method of least squares, determine the straight line $y = ax + b$ which best fits the data in the last table.

   (b) Repeat the method above to estimate c and d, where $\ln(FA) = cx + d$.

(c) The Norwegian government had a stated goal of eventually giving 1% of its GNP as foreign aid. If the time trends of the two variables had continued as they did during the years 1970–1973, when would this goal have been reached?

(SM) **5.** *(Duopoly)* Each of two firms A and B produces its own brand of a commodity such as mineral water in amounts denoted by x and y, which are sold at prices p and q per unit, respectively. Each firm determines its own price and produces exactly as much as is demanded. The demands for the two brands are given by

$$x = 29 - 5p + 4q \text{ and } y = 16 + 4p - 6q$$

Firm A has total costs $5 + x$, whereas firm B has total costs $3 + 2y$. (Assume that the functions to be maximized have maxima, and at positive prices.)

(a) Initially, the two firms collude in order to maximize their combined profit, as one monopolist would. Find the prices (p, q), the production levels (x, y), and the profits of firms A and B.

(b) Then an anti-trust authority prohibits collusion, so each producer maximizes its own profit, taking the other's price as given. If q is fixed, how will A choose p as a function $p = p_A(q)$ of q? If p is fixed, how will B choose q as a function $q = q_B(p)$ of p?

(c) Under the assumptions in part (b), what constant equilibrium prices are possible? What are the production levels and profits in this case?

(d) Draw a diagram with p along the horizontal axis and q along the vertical axis, and draw the "reaction" curves $p_A(q)$ and $q_B(p)$. Show on the diagram how the two firms' prices change over time if A breaks the cooperation first by maximizing its profit, taking B's initial price as fixed, then B answers by maximizing its profit with A's price fixed, then A responds, and so on.

8.5   The Extreme Value Theorem

As with functions of one variable, it is easy to find examples of functions of several variables that do not have any maximum or minimum points. The extreme value theorem, Theorem 8.4.1, however, was very useful for providing sufficient conditions to ensure that extreme points do exist for functions of one variable. It can be directly generalized to functions of several variables. In order to formulate the theorem, however, we need a few new concepts.

For many of the results concerning functions of one variable, it was important to distinguish between different kinds of domain for the functions. For functions of several variables, the distinction between different kinds of domain is no less important. In the one-variable case, most functions were defined over intervals, and there are not many different kinds of interval. For functions of several variables, however, there are many different kinds of domain. Fortunately, the distinctions that are relevant to the extreme value theorem can be made using only the concepts of open, closed, and bounded sets.

A point (a, b) is called an *interior point* of a set S in the plane if there exists a circle centred at (a, b) such that all points strictly inside the circle lie in S. (See Fig. 8.5.1.) A set is called *open* if it consists only of interior points, as in the second set illustrated in Fig. 8.5.1, where we indicate boundary points that belong to the set by a solid curve, and those that do not by a dashed curve. The point (a, b) is called a *boundary point* of a set S if *every* circle centred at (a, b) contains points of S as well as points in its complement, as illustrated in the first figure.

A boundary point of S does not necessarily lie in S. If S contains all its boundary points, then S is called *closed*—this is the case for the third set in Fig. 8.5.1. Note that a set that contains some but not all of its boundary points, like the last of those illustrated in Fig. 8.5.1, is neither open nor closed. In fact, a set is closed if and only if its complement is open.[11]

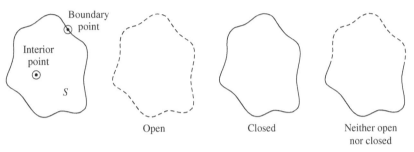

Figure 8.5.1 Open and closed sets

These illustrations give only very loose indications of what it means for a set to be either open or closed. Of course, if a set is not even precisely defined, it is impossible to decide conclusively whether it is open or closed.

In many of the optimization problems considered in economics, sets are defined by one or more inequalities, and boundary points occur where one or more of these inequalities are satisfied with equality. For instance, provided that p, q, and m are positive parameters, the "budget" set of points (x, y) that satisfy the inequalities

$$px + qy \leq m, \quad x \geq 0, \quad y \geq 0 \tag{$*$}$$

is closed. This set is a triangle, as shown in Fig. 4.4.12. Its boundary consists of the three sides of the triangle. Each of the three sides corresponds to having one of the inequalities in ($*$) be satisfied with equality. On the other hand, the set that results from replacing $\leq$ by $<$ and $\geq$ by $>$ in ($*$) is open.

In general, if $g(x, y)$ is a continuous function and c is a real number, then the sets

$$\{(x, y) : g(x, y) \geq c\}, \quad \{(x, y) : g(x, y) \leq c\}, \quad \{(x, y) : g(x, y) = c\}$$

are all closed. If $\geq$ is replaced by $>$, or $\leq$ is replaced by $<$, or $=$ by $\neq$, then the corresponding set becomes open.

A set in the plane is *bounded* if the whole set is contained within a sufficiently large circle. The sets in Fig. 8.5.1 and the budget triangle in Fig. 4.4.12 are all bounded. On the other hand, the set of all (x, y) satisfying $x \geq 1$ and $y \geq 0$, which appears in Fig. 11.1.1,

---

[11] In every day usage the words "open" and "closed" are antonyms: a shop is either open or closed. In topology, however, a set that contains some but not all its boundary points is neither open nor closed. To make matters even odder, in topology there always exist sets that are *both* open *and* closed. This is explained in FMEA.

is a closed but unbounded set. It is closed because it contains all its boundary points, but it is unbounded because no circle of finite radius can enclose it. This example shows that closed sets need not be bounded. The opposite implication does not hold true either: the set depicted in Fig. 11.1.2 is neither open nor closed, but it is bounded. Importantly, a set in the plane that is both closed and bounded is often called *compact*.

We are now ready to formulate the main result in this section.

THEOREM 8.5.1 (EXTREME VALUE THEOREM)

Suppose the function $f(x, y)$ is continuous throughout a nonempty, closed and bounded set S in the plane. Then there exist both a point (a, b) in S where f has a minimum and a point (c, d) in S where it has a maximum—that is,

$$f(a, b) \leq f(x, y) \leq f(c, d)$$

for all (x, y) in S

Theorem 8.5.1 is a pure existence theorem. It tells us nothing about *how to find* the extreme points. Its proof is found in most advanced calculus books and in FMEA. Also, even though the conditions of the theorem are *sufficient* to ensure the existence of extreme points, they are far from necessary, as discussed in Section 8.4.

Finding Maxima and Minima

Sections 8.1 and 8.2 presented some simple cases where we could find the maximum and minimum points of a function of two variables by finding its critical points. The procedure set out in the following frame covers many additional optimization problems.

FINDING MAXIMA AND MINIMA

In order to find the maximum and minimum values of a differentiable function $f(x, y)$ defined on a closed, bounded set S in the plane:

(i) Find all critical points of f in the interior of S.

(ii) Find the largest value and the smallest value of f on the boundary of S, along with the associated points. If it is convenient, subdivide the boundary into several pieces and find the largest and smallest value on each piece.

(iii) Compute the values of the function at all the points found in (i) and (ii). The largest function value is the maximum value of f in S; the smallest one is the minimum value of f in S.

We try out this procedure on the function whose graph is depicted in Fig. 8.5.2.[12] The function has a rectangular domain S of points (x, y) in the xy-plane. The only critical point

---

[12] Because the function is not specified analytically, we can only give a rough geometric argument.

of f is (x_0, y_0), which corresponds to the point P of the graph. The boundary of S consists of four straight-line segments. The point R vertically above one corner point of S represents the maximum value of f along the boundary; similarly, Q represents the minimum value of f along the boundary. The only candidates for a maximum/minimum are, therefore, the three points P, Q, and R. By comparing the values of f at these points, we see that P represents the minimum value, whereas R represents the maximum value of f in S.

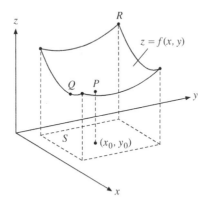

Figure 8.5.2 Finding maxima and minima

As an aspiring economist, doubtless you will be glad to hear that most optimization problems in economics, especially those appearing in textbooks, rarely create enough difficulties to call for the full recipe. Usually, there is an interior optimum that can be found by equating all the first-order partial derivatives to zero. Conditions that are sufficient for this easier approach to work were already discussed in Section 8.2. Nevertheless, we consider an example of a harder problem which illustrates how the whole recipe is sometimes needed. This recipe is also needed in several of the problems for this section. In particular, Exercise 3 gives an economic application.

EXAMPLE 8.5.1   Find the extreme values for $f(x, y)$ defined over S, when

$$f(x, y) = x^2 + y^2 + y - 1 \ \text{ and } \ S = \{(x, y) : x^2 + y^2 \le 1\}$$

Solution: Set S consists of all the points on or inside the circle of radius 1 centred at the origin, as shown in Fig. 8.5.3. The continuous function f will attain both a maximum and a minimum over S, by the extreme value theorem.

According to the preceding recipe, we start by finding all the critical points in the interior of S. These critical points satisfy the two equations

$$f_1'(x, y) = 2x = 0 \ \text{ and } \ f_2'(x, y) = 2y + 1 = 0$$

It follows that $(x, y) = (0, -1/2)$ is the only critical point, and it is in the interior of S, with $f(0, -1/2) = -5/4$.

The boundary of S consists of the circle $x^2 + y^2 = 1$. Note that if (x, y) lies on this circle, then in particular both x and y lie in the interval $[-1, 1]$. Inserting $x^2 + y^2 = 1$ into the

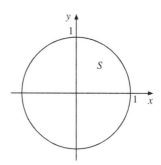

Figure 8.5.3 The domain in Example 8.5.1

expression for $f(x, y)$ shows that, *along the boundary of S*, the value of f is determined by the following function of one variable:

$$g(y) = 1 + y - 1 = y, \text{ defined for } y \in [-1, 1]$$

The maximum value of g is 1 for $y = 1$, and then $x = 0$. The minimum value is -1 when $y = -1$, and then again $x = 0$.

We have now found the only three possible candidates for extreme points, namely, $(0, -1/2)$, $(0, 1)$, and $(0, -1)$. But $f(0, -1/2) = -5/4$, $f(0, 1) = 1$, and $f(0, -1) = -1$. We conclude that the *maximum value* of f in S is 1, which is attained at $(0, 1)$, whereas the *minimum value* is $-5/4$, attained at $(0, -1/2)$.

EXERCISES FOR SECTION 8.5

1. Let $f(x, y) = 4x - 2x^2 - 2y^2$, $S = \{(x, y) : x^2 + y^2 \le 25\}$.

   (a) Compute $f_1'(x, y)$ and $f_2'(x, y)$, then find the only critical point for f.

   (b) Find the extreme points for f over S.

(SM) 2. Find the maximum and minimum points for the following:

   (a) $f(x, y) = x^3 + y^3 - 9xy + 27$ subject to $0 \le x \le 4$ and $0 \le y \le 4$.

   (b) $f(x, y) = x^2 + 2y^2 - x$ subject to $x^2 + y^2 \le 1$.

(SM) 3. In one study of the quantities x and y of natural gas that Western Europe should import from Norway and Siberia, respectively, it was assumed that the benefits were given by the function

$$f(x, y) = 9x + 8y - 6(x + y)^2$$

Because of capacity constraints, x and y must satisfy $0 \le x \le 5$ and $0 \le y \le 3$. Finally, for political reasons, it was felt that imports from Norway should not provide too small a fraction of total imports at the margin, so that $x \ge 2(y - 1)$, or equivalently $-x + 2y \le 2$. In the xy-plane, draw the set S of all points satisfying the three constraints, and then find the quantities that maximize the benefits, subject to the three constraints.

4. Consider the function $f(x, y) = ax^2y + bxy + 2xy^2 + c$.

   (a) Determine values of the constants a, b, and c such that f has a local minimum at the point $(2/3, 1/3)$ with local minimum value $-1/9$.

   (b) With the values of a, b, and c found in part (a), find the maximum and minimum values of f over the set $S = \{(x, y) : x \geq 0, y \geq 0, 2x + y \leq 4\}$.

SM **5.** Consider the function $f(x, y) = xe^{-x}(y^2 - 4y)$.

   (a) Find all critical points of f and classify them by using the second-derivative test.

   (b) Show that f has neither a global maximum nor a global minimum.

   (c) Let $S = \{(x, y) : 0 \leq x \leq 5, \ 0 \leq y \leq 4\}$. Prove that f has global maximum and minimum points in S and find them.

   (d) Find the slope of the tangent to the level curve $xe^{-x}(y^2 - 4y) = e - 4$ at the point where $x = 1$ and $y = 4 - e$.

6. Determine whether each of the following sets is open, closed, bounded, or compact:

   (a) $\{(x, y) : 5x^2 + 5y^2 \leq 9\}$ (b) $\{(x, y) : x^2 + y^2 > 9\}$ (c) $\{(x, y) : x^2 + y^2 \leq 9\}$

   (d) $\{(x, y) : 2x + 5y \geq 6\}$ (e) $\{(x, y) : 5x + 8y = 8\}$ (f) $\{(x, y) : 5x + 8y > 8\}$

7. [HARDER] Give an example of a discontinuous function g of one variable such that the set $\{x : g(x) \leq 1\}$ is not closed.

8.6 The General Case

So far, this chapter has considered optimization problems for functions of two variables. In order to be prepared to understand modern economic theory we need to extend the analysis to an arbitrary number of variables.

There are almost obvious extensions of the definitions of maximum and minimum points, extreme points, etc. If $f(\mathbf{x}) = f(x_1, \ldots, x_n)$ is a function defined over a set S in $\mathbb{R}^n$, then $\mathbf{c} = (c_1, \ldots, c_n)$ is a (global) *maximum point* for f in S if

$$f(\mathbf{x}) \leq f(\mathbf{c}) \quad \text{for all } \mathbf{x} \text{ in } S \tag{8.6.1}$$

If this is the case, then $-f(\mathbf{x}) \geq -f(\mathbf{c})$ for all $\mathbf{x}$ in S. Thus, $\mathbf{c}$ maximizes f over S if and only if $\mathbf{c}$ minimizes $-f$ over S. We can use this simple observation to convert maximization problems into minimization problems and vice versa.[13]

The concepts of interior and boundary points, and of open, closed, and bounded sets, are also easy to generalize. First, define the *distance* between the points $\mathbf{x} = (x_1, \ldots, x_n)$ and $\mathbf{y} = (y_1, \ldots, y_n)$ in $\mathbb{R}^n$ by

$$\|\mathbf{x} - \mathbf{y}\| = \sqrt{(x_1 - y_1)^2 + (x_2 - y_2)^2 + \cdots + (x_n - y_n)^2} \tag{8.6.2}$$

---

[13]   Recall Fig. 8.1.1, which illustrates this for the case of functions of one variable.

For $n = 1, 2$, and 3 this reduces to the distance concept discussed earlier. In particular, if $\mathbf{y} = \mathbf{0}$, then

$$\|\mathbf{x}\| = \sqrt{x_1^2 + x_2^2 + \cdots + x_n^2}$$

is the distance between $\mathbf{x}$ and the origin. The number $\|\mathbf{x}\|$ is also called the *norm* or *length* of the vector $\mathbf{x}$.

The *open ball with centre at* $\mathbf{a} = (a_1, \ldots, a_n)$ *and radius* r is the set of all points $\mathbf{x} = (x_1, \ldots, x_n)$ in $\mathbb{R}^n$ such that $\|\mathbf{x} - \mathbf{a}\| < r$. The definitions in Section 8.5 of interior point, open set, boundary point, closed set, bounded set, and compact set all become valid for sets in $\mathbb{R}^n$, provided we replace the word "circle" by "ball". If A is an arbitrary set in $\mathbb{R}^n$, we define the *interior* of A as the set of interior points in A. If A is open, the interior of A is equal to the set itself.[14]

If $g(\mathbf{x}) = g(x_1, \ldots, x_n)$ is a continuous function, and c is a real number, then each of the three sets $\{\mathbf{x} : g(\mathbf{x}) \geq c\}$, $\{\mathbf{x} : g(\mathbf{x}) \leq c\}$, and $\{\mathbf{x} : g(\mathbf{x}) = c\}$ is closed. If $\geq$ is replaced by $>$, $\leq$ by $<$, or $=$ by $\neq$, the corresponding set is open.

A *critical* (or *stationary*) *point* for a function of n variables is a point where all the first-order derivatives are 0. We have the following important generalization of Theorem 8.1.1:

THEOREM 8.6.1   (NECESSARY CONDITIONS FOR INTERIOR EXTREMA)

Suppose that f is defined in a set S in $\mathbb{R}^n$ and let $\mathbf{c} = (c_1, \ldots, c_n)$ be an interior point in S where f is differentiable. A necessary condition for $\mathbf{c}$ to be a maximum or minimum point for f is that $\mathbf{c}$ is a critical point for f—that is, $\mathbf{x} = \mathbf{c}$ satisfies the n first-order conditions stating that, for each $i = 1, \ldots, n$,

$$f_i'(\mathbf{x}) = 0 \tag{8.6.3}$$

We already have everything we need to prove this theorem.

Fix $i = 1, \ldots, n$, and define the function

$$g(x) = f(c_1, \ldots, c_{i-1}, x_i, c_{i+1}, \ldots, c_n)$$

whose domain consists of all those x_i such that $(c_1, \ldots, c_{i-1}, x, c_{i+1}, \ldots, c_n)$ belongs to S. If $\mathbf{c} = (c_1, \ldots, c_n)$ is a maximum point for f, then the function g of one variable must attain a maximum at $x = c_i$. Because $\mathbf{c}$ is an interior point of S, it follows that c_i is also an interior point in the domain of g. Hence, according to Theorem 8.1.1, we must have $g'(c_i) = 0$. But $g'(c_i) = f_i'(c_1, \ldots, c_n)$, so the conclusion follows. The argument when $\mathbf{c}$ is a minimum is identical.

The extreme value theorem is valid also for functions of n variables:

---

[14]   These topological definitions and results are dealt with in some detail in FMEA.

THEOREM 8.6.2 (EXTREME VALUE THEOREM)

Suppose that function f is continuous throughout a nonempty, closed and bounded set S in $\mathbb{R}^n$. Then there exist both a point $\mathbf{a}$ in S where f has a minimum and a point $\mathbf{c}$ in S where f has a maximum—that is, for all $\mathbf{x}$ in S, one has

$$f(\mathbf{a}) \leq f(\mathbf{x}) \leq f(\mathbf{c})$$

If $f(\mathbf{x})$ is defined over a set S in $\mathbb{R}^n$, then the maximum and minimum points, if there are any, must lie either in the interior of S or on the boundary of S. According to Theorem 8.6.1, if f is differentiable, then any maximum or minimum point in the interior must satisfy the first-order conditions. Consequently, the recipe in Section 8.5 is also valid for any function of n variables defined on a closed and bounded set in $\mathbb{R}^n$.

Both the local and the global second-order conditions for the two-variable case can be generalized to functions of n variables, though they become considerably more complicated. This will be discussed in FMEA.

A Useful Result

One simple result is nevertheless of considerable interest in theoretical economics. It is this: *maximizing a function is equivalent to maximizing a strictly increasing transformation of that function.* For instance, suppose we want to find all pairs (x, y) that maximize $f(x, y)$ over a set S in the xy-plane. Instead (provided the constant $a > 0$) we can find those (x, y) that maximize over S any one of the following objective functions:

(a) $af(x, y) + b$;   (b) $e^{f(x,y)}$;   (c) $\ln f(x, y)$ (in case $f(x, y) > 0$ throughout S).

The maximum *points* are exactly the same. But the maximum *values* are, of course, quite different. As a concrete example, because the transformation $u \mapsto \ln u$ is strictly increasing when $u > 0$, the following two problems have exactly the same solutions for x and y:

(i) $\max e^{x^2 + 2xy^2 - y^3}$ subject to $(x, y) \in S$;   (ii) $\max x^2 + 2xy^2 - y^3$ subject to $(x, y) \in S$.

In general, it is easy to prove the following result:

THEOREM 8.6.3

Suppose $f(\mathbf{x}) = f(x_1, \ldots, x_n)$ is defined over a set S in $\mathbb{R}^n$. Let F be a function of one variable defined over the range of f, and let $\mathbf{c}$ be a point in S. Define g over S by $g(\mathbf{x}) = F(f(\mathbf{x}))$.

(a) If F is increasing and $\mathbf{c}$ maximizes (minimizes) f over S, then the same point $\mathbf{c}$ also maximizes (resp. minimizes) g over S.

(b) If F is strictly increasing, then $\mathbf{c}$ maximizes (minimizes) f over S if and only if $\mathbf{c}$ maximizes (resp. minimizes) g over S.

We give a proof only for the maximization case, since the minimization case is entirely similar.

(a) Because c maximizes f over S, we have $f(\mathbf{x}) \leq f(\mathbf{c})$ for all $\mathbf{x}$ in S. But then $g(\mathbf{x}) = F(f(\mathbf{x})) \leq F(f(\mathbf{c})) = g(\mathbf{c})$ for all $\mathbf{x}$ in S, because F is increasing. It follows that c maximizes g over S.

(b) If F is also strictly increasing and $f(\mathbf{x}) > f(\mathbf{c})$, then it must be true that $g(\mathbf{x}) = F(f(\mathbf{x})) > F(f(\mathbf{c})) = g(\mathbf{c})$. So $g(\mathbf{x}) \leq g(\mathbf{c})$ for all $\mathbf{x}$ in S implies that $f(\mathbf{x}) \leq f(\mathbf{c})$ for all $\mathbf{x}$ in S.

Note how extremely simple the argument was. No continuity or differentiability assumptions were required, and, instead, the proof is based only on the concepts of maximum, and of increasing/strictly increasing functions. Some people appear to distrust such simple, direct arguments and replace them by inefficient or even insufficient arguments based on "differentiating everything in sight" in order to use first- or second-order conditions. Such distrust merely makes matters unnecessarily complicated and risks introducing errors.

EXERCISES FOR SECTION 8.6

1. Each of the following functions has a maximum point. Find it.

(a) $f(x, y, z) = 2x - x^2 + 10y - y^2 + 3 - z^2$

(b) $f(x, y, z) = 3 - x^2 - 2y^2 - 3z^2 - 2xy - 2xz$

2. Define $f(x) = e^{-x^2}$.

(a) Let $F(u) = \ln u$. Verify that the two functions $f(x)$ and $F(f(x))$ have maxima at the same values of x.

(b) Let $F(u) = 5$. Then $g(x) = F(f(x)) = 5$. Explain why this example shows that implication (a) in Theorem 8.6.3 cannot be reversed. (Recall that our definition of an increasing function is satisfied by a constant function.)

3. Suppose $g(\mathbf{x}) = F(f(\mathbf{x}))$ where $f : \mathbb{R}^n \to \mathbb{R}$ and $F : \mathbb{R} \to \mathbb{R}$ are differentiable functions, with $F' \neq 0$ everywhere. Prove that $\mathbf{x}$ is a critical point for f if, and only if, it is a critical point for g.

(SM) **4.** Find the first-order partial derivatives of the function of three variables given by

$$f(x, y, z) = -2x^3 + 15x^2 - 36x + 2y - 3z + \int_y^z e^{t^2}\, dt$$

Then determine its eight critical points.

5. Suggest how to simplify the following problems:

(a) max $\frac{1}{2}[e^{x^2+y^2-2x} - e^{-(x^2+y^2-2x)}]$, subject to $(x, y) \in S$

(b) max $Ax_1^{a_1} \cdots x_n^{a_n}$, subject to $x_1 + x_2 + \cdots + x_n = 1$, where $A > 0$ and $x_1 > 0, \ldots, x_n > 0$

8.7   Comparative Statics and the Envelope Theorem

Optimization problems in economics usually involve maximizing or minimizing functions which depend not only on endogenous variables one can choose, but also on one or more exogenous parameters like prices, tax rates, income levels, etc. Although these parameters are held constant during the optimization, they vary according to the economic situation. For example, we may calculate a firm's profit-maximizing input and output quantities while treating the prices it faces as parameters. But then we may want to know how the optimal quantities respond to changes in those prices, or in whatever other exogenous parameters affect the problem we are considering.

Consider first the following simple problem. A function f depends on a single variable x as well as on a single parameter r. We wish to maximize $f(x, r)$ w.r.t. x while keeping r constant:[15]

$$\max_{x} f(x, r)$$

The value of x that maximizes f will usually depend on r, so we denote it by $x^*(r)$. Inserting $x^*(r)$ into $f(x, r)$, we obtain the *value function*:

$$f^*(r) = f(x^*(r), r)$$

What happens to the value function as r changes? Assuming that $f^*(r)$ is differentiable, the chain rule yields

$$\frac{df^*(r)}{dr} = f_1'(x^*(r), r)\frac{dx^*(r)}{dr} + f_2'(x^*(r), r)$$

If f achieves a maximum at an interior point $x^*(r)$ in the domain of variation for x, then the FOC $f_1'(x^*(r), r) = 0$ is satisfied. It follows that

$$\frac{df^*(r)}{dr} = f_2'(x^*(r), r) \tag{8.7.1}$$

Note that when r is changed, then $f^*(r)$ changes for two reasons. First, a change in r changes the value of f^* directly because r is the second variable in $f(x, r)$. Second, a change in r changes the value of the function $x^*(r)$, and hence $f(x^*(r), r)$ is changed indirectly. Equation (8.7.1) shows that the total effect is simply found by computing the partial derivative of $f(x^*(r), r)$ w.r.t. r, ignoring entirely the indirect effect of the dependence of x^* on r. At first sight, this seems very surprising. On further reflection, however, you may realize that the first-order condition for $x^*(r)$ to maximize $f(x, r)$ w.r.t. x implies that any small change in x, whether or not it is induced by a small change in r, must have a negligible effect on the value of $f(x^*, r)$.

EXAMPLE 8.7.1   Suppose that when a firm produces and sells x units of a commodity, it has revenue $R(x) = rx$, where r is a positive parameter, while the cost is $C(x) = x^2$. The profit is then

$$\pi(x, r) = R(x) - C(x) = rx - x^2$$

---

[15] The theory is identical for the case of minimization.

Find the optimal choice x^* of x, and verify (8.7.1) in this case.

Solution: The quadratic profit function has a maximum when $\pi_1' = r - 2x = 0$, that is for $x^* = r/2$. So the maximum profit as a function of r is given by $\pi^*(r) = rx^* - (x^*)^2 = r(r/2) - (r/2)^2 = r^2/4$, and then $d\pi^*/dr = r/2$. Using formula (8.7.1) is much more direct: because $\pi_2'(x, r) = x$, it implies that $d\pi^*/dr = \pi_2'(x^*(r), r) = x^*(r) = \frac{1}{2}r$.

EXAMPLE 8.7.2   In Example 8.6.5 we studied a firm with the profit function $\hat\pi(Q, \tau) = R(Q) - C(Q) - \tau Q$, where τ denoted a tax per unit produced. Let $Q^* = Q^*(\tau)$ denote the optimal choice of Q as a function of the tax rate τ, and let $\pi^*(\tau)$ be the corresponding value function. Because $\hat\pi_2' = -Q$, Eq. (8.7.1) yields

$$\frac{d\pi^*(\tau)}{d\tau} = \hat\pi_2'(Q^*(\tau), \tau) = -Q^*(\tau)$$

which is the same result found earlier.

It is easy to generalize (8.7.1) to the case with many choice variables and many parameters. We let $\mathbf{x} = (x_1, \ldots, x_n)$, and $\mathbf{r} = (r_1, \ldots, r_m)$. Then, assuming that the function $f(\mathbf{x}, \mathbf{r})$ is differentiable, we can formulate the following result:

THEOREM 8.7.1 (ENVELOPE THEOREM)

If $f^*(\mathbf{r}) = \max_\mathbf{x} f(\mathbf{x}, \mathbf{r})$ and if $\mathbf{x}^*(\mathbf{r})$ is the value of $\mathbf{x}$ that maximizes $f(\mathbf{x}, \mathbf{r})$, then

$$\frac{\partial f^*(\mathbf{r})}{\partial r_j} = \frac{\partial f(\mathbf{x}^*(\mathbf{r}), \mathbf{r})}{\partial r_j} \tag{8.7.2}$$

for $j = 1, \ldots, m$, provided that the partial derivative exists.

Again, $f^*(\mathbf{r})$ is the *value function*. It is easy to prove Theorem 8.7.1 by using the first-order conditions to eliminate other terms, as in the argument for Eq.(8.7.1). The same equality holds if we minimize $f(\mathbf{x}, \mathbf{r})$ w.r.t. $\mathbf{x}$ instead of maximizing it, or even if $\mathbf{x}^*(\mathbf{r})$ is any critical point.

Figure 8.7.1 illustrates Eq. (8.7.2) in the case where there is only one parameter r. For each fixed value of $\mathbf{x}$ there is a curve $K_\mathbf{x}$ in the ry-plane, given by the equation $y = f(\mathbf{x}, r)$. Figure 8.7.1 shows some of these curves together with the graph of $f^*(r)$. For all $\tilde{\mathbf{x}}$ and all r we have

$$f(\tilde{\mathbf{x}}, r) \leq \max_\mathbf{x} f(\mathbf{x}, r) = f^*(r)$$

It follows that none of the $K_\mathbf{x}$-curves can ever lie above the curve $y = f^*(r)$. On the other hand, for each value of r there is at least one value $\mathbf{x}^*(r)$ such that $f(\mathbf{x}^*(r), r) = f^*(r)$, namely a choice of $\mathbf{x}$ that solves the maximization problem for the given value of r. For instance, if we fix $r = r_0$ and let $\mathbf{x}_0$ denote $\mathbf{x}^*(r_0)$, then the curve $K_{\mathbf{x}_0}$ will touch the curve $y = f^*(r)$ at the point $(r_0, f^*(r_0))$, as in the figure. Moreover, because $K_{\mathbf{x}_0}$ can never go above this graph, it must have exactly the same tangent as the graph of f^* at the point where

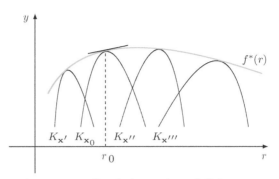

Figure 8.7.1 The curve $y = f^*(r)$ is the envelope of all the curves $y = f(\mathbf{x}, r)$

the curves touch. The slope of this common tangent, therefore, must be not only df^*/dr, the slope of the tangent to the graph of f^* at $(r_0, f^*(r_0))$, but also $\partial f(\mathbf{x}_0, r)/\partial r$, the slope of the tangent to the curve $K_{\mathbf{x}_0}$ at the point $(r_0, f(\mathbf{x}_0, r_0))$. Equation (8.7.2) follows because $K_{\mathbf{x}_0}$ is the graph of $f(\mathbf{x}_0, r)$ when $\mathbf{x}_0$ is fixed.

As Fig. 8.7.1 suggests, the graph of $y = f^*(r)$ is the lowest curve with the property that it lies on or above all the curves $K_{\mathbf{x}}$. So its graph is like an envelope or some "cling film" that is used to enclose or wrap up all these curves. Indeed, a point is on or below the graph if and only if it lies on or below one of the curves $K_{\mathbf{x}}$. For this reason we call the graph of f^* the *envelope* of the family of $K_{\mathbf{x}}$-curves.

EXAMPLE 8.7.3   In Example 8.1.3, $Q = F(K, L)$ denoted a production function with K as capital input and L as labour input. The price per unit of the product was p, the price per unit of capital was r, and the price per unit of labour was w. The profit obtained by using K and L units of the inputs, then producing and selling $F(K, L)$ units of the product, is given by

$$\hat{\pi}(K, L, p, r, w) = pF(K, L) - rK - wL$$

Here profit has been expressed as a new function $\hat{\pi}$ of the parameters p, r, and w, as well as of the choice variables K and L. We keep p, r, and w fixed and maximize $\hat{\pi}$ w.r.t. K and L. The optimal values of K and L are functions of p, r, and w, which we denote by $K^* = K^*(p, r, w)$ and $L^* = L^*(p, r, w)$. The value function for the problem is $\hat{\pi}^*(p, r, w) = \hat{\pi}(K^*, L^*, p, r, w)$. Usually, $\hat{\pi}^*$ is called the firm's *profit function*, though it would be more accurately described as the "maximum profit function". It is found by taking prices as given and choosing the optimal quantities of all inputs and outputs.

According to Theorem 8.7.1, one has

$$\frac{\partial \hat{\pi}^*}{\partial p} = F(K^*, L^*) = Q^*, \quad \frac{\partial \hat{\pi}^*}{\partial r} = -K^*, \quad \frac{\partial \hat{\pi}^*}{\partial w} = -L^* \qquad (*)$$

These three equalities are instances of what is known in production theory as *Hotelling's lemma*. An economic interpretation of the middle equality is this: How much profit is lost if the price of capital increases by a small amount? At the optimum the firm uses K^* units of capital, so the answer is K^* per unit increase in the price. See Exercise 4 for further interesting relationships.

EXERCISES FOR SECTION 8.7

1. A firm produces a single commodity and gets p for each unit sold. The cost of producing x units is $ax + bx^2$ and the tax per unit is t. Assume that the parameters are positive with $p > a + t$. The firm wants to maximize its profit.

   (a) Find the optimal production x^* and the optimal profit π^*.

   (b) Prove that $\partial \pi^* / \partial p = x^*$, and give an economic interpretation.

2. A firm produces $Q = \sqrt{L}$ units of a commodity when labour input is L units. The price obtained per unit of output is P, and the price per unit of labour is w, both positive.

   (a) Write down the profit function π. What choice of labour input $L = L^*$ maximizes profits?

   (b) Consider L^* as a function $L^*(P, w)$ of the two prices, and define the value function

$$\pi^*(P, w) = \pi(L^*(P, w), P, w)$$

   Verify that $\partial \pi^* / \partial P = \pi_P'(L^*, P, w)$ and $\partial \pi^* / \partial w = \pi_w'(L^*, P, w)$, thus confirming the envelope theorem.

(SM) 3. A firm uses capital K, labour L, and land T to produce Q units of a commodity, where

$$Q = K^{2/3} + L^{1/2} + T^{1/3}$$

   Suppose that the firm is paid a positive price p for each unit it produces, and that the positive prices it pays per unit of capital, labour, and land are r, w, and q, respectively.

   (a) Express the firm's profits as a function π of (K, L, T). Then, find the values of K, L, and T, as functions of the four prices, that maximize the firm's profits—assuming a maximum exists.

   (b) Let Q^* denote the optimal number of units produced and K^* the optimal capital stock. Show that $\partial Q^* / \partial r = -\partial K^* / \partial p$.

4. With reference to Example 8.7.3, assuming that F is a C^2 function, prove the symmetry relations:

$$\frac{\partial Q^*}{\partial r} = -\frac{\partial K^*}{\partial p}; \quad \frac{\partial Q^*}{\partial w} = -\frac{\partial L^*}{\partial p}; \quad \frac{\partial L^*}{\partial r} = \frac{\partial K^*}{\partial w}$$

   (*Hint*: First establish that $\dfrac{\partial Q^*}{\partial r} = \dfrac{\partial}{\partial r}\left(\dfrac{\partial \hat{\pi}^*}{\partial p}\right) = \dfrac{\partial}{\partial p}\left(\dfrac{\partial \hat{\pi}^*}{\partial r}\right)$ by combining the first result in Example 8.7.3 with Young's theorem. Then use the other results in Example 8.7.3.)

(SM) 5. With reference to Example 8.1.3, we want to study the factor demand functions—in particular, how the optimal choices of capital and labour respond to price changes.

   (a) Differentiate the first-order conditions (∗) in Example 8.1.3 to verify that

$$F_K'(K^*, L^*)\, dp + pF_{KK}''(K^*, L^*)\, dK + pF_{KL}''(K^*, L^*)\, dL = dr$$
$$F_L'(K^*, L^*)\, dp + pF_{LK}''(K^*, L^*)\, dK + pF_{LL}''(K^*, L^*)\, dL = dw$$

   (b) Use this system to find the partials of K^* and L^* w.r.t. p, r, and w. (*Hint*: You might find it easier first to find $\partial K^* / \partial p$ and $\partial L^* / \partial p$ by putting $dr = dw = 0$, etc. in (a).)

   (c) Assume that the local second-order conditions (8.3.1) are satisfied. What can you say about the signs of the partial derivatives? In particular, show that the factor demand curves are downward sloping as functions of their own factor prices. Verify that $\partial K^* / \partial w = \partial L^* / \partial r$.

SM **6.** A profit-maximizing monopolist produces two commodities whose quantities are denoted by x_1 and x_2. Good 1 is subsidized at the rate of σ per unit and good 2 is taxed at τ per unit. The monopolist's profit function is therefore given by

$$\pi(x_1, x_2) = R(x_1, x_2) - C(x_1, x_2) + \sigma x_1 - \tau x_2$$

where R and C are the firm's revenue and cost functions, respectively. Assume that the partial derivatives of these functions have the following signs

$$R_1' > 0, \ R_2' > 0, \ R_{11}'' < 0, \ R_{12}'' = R_{21}'' < 0, \ R_{22}'' < 0$$
$$C_1' > 0, \ C_2' > 0, \ C_{11}'' > 0, \ C_{12}'' = C_{21}'' > 0, \ C_{22}'' > 0$$

everywhere in their domains.

(a) Find the first-order conditions for maximum profits.

(b) Write down the local second-order conditions for maximum profits.

(c) Suppose that $x_1^* = x_1^*(\sigma, \tau)$, $x_2^* = x_2^*(\sigma, \tau)$ solve the problem. Find the signs of $\partial x_1^*/\partial \sigma$, $\partial x_1^*/\partial \tau$, $\partial x_2^*/\partial \sigma$, and $\partial x_2^*/\partial \tau$, assuming that the local second-order conditions are satisfied.

(d) Show that $\partial x_1^*/\partial \tau = -\partial x_2^*/\partial \sigma$.

REVIEW EXERCISES

1. The function f defined for all (x, y) by $f(x, y) = -2x^2 + 2xy - y^2 + 18x - 14y + 4$ has a maximum. Find the corresponding values of x and y. Use Theorem 8.2.1 to prove that it is a maximum point.

SM **2.** A firm produces two different kinds, A and B, of a commodity. The daily cost of producing Q_1 units of A and Q_2 units of B is $C(Q_1, Q_2) = 0.1(Q_1^2 + Q_1 Q_2 + Q_2^2)$. Suppose that the firm sells all its output at a price per unit of $P_1 = 120$ for A and $P_2 = 90$ for B.

(a) Find the daily production levels that maximize profits.

(b) If P_2 remains unchanged at 90, what new price P_1 per unit of A would imply that the optimal daily production level for A is 400 units?

3. The profit obtained by a firm from producing and selling x and y units of two brands of a commodity is given by $P(x, y) = -0.1x^2 - 0.2xy - 0.2y^2 + 47x + 48y - 600$.

(a) Find the production levels that maximize profits.

(b) A key raw material is rationed so that total production must be restricted to 200 units. Find the production levels that now maximize profits.

SM **4.** Find the critical points of the following functions of (x, y):

(a) $x^3 - x^2 y + y^2$ (b) $xye^{4x^2 - 5xy + y^2}$ (c) $4y^3 + 12x^2 y - 24x^2 - 24y^2$

5. Define $f(x, y, a) = ax^2 - 2x + y^2 - 4ay$, where a is a parameter. For each fixed $a \neq 0$, find the unique critical point $(x^*(a), y^*(a))$ of the function f w.r.t. (x, y). Find also the value function $f^*(a) = f(x^*(a), y^*(a), a)$, and verify the envelope theorem in this case.

(SM) **6.** Suppose the production function in Exercise 8.7.3 is replaced by $Q = K^a + L^b + T^c$, for parameters $a, b, c \in (0, 1)$.

   (a) Assuming that a maximum exists, find the values of K, L, and T that maximize the firm's profits.

   (b) Let π^* denote the optimal profit as a function of the four prices. Compute the partial derivative $\partial \pi^* / \partial r$.

   (c) Verify the envelope theorem in this case.

7. Define $f(x, y)$ for all (x, y) by $f(x, y) = e^{x+y} + e^{x-y} - \frac{3}{2}x - \frac{1}{2}y$.

   (a) Find the first- and second-order partial derivatives of f, then show that $f(x, y)$ is convex.

   (b) Find the minimum point of $f(x, y)$.

(SM) **8.** Consider the function $f(x, y) = x^2 - y^2 - xy - x^3$.

   (a) Find and classify its critical points.

   (b) Find the domain S where f is concave, and find the largest value f in S.

(SM) **9.** Consider the function f defined for all (x, y) by

$$f(x, y) = \tfrac{1}{2}x^2 - x + ay(x - 1) - \tfrac{1}{3}y^3 + a^2y^2$$

where a is a constant.

   (a) Prove that $(x^*, y^*) = (1 - a^3, a^2)$ is a critical point of f.

   (b) Verify the envelope theorem in this case.

   (c) Where in the xy-plane is f convex?

10. In this problem we will generalize several of the economic examples and problems considered so far. Consider a firm that produces two different goods, A and B. If the total cost function is $C(x, y)$, then the profit is

$$\pi(x, y) = px + qy - C(x, y) \qquad (i)$$

where the prices obtained per unit of A and B are p and q respectively.

   (a) Suppose first that the firm has a small share in the markets for both these goods, and so takes p and q as given. Write down and interpret the first-order conditions for $x^* > 0$ and $y^* > 0$ to maximize profits.

   (b) Suppose next that the firm has a monopoly in the sale of both goods. The prices are no longer fixed, but chosen by the monopolist, bearing in mind the demand functions

$$x = f(p, q) \quad \text{and} \quad y = g(p, q) \qquad (ii)$$

   Suppose we solve equations (ii) for p and q to obtain the inverse demand functions

$$p = F(x, y) \quad \text{and} \quad q = G(x, y) \qquad (iii)$$

   Then profit as a function of x and y is

$$\pi(x, y) = xF(x, y) + yG(x, y) - C(x, y) \qquad (iv)$$

   Write down and interpret the first-order conditions for $x^* > 0$ and $y^* > 0$ to maximize profits.

(c) Suppose $p = a - bx - cy$ and $q = \alpha - \beta x - \gamma y$, where b and γ are positive.[16] If the cost function is $C(x, y) = Px + Qy + R$, write down the first-order conditions for maximum profit.

(d) Prove that the (global) second-order conditions are satisfied provided $4\gamma b \geq (\beta + c)^2$.

9

CONSTRAINED OPTIMISATION

Mathematics is removed from this turmoil of human life, but its methods and the relations are a mirror, an incredibly pure mirror, of the relations that link facts of our existence.
—Konrad Knopp (1928)

The previous chapter introduced unconstrained optimization problems with several variables. In economics, however, the variables to be chosen must often satisfy one or more constraints. Accordingly, this chapter considers constrained optimization problems, and studies the method of Lagrange multipliers in some detail. Sections 9.1 to 9.7 treat equality constraints, with Section 9.7 presenting some comparative static results and the envelope theorem. More general constrained optimization problems allowing inequality constraints are introduced in Sections 9.8 to 9.10. A much fuller treatment of constrained optimization can be found in FMEA.

9.1 The Lagrange Multiplier Method

A typical economic example of a constrained optimization problem concerns a consumer who chooses how much of the available income m to spend on a good x whose price is p, and how much income to leave over for expenditure on other goods, which we denote by y. Note that the consumer then faces the budget constraint $px + y = m$. Suppose that preferences are represented by the utility function $u(x, y)$. In mathematical terms the consumer's problem can be expressed as

$$\max u(x, y) \quad \text{s.t.} \quad px + y = m$$

where "s.t." stands for "such that". This is a typical *constrained maximization problem*. In this case, because $y = m - px$, the same problem can be expressed as the *unconstrained maximization* of the function $h(x) = u(x, m - px)$ w.r.t. the single variable x. Indeed, this method of converting a constrained optimization problem involving two variables to a one-variable problem was used in Section 8.2.

When the constraint involves a complicated function, or when there are several equality constraints to consider, this substitution method might be difficult or even impossible to carry out in practice. In such cases, economists make much use of the *Lagrange multiplier method.*[1]

We start with the problem of maximizing a function $f(x, y)$ of two variables, when x and y are restricted to satisfy an equality constraint $g(x, y) = c$. This can be written as

$$\max f(x, y) \quad \text{s.t.} \quad g(x, y) = c \tag{9.1.1}$$

The first step of the method is to introduce a *Lagrange multiplier*, often denoted by λ, which is "associated" with the constraint $g(x, y) = c$. We do this when we define the *Lagrangian* function, $\mathcal{L}$, by

$$\mathcal{L}(x, y) = f(x, y) - \lambda[g(x, y) - c] \tag{9.1.2}$$

in which the expression $g(x, y) - c$, which must be 0 when the constraint is satisfied, has been multiplied by λ. For future reference, note that $\mathcal{L}(x, y) = f(x, y)$ for all (x, y) that satisfy the constraint $g(x, y) = c$.

The Lagrange multiplier is a constant, so the partial derivatives of $\mathcal{L}(x, y)$ w.r.t. x and y are

$$\mathcal{L}'_1(x, y) = f'_1(x, y) - \lambda g'_1(x, y) \quad \text{and} \quad \mathcal{L}'_2(x, y) = f'_2(x, y) - \lambda g'_2(x, y)$$

respectively. As will be explained in Section 9.4, except in rare cases a solution of problem (9.1.1) can only be a point (x, y) where, for a suitable value of λ, the first-order partial derivatives of $\mathcal{L}$ vanish, and also the constraint $g(x, y) = c$ is satisfied. As in Chapters 7 and 8, we refer to these as "first-order" conditions.

Here is a simple economic application.

EXAMPLE 9.1.1   A consumer has the utility function $u(x, y) = xy$ and faces the budget constraint $2x + y = 100$. Find the only solution candidate to the utility maximization problem.

Solution: The problem is

$$\max xy \quad \text{s.t.} \quad 2x + y = 100$$

so its Lagrangian is

$$\mathcal{L}(x, y) = xy - \lambda(2x + y - 100)$$

Including the constraint, the first-order conditions for the solution of the problem are

$$\mathcal{L}'_1(x, y) = y - 2\lambda = 0, \quad \mathcal{L}'_2(x, y) = x - \lambda = 0, \quad \text{and} \quad 2x + y = 100$$

---

[1] Named after its discoverer, the Italian-born French mathematician J. L. Lagrange (1736–1813). The Danish economist Harald Westergaard seems to have been the first to use it in economics, in 1876. As a matter of practice, this method is often used even for problems that are quite easy to express as unconstrained problems. One reason is that Lagrange multipliers have an important economic interpretation. In addition, a similar method works for many more complicated optimization problems, such as those where the constraints are expressed in terms of inequalities, as we will see later.

The first two equations imply that $y = 2\lambda$ and $x = \lambda$. So $y = 2x$. Inserting this into the constraint yields $2x + 2x = 100$. So $x = 25$ and $y = 50$, implying that $\lambda = x = 25$.

This solution can be confirmed by the substitution method. From $2x + y = 100$ we get $y = 100 - 2x$, so the problem is reduced to maximizing the unconstrained function $h(x) = x(100 - 2x) = -2x^2 + 100x$. Since $h'(x) = -4x + 100 = 0$ gives $x = 25$, and $h''(x) = -4 < 0$ for all x, this shows that $x = 25$ *is* a maximum point.

Perhaps surprisingly, in the alternative minimization problem

$$\min f(x,y) \text{ s.t. } g(x,y) = c \tag{9.1.3}$$

function $\mathcal{L}$ is defined identically, by Eq. (9.1.2), and the relevant first-order conditions are the same. Given this, we often write

$$\max(\min) f(x,y) \text{ s.t. } g(x,y) = c$$

when referring to both the maximization and minimization problems.[2]

Example 9.1.1 illustrates the following general method:

THE LAGRANGE MULTIPLIER METHOD

To find the only possible solutions of problems (9.1.1) and (9.1.3), proceed as follows:

(i) Write down the Lagrangian function, as in Eq. (9.1.2), where λ is a constant.

(ii) Differentiate $\mathcal{L}$ w.r.t. x and y, and equate the partial derivatives to 0.

(iii) The two equations in (ii), together with the constraint, yield the following three *first-order conditions*:

$$\mathcal{L}_1'(x,y) = f_1'(x,y) - \lambda g_1'(x,y) = 0$$
$$\mathcal{L}_2'(x,y) = f_2'(x,y) - \lambda g_2'(x,y) = 0$$
$$g(x,y) = c$$

(iv) Solve these three equations simultaneously for the three unknowns x, y, and λ. These triples (x, y, λ) are the solution *candidates*, at least one of which solves the respective problem, if it has a solution.

Importantly, if $g_1'(x,y)$ and $g_2'(x,y)$ both vanish, the method might fail to give the right answer.

Some economists prefer to consider the Lagrangian as a function $\tilde{\mathcal{L}}(x, y, \lambda)$ of three variables. Then, the first-order condition $\tilde{\mathcal{L}}_3'(x, y, \lambda) = 0$ yields the constraint of the problem,

---

[2] The reader may have seen expressions like $\max \min f(x, y)$ in, for instance, game theory courses. Those expressions mean something entirely different.

$g(x, y) = c$. The advantage of this method is that, written in this way, all the three necessary conditions are obtained by equating the partial derivatives of this extended Lagrangian to 0, so that the first-order conditions can be summarized by saying that we need to find a critical point of the Lagrangian. It seems unnatural, however, to rely on differentiation in order to derive such an obvious necessary condition—namely the constraint equation. Moreover, this procedure can easily lead to trouble when treating problems with inequality constraints. For these two reasons, we prefer to avoid it.

EXAMPLE 9.1.2   A single-product firm intends to produce 30 units of output as cheaply as possible. By using K units of capital and L units of labour, it can produce $\sqrt{K} + L$ units. Suppose the prices of capital and labour are, respectively, \$1 and \$20. The firm's problem is, then:

$$\min K + 20L \quad \text{s.t.} \quad \sqrt{K} + L = 30$$

(a) Find the optimal choices of K and L.

(b) What is the additional cost of producing 31 rather than 30 units?

Solution:

(a) The Lagrangian is

$$\mathcal{L} = K + 20L - \lambda(\sqrt{K} + L - 30)$$

so the first-order conditions are:

$$\mathcal{L}'_K = 1 - \lambda/2\sqrt{K} = 0, \ \mathcal{L}'_L = 20 - \lambda = 0, \ \text{and} \ \sqrt{K} + L = 30$$

The second equation gives $\lambda = 20$, which inserted into the first equation yields $1 = 20/2\sqrt{K}$. It follows that $\sqrt{K} = 10$, and hence $K = 100$. Inserted into the constraint this gives $\sqrt{100} + L = 30$, and hence $L = 20$. The 30 units are therefore produced in the cheapest way when the firm uses 100 units of capital and 20 units of labour. The associated cost is $K + 20L = 500$.[3]

(b) Solving the problem with the constraint $\sqrt{K} + L = 31$, we see that still $\lambda = 20$ and $K = 100$, while $L = 31 - 10 = 21$. The associated minimum cost is $100 + 20 \cdot 21 = 520$, so the additional cost is $520 - 500 = 20$. This is precisely equal to the Lagrange multiplier! Thus, in this case the Lagrange multiplier tells us by how much costs increase if the production requirement is increased by one unit from 30 to 31.[4]

EXAMPLE 9.1.3   A consumer who has Cobb–Douglas utility function $u(x, y) = Ax^a y^b$ faces the budget constraint $px + qy = m$, where A, a, b, p, q, and m are all positive constants. Find the only solution candidate to the consumer demand problem

$$\max Ax^a y^b \quad \text{s.t.} \quad px + qy = m \tag{$*$}$$

---

[3] Theorem 9.5.1 will tell us that this is the constrained minimum, because $\mathcal{L}$ is convex in (K, L).

[4] Section 9.2 will tell us why this is not entirely coincidental.

Solution: The Lagrangian is $\mathcal{L}(x, y) = Ax^a y^b - \lambda(px + qy - m)$, so the first-order conditions are

$$\mathcal{L}_1'(x, y) = aAx^{a-1}y^b - \lambda p = 0, \quad \mathcal{L}_2'(x, y) = bAx^a y^{b-1} - \lambda q = 0, \quad \text{and} \quad px + qy = m$$

Solving the first two equations for λ yields

$$\lambda = \frac{aAx^{a-1}y^b}{p} = \frac{bAx^a y^{b-1}}{q}$$

Cancelling the common factor $Ax^{a-1}y^{b-1}$ from the last equality gives $ay/p = bx/q$. Solving this equation for qy yields $qy = (b/a)px$, which inserted into the budget constraint gives $px + (b/a)px = m$. From this equation we find x and then y. The results are the following *demand functions*:

$$x = x(p, q, m) = \frac{a}{a+b}\frac{m}{p} \quad \text{and} \quad y = y(p, q, m) = \frac{b}{a+b}\frac{m}{q} \qquad (**)$$

The solution we have found makes good sense. It follows from $(**)$ that for all $t > 0$ one has $x(tp, tq, tm) = x(p, q, m)$ and $y(tp, tq, tm) = y(p, q, m)$, so the demand functions are homogeneous of degree 0. This is as one should expect because, if (p, q, m) is changed to (tp, tq, tm), then the constraint in $(*)$ is unchanged, and so the optimal choices of x and y are unchanged—as they should be, according to Example 12.7.4.

Note that in the utility function $Ax^a y^b$, the relative sizes of the coefficients a and b indicate the relative importance of x and y in the individual's preferences. For instance, if a is larger than b, then the consumer values a 1% increase in x more than a 1% increase in y. The product px is the amount spent on the first good, and $(**)$ says that the consumer should spend the fraction $a/(a + b)$ of income on this good and the fraction $b/(a + b)$ on the second good.

Formula $(**)$ can be applied immediately to find the correct answer to thousands of exam problems in mathematical economics courses given each year all over the world! But note that the utility function has to be of the Cobb–Douglas type $Ax^a y^b$.[5]

Another warning is in order here: there is an underlying assumption in problem $(*)$ that $x \geq 0$ and $y \geq 0$. Thus, we maximize a continuous function $Ax^a y^b$ over a closed bounded set $S = \{(x, y) : px + qy = m, x \geq 0, y \geq 0\}$. According to the extreme value theorem, 13.5.1, a maximum must exist. Since utility is 0 when $x = 0$ or when $y = 0$, and positive at the point given by $(**)$, this point indeed solves the problem. Without nonnegativity conditions on x and y, however, the problem might fail to have a maximum. Indeed, consider the problem max $x^2 y$ s.t. $x + y = 1$. For real t, the pair $(x, y) = (-t, 1 + t)$ satisfies the constraint, yet $x^2 y = t^2(1 + t) \to \infty$ as $t \to \infty$, so there is no maximum.

EXAMPLE 9.1.4   Examine the general utility maximizing problem with two goods:

$$\max u(x, y) \quad \text{s.t.} \quad px + qy = m \qquad (9.1.4)$$

---

[5] When $u(x, y) = x^a + y^b$, for instance, the solution is *not* given by $(**)$. To check this, assuming that $0 < a < 1$, see: Exercise 9, for the case when $b = 1$; and Exercise 9.5.4, for the case when $a = b$.

Solution: The Lagrangian is $\mathcal{L}(x, y) = u(x, y) - \lambda(px + qy - m)$, so the first-order conditions are

$$\mathcal{L}'_x(x, y) = u'_x(x, y) - \lambda p = 0 \tag{i}$$

$$\mathcal{L}'_y(x, y) = u'_y(x, y) - \lambda q = 0 \tag{ii}$$

$$px + qy = m \tag{iii}$$

From equation (i) we get $\lambda = u'_x(x, y)/p$, and from (ii), $\lambda = u'_y(x, y)/q$. Hence, $u'_x(x, y)/p = u'_y(x, y)/q$, which can be rewritten as

$$\frac{u'_x(x, y)}{u'_y(x, y)} = \frac{p}{q} \tag{9.1.5}$$

The left-hand side of the last equation is the *marginal rate of substitution*, or MRS. Utility maximization thus requires equating the MRS to the price ratio p/q.

A geometric interpretation of Eq. (9.1.5) is that the consumer should choose the point on the budget line at which the slope of the level curve of the utility function, $-u'_x(x, y)/u'_y(x, y)$, is equal to the slope of the budget line, $-p/q$. Thus, at the optimal point the budget line is tangent to a level curve of the utility function, illustrated by point P in Fig. 9.1.1. The level curves of the utility function are the *indifference curves*, along which the utility level is constant by definition. Thus, utility is maximized at a point where the budget line is tangent to an indifference curve. The fact that $\lambda = u'_x(x, y)/p = u'_y(x, y)/q$ at point P means that the marginal utility per dollar is the same for both goods. At any other point (x, y) where, for example, $u'_x(x, y)/p > u'_y(x, y)/q$, the consumer can increase utility by shifting expenditure away from y toward x. Indeed, then the increase in utility per extra dollar spent on x would equal $u'_x(x, y)/p$; this exceeds the decrease in utility per dollar reduction in the amount spent on y, which equals $u'_y(x, y)/q$.

As in Example 9.1.3, the optimal choices of x and y can be expressed as *demand functions* of (p, q, m), which must be homogeneous of degree zero in the three variables together.

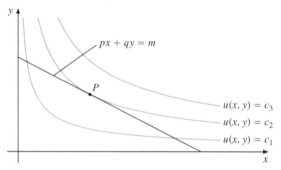

Figure 9.1.1   Assuming that $c_1 < c_2 < c_3$, the solution to problem (9.1.4) is at P

EXERCISES FOR SECTION 9.1[6]

1. Consider the problem: max xy s.t. $x + 3y = 24$.

   (a) Use Lagrange's method to find its only possible solution.

   (b) Check the solution by using the results in Example 9.1.3.

2. Use the Lagrange multiplier method to solve the problem

$$\min -40Q_1 + Q_1^2 - 2Q_1Q_2 - 20Q_2 + Q_2^2 \text{ s.t. } Q_1 + Q_2 = 15$$

3. Use the results in Example 9.1.3 to solve the following problems:

   (a) max $10x^{1/2}y^{1/3}$ s.t. $2x + 4y = m$

   (b) max $x^{1/2}y^{1/2}$ s.t. $50\,000x + 0.08y = 1\,000\,000$

   (c) max $12x\sqrt{y}$ s.t. $3x + 4y = 12$

(SM) 4. Solve the following problems:

   (a) min $f(x, y) = x^2 + y^2$ s.t. $g(x, y) = x + 2y = 4$

   (b) min $f(x, y) = x^2 + 2y^2$ s.t. $g(x, y) = x + y = 12$

   (c) max $f(x, y) = x^2 + 3xy + y^2$ s.t. $g(x, y) = x + y = 100$

5. A person has utility function $u(x, y) = 100xy + x + 2y$. Suppose that the price per unit of x is $2, and that the price per unit of y is $4. The person receives $1\,000 that all has to be spent on the two commodities x and y. Solve the utility maximization problem.

6. An individual has a Cobb–Douglas utility function $U(m, l) = Am^a l^b$, where m is income and l is leisure, and A, a, and b are positive constants, with $a + b \leq 1$. A total of T_0 hours are to be allocated between work W and leisure l, so that $W + l = T_0$. If the hourly wage is w, then $m = wW$, and the individual's problem is

$$\max Am^a l^b \text{ s.t. } \frac{m}{w} + l = T_0$$

   Solve the problem by using (**) in Example 9.1.3.

7. Solve part (b) of Review Exercise 13.3 by using the Lagrange method.

8. A firm produces and sells two commodities. By selling x tons of the first commodity the firm gets a price per ton given by $p = 96 - 4x$. By selling y tons of the other commodity the price per ton is given by $q = 84 - 2y$. The total cost of producing and selling x tons of the first commodity and y tons of the second is given by $C(x, y) = 2x^2 + 2xy + y^2$.

   (a) Show that the firm's profit function is $P(x, y) = -6x^2 - 3y^2 - 2xy + 96x + 84y$.

   (b) Compute the first-order partial derivatives of P, and find its only critical point.

   (c) Suppose that the firm's production activity causes so much pollution that the authorities limit its output to 11 tons in total. Solve the firm's maximization problem in this case. Verify that the production restrictions do reduce the maximum possible value of $P(x, y)$.

---

[6] All the following exercises have only one solution candidate, which is the optimal solution.

(SM) **9.** Consider the utility maximization problem max $x^a + y$ s.t. $px + y = m$, where the constants p, q, and m are positive, and the constant $a \in (0, 1)$.

(a) Find the demand functions, $x^*(p, m)$ and $y^*(p, m)$.

(b) Find the partial derivatives of the demand functions w.r.t. p and m, and check their signs.

(c) How does the optimal expenditure on the x good vary with p?[7]

(d) Put $a = 1/2$. What are the demand functions in this case? Denote the maximal utility as a function of p and m by $U^*(p, m)$, the value function, also called the indirect utility function. Verify that $\partial U^*/\partial p = -x^*(p, m)$.

(SM) **10.** [HARDER] Consider the problem max $U(x, y) = 100 - e^{-x} - e^{-y}$ s.t. $px + qy = m$.

(a) Write down the first-order conditions for the problem and solve them for x, y, and λ as functions of p, q, and m. What assumptions are needed for x and y to be nonnegative?

(b) Verify that x and y are homogeneous of degree 0 as functions of p, q, and m.

9.2 Interpreting the Lagrange Multiplier

Consider again the problem

$$\max(\min) f(x, y) \quad \text{s.t.} \quad g(x, y) = c$$

and suppose x^* and y^* are the values of x and y that solve this problem. In general, x^* and y^* depend on c, so we write $x^* = x^*(c)$ and $y^* = y^*(c)$. We *assume* that these solutions are differentiable functions of c. The associated value of $f(x, y)$ is then also a function of c, with

$$f^*(c) = f(x^*(c), y^*(c)) \tag{9.2.1}$$

Here $f^*(c)$ is called the (optimal) *value function* for the problem. Of course, the associated value of the Lagrange multiplier also depends on c, in general, so we write $\lambda(c)$. Provided that certain regularity conditions are satisfied, we have the remarkable result that

$$\frac{df^*(c)}{dc} = \lambda(c) \tag{9.2.2}$$

Thus, *the Lagrange multiplier* $\lambda = \lambda(c)$ *is the rate at which the optimal value of the objective function changes with respect to changes in the constraint constant c.*

In particular, if dc is a small change in c, then

$$f^*(c + dc) - f^*(c) \approx \lambda(c) \, dc \tag{9.2.3}$$

In economic applications, c often denotes the available stock of some resource, and $f(x, y)$ denotes utility or profit. Then $\lambda(c) \, dc$ measures the approximate change in utility or profit that can be obtained from dc units more.[8] Economists call λ a *shadow price* of the resource.

---

[7] Check the elasticity of $px^*(p, m)$ w.r.t. p.

[8] Or $-dc$ units less, when $dc < 0$.

If $f^*(c)$ is the maximum profit when the resource input is c, then Eq. (9.2.3) says that λ indicates the approximate increase in profit per unit increase in the resource.

Assuming that $f^*(c)$ is differentiable, we can prove Eq. (9.2.2) as follows:

Taking the differential of the value function defined by Eq. (9.2.1) gives

$$df^*(c) = df(x^*, y^*) = f_1'(x^*, y^*)\,dx^* + f_2'(x^*, y^*)\,dy^* \qquad (*)$$

But from the first-order conditions we have $f_1'(x^*, y^*) = \lambda g_1'(x^*, y^*)$ and $f_2'(x^*, y^*) = \lambda g_2'(x^*, y^*)$, so $(*)$ can be written as

$$
\begin{aligned}
df^*(c) &= \lambda g_1'(x^*, y^*)\,dx^* + \lambda g_2'(x^*, y^*)\,dy^* \\
&= \lambda[g_1'(x^*, y^*)\,dx^* + g_2'(x^*, y^*)\,dy^*]
\end{aligned}
\qquad (**)
$$

Moreover, taking the differential of the identity $g(x^*(c), y^*(c)) = c$ yields

$$dg(x^*, y^*) = g_1'(x^*, y^*)\,dx^* + g_2'(x^*, y^*)\,dy^* = dc$$

Substituting the last equality in $(**)$ implies that $df^*(c) = \lambda\,dc$.

EXAMPLE 9.2.1   Consider the following generalization of Example 9.1.1:

$$\max xy \text{ s.t. } 2x + y = m$$

The first-order conditions again give $y = 2x$ with $\lambda = x$. The constraint now becomes $2x + 2x = m$, so $x = m/4$. In the notation introduced above, the solution is $x^*(m) = m/4$ and $y^*(m) = m/2$, with $\lambda(m) = m/4$. The value function is therefore $f^*(m) = (m/4)(m/2) = m^2/8$. It follows that $df^*(m)/dm = m/4 = \lambda(m)$. Hence, (9.2.2) is confirmed. Suppose in particular that $m = 100$, so that $f^*(100) = 100^2/8$. If $m = 100$ increases by 1, the new value is $f^*(101) = 101^2/8$, so $f^*(101) - f^*(100) = 101^2/8 - 100^2/8 = 25.125$. Note that formula (9.2.3) with $dc = 1$ gives $f^*(101) - f^*(100) \approx \lambda(100) \cdot 1 = 25 \cdot 1 = 25$, which is quite close to the exact value, 25.125.

EXAMPLE 9.2.2   Suppose $Q = F(K, L)$ denotes the output of a state-owned firm when the input of capital is K and that of labour is L. Suppose the prices of capital and labour are r and w, respectively, and that the firm is given a total budget of m to spend on the two input factors. The firm wishes to find the choice of inputs it can afford that maximizes output. So it faces the problem

$$\max F(K, L) \text{ s.t. } rK + wL = m$$

Solving this problem by using Lagrange's method, the value of the Lagrange multiplier will tell us approximately the increase in output if m is increased by 1 dollar.

Consider, for example, the specific problem $\max 120KL$ s.t. $2K + 5L = m$. Note that this is, mathematically, a special case of the problem in Example 9.1.3.[9] From $(**)$ in Example 9.1.3, we find the solution $K^* = m/4$ and $L^* = m/10$, with $\lambda = 6m$. The optimal output is

$$Q^*(m) = 120K^*L^* = 120 \cdot \frac{1}{4}m \cdot \frac{1}{10}m = 3m^2$$

so $dQ^*/dm = 6m = \lambda$, and (9.2.2) is confirmed.

---

[9]   Only the notation is different, along with the fact that the consumer has been replaced with a firm.

EXERCISES FOR SECTION 9.2

1. Verify that Eq. (9.2.2) holds for the problem $\max x^3 y$ s.t. $2x + 3y = m$.

2. With reference to Example 9.1.2:

(a) Solve the problem $\min rK + wL$ s.t. $\sqrt{K} + L = Q$, assuming that $Q > w/2r$, where r, w, and Q are positive constants.

(b) Verify Eq. (9.2.2).

3. Consider the problem $\min x^2 + y^2$ s.t. $x + 2y = a$, where a is a constant.

(a) Solve the problem by transforming it into an unconstrained optimization problem with one variable.

(b) Show that the Lagrange method leads to the same solution, and verify Eq. (9.2.2).

(c) Explain the solution by studying the level curves of $f(x, y) = x^2 + y^2$ and the graph of the straight line $x + 2y = a$. Can you give a geometric interpretation of the problem? Does the corresponding maximization problem have a solution?

(SM) **4.** Consider the utility maximization problem $\max U(x, y) = \sqrt{x} + y$ s.t. $x + 4y = 100$.

(a) Using the Lagrange method, find the quantities demanded of the two goods.

(b) Suppose income increases from 100 to 101. What is the exact increase in the optimal value of $U(x, y)$? Compare with the value found in (a) for the Lagrange multiplier.

(c) Suppose we change the budget constraint to $px + qy = m$, but keep the same utility function. Derive the quantities demanded of the two goods if $m > q^2/4p$.

(SM) **5.** Consider the consumer demand problem

$$\max U(x, y) = \alpha \ln(x - a) + \beta \ln(y - b) \quad \text{s.t.} \quad px + qy = m \qquad (*)$$

where α, β, a, b, p, q, and m are positive constants, with $\alpha + \beta = 1$ and $m > ap + bq$.

(a) Show that if x^*, y^* solve problem $(*)$, then expenditure on the two goods is given by the two linear functions

$$px^* = \alpha m + pa - \alpha(pa + qb) \quad \text{and} \quad qy^* = \beta m + qb - \beta(pa + qb) \qquad (**)$$

of the variables (m, p, q).[10]

(b) Let $U^*(p, q, m) = U(x^*, y^*)$ denote the indirect utility function. Show that $\partial U^*/\partial m > 0$ and verify the so-called Roy's identities:

$$\frac{\partial U^*}{\partial p} = -\frac{\partial U^*}{\partial m} x^* \quad \text{and} \quad \frac{\partial U^*}{\partial q} = -\frac{\partial U^*}{\partial m} y^*$$

(SM) **6.** [HARDER] An oil producer starts extracting oil from a well at time $t = 0$, and ends at a time $t = T$ that the producer chooses. Suppose that the output flow at any time t in the interval $[0, T]$ is $xt(T - t)$ barrels per unit of time, where the intensity x can also be chosen. The total amount of

---

[10] This is a special case of the *linear expenditure system* that the Nobel prize winning British economist Richard (J.R.N.) Stone fitted to UK data, as described in the *Economic Journal*, 1954.

oil extracted in the given time span is thus given by the function $g(x, T) = \int_0^T xt(T - t)\,dt$ of x and T. Assume further that the sales price per barrel at time t is $p = 1 + t$, and that the cost per barrel extracted is equal to αT^2, where α is a positive constant. The profit per unit of time is then $(1 + t - \alpha T^2)xt(T - t)$, so that the total profit earned during the time interval $[0, T]$ is a function of x and T given by

$$f(x, T) = \int_0^T (1 + t - \alpha T^2)\, xt\, (T - t)\, dt$$

If the total amount of extractable oil in the field is M barrels, the producer can choose values of x and T such that $g(x, T) = M$. The producer's problem is thus

$$\max f(x, T) \quad \text{s.t.} \quad g(x, T) = M \tag{$*$}$$

Find explicit expressions for $f(x, T)$ and $g(x, T)$ by calculating the given integrals. Then solve problem $(*)$ and verify Eq. (9.2.2).

9.3 Multiple Solution Candidates

In all our examples and problems so far, the recipe for solving constrained optimization problems has produced only one solution candidate. In this section we consider a problem where there are several of them. In such cases, we have to decide which of the candidates actually solves the problem, assuming it has any solution at all.

EXAMPLE 9.3.1   Solve the problems

$$\max(\min) f(x, y) = x^2 + y^2 \quad \text{s.t.} \quad g(x, y) = x^2 + xy + y^2 = 3$$

Solution: For both the maximization and the minimization problems, the Lagrangian is

$$\mathcal{L}(x, y) = x^2 + y^2 - \lambda(x^2 + xy + y^2 - 3)$$

so the three FOCs to consider are

$$\mathcal{L}_1'(x, y) = 2x - \lambda(2x + y) = 0 \tag{i}$$

$$\mathcal{L}_2'(x, y) = 2y - \lambda(x + 2y) = 0 \tag{ii}$$

$$x^2 + xy + y^2 - 3 = 0 \tag{iii}$$

Let us eliminate λ from (i) and (ii). From (i) we get $\lambda = 2x/(2x + y)$ provided that $y \neq -2x$. Inserting this value of λ into (ii) gives

$$2y = \frac{2x}{2x + y}(x + 2y)$$

This reduces to $y^2 = x^2$, and so $y = \pm x$, which leaves us with three possibilities:

1. *Suppose, first, that $y = x$.* Then, (iii) yields $x^2 = 1$, so $x = 1$ or $x = -1$. This gives the two solution candidates $(x, y) = (1, 1)$ and $(-1, -1)$, with $\lambda = 2/3$.

2. *Alternatively, suppose* $y = -x$. Then (iii) yields $x^2 = 3$, so $x = \sqrt{3}$ or $x = -\sqrt{3}$. This gives the two solution candidates $(x, y) = (\sqrt{3}, -\sqrt{3})$ and $(-\sqrt{3}, \sqrt{3})$, with $\lambda = 2$.

3. It only remains to consider the case $y = -2x$. Then from (i) we have $x = 0$ and so $y = 0$. But this contradicts (iii), so this case cannot occur.

We have found the only four points (x, y) that can solve the problem. Furthermore,

$$f(1, 1) = f(-1, -1) = 2 \text{ and } f(\sqrt{3}, -\sqrt{3}) = f(-\sqrt{3}, \sqrt{3}) = 6$$

We conclude that if the problem has solutions, then $(1, 1)$ and $(-1, -1)$ solve the minimization problem, whereas $(\sqrt{3}, -\sqrt{3})$ and $(-\sqrt{3}, \sqrt{3})$ solve the maximization problem.

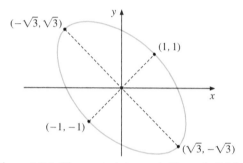

Figure 9.3.1 The constraint curve in Example 9.3.1

Geometrically, the equality constraint determines an ellipse. The problem is therefore to find what points on the ellipse are nearest to or furthest from the origin. See Fig. 9.3.1; it is "geometrically obvious" that such points exist.

EXERCISES FOR SECTION 9.3

(SM) 1. Solve the problems:

(a) $\max(\min) 3xy$ s.t. $x^2 + y^2 = 8$ (b) $\max(\min) x + y$ s.t. $x^2 + 3xy + 3y^2 = 3$

(SM) 2. Solve the problems:[11]

(a) $\max x^2 + y^2 - 2x + 1$ s.t. $x^2 + 4y^2 = 16$ (b) $\min \ln(2 + x^2) + y^2$ s.t. $x^2 + 2y = 2$

3. Consider the problem $\max(\min) f(x, y) = x + y$ s.t. $g(x, y) = x^2 + y = 1$.

(a) Find the solutions to the necessary conditions for these problems.

(b) Explain the solution geometrically by drawing appropriate level curves for $f(x, y)$ together with the graph of the parabola $x^2 + y = 1$. Does the associated minimization problem have a solution?

---

[11] In (b) you should take it for granted that the minimum value exists.

(c) Replace the constraint by $x^2 + y = 1.1$, and solve the problem in this case. Find the corresponding change in the optimal value of $f(x, y) = x + y$, and check to see if this change is approximately equal to $\lambda \cdot 0.1$, as suggested by Eq. (9.2.3).

SM **4.** Consider the problem $\max f(x, y) = 24x - x^2 + 16y - 2y^2$ s.t. $g(x, y) = x^2 + 2y^2 = 44$.

(a) Solve the problem.

(b) What is the approximate change in the optimal value of $f(x, y)$ if 44 is changed to 45?

9.4   Why the Lagrange Method Works

We have explained the Lagrange multiplier method for solving the problem

$$\max f(x, y) \ \text{ s.t. } \ g(x, y) = c \tag{9.4.1}$$

In this section we give a geometric as well as an analytic argument for the method.

A Geometric Argument

The maximization problem in (9.4.1) can be given a geometric interpretation, as shown in Fig. 9.4.1. Here the graph of f is like the surface of an inverted bowl, whereas the equation $g(x, y) = c$ represents a curve in the xy-plane. The curve K on the bowl is the one that lies directly above the curve $g(x, y) = c$. Maximizing $f(x, y)$ without taking the constraint into account gets us to the peak A in Fig. 9.4.1. The solution to problem (9.4.1), however, is at B, which is the highest point on the curve K. If we think of the graph of f as representing a mountain, and K as a mountain path, then we seek the highest point on the path, which is B. Analytically, the problem is to find the coordinates of B.

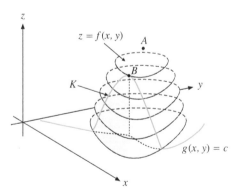

Figure 9.4.1 A constrained optimization problem

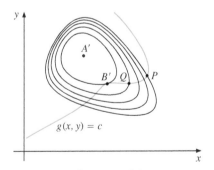

Figure 9.4.2 Geometry of the Lagrange method

Figure 9.4.2 "projects" the information of Fig. 9.4.1 into the xy-plane. The curve $g(x, y) = c$, which appeared in Fig. 9.4.1 too, is the projection of curve K. The figure also shows some of the level curves for f, and also indicates the constraint curve $g(x, y) = c$. Now A' represents the point at which $f(x, y)$ has its unconstrained maximum. The closer a level curve of f is to point A', the higher is the value of f along that level curve. We are seeking that point on the constraint curve $g(x, y) = c$ where f has its highest value. If we start at point P on the constraint curve and move along that curve toward A', we encounter level curves with higher and higher values of f.

Obviously, the point Q indicated in Fig. 9.4.2 is *not* the point on $g(x, y) = c$ at which f has its highest value, because the constraint curve passes *through* the level curve of f at that point. Therefore, we can cross a level curve to higher values of f by proceeding further along the constraint curve. However, when we reach point B', we cannot go any higher. It is intuitively clear that B' is the point where the constraint curve touches a level curve for f, *without intersecting it*. This observation implies that the slope of the tangent to the curve $g(x, y) = c$ at (x, y) is equal to the slope of the tangent to the level curve of f at that point.

The slope of the level curve $F(x, y) = c$ is given by $dy/dx = -F_1'(x, y)/F_2'(x, y)$. Thus, the condition that the slope of the tangent to $g(x\ y) = c$ is equal to the slope of a level curve for $f(x, y)$ can be expressed analytically as:[12]

$$-\frac{g_1'(x, y)}{g_2'(x, y)} = -\frac{f_1'(x, y)}{f_2'(x, y)}$$

or, equivalently, as

$$\frac{f_1'(x, y)}{g_1'(x, y)} = \frac{f_2'(x, y)}{g_2'(x, y)} \tag{9.4.2}$$

It follows that a necessary condition for (x, y) to solve problem (9.4.1) is that the left- and right-hand sides of the last equation in (9.4.2) be equal at (x, y). Let λ denote the common value of these fractions. This is the Lagrange multiplier introduced in Section 9.1. With this definition,

$$f_1'(x, y) - \lambda g_1'(x, y) = 0 \text{ and } f_2'(x, y) - \lambda g_2'(x, y) = 0 \tag{9.4.3}$$

Using the Lagrangian from Eq. (9.1.2), we see that (9.4.3) just tells us that the Lagrangian has a critical point. An analogous argument for the problem of minimizing $f(x, y)$ subject to $g(x, y) = c$ gives the same condition.

The geometric argument above is quite convincing. But the analytic argument that follows is easier to generalize to more than two variables.

An Analytic Argument

So far we have studied the problem of finding the largest or smallest value of $f(x, y)$ subject to the constraint $g(x, y) = c$. Sometimes we are interested in studying the corresponding local maximum (minimum), in the same sense as in Section 8.3: points (x_0, y_0) where $g(x_0, y_0) = c$ and such that $f(x, y) \leq (\geq) f(x_0, y_0)$ for all pairs (x, y) that satisfy $g(x, y) = c$ and lie sufficiently close to (x_0, y_0). Graphically, possible local extrema are illustrated in Fig. 9.4.3.

---

[12] Disregard for the moment cases where any denominator is 0.

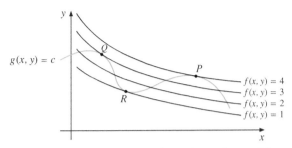

Figure 9.4.3 Q, R, and P all satisfy the first-order conditions

Point R is a local minimum point for $f(x, y)$ subject to $g(x, y) = c$, whereas Q and P are local maximum points. The global maximum of $f(x, y)$ subject to $g(x, y) = c$ is attained only at P. Each of the points P, Q, and R in Fig. 9.4.3 satisfies condition (9.4.3), so the first-order conditions are exactly as before. Let us derive them now in a way that does not rely on geometric intuition.

Except in some special cases, the equation $g(x, y) = c$ with c fixed defines y implicitly as a differentiable function of x near any local extreme point. Denote this function by $y = h(x)$. According to formula (12.3.2), provided that $g_2'(x, y) \neq 0$, one has

$$y' = h'(x) = -\frac{g_1'(x, y)}{g_2'(x, y)}$$

Now, the objective function $z = f(x, y) = f(x, h(x))$ is, in effect, a function of x alone. By calculating dz/dx while taking into account how y depends on x, we obtain a necessary condition for local extreme points by equating dz/dx to 0. But

$$\frac{dz}{dx} = f_1'(x, y) + f_2'(x, y)y' = f_1'(x, y) + f_2'(x, y)h'(x)$$

So substituting the previous expression for $h'(x)$ gives the following necessary condition for (x, y) to solve problem (9.4.1):

$$\frac{dz}{dx} = f_1'(x, y) - f_2'(x, y)\frac{g_1'(x, y)}{g_2'(x, y)} = 0 \tag{9.4.4}$$

Assuming that $g_2'(x, y) \neq 0$, and defining $\lambda = f_2'(x, y)/g_2'(x, y)$, we deduce that the two equations $f_1'(x, y) - \lambda g_1'(x, y) = 0$ and $f_2'(x, y) - \lambda g_2'(x, y) = 0$ must both be satisfied. Hence, the Lagrangian must have a critical point at (x, y). The same result holds, by an analogous argument, provided $g_1'(x, y) \neq 0$. To summarize, one can prove the following precise result:

THEOREM 9.4.1 (LAGRANGE'S THEOREM)

Suppose that $f(x, y)$ and $g(x, y)$ have continuous partial derivatives in a domain A of the xy-plane, and that (x_0, y_0) is both an interior point of A and a local extreme point for $f(x, y)$ subject to the constraint $g(x, y) = c$. Suppose further that $g_1'(x_0, y_0)$ and $g_2'(x_0, y_0)$ are not both 0. Then, there exists a unique number λ such that the Lagrangian has a critical point at (x_0, y_0).

Exercise 3 asks you to show how trouble can result from uncritical use of the Lagrange multiplier method, disregarding the assumptions in Theorem 9.4.1. Exercise 4 asks you to show what can go wrong if $g_1'(x_0, y_0)$ and $g_2'(x_0, y_0)$ are both 0.

In constrained optimization problems in economics, it is often implicitly assumed that the variables are nonnegative. This was certainly the case for the specific utility maximization problem in Example 9.1.3. Because the optimal solutions were positive, nothing was lost by disregarding the nonnegativity constraints. Here is an example showing that sometimes we must take greater care.

EXAMPLE 9.4.1   Consider the utility maximization problem

$$\max xy + x + 2y \text{ s.t. } 2x + y = m, \ x \ge 0 \text{ and } y \ge 0$$

where we have required that the amount of each good is nonnegative. The Lagrangian is $\mathcal{L} = xy + x + 2y - \lambda(2x + y - m)$. So the first-order conditions, disregarding the nonnegativity constraints for the moment, are

$$\mathcal{L}_1' = y + 1 - 2\lambda = 0 \text{ and } \mathcal{L}_2'(x, y) = x + 2 - \lambda = 0$$

By eliminating λ, we find that $y = 2x + 3$. Inserting this into the budget constraint gives $2x + 2x + 3 = m$, so $x = \frac{1}{4}(m - 3)$. We easily find the corresponding value of y, and the suggested solution that emerges is $x^* = \frac{1}{4}(m - 3)$, $y^* = \frac{1}{2}(m + 3)$. Note that in the case when $m < 3$, then $x^* < 0$, so that the expressions we have found for x^* and y^* do not solve the given problem. The solution in this case is, as shown below, $x^* = 0$, $y^* = m$. This implies that when income is low, this consumer would spend everything on just the second commodity.

Let us analyse the problem by converting it to one that is unconstrained. To do this, note how the constraint implies that $y = m - 2x$. In order for both x and y to be nonnegative, one must have $0 \le x \le m/2$ and $0 \le y \le m$. Substituting $y = m - 2x$ into the utility function, we obtain utility as function $U(x)$ of x alone, where

$$U(x) = x(m - 2x) + x + 2(m - 2x) = -2x^2 + (m - 3)x + 2m, \ x \in [0, m/2]$$

This is a quadratic function with $x = \frac{1}{4}(m - 3)$ as the critical point. If $m > 3$, it is an interior critical point for the concave function U, so it is a maximum point. If $m \le 3$, then $U'(x) = -4x + (m - 3) \le 0$ for all $x \ge 0$. Because of the constraint $x \ge 0$, it follows that $U(x)$ must have its largest value for $x = 0$.

Concerning the Lagrange multiplier method, one of the most frequently occurring errors in the economics literature—even in some leading textbooks—is the claim that it transforms a constrained optimization problem into one of finding an unconstrained optimum of the Lagrangian. Exercise 1 shows that this is wrong. What the method does instead is to transform a constrained optimization problem into one of finding the appropriate critical points of the Lagrangian. Sometimes these are maximum points, but often they are not.

To test your understanding of when the Lagrange procedure can be used, it is a good exercise to explain why it certainly works, for instance, in Exercise 9.4.1, but not in either Exercise 9.4.3 or Exercise 9.4.4.

EXERCISES FOR SECTION 9.4

1. Consider the problem max xy s.t. $x + y = 2$. Reduce it to the one-variable problem of maximizing $x(2 - x)$, and show that $(x, y) = (1, 1)$ is the only possible solution. Check that this satisfies the first-order conditions for the constrained maximization problem, with Lagrange multiplier $\lambda = 1$. Show that $(1, 1)$ does not maximize the Lagrangian $\mathcal{L}(x, y) = xy - 1 \cdot (x + y - 2)$. Does this matter?

2. The following text, which attempts to justify the Lagrange method, is taken from a book on mathematics for management. It contains *grave* errors. Sort them out.

"Consider the general problem of finding the extreme points of $z = f(x, y)$ subject to the constraint $g(x, y) = 0$. Clearly the extreme points must satisfy the pair of equations $f'_x(x, y) = 0, f'_y(x, y) = 0$ in addition to the constraint $g(x, y) = 0$. Thus, there are three equations that must be satisfied by the pair of unknowns x, y. Because there are more equations than unknowns, the system is said to be overdetermined and, in general, is difficult to solve. In order to facilitate computation ..."

3. [HARDER] Consider the problem max $f(x, y) = 2x + 3y$ s.t. $g(x, y) = \sqrt{x} + \sqrt{y} = 5$.

   (a) Show that the Lagrange multiplier method suggests the solution $(x, y) = (9, 4)$. Show that this does not solve the constrained maximization problem because $f(9, 4) = 30$, and yet $f(25, 0) = 50$.

   (b) Find the true solution to the problem by studying the level curves of $f(x, y) = 2x + 3y$ along with the graph of the constraint equation. (*Hint:* See Exercise 5.4.2.)

   (c) Which assumption of Theorem 9.4.1 is violated?

SM **4.** [HARDER] Solve the problem

$$\min f(x, y) = (x + 2)^2 + y^2 \text{ s.t. } g(x, y) = y^2 - x(x + 1)^2 = 0$$

Show that the Lagrange multiplier method cannot locate this minimum. (*Hint*: Draw a graph of $g(x, y) = 0$. Note in particular that $g(-1, 0) = 0$.)

9.5   Sufficient Conditions

Theorem 9.4.1 gives *necessary* conditions for the local solution of constrained optimization problems. In order to confirm that we have really found the solution, however, a more careful check is needed. The examples and problems of Section 9.3 have geometric interpretations which strongly suggest we have found the solution. Indeed, if the constraint set is closed and bounded, then Theorem 9.5.1, the extreme value theorem, guarantees that a continuous function *will* attain both maximum and minimum values over this set.[13]

---

[13] A case in point is Example 9.3.1. Here the constraint set, which was graphed in Fig. 9.3.1, *is* closed and bounded. The continuous function $f(x, y) = x^2 + y^2$ will therefore attain both a maximum value and a minimum value over the constraint set. Since there are four points satisfying the first-order conditions, it remains only to check which of them gives f its highest and lowest values.

Concave/Convex Lagrangian

We already know that if (x_0, y_0) solves problem

$$\text{max (min) } f(x, y) \text{ s.t. } g(x, y) = c \tag{9.5.1}$$

then the Lagrangian

$$\mathcal{L}(x, y) = f(x, y) - \lambda[g(x, y) - c] \tag{9.5.2}$$

usually has a critical point at (x_0, y_0), but $\mathcal{L}$ may not have a maximum (minimum) at (x_0, y_0). Suppose, however, that $\mathcal{L}$ happens to reach a global maximum at (x_0, y_0), in the sense that (x_0, y_0) maximizes $\mathcal{L}(x, y)$ among *all* (x, y) in the plane. Then, for all (x, y), one has

$$\mathcal{L}(x_0, y_0) = f(x_0, y_0) - \lambda[g(x_0, y_0) - c] \geq \mathcal{L}(x, y) = f(x, y) - \lambda[g(x, y) - c] \quad (*)$$

If (x_0, y_0) also satisfies the constraint $g(x_0, y_0) = c$, then $(*)$ implies that $f(x_0, y_0) \geq f(x, y)$ for all (x, y) such that $g(x, y) = c$. Hence, (x_0, y_0) really does solve the maximization problem in (9.5.1). A corresponding result is obtained for the minimization problem in (9.5.1), provided that $\mathcal{L}$ reaches a global minimum at (x_0, y_0).

Next, we recall from Theorem 13.2.1 and the definitions of concave and convex functions, that a critical point (x_0, y_0) for a concave (convex) function really does maximize (minimize) the function. Thus we have the following result:

THEOREM 9.5.1 (CONCAVE/CONVEX LAGRANGIAN)

Consider the problems in (9.5.1) and suppose (x_0, y_0) is a critical point for the Lagrangian $\mathcal{L}$, defined in (9.5.2).

(A) If the Lagrangian is concave, then (x_0, y_0) solves the maximization problem.

(B) If the Lagrangian is convex, then (x_0, y_0) solves the minimization problem.

EXAMPLE 9.5.1   Consider a firm that uses positive inputs K and L of capital and labour, respectively, to produce a single output Q according to the Cobb–Douglas production function $Q = F(K, L) = AK^a L^b$, where A, a, and b are positive parameters satisfying $a + b \leq 1$. Suppose that the unit prices per unit of capital and labour are $r > 0$ and $w > 0$, respectively. The cost-minimizing inputs of K and L must solve the problem

$$\text{min } rK + wL \text{ s.t. } AK^a L^b = Q$$

Explain why the Lagrangian is convex, so that a critical point of the Lagrangian must minimize costs. (*Hint*: See Exercise 13.2.8.)

Solution: The Lagrangian is $\mathcal{L} = rK + wL - \lambda(AK^a L^b - Q)$, and the first-order conditions are $r = \lambda A a K^{a-1} L^b$ and $w = \lambda A b K^a L^{b-1}$, implying that $\lambda > 0$. From Exercise 13.2.8, we see that $-\mathcal{L}$ is concave, so $\mathcal{L}$ is convex.

Local Second-Order Conditions

Sometimes we are interested in conditions that are sufficient for (x_0, y_0) to be a local extreme point of $f(x, y)$ subject to $g(x, y) = c$. We start by looking at the expression for dz/dx given by Eq. (9.4.4). The condition $dz/dx = 0$ is necessary for local optimality. If, additionally, $d^2z/dx^2 < 0$, then a critical point of the Lagrangian must solve the local maximization problem. The second derivative d^2z/dx^2 is just the total derivative of dz/dx w.r.t. x. Assuming that both f and g are C^2 functions, and recalling that y is a function of x, it follows from (9.4.4) that

$$\frac{d^2z}{dx^2} = f''_{11} + f''_{12}y' - (f''_{21} + f''_{22}y')\frac{g'_1}{g'_2} - f'_2 \frac{(g''_{11} + g''_{12}y')g'_2 - (g''_{21} + g''_{22}y')g'_1}{(g'_2)^2}$$

But f and g are C^2 functions, so $f''_{12} = f''_{21}$ and $g''_{12} = g''_{21}$. Moreover, $y' = -g'_1/g'_2$. Also $f'_1 = \lambda g'_1$ and $f'_2 = \lambda g'_2$, because these are the first-order conditions. Using these relationships to eliminate y' and f'_2, as well as some elementary algebra, we obtain

$$\frac{d^2z}{dx^2} = \frac{1}{(g'_2)^2}\left[(f''_{11} - \lambda g''_{11})(g'_2)^2 - 2(f''_{12} - \lambda g''_{12})g'_1 g'_2 + (f''_{22} - \lambda g''_{22})(g'_1)^2 \right]$$

We see that $d^2z/dx^2 < 0$ provided the expression in the square brackets is negative. Thus, we have the following result:

THEOREM 9.5.2 (LOCAL SECOND-ORDER CONDITIONS)

Consider the problems in Eq. (9.5.1), and suppose that (x_0, y_0) satisfies the first-order conditions $f'_1(x, y) = \lambda g'_1(x, y)$, $f'_2(x, y) = \lambda g'_2(x, y)$ and $g(x, y) = c$. Define

$$D(x, y, \lambda) = (f''_{11} - \lambda g''_{11})(g'_2)^2 - 2(f''_{12} - \lambda g''_{12})g'_1 g'_2 + (f''_{22} - \lambda g''_{22})(g'_1)^2$$

Then,

(i) If $D(x_0, y_0, \lambda) < 0$, then (x_0, y_0) solves the maximization problem locally.

(ii) If $D(x_0, y_0, \lambda) > 0$, then (x_0, y_0) solves the minimization problem locally.

The conditions on the sign of $D(x_0, y_0, \lambda)$ are called the local *second-order conditions*.

EXAMPLE 9.5.2   Consider the problem

$$\max(\min) f(x, y) = x^2 + y^2 \text{ s.t. } g(x, y) = x^2 + xy + y^2 = 3$$

In Example 9.3.1 we saw that the first-order conditions give the points $(1, 1)$ and $(-1, -1)$ with $\lambda = 2/3$, as well as $(\sqrt{3}, -\sqrt{3})$ and $(-\sqrt{3}, \sqrt{3})$ with $\lambda = 2$. Check the local second-order conditions of Theorem 9.5.2 in this case.

Solution: We find that $f_{11}'' = 2, f_{12}'' = 0, f_{22}'' = 2, g_{11}'' = 2, g_{12}'' = 1$, and $g_{22}'' = 2$. So

$$D(x, y, \lambda) = (2 - 2\lambda)(x + 2y)^2 + 2\lambda(2x + y)(x + 2y) + (2 - 2\lambda)(2x + y)^2$$

Hence $D(1, 1, \frac{2}{3}) = D(-1, -1, \frac{2}{3}) = 24$ and $D(\sqrt{3}, -\sqrt{3}, 2) = D(-\sqrt{3}, \sqrt{3}, 2) = -24$. From the signs of D at the four points satisfying the first-order conditions, we conclude that $(1, 1)$ and $(-1, -1)$ are local minimum points, whereas $(\sqrt{3}, -\sqrt{3})$ and $(-\sqrt{3}, \sqrt{3})$ are local maximum points.[14]

EXERCISES FOR SECTION 9.5

1. Use Theorem 9.5.1 to check that the optimal solution is found in part (a) of Exercise 9.1.3.

2. Consider the problem $\max \ln x + \ln y$ s.t. $px + qy = m$. Compute $D(x, y, \lambda)$, as defined in Theorem 9.5.2, and verify that the second-order conditions in that theorem are satisfied. [15]

3. Compute $D(x, y, \lambda)$ in Theorem 9.5.2 for Problem 9.2.3(a). Conclusion?

(SM) 4. Prove that $U(x, y) = x^a + y^a$, where $a \in (0, 1)$, is concave when $x > 0$ and $y > 0$. Then, solve the problem $\max U(x, y)$ s.t. $px + qy = m$, where p, q, and m are positive constants.

9.6 Additional Variables and Constraints

Constrained optimization problems in economics usually involve more than just two variables. The typical problem with n variables can be written in the form

$$\max(\min) f(x_1, \dots, x_n) \text{ s.t. } g(x_1, \dots, x_n) = c \tag{9.6.1}$$

The Lagrange multiplier method presented in the previous sections can be easily generalized. As before, associate a Lagrange multiplier λ with the constraint and form the Lagrangian

$$\mathcal{L}(x_1, \dots, x_n) = f(x_1, \dots, x_n) - \lambda[g(x_1, \dots, x_n) - c] \tag{9.6.2}$$

Next, find all the first-order partial derivatives of $\mathcal{L}$ and equate them to zero, so that

---

[14] In Example 9.3.1 we proved that these points were actually *global* extrema.
[15] Note that the Lagrangian is concave, as is easily checked, so the unique solution $(x, y) = (m/p, m/2q)$ to the first-order conditions is actually a global constrained maximum for this problem.

$$\mathcal{L}'_1 = f'_1(x_1, \ldots, x_n) - \lambda g'_1(x_1, \ldots, x_n) = 0$$

$$\vdots \qquad\qquad (9.6.3)$$

$$\mathcal{L}'_n = f'_n(x_1, \ldots, x_n) - \lambda g'_n(x_1, \ldots, x_n) = 0$$

These n equations, together with the constraint, form $n + 1$ equations that should be solved simultaneously to determine the $n + 1$ unknowns: $x_1, \ldots, x_n$, and λ.

This method will, in general, fail to give correct necessary conditions if all the first-order partial derivatives of $g(x_1, \ldots, x_n)$ vanish at the critical point of the Lagrangian. Otherwise, the proof is an easy generalization of the analytic argument in Section 9.4 for the first-order conditions. If, say, $\partial g / \partial x_n \neq 0$, we "solve" $g(x_1, \ldots, x_n) = c$ for x_n near the critical point, and thus reduce the problem to an unconstrained extremum problem in the remaining $n - 1$ variables $x_1, \ldots, x_{n-1}$.

EXAMPLE 9.6.1   Solve the consumer's demand problem

$$\max U(x, y, z) = x^2 y^3 z \quad \text{s.t.} \quad x + y + z = 12$$

Solution: With $\mathcal{L}(x, y, z) = x^2 y^3 z - \lambda(x + y + z - 12)$, the first-order conditions are

$$\mathcal{L}'_1 = 2xy^3 z - \lambda = 0, \; \mathcal{L}'_2 = 3x^2 y^2 z - \lambda = 0, \; \text{and} \; \mathcal{L}'_3 = x^2 y^3 - \lambda = 0 \qquad (*)$$

If *any* of the variables x, y, and z is 0, then $x^2 y^3 z = 0$, which is *not* the maximum value. So suppose that x, y, and z are all positive. From the two first equations in $(*)$, we have $2xy^3 z = 3x^2 y^2 z$, so $y = 3x/2$. The first and third equations in $(*)$ likewise imply that $z = x/2$. Inserting $y = 3x/2$ and $z = x/2$ into the constraint yields $x + 3x/2 + x/2 = 12$, so $x = 4$. Then $y = 6$ and $z = 2$. Thus, the only possible solution is $(x, y, z) = (4, 6, 2)$.

EXAMPLE 9.6.2   Solve the problem

$$\min f(x, y, z) = (x - 4)^2 + (y - 4)^2 + \left(z - \tfrac{1}{2}\right)^2 \quad \text{s.t.} \quad x^2 + y^2 = z$$

Can you give a geometric interpretation of the problem?

Solution: The Lagrangian is

$$\mathcal{L}(x, y, z) = (x - 4)^2 + (y - 4)^2 + \left(z - \tfrac{1}{2}\right)^2 - \lambda(x^2 + y^2 - z)$$

and the first-order conditions are:

$$\mathcal{L}'_1(x, y, z) = 2(x - 4) - 2\lambda x = 0 \qquad\qquad \text{(i)}$$

$$\mathcal{L}'_2(x, y, z) = 2(y - 4) - 2\lambda y = 0 \qquad\qquad \text{(ii)}$$

$$\mathcal{L}'_3(x, y, z) = 2\left(z - \tfrac{1}{2}\right) + \lambda = 0 \qquad\qquad \text{(iii)}$$

$$x^2 + y^2 = z \qquad\qquad \text{(iv)}$$

From (i) we see that $x = 0$ is impossible. Equation (i) thus gives $\lambda = 1 - 4/x$. Inserting this into (ii) and (iii) gives $y = x$ and $z = 2/x$. Using these results, Eq. (iv) reduces to $2x^2 = 2/x$, that is, $x^3 = 1$, so $x = 1$. It follows that $(x, y, z) = (1, 1, 2)$ is the only solution candidate for the problem.

The expression $(x - 4)^2 + (y - 4)^2 + (z - 1/2)^2$ measures the square of the distance from the point $(4, 4, 1/2)$ to the point (x, y, z). The set of points (x, y, z) that satisfy $z = x^2 + y^2$ is a surface known as a paraboloid, part of which is shown in Fig. 9.6.1. The minimization problem is therefore to find that point on the paraboloid which has the smallest (square) distance from $(4, 4, 1/2)$. It is "geometrically obvious" that this problem has a solution. On the other hand, the problem of finding the largest distance from $(4, 4, 1/2)$ to a point on the paraboloid does not have a solution, because the distance can be made as large as we like.

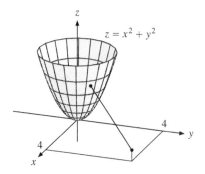

Figure 9.6.1 An illustration of Example 9.6.2

EXAMPLE 9.6.3   The general consumer optimization problem with n goods is

$$\max U(x_1, \ldots, x_n) \text{ s.t. } p_1 x_1 + \cdots + p_n x_n = m \tag{9.6.4}$$

where function U is defined for $x_1 \geq 0, \ldots, x_n \geq 0$. Writing $\mathbf{x} = (x_1, \ldots, x_n)$, the Lagrangian is

$$\mathcal{L}(\mathbf{x}) = U(\mathbf{x}) - \lambda(p_1 x_1 + \cdots + p_n x_n - m)$$

The first-order conditions are

$$\mathcal{L}_i'(\mathbf{x}) = U_i'(\mathbf{x}) - \lambda p_i = 0$$

for each $i = 1, \ldots, n$. By direct computation, we then have

$$\frac{U_1'(\mathbf{x})}{p_1} = \frac{U_2'(\mathbf{x})}{p_2} = \cdots = \frac{U_n'(\mathbf{x})}{p_n} = \lambda \tag{9.6.5}$$

Apart from the last equation, which serves only to determine the Lagrange multiplier λ, we have $n - 1$ equations.[16] In addition, the constraint must hold. Thus, we have n equations to

---

[16] For $n = 2$, there is one equation; for $n = 3$, there are two equations; and so on.

determine the values of $x_1, \ldots, x_n$. From Eq. (9.6.5) it also follows that for every pair of goods j and k

$$\frac{U'_j(\mathbf{x})}{U'_k(\mathbf{x})} = \frac{p_j}{p_k} \qquad (9.6.6)$$

The left-hand side is the MRS of good k for good j, whereas the right-hand side is their price ratio, or rate of exchange of good k for good j. So condition (9.6.6) equates the MRS for each pair of goods to the corresponding price ratio.

Consider the equations in (9.6.5), together with the budget constraint. Assume that this system is solved for $x_1, \ldots, x_n$ and λ, as functions of $\mathbf{p} = (p_1, \ldots, p_n)$ and m, giving $x_i = D_i(\mathbf{p}, m)$, for $i = 1, \ldots, n$. Then $D_i(\mathbf{p}, m)$ gives the amount of the i-th commodity demanded by the individual when facing prices $\mathbf{p}$ and income m. For this reason $D_1, \ldots, D_n$ are called the *individual demand functions*. By the same argument as in Examples 12.7.4 and 9.1.3, the demand functions are homogeneous of degree 0. As one check that you have correctly derived the demand functions, it is a good idea to verify that the functions you find are indeed homogeneous of degree 0, and satisfy the budget constraint.

In the case when the consumer has a Cobb–Douglas utility function, the constrained maximization problem is

$$\max A x_1^{a_1} \cdots x_n^{a_n} \quad \text{s.t.} \quad p_1 x_1 + \cdots + p_n x_n = m \qquad (9.6.7)$$

where we assume that each "taste" parameter $a_i > 0$. Then as in part (a) of Exercise 8, the demand functions are

$$D_i(\mathbf{p}, m) = \frac{a_i}{a_1 + \cdots + a_n} \frac{m}{p_i} \qquad (9.6.8)$$

We see how the pattern of the two-variable case in Example 9.1.3 is repeated, with a constant fraction of income m spent on each good, independent of all prices. Note also that the demand for any good i is completely unaffected by changes in the price of any other good. This is an argument against using Cobb–Douglas utility functions, because we expect realistic demand functions to depend on prices of other goods that are either complements or substitutes.

More Constraints

Occasionally economists need to consider optimization problems with more than one equality constraint, although it is much more common to have many inequality constraints. The corresponding general problem is

$$\max(\min) f(x_1, \ldots, x_n) \quad \text{s.t.} \quad \begin{cases} g_1(x_1, \ldots, x_n) = c_1 \\ \qquad \cdots\cdots\cdots \\ g_m(x_1, \ldots, x_n) = c_m \end{cases} \qquad (9.6.9)$$

The Lagrange multiplier method can be extended to treat problem (9.6.9). To do so, associate a Lagrange multiplier with each constraint, then form the Lagrangian function

$$\mathcal{L}(\mathbf{x}) = f(\mathbf{x}) - \sum_{j=1}^{m} \lambda_j [g_j(\mathbf{x}) - c_j] \qquad (9.6.10)$$

where $\mathbf{x} = (x_1, \ldots, x_n)$. Except in special cases, this Lagrangian must be critical at any optimal point, both local and global. That is, its partial derivative w.r.t. each variable x_i must vanish. Hence, for each $i = 1, 2, \ldots, n$,

$$\frac{\partial \mathcal{L}}{\partial x_i} = \frac{\partial f(\mathbf{x})}{\partial x_i} - \sum_{j=1}^{m} \lambda_j \frac{\partial g_j(\mathbf{x})}{\partial x_i} = 0 \tag{9.6.11}$$

Together with the m equality constraints, these n equations form a total of $n + m$ equations in the $n + m$ unknowns: $x_1, \ldots, x_n$ and $\lambda_1, \ldots, \lambda_m$.

EXAMPLE 9.6.4   Solve the problem

$$\min\ x^2 + y^2 + z^2 \ \text{ s.t. } \begin{cases} x + 2y + z = 30 \\ 2x - y - 3z = 10 \end{cases}$$

Solution: The Lagrangian is

$$\mathcal{L}(x, y, z) = x^2 + y^2 + z^2 - \lambda_1(x + 2y + z - 30) - \lambda_2(2x - y - 3z - 10)$$

The first-order conditions (9.6.11) require that

$$\frac{\partial \mathcal{L}}{\partial x} = 2x - \lambda_1 - 2\lambda_2 = 0 \tag{i}$$

$$\frac{\partial \mathcal{L}}{\partial y} = 2y - 2\lambda_1 + \lambda_2 = 0 \tag{ii}$$

$$\frac{\partial \mathcal{L}}{\partial z} = 2z - \lambda_1 + 3\lambda_2 = 0 \tag{iii}$$

in addition to the two constraints,

$$x + 2y + z = 30 \tag{iv}$$

$$2x - y - 3z = 10 \tag{v}$$

So there are five equations, (i) to (v), to determine the five unknowns: x, y, z, λ_1, and λ_2.

Solving (i) and (ii), simultaneously, for λ_1 and λ_2 gives $\lambda_1 = \frac{2}{5}x + \frac{4}{5}y$ and $\lambda_2 = \frac{4}{5}x - \frac{2}{5}y$. Inserting these expressions for λ_1 and λ_2 into (iii) and rearranging yields

$$x - y + z = 0 \tag{vi}$$

This equation, together with (iv) and (v), constitutes a system of three linear equations in the unknowns x, y, and z. Solving this system by elimination gives $(x, y, z) = (10, 10, 0)$. The corresponding values of the multipliers are $\lambda_1 = 12$ and $\lambda_2 = 4$.

A geometric argument allows us to confirm that we have solved the minimization problem. Each of the two constraints represents a plane in $\mathbb{R}^3$, and the points satisfying both constraints consequently lie on the straight line where the two planes intersect. Now $x^2 + y^2 + z^2$ measures (the square of) the distance from the origin to a point on this straight line, which we want to make as small as possible by choosing the point on the line that is nearest to the origin. No maximum distance can possibly exist, but it is geometrically obvious that there is a minimum distance, and it must be attained at this nearest point.

An alternative method to solve this particular problem is to reduce it to a one-variable optimization problem by using the two constraints to get $y = 20 - x$ and $z = x - 10$, the equations of the straight line where the two planes intersect. Then the square of the distance from the origin is

$$x^2 + y^2 + z^2 = x^2 + (20 - x)^2 + (x - 10)^2 = 3(x - 10)^2 + 200$$

and this function is easily seen to have a minimum when $x = 10$. See also Exercise 5.

EXERCISES FOR SECTION 9.6

1. Consider the problem $\min x^2 + y^2 + z^2$ s.t. $x + y + z = 1$.

   (a) Write down the Lagrangian for this problem, and find the only point (x, y, z) that satisfies the necessary conditions.

   (b) Give a geometric argument for the existence of a solution. Does the corresponding maximization problem have any solution?

2. Use the result in (∗∗) in Example 9.6.3 to solve the utility maximization problem

   $$\max 10x^{1/2}y^{1/3}z^{1/4} \quad \text{s.t.} \quad 4x + 3y + 6z = 390$$

3. A consumer's demands for three goods are chosen to maximize the utility function

   $$U(x, y, z) = x + \sqrt{y} - 1/z$$

   for $x \geq 0$, $y > 0$ and $z > 0$. The budget constraint is $px + qy + rz = m$, where p, q, $r > 0$ and $m \geq \sqrt{pr} + p^2/4q$.

   (a) Write out the first-order conditions for a constrained maximum.

   (b) Find the utility-maximizing demands for all three goods as functions of the four parameters (p, q, r, m).

   (c) Show that the maximized utility is given by the indirect utility function

   $$U^*(p, q, r, m) = \frac{m}{p} + \frac{p}{4q} - 2\sqrt{\frac{r}{p}}$$

   (d) Find $\partial U^*/\partial m$ and comment on your answer.

4. Each week an individual consumes quantities x and y of two goods, and works for l hours. These three quantities are chosen to maximize the utility function

   $$U(x, y, l) = \alpha \ln x + \beta \ln y + (1 - \alpha - \beta) \ln(L - l)$$

   which is defined for $0 \leq l < L$ and for $x, y > 0$. Here α and β are positive parameters satisfying $\alpha + \beta < 1$. The individual faces the budget constraint $px + qy = wl$, where w is the wage per hour. Define $\gamma = (\alpha + \beta)/(1 - \alpha - \beta)$. Find the individual's demands x^*, y^*, and labour supply l^* as functions of p, q, and w.

5. Consider the problem in Example 9.6.4, and let $(x, y, z) = (10 + h, 10 + k, l)$. Show that if (x, y, z) satisfies both constraints, then $k = -h$ and $l = h$. Then show that $x^2 + y^2 + z^2 = 200 + 3h^2$. What do you conclude?

6. An important problem in statistics requires solving

$$\min \ a_1^2 x_1^2 + a_2^2 x_2^2 + \cdots + a_n^2 x_n^2 \ \text{ s.t. } \ x_1 + x_2 + \cdots + x_n = 1$$

where all the constants a_i are nonzero. Solve the problem, taking it for granted that the minimum value exists. What is the solution if one of the $a_i = 0$ for some i?

(SM) **7.** Solve the problem:

$$\max(\min) \ x + y \ \text{ s.t. } \ \begin{cases} x^2 + 2y^2 + z^2 = 1 \\ x + y + z = 1 \end{cases}$$

(SM) **8.** [HARDER] Consider the consumer optimization problem in Example 9.6.3. Find the demand functions when:

(a) $U(x_1, \ldots, x_n) = A x_1^{a_1} \cdots x_n^{a_n}$, with $A > 0$, $a_1 > 0$, $\ldots$, $a_n > 0$.

(b) $U(x_1, \ldots, x_n) = x_1^a + \cdots + x_n^a$, with $0 < a < 1$.

9.7 Comparative Statics

Equation (9.2.2) offers an economic interpretation of the Lagrange multiplier for the case of two variables and one constraint. This can be extended to the problem with n variables and m constraints. Let us rewrite that problem in the form

$$\max(\min) f(\mathbf{x}) \ \text{ s.t. } \ g_j(\mathbf{x}) = c_j, \ \text{ for } j = 1, \ldots, m \tag{9.7.1}$$

Let $\mathbf{x}^* = (x_1^*, \ldots, x_n^*)$ be the values of $\mathbf{x}$ that satisfy the necessary conditions for the solution to (9.7.1). In general, $\mathbf{x}^*$ depends on the values of $\mathbf{c} = (c_1, \ldots, c_m)$. We assume that each $x_i^* = x_i^*(\mathbf{c})$ is a differentiable function. The associated value function, f^*, is then a function of $\mathbf{c}$ as well:

$$f^*(\mathbf{c}) = f(\mathbf{x}^*(\mathbf{c})) \tag{9.7.2}$$

The m Lagrange multipliers associated with $\mathbf{x}^*$, namely $\lambda_1, \ldots, \lambda_m$, also depend on $\mathbf{c}$. Provided that certain regularity conditions are satisfied, we have that for all $j = 1, \ldots, m$,

$$\frac{\partial f^*(\mathbf{c})}{\partial c_j} = \lambda_j(\mathbf{c}) \tag{9.7.3}$$

Hence, *the Lagrange multiplier for the i-th constraint, $\lambda_i = \lambda_i(\mathbf{c})$, is the rate at which the optimal value of the objective function changes w.r.t. changes in the constant c_i.* For this reason λ_i is referred to as the imputed *shadow price* (or *marginal value*) per unit of resource i.

Suppose that we change the components of the vector $\mathbf{c} = (c_1, \ldots, c_m)$ by the respective amounts $d\mathbf{c} = (dc_1, \ldots, dc_m)$. According to linear approximation (12.8.2), if $dc_1, \ldots, dc_m$ are all small in absolute value, Eq. (9.7.3) yields

$$f^*(\mathbf{c} + d\mathbf{c}) - f^*(\mathbf{c}) \approx \lambda_1(\mathbf{c}) \, dc_1 + \cdots + \lambda_m(\mathbf{c}) \, dc_m \tag{9.7.4}$$

EXAMPLE 9.7.1   Consider Example 9.6.4, and suppose we change the first constraint to $x + 2y + z = 31$ and the second constraint to $2x - y - 3z = 9$. Estimate the corresponding change in the value function by using (9.7.4). Find also the new exact value of the value function.

Solution: Using the notation introduced above and the results in Example 9.6.4, we have $c_1 = 30$, $c_2 = 10$, $dc_1 = 1$, $dc_2 = -1$, $\lambda_1(30, 10) = 12$, $\lambda_2(30, 10) = 4$, and $f^*(c_1, c_2) = f^*(30, 10) = 10^2 + 10^2 + 0^2 = 200$. Then, approximation (9.7.4) yields

$$f^*(30 + 1, 10 - 1) - f^*(30, 10) \approx \lambda_1(30, 10)\,dc_1 + \lambda_2(30, 10)\,dc_2$$

$$= 12 \cdot 1 + 4 \cdot (-1) = 8$$

Thus, $f^*(31, 9) \approx 200 + 8 = 208$.

To find the exact value of $f^*(31, 9)$, observe that (vi) in Example 9.6.4 is still valid. Thus, we have the three equations $x + 2y + z = 31, 2x - y - 3z = 9, x - y + z = 0$, whose solutions for x, y, and z are $151/15$, $31/3$, and $4/15$, respectively. We find that $f^*(31, 9) = 15\,614/75 \approx 208.19$.

The Envelope Theorem

Using vector notation with $\mathbf{x} = (x_1, \ldots, x_n)$ and $\mathbf{r} = (r_1, \ldots, r_k)$, consider the following, more general version of problem (9.7.1):

$$\max(\min)_{\mathbf{x}} f(\mathbf{x}, \mathbf{r}) \quad \text{s.t.} \quad g_j(\mathbf{x}, \mathbf{r}) = 0, \quad \text{for } j = 1, \ldots, m \qquad (9.7.5)$$

Here, both the objective function f and each of the m different constraint functions g_j depend not only on the vector $\mathbf{x}$ of variables to be chosen, but also on the parameter vector $\mathbf{r}$. Suppose that $\lambda_j = \lambda_j(\mathbf{r})$, for $j = 1, \ldots, m$, are the Lagrange multipliers obtained from the first-order conditions for problem (9.7.5). Also, we use the generalized definition

$$\mathcal{L}(\mathbf{x}, \mathbf{r}) = f(\mathbf{x}, \mathbf{r}) - \sum_{j=1}^{m} \lambda_j g_j(\mathbf{x}, \mathbf{r})$$

of the corresponding Lagrangian. By analogy with Eq. (9.7.2), let $\mathbf{x}^*(\mathbf{r})$ denote the optimal choice of $\mathbf{x}$ when the parameter vector is $\mathbf{r}$, and define the value function

$$f^*(\mathbf{r}) = f(\mathbf{x}^*(\mathbf{r}), \mathbf{r}) \qquad (9.7.6)$$

Then the following result holds:

THEOREM 9.7.1 (THE ENVELOPE THEOREM)

If $f^*(\mathbf{r})$ and $\mathbf{x}^*(\mathbf{r})$ are differentiable, then

$$\frac{\partial f^*(\mathbf{r})}{\partial r_h} = \frac{\partial \mathcal{L}(\mathbf{x}^*(\mathbf{r}), \mathbf{r})}{\partial r_h} \qquad (9.7.7)$$

for each $h = 1, \ldots, k$.

This is a very useful general result that should be studied carefully. When any parameter is changed, then $f^*(\mathbf{r})$ changes for two reasons: first, a change in r_h changes the vector $\mathbf{r}$ and thus changes $f(\mathbf{x}^*(\mathbf{r}), \mathbf{r})$ directly; and, second, a change in r_h changes, in general, all the functions $x_1^*(\mathbf{r}), \ldots, x_n^*(\mathbf{r})$, which changes $f(\mathbf{x}^*(\mathbf{r}), \mathbf{r})$ indirectly. Theorem 9.7.1 shows that the total effect on the value function of a small change in r_h is found by computing the *partial* derivative of $\mathcal{L}(\mathbf{x}, \mathbf{r})$ w.r.t. r_h, and evaluating it at $\mathbf{x}^*(\mathbf{r})$, ignoring the indirect effect of the dependence of $\mathbf{x}^*$ on $\mathbf{r}$ altogether. The reason is that, because of FOCs (9.6.11), any small change in $\mathbf{x}$ that preserves the equality constraints of problem (9.7.5) will have a negligible effect on the value of $f(\mathbf{x}^*, \mathbf{r})$, so Eq. (9.7.7) holds.

EXAMPLE 9.7.2   In Example 9.6.3, let $U^*(\mathbf{p}, m)$ denote the *indirect utility function* whose value is the maximum utility obtainable by the consumer when prices are $\mathbf{p} = (p_1, \ldots, p_n)$ and the income is m. Let λ denote the Lagrange multiplier associated with the budget constraint. Using Eq. (9.7.3), we see that

$$\lambda = \frac{\partial U^*}{\partial m} \tag{9.7.8}$$

Thus, λ is the rate of increase in maximum utility as income increases. For this reason, λ is generally called the *marginal utility of income*.

Including the vector $(\mathbf{p}, m)$ of all parameters, the Lagrangian takes the form

$$\mathcal{L}(\mathbf{x}, \mathbf{p}, m) = U(\mathbf{x}) - \lambda(p_1 x_1 + \cdots + p_n x_n - m)$$

Obviously, $\partial \mathcal{L}/\partial m = \lambda$ and $\partial \mathcal{L}/\partial p_i = -\lambda x_i$. Hence, from (9.7.7) we get

$$\frac{\partial U^*(\mathbf{p}, m)}{\partial m} = \frac{\partial \mathcal{L}(\mathbf{x}, \mathbf{p}, m)}{\partial m} = \lambda$$

which repeats (9.7.8). Moreover,

$$\frac{\partial U^*(\mathbf{p}, m)}{\partial p_i} = \frac{\partial \mathcal{L}(\mathbf{x}, \mathbf{p}, m)}{\partial p_i} = -\lambda x_i^*$$

which is called *Roy's identity*.[17] This formula has a nice interpretation: the marginal disutility of a price increase is the marginal utility of income, λ, multiplied by the quantity demanded, x_i^*. Intuitively, this is because, for a small price change, the loss of real income is approximately equal to the change in price multiplied by the quantity demanded.

As an illustration of Roy's identity, consider the consumer optimization problem with a Cobb–Douglas utility function, as in Eq. (9.6.7). Substituting the demands given by Eq. (9.6.8) into the utility function, we obtain the indirect utility function

$$U^*(\mathbf{p}, m) = A \left(\frac{a_1 m}{a p_1} \right)^{a_1} \cdots \left(\frac{a_n m}{a p_n} \right)^{a_n} = \frac{B m^a}{P(p_1, \ldots, p_n)}$$

where we have used the notation $a = a_1 + a_2 + \cdots + a_n$, while B denotes the constant $A a_1{}^{a_1} \cdots a_n{}^{a_n}/a^a$, and $P = P(p_1, \ldots, p_n)$ denotes the function $p_1^{a_1} \cdots p_n^{a_n}$.[18]

---

[17] Named after the French economist René Roy (1894–1977). His name should be pronounced accordingly.

[18] Note that P is homogeneous of degree a. This *price index* is also a Cobb–Douglas function whose powers match those of the original utility function.

This formula for the indirect utility function implies that $\partial U^*/\partial m = Bam^{a-1}/P$, and also that

$$\frac{\partial U^*}{\partial p_i} = -\frac{Bm^a}{P^2}\frac{\partial P}{\partial p_i} = -\frac{Bm^a}{P^2}\frac{a_iP}{p_i} = -\frac{Bam^{a-1}}{P}\frac{a_im}{ap_i} = -\frac{\partial U^*}{\partial m}D_i(\mathbf{p}, m)$$

This confirms Roy's identity for the case of a Cobb–Douglas utility function.

EXAMPLE 9.7.3   A firm uses K units of capital and L units of labour to produce $F(K,L)$ units of a commodity. The prices of capital and labour are r and w, respectively. Consider the cost minimization problem

$$\min C(K,L) = rK + wL \ \text{ s.t. } \ F(K,L) = Q$$

where we want to find the values of K and L that minimize the cost of producing Q units. Let $C^* = C^*(r, w, Q)$ be the value function for the problem. Find $\partial C^*/\partial r$, $\partial C^*/\partial w$, and $\partial C^*/\partial Q$.

Solution: Including the output requirement Q and the price parameters r and w, the Lagrangian is

$$\mathcal{L}(K, L, r, w, Q) = rK + wL - \lambda(F(K,L) - Q)$$

whose partial derivatives are $\partial \mathcal{L}/\partial r = K$, $\partial \mathcal{L}/\partial w = L$, and $\partial \mathcal{L}/\partial Q = \lambda$. According to Theorem 9.7.1,

$$\frac{\partial C^*}{\partial r} = K^*, \quad \frac{\partial C^*}{\partial w} = L^*, \quad \text{and} \quad \frac{\partial C^*}{\partial Q} = \lambda \tag{$*$}$$

The first two equalities are instances of *Shephard's lemma*. The last equation shows that λ must equal *marginal cost*, the rate at which minimum cost increases w.r.t. changes in output.

To conclude, we present a proof of Theorem 9.7.1.:

Using the chain rule to differentiate the right-hand side of Eq. (9.7.6) w.r.t. r_h yields

$$\frac{\partial f^*(\mathbf{r})}{\partial r_h} = \sum_{i=1}^{n} \frac{\partial f(\mathbf{x}^*(\mathbf{r}), \mathbf{r})}{\partial x_i} \frac{\partial x_i^*(\mathbf{r})}{\partial r_h} + \frac{\partial f(\mathbf{x}^*(\mathbf{r}), \mathbf{r})}{\partial r_h} \tag{i}$$

But the corresponding partial derivative of the Lagrangian, evaluated at $(\mathbf{x}^*(\mathbf{r}), \mathbf{r})$, is

$$\frac{\partial \mathcal{L}(\mathbf{x}^*(\mathbf{r}), \mathbf{r})}{\partial r_h} = \frac{\partial f(\mathbf{x}^*(\mathbf{r}), \mathbf{r})}{\partial r_h} - \sum_{j=1}^{m} \lambda_j \frac{\partial g_j(\mathbf{x}^*(\mathbf{r}), \mathbf{r})}{\partial r_h} \tag{ii}$$

Subtracting each side of (ii) from the corresponding side of (i), we obtain

$$\frac{\partial f^*(\mathbf{r})}{\partial r_h} - \frac{\partial \mathcal{L}(\mathbf{x}^*(\mathbf{r}), \mathbf{r})}{\partial r_h} = \sum_{i=1}^{n} \frac{\partial f(\mathbf{x}^*(\mathbf{r}), \mathbf{r})}{\partial x_i} \frac{\partial x_i^*(\mathbf{r})}{\partial r_h} + \sum_{j=1}^{m} \lambda_j \frac{\partial g_j(\mathbf{x}^*(\mathbf{r}), \mathbf{r})}{\partial r_h} \tag{iii}$$

Differentiating each constraint $g_j(\mathbf{x}^*(\mathbf{r}), \mathbf{r}) = 0$ w.r.t. r_h, however, yields

$$\sum_{i=1}^{n} \frac{\partial g_j(\mathbf{x}^*(\mathbf{r}), \mathbf{r})}{\partial x_i} \frac{\partial x_i^*(\mathbf{r})}{\partial r_h} + \frac{\partial g_j(\mathbf{x}^*(\mathbf{r}), \mathbf{r})}{\partial r_h} = 0 \tag{iv}$$

Using (iv) to substitute for each term $\partial g_j(\mathbf{x}^*(\mathbf{r}), \mathbf{r})/\partial r_h$ in (iii) gives

$$\frac{\partial f^*(\mathbf{r})}{\partial r_h} - \frac{\partial \mathcal{L}(\mathbf{x}^*(\mathbf{r}), \mathbf{r})}{\partial r_h} = \sum_{i=1}^{n} \left\{ \left[\frac{\partial f(\mathbf{x}^*(\mathbf{r}), \mathbf{r})}{\partial x_i} - \sum_{j=1}^{m} \lambda_j \frac{\partial g_j(\mathbf{x}^*(\mathbf{r}), \mathbf{r})}{\partial x_i} \right] \frac{\partial x_i^*(\mathbf{r})}{\partial r_h} \right\} \quad \text{(v)}$$

The terms in square brackets, however, are equal to the partial derivatives $\partial \mathcal{L}/\partial x_i$ which the first-order conditions (9.6.11) require to be zero at the optimum $(\mathbf{x}^*(\mathbf{r}), \mathbf{r})$. Hence Eq. (v) reduces to

$$\frac{\partial f^*(\mathbf{r})}{\partial r_h} - \frac{\partial \mathcal{L}(\mathbf{x}^*(\mathbf{r}), \mathbf{r})}{\partial r_h} = 0$$

thus proving Eq. (9.7.7).

Note that this proof used only the first-order conditions (9.6.11) for the problem set out in (9.7.5). Therefore, the results in Theorem 9.7.1 are equally valid if we minimize rather than maximize $f(\mathbf{x}, \mathbf{r})$. Note also that we did *not* prove that f^* is differentiable. Sufficient conditions for this are discussed in FMEA.

EXERCISES FOR SECTION 9.7

1. Consider the utility maximization problem $\max x + a \ln y$ s.t. $px + qy = m$, where $0 \le a < m/p$.

   (a) Find the solution (x^*, y^*).

   (b) Find the indirect utility function $U^*(p, q, m, a)$, and compute its partial derivatives w.r.t. p, q, m, and a.

   (c) Verify the envelope theorem.

SM 2. Consider the problem $\min x + 4y + 3z$ s.t. $x^2 + 2y^2 + \frac{1}{3}z^2 = b$, where $b > 0$. Suppose that the problem has a solution, and find it. Then verify Eq. (9.7.3).

3. A firm has L units of labour at its disposal. Its outputs are three different commodities. Producing x, y, and z units of these commodities requires αx^2, βy^2, and γz^2 units of labour, respectively.

   (a) Solve the problem $\max ax + by + cz$ s.t. $\alpha x^2 + \beta y^2 + \gamma z^2 = L$, where a, b, c, α, β, and γ are positive constants.

   (b) Put $a = 4$, $b = c = 1$, $\alpha = 1$, $\beta = \frac{1}{4}$, and $\gamma = \frac{1}{5}$, and show that in this case the problem in (a) has the solution $x = \frac{4}{5}\sqrt{L}$, $y = \frac{4}{5}\sqrt{L}$, and $z = \sqrt{L}$.

   (c) What happens to the maximum value of $4x + y + z$ when L increases from 100 to 101? Find both the exact change and the appropriate linear approximation based on the interpretation of the Lagrange multiplier.

SM 4. Consider the two problems[19]

$$\max(\min) f(x, y, z) = x^2 + y^2 + z \quad \text{s.t.} \quad g(x, y, z) = x^2 + 2y^2 + 4z^2 = 1$$

   (a) Solve them both for the specified constraint.

   (b) Suppose the constraint is changed to $x^2 + 2y^2 + 4z^2 = 1.02$. What is the approximate change in the maximum value of $f(x, y, z)$?

---

[19] The graph of the constraint is the surface of an ellipsoid in $\mathbb{R}^3$, a closed and bounded set.

SM 5. With reference to Example 9.7.3, let $F(K,L) = K^{1/2}L^{1/4}$ and solve the problem, finding explicit expressions for K^*, L^*, C^*, and λ. Verify the equalities $(*)$ in the example.

6. With reference to Example 9.7.3, assuming that the cost function C^* is continuously differentiable twice, prove the symmetry relation $\partial K^*/\partial w = \partial L^*/\partial r$.

7. Consider the utility maximization problem $\max \sqrt{x} + ay$ s.t. $px + qy = m$, where $m > q^2/4a^2p$.

(a) Find the demand functions $x^*(p,q,m,a)$ and $y^*(p,q,m,a)$, as well as the indirect utility function $U^*(p,q,m,a)$.

(b) Find all four partials of $U^*(p,q,m,a) = x^* + ay^*$ and verify the envelope theorem.

9.8   Nonlinear Programming: A Simple Case

So far this chapter has considered how to maximize or minimize a function subject to equality constraints. The final two sections concern "nonlinear programming" problems which involve *inequality* constraints. Some particularly simple inequality constraints are those requiring certain variables to be nonnegative. These often have to be imposed for the solution to make economic sense. In addition, bounds on resource availability are often expressed as inequalities rather than equalities.

In this section we consider the simple *nonlinear programming problem*

$$\max f(x,y) \text{ s.t. } g(x,y) \leq c \tag{9.8.1}$$

with just one inequality constraint. Thus, we seek the largest value attained by $f(x,y)$ in the *admissible* or *feasible* set S of all pairs (x,y) satisfying $g(x,y) \leq c$. Problems where one wants to minimize $f(x,y)$ subject to $(x,y) \in S$ can be handled by instead studying the problem of maximizing $-f(x,y)$ subject to $(x,y) \in S$.

Problem (9.8.1) can be solved using the methods explained in Chapter 8. This involves examining not only the critical points of f in the interior of the admissible set S, but also the behaviour of f on the boundary of S. However, since the 1950s, economists have generally tackled such problems by using an extension of the Lagrangian multiplier method due originally to H.W. Kuhn and A.W. Tucker.

To apply their method, we begin by writing down a recipe giving all the points (x,y) that can possibly solve problem (9.8.1), except in some bizarre cases. The recipe closely resembles the one we used to solve problem (9.1.3).

THE KUHN–TUCKER METHOD

To find the only possible solutions to problem (9.8.1), proceed as follows:

(i) Associate a constant Lagrange multiplier λ with the constraint $g(x,y) \leq c$, and define the Lagrangian

$$\mathcal{L}(x,y) = f(x,y) - \lambda[g(x,y) - c]$$

(ii) Find the critical points of $\mathcal{L}(x,y)$, by equating its partial derivatives to zero:

$$\mathcal{L}_1'(x,y) = f_1'(x,y) - \lambda g_1'(x,y) = 0 \qquad (9.8.2a)$$

$$\mathcal{L}_2'(x,y) = f_2'(x,y) - \lambda g_2'(x,y) = 0 \qquad (9.8.2b)$$

(iii) Introduce the *complementary slackness condition*:

$$\lambda \geq 0, \text{ with } \lambda = 0 \text{ if } g(x,y) < c \qquad (9.8.3)$$

(iv) Require (x,y) to satisfy the constraint

$$g(x,y) \leq c \qquad (9.8.4)$$

(v) Find all the points (x,y) that, together with associated values of λ, satisfy all the conditions (9.8.2a) to (9.8.4). These are the solution candidates, at least one of which solves the problem, if it has a solution.

If $g = c$ and $g_1' = g_2' = 0$ at the maximum of the problem, this method may fail.

Note that the conditions (9.8.2a) and (9.8.2b) are exactly the same as those used in the Lagrange multiplier method of Section 9.1. Condition (9.8.4) obviously has to be satisfied, so the only new feature is condition (9.8.3), which can be rather tricky. It requires that λ be nonnegative, and moreover that $\lambda = 0$ if $g(x,y) < c$. Thus, if $\lambda > 0$, we must have $g(x,y) = c$. An alternative formulation of this condition, then, is that

$$\lambda \geq 0, \text{ with } \lambda \cdot [g(x,y) - c] = 0 \qquad (9.8.5)$$

Later we shall see that even in nonlinear programming, the Lagrange multiplier can be interpreted as a "price" per unit associated with increasing the right-hand side c of the "resource constraint" $g(x,y) \leq c$. With this interpretation, prices are nonnegative, and if the resource constraint is not binding, because $g(x,y) < c$ at the optimum, this means that the price associated with increasing c by one unit is 0.

The two inequalities $\lambda \geq 0$ and $g(x,y) \leq c$ are *complementary* in the sense that at most one can be "slack"—that is, at most one can hold with inequality. Equivalently, at least one must be an equality. Failure to observe that it *is* possible to have *both $\lambda = 0$ and $g(x,y) = c$* in the complementary slackness condition is probably the most common error when solving nonlinear programming problems.

Parts (ii) and (iii) of the method above are together called the *Kuhn–Tucker conditions*. Note that these are (essentially) *necessary* conditions for the solution of Problem (9.8.1). In general, though, they are far from sufficient: indeed, suppose that one can find a point (x_0, y_0) where f is critical and $g(x_0, y_0) < c$; then the Kuhn–Tucker conditions will automatically be satisfied by (x_0, y_0) together with the Lagrange multiplier $\lambda = 0$, yet then (x_0, y_0) could be a local or global minimum or maximum, or a saddle point.

We say that these Kuhn–Tucker conditions are only *essentially* necessary because there may not always be a Lagrange multiplier for which the Kuhn–Tucker conditions hold. The exceptions are some rather rare constrained optimization problems that fail to satisfy a special technical condition called the "constraint qualification". For details, see FMEA.

With equality constraints, setting the partial derivative $\partial \mathcal{L}/\partial \lambda$ equal to zero just recovers the constraint $g(x,y) = c$. Yet with an inequality constraint, one can have $\partial \mathcal{L}/\partial \lambda = -g(x,y) + c > 0$ if the constraint is slack or inactive at an optimum. It was for this reason that we advised against differentiating the Lagrangian w.r.t. the multiplier λ, even though many other books advocate this procedure.

In Theorem 9.5.1 we proved that if the Lagrangian is concave, then the first-order conditions in problem (9.1.1) are sufficient for optimality. The corresponding result is also valid for problem (9.8.1):

THEOREM 9.8.1 (SUFFICIENT CONDITIONS)

Consider the problem set out in (9.8.1), and suppose that (x_0, y_0) satisfies conditions (9.8.2a) to (9.8.4) for the Lagrangian

$$\mathcal{L}(x,y) = f(x,y) - \lambda[g(x,y) - c]$$

If the Lagrangian is concave, then (x_0, y_0) solves the problem.

The proof of this result is actually quite instructive:

Any pair (x_0, y_0) that satisfies conditions (9.8.2a) and (9.8.2b) must be a critical point of the Lagrangian. By Theorem 13.2.1, if the Lagrangian is concave, this (x_0, y_0) will give a maximum. So

$$\mathcal{L}(x_0, y_0) = f(x_0, y_0) - \lambda[g(x_0, y_0) - c] \geq \mathcal{L}(x,y) = f(x,y) - \lambda[g(x,y) - c]$$

Rearranging the terms, we obtain

$$f(x_0, y_0) - f(x,y) \geq \lambda[g(x_0, y_0) - g(x,y)] \tag{$*$}$$

If $g(x_0, y_0) < c$, then by (9.8.3), we have $\lambda = 0$, so $(*)$ implies that $f(x_0, y_0) \geq f(x,y)$ for all (x,y). On the other hand, if $g(x_0, y_0) = c$ and $g(x,y) \leq c$, then $\lambda[g(x_0, y_0) - g(x,y)] = \lambda[c - g(x,y)]$. Because $\lambda \geq 0$ and $c - g(x,y) \geq 0$ for all (x,y) satisfying the inequality constraint, so, again the inequality constraint $(*)$ implies that $f(x_0, y_0) \geq f(x,y)$. Hence, (x_0, y_0) solves Problem (9.8.1).

Note that, as in the argument preceding Theorem 9.5.1, this proof shows that if the Lagrangian achieves a global maximum at a point (x_0, y_0) that satisfies conditions (9.8.3) and (9.8.4), then (x_0, y_0) solves the problem, whether or not the Lagrangian is concave. In this sense, the concavity hypothesis of Theorem 9.8.1 is a useful but unnecessarily strong sufficient condition.

EXAMPLE 9.8.1   A firm has a total of L units of labour to allocate to the production of two goods. These can be sold at fixed positive prices a and b respectively. Producing x units of the first good requires αx^2 units of labour, whereas producing y units of the second good requires

βy^2 units of labour, where α and β are positive constants. Find what output levels of the two goods maximize the revenue that the firm can earn by using this fixed amount of labour.

Solution: The firm's problem is max $ax + by$ s.t. $\alpha x^2 + \beta y^2 \leq L$. The Lagrangian is

$$\mathcal{L}(x, y) = ax + by - \lambda(\alpha x^2 + \beta y^2 - L)$$

and the necessary conditions for (x^*, y^*) to solve the problem are

$$\mathcal{L}'_x = a - 2\lambda\alpha x^* = 0 \tag{i}$$

$$\mathcal{L}'_y = b - 2\lambda\beta y^* = 0 \tag{ii}$$

plus the complementary slackness condition

$$\lambda \geq 0, \ \text{with} \ \lambda = 0 \ \text{if} \ \alpha(x^*)^2 + \beta(y^*)^2 < L \tag{iii}$$

and the resource constraint. Because a and b are positive, we see that λ, x^*, and y^* are all positive, with

$$x^* = \frac{a}{2\alpha\lambda} \ \text{and} \ y^* = \frac{b}{2\beta\lambda} \tag{$*$}$$

Because $\lambda > 0$, condition (iii) implies that $\alpha(x^*)^2 + \beta(y^*)^2 = L$. Inserting the expressions for x^* and y^* into the resource constraint yields $a^2/4\alpha\lambda^2 + b^2/4\beta\lambda^2 = L$. It follows that

$$\lambda = \tfrac{1}{2}L^{-1/2}\sqrt{a^2/\alpha + b^2/\beta} \tag{$**$}$$

Our recipe has produced the solution candidate with x^* and y^* given by ($*$), and λ as in ($**$). The Lagrangian $\mathcal{L}$ is obviously concave, so we have found the solution.

EXAMPLE 9.8.2   Solve the problem

$$\max f(x, y) = x^2 + y^2 + y - 1 \ \text{s.t.} \ g(x, y) = x^2 + y^2 \leq 1$$

Solution: The Lagrangian is

$$\mathcal{L}(x, y) = x^2 + y^2 + y - 1 - \lambda(x^2 + y^2 - 1)$$

so the first-order conditions are:

$$\mathcal{L}'_1(x, y) = 2x - 2\lambda x = 0 \tag{i}$$

$$\mathcal{L}'_2(x, y) = 2y + 1 - 2\lambda y = 0 \tag{ii}$$

The complementary slackness condition is

$$\lambda \geq 0, \ \text{with} \ \lambda = 0 \ \text{if} \ x^2 + y^2 < 1 \tag{iii}$$

We want to find all pairs (x, y) that satisfy these conditions for some suitable value of λ.

Conditions (i) and (ii) can be written as $2x(1 - \lambda) = 0$ and $2y(1 - \lambda) = -1$, respectively. The second of these implies that $\lambda \neq 1$, so the first implies that $x = 0$.

Suppose $x^2 + y^2 = 1$ and so $y = \pm 1$ because $x = 0$. Try $y = 1$ first. Then, (ii) implies $\lambda = 3/2$ and so (iii) is satisfied. Thus, $(0, 1)$ *with* $\lambda = 3/2$ *is a first candidate for optimality*, because all the conditions (i)–(iii) are satisfied. Next, try $y = -1$. Then condition (ii) yields $\lambda = 1/2$ and (iii) is again satisfied. Thus, $(0, -1)$ *with* $\lambda = 1/2$ *is a second candidate for optimality*.

Consider, finally, the case when $x = 0$ and also $x^2 + y^2 = y^2 < 1$—that is, $-1 < y < 1$. Then (iii) implies that $\lambda = 0$, and so (ii) yields $y = -1/2$. Hence, $(0, -1/2)$ *with* $\lambda = 0$ *is a third candidate for optimality*.

We conclude that there are three candidates for optimality. Now

$$f(0, 1) = 1, \ f(0, -1) = -1, \ \text{and} \ f(0, -1/2) = -5/4$$

Because we want to maximize a continuous function over a closed, bounded set, by the extreme value theorem there is a solution to the problem. Because the only possible solutions are the three points already found, we conclude that $(x, y) = (0, 1)$ solves the maximization problem.[20]

Why Does the Kuhn–Tucker Method Work?

Suppose (x^*, y^*) solves problem (9.8.1). Then, either $g(x^*, y^*) < c$, in which case the constraint $g(x^*, y^*) \le c$ is said to be *inactive* or *slack* at (x^*, y^*), or else $g(x^*, y^*) = c$, in which case the same inequality constraint is said to be *active* or *binding* at (x^*, y^*). The two different cases are illustrated for two different values of c in Figs 9.8.1 and 9.8.2, which both display the same four level curves of the objective function f as well. This function is assumed to increase as the level curves shrink. In Fig. 9.8.1, the solution (x^*, y^*) to problem (9.8.1) is an interior point P of the shaded admissible set. On the other hand, in Fig. 9.8.2, the solution (x^*, y^*) is at the boundary of the shaded admissible set.

In case the solution (x^*, y^*) satisfies $g(x^*, y^*) < c$, as in Fig. 9.8.1, the point (x^*, y^*) is usually an interior maximum of the function f. Then it is a critical point at which $f'_1(x^*, y^*) = f'_2(x^*, y^*) = 0$. In this case, if we set $\lambda = 0$, then conditions (9.8.2a) to (9.8.4) are all satisfied.

On the other hand, in the case when the constraint is binding at (x^*, y^*), as in Fig. 9.8.2, the point (x^*, y^*) solves the problem

$$\max f(x, y) \ \text{s.t.} \ g(x, y) = c$$

with an equality constraint. Provided that the conditions of Theorem 9.4.1 are all satisfied, there will exist a unique Lagrange multiplier λ such that the Lagrangian satisfies the first-order conditions (9.8.2a) and (9.8.2b) at (x^*, y^*). It remains to be shown that this Lagrange multiplier λ satisfies $\lambda \ge 0$, thus ensuring that (9.8.3) is also satisfied at (x^*, y^*).

To prove that $\lambda \ge 0$, consider the following two problems

$$\max f(x, y) \ \text{s.t.} \ g(x, y) \le b \ \text{and} \ \max f(x, y) \ \text{s.t.} \ g(x, y) = b$$

---

[20] The point $(0, -1/2)$ solves the corresponding minimization problem. We solved both these problems in Example 13.5.1.

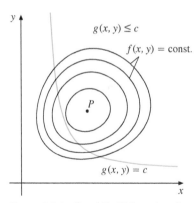

Figure 9.8.1 $P = (x^*, y^*)$ is an interior point of the admissible set

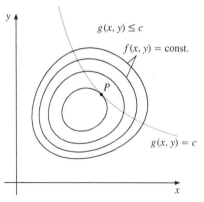

Figure 9.8.2 Constraint $g(x, y) \leq c$ is binding at $P = (x^*, y^*)$

where the constant c has been replaced by the variable parameter b. Let $v(b)$ and $f^*(b)$, respectively, be the value functions of the two problems. Recall from (9.2.2) that $\lambda = df^*(c)/dc$ if f^* is differentiable at c. We shall now show that $f^*(b) \leq f^*(c)$ whenever $b \leq c$, thus implying that

$$\lambda = \lim_{b \to c} \frac{f^*(b) - f^*(c)}{b - c} = \lim_{b \to c^-} \frac{f^*(b) - f^*(c)}{b - c} \geq 0$$

at least when f^* is differentiable, because both the numerator and the denominator of the last limit are nonpositive.

Indeed, our construction implies that $f^*(b) \leq v(b)$ for all b, because the equality constraint $g(x, y) = b$ is more stringent than $g(x, y) \leq b$, and imposing a more stringent constraint never allows a higher maximum value. But also, in case $b < c$, the constraint $g(x, y) \leq b$ is more stringent than $g(x, y) \leq c$, from which it follows that $v(b) \leq v(c)$. Finally, because we are discussing the case when the constraint $g(x^*, y^*) = c$ binds at the solution to problem (9.8.1), we must have $v(c) = f^*(c)$. Thus,

$$f^*(b) \leq v(b) \leq v(c) = f^*(c)$$

is satisfied whenever $b \leq c$, as required.

EXERCISES FOR SECTION 9.8

1. Consider the problem max $-x^2 - y^2$ s.t. $x - 3y \leq -10$.

   (a) Find the pair (x^*, y^*) that solves the problem.

   (b) The same pair (x^*, y^*) also solves the minimization problem min$(x^2 + y^2)$ s.t. $x - 3y \leq -10$. Sketch the admissible set S and explain the solution geometrically.

2. Consider the consumer demand problem max $\sqrt{x} + \sqrt{y}$ s.t. $px + qy \leq m$.

   (a) Find the demand functions.

   (b) Are the demand functions homogeneous of degree 0?

3. Consider the problem max $4 - \frac{1}{2}x^2 - 4y$ s.t. $6x - 4y \leq a$.

   (a) Write down the Kuhn–Tucker conditions.

   (b) Solve the problem.

   (c) With $V(a)$ as the value function, verify that $V'(a) = \lambda$, where λ is the Lagrange multiplier in (b).

4. Consider the problem max $x^2 + 2y^2 - x$ s.t. $x^2 + y^2 \leq 1$.

   (a) Write down the Lagrangian and conditions (9.8.2a) and (9.8.2b).

   (b) Find the five pairs (x, y) that satisfy all the necessary conditions.

   (c) Find the solution to the problem.

(SM) 5. Consider the problem max $f(x, y) = 2 - (x - 1)^2 - e^{y^2}$ s.t. $x^2 + y^2 \leq a$, where a is a positive constant.

   (a) Write down the Kuhn–Tucker conditions for the solution of the problem, distinguishing between the cases $a \in (0, 1)$ and $a \geq 1$, then find the only solution candidate.

   (b) Prove optimality by using Theorem 9.8.1.

   (c) Let $f^*(a)$ be the value function for the problem. Verify that $df^*(a)/da = \lambda$.

6. Suppose a firm earns revenue $R(Q) = aQ - bQ^2$ and incurs cost $C(Q) = \alpha Q + \beta Q^2$ as functions of output $Q \geq 0$, where a, b, α, and β are positive parameters. The firm maximizes profit $\pi(Q) = R(Q) - C(Q)$ subject to the constraint $Q \geq 0$. Solve this one-variable problem by the Kuhn–Tucker method, and find conditions for the constraint to bind at the optimum.

9.9 Multiple Inequality Constraints

A fairly general nonlinear programming problem is the following:

$$\max f(x_1, \ldots, x_n) \text{ s.t. } \begin{cases} g_1(x_1, \ldots, x_n) \leq c_1 \\ \qquad \cdots\cdots\cdots \\ g_m(x_1, \ldots, x_n) \leq c_m \end{cases} \tag{9.9.1}$$

The set of vectors $\mathbf{x} = (x_1, \ldots, x_n)$ that satisfy all the constraints is called the *admissible set* or the *feasible set*. Here is a recipe for solving this problem:

THE KUHN–TUCKER METHOD

To find the only possible solutions to problem (9.9.1), proceed as follows:

(i) Associate Lagrange multipliers $\lambda_1, \ldots, \lambda_m$ with the m constraints, and then write down the Lagrangian

$$\mathcal{L}(\mathbf{x}) = f(\mathbf{x}) - \sum_{j=1}^{m} \lambda_j(g_j(\mathbf{x}) - c_j)$$

(ii) Find the critical points of $\mathcal{L}(\mathbf{x})$ by finding each partial derivative and then solving the equation

$$\frac{\partial \mathcal{L}(\mathbf{x})}{\partial x_i} = \frac{\partial f(\mathbf{x})}{\partial x_i} - \sum_{j=1}^{m} \lambda_j \frac{\partial g_j(\mathbf{x})}{\partial x_i} = 0$$

for each $i = 1, \ldots, n$.

(iii) Impose the complementary slackness conditions:

$$\lambda_j \geq 0, \quad \text{with } \lambda_j = 0 \text{ if } g_j(\mathbf{x}) < c_j$$

for each $j = 1, \ldots, m$.

(iv) Require $\mathbf{x}$ to satisfy all the constraints $g_j(\mathbf{x}) \leq c_j$.

(v) Find all the vectors $\mathbf{x}$ that, together with associated values of $\lambda_1, \ldots, \lambda_m$, satisfy conditions (ii), (iii), and (v). These are the solution candidates, at least one of which solves the problem, if it has a solution.

Note that, as with Eq. (9.8.5), the constraints in steps (iii) and (iv) can be combined into the requirement that

$$\lambda_j \geq 0, \quad g_j(\mathbf{x}) \leq c_j, \quad \text{and} \quad \lambda_j[g_j(\mathbf{x}) - c_j] = 0 \tag{9.9.2}$$

This may be easier to remember and make the derivations easier to express.

If the Lagrangian $\mathcal{L}(\mathbf{x})$ is concave in $\mathbf{x}$, then conditions (iii) to (v) are sufficient for optimality.[21] If $\mathcal{L}(\mathbf{x})$ is not concave, still any vector $\mathbf{x}$ which happens to maximize the Lagrangian while also satisfying (iv) and (v) must be an optimum.[22]

Recall that minimizing $f(\mathbf{x})$ is equivalent to maximizing $-f(\mathbf{x})$. Also an inequality constraint of the form $g_j(\mathbf{x}) \geq c_j$ can be rewritten as $-g_j(\mathbf{x}) \leq -c_j$, whereas an equality constraint $g_j(\mathbf{x}) = c_j$ is equivalent to the double inequality constraint $g_j(\mathbf{x}) \leq c_j$ and $-g_j(\mathbf{x}) \leq -c_j$. In this way, most constrained optimization problems can be expressed in the form (9.9.1).

EXAMPLE 9.9.1   Consider the nonlinear programming problem

$$\max x + 3y - 4e^{-x-y} \quad \text{s.t.} \quad \begin{cases} 2 - x \geq 2y \\ x - 1 \leq -y \end{cases}$$

(a) Write down the necessary Kuhn–Tucker conditions for a point (x^*, y^*) to be a solution of the problem. Are the conditions sufficient for optimality?

(b) Solve the problem.

---

[21] Concavity and convexity for functions of several variables are discussed extensively in FMEA.

[22] As before, in order for the conditions to be truly necessary, a constraint qualification is needed. Once again, see FMEA for details.

Solution:

(a) The first step is to write the problem in the same form as (9.9.1):

$$\max x + 3y - 4e^{-x-y} \ \text{s.t.} \ \begin{cases} x + 2y \le 2 \\ x + y \le 1 \end{cases}$$

The Lagrangian is

$$\mathcal{L}(x, y) = x + 3y - 4e^{-x-y} - \lambda_1(x + 2y - 2) - \lambda_2(x + y - 1)$$

Hence, the Kuhn–Tucker conditions for (x^*, y^*) to solve the problem are:

$$\mathcal{L}'_1 = 1 + 4e^{-x^*-y^*} - \lambda_1 - \lambda_2 = 0 \tag{i}$$

$$\mathcal{L}'_2 = 3 + 4e^{-x^*-y^*} - 2\lambda_1 - \lambda_2 = 0 \tag{ii}$$

$$\lambda_1 \ge 0, \ \text{with} \ \lambda_1 = 0 \ \text{if} \ x^* + 2y^* < 2 \tag{iii}$$

$$\lambda_2 \ge 0, \ \text{with} \ \lambda_2 = 0 \ \text{if} \ x^* + y^* < 1 \tag{iv}$$

The Hessian matrix of $\mathcal{L}(x, y)$ satisfies $\mathcal{L}''_{11} = \mathcal{L}''_{22} = \mathcal{L}''_{12} = -4e^{-x-y}$, implying that $\mathcal{L}''_{11} = \mathcal{L}''_{22} < 0$ and $\mathcal{L}''_{11}\mathcal{L}''_{22} - (\mathcal{L}''_{12})^2 = 0$, so the Lagrangian is concave. Hence these Kuhn–Tucker conditions are sufficient for optimality.

(b) Subtracting (ii) from (i) we get $-2 + \lambda_1 = 0$ and so $\lambda_1 = 2$. But then (iii) together with $x^* + 2y^* \le 2$ yields $x^* + 2y^* = 2$.

Suppose $\lambda_2 = 0$. Then from (i), $4e^{-x^*-y^*} = 1$, so $-x^* - y^* = \ln(1/4)$, and then $x^* + y^* = \ln 4 > 1$, a contradiction.

Thus $\lambda_2 > 0$. Then from (iv) and $x^* + y^* \le 1$ we deduce $x^* + y^* = 1$. Since $x^* + 2y^* = 2$, we see that $x^* = 0$ and $y^* = 1$. Inserting these values for x^* and y^* into (i) and (ii) we find that $\lambda_2 = e^{-1}(4 - e)$, which is positive. We conclude that the solution is: $x^* = 0$ and $y^* = 1$, with $\lambda_1 = 2$, $\lambda_2 = e^{-1}(4 - e)$.

EXAMPLE 9.9.2   A worker chooses both consumption c and labour supply l in order to maximize the utility function $\alpha \ln c + (1 - \alpha) \ln(1 - l)$ over consumption, c, and leisure, $1 - l$, where $0 < \alpha < 1$. The worker's budget constraint is $c \le wl + m$, where m is unearned income. In addition, the worker must choose $l \ge 0$. Solve the worker's constrained maximization problem.

Solution: The worker's problem is

$$\max \ \alpha \ln c + (1 - \alpha) \ln(1 - l) \ \text{s.t.} \ c \le wl + m \ \text{and} \ l \ge 0$$

The Lagrangian is

$$\mathcal{L}(c, l) = \alpha \ln c + (1 - \alpha) \ln(1 - l) - \lambda(c - wl - m) + \mu l$$

and the Kuhn–Tucker conditions for (c^*, l^*) to solve the problem are

$$\mathcal{L}'_c = \frac{\alpha}{c^*} - \lambda = 0 \tag{i}$$

$$\mathcal{L}'_l = \frac{-(1 - \alpha)}{1 - l^*} + \lambda w + \mu = 0 \tag{ii}$$

$$\lambda \geq 0, \quad \text{with } \lambda = 0 \text{ if } c^* < wl^* + m \tag{iii}$$

$$\mu \geq 0, \quad \text{with } \mu = 0 \text{ if } l^* > 0 \tag{iv}$$

From (i) we have $\lambda = \alpha/c^* > 0$. Then (iii) together with the first constraint yield

$$c^* = wl^* + m \tag{v}$$

Case I: $\mu = 0$. Then, from (ii) we get $l^* = 1 - (1-\alpha)/\lambda w$. Then (i) and (v) imply that $\lambda = 1/(w+m)$, so $c^* = \alpha(w+m)$ and $l^* = \alpha - (1-\alpha)m/w$. The Kuhn–Tucker conditions are all satisfied provided that $l^* \geq 0$, which holds if and only if $m \leq \alpha w/(1-\alpha)$.

Case II: $\mu > 0$. Then, $l^* = 0$, $c^* = m$, and $\lambda = \alpha/c^* = \alpha/m$. From (ii) it follows that $\mu = 1 - \alpha - \alpha w/m$, and $\mu > 0$ if, and only if, $m > \alpha w/(1-\alpha)$.

In the last two examples it was not too hard to find which constraints bind—that is, hold with equality—at the optimum. But with more complicated nonlinear programming problems, this can be harder. A general method for finding all candidates for optimality in a nonlinear programming problem with two constraints can be formulated as follows: First, examine the case where both constraints bind. Next, examine the two cases where only one constraint binds. Finally, examine the case where neither constraint binds. In each case, find all vectors **x**, with associated non-negative values of the Lagrange multipliers, that satisfy all the relevant conditions—if any do. Then calculate the value of the objective function for these values of **x**, and retain those **x** with the highest values. Except for perverse problems, this procedure will find the optimum. The next example illustrates how it works in practice.

EXAMPLE 9.9.3   Suppose your utility of consuming x_1 units of good A and x_2 units of good B is $U(x_1, x_2) = \ln x_1 + \ln x_2$, that the prices per unit of A and B are \$10 and \$5, respectively, and that you have \$350 to spend on the two goods. Suppose it takes 0.1 hours to consume one unit of A and 0.2 hours to consume one unit of B, and you have eight hours to spend on consuming the two goods. How much of each good should you buy in order to maximize your utility?

Solution: The problem is

$$\max U(x_1, x_2) = \ln x_1 + \ln x_2 \text{ s.t. } \begin{cases} 10x_1 + 5x_2 \leq 350 \\ 0.1x_1 + 0.2x_2 \leq 8 \end{cases}$$

The Lagrangian is

$$\mathcal{L} = \ln x_1 + \ln x_2 - \lambda_1(10x_1 + 5x_2 - 350) - \lambda_2(0.1x_1 + 0.2x_2 - 8)$$

and the necessary conditions are that there exist numbers λ_1 and λ_2 such that

$$\mathcal{L}'_1 = 1/x_1^* - 10\lambda_1 - 0.1\lambda_2 = 0 \tag{i}$$

$$\mathcal{L}'_2 = 1/x_2^* - 5\lambda_1 - 0.2\lambda_2 = 0 \tag{ii}$$

$$\lambda_1 \geq 0, \quad \text{with } \lambda_1 = 0 \text{ if } 10x_1^* + 5x_2^* < 350 \qquad \text{(iiii)}$$

$$\lambda_2 \geq 0, \quad \text{with } \lambda_2 = 0 \text{ if } 0.1x_1^* + 0.2x_2^* < 8 \qquad \text{(iv)}$$

We start the systematic procedure:

Case 1: Both constraints bind. Then

$$10x_1^* + 5x_2^* = 350 \qquad \text{(v)}$$

and $0.1x_1^* + 0.2x_2^* = 8$. The solution is $(x_1^*, x_2^*) = (20, 30)$. Inserting these values into (i) and (ii) yields the system $10\lambda_1 + 0.1\lambda_2 = 1/20$ and $5\lambda_1 + 0.2\lambda_2 = 1/30$, with solution $(\lambda_1, \lambda_2) = (1/225, 1/18)$. In particular, both λ_1 and λ_2 are nonnegative. So we have found a candidate for optimality because all the Kuhn–Tucker conditions are satisfied.

Case 2: Constraint 1 binds, 2 does not. Then (v) holds and $0.1x_1^* + 0.2x_2^* < 8$. From (iv) we obtain $\lambda_2 = 0$. Now (i) and (ii) give $x_2^* = 2x_1^*$. Inserting this into (v), we get $x_1^* = 17.5$ and then $x_2^* = 2x_1^* = 35$. But then $0.1x_1^* + 0.2x_2^* = 8.75$, which violates the second constraint. So there is no candidate for optimality in this case.

Case 3: Constraint 2 binds, 1 does not. Then $10x_1^* + 5x_2^* < 350$ and $0.1x_1^* + 0.2x_2^* = 8$. From (iii), $\lambda_1 = 0$, and (i) and (ii) yield $0.1x_1^* = 0.2x_2^*$. Inserted into $0.1x_1^* + 0.2x_2^* = 8$ this yields $x_2^* = 20$ and so $x_1^* = 40$. But then $10x_1^* + 5x_2^* = 500$, violating the first constraint. So there is no candidate for optimality in this case either.

Case 4: None of the constraints bind. Then $\lambda_1 = \lambda_2 = 0$, in which case (i) and (ii) make no sense.

We conclude that there is only one candidate for optimality, which is $(x_1^*, x_2^*) = (20, 30)$. Since the Lagrangian is easily seen to be concave, we have found the solution.

Properties of the Value Function

As in previous problems, the value function of problem (9.9.1) is defined by $f^*(\mathbf{c}) = f(\mathbf{x}^*(\mathbf{c}))$, where $\mathbf{x}^*(\mathbf{c})$ is the solution to the problem and $\mathbf{c} = (c_1, \ldots, c_m)$. The following properties of f^* are very useful:

$$f^*(\mathbf{c}) \text{ is nondecreasing in each variable } c_1, \ldots, c_m \qquad (9.9.3)$$

$$\text{If } \partial f^*(\mathbf{c})/\partial c_j \text{ exists, then it is equal to } \lambda_j(\mathbf{c}), \text{ for } j = 1, \ldots, m \qquad (9.9.4)$$

Here, (9.9.3) follows immediately because if c_j increases, and all the other c_k are fixed, then the admissible set becomes larger; hence, $f^*(\mathbf{c})$ cannot decrease. Concerning property (9.9.4), each $\lambda_j(\mathbf{c})$ is a Lagrange multiplier coming from the Kuhn–Tucker conditions.

However, there is a catch: the value function f^* need not be differentiable. Even if f and $g_1, \ldots, g_m$ are all differentiable, the value function can have sudden changes of slope. Such cases are studied in FMEA.

1. Consider the problem max $\frac{1}{2}x - y$ s.t. $x + e^{-x} \leq y$ and $x \geq 0$.

   (a) Write down the Lagrangian and the necessary Kuhn–Tucker conditions.

   (b) Find the solution to the problem.

(SM) 2. Solve the following consumer demand problem where, in addition to the budget constraint, there is an upper limit $\bar{x}$ which rations how much of the first good can be bought:

$$\max \alpha \ln x + (1 - \alpha) \ln y \quad \text{s.t.} \quad px + qy \leq m \text{ and } x \leq \bar{x}$$

(SM) 3. Consider the problem max $x + y - e^x - e^{x+y}$ s.t. $x + y \geq 4$, $x \geq -1$ and $y \geq 1$.

   (a) Sketch the admissible set S.

   (b) Find all pairs (x, y) that satisfy all the necessary conditions.

   (c) Find the solution to the problem.

(SM) 4. Consider the problem max $x + ay$ s.t. $x^2 + y^2 \leq 1$ and $x + y \geq 0$, where a is a constant.

   (a) Sketch the admissible set and write down the necessary conditions.

   (b) Find the solution for all values of the constant a.

(SM) 5. Solve the following problem, assuming it has a solution:

$$\max y - x^2 \quad \text{s.t.} \quad y \geq 0, \ y - x \geq -2 \text{ and } y^2 \leq x$$

(SM) 6. Consider the problem max $-\left(x + \frac{1}{2}\right)^2 - \frac{1}{2}y^2$ s.t. $e^{-x} - y \leq 0$ and $y \leq \frac{2}{3}$.

   (a) Sketch the admissible set.

   (b) Write down the Kuhn–Tucker conditions, and find the solution of the problem.

7. Consider the problem max $xz + yz$ s.t. $x^2 + y^2 + z^2 \leq 1$.

   (a) Write down the Kuhn–Tucker conditions.

   (b) Solve the problem.

9.10 Nonnegativity Constraints

Consider the general nonlinear programming problem (9.9.1) once again. Often, variables involved in economic optimization problems must be nonnegative by their very nature. It is not difficult to incorporate such constraints in the formulation of (9.9.1). If $x_1 \geq 0$, for example, this can be represented by the new constraint $h_1(x_1, \ldots, x_n) = -x_1 \leq 0$, and we introduce an additional Lagrange multiplier to go with it. But in order not to have too many Lagrange multipliers, the necessary conditions for the solution of nonlinear programming problems with nonnegativity constraints are sometimes formulated in a slightly different way.

Consider first the problem

$$\max f(x, y) \quad \text{s.t.} \quad g(x, y) \leq c, \ x \geq 0, \ \text{and} \ y \geq 0 \tag{9.10.1}$$

Here we introduce the functions $h_1(x, y) = -x$ and $h_2(x, y) = -y$, so that the constraints in problem (9.10.1) become $g(x, y) \leq c$, $h_1(x, y) \leq 0$, and $h_2(x, y) \leq 0$. Applying the recipe for solving (9.9.1), we introduce the Lagrangian

$$\mathcal{L}(x, y) = f(x, y) - \lambda[g(x, y) - c] - \mu_1(-x) - \mu_2(-y)$$

The Kuhn–Tucker conditions are

$$\mathcal{L}_1' = f_1'(x, y) - \lambda g_1'(x, y) + \mu_1 = 0 \tag{i}$$

$$\mathcal{L}_2' = f_2'(x, y) - \lambda g_2'(x, y) + \mu_2 = 0 \tag{ii}$$

$$\lambda \geq 0, \quad \text{with} \ \lambda = 0 \ \text{if} \ g(x, y) < c \tag{iii}$$

$$\mu_1 \geq 0, \quad \text{with} \ \mu_1 = 0 \ \text{if} \ x > 0 \tag{iv}$$

$$\mu_2 \geq 0, \quad \text{with} \ \mu_2 = 0 \ \text{if} \ y > 0 \tag{v}$$

From (i), we have $f_1'(x, y) - \lambda g_1'(x, y) = -\mu_1$. From (iv), we have $-\mu_1 \leq 0$ and $-\mu_1 = 0$ if $x > 0$. Thus, (i) and (iv) are together equivalent to

$$f_1'(x, y) - \lambda g_1'(x, y) \leq 0, \ \text{with equality if} \ x > 0 \tag{vi}$$

In the same way, (ii) and (v) are together equivalent to

$$f_2'(x, y) - \lambda g_2'(x, y) \leq 0, \ \text{with equality if} \ y > 0 \tag{vii}$$

So the new Kuhn–Tucker conditions are (vi), (vii), and (iii). Note that after replacing (i) and (iv) by (vi), as well as (ii) and (v) by (vii), only the multiplier λ associated with $g(x, y) \leq c$ remains.

The same idea can obviously be extended to the n-variable problem

$$\max f(\mathbf{x}) \quad \text{s.t.} \quad \begin{cases} g_1(\mathbf{x}) \leq c_1 \\ \ldots\ldots\ldots \\ g_m(\mathbf{x}) \leq c_m \end{cases} \quad x_1 \geq 0, \ \ldots, \ x_n \geq 0 \tag{9.10.2}$$

Briefly formulated, the necessary conditions for the solution of problem (9.10.2) are that, for each $i = 1, \ldots, n$,

$$\frac{\partial f(\mathbf{x})}{\partial x_i} - \sum_{j=1}^{m} \lambda_j \frac{\partial g_j(\mathbf{x})}{\partial x_i} \leq 0, \ \text{with equality if} \ x_i > 0 \tag{9.10.3}$$

and that

$$\lambda_j \geq 0, \ \text{with} \ \lambda_j = 0 \ \text{if} \ g_j(\mathbf{x}) < c_j \tag{9.10.4}$$

for all $j = 1, \ldots, m$.

EXAMPLE 9.10.1   Consider the utility maximization problem

$$\max\ x + \ln(1+y)\ \text{ s.t. } px + y \le m,\ x \ge 0 \text{ and } y \ge 0$$

where consumption of both commodities is explicitly required to be nonnegative.

(a) Write down the necessary Kuhn–Tucker conditions for a point (x^*, y^*) to be a solution.

(b) Find the solution to the problem, for all positive values of p and m.

Solution:

(a) The Lagrangian is

$$\mathcal{L}(x, y) = x + \ln(1+y) - \lambda(px + y - m)$$

and the Kuhn–Tucker conditions for (x^*, y^*) to be a solution are that there exists a λ such that

$$\mathcal{L}'_1(x^*, y^*) = 1 - p\lambda \le 0, \text{ with } 1 - p\lambda = 0 \text{ if } x^* > 0 \tag{i}$$

$$\mathcal{L}'_2(x^*, y^*) = \frac{1}{1+y^*} - \lambda \le 0, \text{ with } \frac{1}{1+y^*} - \lambda = 0 \text{ if } y^* > 0 \tag{ii}$$

$$\lambda \ge 0, \text{ with } \lambda = 0 \text{ if } px^* + y^* < m \tag{iii}$$

Also, $x^* \ge 0$, $y^* \ge 0$, and the budget constraint has to be satisfied, so $px^* + y^* \le m$.

(b) Note that the Lagrangian is concave, so a point that satisfies the Kuhn–Tucker conditions will be a maximum point. It is clear from (i) that λ cannot be 0. Therefore $\lambda > 0$, so (iii) and $px^* + y^* \le m$ imply that

$$px^* + y^* = m \tag{iv}$$

Regarding which constraints $x \ge 0$ and $y \ge 0$ bind, there are four cases to consider:

Case 1: Suppose $x^* = 0$, $y^* = 0$. Since $m > 0$, this is impossible because of (iv).

Case 2: Suppose $x^* > 0$, $y^* = 0$. From (ii) and $y^* = 0$ we get $\lambda \ge 1$. Then (i) implies that $p = 1/\lambda \le 1$. Equation (iv) gives $x^* = m/p$, so we get one candidate for a maximum point:
$$(x^*, y^*) = (m/p, 0) \text{ and } \lambda = 1/p, \text{ if } 0 < p \le 1$$

Case 3: Suppose $x^* = 0$, $y^* > 0$. By (iv) we have $y^* = m$. Then (ii) yields $\lambda = 1/(1+y^*)$ $= 1/(1+m)$. From (i) we get $p \ge 1/\lambda = m + 1$. This gives one more candidate:
$$(x^*, y^*) = (0, m) \text{ and } \lambda = 1/(1+m), \text{ if } p \ge m + 1$$

Case 4: Suppose $x^* > 0$, $y^* > 0$. With equality in both (i) and (ii), $\lambda = 1/p = 1/(1+y^*)$. It follows that $y^* = p - 1$, and then $p > 1$ because $y^* > 0$. Equation (iv) implies that $px^* = m - y^* = m - p + 1$, so $x^* = (m + 1 - p)/p$. Since $x^* > 0$, we must have $p < m + 1$. Thus we get one last candidate
$$(x^*, y^*) = \left(\frac{m + 1 - p}{p}, p - 1\right) \text{ and } \lambda = 1/p, \text{ if } 1 < p < m + 1$$

Putting all this together, we see that the solution of the problem is: (a) If $0 < p \le 1$, then $(x^*, y^*) = (m/p, 0)$, with $\lambda = 1/p$, from Case 2. (b) If $1 < p < m + 1$, then $(x^*, y^*) = ((m + 1 - p)/p, p - 1)$, with $\lambda = 1/p$, from Case 4. (c) If $p \ge m + 1$, then $(x^*, y^*) = (0, m)$, with $\lambda = 1/(m + 1)$, from Case 3.

Note that, except in the intermediate case (b) when $1 < p < m + 1$, it is optimal to spend everything on only the cheaper of the two goods—either x in case (a), or y in case (c).

EXAMPLE 9.10.2   (**Peak load pricing**) Consider a producer who generates electricity by burning a fuel such as coal or natural gas. The demand for electricity varies between peak periods, during which all the generating capacity is used, and off-peak periods when there is spare capacity. We consider a certain time interval (say, a year) divided into n periods of equal length. Suppose the amounts of electric power sold in these n periods are $x_1, x_2, \ldots, x_n$. Assume that a regulatory authority fixes the corresponding prices at levels equal to $p_1, p_2, \ldots, p_n$. The total operating cost over all n periods is given by the function $C(\mathbf{x})$, where $\mathbf{x} = (x_1, \ldots, x_n)$, and k is the output capacity in each period. Let $D(k)$ denote the cost of maintaining output capacity at level k. The producer's total profit is then

$$\pi(\mathbf{x}, k) = \sum_{i=1}^{n} p_i x_i - C(\mathbf{x}) - D(k)$$

Because the producer cannot exceed capacity k in any period, it faces the constraints

$$x_1 \le k, \ldots, x_n \le k \tag{i}$$

We consider the problem of finding $x_1 \ge 0, \ldots, x_n \ge 0$ and $k \ge 0$ such that profit is maximized subject to the capacity constraints (i).

This is a nonlinear programming problem with $n + 1$ variables and n constraints. The Lagrangian is

$$\mathcal{L}(\mathbf{x}, k) = \sum_{i=1}^{n} p_i x_i - C(\mathbf{x}) - D(k) - \sum_{i=1}^{n} \lambda_i (x_i - k)$$

Following (9.10.3) and (9.10.4), the choice $(\mathbf{x}^0, k^0) \ge 0$ can solve the problem only if there exist Lagrange multipliers $\lambda_1 \ge 0, \ldots, \lambda_n \ge 0$ such that

$$\frac{\partial \mathcal{L}}{\partial x_i} = p_i - C_i'(\mathbf{x}^0) - \lambda_i \le 0 \text{ with equality if } x_i^0 > 0, \text{ for } i = 1, \ldots, n \tag{i}$$

$$\frac{\partial \mathcal{L}}{\partial k} = -D'(k^0) + \sum_{i=1}^{n} \lambda_i \le 0 \text{ with equality if } k^0 > 0 \tag{ii}$$

$$\lambda_i \ge 0, \text{ with } \lambda_i = 0 \text{ if } x_i^0 < k^0, \text{ for } i = 1, \ldots, n \tag{iii}$$

Suppose that i is such that $x_i^0 > 0$. Then (i) implies that

$$p_i = C_i'(\mathbf{x}^0) + \lambda_i \tag{iv}$$

If period i is an off-peak period, then $x_i^0 < k^0$ and so $\lambda_i = 0$ by (iii). From (iv) it follows that $p_i = C_i'(x_1^0, \ldots, x_n^0)$. Thus, we see that *the profit-maximizing pattern of output $\mathbf{x}^0$ will bring* *about equality between the regulator's price in any off-peak period and the corresponding marginal operating cost.*

On the other hand, λ_j might be positive in a peak period when $x_j^0 = k^0$. If $k^0 > 0$, it follows from (ii) that $\sum_{i=1}^{n} \lambda_i = D'(k^0)$. We conclude that the output pattern will be such that *in peak periods the price set by the regulator will exceed the marginal operating cost by an additional amount λ_j, which is really the "shadow price" of the capacity constraint $x_j^0 \le k^0$. The sum of these shadow prices over all peak periods is equal to the marginal capacity cost.*

EXERCISES FOR SECTION 9.10

1. Consider the utility maximization problem max $x + \ln(1 + y)$ s.t. $16x + y \le 495, x \ge 0, y \ge 0$.

   (a) Write down the necessary Kuhn–Tucker conditions, with nonnegativity constraints, for a point to be a solution.

   (b) Find the solution to the problem.

   (c) Estimate by how much utility will increase if income is increased from 495 to 500.

SM 2. Solve the following problem, assuming it has a solution:

$$\max\ xe^{y-x} - 2ey \quad \text{s.t.}\quad y \le 1 + x/2,\ x \ge 0,\ \text{and } y \ge 0$$

SM 3. Suppose that optimal capacity utilization by a firm requires that its output quantities x_1 and x_2, along with its capacity level k, should be chosen to solve the problem

$$\max\ x_1 + 3x_2 - x_1^2 - x_2^2 - k^2 \quad \text{s.t.}\quad x_1 \le k,\ x_2 \le k,\ x_1 \ge 0,\ x_2 \ge 0,\ k \ge 0$$

Show that $k = 0$ cannot be optimal, and then find the solution.

REVIEW EXERCISES

1. Consider the problem max $f(x, y) = 3x + 4y$ s.t. $g(x, y) = x^2 + y^2 = 225$.

   (a) Solve it using the Lagrange multiplier method.

   (b) Suppose 225 is changed to 224. What is the approximate change in the optimal value of f?

2. Use result $(\ast\ast)$ in Example 9.1.3 to write down the solution to the problem of maximizing $f(x, y)$ subject to $px + qy = m$, in each of the following cases, assuming $x \ge 0$ and $y \ge 0$:

   (a) $f(x, y) = 25x^2 y^3$ (b) $f(x, y) = x^{1/5} y^{2/5}$ (c) $f(x, y) = 10\sqrt{x}\sqrt[3]{y}$

SM 3. By selling x tons of one commodity the firm gets a price per ton given by $p(x)$. By selling y tons of another commodity the price per ton is $q(y)$. The cost of producing and selling x tons of the first commodity and y tons of the second is given by $C(x, y)$.

(a) Write down the firm's profit function and find necessary conditions for $x^* > 0$ and $y^* > 0$ to solve the problem. Give economic interpretations of the necessary conditions.

(b) Suppose that the firm's production activity causes so much pollution that the authorities limit its output to no more than m tons of total output. Write down the necessary conditions for $\hat{x} > 0$ and $\hat{y} > 0$ to solve the problem.

4. Suppose $U(x, y)$ denotes the utility enjoyed by a person when having x hours of leisure per day (24 hours) and y units per day of other goods. The person gets an hourly wage of w and pays an average price of p per unit of the other goods, so that

$$py = w(24 - x) \qquad (*)$$

assuming that the person spends all that is earned.

(a) Show that maximizing $U(x, y)$ subject to the constraint $(*)$ leads to the equation

$$pU_1'(x, y) = wU_2'(x, y) \qquad (**)$$

(b) Suppose that the equations $(*)$ and $(**)$ define x and y as differentiable functions $x(p, w)$, $y(p, w)$ of p and w. Show that, with appropriate conditions on $U(x, y)$,

$$\frac{\partial x}{\partial w} = \frac{(24 - x)(wU_{22}'' - pU_{12}'') + pU_2'}{p^2 U_{11}'' - 2pw U_{12}'' + w^2 U_{22}''}$$

SM 5. Consider the problems

$$\max(\min) \, x^2 + y^2 - 2x + 1 \quad \text{s.t.} \quad \tfrac{1}{4}x^2 + y^2 = b$$

where b is a constant.[23]

(a) Solve the problem in case $b > \frac{4}{9}$.

(b) If $f^*(b)$ denotes the value function for the maximization problem, verify that $df^*(b)/db = \lambda$ when $b > \frac{4}{9}$, where λ is the corresponding Lagrange multiplier.

6. Consider the utility maximization problem (9.1.4) with a "separable" utility function $u(x, y) = v(x) + w(y)$, where $v'(x) > 0$, $w'(y) > 0$, $v''(x) \leq 0$, and $w''(y) \leq 0$.

(a) State the first-order conditions for utility maximization.

(b) Why are these conditions sufficient for optimality?

SM 7. Consider the problem

$$\min \, x^2 - 2x + 1 + y^2 - 2y \quad \text{s.t.} \quad (x + y)\sqrt{x + y + b} = 2\sqrt{a}$$

where a and b are positive constants and x and y are positive.

(a) Suppose that (x, y) solves the problem. Show that x and y must then satisfy the equations

$$x = y \text{ and } 2x^3 + bx^2 = a \qquad (*)$$

(b) The equations in $(*)$ define x and y as differentiable functions of a and b. Find expressions for $\partial x/\partial a$, $\partial^2 x/\partial a^2$, and $\partial x/\partial b$.

---

[24] The constraint has a graph that is an ellipse in the xy-plane, so it defines a closed and bounded set.

(SM) **8.** For all $a > 0$, solve the problem max $10 - (x - 2)^2 - (y - 1)^2$ s.t. $x^2 + y^2 \leq a$.

(SM) **9.** Consider the nonlinear programming problem

$$\max xy \quad \text{s.t.} \quad \begin{cases} x^2 + ry^2 \leq m \\ x \geq 1 \end{cases}$$

where r and m are positive constants, with $m > 1$.

(a) Write down the necessary Kuhn–Tucker conditions for a point to be a solution of the problem.

(b) Solve the problem.

(c) Let $V(r, m)$ denote the value function. Compute $\partial V(r, m)/\partial m$, and comment on its sign.

(d) Verify that $\partial V(r, m)/\partial r = \partial \mathcal{L}/\partial r$, where $\mathcal{L}$ is the Lagrangian.

10. Suppose the firm of Example 8.5.1 earns revenue $R(Q)$ and incurs cost $C(Q)$ as functions of output $Q \geq 0$, where $R'(Q) > 0$, $C'(Q) > 0$, $R''(Q) < 0$, and $C''(Q) > 0$ for all $Q \geq 0$. The firm maximizes profit $\pi(Q) = R(Q) - C(Q)$ subject to $Q \geq 0$. Write down the first-order conditions for the solution to this problem, and find sufficient conditions for the constraint to bind at the optimum.

11. A firm uses K and L units of two inputs to produce $\sqrt{KL}$ units of a product, where $K > 0, L > 0$. The input factor costs are r and w per unit, respectively. The firm wants to minimize the costs of producing at least Q units.

(a) Formulate the nonlinear programming problem that emerges. Reformulate it as a maximization problem, then write down the Kuhn–Tucker conditions for the optimum. Solve these conditions to determine K^* and L^* as functions of (r, w, Q).

(b) Define the minimum cost function as $c^*(r, w, Q) = rK^* + wL^*$. Verify that $\partial c^*/\partial r = K^*$ and $\partial c^*/\partial w = L^*$, then give these results economic interpretations.

Section 5

Dynamic Analysis

INTEGRATION AND DIFFERENTIAL EQUATIONS

Is it right I ask; is it even prudence; to bore thyself and bore the students?
—Mephistopheles to Faust, in Johann Wolfgang von Goethe's *Faust*

The main topic of the preceding three chapters was differentiation, which can be applied to many interesting economic problems. Economists, however, especially when doing statistics, often face the mathematical problem of finding a function from information about its derivative. This process of reconstructing a function from its derivative can be regarded as the "inverse" of differentiation. Mathematicians call this process *integration*.

There are simple formulas that have been known since ancient times for calculating the area of any triangle, and so of any polygon that, by definition, is entirely bounded by straight lines. Over 4000 years ago, however, the Babylonians were concerned with accurately measuring the area of plane surfaces, like circles, that are not bounded by straight lines. Solving this kind of area problem is intimately related to integration, as will be explained in Section 10.2.

Apart from providing an introduction to integration, this chapter will also discuss some important applications of integrals that economists are expected to know. A brief introduction to some simple differential equations concludes the chapter.

10.1 Indefinite Integrals

Suppose we do not know the function F, but we do know that its derivative is x^2, so that $F'(x) = x^2$. What is F? Since the derivative of x^3 is $3x^2$, we see that $\frac{1}{3}x^3$ has x^2 as its derivative. But so does $\frac{1}{3}x^3 + C$ where C is an arbitrary constant, since additive constants disappear with differentiation.

In fact, let $G(x)$ denote an arbitrary function having x^2 as its derivative. Then the derivative of $G(x) - \frac{1}{3}x^3$ is equal to 0 for all x. But, by (5.3.3), a function that has derivative equal to 0 for all x must be constant. This shows that

$$F'(x) = x^2 \iff F(x) = \tfrac{1}{3}x^3 + C$$

with C as an arbitrary constant.

EXAMPLE 10.1.1   Assume that the marginal cost function of a firm is $C'(Q) = 2Q^2 + 2Q + 5$, and that the fixed costs are 100. Find the cost function $C(Q)$.

Solution: Considering separately each of the three terms in the expression for $C'(Q)$, we realize that the cost function must have the form $C(Q) = \frac{2}{3}Q^3 + Q^2 + 5Q + c$, because if we differentiate this function we obtain precisely $2Q^2 + 2Q + 5$. But the fixed costs are 100, which means that $C(0) = 100$. Inserting $Q = 0$ into the proposed formula for $C(Q)$ yields $c = 100$. Hence, the required cost function must be $C(Q) = \frac{2}{3}Q^3 + Q^2 + 5x + 100$.

Suppose $f(x)$ and $F(x)$ are two functions of x having the property that $f(x) = F'(x)$ for all x in some interval I. We pass from F to f by taking the derivative, so the reverse process of passing from f to F could appropriately be called taking the *antiderivative*. But following usual mathematical practice, we call F an *indefinite integral* of f over the interval I, and denote it by $\int f(x)\,dx$. Two functions having the same derivative throughout an interval must differ by a constant, so:

THE INDEFINITE INTEGRAL

If $F'(x) = f(x)$, then

$$\int f(x)\,dx = F(x) + C \tag{10.1.1}$$

where C is an arbitrary constant.

For instance, the solution to Example 10.1.1 implies that

$$\int (2x^2 + 2x + 5)\,dx = \frac{2}{3}x^3 + x^2 + 5x + C$$

The symbol $\int$ is the *integral sign*, and the function $f(x)$ appearing in (10.1.1) is the *integrand*. Then we write dx to indicate that x is the *variable of integration*. Finally, C is a *constant of integration* We read (10.1.1) this way: The indefinite integral of $f(x)$ w.r.t. x is $F(x)$ plus a constant. We call it an *indefinite* integral because $F(x) + C$ is not to be regarded as one definite function, but as a whole class of functions, all having the same derivative f.

Differentiating each side of (10.1.1) shows directly that

$$\frac{d}{dx}\int f(x)\,dx = f(x) \tag{10.1.2}$$

namely, that the derivative of an indefinite integral equals the integrand. Also, (10.1.1) can obviously be rewritten as

$$\int F'(x)\,dx = F(x) + C \tag{10.1.3}$$

Thus, *integration and differentiation cancel each other out.*

Some Important Integrals

There are some important integration formulas which follow immediately from the corresponding rules for differentiation. Let a be a fixed number, different from -1. Because the derivative of $x^{a+1}/(a+1)$ is x^a, one has

If $a \neq -1$, then

$$\int x^a \, dx = \frac{1}{a+1} x^{a+1} + C \tag{10.1.4}$$

This very important result states that the indefinite integral of any power of x, except x^{-1}, is obtained by increasing the exponent of x by 1, then dividing by the new exponent, and finally adding a constant of integration. Here are three prominent examples.

EXAMPLE 10.1.2

(a) $\int x \, dx = \int x^1 \, dx = \dfrac{1}{1+1} x^{1+1} + C = \dfrac{1}{2} x^2 + C$

(b) $\int \frac{1}{x^3} \, dx = \int x^{-3} \, dx = \dfrac{1}{-3+1} x^{-3+1} + C = -\dfrac{1}{2x^2} + C$

(c) $\int \sqrt{x} \, dx = \int x^{1/2} \, dx = \dfrac{1}{\frac{1}{2}+1} x^{\frac{1}{2}+1} + C = \dfrac{2}{3} x^{3/2} + C$

When $a = -1$, the formula in (10.1.4) is not valid, because the right-hand side involves division by zero and so becomes meaningless. The integrand is then $1/x$, and the problem is thus to find a function having $1/x$ as its derivative. Now $F(x) = \ln x$ has this property, but it is only defined for $x > 0$. Note, however, that $\ln(-x)$ is defined for $x < 0$, and according to the chain rule, its derivative is $[1/(-x)](-1) = 1/x$. Recall too that $|x| = x$ when $x \geq 0$ and $|x| = -x$ when $x < 0$. Thus, whether $x > 0$ or $x < 0$, we have:

$$\int \frac{1}{x} \, dx = \ln |x| + C \tag{10.1.5}$$

Consider next the exponential function. The derivative of e^x is e^x. Thus $\int e^x \, dx = e^x + C$. More generally, since the derivative of $(1/a)e^{ax}$ is e^{ax}, we have:

If $a \neq 0$, then

$$\int e^{ax} \, dx = \frac{1}{a} e^{ax} + C \tag{10.1.6}$$

For $a > 0$ we can write $a^x = e^{(\ln a)x}$. As a special case of (10.1.6), when $\ln a \neq 0$ because $a \neq 1$, we obtain:

When $a > 0$ and $a \neq 1$,

$$\int a^x \, dx = \frac{1}{\ln a} a^x + C \qquad (10.1.7)$$

The above were examples of how knowing the derivative of a function given by a formula automatically gives us a corresponding indefinite integral. Indeed, suppose it were possible to construct a complete table with every formula that we knew how to differentiate in the first column, and the corresponding derivative in the second column. For example, corresponding to the entry $y = x^2 e^x$ in the first column, there would be $y' = 2xe^x + x^2 e^x$ in the second column. Because integration is the reverse of differentiation, we infer the corresponding integration result that $\int (2xe^x + x^2 e^x) \, dx = x^2 e^x + C$ for a constant C.

Even after this superhuman effort, you would look in vain for e^{-x^2} in the second column of this table. The reason is that there is no "elementary" function that has e^{-x^2} as its derivative. Indeed, the integral of e^{-x^2} is used in the definition of a new very special "error function" that plays a prominent role in statistics because of its relationship to the "normal distribution" — see Exercises 4.9.5 and 10.7.12. A list of a few such impossible "integrals" is given in (10.3.9).

Using the proper rules systematically allows us to *differentiate* very complicated functions. On the other hand, finding the indefinite integral of even quite simple functions can be very difficult, or even impossible. Where it is possible, mathematicians have developed a number of *integration methods* to help in the task. Some of these methods will be explained in the rest of this chapter.

It is usually quite easy, however, to check whether a proposed indefinite integral is correct. We simply differentiate the proposed function to see if its derivative really is equal to the integrand.

EXAMPLE 10.1.3   Verify that, for $x > 0$, $\int \ln x \, dx = x \ln x - x + C$.

Solution: We put $F(x) = x \ln x - x + C$. Then

$$F'(x) = 1 \cdot \ln x + x \cdot (1/x) - 1 = \ln x + 1 - 1 = \ln x$$

which shows that the integral formula is correct.

Some General Rules

The two differentiation rules (5.7.1) and (5.7.2) immediately imply that $(aF(x))' = aF'(x)$ and $(F(x) + G(x))' = F'(x) + G'(x)$. These equalities then imply the following:

BASIC INTEGRATION RULES

$$\int af(x)\,dx = a \int f(x)\,dx, \text{ where } a \neq 0 \text{ is a constant} \qquad (10.1.8)$$

$$\int [f(x) + g(x)]\,dx = \int f(x)\,dx + \int g(x)\,dx \qquad (10.1.9)$$

Rule (10.1.8) says that a constant factor can be moved outside the integral, while rule (10.1.9) shows that the integral of a sum is the sum of the integrals. Repeated use of these two rules yields:

$$\int \left[a_1 f_1(x) + \cdots + a_n f_n(x) \right] dx = a_1 \int f_1(x)\,dx + \cdots + a_n \int f_n(x)\,dx \qquad (10.1.10)$$

EXAMPLE 10.1.4   Use (10.1.10) to evaluate: (a) $\int (3x^4 + 5x^2 + 2)\,dx$; (b) $\int \left(\dfrac{3}{x} - 8e^{-4x} \right) dx$.

Solution:

(a)
$$\int (3x^4 + 5x^2 + 2)\,dx = 3 \int x^4\,dx + 5 \int x^2\,dx + 2 \int 1\,dx$$

$$= 3 \left(\frac{1}{5}x^5 + C_1 \right) + 5 \left(\frac{1}{3}x^3 + C_2 \right) + 2(x + C_3)$$

$$= \frac{3}{5}x^5 + \frac{5}{3}x^3 + 2x + 3C_1 + 5C_2 + 2C_3$$

$$= \frac{3}{5}x^5 + \frac{5}{3}x^3 + 2x + C$$

Because C_1, C_2, and C_3 are arbitrary constants, $3C_1 + 5C_2 + 2C_3$ is also an arbitrary constant. So in the last line we have replaced it by just one constant C. In future examples of this kind, we will usually drop the two middle lines of the equations.

(b) $\int \left(3/x - 8e^{-4x} \right) dx = 3 \int (1/x)\,dx + (-8) \int e^{-4x}\,dx = 3 \ln |x| + 2e^{-4x} + C$

So far, we have always used x as the variable of integration. In applications, the variables often have other labels, but this makes no difference to the rules of integration.

EXAMPLE 10.1.5   Evaluate:

(a) $\int (B/r^{2.5})\,dr$ (b) $\int (a + bq + cq^2)\,dq$ (c) $\int (1 + t)^5\,dt$

Solution:

(a) Writing $B/r^{2.5}$ as $Br^{-2.5}$, formula (10.1.4) can be used with r replacing x, and so

$$\int \frac{B}{r^{2.5}}\,dr = B \int r^{-2.5}\,dr = B\frac{1}{-2.5 + 1}r^{-2.5+1} + C = -\frac{B}{1.5r^{1.5}} + C$$

(b) $\int (a + bq + cq^2)\, dq = aq + \frac{1}{2}bq^2 + \frac{1}{3}cq^3 + C$

(c) $\int (1 + t)^5\, dt = \frac{1}{6}(1 + t)^6 + C$

EXERCISES FOR SECTION 10.1

1. Find the following integrals by using formula (10.1.4):

(a) $\int x^{13}\, dx$ 　　(b) $\int x\sqrt{x}\, dx$ 　　(c) $\int \frac{1}{\sqrt{x}}\, dx$ 　　(d) $\int \sqrt{x\sqrt{x\sqrt{x}}}\, dx$

(e) $\int e^{-x}\, dx$ 　　(f) $\int e^{x/4}\, dx$ 　　(g) $\int 3e^{-2x}\, dx$ 　　(h) $\int 2^x\, dx$

2. In the manufacture of a product, the marginal cost of producing x units is $C'(x)$ and fixed costs are $C(0)$. Find the total cost function $C(x)$ when:

(a) $C'(x) = 3x + 4$ and $C(0) = 40$ 　　　　(b) $C'(x) = ax + b$ and $C(0) = C_0$

(SM) 3. Find the following integrals:

(a) $\int (t^3 + 2t - 3)\, dt$ 　　(b) $\int (x - 1)^2\, dx$ 　　(c) $\int (x - 1)(x + 2)\, dx$

(d) $\int (x + 2)^3\, dx$ 　　(e) $\int \left(e^{3x} - e^{2x} + e^x\right) dx$ 　　(f) $\int \frac{x^3 - 3x + 4}{x}\, dx$

(SM) 4. Find the following integrals:

(a) $\int \frac{(y - 2)^2}{\sqrt{y}}\, dy$ 　　(b) $\int \frac{x^3}{x + 1}\, dx$ 　　(c) $\int x(1 + x^2)^{15}\, dx$

(*Hints:* In part (a), first expand $(y - 2)^2$, and then divide each term by $\sqrt{y}$. In part (b), use polynomial division. In part (c), what is the derivative of $(1 + x^2)^{16}$?)

5. Show that

(a) $\int x^2 \ln x\, dx = \frac{1}{3}x^3 \ln x - \frac{1}{9}x^3 + C$

(b) $\int \sqrt{x^2 + 1}\, dx = \frac{1}{2}x\sqrt{x^2 + 1} + \frac{1}{2}\ln\left(x + \sqrt{x^2 + 1}\right) + C$

6. Suppose that $f(0) = 2$ and that the *derivative* of f has the graph given in Fig. 10.1.1. First suggest a formula for $f'(x)$, then sketch the graph of $f(x)$, and finally find an explicit function $f(x)$ which has this graph.

7. Suppose that $f(0) = 0$ and that the *derivative* of f has the graph given in Fig. 10.1.2. Sketch the graph of $f(x)$ and find an explicit function $f(x)$ which has this graph.

8. Prove that $\int 2x \ln(x^2 + a^2)\, dx = (x^2 + a^2) \ln(x^2 + a^2) - x^2 + C$.

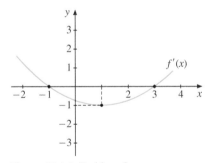

Figure 10.1.1 Problem 6

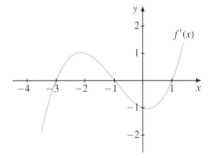

Figure 10.1.2 Problem 7

9. (a) Show that if $a \neq 0$ and $p \neq -1$ then $\int (ax+b)^p \, dx = \dfrac{1}{a(p+1)}(ax+b)^{p+1} + C$.

(b) Use part (a) to evaluate: (i) $\int (2x+1)^4 \, dx$; (ii) $\int \sqrt{x+2}\, dx$; and (iii) $\int \dfrac{1}{\sqrt{4-x}}\, dx$.

(c) Find $F(x)$ if: (i) $F'(x) = \frac{1}{2}e^x - 2x$ and $F(0) = \frac{1}{2}$; (ii) $F'(x) = x(1-x^2)$ and $F(1) = \frac{5}{12}$.

10. Find the general form of a function f whose second derivative is x^2. If we require in addition that $f(0) = 1$ and $f'(0) = -1$, what is $f(x)$?

SM 11. Suppose that $f''(x) = x^{-2} + x^3 + 2$ for $x > 0$, and $f(1) = 0$, $f'(1) = 1/4$. Find $f(x)$.

10.2 Area and Definite Integrals

This section will show how the concept of the integral can be used to calculate the area of many plane regions. This problem has been important in economics for over 4000 years. Like all major rivers, the Tigris and Euphrates in Mesopotamia (now part of Iraq) and the Nile in Egypt would occasionally change course as a result of severe floods. Some farmers would gain new land from the river, while others would lose land. Since taxes were often assessed on land area, it became necessary to re-calculate the area of a parcel of land whose boundary might be an irregularly shaped river bank.

Rather later, but still around 360 *b.c.*, the Greek mathematician Eudoxos developed a general *method of exhaustion* for determining the areas of irregularly shaped plane regions. The idea was to exhaust the area by inscribing within it an expanding sequence of polygonal regions, whose area can be calculated exactly by summing the areas of a finite collection of triangles. Provided this sequence does indeed "exhaust" the area by including every point in the limit, we can define the *area* of the region as the limit of the increasing sequence of areas of the inscribed polygonal regions. Moreover, one can bound the error of any finite approximation by circumscribing the region within a decreasing sequence of polygonal regions, whose intersection is the region itself.

Eudoxos and Archimedes, amongst others, used the method of exhaustion in order to determine quite accurate approximations to the areas of a number of specific plane regions, especially for a circular disk. The method was able to provide exact answers, however, only for a limited number of special cases, largely because of the algebraic problems encountered. Nearly 1900 years passed after Eudoxos before an exact method could be devised, combining what we now call integration with the new differential calculus due to Newton and Leibniz. Besides allowing areas to be measured with complete accuracy, their ideas have many other applications. Demonstrating the precise logical relationship between differentiation and integration is one of the main achievements of mathematical analysis. It has even been argued that this discovery is the single most important in all of science.

The problem to be considered and solved in this section is illustrated in Fig. 10.2.1: *How do we compute the area A under the graph of a continuous and nonnegative function f over the interval* $[a, b]$?

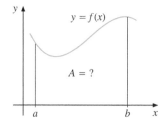

Figure 10.2.1 Area A under the graph

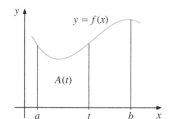

Figure 10.2.2 Area $A(t)$ under the graph up to t

Let t be an arbitrary point in $[a, b]$, and let $A(t)$ denote the area under the curve $y = f(x)$ over the interval $[a, t]$, as shown in Fig. 10.2.2. Clearly, $A(a) = 0$, because there is no area from a to a. On the other hand, the area in Fig. 10.2.1 is $A = A(b)$. It is obvious from Fig. 10.2.2 that, because f is always positive, $A(t)$ increases as t increases. Suppose we increase t by a positive amount Δt. Then $A(t + \Delta t)$ is the area under the curve $y = f(x)$ over the interval $[a, t + \Delta t]$. Hence, $A(t + \Delta t) - A(t)$ is the area ΔA under the curve over the interval $[t, t + \Delta t]$, as shown in Fig. 10.2.3.

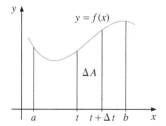

Figure 10.2.3 Change in area, ΔA

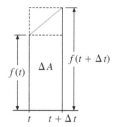

Figure 10.2.4 Approximating ΔA

In Fig. 10.2.4, the area ΔA has been magnified. It cannot be larger than the area of the rectangle with base Δt and height $f(t + \Delta t)$, nor smaller than the area of the rectangle with base Δt and height $f(t)$. Hence, for all $\Delta t > 0$, one has

$$f(t)\Delta t \leq A(t + \Delta t) - A(t) \leq f(t + \Delta t)\Delta t \qquad (*)$$

Because $\Delta t > 0$, this implies

$$f(t) \le \frac{A(t + \Delta t) - A(t)}{\Delta t} \le f(t + \Delta t) \qquad (**)$$

Let us consider what happens to $(**)$ as $\Delta t \to 0$. The interval $[t, t + \Delta t]$ shrinks to the single point t, and by continuity of f, the value $f(t + \Delta t)$ approaches $f(t)$. The Newton quotient $[A(t + \Delta t) - A(t)]/\Delta t$ is squeezed between $f(t)$ and a quantity $f(t + \Delta t)$ that tends to $f(t)$. This quotient must therefore tend to $f(t)$ in the limit as $\Delta t \to 0$.

So we arrive at the remarkable conclusion that the function $A(t)$, which measures the area under the graph of f over the interval $[a, t]$, is differentiable, with derivative given by

$$A'(t) = f(t), \quad \text{for all } t \text{ in } (a, b) \qquad (***)$$

This proves that:

The derivative of the area function $A(t)$ is the curve's "height" function $f(t)$, and the area function is therefore one of the indefinite integrals of $f(t)$.[1]

Let us now use x as the free variable, and suppose that $F(x)$ is an arbitrary indefinite integral of $f(x)$. Then $A(x) = F(x) + C$ for some constant C. Recall that $A(a) = 0$. Hence, $0 = A(a) = F(a) + C$, so $C = -F(a)$. Therefore,

$$A(x) = F(x) - F(a), \quad \text{where } F(x) = \int f(x)\, dx \qquad (10.2.1)$$

Suppose $G(x)$ is another function with $G'(x) = f(x)$. Then $G(x) = F(x) + C_1$ for some other constant C_1, and so $G(x) - G(a) = F(x) + C_1 - (F(a) + C_1) = F(x) - F(a)$. This argument tells us that the area we compute using (10.2.1) is independent of which indefinite integral of f we choose.

EXAMPLE 10.2.1   Calculate the area under the parabola $f(x) = x^2$ over the interval $[0, 1]$.

Solution: The area in question is the shaded region in Fig. 10.2.5. The area is equal to $A = F(1) - F(0)$ where $F(x)$ is an indefinite integral of x^2. Now, $\int x^2\, dx = \frac{1}{3}x^3 + C$, so we choose $F(x) = \frac{1}{3}x^3$. Thus the required area is

$$A = F(1) - F(0) = \frac{1}{3} \cdot 1^3 - \frac{1}{3} \cdot 0^3 = \frac{1}{3}$$

Figure 10.2.5 suggests that this answer is reasonable, because the shaded region appears to have roughly 1/3 the area of a square whose side is of length 1.

---

[1] The function f in the figures is increasing in the interval $[t, t + \Delta t]$. It is easy to see that the same conclusion is obtained whenever the function f is continuous on the closed interval $[t, t + \Delta t]$. On the left-hand side of $(*)$, just replace $f(t)$ by $f(c)$, where c is a minimum point of the continuous function f in the interval; and on the right-hand side, replace $f(t + \Delta t)$ by $f(d)$, where d is a maximum point of f in $[t, t + \Delta t]$. By continuity, both $f(c)$ and $f(d)$ must tend to $f(t)$ as $\Delta t \to 0$. So $(***)$ holds also for general continuous functions f.

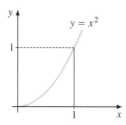

Figure 10.2.5 $y = x^2$

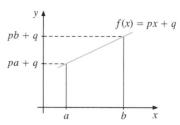

Figure 10.2.6 $y = px + q$

The argument leading to (10.2.1) is based on rather intuitive considerations. Formally, mathematicians choose to *define* the area under the graph of a continuous and nonnegative function f over the interval $[a, b]$ as the number $F(b) - F(a)$, where $F'(x) = f(x)$. The concept of area that emerges agrees with the usual concept for regions bounded by straight lines. The next example verifies this in a special case.

EXAMPLE 10.2.2   Find the area A under the straight line $f(x) = px + q$ over the interval $[a, b]$, where $a, b, p,$ and q are all positive, with $b > a$.

Solution: The area is shown shaded in Fig. 10.2.6. It is equal to $F(b) - F(a)$ where $F(x)$ is an indefinite integral of $px + q$. Now, $\int (px + q)\,dx = \frac{1}{2}px^2 + qx + C$. The obvious choice of an indefinite integral is $F(x) = \frac{1}{2}px^2 + qx$, and so

$$A = F(b) - F(a) = \left(\frac{1}{2}pb^2 + qb\right) - \left(\frac{1}{2}pa^2 + qa\right) = \frac{1}{2}p(b^2 - a^2) + q(b - a)$$

As Fig. 10.2.6 shows, the area A is the sum of a rectangle whose area is $(b - a)(pa + q)$, and a triangle whose area is $\frac{1}{2}p(b - a)^2$, which you should check gives the same answer.

The Definite Integral

Let f be a continuous function defined in the interval $[a, b]$. Suppose that the function F is continuous in $[a, b]$ and has a derivative with $F'(x) = f(x)$ for every x in (a, b). Then the difference $F(b) - F(a)$ is called the *definite integral* of f over $[a, b]$. We observed above that this difference does not depend on which of the indefinite integrals of f we choose as F. The definite integral of f over $[a, b]$ is therefore a *number* that depends only on the function f and the numbers a and b. We denote this number by

$$\int_a^b f(x)\,dx \tag{10.2.2}$$

This notation makes explicit the function $f(x)$ we integrate and the interval of integration $[a, b]$. The numbers a and b are called, respectively, the *lower* and *upper limit of integration*.

The variable x in Eq. (10.2.2) is a *dummy variable* in the sense that it could be replaced by any other variable that does not occur elsewhere in the expression. For instance,

$$\int_a^b f(x)\,\mathrm{d}x = \int_a^b f(y)\,\mathrm{d}y = \int_a^b f(\xi)\,\mathrm{d}\xi$$

are all equal to $F(b) - F(a)$. But do not write anything like $\int_a^y f(y)\,\mathrm{d}y$, with the same variable as both the upper limit and the dummy variable of integration, because that is meaningless.

The difference $F(b) - F(a)$ is denoted by $\big|_a^b F(x)$, or by $[F(x)]_a^b$. Thus:

THE DEFINITE INTEGRAL

$$\int_a^b f(x)\,\mathrm{d}x = \bigg|_a^b F(x) = F(b) - F(a) \tag{10.2.3}$$

where F is any indefinite integral of f over an interval containing both a and b.

EXAMPLE 10.2.3   Evaluate the definite integrals: (a) $\int_2^5 e^{2x}\,\mathrm{d}x$; (b) $\int_{-2}^2 \left(x - x^3 - x^5\right)\,\mathrm{d}x$.

Solution:

(a) Here $\int e^{2x}\,\mathrm{d}x = \tfrac{1}{2}e^{2x} + C$, so $\int_2^5 e^{2x}\,\mathrm{d}x = \big|_2^5 \tfrac{1}{2}e^{2x} = \tfrac{1}{2}e^{10} - \tfrac{1}{2}e^4 = \tfrac{1}{2}e^4(e^6 - 1)$.

(b) $\int_{-2}^2 (x - x^3 - x^5)\,\mathrm{d}x = \big|_{-2}^2 \left(\tfrac{1}{2}x^2 - \tfrac{1}{4}x^4 - \tfrac{1}{6}x^6\right) = \left(2 - 4 - \tfrac{64}{6}\right) - \left(2 - 4 - \tfrac{64}{6}\right) = 0$.

After reading the next subsection and realizing that the graph of $f(x) = x - x^3 - x^5$ is symmetric about the origin, you should understand better why the answer to part (b) must be 0.

Definition (10.2.1) does not necessarily require $a < b$. However, if $a > b$ and $f(x)$ is positive throughout the interval $[b, a]$, then $\int_a^b f(x)\,\mathrm{d}x$ is a negative number. Note, also, that in (10.2.1) we have defined the definite integral without necessarily giving it a geometric interpretation as the area under a curve. In fact, depending on the context, it can have different interpretations. For instance, if $f(r)$ is an income density function, as in Section 10.4 below, then $\int_a^b f(r)\mathrm{d}r$ is the proportion of people with income between a and b.

Although the notation for definite and indefinite integrals is similar, the two integrals are entirely different. In fact, $\int_a^b f(x)\,\mathrm{d}x$ denotes a single number, whereas $\int f(x)\,\mathrm{d}x$ represents any one of the infinite set of functions that all have $f(x)$ as their derivative.

The Area when $f(x)$ is Negative

If $f(x) \geq 0$ over $[a, b]$, then $\int_a^b f(x)\,\mathrm{d}x$ is the area below the graph of f over $[a, b]$. If f is defined in $[a, b]$ and $f(x) \leq 0$ for all x in $[a, b]$, then the graph of f, the x-axis, and the lines $x = a$ and $x = b$ still enclose an area, shown as area A in Fig. 10.2.7. Defining $g(x) = -f(x)$,

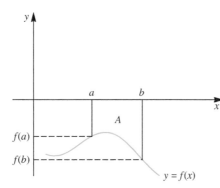

Figure 10.2.7 $f(x) \leq 0$

Figure 10.2.8 $g(x) = -f(x) \geq 0$

we have $g(x) \geq 0$, so that $\int_a^b g(x)\,dx$ measures the area below the graph of g over $[a, b]$. But it follows, by construction, that this is the same as area A, as depicted in Fig. 10.2.8. It follows, then, that the area over f and under $[a, b]$ is $\int_a^b (-f)(x)\,dx$, with a minus sign before the integrand because the area of a region must be positive (or zero), whereas the definite integral of f is negative. Shortly, in Section 10.3, we will see that we can equivalently put the minus sign in front of the integral: see rule (10.3.3).

EXAMPLE 10.2.4   Figure 10.2.9 shows the graph of $f(x) = e^{x/3} - 3$. Evaluate the shaded area A between the x-axis and this graph over the interval $[0, b]$, where $b = 3 \ln 3$ is chosen because there $f(b) = 0$.

Solution: Because $f(x) \leq 0$ in the interval $[0, 3 \ln 3]$, we obtain

$$A = -\int_0^{3\ln 3} \left(e^{x/3} - 3\right) dx = -\bigg|_0^{3\ln 3} (3e^{x/3} - 3x) = -(3e^{\ln 3} - 3 \cdot 3\ln 3) + 3e^0$$

$$= -9 + 9\ln 3 + 3 = 9\ln 3 - 6 \approx 3.89$$

Is the answer reasonable? Yes, because the shaded set in Fig. 10.2.9 seems to have an area somewhat less than that of the triangle enclosed by the points $(0, 0)$, $(0, -2)$, and $(4, 0)$, whose area is 4, and a little more than the area of the inscribed triangle with vertices $(0, 0)$, $(0, -2)$, and $(3\ln 3, 0)$, whose area is $3\ln 3 \approx 3.30$.

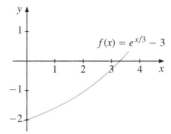

Figure 10.2.9 $e^{x/3} - 3$

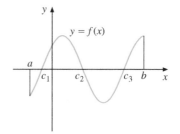

Figure 10.2.10 A function that takes positive and negative values

Suppose the function f is defined and continuous in $[a, b]$, and that it is positive in some subintervals, negative in others, as shown in Fig. 10.2.10. Let c_1, c_2, c_3 denote three roots of the equation $f(x) = 0$—that is, three points where the graph crosses the x-axis. The definite integral $\int_a^b f(x)\,dx$ is the sum of the two shaded areas above the x-axis, minus the sum of the two shaded areas below the x-axis. The total area bounded by the graph of f, the x-axis, and the lines $x = a$ and $x = b$, on the other hand, is calculated by computing the positive areas in each subinterval $[a, c_1]$, $[c_1, c_2]$, $[c_2, c_3]$, and $[c_3, b]$ in turn according to the previous definitions, and then adding these areas. Specifically, the total shaded area is

$$ -\int_a^{c_1} f(x)\,dx + \int_{c_1}^{c_2} f(x)\,dx - \int_{c_2}^{c_3} f(x)\,dx + \int_{c_3}^{b} f(x)\,dx $$

In fact, this illustrates a general result: the area between the graph of a function f and the x-axis is given by the definite integral $\int_a^b |f(x)|\,dx$ of the absolute value of the integrand $f(x)$, which equals the area under the graph of the nonnegative-valued function $|f(x)|$.

EXERCISES FOR SECTION 10.2

1. Compute the areas under the graphs, over $[0, 1]$, of: (a) $f(x) = x^2$; (b) $f(x) = x^{10}$.

2. Compute the area bounded by the graph of the function over the indicated interval. In (c), sketch the graph and indicate by shading the area in question.

(a) $f(x) = 3x^2$, in $[0, 2]$ (b) $f(x) = x^6$, in $[0, 1]$

(c) $f(x) = e^x$, in $[-1, 1]$ (d) $f(x) = 1/x^2$, in $[1, 10]$

3. Compute the area bounded by the graph of $f(x) = 1/x^3$, the x-axis, and the two lines $x = -2$ and $x = -1$. Make a drawing. (*Hint:* $f(x) < 0$ in $[-2, -1]$.)

4. Compute the area bounded by the graph of $f(x) = \frac{1}{2}(e^x + e^{-x})$, the x-axis, and the lines $x = -1$ and $x = 1$.

(SM) **5.** Evaluate the following integrals:

(a) $\displaystyle\int_0^1 x\,dx$ (b) $\displaystyle\int_1^2 (2x + x^2)\,dx$ (c) $\displaystyle\int_{-2}^3 \left(\frac{1}{2}x^2 - \frac{1}{3}x^3\right)dx$

(d) $\displaystyle\int_0^2 (t^3 - t^4)\,dt$ (e) $\displaystyle\int_1^2 \left(2t^5 - \frac{1}{t^2}\right)dt$ (f) $\displaystyle\int_2^3 \left(\frac{1}{t-1} + t\right)dt$

(SM) **6.** Let $f(x) = x(x - 1)(x - 2)$.

(a) Calculate $f'(x)$. Where is $f(x)$ increasing?

(b) Sketch the graph and calculate $\int_0^1 f(x)\,dx$.

7. The profit of a firm as a function of its output $x > 0$ is given by

$$f(x) = 4000 - x - \frac{3\,000\,000}{x}$$

   (a) Find the level of output that maximizes profit. Sketch the graph of f.

   (b) The actual output varies between 1000 and 3000 units. Compute the average profit

$$I = \frac{1}{2000} \int\limits_{1000}^{3000} f(x)\,dx$$

8. Evaluate the integrals

   (a) $\displaystyle\int\limits_{1}^{3} \frac{3x}{10}\,dx$ (b) $\displaystyle\int\limits_{-3}^{-1} \xi^2\,d\xi$ (c) $\displaystyle\int\limits_{0}^{1} \alpha e^{\beta\tau}\,d\tau$, with $\beta \neq 0$ (d) $\displaystyle\int\limits_{-2}^{-1} \frac{1}{y}\,dy$

10.3 Properties of Definite Integrals

From the definition of the definite integral, a number of properties can be derived.

PROPERTIES OF DEFINITE INTEGRALS

If f is a continuous function in an interval that contains the points a, b, and c, then

$$\int\limits_{a}^{b} f(x)\,dx = -\int\limits_{b}^{a} f(x)\,dx \tag{10.3.1}$$

$$\int\limits_{a}^{a} f(x)\,dx = 0 \tag{10.3.2}$$

$$\int\limits_{a}^{b} \alpha f(x)\,dx = \alpha \int\limits_{a}^{b} f(x)\,dx, \quad \text{where } \alpha \text{ is an arbitrary number} \tag{10.3.3}$$

and

$$\int\limits_{a}^{b} f(x)\,dx = \int\limits_{a}^{c} f(x)\,dx + \int\limits_{c}^{b} f(x)\,dx \tag{10.3.4}$$

When the definite integral is interpreted as an area, (10.3.4) is the additivity property of areas, as illustrated in Fig. 10.3.1. Of course, rule (10.3.4) easily generalizes to the case in which we partition the interval $[a, b]$ into an arbitrary finite number of subintervals.

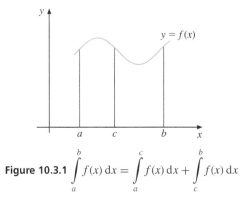

Figure 10.3.1 $\displaystyle\int\limits_a^b f(x)\,dx = \int\limits_a^c f(x)\,dx + \int\limits_c^b f(x)\,dx$

Equations (10.3.3) and (10.3.4) are counterparts for definite integrals of, respectively, the constant multiple property (10.1.8) and the summation property (10.1.9) for indefinite integrals. In fact, if f and g are continuous in $[a, b]$, and if α and β are real numbers, then it is easy to prove that

$$\int\limits_a^b [\alpha f(x) + \beta g(x)]\,dx = \alpha \int\limits_a^b f(x)\,dx + \beta \int\limits_a^b g(x)\,dx \qquad (10.3.5)$$

Again, this rule can obviously be extended to more than two functions.

Differentiation with Respect to the Limits of Integration

Suppose that $F'(x) = f(x)$ for all x in an open interval (a, b). Suppose too that $a < t < b$. It follows that $\int_a^t f(x)\,dx = \big|_a^t F(x) = F(t) - F(a)$, so

$$\frac{d}{dt}\int\limits_a^t f(x)\,dx = F'(t) = f(t) \qquad (10.3.6)$$

In words: *The derivative of the definite integral with respect to the upper limit of integration is equal to the integrand evaluated at that limit.*

Correspondingly, $\int_t^b f(x)\,dx = \big|_t^b F(x) = F(b) - F(t)$, so that

$$\frac{d}{dt}\int\limits_t^b f(x)\,dx = -F'(t) = -f(t) \qquad (10.3.7)$$

In words: *The derivative of the definite integral with respect to the lower limit of integration is equal to minus the integrand evaluated at that limit.*

These results are not surprising: Suppose that $f(x) \geq 0$ and $t < b$. We can interpret $\int_t^b f(x)\,dx$ as the area below the graph of f over the interval $[t, b]$. Then the interval shrinks as t increases, and the area will decrease by the value of the integrand at the lower limit.

The results in (10.3.6) and (10.3.7) can be generalized. In fact, if $a(t)$ and $b(t)$ are differentiable and $f(x)$ is continuous, then

$$\frac{d}{dt} \int_{a(t)}^{b(t)} f(x)\, dx = f(b(t))b'(t) - f(a(t))a'(t) \tag{10.3.8}$$

To prove this formula, suppose F is an indefinite integral of f, so that $F'(x) = f(x)$. Then $\int_u^v f(x)\, dx = F(v) - F(u)$, so in particular,

$$\int_{a(t)}^{b(t)} f(x)\, dx = F(b(t)) - F(a(t))$$

Using the chain rule to differentiate the right-hand side of this equation w.r.t. t, we obtain $F'(b(t))b'(t) - F'(a(t))a'(t)$. But $F'(b(t)) = f(b(t))$ and $F'(a(t)) = f(a(t))$, so Eq.(10.3.8) holds.[2]

Continuous Functions are Integrable

Suppose $f(x)$ is a continuous function in $[a, b]$. Then we defined $\int_a^b f(x)\, dx$ as the number $F(b) - F(a)$, provided that $F(x)$ is some function whose derivative is $f(x)$. In some cases, we are able to find an explicit expression for $F(x)$. But this is not always the case. For example, it is impossible to find an explicit standard function of x whose derivative is the positive valued function $f(x) = (1/\sqrt{2\pi})e^{-x^2/2}$, the standard normal density function in statistics, whose graph is shown in the answer to Exercise 4.9.5. Yet $f(x)$ is continuous on any interval $[a, b]$ of the real line, so the area under the graph of f over this interval definitely exists and is equal to $\int_a^b f(x)\, dx$.

In fact, one can prove that any continuous function has an antiderivative. Here are some integrals that really are impossible to "solve", except by introducing special new functions:

$$\int e^{x^2}\, dx, \quad \int e^{-x^2}\, dx, \quad \int \frac{e^x}{x}\, dx, \quad \int \frac{1}{\ln x}\, dx, \quad \text{and} \quad \int \frac{1}{\sqrt{x^4 + 1}}\, dx \tag{10.3.9}$$

The Riemann Integral

The kind of integral discussed so far, which is based on the antiderivative, is called the *Newton–Leibniz, or N–L, integral*. Several other kinds of integral are considered by mathematicians. For continuous functions, they all give the same result as the N–L integral. We briefly sketch the so-called *Riemann integral*. The idea behind the definition is closely related to the exhaustion method that was described in Section 10.2.

Let f be a *bounded* function in the interval $[a, b]$, and let n be a natural number. Subdivide $[a, b]$ into n parts by choosing points $a = x_0 < x_1 < x_2 < \cdots < x_{n-1} < x_n = b$. Let $\Delta x_i = x_{i+1} - x_i$, $i = 0, 1, \ldots, n - 1$, and choose an arbitrary number ξ_i in each interval $[x_i, x_{i+1}]$. Then the sum

$$f(\xi_0)\Delta x_0 + f(\xi_1)\Delta x_1 + \cdots + f(\xi_{n-1})\Delta x_{n-1} \tag{10.3.10}$$

---

[2] Formula (10.3.8) is a special case of Leibniz's formula discussed in FMEA, Section 3.3.

is called *a Riemann sum* associated with the function f. You should draw a figure to help understand this construction.

The sum (10.3.10) depends on f as well as on the subdivision and on the choice of the different points ξ_i. Suppose however that, when n approaches infinity and simultaneously the largest of the numbers $\Delta x_0, \Delta x_1, \ldots, \Delta x_{n-1}$ approaches 0, the limit of the sum exists. Then f is called *Riemann, or R, integrable* in the interval $[a, b]$, and we put

$$\int_a^b f(x)\,dx = \lim \sum_{i=0}^{n-1} f(\xi_i)\Delta x_i$$

Textbooks on mathematical analysis show that the value of the integral is independent of how the ξ_i are chosen. They also show that every continuous function is R integrable, and that the R integral in this case satisfies (10.2.3). The N–L integral and the R integral thus coincide for continuous functions. But the R integral is defined for some (discontinuous) functions whose N–L integral does not exist.

EXERCISES FOR SECTION 10.3

1. Evaluate the following integrals:

(a) $\displaystyle\int_0^5 (x + x^2)\,dx$ (b) $\displaystyle\int_{-2}^2 (e^x - e^{-x})\,dx$ (c) $\displaystyle\int_2^{10} \frac{1}{x-1}\,dx$ (d) $\displaystyle\int_0^1 2xe^{x^2}\,dx$

(e) $\displaystyle\int_{-4}^4 (x-1)^3\,dx$ (f) $\displaystyle\int_1^2 (x^5 + x^{-5})\,dx$ (g) $\displaystyle\int_0^4 \frac{1}{2}\sqrt{x}\,dx$ (h) $\displaystyle\int_1^2 \frac{1 + x^3}{x^2}\,dx$

2. If $\int_a^b f(x)\,dx = 8$ and $\int_a^c f(x)\,dx = 4$, what is $\int_c^b f(x)\,dx$?

3. If $\int_0^1 (f(x) - 2g(x))\,dx = 6$ and $\int_0^1 (2f(x) + 2g(x))\,dx = 9$, find $I = \int_0^1 (f(x) - g(x))\,dx$.

(SM) **4.** Let p, q, and r be positive constants. Evaluate the integral $\int_0^1 x^p(x^q + x^r)\,dx$.

(SM) **5.** Find the function $f(x)$ if $f'(x) = ax^2 + bx$, and the following three equations all hold:

(i) $f'(1) = 6$ (ii) $f''(1) = 18$ (iii) $\int_0^2 f(x)\,dx = 18$

(SM) **6.** Evaluate the following integrals, assuming, in (d), that all constants are positive:

(a) $\displaystyle\int_0^3 \left(\frac{1}{3}e^{3t-2} + (t+2)^{-1}\right) dt$ (b) $\displaystyle\int_0^1 (x^2 + 2)^2\,dx$

(c) $\displaystyle\int_0^1 \frac{x^2 + x + \sqrt{x+1}}{x+1}\,dx$ (d) $\displaystyle\int_1^b \left(A\frac{x+b}{x+c} + \frac{d}{x}\right) dx$

7. Let $F(x) = \int_0^x (t^2 + 2)\,dt$ and $G(x) = \int_0^{x^2} (t^2 + 2)\,dt$. Find $F'(x)$ and $G'(x)$.

8. Define $H(t) = \int_0^{t^2} K(\tau) e^{-\rho\tau} \, d\tau$, where $K(\tau)$ is a given continuous function and ρ is a constant. Find $H'(t)$.

9. Find:

(a) $\dfrac{d}{dt} \displaystyle\int_0^t x^2 \, dx$

(b) $\dfrac{d}{dt} \displaystyle\int_t^3 e^{-x^2} \, dx$

(c) $\dfrac{d}{dt} \displaystyle\int_{-t}^t \dfrac{1}{\sqrt{x^4 + 1}} \, dx$

(d) $\dfrac{d}{d\lambda} \displaystyle\int_{-\lambda}^2 (f(t) - g(t)) \, dt$

10. Find the area between the two parabolas defined by the equations $y + 1 = (x - 1)^2$ and $3x = y^2$. (*Hint:* The points of intersection have integer coordinates.)

(SM) **11.** [HARDER] A theory of investment has used a function W defined for all $T > 0$ by

$$W(T) = \frac{K}{T} \int_0^T e^{-\rho t} \, dt$$

where K and ρ are positive constants. Evaluate the integral, then prove that $W(T)$ takes values in the interval $(0, K)$ and is strictly decreasing. (*Hint:* See Exercise 6.11.11.)

(SM) **12.** [HARDER] Consider the function f defined, for $x > 0$, by $f(x) = 4 \ln(\sqrt{x + 4} - 2)$.

(a) Show that f has an inverse function g, and find a formula for g.

(b) Draw the graphs of f and g in the same coordinate system.

(c) Give a geometric interpretation of $A = \int_5^{10} 4 \ln(\sqrt{x + 4} - 2) \, dx$, and explain why

$$A = 10a - \int_0^a (e^{x/2} + 4e^{x/4}) \, dx$$

where $a = f(10)$. Use this equality to express A in terms of a.

10.4 Economic Applications

We motivated the definite integral as a tool for computing the area under a curve. However, the integral has many other important interpretations. In statistics, many important probability distributions are expressed as integrals of continuous probability density functions. This section presents some other examples showing why integrals are important in economics.

Extraction from an Oil Well

Assume that at time $t = 0$ an oil producer starts extracting oil from a well that contains K barrels at that time. Let us define $x(t)$ as the number of barrels of oil that is left at time t.

In particular, $x(0) = K$. Assuming it is impractical to put oil back into the well, $x(t)$ is a decreasing function of t. The amount of oil that is extracted in a time interval $[t, t + \Delta t]$, where $\Delta t > 0$, is $x(t) - x(t + \Delta t)$. Extraction per unit of time is, therefore,

$$\frac{x(t) - x(t + \Delta t)}{\Delta t} = -\frac{x(t + \Delta t) - x(t)}{\Delta t} \tag{$*$}$$

If we assume that $x(t)$ is differentiable, then as $\Delta t \to 0$ the fraction $(*)$ tends to $-\dot{x}(t)$. Letting $u(t)$ denote the *rate of extraction* at time t, we have $\dot{x}(t) = -u(t)$, with $x(0) = K$. The solution to this equation is

$$x(t) = K - \int_0^t u(\tau)\,d\tau \tag{$**$}$$

Indeed, we check $(**)$ as follows. First, setting $t = 0$ gives $x(0) = K$. Moreover, differentiating $(**)$ w.r.t. t according to rule (10.3.6) yields $\dot{x}(t) = -u(t)$.

The result $(**)$ may be interpreted as follows: The amount of oil left at time t is equal to the initial amount K, minus the total amount that has been extracted during the time span $[0, t]$, namely $\int_0^t u(\tau)\,d\tau$.

If the rate of extraction is constant, with $u(t) = \bar{u}$, then $(**)$ yields

$$x(t) = K - \int_0^t \bar{u}\,d\tau = K - \Big|_0^t \bar{u}\tau = K - \bar{u}t$$

In particular, the well will be empty when $x(t) = 0$, or when $K - \bar{u}t = 0$, that is when $t = K/\bar{u}$. (Of course, this particular answer could have been found more directly, without recourse to integration.)

The example illustrates two concepts that it is important to distinguish in many economic arguments. The quantity $x(t)$ is a *stock*, measured in barrels. On the other hand, $u(t)$ is a *flow*, measured in barrels *per unit of time*.

Income Distribution

In many countries, data collected by income tax authorities can be used to reveal some properties of the income distribution within a given year, as well as how the distribution changes from year to year. Suppose we measure annual income in dollars and let $F(r)$ denote the proportion of individuals that receive no more than r dollars in a particular year. Thus, if there are n individuals in the population, $nF(r)$ is the number of individuals with income no greater than r. If r_0 is the lowest and r_1 is the highest (registered) income in the group, we are interested in the function F defined on the interval $[r_0, r_1]$. By definition, F is not continuous and therefore also not differentiable in $[r_0, r_1]$, because r has to be a multiple of \$0.01 and $F(r)$ has to be a multiple of $1/n$. However, if the population consists of a large number of individuals, then it is usually possible to find a "smooth" function that gives a good approximation to the true income distribution. Assume, therefore, that F is a function with a continuous derivative denoted by f, so that $f(r) = F'(r)$ for all r in (r_0, r_1).

According to the definition of the derivative, we have

$$f(r)\Delta r \approx F(r + \Delta r) - F(r)$$

for all small Δr. Thus, $f(r)\Delta r$ is approximately equal to the proportion of individuals who have incomes between r and $r + \Delta r$. The function f is called an *income density function*, and F is the associated *cumulative distribution function*.[3]

Suppose that f is a continuous income distribution for a certain population with incomes in the interval $[r_0, r_1]$. If $r_0 \le a \le b \le r_1$, then the previous discussion and the definition of the definite integral imply that $\int_a^b f(r)dr$ is the proportion of individuals with incomes in $[a, b]$. Thus,

$$N = n \int_a^b f(r)\, dr \tag{10.4.1}$$

is the *number of individuals* with incomes in $[a, b]$.

We will now find an expression for the combined income of those who earn between a and b dollars. Let $M(r)$ denote the total income of those who earn no more than r dollars during the year, and consider the income interval $[r, r + \Delta r]$. There are approximately $nf(r)\Delta r$ individuals with incomes in this interval. Each of them has an income approximately equal to r, so that the total income of these individuals, $M(r + \Delta r) - M(r)$, is approximately equal to $nrf(r)\Delta r$. So we have

$$\frac{M(r + \Delta r) - M(r)}{\Delta r} \approx nrf(r)$$

The approximation improves (in general) as Δr decreases. By taking the limit as $\Delta r \to 0$, we obtain $M'(r) = nrf(r)$. Integrating over the interval from a to b gives $M(b) - M(a) = n\int_a^b rf(r)dr$. Hence,

$$M = n \int_a^b rf(r)\, dr \tag{10.4.2}$$

is the *total income* of individuals with income in $[a, b]$.

The argument that leads to (10.4.2) can be made more exact: $M(r + \Delta r) - M(r)$ is the total income of those who have income in the interval $[r, r + \Delta r]$, when $\Delta r > 0$. In this income interval, there are $n[F(r + \Delta r) - F(r)]$ individuals each of whom earns at least r and at most $r + \Delta r$. Thus,

$$nr\,[F(r + \Delta r) - F(r)] \le M(r + \Delta r) - M(r) \le n(r + \Delta r)\,[F(r + \Delta r) - F(r)] \tag{$*$}$$

If $\Delta r > 0$, division by Δr yields

$$nr\frac{F(r + \Delta r) - F(r)}{\Delta r} \le \frac{M(r + \Delta r) - M(r)}{\Delta r} \le n(r + \Delta r)\frac{F(r + \Delta r) - F(r)}{\Delta r} \tag{$**$}$$

---

[3] Readers who know some statistics may see the analogy with probability density functions and with cumulative (probability) distribution functions.

(If $\Delta r < 0$, then the inequalities in $(*)$ are left unchanged, whereas those in $(**)$ are reversed.) Letting $\Delta r \to 0$ gives $nrF'(r) \leq M'(r) \leq nrF'(r)$, so that $M'(r) = nrF'(r) = nrf(r)$.

The ratio between the total income and the number of individuals belonging to a certain income interval $[a, b]$ is called the mean income for the individuals in this income interval. Therefore, the *mean income* of individuals with incomes in the interval $[a, b]$ is:

$$m = \frac{\int_a^b rf(r)\, dr}{\int_a^b f(r)\, dr} \tag{10.4.3}$$

A function that approximates actual income distributions quite well, particularly for large incomes, is the *Pareto distribution*. In this case, the proportion of individuals who earn at most r dollars is given by

$$f(r) = \frac{B}{r^\beta} \tag{10.4.4}$$

Here B and β are positive constants. Empirical estimates of β are usually in the range $2.4 < \beta < 2.6$. For values of r close to 0, the formula is of no use. In fact, the integral $\int_0^a f(r)\, dr$ diverges to ∞, as will be seen using the arguments of Section 10.7.

EXAMPLE 10.4.1   Consider a population of n individuals in which the income density function for those with incomes between a and b is given by $f(r) = B/r^{2.5}$. Here $b > a > 0$, and B is positive. Determine the mean income of this group.

Solution: According to (10.4.1), the total number of individuals in this group is

$$N = n \int_a^b Br^{-2.5}\, dr = nB \Big|_a^b \left(-\tfrac{2}{3} r^{-1.5}\right) = \tfrac{2}{3} nB \left(a^{-1.5} - b^{-1.5}\right)$$

According to (10.4.2), the total income of these individuals is

$$M = n \int_a^b rBr^{-2.5}\, dr = nB \int_a^b r^{-1.5}\, dr = -2nB \Big|_a^b r^{-0.5} = 2nB \left(a^{-0.5} - b^{-0.5}\right)$$

So the mean income of the group is

$$m = \frac{M}{N} = 3\frac{a^{-0.5} - b^{-0.5}}{a^{-1.5} - b^{-1.5}}$$

by (10.4.3). Suppose that b is very large. Then $b^{-0.5}$ and $b^{-1.5}$ are both close to 0, and so $m \approx 3a$. The mean income of those who earn at least a is therefore approximately $3a$.

The Influence of Income Distribution on Demand

Obviously each consumer's demand for a particular commodity depends on its price p. In addition, economists soon learn that it depends on the consumer's income r as well. Here, we consider the total demand quantity for a group of consumers whose individual demands are given by the same continuous function $D(p, r)$ of the single price p, as well as of individual income r whose distribution is given by a continuous density function $f(r)$ on the interval $[a, b]$.

Given a particular price p, let $T(r)$ denote the total demand for the commodity by all individuals whose income does not exceed r. Consider the income interval $[r, r + \Delta r]$. There are approximately $nf(r)\Delta r$ individuals with incomes in this interval. Because each of them demands approximately $D(p, r)$ units of the commodity, the total demand of these individuals will be approximately $nD(p, r)f(r)\Delta r$. However, the actual total demand of individuals with incomes in the interval $[r, r + \Delta r]$ is $T(r + \Delta r) - T(r)$, by definition. So we must have $T(r + \Delta r) - T(r) \approx nD(p, r)f(r)\Delta r$, and thus

$$\frac{T(r + \Delta r) - T(r)}{\Delta r} \approx nD(p, r)f(r)$$

The approximation improves, in general, as Δr decreases. Taking the limit as $\Delta r \to 0$, we obtain $T'(r) = nD(p, r)f(r)$. By definition of the definite integral,

$$T(b) - T(a) = n \int_a^b D(p, r)f(r)\, dr$$

But $T(b) - T(a)$ is the desired measure of total demand for the commodity by all the individuals in the group. In fact, this total demand will depend on the price p. So we denote it by $x(p)$, and thus we have that total demand is

$$x(p) = \int_a^b nD(p, r)f(r)\, dr \qquad (10.4.5)$$

EXAMPLE 10.4.2   Let the income distribution function be that of Example 10.4.1, and let $D(p, r) = Ap^{-1.5}r^{2.08}$. Compute the total demand.

Solution: Using (10.4.5) gives

$$x(p) = \int_a^b nAp^{-1.5}r^{2.08}Br^{-2.5}\, dr = nABp^{-1.5} \int_a^b r^{-0.42}\, dr$$

Hence,

$$x(p) = nABp^{-1.5} \times \Big|_a^b \frac{1}{0.58}r^{0.58} = \frac{nAB}{0.58}p^{-1.5}(b^{0.58} - a^{0.58})$$

Consumer and Producer Surplus

Economists are interested in studying how much consumers and producers as a whole benefit (or lose) when market conditions change. A common (but theoretically questionable) measure of these benefits used by many applied economists is the total amount of consumer and producer surplus defined below.[4] At the equilibrium point E in Fig. 10.4.1, demand

---

[4] See, for example, H. Varian: *Intermediate Microeconomics: A Modern Approach*, 8th ed., Norton, 2009 for a more detailed treatment.

quantity is equal to supply. The corresponding equilibrium price P^* is the one which induces consumers to purchase (demand) precisely the same aggregate amount that producers are willing to offer (supply) at that price, as in Example 4.5.3. According to the demand curve in Fig. 10.4.1, there are consumers who are willing to pay more than P^* per unit. In fact, even if the price is almost as high as P_1, some consumers still wish to buy some units at that price. The total amount "saved" by all such consumers is called the *consumer surplus*, denoted by CS.

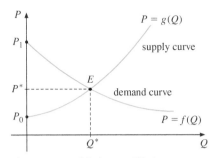

Figure 10.4.1 Market equilibrium

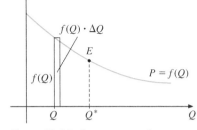

Figure 10.4.2 Consumer surplus, CS

Consider the small rectangle indicated in Fig. 10.4.2. It has base ΔQ and height $f(Q)$, so its area is $f(Q) \cdot \Delta Q$. It is approximately the maximum additional amount that consumers as a whole are willing to pay for an extra ΔQ units at price $f(Q)$, after they have already bought Q units. For those willing to buy the commodity at price P^* or higher, the total amount they are willing to pay is the total area below the demand curve over the interval $[0, Q^*]$, that is $\int_0^{Q^*} f(Q)\,\mathrm{d}Q$. This area is shaded in Fig. 10.4.2. If all consumers together buy Q^* units of the commodity, the total cost is P^*Q^*. This represents the area of the rectangle with base Q^* and height P^*. It can therefore be expressed as the integral $\int_0^{Q^*} P^*\,\mathrm{d}Q$. The consumer surplus is defined as the integral

$$\mathrm{CS} = \int_0^{Q^*} [f(Q) - P^*]\,\mathrm{d}Q \tag{10.4.6}$$

which equals the total amount consumers are willing to pay for Q^*, minus what they actually pay. In Fig. 10.4.3, $\int_0^{Q^*} f(Q)\,\mathrm{d}Q$ is the area OP_1EQ^*, whereas OP^*EQ^* is P^*Q^*. So CS is equal to the area P^*P_1E between the demand curve and the horizontal line $P = P^*$. This is also the area to the left of the demand curve—that is between the demand curve and the P-axis. So the consumer surplus CS is the lighter-shaded area in Fig. 10.4.3.

Most producers also derive positive benefit or "surplus" from selling at the equilibrium price P^* because they would be willing to supply the commodity for less than P^*. In Fig. 10.4.3, even if the price is almost as low as P_0, some producers are still willing to supply the commodity. Consider the total surplus of all the producers who receive more than the price at which they are willing to sell. We call this the *producer surplus*, denoted by PS. Geometrically it is represented by the darker-shaded area in Fig. 10.4.3. Analytically,

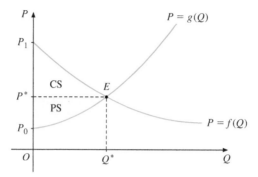

Figure 10.4.3 Consumer and producer surplus, CS and PS

it is defined by

$$PS = \int_0^{Q^*} [P^* - g(Q)] \, dQ \qquad (10.4.7)$$

since this is the total revenue producers actually receive, minus what would make them willing to supply Q^*. In Fig. 10.4.3, the area OP^*EQ^* is again P^*Q^*, and $\int_0^{Q^*} g(Q) \, dQ$ is the area OP_0EQ^*. So PS is equal to the area P^*P_0E between the supply curve and the line $P = P^*$. This is also the area to the left of the supply curve—that is between the supply curve and the P-axis.

EXAMPLE 10.4.3   Suppose that the demand curve is $P = f(Q) = 50 - 0.1Q$ and the supply curve is $P = g(Q) = 0.2Q + 20$. Find the equilibrium price and compute the consumer and producer surplus.

Solution: The equilibrium quantity is determined by the equation $50 - 0.1Q^* = 0.2Q^* + 20$, which gives $Q^* = 100$. Then $P^* = 0.2Q^* + 20 = 40$. Hence,

$$CS = \int_0^{100} [50 - 0.1Q - 40] \, dQ = \int_0^{100} [10 - 0.1Q] \, dQ = \Big|_0^{100} (10Q - 0.05Q^2) = 500$$

and

$$PS = \int_0^{100} [40 - (0.2Q + 20)] \, dQ = \int_0^{100} [20 - 0.2Q] \, dQ = \Big|_0^{100} (20Q - 0.1Q^2) = 1000$$

EXERCISES FOR SECTION 10.4

1. Assume that the rate of extraction $u(t)$ from an oil well decreases exponentially over time, with $u(t) = \bar{u}e^{-at}$, where $\bar{u}$ and a are positive constants. Given the initial stock $x(0) = K$, find an expression $x(t)$ for the remaining amount of oil at time t. Under what condition will the well never be exhausted?

(SM) **2.** Follow the pattern in Examples 10.4.1 and 10.4.2, and:

(a) Find the mean income m over the interval $[b, 2b]$ when $f(r) = Br^{-2}$, assuming that there are n individuals in the population.

(b) Assume that the individuals' demand function is $D(p, r) = Ap^{\gamma} r^{\delta}$ with $A > 0$ $\gamma < 0$, $\delta > 0$, $\delta \neq 1$. Compute the total demand $x(p)$ by using formula (10.4.5).

3. Solve the equation $S = \int_0^T e^{rt} \, dt$ for T.

4. Let $K(t)$ denote the capital stock of an economy at time t. Then *net investment* at time t, denoted by $I(t)$, is given by the rate of increase $\dot{K}(t)$ of $K(t)$.

(a) If $I(t) = 3t^2 + 2t + 5$ ($t \geq 0$), what is the total increase in the capital stock during the interval from $t = 0$ to $t = 5$?

(b) If $K(t_0) = K_0$, find an expression for the total increase in the capital stock from time $t = t_0$ to $t = T$ when the investment function $I(t)$ is as in part (a).

5. An oil company is planning to extract oil from one of its fields, starting today at $t = 0$, where t is time measured in years. It has a choice between two extraction profiles f and g giving the rates of flow of oil, measured in barrels per year. Both extraction profiles last for 10 years, with $f(t) = 10t^2 - t^3$ and $g(t) = t^3 - 20t^2 + 100t$ for t in $[0, 10]$.

(a) Sketch the two profiles in the same coordinate system.

(b) Show that $\int_0^t g(\tau) \, d\tau \geq \int_0^t f(\tau) \, d\tau$ for all t in $[0, 10]$.

(c) The company sells its oil at a price per unit given by $p(t) = 1 + 1/(t + 1)$. Total revenues from the two profiles are then given by $\int_0^{10} p(t) f(t) \, dt$ and $\int_0^{10} p(t) g(t) \, dt$ respectively. Compute these integrals. Which of the two extraction profiles earns the higher revenue?

6. Suppose that the inverse demand and supply curves for a particular commodity are, respectively, $P = f(Q) = 200 - 0.2Q$ and $P = g(Q) = 20 + 0.1Q$. Find the equilibrium price and quantity, and compute the consumer and producer surplus.

7. Suppose the inverse demand and supply curves for a particular commodity are, respectively, $P = f(Q) = 6000/(Q + 50)$ and $P = g(Q) = Q + 10$. Find the equilibrium price and quantity, and compute the consumer and producer surplus.

10.5 Integration by Parts

Mathematicians, statisticians and economists often need to evaluate integrals like $\int x^3 e^{2x} \, dx$, whose integrand is a product of two functions. We know that $\frac{1}{4}x^4$ has x^3 as its derivative and that $\frac{1}{2}e^{2x}$ has e^{2x} as its derivative, but $(\frac{1}{4}x^4)(\frac{1}{2}e^{2x})$ certainly does not have $x^3 e^{2x}$ as its derivative. In general, because the derivative of a product is *not* the product of the derivatives, the integral of a product is not the product of the integrals.

The correct rule for differentiating a product allows us to derive an important and useful rule for integrating products. The product rule for differentiation, Eq. (5.7.2), states that

$$(f(x)g(x))' = f'(x)g(x) + f(x)g'(x) \tag{$*$}$$

Now take the indefinite integral of each side in $(*)$, and then use the rule for integrating a sum. The result is

$$f(x)g(x) = \int f'(x)g(x)\,dx + \int f(x)g'(x)\,dx$$

where the constants of integration have been left implicit in the indefinite integrals on the right-hand side of this equation. Rearranging this last equation yields the following formula:

FORMULA FOR INTEGRATION BY PARTS

$$\int f(x)g'(x)\,dx = f(x)g(x) - \int f'(x)g(x)\,dx \tag{10.5.1}$$

At first sight, this formula does not look at all helpful. Yet the examples that follow show how this impression is quite wrong, once one has learned to use the formula properly.

Indeed, suppose we are asked to integrate a function $H(x)$ that can be written in the form $f(x)g'(x)$. By using (10.5.1), the problem can be transformed into that of integrating $f'(x)g(x)$. Usually, a function $H(x)$ can be written as $f(x)g'(x)$ in several different ways. The point is, therefore, to choose f and g so that it is easier to find $\int f'(x)g(x)\,dx$ than it is to find $\int f(x)g'(x)\,dx$.

EXAMPLE 10.5.1   Use integration by parts to evaluate $\int xe^x\,dx$.

Solution: In order to use (10.5.1), we must write the integrand in the form $f(x)g'(x)$. Let $f(x) = x$ and $g'(x) = e^x$, implying that $g(x) = e^x$. Then $f(x)g'(x) = xe^x$, so (10.5.1) gives

$$\int \underbrace{x \cdot e^x}_{f(x)g'(x)}\,dx = \underbrace{x \cdot e^x}_{f(x)g(x)} - \int \underbrace{1 \cdot e^x}_{f'(x)g(x)}\,dx = xe^x - \int e^x\,dx = xe^x - e^x + C$$

The derivative of $xe^x - e^x + C$ is indeed $e^x + xe^x - e^x = xe^x$, so the integration has been carried out correctly.

An appropriate choice of f and g enabled us to evaluate the integral. Let us see what happens if we interchange the roles of f and g, and try $f(x) = e^x$ and $g'(x) = x$ instead. Then $g(x) = \frac{1}{2}x^2$. Again $f(x)g'(x) = e^x x = xe^x$, and by (10.5.1):

$$\int \underbrace{e^x \cdot x}_{f(x)g'(x)}\,dx = \underbrace{e^x \cdot \frac{1}{2}x^2}_{f(x)g(x)} - \int \underbrace{e^x \cdot \frac{1}{2}x^2}_{f'(x)g(x)}\,dx$$

In this case, the integral on the right-hand side is more complicated than the original one. Thus, this second choice of f and g does not simplify the integral.

The example illustrates that we must be careful how we split the integrand. Insights into making a good choice, if there is one, come only with practice.

Sometimes integration by parts works not by producing a simpler integral, but one that is similar, as in part (a) of the next example.

EXAMPLE 10.5.2   Evaluate the following: (a) $I = \int (1/x) \ln x \, dx$; and (b) $J = \int x^3 e^{2x} \, dx$.

Solution:

(a) Choosing $f(x) = 1/x$ and $g'(x) = \ln x$ leads nowhere. Choosing $f(x) = \ln x$ and $g'(x) = 1/x$ works better:

$$I = \int \frac{1}{x} \ln x \, dx = \int \underbrace{\ln x \cdot \frac{1}{x}}_{f(x)g'(x)} \, dx = \underbrace{\ln x \cdot \ln x}_{f(x)g(x)} - \int \underbrace{\frac{1}{x} \cdot \ln x}_{f'(x)g(x)} \, dx$$

In this case, the last integral is exactly the one we started with, namely I. So it must be true that $I = (\ln x)^2 - I + C_1$ for some constant C_1. Solving for I yields $I = \frac{1}{2}(\ln x)^2 + \frac{1}{2}C_1$. Putting $C = \frac{1}{2}C_1$, we conclude that

$$\int \frac{1}{x} \ln x \, dx = \frac{1}{2}(\ln x)^2 + C$$

(b) We begin by arguing rather loosely as follows. Differentiation makes x^3 simpler by reducing the power in the derivative $3x^2$ from 3 to 2. On the other hand, e^{2x} becomes about equally simple whether we differentiate or integrate it. Therefore, we choose $f(x) = x^3$ and $g'(x) = e^{2x}$, so that integration by parts tells us to differentiate f and integrate g'. This yields $f'(x) = 3x^2$ and we can choose $g(x) = \frac{1}{2}e^{2x}$. Therefore,

$$J = \int x^3 e^{2x} \, dx = x^3 \left(\frac{1}{2}e^{2x}\right) - \int (3x^2) \left(\frac{1}{2}e^{2x}\right) \, dx = \frac{1}{2}x^3 e^{2x} - \frac{3}{2} \int x^2 e^{2x} \, dx \quad (*)$$

The last integral *is* somewhat simpler than the one we started with, because the power of x has been reduced. Integrating by parts once more yields

$$\int x^2 e^{2x} \, dx = x^2 \left(\frac{1}{2}e^{2x}\right) - \int (2x) \left(\frac{1}{2}e^{2x}\right) \, dx = \frac{1}{2}x^2 e^{2x} - \int x e^{2x} \, dx \quad (**)$$

Using integration by parts a third and final time gives

$$\int x e^{2x} \, dx = x \left(\frac{1}{2}e^{2x}\right) - \int \frac{1}{2}e^{2x} \, dx = \frac{1}{2}x e^{2x} - \frac{1}{4}e^{2x} + C_1 \quad (***)$$

Successively inserting the results of $(***)$ and $(**)$ into $(*)$ yields, with $3C_1/2 = C$:

$$J = \frac{1}{2}x^3 e^{2x} - \frac{3}{4}x^2 e^{2x} + \frac{3}{4}x e^{2x} - \frac{3}{8}e^{2x} + C$$

It is a good idea to double-check your work by verifying that $dJ/dx = x^3 e^{2x}$.

There is a corresponding result for definite integrals. From the definition of the definite integral and the product rule for differentiation, we have

$$\int_a^b \left[f'(x)g(x) + f(x)g'(x)\right] \, dx = \int_a^b \frac{d}{dx}[f(x)g(x)] \, dx = \Big|_a^b f(x)g(x)$$

implying that

$$\int_a^b f(x)g'(x)\,dx = \left| f(x)g(x) \right|_a^b - \int_a^b f'(x)g(x)\,dx \tag{10.5.2}$$

EXAMPLE 10.5.3   Evaluate $\int_0^{10}(1+0.4t)e^{-0.05t}\,dt$.

Solution: Put $f(t) = 1 + 0.4t$ and $g'(t) = e^{-0.05t}$. Then we can choose $g(t) = -20e^{-0.05t}$, and (10.5.2) yields

$$\int_0^{10}(1+0.4t)e^{-0.05t}\,dt = \left| (1+0.4t)(-20)e^{-0.05t} \right|_0^{10} - \int_0^{10}(0.4)(-20)e^{-0.05t}\,dt$$

$$= -100e^{-0.5} + 20 + 8\int_0^{10} e^{-0.05t}\,dt$$

$$= -100e^{-0.5} + 20 - 160(e^{-0.5} - 1) \approx 22.3$$

EXERCISES FOR SECTION 10.5

(SM) **1.** Use integration by parts to evaluate the following:

(a) $\int xe^{-x}\,dx$ (b) $\int 3xe^{4x}\,dx$ (c) $\int (1+x^2)e^{-x}\,dx$ (d) $\int x\ln x\,dx$

(SM) **2.** Use integration by parts to evaluate the following:

(a) $\int_{-1}^{1} x\ln(x+2)\,dx$ (b) $\int_0^2 x2^x\,dx$ (c) $\int_0^1 x^2 e^x\,dx$ (d) $\int_0^3 x\sqrt{1+x}\,dx$

In part (d) you should graph the integrand and decide if your answer is reasonable.

3. Use integration by parts to evaluate the following:

(a) $\int_1^4 \sqrt{t}\ln t\,dt$ (b) $\int_0^2 (x-2)e^{-x/2}\,dx$ (c) $\int_0^3 (3-x)3^x\,dx$

4. Of course, $f(x) = 1 \cdot f(x)$ for any function $f(x)$. Use this fact and integration by parts to prove that $\int f(x)\,dx = xf(x) - \int xf'(x)\,dx$. Apply this formula to $f(x) = \ln x$. Compare with Example 10.1.3.

5. Given $\rho \neq -1$, show that $\displaystyle\int x^\rho \ln x\,dx = \frac{x^{\rho+1}}{\rho+1}\ln x - \frac{x^{\rho+1}}{(\rho+1)^2} + C.$

(SM) **6.** Evaluate the following integrals, for $r \neq 0$:

(a) $\displaystyle\int_0^T bte^{-rt}\,dt$ (b) $\displaystyle\int_0^T (a+bt)e^{-rt}\,dt$ (c) $\displaystyle\int_0^T (a-bt+ct^2)e^{-rt}\,dt$

10.6   Integration by Substitution

In this section we shall see how the chain rule for differentiation leads to an important method for evaluating many complicated integrals. We start with some simple examples.

EXAMPLE 10.6.1   Evaluate the integrals:

(a) $\displaystyle\int (x^2 + 10)^{50}\, 2x\, dx$ (b) $\displaystyle\int_0^a xe^{-cx^2}\, dx$, where $c \neq 0$

Solution:

(a) Attempts to use integration by parts fail. Expanding $(x^2 + 10)^{50}$ to get a polynomial of 51 terms, and then integrating term by term, would work in principle, but would be extremely cumbersome. Instead, let us introduce $u = x^2 + 10$ as a new variable. Using differential notation, we see that $du = 2x\, dx$. Inserting these into the integral in (a) yields $\int u^{50}\, du$. This integral is easy, $\int u^{50}\, du = \frac{1}{51} u^{51} + C$. Because $u = x^2 + 10$, it appears that

$$\int (x^2 + 10)^{50}\, 2x\, dx = \frac{1}{51}(x^2 + 10)^{51} + C$$

By the chain rule, the derivative of $\frac{1}{51}(x^2 + 10)^{51} + C$ is precisely $(x^2 + 10)^{50}\, 2x$, so the result *is* confirmed.

(b) First, we consider the indefinite integral $\int xe^{-cx^2}\, dx$ and substitute $u = -cx^2$. Then $du = -2cx\, dx$, and thus $x\, dx = -du/2c$. Therefore

$$\int xe^{-cx^2}\, dx = \int -\frac{1}{2c} e^u\, du = -\frac{1}{2c} e^u + C = -\frac{1}{2c} e^{-cx^2} + C$$

The definite integral is

$$\int_0^a xe^{-cx^2}\, dx = -\frac{1}{2c} \times \Big|_0^a e^{-cx^2} = \frac{1}{2c}(1 - e^{-ca^2})$$

In both of these examples, the integrand could be written in the form $f(u)u'$, where $u = g(x)$. In part (a) of Example 10.6.1 we put $f(u) = u^{50}$ with $u = g(x) = x^2 + 10$. In part (b), we put $f(u) = e^u$ with $u = g(x) = -cx^2$. Then the integrand is a constant, $-1/(2c)$, multiplied by $f(g(x))g'(x)$. Let us try the same method on the more general integral

$$\int f(g(x))g'(x)\, dx$$

If we put $u = g(x)$, then $du = g'(x)\, dx$, and so the integral reduces to $\int f(u)\, du$. Suppose we could find an antiderivative function $F(u)$ such that $F'(u) = f(u)$. Then, we would have $\int f(u)\, du = F(u) + C$, which implies that $\int f(g(x))g'(x)\, dx = F(g(x)) + C$. Does this purely formal method always give the right result? To convince you that it does, we use the chain rule to differentiate $F(g(x)) + C$ w.r.t. x. The derivative is $F'(g(x))g'(x)$, which is precisely equal to $f(g(x))g'(x)$, thus confirming the following rule:

CHANGE OF VARIABLE

Suppose that g is continuously differentiable, and $f(u)$ is continuous at all points u belonging to the relevant range of g. Then,

$$\int f(g(x))g'(x)\,dx = \int f(u)\,du \tag{10.6.1}$$

where $u = g(x)$.

EXAMPLE 10.6.2   Evaluate $\int 8x^2(3x^3 - 1)^{16}\,dx$.

Solution: Substitute $u = 3x^3 - 1$. Then $du = 9x^2\,dx$, so that $8x^2\,dx = \frac{8}{9}\,du$. Hence

$$\int 8x^2(3x^3 - 1)^{16}\,dx = \frac{8}{9}\int u^{16}\,du = \frac{8}{9}\cdot\frac{1}{17}u^{17} + C = \frac{8}{153}(3x^3 - 1)^{17} + C$$

The definite integral in part (b) of Example 10.6.1 can be evaluated more simply by "carrying over" the limits of integration. We substituted $u = -cx^2$. As x varies from 0 to a, so u varies from 0 to $-ca^2$. This allows us to write:

$$\int_0^a xe^{-cx^2}\,dx = \int_0^{-ca^2} -\frac{1}{2c}e^u\,du = -\frac{1}{2c}\times\left.\right|_0^{-ca^2} e^u = \frac{1}{2c}(1 - e^{-ca^2})$$

This method of carrying over the limits of integration can be used in general. In fact, for $u = g(x)$,

$$\int_a^b f(g(x))g'(x)\,dx = \int_{g(a)}^{g(b)} f(u)\,du \tag{10.6.2}$$

The argument is simple: Provided that $F'(u) = f(u)$, we obtain

$$\int_a^b f(g(x))g'(x)\,dx = \left.\right|_a^b F(g(x)) = F(g(b)) - F(g(a)) = \int_{g(a)}^{g(b)} f(u)\,du$$

EXAMPLE 10.6.3   Evaluate the integral $\displaystyle\int_1^e \frac{1 + \ln x}{x}\,dx$.

Solution: We suggest the substitution $u = 1 + \ln x$. Then $du = (1/x)\,dx$. Also, if $x = 1$ then $u = 1$; and if $x = e$, then $u = 2$. So, we have

$$\int_1^e \frac{1 + \ln x}{x}\,dx = \int_1^2 u\,du = \frac{1}{2}\left.\right|_1^2 u^2 = \frac{1}{2}(4 - 1) = \frac{3}{2}$$

More Complicated Cases

The examples of integration by substitution considered so far were rather simple. More challenging applications of this integration method are studied in this subsection.

EXAMPLE 10.6.4   Find a substitution that allows $\int \dfrac{x - \sqrt{x}}{x + \sqrt{x}}\, dx$ to be evaluated, assuming $x > 0$.

Solution: Because $\sqrt{x}$ occurs in both the numerator and the denominator, we try to simplify the integral by substituting $u = \sqrt{x}$. Then $x = u^2$ and $dx = 2u\,du$, so we get

$$\int \frac{x - \sqrt{x}}{x + \sqrt{x}}\, dx = \int \frac{u^2 - u}{u^2 + u}\, 2u\,du \;=\; 2\int \frac{u^2 - u}{u + 1}\, du \;=\; 2\int \left(u - 2 + \frac{2}{u + 1} \right) du$$

$$= u^2 - 4u + 4\ln|u + 1| + C$$

where we have performed the polynomial division $(u^2 - u) \div (u + 1)$ with a remainder, as in Section 3.7, in order to derive the third equality. Replacing u by $\sqrt{x}$ in the last expression yields the answer

$$\int \frac{x - \sqrt{x}}{x + \sqrt{x}}\, dx = x - 4\sqrt{x} + 4\ln\left(\sqrt{x} + 1 \right) + C$$

where we use the fact that $\sqrt{x} + 1 > 0$ for all x.

The last example shows the method that is used most frequently. We can summarize it as follows:

A GENERAL METHOD

In order to find $\int G(x)\, dx$

1. Pick out a "part" of $G(x)$ and introduce this "part" as a new variable, $u = g(x)$.
2. Compute $du = g'(x)\, dx$.
3. Using the substitution $u = g(x)$, $du = g'(x)\, dx$, transform, if possible, $\int G(x)\, dx$ to an integral of the form $\int f(u)\, du$.
4. Find, if possible, $\int f(u)\, du = F(u) + C$.
5. Replace u by $g(x)$.

Then the final answer is $\int G(x)\, dx = F(g(x)) + C$.

At the third step of this procedure, it is crucial that the substitution results in an integrand $f(u)$ that only contains u (and du), without any x's. Probably the most common error when integrating by substitution is to replace dx by du, rather than use the correct formula $du = g'(x)\, dx$.

Note that if one particular substitution does not work, one can try another. But as explained in Section 10.3, there is always the possibility that no substitution at all will work.

EXAMPLE 10.6.5   Find the following: (a) $\int x^3 \sqrt{1+x^2}\, dx$; and (b) $\int_0^1 x^3 \sqrt{1+x^2}\, dx$.

Solution:

(a) We follow steps 1 to 5:

1. We pick a "part" of $x^3\sqrt{1+x^2}$ as a new variable. Let us try $u = \sqrt{1+x^2}$.
2. When $u = \sqrt{1+x^2}$, then $u^2 = 1+x^2$ and so $2u\, du = 2x\, dx$, implying that $u\, du = x\, dx$. Note that this is easier than differentiating u directly.
3. $\int x^3\sqrt{1+x^2}\, dx = \int x^2\sqrt{1+x^2}\, x\, dx = \int (u^2 - 1)uu\, du = \int (u^4 - u^2)\, du$
4. $\int (u^4 - u^2)\, du = \frac{1}{5}u^5 - \frac{1}{3}u^3 + C$
5. $\int x^3\sqrt{1+x^2}\, dx = \frac{1}{5}(\sqrt{1+x^2})^5 - \frac{1}{3}(\sqrt{1+x^2})^3 + C$

(b) We combine the results in steps 3 and 4 of part (a), while noting that $u = 1$ when $x = 0$ and $u = \sqrt{2}$ when $x = 1$. The implication is

$$
\int\limits_0^1 x^3\sqrt{1+x^2}\, dx = \Big|_1^{\sqrt{2}} \left(\frac{1}{5}u^5 - \frac{1}{3}u^3 \right) = \frac{4\sqrt{2}}{5} - \frac{2\sqrt{2}}{3} - \frac{1}{5} + \frac{1}{3} = \frac{2}{15}(\sqrt{2} + 1)
$$

In this example the substitution $u = 1+x^2$ also works.

Integrating Rational Functions and Partial Fractions

In Section 3.7 we defined a rational function as the ratio $P(x)/Q(x)$ of two polynomials. Just occasionally economists need to integrate such functions. So we will merely give two examples that illustrate a procedure one can use more generally. One example has already appeared in part (b) of Exercise 10.1.4., where the integrand was the rational function $x^3/(x+1)$. As explained in Section 3.7, this fraction can be simplified by polynomial division with a remainder into a form that can be integrated directly.

That first example was particularly simple because the denominator is a polynomial of degree 1 in x. When degree of the denominator exceeds 1, however, it is generally necessary to combine polynomial division with a *partial fraction expansion* of the remainder. Here is an example:

EXAMPLE 10.6.6   Calculate the integral $\displaystyle\int \frac{x^4 + 3x^2 - 4}{x^2 + 2x}\, dx$.

Solution: We apply polynomial division to the integrand, which yields

$$
\frac{x^4 + 3x^2 - 4}{x^2 + 2x} = x^2 - 2x + 7 - \frac{14x + 4}{x^2 + 2x}
$$

We can easily integrate the first three terms of the right-hand side, to obtain $\int (x^2 - 2x + 7)\, dx = \frac{1}{3}x^3 - x^2 + 7x + C_0$. The fourth term, however, has a denominator equal to the product of the two degree-one factors x and $x + 2$. To obtain an integrand we can integrate, we expand this term as

$$\frac{14x + 4}{x(x + 2)} = \frac{A}{x} + \frac{B}{x + 2}$$

— i.e., the sum of two partial fractions, where A and B are constants to be determined. Multiplying each side of the equation by the common denominator $x(x + 2)$ gives $14x + 4 = A(x + 2) + Bx$, or equivalently $(14 - A - B)x + 4 - 2A = 0$. To make this true for all $x \neq 0$ and all $x \neq -2$ (points where the fraction is undefined), we require that both the coefficient $14 - A - B$ of x and the constant $4 - 2A$ are 0. Solving these two simultaneous equations gives $A = 2$ and $B = 12$. Finally, therefore, we can integrate the fourth remainder term of the integrand to obtain

$$\int \frac{14x + 4}{x^2 + 2x}\, dx = \int \frac{2}{x}\, dx + \int \frac{12}{x + 2}\, dx = 2 \ln |x| + 12 \ln |x + 2| + C$$

Hence, the overall answer is

$$\int \frac{x^4 + 3x^2 - 4}{x^2 + 2x}\, dx = \frac{1}{3}x^3 - x^2 + 7x + 2 \ln |x| + 12 \ln |x + 2| + C$$

This answer, of course, can be verified by differentiation.

EXERCISES FOR SECTION 10.6

1. Find the following integrals by using (10.6.1):

(a) $\displaystyle\int (x^2 + 1)^8 2x\, dx$ (b) $\displaystyle\int (x + 2)^{10}\, dx$ (c) $\displaystyle\int \frac{2x - 1}{x^2 - x + 8}\, dx$

(SM) **2.** Find the following integrals by means of an appropriate substitution:

(a) $\displaystyle\int x(2x^2 + 3)^5\, dx$ (b) $\displaystyle\int x^2 e^{x^3 + 2}\, dx$ (c) $\displaystyle\int \frac{\ln(x + 2)}{2x + 4}\, dx$

(d) $\displaystyle\int x\sqrt{1 + x}\, dx$ (e) $\displaystyle\int \frac{x^3}{(1 + x^2)^3}\, dx$ (f) $\displaystyle\int x^5\sqrt{4 - x^3}\, dx$

3. Find the following integrals:

(a) $\displaystyle\int_0^1 x\sqrt{1 + x^2}\, dx$ (b) $\displaystyle\int_1^e \frac{\ln y}{y}\, dy$ (c) $\displaystyle\int_1^3 \frac{1}{x^2} e^{2/x}\, dx$ (d) $\displaystyle\int_5^8 \frac{x}{x - 4}\, dx$

Hint: In (d), use both integration by substitution and expansion of partial fractions, as alternative methods to find the integral.

4. Solve, for $x > 2$, the equation: $\displaystyle\int_3^x \frac{2t - 2}{t^2 - 2t}\, dt = \ln\left(\frac{2}{3}x - 1\right)$.

5. Show that $\displaystyle\int_{t_0}^{t_1} S'(x(t))x(t)\,dt = S(x(t_1)) - S(x(t_0))$.

(SM) **6.** [HARDER] Calculate the following integrals:

(a) $\displaystyle\int_0^1 (x^4 - x^9)(x^5 - 1)^{12}\,dx$ (b) $\displaystyle\int (\ln x/\sqrt{x})\,dx$ (c) $\displaystyle\int_0^4 \frac{1}{\sqrt{1 + \sqrt{x}}}\,dx$

(SM) **7.** [HARDER] Calculate the following integrals:

(a) $\displaystyle\int_1^4 \frac{e^{\sqrt{x}}}{\sqrt{x}(1 + e^{\sqrt{x}})}\,dx$ (b) $\displaystyle\int_0^{1/3} \frac{1}{e^x + 1}\,dx$ (c) $\displaystyle\int_{8.5}^{41} \frac{1}{\sqrt{2x-1} - \sqrt[4]{2x-1}}\,dx$

Hints: For (b), substitute $t = e^{-x}$; for (c), substitute $z^4 = 2x - 1$.

8. [HARDER] Use one substitution that eliminates both fractional exponents in $x^{1/2}$ and $x^{1/3}$ in order to find the integral $\displaystyle I = \int \frac{x^{1/2}}{1 - x^{1/3}}\,dx$.

9. [HARDER] Use the method of partial fractions suggested in Example 10.6.6 in order to write $f(x) = \dfrac{cx + d}{(x - a)(x - b)}$ as a sum of two fractions. Then use the result to integrate:

(a) $\displaystyle\int \frac{x}{(x + 1)(x + 2)}\,dx$ (b) $\displaystyle\int \frac{1 - 2x}{x^2 - 2x - 15}\,dx$

10.7   Infinite Intervals of Integration

In part (b) of Example 10.6.1, we proved that

$$\int_0^a xe^{-cx^2}\,dx = \frac{1}{2c}(1 - e^{-ca^2})$$

Suppose c is a positive number and let a tend to infinity. Then the right-hand expression tends to $1/(2c)$. This makes it seem natural to write

$$\int_0^\infty xe^{-cx^2}\,dx = \frac{1}{2c}$$

In statistics and economics it is common to encounter such integrals over an infinite interval. In general, suppose f is a function that is continuous for all $x \geq a$. Then $\int_a^b f(x)\,dx$ is defined for each $b \geq a$. If the limit of this integral as $b \to \infty$ exists (and is finite), then we say that f is *integrable over* $[a, \infty)$, and define

$$\int_a^\infty f(x)\,dx = \lim_{b\to\infty} \int_a^b f(x)\,dx \qquad (10.7.1)$$

The *improper integral* $\int_a^\infty f(x)\,dx$ is then said to *converge*. If the limit does *not* exist, however, the improper integral is said to *diverge*. If $f(x) \geq 0$ in $[a, \infty)$, we interpret the integral (10.7.1) as the *area* below the graph of f over the infinite interval $[a, \infty)$.

Analogously, we define

$$\int_{-\infty}^b f(x)\,dx = \lim_{a\to-\infty} \int_a^b f(x)\,dx \qquad (10.7.2)$$

when f is continuous in $(-\infty, b]$. If this limit exists, the improper integral is said to converge. Otherwise, it diverges.

EXAMPLE 10.7.1   The *exponential distribution* in statistics is defined by the density function $f(x) = \lambda e^{-\lambda x}$, where $x \geq 0$ and λ is a positive constant. The area below the graph of f over $[0, \infty)$ is illustrated in Fig. 10.7.1. Show that this area is equal to 1.

Solution: For $b > 0$, the area below the graph of f over $[0, b]$ is equal to

$$\int_0^b \lambda e^{-\lambda x}\,dx = \Big|_0^b \left(-e^{-\lambda x}\right) = -e^{-\lambda b} + 1$$

As $b \to \infty$, so $-e^{-\lambda b} + 1$ approaches 1. Therefore,

$$\int_0^\infty \lambda e^{-\lambda x}\,dx = \lim_{b\to\infty} \int_0^b \lambda e^{-\lambda x}\,dx = \lim_{b\to\infty} \left(-e^{-\lambda b} + 1\right) = 1$$

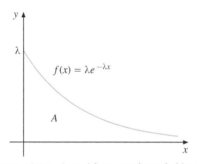

Figure 10.7.1 Area A has an unbounded base but the height decreases to 0 so rapidly that the total area is 1

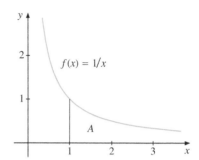

Figure 10.7.2 "$A = \int_1^\infty (1/x)\,dx = \infty$." $1/x$ does not approach 0 sufficiently fast, so the improper integral diverges

EXAMPLE 10.7.2   For $a > 1$, show that

$$\int_1^\infty \frac{1}{x^a}\, dx = \frac{1}{a-1} \qquad\qquad (*)$$

Then study the case $a \leq 1$.

Solution: For $a \neq 1$ and $b > 1$,

$$\int_1^b \frac{1}{x^a}\, dx = \int_1^b x^{-a}\, dx = \Big|_1^b \frac{1}{1-a} x^{1-a} = \frac{1}{1-a}(b^{1-a} - 1) \qquad (**)$$

For $a > 1$, one has $b^{1-a} = 1/b^{a-1} \to 0$ as $b \to \infty$. Hence, $(*)$ follows from $(**)$ by letting $b \to \infty$. For $a = 1$, the right-hand side of $(**)$ is undefined. Nevertheless, $\int_1^b (1/x)\, dx = \ln b - \ln 1 = \ln b$, which tends to ∞ as b tends to ∞, so $\int_1^\infty (1/x)\, dx$ diverges—see Fig. 10.7.2. For $a < 1$, the last expression in $(**)$ tends to ∞ as b tends to ∞. Hence, the integral diverges in this case also.

If both limits of integration are infinite, the improper integral of a continuous function f on $(-\infty, \infty)$ is defined by

$$\int_{-\infty}^\infty f(x)\, dx = \int_{-\infty}^0 f(x)\, dx + \int_0^\infty f(x)\, dx \qquad (10.7.3)$$

If *both* integrals on the right-hand side converge, the improper integral $\int_{-\infty}^\infty f(x)\, dx$ is said to *converge*; otherwise, it *diverges*. Instead of using 0 as the point of subdivision, one could use an arbitrary fixed real number c. The value assigned to the integral will always be the same, provided that the integral does converge.

It is important to note that definition (10.7.3) requires both integrals on the right-hand side to converge. Note in particular that

$$\lim_{b \to \infty} \int_{-b}^b f(x)\, dx \qquad\qquad (10.7.4)$$

is *not* the definition of $\int_{-\infty}^{+\infty} f(x)\, dx$. Exercise 4 provides an example in which (10.7.3) exists, yet the integral in (10.7.4) diverges because $\int_{-b}^0 f(x)\, dx \to -\infty$ as $b \to \infty$, and $\int_0^b f(x)\, dx \to \infty$ as $b \to \infty$. So (10.7.4) is not an acceptable definition, whereas (10.7.3) is.

The following result is very important in statistics. It is also related to Exercise 12.

EXAMPLE 10.7.3   For $c > 0$, prove that the following integral converges, and find its value:

$$\int_{-\infty}^{+\infty} xe^{-cx^2}\, dx$$

Solution: In the introduction to this section we proved that $\int_0^\infty x e^{-cx^2}\, dx = 1/2c$. In the same way we see that

$$\int_{-\infty}^0 x e^{-cx^2}\, dx = \lim_{a \to -\infty} \int_a^0 x e^{-cx^2}\, dx = \lim_{a \to -\infty} \left|_a^0 -\frac{1}{2c} e^{-cx^2}\right. = -\frac{1}{2c}$$

It follows that

$$\int_{-\infty}^\infty x e^{-cx^2}\, dx = -\frac{1}{2c} + \frac{1}{2c} = 0 \tag{10.7.5}$$

In fact, the function $f(x) = x e^{-cx^2}$ satisfies $f(-x) = -f(x)$ for all x, and so its graph is symmetric about the origin. Therefore the integral $\int_{-\infty}^0 x e^{-cx^2}\, dx$ must also exist and be equal to $-1/2c$.

Integrals of Unbounded Functions

We turn next to improper integrals where the *integrand* is not bounded. Consider first the function $f(x) = 1/\sqrt{x}$, with $x \in (0, 2]$—see Fig. 10.7.3. Note that $f(x) \to \infty$ as $x \to 0^+$. The function f is continuous in the interval $[h, 2]$ for any fixed number h in $(0, 2)$. Therefore, the definite integral of f over the interval $[h, 2]$ exists, and in fact

$$\int_h^2 \frac{1}{\sqrt{x}}\, dx = \left|_h^2 2\sqrt{x}\right. = 2\sqrt{2} - 2\sqrt{h}$$

The limit of this expression as $h \to 0^+$ is $2\sqrt{2}$. Then, by definition,

$$\int_0^2 \frac{1}{\sqrt{x}}\, dx = 2\sqrt{2}$$

The improper integral is said to converge in this case, and the area below the graph of f over the interval $(0, 2]$ is $2\sqrt{2}$. The area over the interval $(h, 2]$ is shown in Fig. 10.7.3. As $h \to 0$ the shaded area becomes unbounded, but the graph of f approaches the y-axis so quickly that the total area is finite.

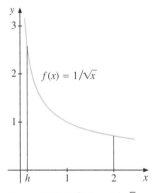

Figure 10.7.3 $f(x) = 1/\sqrt{x}$

More generally, suppose that f is a continuous function in the interval $(a, b]$, but $f(x)$ is not defined at $x = a$. Then we can define

$$\int_a^b f(x)\,\mathrm{d}x = \lim_{h \to 0^+} \int_{a+h}^b f(x)\,\mathrm{d}x \tag{10.7.6}$$

if the limit exists, and the improper integral of f is said to *converge* in this case. If $f(x) \geq 0$ in $(a, b]$, we identify the integral as the *area under the graph* of f over the interval $(a, b]$.

In the same way, if f is not defined at b, we can define

$$\int_a^b f(x)\,\mathrm{d}x = \lim_{h \to 0^+} \int_a^{b-h} f(x)\,\mathrm{d}x \tag{10.7.7}$$

if the limit exists, in which case the improper integral of f is said to *converge*.

Suppose f is continuous in (a, b). We may not even have f defined at a or b. For instance, suppose $f(x) \to -\infty$ as $x \to a^+$ and $f(x) \to +\infty$ as $x \to b^-$. In this case, f is said to be *integrable* in (a, b), and we can define

$$\int_a^b f(x)\,\mathrm{d}x = \int_a^c f(x)\,\mathrm{d}x + \int_c^b f(x)\,\mathrm{d}x \tag{10.7.8}$$

provided that both integrals on the right-hand side of (10.7.8) converge. Here c is an arbitrary fixed number in (a, b), and neither the convergence of the integral nor its value depends on the choice of c. If either of the integrals on the right-hand side of (10.7.8) does not converge, the left-hand side is not well defined.

A Test for Convergence

The following convergence test for integrals is occasionally useful because it does not require that the integral be evaluated.

THEOREM 10.7.1 (A COMPARISON TEST FOR CONVERGENCE)

Suppose that for all $x \geq a$, f and g are continuous, and $|f(x)| \leq g(x)$. If $\int_a^\infty g(x)\,\mathrm{d}x$ converges, then $\int_a^\infty f(x)\,\mathrm{d}x$ also converges, and

$$\left| \int_a^\infty f(x)\,\mathrm{d}x \right| \leq \int_a^\infty g(x)\,\mathrm{d}x$$

Considering the case in which $f(x) \geq 0$, Theorem 10.7.1 can be interpreted as follows: If the area below the graph of g is finite, then the area below the graph of f is finite as well, because at no point in $[a, \infty)$ does the graph of f lie above the graph of g. This result seems quite plausible, especially after drawing a suitable figure, so we shall not give an analytical proof. A corresponding theorem holds for the case where the lower limit of integration is $-\infty$. Also, similar comparison tests can be proved for unbounded functions defined on bounded intervals.

EXAMPLE 10.7.4   Integrals of the form

$$\int_{t_0}^{\infty} U(c(t))e^{-\alpha t}\, dt \qquad (*)$$

often appear in economic growth theory. Here, $c(t)$ denotes consumption at time t, whereas U is an instantaneous utility function, and α is a positive discount rate. Suppose that there exist numbers M and β, with $\beta < \alpha$, such that

$$|U(c(t))| \leq Me^{\beta t} \qquad (**)$$

for all $t \geq t_0$ and for each possible consumption level $c(t)$ at time t. Thus, the absolute value of the utility of consumption is growing at a rate less than the discount rate α. Prove that then $(*)$ converges.

Solution: From $(**)$, we have

$$\left| U(c(t))e^{-\alpha t} \right| \leq Me^{-(\alpha-\beta)t}$$

for all $t \geq t_0$. Moreover,

$$\int_{t_0}^{T} Me^{-(\alpha-\beta)t}\, dt = \Big|_{t_0}^{T} -\frac{M}{\alpha-\beta}e^{-(\alpha-\beta)t} = \frac{M}{\alpha-\beta}\left[e^{-(\alpha-\beta)t_0} - e^{-(\alpha-\beta)T} \right]$$

Because $\alpha - \beta > 0$, the last expression tends to

$$[M/(\alpha-\beta)]\, e^{-(\alpha-\beta)t_0}$$

as $T \to \infty$. From Theorem 10.7.1 it follows that $(*)$ converges.

EXAMPLE 10.7.5   The function $f(x) = e^{-x^2}$ is extremely important in statistics. When multiplied by a suitable constant, $1/\sqrt{\pi}$, it is the density function associated with a *Gaussian*, or *normal*, distribution. We want to show that the improper integral

$$\int_{-\infty}^{+\infty} e^{-x^2}\, dx \qquad (*)$$

converges. Recall from Section 10.1 that the indefinite integral of $f(x) = e^{-x^2}$ cannot be expressed in terms of "elementary" functions. Because $f(x) = e^{-x^2}$ is symmetric about the y-axis, one has $\int_{-\infty}^{\infty} e^{-x^2}\, dx = 2\int_{0}^{\infty} e^{-x^2}\, dx$, so it suffices to prove that $\int_{0}^{\infty} e^{-x^2}\, dx$ converges. To show this, subdivide the interval of integration so that

$$\int_{0}^{\infty} e^{-x^2}\, dx = \int_{0}^{1} e^{-x^2}\, dx + \int_{1}^{\infty} e^{-x^2}\, dx \qquad (**)$$

Of course, $\int_0^1 e^{-x^2}\,dx$ presents no problem because it is the integral of a continuous function over a bounded interval. For $x \geq 1$, one has $x^2 \geq x$ and so $0 \leq e^{-x^2} \leq e^{-x}$. Now $\int_1^\infty e^{-x}\,dx$ converges (to $1/e$), so according to Theorem 10.7.1, the integral $\int_1^\infty e^{-x^2}\,dx$ must also converge. From $(**)$, it follows that $\int_0^\infty e^{-x^2}\,dx$ converges. Thus, the integral $(*)$ does converge, but we have not found its value. In fact, one can use a more advanced technique of integration to prove that

$$\int\limits_{-\infty}^{+\infty} e^{-x^2}\,dx = \sqrt{\pi} \qquad\qquad (10.7.9)$$

as discussed in FMEA.

EXERCISES FOR SECTION 10.7

1. Determine the following integrals, if they converge. Indicate those that diverge.

(a) $\displaystyle\int_1^\infty \frac{1}{x^3}\,dx$ (b) $\displaystyle\int_1^\infty \frac{1}{\sqrt{x}}\,dx$ (c) $\displaystyle\int_{-\infty}^0 e^x\,dx$ (d) $\displaystyle\int_0^a \frac{x}{\sqrt{a^2 - x^2}}\,dx$, where $a > 0$

2. In statistics, the *uniform*, or *rectangular*, *distribution* on the interval $[a, b]$ is described by the density function f defined for all x by $f(x) = 1/(b - a)$ for $x \in [a, b]$, and $f(x) = 0$ for $x \notin [a, b]$. Find the following:

(a) $\displaystyle\int_{-\infty}^{+\infty} f(x)\,dx$ (b) $\displaystyle\int_{-\infty}^{+\infty} x f(x)\,dx$ (c) $\displaystyle\int_{-\infty}^{+\infty} x^2 f(x)\,dx$

(SM) 3. In connection with Example 10.7.1, find the following:

(a) $\displaystyle\int_0^\infty x\lambda e^{-\lambda x}\,dx$ (b) $\displaystyle\int_0^\infty (x - 1/\lambda)^2\,\lambda e^{-\lambda x}\,dx$ (c) $\displaystyle\int_0^\infty (x - 1/\lambda)^3\,\lambda e^{-\lambda x}\,dx$

The three numbers you obtain are called respectively the *expectation*, the *variance*, and the *third central moment* of the exponential distribution.

4. Prove that $\int_{-\infty}^{+\infty} x/(1 + x^2)\,dx$ diverges, but that $\lim_{b\to\infty} \int_{-b}^b x/(1 + x^2)\,dx$ converges.

(SM) 5. The function f is defined for $x > 0$ by $f(x) = (\ln x)/x^3$.

(a) Find the maximum and minimum points of f, if there are any.

(b) Examine the convergence of $\int_0^1 f(x)\,dx$ and $\int_1^\infty f(x)\,dx$.

6. Use Theorem 10.7.1 to prove the convergence of $\displaystyle\int_1^\infty \frac{1}{1 + x^2}\,dx$.

(SM) 7. Show that $\displaystyle\int_{-2}^3 \left(\frac{1}{\sqrt{x + 2}} + \frac{1}{\sqrt{3 - x}} \right) dx = 4\sqrt{5}$.

8. The integral

$$z = \int_0^\infty e^{-rs} D(s)\, ds$$

represents the present discounted value, at interest rate r, of the time-dependent stream of depreciation allowances $D(s)$, for $0 \leq s < \infty$. Find z as a function of τ in the following cases:[5]

(a) $D(s) = 1/\tau$ for $0 \leq s \leq \tau$; $D(s) = 0$ for $s > \tau$.

(b) $D(s) = 2(\tau - s)/\tau^2$ for $0 \leq s \leq \tau$; $D(s) = 0$ for $s > \tau$.

9. Suppose you evaluate $\int_{-1}^{+1}(1/x^2)\, dx$ by using the definition of the definite integral without thinking carefully. Show that you get a negative answer even though the integrand is never negative. What has gone wrong?

10. Prove that the integral $\int_0^1 (\ln x/\sqrt{x})\, dx$ converges and find its value. (*Hint*: See part (b) of Exercise 10.6.6.)

11. Find the integral

$$I_k = \int_1^\infty \left(\frac{k}{x} - \frac{k^2}{1 + kx} \right) dx$$

where k is a positive constant. Find the limit of I_k as $k \to \infty$, if it exists.

(SM) 12. [HARDER] In statistics, the normal, or Gaussian, density function with mean μ and variance σ^2 is defined by

$$f(x) = \frac{1}{\sigma\sqrt{2\pi}} \exp\left[-(x - \mu)^2/2\sigma^2\right]$$

in the interval $(-\infty, \infty)$.[6] Prove that:

(a) $\displaystyle\int_{-\infty}^{+\infty} f(x)\, dx = 1$ (b) $\displaystyle\int_{-\infty}^{+\infty} xf(x)\, dx = \mu$ (c) $\displaystyle\int_{-\infty}^{+\infty} (x - \mu)^2 f(x)\, dx = \sigma^2$

(*Hint*: Use the substitution $u = (x - \mu)/\sqrt{2}\sigma$, together with Eqs (10.7.9) and (10.7.5).)

10.8 A Glimpse at Differential Equations

In economic growth theory, in studies of the extraction of natural resources, in many models in environmental economics, and in several other areas of economics, one encounters equations where the unknowns are functions, and where the derivatives of these functions

---

[5] The first case models constant depreciation over τ years; the second is known as straight-line depreciation.

[6] The formula for this function, along with its bell-shaped graph and a portrait of its inventor Carl Friedrich Gauss (1777–1855), all appeared on the German 10 Deutsche mark banknote that was used between 1991 and 2001, in the decade before the euro currency started to circulate instead.

also appear. Equations of this general type are called *differential equations*, and their study is one of the most fascinating fields of mathematics. Here we shall consider only a few simple types of such equations. We denote the independent variable by t, because most of the differential equations in economics have time as the independent variable.

We have already solved the simplest type of differential equation: Let $f(t)$ be a given function. Find all functions that have $f(t)$ as their derivative—that is, find all functions that solve $\dot{x}(t) = f(t)$ for $x(t)$, where $\dot{x}$ denotes the derivative of x w.r.t. time t. We already know that the answer is an indefinite integral:

$$\dot{x}(t) = f(t) \Leftrightarrow x(t) = \int f(t)\,dt + C$$

We call $x(t) = \int f(t)\,dt + C$ the *general* solution of the equation $\dot{x}(t) = f(t)$.

Consider next some more challenging types of differential equation.

The Exponential Growth Law

Let $x(t)$ denote an economic quantity such as the GDP of China. The ratio $\dot{x}(t)/x(t)$ has previously been called the *relative rate of change* of this quantity. Several economic models postulate that the relative rate of change is approximately a constant, r. Thus, for all t

$$\dot{x}(t) = rx(t) \tag{10.8.1}$$

Which functions have a constant relative rate of change? For $r = 1$ the differential equation is $\dot{x} = x$, and we know that the derivative of $x = e^t$ is again $\dot{x} = e^t$. More generally, the function $x = Ae^t$ satisfies the equation $\dot{x} = x$ for all values of the constant A. By trial and error you will probably be able to come up with $x(t) = Ae^{rt}$ as a solution of (10.8.1). In any case, it is easy to verify: If $x = Ae^{rt}$, then $\dot{x}(t) = Are^{rt} = rx(t)$. Moreover, we can prove that no other function satisfies (10.8.1): Indeed, multiply Eq. (10.8.1) by the positive function e^{-rt} and collect all terms on the left-hand side. This gives

$$\dot{x}(t)e^{-rt} - rx(t)e^{-rt} = 0 \tag{10.8.2}$$

Equation (10.8.2) must have precisely the same solutions as 10.8.1. But the left-hand side of this equation is the derivative of the product $x(t)e^{-rt}$. So Eq. (10.8.2) can be rewritten as $\frac{d}{dt}[x(t)e^{-rt}] = 0$. It follows that $x(t)e^{-rt}$ must equal a constant A. Hence, $x(t) = Ae^{rt}$. If the value of $x(t)$ at $t = 0$ is x_0, then $x_0 = Ae^0 = A$. We conclude that:

$$\dot{x}(t) = rx(t) \text{ with } x(0) = x_0 \Leftrightarrow x(t) = x_0 e^{rt} \tag{10.8.3}$$

EXAMPLE 10.8.1   Let $S(t)$ denote the sales volume of a particular commodity, per unit of time, evaluated at time t. In a stable market where no sales promotion is carried out, the decrease in $S(t)$ per unit of time is proportional to $S(t)$. Thus sales decelerate at the constant proportional rate $a > 0$, implying that $\dot{S}(t) = -aS(t)$.

(a) Find an expression for $S(t)$ when sales at time 0 are S_0.

(b) Solve the equation $S_0 e^{-at} = \frac{1}{2} S_0$ for t. Interpret the answer.

Solution:

(a) This is an equation of type (10.8.1) with $x = S$ and $r = -a$. According to (10.8.3), the solution is $S(t) = S_0 e^{-at}$.

(b) From $S_0 e^{-at} = \frac{1}{2} S_0$, we obtain $e^{-at} = \frac{1}{2}$. Taking the natural logarithm of each side yields $-at = \ln(1/2) = -\ln 2$. Hence $t = \ln 2/a$. This is the time it takes before sales fall to half their initial level.

Equation (10.8.1) has often been called the *law for natural growth*. Whatever it may be called, this law is probably the most important differential equation that economists have to know.

Suppose that $x(t)$ denotes the number of individuals in a population at time t. The population could be, for instance, a particular colony of bacteria, or polar bears in the Arctic. We call $\dot{x}(t)/x(t)$ the *per capita growth rate* of the population. If there is neither immigration nor emigration, then the per capita rate of increase will be equal to the difference between the per capita birth and death rates. These rates will depend on many factors such as food supply, age distribution, available living space, predators, disease, and parasites, among other things.

Equation (10.8.1) specifies a simple model of population growth, following what is often called *Malthus's law*. According to (10.8.3), if the per capita growth rate is constant, then the population must grow exponentially. In reality, of course, exponential growth can go on only for a limited time. Let us consider some alternative models for population growth.

Another way to solve (10.8.1) is to take logarithms. Note that $d \ln x/dt = \dot{x}/x = r$, so $\ln x(t) = \int r \, dt = rt + C$. This implies that $x(t) = e^{rt+C} = e^{rt} e^C = A e^{rt}$, where $A = e^C$. In fact, a generalized version of Eq. (10.8.1) allows for the growth rate to be a function of time:

$$\dot{x}(t) = r(t)x(t) \tag{10.8.4}$$

Provided that $x(t) \neq 0$, this can be rearranged to get

$$\frac{d}{dt} \ln x(t) = \frac{\dot{x}(t)}{x(t)} = r(t)$$

whose solution is $\ln x(t) - \ln x(0) = R(t)$ or, taking exponentials, $x(t) = x(0) e^{R(t)}$ where $R(t) = \int_0^t r(s) \, ds$.

In applications, it is sometimes useful to have an "initial value" for a differential equation at a period t other than $t = 0$. This is easily done, as $t = 0$ is essentially no more than a convention. That is, if the evolution of x is given by Eq. (10.8.1), we know from (10.8.3) that for any t_0 and any t,

$$x(t_0) = x_0 e^{rt_0} \quad \text{and} \quad x(t) = x_0 e^{rt}$$

Now, the latter is equivalent to

$$x(t) = x_0 e^{r(t-t_0+t_0)} = x_0 e^{r(t-t_0)} e^{t_0} = (x_0 e^{t_0}) e^{r(t-t_0)} = x(t_0) e^{r(t-t_0)}$$

where one uses t_0 as the initial reference point of the equation.

Growth Towards an Upper Limit

Suppose the population size $x(t)$ cannot exceed some carrying capacity K, and that the rate of change of population is proportional to its deviation from this carrying capacity:

$$\dot{x}(t) = a(K - x(t)) \qquad (*)$$

With a little trick, it is easy to find all the solutions to this equation. Define a new function $u(t) = K - x(t)$, which at each time t measures the deviation of the population size from the carrying capacity K. Then $\dot{u}(t) = -\dot{x}(t)$. Inserting this into $(*)$ gives $-\dot{u}(t) = au(t)$, or $\dot{u}(t) = -au(t)$. This is an equation like (10.8.1). The solution is $u(t) = Ae^{-at}$, so that $K - x(t) = Ae^{-at}$, hence $x(t) = K - Ae^{-at}$. If $x(0) = x_0$, then $x_0 = K - A$, and so $A = K - x_0$. It follows that:

$$\dot{x}(t) = a(K - x(t)) \text{ with } x(0) = x_0 \iff x(t) = K - (K - x_0)e^{-at} \qquad (10.8.5)$$

In Exercise 3 we shall see that the same equation describes the population in countries where the indigenous population has a fixed relative rate of growth, but where there is immigration each year. The same equation can also represent several other phenomena, some of which are discussed in the problems for this section.

EXAMPLE 10.8.2   Suppose that a population has a carrying capacity of $K = 200$ (million) and that at time $t = 0$ there are 50 (million). Let $x(t)$ denote the population in millions at time t. Suppose that $a = 0.05$ and solve Eq. $(*)$ in this case. Sketch a graph of the solution.

Solution: Using Eq. (10.8.5) we find that

$$x(t) = 200 - (200 - 50)e^{-0.05t} = 200 - 150e^{-0.05t}$$

The graph is drawn in Fig. 10.8.1.

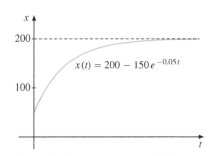

Figure 10.8.1 Growth to level 200

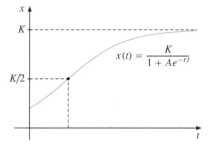

Figure 10.8.2 Logistic growth up to level K

Logistic Growth

Instead of the differential equation $(*)$, a more realistic assumption is that the relative rate of increase is approximately constant while the population is small, but that it converges to zero as the population approaches its carrying capacity K. A special form of this assumption is expressed by the equation

$$\dot{x}(t) = rx(t)\left(1 - \frac{x(t)}{K}\right) \tag{10.8.6}$$

Indeed, when the population $x(t)$ is small in proportion to K, so that $x(t)/K$ is small, then $\dot{x}(t) \approx rx(t)$, which implies that $x(t)$ increases (approximately) exponentially. As $x(t)$ becomes larger, however, the factor $1 - x(t)/K$ increases in significance. In general, we claim that if $x(t)$ satisfies (10.8.6) and is not identically equal to 0, then $x(t)$ must have the form

$$x(t) = \frac{K}{1 + Ae^{-rt}} \tag{10.8.7}$$

for some constant A. The function x given in (10.8.7) is called a *logistic function*.

In order to prove Eq. (10.8.7), we use a little trick:

Suppose that $x = x(t)$ is not 0 and introduce the new variable $u = u(t) = -1 + K/x$. Then $\dot{u} = -K\dot{x}/x^2 = -Kr/x + r = -r(-1 + K/x) = -ru$. Hence $u = u(t) = Ae^{-rt}$ for some constant A. But then $-1 + K/x(t) = Ae^{-rt}$, and solving this equation for $x(t)$ yields (10.8.7).

Suppose the population consists of x_0 individuals at time $t = 0$, and thus $x(0) = x_0$. Then Eq. (10.8.7) gives $x_0 = K/(1 + A)$, so that $A = (K - x_0)/x_0$. All in all, we have shown that the unique solution to (10.8.6) with $x(0) = x_0$ is

$$x(t) = \frac{K}{1 + Ae^{-rt}}, \quad \text{where} \quad A = \frac{K - x_0}{x_0} \tag{10.8.8}$$

If $0 < x_0 < K$, it follows from (10.8.8) that $x(t)$ is strictly increasing and that $x(t) \to K$ as $t \to \infty$, assuming $r > 0$. We say in this case that there is *logistic growth* up to the level K. The graph of the solution is shown in Fig. 10.8.2. It has an inflection point at the height $K/2$ above the t-axis. We verify this by differentiating Eq. (10.8.6) w.r.t. t. The result is $\ddot{x} = r\dot{x}(1 - x/K) + rx(-\dot{x}/K) = r\dot{x}(1 - 2x/K) = 0$. So $\ddot{x} = 0$ when $x = K/2$, and $\ddot{x}$ changes sign at this point.

Equations of type (10.8.6), and hence logistic functions of the form (10.8.7), appear in many economic models. Some of them are discussed in the problems. The simple differential equations studied here are so important that we present them and their general solutions in a form which makes it easier to see their structure. As is often done in the theory of differential equations, we suppress the symbol for time dependence.

SOLUTIONS OF SOME SIMPLE DIFFERENTIAL EQUATIONS

$$\dot{x} = ax \text{ for all } t \iff x = Ae^{at} \text{ for some constant } A \tag{10.8.9}$$

$$\dot{x} + ax = b \text{ for all } t \iff x = Ae^{-at} + \frac{b}{a} \text{ for some constant } A \tag{10.8.10}$$

$$\dot{x} + ax = bx^2 \text{ for all } t \iff x = \frac{a}{b - Ae^{at}} \text{ for some constant } A \tag{10.8.11}$$

Note that in (10.8.10) we must assume that $a \neq 0$, while in (10.8.11) the function $x(t) = 0$, for all t, is also a solution.

EXERCISES FOR SECTION 10.8

1. Which of the following functions have a constant relative rate of increase, $\dot{x}/x$?

   (a) $x = 5t + 10$ (b) $x = \ln(t + 1)$ (c) $x = 5e^t$

   (d) $x = -3 \cdot 2^t$ (e) $x = e^{t^2}$ (f) $x = e^t + e^{-t}$

2. Suppose that a firm's capital stock $K(t)$ satisfies the differential equation $\dot{K}(t) = I - \delta K(t)$, where investment I is constant, and $\delta K(t)$ denotes depreciation, with δ a positive constant.

   (a) Find the solution of the equation if the capital stock at time $t = 0$ is K_0.

   (b) Let $\delta = 0.05$ and $I = 10$. Explain what happens as $t \to \infty$ when: (i) $K_0 = 150$; (ii) $K_0 = 250$.

3. Let $N(t)$ denote the number of people in a country whose homes have broadband internet. Suppose that the rate at which new people get access is proportional to the number of people who still have no access. If the population size is P, the differential equation for $N(t)$ is, therefore, $\dot{N}(t) = k(P - N(t))$, where k is a positive constant. Find the solution of this equation if $N(0) = 0$. Then find the limit of $N(t)$ as $t \to \infty$.

4. A country's annual natural rate of population growth (births minus deaths) is 2%. In addition there is a net immigration of 40 000 persons per year. Write down a differential equation for the function $N(t)$ which denotes the number of persons in the country at time t (year). Suppose that the population at time $t = 0$ is 2 000 000. Find $N(t)$.

5. As in Examples 4.5.1 and 4.9.1, let $P(t)$ denote Europe's population in millions t years after 1960. According to UN estimates, $P(0) = 606$ and $P(10) = 657$. Suppose that $P(t)$ grows exponentially, with $P(t) = 606e^{kt}$. Compute k and then find $P(15)$, $P(40)$, and $P(55)$, which are estimates of the population in 1975, in 2000, and in 2015.

6. When a colony of bacteria is subjected to strong ultraviolet light, they die as their DNA is destroyed. In a laboratory experiment it was found that the number of living bacteria decreased approximately exponentially with the length of time they were exposed to ultraviolet light. Suppose that 70.5% of the bacteria still survive after 7 seconds of exposure. What percentage will be alive after 30 seconds? How long does it take to kill 95% of the bacteria?

7. Solve the following differential equations by using one of (10.8.9)–(10.8.11):

   (a) $\dot{x} = -0.5x$ (b) $\dot{K} = 0.02K$ (c) $\dot{x} = -0.5x + 5$

   (d) $\dot{K} - 0.2K = 100$ (e) $\dot{x} + 0.1x = 3x^2$ (f) $\dot{K} = K(-1 + 2K)$

8. A study of the mechanization of British agriculture from 1950 onwards estimated that y, the number of tractors in use (measured in thousands) as a function of t (measured in years, so that $t = 0$ corresponds to 1950), was approximately given by $y(t) = 250 + x(t)$, where $x = x(t)$ satisfied the logistic differential equation $\dot{x} = 0.34x(1 - x/230)$, and $x(0) = 25$.

(a) Find an expression for $y(t)$.

(b) Find the limit of $y(t)$ as $t \to \infty$, and draw the graph.

9. In a model of how influenza spreads, let $N(t)$ denote the number of persons who develop influenza t days after all members of a group of 1000 people have been in contact with a carrier of infection. Assume that $\dot{N}(t) = 0.39N(t)[1 - N(t)/1000]$, and $N(0) = 1$.

(a) Find a formula for $N(t)$. How many develop influenza after 20 days?

(b) How many days does it take until 800 people are sick?

(c) Will all 1000 people eventually get influenza?

(SM) 10. The logistic function (10.8.6) has been used for describing the stock of certain fish populations. Suppose such a population is harvested at a rate proportional to the stock, so that

$$\dot{x}(t) = rx(t)\left[1 - \frac{x(t)}{K}\right] - fx(t)$$

(a) Solve this equation, when the population at time $t = 0$ is x_0.

(b) Suppose $f > r$. Examine the limit of $x(t)$ as $t \to \infty$.

11. [HARDER] According to *Newton's law of cooling*, the rate at which a warm object cools is proportional to the difference between the temperature of the object and the "ambient" temperature of its surroundings. If the temperature of the object at time t and the (constant) ambient temperature is C, then $\dot{T}(t) = k(C - T(t))$. Note that this is an equation of the type given in (10.8.5.) At 12 noon, the police enter a room and discover a dead body. Immediately they measure its temperature, which is 35° Celsius. At 1 pm they take the temperature again, which is now 32°. The temperature in the room is constant at 20°. When did the person die? (*Hint*: Let the temperature be $T(t)$, where t is measured in hours and 12 noon corresponds to $t = 0$.)

10.9 Separable and Linear Differential Equations

In this final section of the chapter we consider two general types of differential equation that are frequently encountered in economics. The discussion will be brief—for a more extensive treatment we refer the reader to FMEA.

Separable Equations

A differential equation of the type

$$\dot{x} = f(t)g(x) \tag{10.9.1}$$

is called *separable*. The unknown function is $x = x(t)$, and its rate of change $\dot{x}$ is given as the product of a function only of t and a function only of x. A simple case is $\dot{x} = tx$, which is obviously separable, while $\dot{x} = t + x$ is not. In fact, all the differential equations studied in the previous section were separable equations of the type $\dot{x} = g(x)$, with $f(t) \equiv 1$.

Equation (10.8.11), for instance, is separable, since $\dot{x} + ax = bx^2$ can be rewritten as $\dot{x} = g(x)$ where $g(x) = -ax + bx^2$.

The following general method for solving separable equations is justified in FMEA.

RECIPE FOR SOLVING SEPARABLE DIFFERENTIAL EQUATIONS

(i) Write Eq. (10.9.1) as

$$\frac{dx}{dt} = f(t)g(x)$$

(ii) Separate the variables:

$$\frac{1}{g(x)}\,dx = f(t)\,dt$$

(iii) Integrate each side:

$$\int \frac{1}{g(x)}\,dx = \int f(t)\,dt$$

(iv) Evaluate the two integrals, if possible, and you obtain a solution of (∗), possibly in implicit form. Solve for x, if possible.

Note that in step (ii) we divided by $g(x)$. In fact, if $g(x)$ has a zero at $x = a$, so that $g(a) = 0$, then $x(t) \equiv a$ will be a particular solution of the equation, because the right- and left-hand sides of the equation are both 0 for all t. For instance, in the logistic equation (10.8.6), both $x(t) = 0$ and $x(t) = K$ are particular solutions.

EXAMPLE 10.9.1   Solve the differential equation

$$\frac{dx}{dt} = e^t x^2$$

and find the solution curve, which is also called the *integral curve*, that passes through the point $(t, x) = (0, 1)$.

Solution: We observe first that $x(t) \equiv 0$ is one (trivial) solution. To find the other solutions we follow the last three parts of the recipe:

Separate: $(1/x^2)\,dx = e^t\,dt$;

Integrate: $\int (1/x^2)\,dx = \int e^t\,dt$;

Evaluate: $-1/x = e^t + C$.

It follows that:

$$x = \frac{-1}{e^t + C} \tag{∗}$$

To find the integral curve through $(0, 1)$, we must determine the correct value of C. Because we require $x = 1$ for $t = 0$, it follows from (∗) that $1 = -1/(1 + C)$, so $C = -2$. Thus, the integral curve passing through $(0, 1)$ is $x = 1/(2 - e^t)$.

EXAMPLE 10.9.2   (**Economic Growth**[7]). Let $X = X(t)$ denote the national product, $K = K(t)$ the capital stock, and $L = L(t)$ the number of workers in a country at time t. Suppose that, for all $t \geq 0$,

(a) $X = \sqrt{K}\sqrt{L}$ (b) $\dot{K} = 0.4X$ (c) $L = e^{0.04t}$

Derive from these equations a single differential equation for $K = K(t)$, and find the solution of that equation when $K(0) = 10\,000$.[8]

Solution: From equations (a)–(c), we derive the single differential equation

$$\dot{K} = \frac{\mathrm{d}K}{\mathrm{d}t} = 0.4\sqrt{K}\sqrt{L} = 0.4e^{0.02t}\sqrt{K}$$

This is clearly separable. Using the recipe yields the successive equations:

(ii) $\frac{1}{\sqrt{K}}\,\mathrm{d}K = 0.4e^{0.02t}\,\mathrm{d}t$;   (iii) $\int \frac{1}{\sqrt{K}}\,\mathrm{d}K = \int 0.4e^{0.02t}\,\mathrm{d}t$;   (iv) $2\sqrt{K} = 20e^{0.02t} + C$.

If $K = 10\,000$ for $t = 0$, then $2\sqrt{10\,000} = 20 + C$, so $C = 180$. Then $\sqrt{K} = 10e^{0.02t} + 90$, and so the required solution is

$$K(t) = (10e^{0.02t} + 90)^2 = 100(e^{0.02t} + 9)^2$$

The capital–labour ratio has a somewhat bizarre limiting value in this model: as $t \to \infty$, so

$$\frac{K(t)}{L(t)} = 100 \times \frac{(e^{0.02t} + 9)^2}{e^{0.04t}} = 100\left[\frac{e^{0.02t} + 9}{e^{0.02t}}\right]^2 = 100(1 + 9e^{-0.02t})^2 \to 100$$

EXAMPLE 10.9.3   Solve the separable differential equation $(\ln x)\dot{x} = e^{1-t}$.

Solution: Following the recipe yields

(i) $\ln x \dfrac{\mathrm{d}x}{\mathrm{d}t} = e^{1-t}$;

(ii) $\ln x\,\mathrm{d}x = e^{1-t}\,\mathrm{d}t$;

(iii) $\int \ln x\,\mathrm{d}x = \int e^{1-t}\,\mathrm{d}t$;

(iv) $x \ln x - x = -e^{1-t} + C$, using the result in Example 10.1.3.

The desired functions $x = x(t)$ are those that satisfy the last equation for all t.

We usually say that we have solved a differential equation even if the unknown function, as shown in Example 10.9.3, cannot be expressed explicitly. The important point is that we have expressed the unknown function in an equation that does not include the derivative of that function.

---

[7] This is a special case of the Solow–Swan growth model. See Example 5.7.3 in FMEA.
[8] In (a) we have a Cobb–Douglas production function; (b) says that aggregate investment is proportional to output; (c) implies that the labour force grows exponentially.

First-Order Linear Equations

A *first-order linear differential equation* is one that can be written in the form

$$\dot{x} + a(t)x = b(t) \tag{10.9.2}$$

where $a(t)$ and $b(t)$ denote known continuous functions of t in a certain interval, and $x = x(t)$ is the unknown function. Equation (10.9.2) is called "linear" because the left-hand side is a linear function of x and $\dot{x}$.[9]

When $a(t)$ and $b(t)$ are constants, the solution was given in (10.8.10):

$$\dot{x} + ax = b \Leftrightarrow x = Ce^{-at} + \frac{b}{a} \tag{10.9.3}$$

where C is a constant. We found the solution of this equation by introducing a new variable. In fact, the equation is separable, so the recipe for separable equations will also lead us to the solution. If we let $C = 0$ we obtain the constant solution $x(t) = b/a$. We say that $x = b/a$ is an *equilibrium state*, or a *stationary state*, for the equation. Observe how this solution can be obtained from $\dot{x} + ax = b$ by letting $\dot{x} = 0$ and then solving the resulting equation for x. If the constant a is positive, then the solution $x = Ce^{-at} + b/a$ converges to b/a as $t \to \infty$. In this case, the equation is said to be *stable*, because every solution of the equation converges to an equilibrium as t approaches infinity.[10]

EXAMPLE 10.9.4   Find the solution of $\dot{x} + 3x = -9$, and determine whether the equation is stable.

Solution: By (10.9.3), the solution is $x = Ce^{-3t} - 3$. Here the equilibrium state is $x = -3$, and the equation is stable because $a = 3 > 0$, and $x \to -3$ as $t \to \infty$.

EXAMPLE 10.9.5   **(A price adjustment mechanism).** Let $D(P) = a - bP$ and $S(P) = \alpha + \beta P$ denote, respectively, the demand and the supply of a certain commodity, when the price is P. Here a, b, α, and β are positive constants. Assume that the price $P = P(t)$ varies with time, and that $\dot{P}$ is proportional to excess demand $D(P) - S(P)$. Thus,

$$\dot{P} = \lambda[D(P) - S(P)]$$

where λ is a positive constant. Inserting the expressions for $D(P)$ and $S(P)$ into this equation gives $\dot{P} = \lambda(a - bP - \alpha - \beta P)$. Rearranging, we then obtain

$$\dot{P} + \lambda(b + \beta)P = \lambda(a - \alpha)$$

According to (10.9.3), the solution is

$$P = Ce^{-\lambda(b+\beta)t} + \frac{a - \alpha}{b + \beta}$$

Because $\lambda(b + \beta)$ is positive, as t tends to infinity, P converges to the equilibrium price $P^e = (a - \alpha)/(b + \beta)$, for which $D(P^e) = S(P^e)$. Thus, the equation is stable.

---

[9] It is called "first-order" because it only involves the first derivative of x, and not higher-order derivatives.

[10] Stability theory is an important issue for differential equations appearing in economics. For an extensive discussion see, for instance, FMEA.

Variable Right-Hand Side

Consider next the case where the right-hand side is not constant:

$$\dot{x} + ax = b(t) \tag{10.9.4}$$

When $b(t)$ is not constant, this equation is not separable. A clever trick helps us find the solution. We multiply each side of the equation by the positive factor e^{at}, called an *integrating factor*. This gives the equivalent equation

$$\dot{x}e^{at} + axe^{at} = b(t)e^{at} \tag{$*$}$$

This idea may not be obvious beforehand, but it works well because the left-hand side of $(*)$ happens to be the exact derivative of the product xe^{at}. Thus $(*)$ is equivalent to

$$\frac{\mathrm{d}}{\mathrm{d}t}(xe^{at}) = b(t)e^{at} \tag{$**$}$$

According to the definition of the indefinite integral, Eq. $(**)$ holds for all t in an interval if, and only if, $xe^{at} = \int b(t)e^{at}\,\mathrm{d}t + C$ for some constant C. Multiplying this equation by e^{-at} gives the solution for x. Briefly formulated:

$$\dot{x} + ax = b(t) \iff x = Ce^{-at} + e^{-at}\int e^{at}b(t)\,\mathrm{d}t \tag{10.9.5}$$

EXAMPLE 10.9.6   Find the solution of $\dot{x} + x = t$, and determine the solution curve passing through $(0,0)$.

Solution: According to (10.9.5), with $a = 1$ and $b(t) = t$, the solution is given by

$$x = Ce^{-t} + e^{-t}\int te^{t}\,\mathrm{d}t = Ce^{-t} + e^{-t}(te^{t} - e^{t}) = Ce^{-t} + t - 1$$

where, following Example 10.5.1, we used integration by parts to evaluate $\int te^{t}\,\mathrm{d}t$. If $x = 0$ when $t = 0$, we get $0 = C - 1$, so $C = 1$ and the required solution is $x = e^{-t} + t - 1$.

EXAMPLE 10.9.7   (**Economic growth**). Consider the following model of economic growth:

(a) $X(t) = 0.2K(t)$ (b) $\dot{K}(t) = 0.1X(t) + H(t)$ (c) $N(t) = 50e^{0.03t}$

This model is meant to capture the features of a developing country. Here, $X(t)$ is annual GDP, $K(t)$ is capital stock, $H(t)$ is the net inflow of foreign investment per year, and $N(t)$ is the size of the population, all measured at time t. In (i) we assume that the volume of production is simply proportional to the capital stock, with the factor of proportionality 0.2 being called the *average productivity of capital*. In (ii) we assume that the total growth of capital per year is equal to internal savings plus net foreign investment. We assume that savings are proportional to production, with the factor of proportionality 0.1 being called the *savings rate*. Finally, (iii) tells us that population increases at a constant proportional rate of growth 0.03.

Assume that $H(t) = 10e^{0.04t}$ and derive from these equations a differential equation for $K(t)$. Find its solution given that $K(0) = 200$. Find also an expression for $x(t) = X(t)/N(t)$, which is domestic product per capita.

Solution: From (a) and (b), it follows that $K(t)$ must satisfy the linear equation

$$\dot{K}(t) - 0.02K(t) = 10e^{0.04t}$$

Using (10.9.5) we obtain

$$K(t) = Ce^{0.02t} + e^{0.02t} \int e^{-0.02t} 10e^{0.04t} \, dt \ = \ Ce^{0.02t} + 10e^{0.02t} \int e^{0.02t} \, dt$$

$$= Ce^{0.02t} + (10/0.02)e^{0.04t} \ = \ Ce^{0.02t} + 500e^{0.04t}$$

For $t = 0$, $K(0) = 200 = C + 500$, so $C = -300$. Thus, the solution is

$$K(t) = 500e^{0.04t} - 300e^{0.02t} \tag{*}$$

Per capita production is $x(t) = X(t)/N(t) = 0.2K(t)/50e^{0.03t} = 2e^{0.01t} - 1.2e^{-0.01t}$.

The solution procedure for the general linear differential equation (10.9.2) is somewhat more complicated, and again we refer the interested reader to FMEA for a detailed treatment. For the moment, notice that if x evolves according to Eq. (10.9.2), and we have a function $A(t)$ such that $A'(t) = a(t)$, we can apply the same trick as before: by multiplying both sides of (10.9.2) by $e^{A(t)}$, we get

$$\dot{x}e^{A(t)} + a(t)xe^{A(t)} = b(t)e^{A(t)}$$

Since the left-hand side of this equation is the derivative of $xe^{A(t)}$, we have

$$\frac{d}{dt}(xe^{A(t)}) = b(t)e^{A(t)}$$

Hence $xe^{A(t)} = C + \int b(t)e^{A(t)} \, dt$, implying that

$$x = Ce^{-A(t)} + e^{-A(t)} \int e^{A(t)}b(t) \, dt$$

which is a generalization of Eq. (10.9.5).

EXERCISES FOR SECTION 10.9

1. Solve the equation $x^4\dot{x} = 1 - t$. Find the integral curve through $(t, x) = (1, 1)$.

SM 2. Solve the following differential equations:

(a) $\dot{x} = e^{2t}/x^2$

(b) $\dot{x} = e^{-t+x}$

(c) $\dot{x} - 3x = 18$

(d) $\dot{x} = (1+t)^6/x^6$

(e) $\dot{x} - 2x = -t$

(f) $\dot{x} + 3x = te^{t^2-3t}$

3. Suppose that $y = \alpha k e^{\beta t}$ denotes production as a function of capital k, where the factor $e^{\beta t}$ is due to technical progress. Suppose that a constant fraction $s \in (0, 1)$ is saved, and that capital accumulation is equal to savings, so that we have the separable differential equation

$$\dot{k} = s\alpha k e^{\beta t}, \quad k(0) = k_0$$

The constants α, β, and k_0 are positive. Find the solution.

4. Suppose $Y = Y(t)$ is GDP, $C(t)$ is consumption, and $\bar{I}$ is investment, which is constant. Suppose $\dot{Y} = \alpha(C + \bar{I} - Y)$ and $C = aY + b$, where a, b, and α are positive constants with $a < 1$.

   (a) Derive a differential equation for Y.

   (b) Find its solution when $Y(0) = Y_0$ is given. What happens to $Y(t)$ as $t \to \infty$?

(SM) 5. In a growth model, production Q is a function of capital, K, and labour, L. Suppose that: (i) $\dot{K} = \gamma Q$; (ii) $Q = K^\alpha L$; and (iii) $\dot{L}/L = \beta$. Assuming that $L(0) = L_0$, $\beta \neq 0$ and $\alpha \in (0, 1)$, derive a differential equation for K and solve this equation when $K(0) = K_0$.

6. Find $x(t)$, when $\text{El}_t\, x(t) = a$ for all t, where $\text{El}_t\, x(t)$ denotes the elasticity of $x(t)$ w.r.t.t. Assume that both t and x are positive and that a is a constant.

REVIEW EXERCISES

1. Find the following integrals:

   (a) $\displaystyle\int (-16)\, dx$ (b) $\displaystyle\int 5^5\, dx$ (c) $\displaystyle\int (3 - y)\, dy$ (d) $\displaystyle\int (r - 4r^{1/4})\, dr$

   (e) $\displaystyle\int x^8\, dx$ (f) $\displaystyle\int x^2\sqrt{x}\, dx$ (g) $\displaystyle\int \frac{1}{p^5}\, dp$ (h) $\displaystyle\int (x^3 + x)\, dx$

2. Find the following integrals:

   (a) $\displaystyle\int 2e^{2x}\, dx$ (b) $\displaystyle\int (x - 5e^{\frac{2}{5}x})\, dx$ (c) $\displaystyle\int (e^{-3x} + e^{3x})\, dx$ (d) $\displaystyle\int \frac{2}{x + 5}\, dx$

3. Evaluate the following integrals:

   (a) $\displaystyle\int_0^{12} 50\, dx$ (b) $\displaystyle\int_0^2 (x - \frac{1}{2}x^2)\, dx$ (c) $\displaystyle\int_{-3}^3 (u + 1)^2\, du$

   (d) $\displaystyle\int_1^5 \frac{2}{z}\, dz$ (e) $\displaystyle\int_2^{12} \frac{3\, dt}{t + 4}\, dt$ (f) $\displaystyle\int_0^4 v\sqrt{v^2 + 9}\, dv$

(SM) **4.** Find the following integrals:

$$\text{(a)} \int_1^\infty \frac{5}{x^5}\,dx \qquad \text{(b)} \int_0^1 x^3(1+x^4)^4\,dx \qquad \text{(c)} \int_0^\infty \frac{-5t}{e^t}\,dt \qquad \text{(d)} \int_1^e (\ln x)^2\,dx$$

$$\text{(e)} \int_0^2 x^2\sqrt{x^3+1}\,dx \qquad \text{(f)} \int_{-\infty}^0 \frac{e^{3z}}{e^{3z}+5}\,dz \qquad \text{(g)} \int_{1/2}^{e/2} x^3\ln(2x)\,dx \qquad \text{(h)} \int_1^\infty \frac{e^{-\sqrt{x}}}{\sqrt{x}}\,dx$$

(SM) **5.** Find the following integrals:

$$\text{(a)} \int_0^{25} \frac{1}{9+\sqrt{x}}\,dx \qquad \text{(b)} \int_2^7 t\sqrt{t+2}\,dt \qquad \text{(c)} \int_0^1 57x^2\sqrt[3]{19x^3+8}\,dx$$

6. Find $F'(x)$ if: (a) $F(x) = \int_4^x \left(\sqrt{u} + \frac{x}{\sqrt{u}}\right)\,du$;   (b) $F(x) = \int_{\sqrt{x}}^x \ln u\,du.$

7. With $C(Y)$ as the consumption function, suppose the marginal propensity to consume is $C'(Y) = 0.69$, for all Y. Find $C(Y)$, if $C(0) = 1000$.

8. In manufacturing a product, the marginal cost of producing x units is $C'(x) = \alpha e^{\beta x} + \gamma$, with $\beta \neq 0$, whereas fixed costs are C_0. Find the total cost function $C(x)$.

9. Suppose f and g are continuous functions on $[-1,3]$ and that $\int_{-1}^3 (f(x)+g(x))\,dx = 6$ and

$$\int_{-1}^3 (3f(x)+4g(x))\,dx = 9. \text{ Find } I = \int_{-1}^3 (f(x)+g(x))\,dx.$$

(SM) **10.** For the following two cases, find the equilibrium price and quantity and calculate the consumer and producer surplus when the inverse demand curve is $f(Q)$ and the inverse supply curve is $g(Q)$:

(a) $f(Q) = 100 - 0.05Q$ and $g(Q) = 10 + 0.1Q.$

(b) $f(Q) = \dfrac{50}{Q+5}$ and $g(Q) = 4.5 + 0.1Q.$

(SM) **11.** Define f for $t > 0$ by $f(t) = 4(\ln t)^2/t.$

(a) Find $f'(t)$ and $f''(t)$.

(b) Find possible local extreme points, and sketch the graph of f.

(c) Calculate the area below the graph of f over the interval $[1, e^2]$.

12. Solve the following differential equations:

(a) $\dot{x} = -3x$ \qquad\qquad (b) $\dot{x} + 4x = 12$ \qquad\qquad (c) $\dot{x} - 3x = 12x^2$

(d) $5\dot{x} = -x$ \qquad\qquad (e) $3\dot{x} + 6x = 10$ \qquad\qquad (f) $\dot{x} - \frac{1}{2}x = x^2$

(SM) **13.** Solve the following differential equations:

(a) $\dot{x} = tx^2$ 　　　　(b) $2\dot{x} + 3x = -15$ 　　　　(c) $\dot{x} - 3x = 30$

(d) $\dot{x} + 5x = 10t$ 　　　(e) $\dot{x} + \frac{1}{2}x = e^t$ 　　　　(f) $\dot{x} + 3x = t^2$

14. Let $V(x)$ denote the number of litres of fuel left in an aircraft's fuel tank if it has flown x km. Suppose that $V(x)$ satisfies the following differential equation: $V'(x) = -aV(x) - b$. Here, the fuel consumption per km is a constant $b > 0$. The term $-aV(x)$, with $a > 0$, is due to the weight of the fuel.

(a) Find the solution of the equation with $V(0) = V_0$.

(b) How many km, x^*, can the plane fly if it takes off with V_0 litres in its tank?

(c) What is the minimum number of litres, V_m, needed at the outset if the plane is to fly $\hat{x}$ km?

(d) Let $b = 8$, $a = 0.001$, $V_0 = 12\,000$, and $\hat{x} = 1200$. Find x^* and V_m in this case.

15. As discussed in Section 10.4, assume that a population of n individuals has an income density function $f(r) = (1/m)e^{-r/m}$ for r in $[0, \infty)$, where m is a positive constant.

(a) Show that m is the mean income.

(b) Suppose the demand function is $D(p, r) = ar - bp$. Compute the total demand $x(p)$ when the income distribution is as above.